REREADING AMERICA

DATE DUE

REREADING AMERICA

Cultural Contexts for Critical Thinking and Writing

NINTH EDITION

EDITED BY

Gary Colombo
Los Angeles City College

Robert Cullen
San Jose State University

Bonnie Lisle
University of California, Los Angeles

Bedford/St. Martin's   Boston ◆ New York

For Bedford/St. Martin's

Senior Developmental Editor: Ellen Darion
Senior Production Editor: Anne Noonan
Production Supervisor: Samuel Jones
Executive Marketing Manager: Molly Parke
Associate Editor: Alyssa Demirjian
Editorial Assistant: Laura Horton
Copy Editor: Hilly van Loon
Permissions Manager: Kalina K. Ingham
Senior Art Director: Anna Palchik
Text Design: Tom Carling
Cover Design: Billy Boardman
Cover Art: America's America, 72 × 54. An original painting by Giovanni DeCunto (America, b. 1949)
Composition: Achorn International, Inc.
Printing and Binding: RR Donnelley and Sons

President, Bedford/St. Martin's: Denise B. Wydra
Presidents, Macmillan Higher Education: Joan E. Feinberg and Tom Scotty
Editor in Chief: Karen S. Henry
Director of Marketing: Karen R. Soeltz
Production Director: Susan W. Brown
Associate Production Director: Elise S. Kaiser
Managing Editor: Elizabeth M. Schaaf

8 7 6 5 4 3
f e d c b

For information, write: Bedford/St. Martin's, 75 Arlington Street, Boston, MA 02116 (617-399-4000)

ISBN 978-1-4576-0671-7

Acknowledgments

Acknowledgments and copyrights are continued at the back of the book on pages 767–772, which constitute an extension of the copyright page. It is a violation of the law to reproduce these selections by any means whatsoever without the written permission of the copyright holder.

PREFACE FOR INSTRUCTORS

ABOUT *REREADING AMERICA*

Designed for first-year writing and critical thinking courses, *Rereading America* anthologizes a diverse set of readings focused on the myths that dominate U.S. culture. This central theme brings together thought-provoking selections on a broad range of topics — family, education, success, race, gender roles, and freedom — topics that raise controversial issues meaningful to college students of all backgrounds. We've drawn these readings from many sources, both within the academy and outside of it; the selections are both multicultural and cross-curricular and thus represent an unusual variety of voices, styles, and subjects.

The readings in this book speak directly to students' experiences and concerns. Every college student has had some brush with prejudice, and most have something to say about education, the family, or the gender stereotypes they see in films and on television. The issues raised here help students link their personal experiences with broader cultural perspectives and lead them to analyze, or "read," the cultural forces that have shaped and continue to shape their lives. By linking the personal and the cultural, students begin to recognize that they are not academic outsiders — they too have knowledge, assumptions, and intellectual frameworks that give them authority in academic culture. Connecting personal knowledge and academic discourse helps students see that they are able to think, speak, and write academically and that they don't have to absorb passively what the "experts" say.

FEATURES OF THE NINTH EDITION

A Cultural Approach to Critical Thinking. Like its predecessors, the ninth edition of *Rereading America* is committed to the premise that learning to think critically means learning to identify and see beyond dominant cultural myths — collective and often unconsciously held beliefs that influence our thinking, reading, and writing. Instead of treating cultural diversity as just another topic to be studied or "appreciated," *Rereading America* encourages students to grapple with the real differences in perspective that arise in a pluralistic society like ours. This method helps students to break through conventional assumptions and patterns of thought that hinder fresh critical responses and inhibit dialogue. It helps them recognize that even the most apparently "natural" fact or obvious idea results from a process of social construction. And it helps them to develop the intellectual independence essential to critical thinking, reading, and writing.

Classic and Conservative Perspectives. To provide students with the historical context they often need, each chapter in this edition of *Rereading America* includes a "classic" expression of the myth under examination. Approaching the myth of success, for example, by way of Horatio Alger's *Ragged Dick* — or the myth of racial superiority by way of Thomas Jefferson's infamous diatribe against "race mixing" — gives students a better sense of the myth's origins and impact. We've also included at least one contemporary conservative revision of the myth in each chapter, so you'll find in this edition readings by cultural critics who stand to the right of center, writers like Patrick J. Buchanan, John Taylor Gatto, Charles Murray, and Katherine Mangu-Ward.

New Issues. As growing interest in the Occupy, Tea Party, and Libertarian movements suggests, the issue of freedom has recently moved to the center of American political debate. The ninth edition of *Rereading America* offers a new chapter that invites students to explore what it means to be free in twenty-first century America: Chapter Six, "Land of Liberty: American Myths of Freedom," offers a selection of voices from some of the nation's most outspoken critics and a wide variety of topics for discussion and debate. Students have the opportunity to revisit the Declaration of Independence and the Bill of Rights, and — with Naomi Wolf as their guide — to reassess how these classic statements of American liberty affect them personally. Selections by Juan Williams, Anne Applebaum, Katherine Mangu-Ward, and ACLU President Susan N. Herman challenge students to confront current threats to freedom, including corporate censorship, political correctness, bureaucratic over-regulation, and government surveillance. Renowned philosopher Martha C. Nussbaum gives students the chance to consider whether the principle of individual liberty should apply to the sale of sexual services between consenting adults. New selections by social critics like Lori Andrews, Michelle Alexander, Kevin Bales, and Ron Soodalter invite students to assess what freedom means in a nation where data-mining companies track our every move, large segments of the black and brown populations are permanently incarcerated, and slavery continues to flourish in our homes, cities, and factory farms. The chapter's Visual Portfolio features images documenting the conflicts that arise in a country founded on the concept of personal liberty — ranging from Martin Luther King Jr. marching for economic freedom in 1963 to the pepper spraying of University of California students during the Occupy Wall Street protests of 2011. In the chapter's final selection, activists Eric Liu and Nick Hanauer offer a new vision of citizenship based on our participation as free individuals in powerful social networks. Your students will also find valuable supplemental materials in the chapter's e-Pages, including the video "Declaration of Interdependence" and an additional reading by AIDS activist Chris Norwood on the rise of the medical-industrial complex.

Timely New Readings. To keep *Rereading America* up to date, we've worked hard to bring you the best new voices speaking on issues of race, gender, class, family, education, and freedom. As in past editions, we've retained old favorites like Malcolm X, Barbara Ehrenreich, Jamaica Kincaid, Jonathan Kozol, Jean Anyon, Toni Cade Bambara, Gary Soto, and Mike Rose. But you'll also find a host of new selections by authors such as Katherine S. Newman, Theodore B. Olson, Andrew Delbanco, Timothy Noah, JoYin C Shih, David Treuer, Kay Givens McGowan, Hanna Rosin, Peggy Orenstein, Naomi Wolf, Michelle Alexander, Erin Aubry Kaplan, and Martha C. Nussbaum. And like earlier versions, this edition of *Rereading America* includes a healthy mix of personal and academic writing, representing a wide variety of genres, styles, and rhetorical strategies.

e-Pages for *Rereading America*. To help extend what students read and learn in *Rereading America* to the kinds of media they are most familiar with and excited by, we have added additional online readings and videos that expand on the selections found in the text. Linked to Chapter Two, "Learning Power: The Myth of Education and Empowerment," for example, you'll find a short video, *The Commercial Campus*, on the rise of commercialism on college campuses, along with Richard Rodriguez's classic essay "The Achievement of Desire." The e-Pages videos in particular capture the immense diversity of American lives and the impressive ability of ordinary Americans to challenge cultural myths: you will meet a gay college student who has survived bullying, a biracial mother and her Caucasian husband, a group of Native American students who use YouTube to resist mainstream media portrayals, and many others. You and your students can access these additional materials for all six chapters of *Rereading America* at bedfordstmartins.com/rereading/epages.

Visual Portfolios. In addition to frontispieces and cartoons, we've included a Visual Portfolio of myth-related images in every chapter of *Rereading America*. These collections of photographs and reproductions of famous paintings invite students to examine how visual "texts" are constructed and how, like written texts, they are susceptible to multiple readings and rereadings. Each portfolio is accompanied by a series of questions that encourage critical analysis and connect portfolio images to ideas and themes in chapter reading selections. As in earlier editions, the visual frontispieces that open each chapter are integrated into the prereading assignments found in the chapter introductions. The cartoons, offered as a bit of comic relief and as opportunities for visual thinking, are paired with appropriate readings thoughout the text.

Focus on Media. We've continued the practice of including selections focusing on the media. Chapter Three includes a selection by Diana Kendall on the media's role in disseminating myths of material success. Chapter Four offers analyses of gender issues in the media, including Jean Kilbourne on images of women in advertising and Joan Morgan on black feminism and hip-hop culture. In Chapter Six, "Land of Liberty: American Myths of Freedom," Lori Andrews explores how data-mining companies have become a major threat to the privacy of all Americans by tracking all of our online activities and using the information they glean to create virtual models of each of us — models that can shape the content we see and the opportunities we have access to on the Internet.

Focus on Struggle and Resistance. Most multicultural readers approach diversity in one of two ways: either they adopt a pluralist approach and conceive of American society as a kind of salad bowl of cultures, or, in response to worries about the lack of "objectivity" in the multicultural curriculum, they take what might be called the "talk show" approach and present American culture as a series of pro-and-con debates on a number of social issues. The ninth edition of *Rereading America,* like its predecessors, follows neither of these approaches. Pluralist readers, we feel, make a promise that's impossible to keep: no single text, and no single course, can do justice to the many complex cultures that inhabit the United States. Thus the materials selected for *Rereading America* aren't meant to offer a taste of what "family" means for Native Americans, or the flavor of gender relations among immigrants. Instead, we've included selections like Melvin Dixon's "Aunt Ida Pieces a Quilt" or Harlon Dalton's "Horatio Alger" because they offer us fresh critical perspectives on the common myths that shape our ideas, values, and beliefs. Rather than seeing this anthology as a mosaic or kaleidoscope of cultural fragments that combine to form a beautiful picture, it's more accurate to think of *Rereading America* as a handbook that helps students explore the ways that the dominant culture shapes their ideas, values, and beliefs.

This notion of cultural dominance is studiously avoided in most recent multicultural anthologies. "Salad bowl" readers generally sidestep the issue of cultural dynamics: intent on celebrating America's cultural diversity, they offer a relatively static picture of a nation fragmented into a kind of cultural archipelago. "Talk show" readers admit the idea of conflict, but they distort the reality of cultural dynamics by presenting cultural conflicts as a matter of rational — and equally balanced — debate. All of the materials anthologized in *Rereading America* address the cultural struggles that animate American society — the tensions that result from the expectations established by our dominant cultural myths and the diverse realities that these myths often contradict.

Extensive Apparatus. *Rereading America* offers a wealth of features to help students hone their analytic abilities and to aid instructors as they plan class discussions, critical thinking activities, and writing assignments. These include:

- *A Comprehensive Introductory Essay* The book begins with a comprehensive essay, "Thinking Critically, Challenging Cultural Myths," that introduces students to the relationships between thinking, cultural diversity, and the notion of dominant cultural myths, and shows how such myths can influence their academic performance. We've also included a section devoted to active reading, which offers suggestions for prereading, prewriting, note taking, text marking, and keeping a reading journal. Another section helps students work with the many visual images included in the book.

- *"Fast Facts" Begin Each Chapter* Several provocative statistics before each chapter introduction provide context for students and prompt discussion. For example, "According to a 2010 McClatchy poll, 51% of Americans would be willing to give up some of their First Amendment rights to make the country safe from terrorism."

- *Detailed Chapter Introductions* An introductory essay at the beginning of each chapter offers students a thorough overview of each cultural myth, placing it in historical context, raising some of the chapter's central questions, and orienting students to the chapter's internal structure.

- *Prereading Activities* Following each chapter introduction you'll find prereading activities designed to encourage students to reflect on what they already know about the cultural myth in question. Often connected to the images that open every chapter, these prereading activities help students to engage the topic even before they begin to read.

- *Questions to Stimulate Critical Thinking* Three groups of questions following each selection encourage students to consider the reading carefully in several contexts: "Engaging the Text" focuses on close reading of the selection itself; "Exploring Connections" puts the selection into dialogue with other selections throughout the book; "Extending the Critical Context" invites students to connect the ideas they read about here with sources of knowledge outside the anthology, including library and Internet research, personal experience, interviews, ethnographic-style observations, and so forth. As in past editions, we've included a number of questions linking readings with contemporary television shows and feature films for instructors who want to address the interplay of cultural myths and the mass media.

- *"Further Connections" Close Each Chapter* These questions and assignments help students make additional connections among readings. They also provide suggestions for exploring issues through research and include ideas for community projects.

ACKNOWLEDGMENTS

Critical thinking is always a collaborative activity, and the kind of critical thinking involved in the creation of a text like *Rereading America* represents collegial collaboration at its very best. Since publication of the last edition, we've heard from instructors across the country who have generously offered suggestions for new classroom activities and comments for further refinements and improvements. Among the many instructors who shared their insights with us as we reworked this edition, we'd particularly like to thank the following: Janice Agee, Sacramento City College; Fredric J. Ball, Southwestern College; Chantell M. Barnhill, Indiana University, South Bend; Norka Blackman-Richards, Queens College — The City University of New York; Candace Boeck, San Diego State University; Mark Brock-Cancellieri, Stevenson University; Audrey Cameron, North Idaho College; Catheryn Cheal, Oakland University; Kirsti Cole, Minnesota State University, Mankato; Sean P. Connolly, Tulane University; Jackson Connor, Guilford College; Myrto Drizou, State University of New York at Buffalo; David Estrada, Fullerton College; Jacquelyn Lee Gardner,

Western Michigan University; Rochelle Gregory, North Central Texas College; Gwyn Fallbrooke, University of Minnesota; Philip Fishman, Barry University; Naomi E. Hahn, Illinois College; Rick Hansen, California State University, Fresno; Nels P. Highberg, University of Hartford; Amy Lynn Ingalls, Three Rivers Community College; Asao B. Inoue, California State University, Fresno; Amanda Katz, Worcester State University; O. Brian Kaufman, Quinesbaug Valley Community College; Barbara Kilgust, Carroll University; Carolyn Kremers, University of Alaska, Fairbanks; Catherine Lamas, East Los Angeles College; Sharon A. Lefevre, Community College of Philadelphia; Alisea Williams McLeod, Indiana University South Bend; Tanya Millner-Harlee, Manchester Community College; Ilona Missakian, Rio Hondo College; Roxanne Munch, Joliet Junior College; Katrina J. Pelow, Kent State University; M. Karen Powers, Kent State University at Tuscarawas; Kevin Quirk, DePaul University; Alex Reid, State University of New York at Buffalo; Brad C. Southard, Appalachian State University; Terry Spaise, University of California, Riverside; Sarah Stanley, University of Alaska, Fairbanks.

For their help with the eighth edition, we'd like to thank Lysbeth Benkert-Rasmussen, Northern State University; Harilaos Costarides, City College of San Francisco; Sharon Delmendo, St. John Fisher College; Deanne Fernandez, San Diego State University; Art Goldman, East L.A. College; Kim Greenfield, Lorain County Community College; Tim Gustafson, University of Minnesota; Adam Heidenreich, Joliet Junior College; Jeffrey Hillard, College of Mount St. Joseph; Robert S. Imbur, The University of Toledo; Deveryle James, University at Buffalo; Kerry J. Lane, Joliet Junior College; Kristin LaTour, Joliet Junior College; Scott A. Leonard, Youngstown State University; Carol Nowotny-Young, University of Arizona; Laura Patterson, Seton Hill University; Michael Ronan, Houston Community College; Carolyn E. Rubin-Trimble, University of Houston–Downtown; Steven Wolfe, Houston Community College.

For their help with the seventh edition, we'd like to thank José Amaya, Iowa State University; Michael A. Arnzen, Seton Hill University; Alvin Clarke, Iowa State University; Scott DeShong, Quinebaug Valley Community College; Stephen Evans, University of Kansas; Irene Faass, Iowa State University; Eileen Ferretti, Kingsborough Community College; Susan E. Howard, University of Houston, Downtown; Emily Isaacs, Montclair State University; Laureen Katana, Community College of Philadelphia; Misty Krueger, University of Tennessee; Robb Kunz, Utah State University; Mark Lidman, Maple Woods Community College; Seri Luangphinith, University of Hawai'i at Hilo; Michael Morris, Eastfield College; Roxanne Munch, Joliet Junior College; Beverly Neiderman, Kent State University; Carol Nowotny-Young, University of Arizona; Ellen O'Brien, Roosevelt University; Ildiko Olasz, Michigan State University; Cecilia Ornelas, California State University, Fullerton; Ted Otteson, University of Missouri, Kansas City; Carol Perdue, Green River Community College; Evelyn Pezzulich, Bridgewater State College; Mary Anne Quick, Bristol Community College; Elizabeth Rich, Saginaw Valley State University; Therese Rizzo, University of Delaware; Carolyn Rubin-Trimble, University of Houston–Downtown; Lori Taylor, SUNY University at Buffalo; Linda Tucker, Southern Arkansas University; Phoebe Wiley, Frostburg

State University; Malcolm Williams, University of Houston, Downtown; Elizabeth Wright, Pennsylvania State University, Hazleton.

We are also grateful to those reviewers who helped shape previous editions.

As always, we'd also like to thank all the kind folks at Bedford / St. Martin's, who do their best to make the effort of producing a book like this a genuine pleasure. Our publishers, former presidents Charles Christensen and Joan Feinberg and president Denise Wydra, deserve special praise for the support they've shown us over the years and for the wise counsel they've offered in the occasional hour of need. We're delighted to have worked once again with our editor, Ellen Darion, who also edited the first edition of *Rereading America*; her patience, professionalism, and sense of humor have helped us immensely throughout the process of producing this new edition of the book. We also want to thank associate editor Alyssa Demirjian, who found and helped create powerful e-Pages content and art; Anne Noonan, who served as production editor on this edition; Hilly van Loon, who expertly copyedited the manuscript; Billy Boardman, who produced our new cover; Natalie Giboney Turner, for clearing text permissions; Julie Tesser, for researching and tracking down art; and editorial assistant Laura Horton, who helped out with many of the hundreds of details that go into a project such as this. Finally, we'd like to acknowledge our spouses, Elena Barcia, Liz Silver, and Roy Weitz, for their love and support.

Gary Colombo
Robert Cullen
Bonnie Lisle

YOU GET MORE DIGITAL CHOICES FOR *REREADING AMERICA*

Rereading America doesn't stop with a book. Online, you'll find both free and affordable premium resources to help students get even more out of the book and your course. You'll also find convenient instructor resources, such as downloadable sample syllabi, classroom activities, and even a nationwide community of teachers. To learn more about or to order any of the products below, contact your Bedford/St. Martin's sales representative, e-mail sales support (sales_support@bfwpub.com), or visit the Web site at bedfordstmartins.com.

Student Site for *Rereading America* at bedfordstmartins.com/rereading

Send students to free and open resources, choose flexible premium resources to supplement your print text, or upgrade to an expanding collection of innovative digital content.

Free and open resources for *Rereading America* provide students with easy-to-access reference materials, visual tutorials, and support for working with sources.

- Three free tutorials from *ix visual exercises* by Cheryl Ball and Kristin Arola

- *TopLinks* with reliable online sources for exploring issues and topics for writing

- *The Bedford Bibliographer*: a tool for collecting source information and making a bibliography in MLA, APA, and *Chicago* styles

e-Pages for *Rereading America*

Designed to take advantage of what the Web can do, the e-Pages include compelling additional selections exploring cultural myths, including six videos addressing the six chapter themes in *Rereading America*. For a complete list of e-Pages, see the book's table of contents. Instructors can also use the free tools accompanying the e-Pages to upload a syllabus, readings, and assignments to share with the class.

You and your students can access the e-Pages from a tab on the *Student Site for Rereading America* at bedfordstmartins.com/rereading/epages. Students receive access automatically with the purchase of a new book. If the activation code printed on the inside front cover of the student edition has already been revealed and is expired, students can purchase access at the *Student Site*. Instructors receive access information in a separate e-mail with access to all of the resources on the *Student Site*. You can also log in or request access information at the *Student Site*.

Let students choose their format. Students can purchase *Rereading America* in other popular e-Book formats for computers, tablets, and e-Readers. For more details, visit bedfordstmartins.com/ebooks.

VideoCentral is a growing collection of videos for the writing class that captures real-world, academic, and student writers talking about how and why they write. *VideoCentral* can be packaged for free with *Rereading America*. An activation code is required. To order *VideoCentral* packaged with the print book, use ISBN 1-457-64187-9 or 978-1-457-64187-9.

Re:Writing Plus gathers all of Bedford/St. Martin's' premium digital content for composition into one online collection. It includes hundreds of model documents, the first peer review game, and *VideoCentral*. *Re:Writing Plus* can be purchased separately or packaged with the print book at a significant discount. An activation code is required. To order *Re:Writing Plus* packaged with *Rereading America*, use ISBN 1-457-64188-7 or 978-1-457-64188-6.

i-series

Add more value to your text by choosing one of the following three tutorial series, free when packaged with *Rereading America*. This popular series presents multimedia tutorials in a flexible format because there are things you can't do in a book. To learn more about package options or any of the products below, contact your Bedford/St. Martin's sales representative or visit bedfordstmartins.com.

ix visualizing composition 2.0 (available online) helps students put into practice key rhetorical and visual concepts. To order *ix visualizing composition* packaged with the print book, use ISBN 1-457-64189-5 or 978-1-457-64189-3.

i-claim: visualizing argument 2.0 (available online) shows students how to analyze and compose arguments in words, images, and sounds with six tutorials, an illustrated glossary, and over seventy multimedia arguments. To order *i-claim: visualizing argument* packaged with the print book, use ISBN 1-457-64320-0 or 978-1-457-64320-0.

i-cite: visualizing sources (available online as part of *Re:Writing Plus*) brings research to life through an animated introduction, four tutorials, and hands-on source practice. To order *i-cite: visualizing sources* packaged with the print book, use ISBN 1-457-64312-X or 978-1-457-64312-5.

Instructor Resources

You have a lot to do in your course. Bedford/St. Martin's wants to make it easy for you to find the support you need — and to get it quickly.

The Instructor's Manual for *Rereading America* is available in PDF that can be downloaded from bedfordstmartins.com/rereadingamerica. In addition to chapter overviews and teaching tips, the *Instructor's Manual* includes sample syllabi and suggestions for classroom activities.

Teaching Central (bedfordstmartins.com/teachingcentral) offers the entire list of Bedford/St. Martin's print and online professional resources in one place. You'll find landmark reference works, sourcebooks on pedagogical issues, award-winning collections, and practical advice for the classroom — all free for instructors.

Bits (bedfordbits.com) collects creative ideas for teaching a range of composition topics in an easily searchable blog. A community of teachers — leading scholars, authors, and editors — discuss revision, research, grammar and style, technology, peer review, and much more. Take, use, adapt, and pass the ideas around. Then come back to the site to comment or share your own suggestion.

Bedford Coursepacks allow you to easily integrate our most popular content into your own course management system. For details, visit bedfordstmartins .com/coursepacks.

CONTENTS

For readings that go beyond the printed page, see
bedfordstmartins.com/rereading/epages

2

LEARNING POWER   103

The Myth of Education and Empowerment

🄴 bedfordstmartins.com/rereading/epages

bedfordstmartins.com/rereading/epages

:e: bedfordstmartins.com/rereading/epages

4

TRUE WOMEN AND REAL MEN 375

Myths of Gender

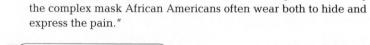

5

CREATED EQUAL   493

The Myth of the Melting Pot

6

Land of Liberty 617

American Myths of Freedom

bedfordstmartins.com/rereading/epages

THINKING CRITICALLY, CHALLENGING CULTURAL MYTHS

BECOMING A COLLEGE STUDENT

Beginning college can be a disconcerting experience. It may be the first time you've lived away from home and had to deal with the stresses and pleasures of independence. There's increased academic competition, increased temptation, and a whole new set of peer pressures. In the dorms you may find yourself among people whose backgrounds make them seem foreign and unapproachable. If you commute, you may be struggling against a feeling of isolation that you've never faced before. And then there are increased expectations. For an introductory history class you may read as many books as you covered in a year of high school coursework. In anthropology, you might be asked to conduct ethnographic research — when you've barely heard of an ethnography before, much less written one. In English, you may tackle more formal analytic writing in a single semester than you've ever done in your life.

College typically imposes fewer rules than high school, but also gives you less guidance and makes greater demands — demands that affect the quality as well as the quantity of your work. By your first midterm exam, you may suspect that your previous academic experience is irrelevant, that nothing you've done in school has prepared you to think, read, or write in the ways your professors expect. Your sociology instructor says she doesn't care whether you can remember all the examples in the textbook as long as you can apply the theoretical concepts to real situations. In your composition class, the perfect five-paragraph essay you turn in for your first assignment is dismissed as "superficial, mechanical, and dull." Meanwhile, the lecturer in your political science or psychology course is rejecting ideas about country, religion, family, and self that have always been a part of your deepest beliefs. How can you cope with these new expectations and challenges?

There is no simple solution, no infallible five-step method that works for everyone. As you meet the personal challenges of college, you'll grow as a human being. You'll begin to look critically at your old habits, beliefs, and values, to see them in relation to the new world you're entering. You may have to re-examine your relationships to family, friends, neighborhood, and heritage. You'll have to sort out your strengths from your weaknesses and make tough choices about who you are and who you want to become. Your academic work demands the same process of serious self-examination. To excel in college work you need to grow intellectually — to become a critical thinker.

WHAT IS CRITICAL THINKING?

What do instructors mean when they tell you to think critically? Most would say that it involves asking questions rather than memorizing information. Instead of simply collecting the "facts," a critical thinker probes them, looking for underlying assumptions and ideas. Instead of focusing on dates and events in history or symptoms in psychology, she probes for motives, causes — an explanation of how these things came to be. A critical thinker cultivates the ability to imagine and value points of view different from her own — then strengthens, refines, enlarges, or reshapes her ideas in light of those other perspectives. She is at once open and skeptical: receptive to new ideas yet careful to test them against previous experience and knowledge. In short, a critical thinker is an active learner, someone with the ability to shape, not merely absorb, knowledge.

All this is difficult to put into practice, because it requires getting outside your own skin and seeing the world from multiple perspectives. To see why critical thinking doesn't come naturally, take another look at the cover of this book. Many would scan the title, *Rereading America,* take in the surface meaning — to reconsider America — and go on to page one. There isn't much to question here; it just "makes sense." But what happens with the student who brings a different perspective? For example, a student from El Salvador might justly complain that the title reflects an ethnocentric view of what it means to be an American. After all, since America encompasses all the countries of North, South, and Central America, he lived in "America" long before arriving in the United States. When this student reads the title, then, he actually does *reread* it; he reads it once in the "commonsense" way but also from the perspective of someone who has lived in a country dominated by U.S. intervention and interests. This double vision or double perspective frees him to look beyond the "obvious" meaning of the book and to question its assumptions.

Of course you don't have to be bicultural to become a proficient critical thinker. You can develop a genuine sensitivity to alternative perspectives even if you've never lived outside your hometown. But to do so you need to recognize that there are no "obvious meanings." The automatic equation that the native-born student makes between "America" and the United States seems to make sense only because our culture has traditionally endorsed the idea that the United States *is* America and, by implication, that other countries in this hemisphere are somehow inferior — not the genuine article. We tend to accept this equation and its unfortunate implications because we are products of our culture.

THE POWER OF CULTURAL MYTHS

Culture shapes the way we think; it tells us what "makes sense." It holds people together by providing us with a shared set of customs, values, ideas, and beliefs, as well as a common language. We live enmeshed in this cultural web: it influences the way we relate to others, the way we look, our tastes, our habits; it enters our dreams and desires. But as culture binds us together it also selectively blinds us. As we grow up, we accept ways of looking at the world, ways of thinking and being that might best be characterized as cultural frames of reference or cultural myths. These myths help us understand our place in the world — our place as prescribed by our culture. They define our relationships to friends and lovers, to the past and future, to nature, to power, and to nation. Becoming a critical thinker means learning how to look beyond these cultural myths and the assumptions embedded in them.

You may associate the word "myth" primarily with the myths of the ancient Greeks. The legends of gods and heroes like Athena, Zeus, and Oedipus embodied the central ideals and values of Greek civilization — notions like civic responsibility, the primacy of male authority, and humility before the gods. The stories were "true" not in a literal sense but as reflections of important cultural beliefs. These myths assured the Greeks of the nobility of their origins; they provided models for the roles that Greeks would play in their public and private lives; they justified inequities in Greek society; they helped the Greeks understand human life and destiny in terms that "made sense" within the framework of that culture.

Our cultural myths do much the same. Take, for example, the American dream of success. Since the first European colonists came to the "New World" some four centuries ago, America has been synonymous with the idea of individual opportunity. For generations, immigrants have been lured across the ocean to make their fortunes in a land where the streets were said to be paved with gold. Of course we don't always agree on what success means or how it should be measured. Some calculate the meaning of success in terms of six-figure salaries or the acreage of their country estates. Others discover success in the attainment of a dream — whether it's graduating from college, achieving excellence on the playing field, or winning new rights and opportunities for less fortunate fellow citizens. For some Americans, the dream of success is the very foundation of everything that's right about life in the United States. For others, the American dream is a cultural mirage that keeps workers happy in low-paying jobs while their bosses pocket the profits of an unfair system. But whether you embrace or reject the dream of success, you can't escape its influence. As Americans, we are steeped in a culture that prizes individual achievement; growing up in the United States, we are told again and again by parents, teachers, advertisers, Hollywood writers, politicians, and opinion makers that we, too, can achieve our dream — that we, too, can "Just Do It" if we try. You might aspire to become an Internet tycoon, or you might rebel and opt for a simple life, but you can't ignore the impact of the myth. We each define success in our own way, but ultimately, the myth of success defines who we are and what we think, feel, and believe.

Cultural myths gain such enormous power over us by insinuating them-selves into our thinking before we're aware of them. Most are learned at a deep, even unconscious level. Gender roles are a good example. As children we get gender role models from our families, our schools, our churches, and other important institutions. We see them acted out in the relationships between family members or portrayed on television, in the movies, or in song lyrics. Before long, the culturally determined roles we see for women and men appear to us as "self-evident": it seems "natural" for a man to be strong, responsible, competitive, and heterosexual, just as it may seem "unnatural" for a man to shun competitive activity or to take a romantic interest in other men. Our most dominant cultural myths shape the way we perceive the world and blind us to alternative ways of seeing and being. When something violates the expec-tations that such myths create, it may even be called unnatural, immoral, or perverse.

CULTURAL MYTHS AS OBSTACLES
TO CRITICAL THINKING

Cultural myths can have more subtle effects as well. In academic work they can reduce the complexity of our reading and thinking. A few years ago, for example, a professor at Los Angeles City College noted that he and his stu-dents couldn't agree in their interpretations of the following poem by Theodore Roethke:

My Papa's Waltz

The whiskey on your breath
Could make a small boy dizzy;
But I hung on like death:
Such waltzing was not easy.

We romped until the pans
Slid from the kitchen shelf;
My mother's countenance
Could not unfrown itself.

The hand that held my wrist
Was battered on one knuckle;
At every step you missed
My right ear scraped a buckle.

You beat time on my head
With a palm caked hard by dirt,
Then waltzed me off to bed
Still clinging to your shirt.

The instructor read this poem as a clear expression of a child's love for his blue-collar father, a rough-and-tumble man who had worked hard all his life ("a palm caked hard by dirt"), who was not above taking a drink of whiskey to ease his mind, but who also found the time to "waltz" his son off to bed. The students didn't see this at all. They saw the poem as a story about an abusive father and heavy drinker. They seemed unwilling to look beyond the father's roughness and the whiskey on his breath, equating these with drunken violence. Although the poem does suggest an element of fear mingled with the boy's excitement ("I hung on like death"), the class ignored its complexity — the mixture of fear, love, and boisterous fun that colors the son's memory of his father. It's possible that some students might overlook the positive traits in the father in this poem because they have suffered child abuse themselves. But this couldn't be true for all the students in the class. The difference between these interpretations lies, instead, in the influence of cultural myths. After all, in a culture now dominated by images of the family that emphasize "positive" parenting, middle-class values, and sensitive fathers, it's no wonder that students refused to see this father sympathetically. Our culture simply doesn't associate good, loving families with drinking or with even the suggestion of physical roughness.

Years of acculturation — the process of internalizing cultural values — leave us with a set of rigid categories for "good" and "bad" parents, narrow conceptions of how parents should look, talk, and behave toward their children. These cultural categories work like mental pigeonholes: they help us sort out and evaluate our experiences rapidly, almost before we're consciously aware of them. They give us a helpful shorthand for interpreting the world; after all, we can't stop to ponder every new situation we meet as if it were a puzzle or a philosophical problem. But while cultural categories help us make practical decisions in everyday life, they also impose their inherent rigidity on our thinking and thus limit our ability to understand the complexity of our experience. They reduce the world to dichotomies — simplified either/or choices: either women or men, either heterosexuals or homosexuals, either nature or culture, either animal or human, either "alien" or American, either them or us.

Rigid cultural beliefs can present serious obstacles to success for first-year college students. In a psychology class, for example, students' cultural myths may so color their thinking that they find it nearly impossible to comprehend Freud's ideas about infant sexuality. Ingrained assumptions about childhood innocence and sexual guilt may make it impossible for them to see children as sexual beings — a concept absolutely basic to an understanding of the history of psychoanalytic theory. Yet college-level critical inquiry thrives on exactly this kind of revision of common sense: academics prize the unusual, the subtle, the ambiguous, the complex — and expect students to appreciate them as well. Good critical thinkers in all academic disciplines welcome the opportunity to challenge conventional ways of seeing the world; they seem to take delight in questioning everything that appears clear and self-evident.

QUESTIONING: THE BASIS OF CRITICAL THINKING

By questioning the myths that dominate our culture, we can begin to resist the limits they impose on our vision. In fact, they invite such questioning. Often our personal experience fails to fit the images the myths project: a young woman's ambition to be a test pilot may clash with the ideal of femininity our culture promotes; a Cambodian immigrant who has suffered from racism in the United States may question our professed commitment to equality; a student in the vocational track may not see education as the road to success that we assume it is; and few of our families these days fit the mythic model of husband, wife, two kids, a dog, and a house in the suburbs.

Moreover, because cultural myths serve such large and varied needs, they're not always coherent or consistent. Powerful contradictory myths coexist in our society and our own minds. For example, while the myth of "the melting pot" celebrates equality, the myth of individual success pushes us to strive for inequality — to "get ahead" of everyone else. Likewise, our attitudes toward education are deeply paradoxical: on one level, Americans tend to see schooling as a valuable experience that unites us in a common culture and helps us bring out the best in ourselves; yet at the same time, we suspect that formal classroom instruction stifles creativity and chokes off natural intelligence and enthusiasm. These contradictions infuse our history, literature, and popular culture; they're so much a part of our thinking that we tend to take them for granted, unaware of their inconsistencies.

Learning to recognize contradictions lies at the very heart of critical thinking, for intellectual conflict inevitably generates questions. Can both (or all) perspectives be true? What evidence do I have for the validity of each? Is there some way to reconcile them? Are there still other alternatives? Questions like these represent the beginning of serious academic analysis. They stimulate the reflection, discussion, and research that are the essence of good scholarship. Thus whether we find contradictions between myth and lived experience, or between opposing myths, the wealth of powerful, conflicting material generated by our cultural mythology offers a particularly rich context for critical inquiry.

THE STRUCTURE OF *REREADING AMERICA*

We've designed this book to help you develop the habits of mind you'll need to become a critical thinker — someone who recognizes the way that cultural myths shape thinking and can move beyond them to evaluate issues from multiple perspectives. Each of the book's six chapters addresses one of the dominant myths of American culture. We begin with the myth that's literally closest to home — the myth of the model family. In Chapter One, "Harmony at Home," we begin with readings that show what makes the mythical nuclear family so appealing and yet so elusive. Subsequent readings, visual images, and e-Pages selections dissect the myth, exploring and explaining working-class families, tribal families, flexible kinship structures, multiracial families, and "accordion" families which stretch to accommodate adult children; the chapter also includes a cluster of readings addressing the raging cultural debate over marriage equality for lesbian and gay couples. Next we turn to a topic that every student should have a lot to say about — the myth of educational empowerment. Chapter Two, "Learning Power," gives you the chance to reflect on how the "hidden curriculum" of schooling has shaped your own attitudes toward learning. We begin our exploration of American cultural myths by focusing on home and education because most students find it easy to make personal connections with these topics and because they both involve institutions — families and schools — that are surrounded by a rich legacy of cultural stories and myths. These two introductory chapters are followed by consideration of what is perhaps the most famous of all American myths, the American Dream. Chapter Three, "Money and Success," addresses the idea of unlimited personal opportunity that brought millions of immigrants to our shores and set the story of America in motion. It invites you to weigh some of the human costs of the dream and to reconsider your own definition of a successful life.

The second portion of the book focuses on three cultural myths that offer greater intellectual and emotional challenges because they touch on highly charged social issues. Chapter Four, "True Women and Real Men," considers the socially constructed categories of gender — the traditional roles that enforce differences between women and men. This chapter also explores the perspectives of Americans who defy conventional gender boundaries. The book's fifth chapter, "Created Equal," examines two myths that have powerfully shaped racial and ethnic relations in the United States: the myth of the melting pot, which celebrates cultural homogenization, and the myth of racial and ethnic superiority, which promotes separateness and inequality. This chapter probes the nature of prejudice, explores the ways that prejudicial attitudes are created, and examines ethnic identities within a race-divided society. Each of these two chapters questions how our culture divides and defines our world, how it artificially channels our experience into oppositions like black and white, male and female, straight and gay. The book's sixth and final chapter, "Land of Liberty," invites you to explore the meaning of freedom in twenty-first-century America. In this chapter, you'll encounter readings that challenge you to evaluate the state of freedom in the United States today and to survey some recent threats to our most important civil liberties — threats like corporate censorship, "nanny-state" overregulation, post-9/11 government surveillance, Internet "data mining," and the continuing growth of state power. You'll also have the chance to consider exactly how free Americans are, living in a country that has the highest incarceration rate in the world and that is a prime destination for the modern slave trade. The chapter offers a selection of voices from some of the nation's most outspoken critics and a wide variety of topics for discussion and debate — from the threat of political correctness to the legalization of prostitution.

THE SELECTIONS

Our identities — who we are and how we relate to others — are deeply entangled with the cultural values we have internalized since infancy. Cultural myths become so closely identified with our personal beliefs that rereading them actually means rereading ourselves, rethinking the way we see the world. Questioning long-held assumptions can be an exhilarating experience, but it can be distressing too. Thus you may find certain selections in *Rereading America* difficult, controversial, or even downright offensive. They are meant to challenge you and to provoke classroom debate. But as you discuss the ideas you encounter in this book, remind yourself that your classmates may bring with them very different, and equally profound, beliefs. Keep an open mind, listen carefully, and treat other perspectives with the same respect you'd expect other people to show for your own. It's by encountering new ideas and engaging with others in open dialogue that we learn to grow.

Because *Rereading America* explores cultural myths that shape our thinking, it doesn't focus on the kind of well-defined public issues you might expect to find in a traditional composition anthology. You won't be reading arguments for and against affirmative action, bilingual education, or the death penalty here. Although we do include conservative as well as liberal—and even radical—perspectives, we've deliberately avoided the traditional pro-and-con approach because we want you to aim deeper than that; we want you to focus on the subtle cultural beliefs that underlie, and frequently determine, the debates that are waged on public issues. We've also steered clear of the "issues approach" because we feel it reinforces simplistic either/or thinking. Polarizing American culture into a series of debates doesn't encourage you to examine your own beliefs or explore how they've been shaped by the cultures you're part of. To begin to appreciate the influence of your own cultural myths, you need new perspectives: you need to stand outside the ideological machinery that makes American culture run to begin to appreciate its power. That's why we've included many strongly dissenting views: there are works by community activists, gay-rights activists, socialists, libertarians, and more. You may find that their views confirm your own experience of what it means to be an American, or you may find that you bitterly disagree with them. We only hope that you will use the materials here to gain some insight into the values and beliefs that shape our thinking and our national identity. This book is meant to complicate the mental categories that our cultural myths have established for us. Our intention is not to present a new "truth" to replace the old but to expand the range of ideas you bring to all your reading and writing in college. We believe that learning to see and value other perspectives will enable you to think more critically—to question, for yourself, the truth of any statement.

You may also note that several selections in *Rereading America* challenge the way you think writing is supposed to look or sound. You won't find many "classic" essays in this book, the finely crafted reflective essays on general topics that are often held up as models of "good writing." It's not that we reject this type of essay in principle. It's just that most writers who stand outside mainstream culture seem to have little use for it.

Our selections, instead, come from a wide variety of sources: professional books and journals from many disciplines, popular magazines, college textbooks, autobiographies, oral histories, and literary works. We've included this variety partly for the very practical reason that you're likely to encounter texts like these in your college coursework. But we also see textual diversity, like ethnic and political diversity, as a way to multiply perspectives and stimulate critical analysis. For example, an academic article like Jean Anyon's study of social class and school curriculum might give you a new way of understanding

Mike Rose's personal narrative about his classroom experiences. On the other hand, you may find that some of the teachers Rose encounters don't neatly fit Anyon's theoretical model. Do such discrepancies mean that Anyon's argument is invalid? That her analysis needs to be modified to account for these teachers? That the teachers are simply exceptions to the rule? You'll probably want to consider your own classroom experience as you wrestle with such questions. Throughout the book, we've chosen readings that "talk to each other" in this way and that draw on the cultural knowledge you bring with you. These readings invite you to join the conversation; we hope they raise difficult questions, prompt lively discussion, and stimulate critical inquiry.

THE POWER OF DIALOGUE

Good thinking, like good writing and good reading, is an intensely social activity. Thinking, reading, and writing are all forms of relationship — when you read, you enter into dialogue with an author about the subject at hand; when you write, you address an imaginary reader, testing your ideas against probable responses, reservations, and arguments. Thus you can't become an accomplished writer simply by declaring your right to speak or by criticizing as an act of principle: real authority comes when you enter into the discipline of an active exchange of opinions and interpretations. Critical thinking, then, is always a matter of dialogue and debate — discovering relationships between apparently unrelated ideas, finding parallels between your own experiences and the ideas you read about, exploring points of agreement and conflict between yourself and other people.

We've designed the readings and questions in this text to encourage you to make just these kinds of connections. You'll notice, for example, that we often ask you to divide into small groups to discuss readings, and we frequently suggest that you take part in projects that require you to collaborate with your classmates. We're convinced that the only way you can learn critical reading, thinking, and writing is by actively engaging others in an intellectual exchange. So we've built into the text many opportunities for listening, discussion, and debate.

The questions that follow each selection should guide you in critical thinking. Like the readings, they're intended to get you started, not to set limits; we strongly recommend that you also devise your own questions and pursue them either individually or in study groups. We've divided our questions into three categories. Here's what to expect from each:

- Those labeled "Engaging the Text" focus on the individual selection they follow. They're designed to highlight important issues in the reading, to help you begin questioning and evaluating what you've read, and sometimes to remind you to consider the author's choices of language, evidence, structure, and style.

- The questions labeled "Exploring Connections" will lead you from the selection you've just finished to one or more other readings in this book.

When you think critically about these connecting questions, though, you'll see some real collisions of ideas and perspectives, not just polite and predictable "differences of opinion."

- The final questions for each reading, "Extending the Critical Context," invite you to extend your thinking beyond the book—to your family, your community, your college, the media, the Internet, or the more traditional research environment of the library. The emphasis here is on creating new knowledge by applying ideas from this book to the world around you and by testing these ideas in your world.

ACTIVE READING

You've undoubtedly read many textbooks, but it's unlikely that you've had to deal with the kind of analytic, argumentative, and scholarly writing you'll find in college and in *Rereading America*. These different writing styles require a different approach to reading as well. In high school you probably read to "take in" information, often for the sole purpose of reproducing it later on a test. In college you'll also be expected to recognize larger issues, such as the author's theoretical slant, her goals and methods, her assumptions, and her relationship to other writers and researchers. These expectations can be especially difficult in the first two years of college, when you take introductory courses that survey large, complex fields of knowledge. With all these demands on your attention, you'll need to read actively to keep your bearings. Think of active reading as a conversation between you and the text: instead of listening passively as the writer talks, respond to what she says with questions and comments of your own. Here are some specific techniques you can practice to become a more active reader.

Prereading and Prewriting

It's best with most college reading to "preread" the text. In prereading, you briefly look over whatever information you have on the author and the selection itself. Reading chapter introductions and headnotes like those provided in this book can save you time and effort by giving you information about the author's background and concerns, the subject or thesis of the selection, and its place in the chapter as a whole. Also take a look at the title and at any headings or subheadings in the piece. These will give you further clues about an article's general scope and organization. Next, quickly skim the entire selection, paying a bit more attention to the first few paragraphs and the conclusion. Now you should have a pretty good sense of the author's position—what she's trying to say in this piece of writing.

At this point you may do one of several things before you settle down to in-depth reading. You may want to jot down in a few lines what you think the author is doing. Or you may want to make a list of questions you can ask about this topic based on your prereading. Or you may want to freewrite a page or so on the subject. Informally writing out your own ideas will prepare you for more in-depth reading by recalling what you already know about the topic.

We emphasize writing about what you've read because reading and writing are complementary activities: being an avid reader will help you as a writer by familiarizing you with a wide range of ideas and styles to draw on; likewise, writing about what you've read will give you a deeper understanding of your reading. In fact, the more actively you "process" or reshape what you've read, the better you'll comprehend and remember it. So you'll learn more effectively by marking a text as you read than by simply reading; taking notes as you read is even more effective than marking, and writing about the material for your own purposes (putting it in your own words and connecting it with what you already know) is better still.

Marking the Text and Taking Notes

After prereading and prewriting, you're ready to begin critical reading in earnest. As you read, be sure to highlight ideas and phrases that strike you as especially significant — those that seem to capture the gist of a particular paragraph or section, or those that relate directly to the author's purpose or argument. While prereading can help you identify central ideas, you may find that you need to reread difficult sections or flip back and skim an earlier passage if you feel yourself getting lost. Many students think of themselves as poor readers if they can't whip through an article at high speed without pausing. However, the best readers read recursively — that is, they shuttle back and forth, browsing, skimming, and rereading as necessary, depending on their interest, their familiarity with the subject, and the difficulty of the material. This shuttling actually parallels what goes on in your mind when you read actively, as you alternately recall prior knowledge or experience and predict or look for clues about where the writer is going next.

Keep a record of your mental shuttling by writing comments in the margins as you read. It's often useful to gloss the contents of each paragraph or section, to summarize it in a word or two written alongside the text. This note will serve as a reminder or key to the section when you return to it for further thinking, discussion, or writing. You may also want to note passages that puzzled you. Or you may want to write down personal reactions or questions stimulated by the reading. Take time to ponder why you felt confused or annoyed or affirmed by a particular passage. Let yourself wonder "out loud" in the margins as you read.

The following section illustrates one student's notes on a few stanzas of Inés Hernández-Ávila's "Para Teresa" (p. 198). In this example, you can see that the reader puts glosses or summary comments to the left of the poem and questions or personal responses to the right. You should experiment and create your own system of note taking, one that works best for the way you read. Just remember that your main goals in taking notes are to help you understand the author's overall position, to deepen and refine your responses to the selection, and to create a permanent record of those responses.

PARA TERESA[1]

INÉS HERNÁNDEZ-ÁVILA

This poem explores and attempts to resolve an old conflict between its speaker and her schoolmate, two Chicanas at "Alamo which-had-to-be-its-name" Elementary School who have radically different ideas about what education means and does. Inés Hernández-Ávila is a cofounder of the Native American and Indigenous Studies Association and Chair of the Department of Native American Studies at the University of California, Davis. This poem appeared in her collection *Con Razón, Corazón* (1987).

Writes   A tí-Teresa   — *Why in Spanish?*
to   Te dedico las palabras estás
Teresa   que (explotan) de mi corazón[2] — *Why do her words explode?*

That day during lunch hour
at Alamo which-had-to-be-its-name !*Why?*
The day   Elementary
of their   my dear raza   — *Feels close to T. (?)*
confron- That day in the bathroom
tation   Door guarded
Myself cornered
I was accused by you, Teresa
Tú y las demás de tus amigas
Pachucas todas
Eran Uds. cinco.[3]

Me gritaban que porque me creía tan grande[4]
What was I trying to do, you growled
T.'s   Show you up?   *Teachers must be*
accusa- Make the teachers like me, pet me, *white / Anglo.*
tion   Tell me what a credit (to my people) I was?
I was playing right into their hands, you challenged
And you would have none of it. *Speaker is a "good*
I was to stop.   *student."*

[1]*Para Teresa:* For Teresa. [All notes are Hernández-Ávila's.]
[2]*A . . . corazón:* To you, Teresa, I dedicate these words that explode from my heart.
[3]*Tú . . . cinco:* You and the rest of your friends, all Pachucas, there were five of you.
[4]*Me . . . grande:* You were screaming at me, asking me why I thought I was so hot.

Keeping a Reading Journal

You may also want (or be required) to keep a reading journal in response to the selections you cover in *Rereading America*. In such a journal you'd keep all the freewriting that you do either before or after reading. Some students find it helpful to keep a double-entry journal, writing initial responses on the left side of the page and adding later reflections and reconsiderations on the right. You may want to use your journal as a place to explore personal reactions to your reading. You can do this by writing out imaginary dialogues — between two writers who address the same subject, between yourself and the writer of the selection, or between two parts of yourself. You can use the journal as a place to rewrite passages from a poem or essay in your own voice and from your own point of view. You can write letters to an author you particularly like or dislike or to a character in a story or poem. You might even draw a cartoon that comments on one of the reading selections.

Many students don't write as well as they could because they're afraid to take risks. They may have been repeatedly penalized for breaking "rules" of grammar or essay form; their main concern in writing becomes avoiding trouble rather than exploring ideas or experimenting with style. But without risk and experimentation, there's little possibility of growth. One of the benefits of journal writing is that it gives you a place to experiment with ideas, free from worries about "correctness." Here are two examples of student journal entries, in response to "Para Teresa" (we reprint the entries as they were written):

Entry 1: Internal Dialogue

Me 1: I agree with Inés Hernández-Ávila's speaker. Her actions were justifiable in a way that if you can't fight 'em, join 'em. After all, Teresa is just making the situation worse for her because not only is she sabotaging the teacher-student relationship, she's also destroying her chance for a good education.

Me 2: Hey, Teresa's action was justifiable. Why else would the speaker admit at the end of the poem that what Teresa did was fine, thus she respects Teresa more?

Me 1: The reason the speaker respected Teresa was because she (Teresa) was still keeping her culture alive, although through different means. It wasn't her action that the speaker respected, it was the representation of it.

Me 2: The reason I think Teresa acted the way she did was because she felt she had something to prove to society. She wanted to show that no one could push her people around; that her people were tough.

Entry 2: Personal Response

"Con cố gắng học gioi, cho Bá Má,
Rồi sau nây dồi sống cua con sẽ thõai mái lám."*
What if I don't want to?
What if I can't?
Sometimes I feel my parents don't understand what

*"Con . . . lám": "Daughter, study hard (for us, your Mom and Dad), so your future will be bright and easy."

I'm going through.
To them, education is money.
And money is success.
They don't see beyond that.
Sometimes I want to fail my classes purposely to
See their reaction, but that is too cruel.
They have taught me to value education.
Education makes you a person, makes you somebody, they say.
I agree.
They are proud I am going to UCLA.
They brag to their friends, our Vietnamese community, people
I don't even know.

. . .

They believe in me, but I doubt myself. . . .

You'll notice that neither of these students talks directly about "Para Teresa" as a poem. Instead, each uses it as a point of departure for her own reflections on ethnicity, identity, and education. Although we've included a number of literary works in *Rereading America*, we don't expect you to do literary analysis. We want you to use these pieces to stimulate your own thinking about the cultural myths they address. So don't feel you have to discuss imagery in Inés Hernández-Ávila's "Para Teresa" or characterization in Toni Cade Bambara's "The Lesson" in order to understand and appreciate them.

WORKING WITH VISUAL IMAGES

The myths we examine in *Rereading America* make their presence felt not only in the world of print — essays, stories, poems, memoirs — but in every aspect of our culture. Consider, for example, the myth of "the American family." If you want to design a minivan, a restaurant, a cineplex, a park, a synagogue, a personal computer, or a tax code, you had better have some idea of what families are like and how they behave. Most important, you need a good grasp of what Americans *believe* about families, about the mythology of the American family. The Visual Portfolio in each chapter, while it maintains our focus on myths, also carries you beyond the medium of print and thus lets you practice your analytic skills in a different arena.

Although we are all surrounded by visual stimuli, we don't always think critically about what we see. Perhaps we are numbed by constant exposure to a barrage of images on TV, in magazines and newspapers, in video games and films. In any case, here are a few tips on how to get the most out of the images we have collected for this book. Take the time to look at the images carefully; first impressions are important, but many of the photographs contain details that might not strike you immediately. Once you have noted the immediate impact of an image, try focusing on separate elements such as background, foreground, facial expressions, and body language. Read any text that appears in the photograph, even if it's on a T-shirt or a belt buckle. Remember that many photographs are carefully *constructed*, no matter how "natural" they may look. In a photo for a magazine advertisement, for example, everything is meticulously chosen and arranged: certain actors or models are cast for their roles;

they wear makeup; their clothes are really costumes; the location or setting of the ad is designed to reinforce its message; lighting is artificial; and someone is trying to sell you something.

Also be sure to consider the visual images contextually, not in isolation. How does each resemble or differ from its neighbors in the portfolio? How does it reinforce or challenge cultural beliefs or stereotypes? Put another way, how can it be understood in the context of the myths examined in *Rereading America*? Each portfolio is accompanied by a few questions to help you begin this type of analysis. You can also build a broader context for our visual images by collecting your own, then working in small groups to create a portfolio or collage.

Finally, remember that both readings and visual images are just starting points for discussion. You have access to a wealth of other perspectives and ideas among your family, friends, classmates; in your college library; in your personal experience; and in your imagination. We urge you to consult them all as you grapple with the perspectives you encounter in this text.

HARMONY AT HOME
The Myth of the Model Family

The Donna Reed Show.

FAST FACTS

1. Experts estimate that 40% to 50% of existing marriages will end in divorce.

2. More than half the births to American women under age 30 occur outside marriage.

3. Roughly 80% of mothers aged 25 to 54 are in the labor force.

4. Nearly 14 million American households are headed by women with no husband present. Nearly 70% of American households are childless.

5. More than 40% of American children live in families that don't contain their married, biological parents.

6. In January 2013, same-sex marriage was legal in nine states, with many more states offering substantial legal rights through civil unions or domestic partnerships.

7. Among "Millennials"—those born after 1980—only 30% say having a successful marriage is "one of the most important things" in life.

Sources: (1), (4) U.S. Census Bureau. (2) Child Trends, reported in the *New York Times*, 1/18/2012. (3) U.S. Current Population Survey. (5) Center for Marriage and Families Research Brief #13, 2008. (7) Pew Research Center.

THE NEED TO REREAD COMMONPLACE IDEAS is nowhere more apparent than in the ongoing culture war over the American family. Everyone is in favor of "family," but our definitions and values can differ dramatically. While legal and political battles over same-sex marriage are being fought across the nation, the new century has brought many other developments as well. We've seen the world's first pregnant man (female-to-male transgender Thomas Beatie), and many couples are embracing cutting-edge medical technologies to help them have a family or to control its size or makeup. At the same time, a conservative Christian movement is using biblical authority to promote prolific childbearing — eight or ten or twelve children per family. "Boomerang kids" — children in their twenties or thirties who live in their parents' households — have become increasingly common, complicating stereotypical views of "normal" family life and prompting debates about what it really means to be an adult. We have ambitious "tiger moms," overprotective "helicopter moms," and moms who breastfeed their children until age three or older.

Amidst such changes, the traditional vision of the ideal nuclear family—Dad, Mom, a couple of kids, maybe a dog, and a spacious suburban home—remains surprisingly strong. The cliché is also a potent myth, a dream that millions of Americans work to fulfill. The image is so compelling that it's easy to forget what a short time it's been around, especially compared with the long history of the family itself.

In fact, what we call the "traditional" family, headed by a breadwinner-father and a housewife-mother, has existed for little more than two hundred years, and the suburbs only came into being in the 1950s. But the family as a social institution was legally recognized in Western culture at least as far back as the Code of Hammurabi, created in ancient Mesopotamia some four thousand years ago. To appreciate how profoundly concepts of family life have changed, consider the absolute power of the Mesopotamian father, the patriarch: the law allowed him to use any of his dependents, including his wife, as collateral for loans or even to sell family members outright to pay his debts.

Although patriarchal authority was less absolute in Puritan America, fathers remained the undisputed heads of families. Seventeenth-century Connecticut, Massachusetts, and New Hampshire enacted laws condemning rebellious children to severe punishment and, in extreme cases, to death. In the early years of the American colonies, as in Western culture stretching back to Hammurabi's time, unquestioned authority within the family served as both the model for and the basis of state authority. Just as family members owed complete obedience to the father, so all citizens owed unquestioned loyalty to the king and his legal representatives. In his influential volume *Democracy in America* (1835), French aristocrat Alexis de Tocqueville describes the relationship between the traditional European family and the old political order:

> Among aristocratic nations, social institutions recognize, in truth, no one in the family but the father; children are received by society at his hands; society governs him, he governs them. Thus, the parent not only has a natural right, but acquires a political right to command them; he is the author and the support of his family; but he is also its constituted ruler.

By the mid-eighteenth century, however, new ideas about individual freedom and democracy were stirring the colonies. And by the time Tocqueville visited the United States in 1831, they had evidently worked a revolution in the family as well as in the nation's political structure: he observes, "When the condition of society becomes democratic, and men adopt as their general principle that it is good and lawful to judge of all things for one's self, . . . the power which the opinions of a father exercise over those of his sons diminishes, as well as his legal power." To Tocqueville, this shift away from strict patriarchal rule signaled a change in the emotional climate of families: "as manners and laws become more democratic, the relation of father and son becomes more intimate and more affectionate; rules and authority are less talked of, confidence and tenderness are oftentimes increased, and it would seem that the natural bond is drawn closer." In his view, the American family heralded a new era in human relations. Freed from the rigid hierarchy of the past, parents and children could meet as near equals, joined by "filial love and fraternal affection."

This vision of the democratic family — a harmonious association of parents and children united by love and trust — has mesmerized popular culture in the United States. From the nineteenth century to the present, popular novels, magazines, music, and advertising images have glorified the comforts of loving domesticity. For several decades we have absorbed our strongest impressions of the family from television. In the 1950s we watched the Andersons on *Father Knows Best*, the Stones on *The Donna Reed Show*, and the real-life Nelson family on *The Adventures of Ozzie & Harriet*. Over the next three decades the model stretched to include single parents, second marriages, and interracial adoptions on *My Three Sons*, *The Brady Bunch*, and *Diff'rent Strokes*, but the underlying ideal of wise, loving parents and harmonious happy families remained unchanged. Over the last twenty years our collective vision of the family has grown darker; prominent television families have included gangsters on *The Sopranos*, a drug-dealing mother on *Weeds*, drug abusers on *Nurse Jackie*, a drunk deadbeat dad on *Shameless*, and innumerable nontraditional family structures, including one consisting of "two and a half men." Although not every television family is dysfunctional, clearly the 1950s myth of the happy nuclear family scarcely reflects the complexities of current American life. Just as clearly, our never-ending fascination with television families underscores the cultural importance of family dynamics and family boundaries.

This chapter examines the myth of the model family and explores alternative visions of family life, including marriage equality for gay and lesbian couples. The mythical American family is well portrayed in the frontispiece to this chapter (*The Donna Reed Show*, p. 17) and in Norman Rockwell's *Freedom from Want* (p. 58); both images show happy, healthy, modestly affluent nuclear families. The myth also plays a major role in the chapter's first reading selection, "Looking for Work," in which Gary Soto recalls his boyhood desire to live the myth and recounts his humorous attempts to transform his working-class Chicano family into a facsimile of the Cleavers on *Leave It to Beaver*. Stephanie Coontz, in "What We Really Miss About the 1950s," then takes a close analytical look at the 1950s family, explaining its lasting appeal to some Americans but also documenting its dark side.

The next selections use literary, sociological, and visual approaches to explore the meanings of family. "Aunt Ida Pieces a Quilt," a short poem by Melvin Dixon, tells the story of an extended African American family helping one another cope with the loss of Ida's nephew to AIDS. "The Color of Family Ties: Race, Class, Gender, and Extended Family Involvement," by Naomi Gerstel and Natalia Sarkisian, moves us from individual experience to sociological analysis, as the authors challenge common misconceptions by carefully examining how ethnicity and social class shape the behaviors of American families. Next, the chapter's Visual Portfolio offers you a chance to practice interpreting images; the photographs in this collection suggest some of the complex ways the contemporary American family intersects with gender, ethnicity, and social class.

After the Visual Portfolio, the chapter turns to the hotly contested cultural battle over same-sex marriage. We begin with "Proposition 8: The California Marriage Protection Act," the ballot measure that amended California's Constitution to define marriage as valid only between a man and a woman and that has served as a model for similar measures in many states. Next, "Prop 8 Hurt My Family — Ask Me How," a report from Marriage Equality USA, describes the harassment that Prop 8 proponents and their families were subjected to during the 2008 campaign, including homophobic slurs and threats of physical violence. In the final selection on this topic, attorney Theodore Olson argues that contrary to popular opinion, gay marriage is actually in line with conservative values; Olson is an expert on constitutional law and helped bring the case for same-sex marriage before the U.S. Supreme Court.

The chapter concludes with two selections about other ways the American family may be evolving. In an excerpt from her book *The Accordion Family*, Katherine Newman examines the growing trend of adults in their twenties or thirties to live in their parents' households — a trend that began decades ago but is now rapidly accelerating. Finally, in "Quality Time, Redefined," Alex Williams looks at how the increasing use of laptops, smartphones, and other technologies is changing personal interactions within the family. Is a family "together" if they are all plugged into their own virtual worlds?

In the e-Pages for *Rereading America*, you'll find two selections about nontraditional families that seem to function very well. "An Indian Story," by Roger Jack, paints a warm, magical portrait of the bond between a Native American boy and his caretaker aunt. Finally, the video *Just a Family* features three generations speaking about their experiences of life in a multiracial family. See bedfordstmartins.com/rereading/epages for these two selections.

Sources

Lerner, Gerda. *The Creation of Patriarchy*. New York: Oxford University Press, 1986. Print.

Mintz, Steven, and Susan Kellogg. *Domestic Revolutions: A Social History of American Life*. New York: Free Press, 1988. Print.

Tocqueville, Alexis de. *Democracy in America*. 1835. New York: Vintage Books, 1990. Print.

BEFORE READING

- Spend ten minutes or so jotting down every word, phrase, or image you associate with the idea of "family." Write as freely as possible, without censoring your thoughts or worrying about grammatical correctness. Working in small groups, compare lists and try to categorize your responses. What assumptions about families do they reveal?

- Draw a visual representation of your family. This could take the form of a graph, chart, diagram, map, cartoon, symbolic picture, or literal portrait. Don't worry if you're not a skillful artist: the main point is to convey an idea, and even stick figures can speak eloquently. When you're finished, write a journal entry about your drawing. Was it easier to depict some feelings or ideas visually than it would have been to describe them in words? Did you find some things about your family difficult or impossible to convey visually? Does your drawing "say" anything that surprises you?

- Write a journal entry about how you think attending college has changed, or will change, your relationship to your family.

LOOKING FOR WORK

GARY SOTO

"Looking for Work" is the narrative of a nine-year-old Mexican American boy who wants his family to imitate the "perfect families" he sees on TV. Much of the humor in this essay comes from the author's perspective as an adult looking back at his childhood self, but Soto also respects the child's point of view. In the marvelous details of this midsummer day, Soto captures the interplay of seductive myth and complex reality. Gary Soto (b. 1952) grew up "on the industrial side of Fresno, right smack against a junkyard and the junkyard's cross-eyed German shepherd." Having discovered poetry almost by chance in a city college library, he has now published eleven volumes of his own for adult readers, in addition to many volumes of fiction, nonfiction, and poetry for children and young adult readers. His *New and Selected Poems* (1995) was a finalist for both the *Los Angeles Times* Book Award and the National Book Award. Recent publications include *Facts of Life: Stories* (2008), *Partly Cloudy: Poems of Love and Longing* (2009), and the novella *When Dad Came Back* (2011).

ONE JULY, WHILE KILLING ANTS ON THE KITCHEN SINK with a rolled newspaper, I had a nine-year-old's vision of wealth that would save us from ourselves. For weeks I had drunk Kool-Aid and watched morning reruns of *Father Knows Best*, whose family was so uncomplicated in its routine that I very much wanted to imitate it. The first step was to get my brother and sister to wear shoes at dinner.

"Come on, Rick—come on, Deb," I whined. But Rick mimicked me and the same day that I asked him to wear shoes he came to the dinner table in only his swim trunks. My mother didn't notice, nor did my sister, as we sat to eat our beans and tortillas in the stifling heat of our kitchen. We all gleamed like cellophane, wiping the sweat from our brows with the backs of our hands as we talked about the day: Frankie our neighbor was beat up by Faustino; the swimming pool at the playground would be closed for a day because the pump was broken.

Such was our life. So that morning, while doing-in the train of ants which arrived each day, I decided to become wealthy, and right away! After downing a bowl of cereal, I took a rake from the garage and started up the block to look for work.

We lived on an ordinary block of mostly working class people: warehousemen, egg candlers,[1] welders, mechanics, and a union plumber. And there were many retired people who kept their lawns green and

---

[1] *egg candler:* One who inspects eggs by holding them up to a light. [All notes are the editors'.]

the gutters uncluttered of the chewing gum wrappers we dropped as we rode by on our bikes. They bent down to gather our litter, muttering at our evilness.

At the corner house I rapped the screen door and a very large woman in a muu-muu answered. She sized me up and then asked what I could do.

"Rake leaves," I answered smiling.

"It's summer, and there ain't no leaves," she countered. Her face was pinched with lines; fat jiggled under her chin. She pointed to the lawn, then the flower bed, and said: "You see any leaves there—or there?" I followed her pointing arm, stupidly. But she had a job for me and that was to get her a Coke at the liquor store. She gave me twenty cents, and after ditching my rake in a bush, off I ran. I returned with an unbagged Pepsi, for which she thanked me and gave me a nickel from her apron.

I skipped off her porch, fetched my rake, and crossed the street to the next block where Mrs. Moore, mother of Earl the retarded man, let me weed a flower bed. She handed me a trowel and for a good part of the morning my fingers dipped into the moist dirt, ripping up runners of Bermuda grass. Worms surfaced in my search for deep roots, and I cut them in halves, tossing them to Mrs. Moore's cat who pawed them playfully as they dried in the sun. I made out Earl whose face was pressed to the back window of the house, and although he was calling to me I couldn't understand what he was trying to say. Embarrassed, I worked without looking up, but I imagined his contorted mouth and the ring of keys attached to his belt—keys that jingled with each palsied step. He scared me and I worked quickly to finish the flower bed. When I did finish Mrs. Moore gave me a quarter and two peaches from her tree, which I washed there but ate in the alley behind my house.

I was sucking on the second one, a bit of juice staining the front of my T-shirt, when Little John, my best friend, came walking down the alley with a baseball bat over his shoulder, knocking over trash cans as he made his way toward me.

Little John and I went to St. John's Catholic School, where we sat among the "stupids." Miss Marino, our teacher, alternated the rows of good students with the bad, hoping that by sitting side-by-side with the bright students the stupids might become more intelligent, as though intelligence were contagious. But we didn't progress as she had hoped. She grew frustrated when one day, while dismissing class for recess, Little John couldn't get up because his arms were stuck in the slats of the chair's backrest. She scolded us with a shaking finger when we knocked over the globe, denting the already troubled Africa. She muttered curses when Leroy White, a real stupid but a great softball player with the gift to hit to all fields, openly chewed his host[2] when he made

[2]*his host:* The wafer that embodies, in the Catholic sacrament of Communion, the bread of the Last Supper and the body of Christ.

his First Communion; his hands swung at his sides as he returned to the pew looking around with a big smile.

Little John asked what I was doing, and I told him that I was taking a break from work, as I sat comfortably among high weeds. He wanted to join me, but I reminded him that the last time he'd gone door-to-door asking for work his mother had whipped him. I was with him when his mother, a New Jersey Italian who could rise up in anger one moment and love the next, told me in a polite but matter-of-fact voice that I had to leave because she was going to beat her son. She gave me a home-made popsicle, ushered me to the door, and said that I could see Little John the next day. But it was sooner than that. I went around to his bedroom window to suck my popsicle and watch Little John dodge his mother's blows, a few hitting their mark but many whirring air.

It was midday when Little John and I converged in the alley, the sun blazing in the high nineties, and he suggested that we go to Roosevelt High School to swim. He needed five cents to make fifteen, the cost of admission, and I lent him a nickel. We ran home for my bike and when my sister found out that we were going swimming, she started to cry because she didn't have the fifteen cents but only an empty Coke bottle. I waved for her to come and three of us mounted the bike—Debra on the cross bar, Little John on the handle bars and holding the Coke bottle which we would cash for a nickel and make up the difference that would allow all of us to get in, and me pumping up the crooked streets, dodging cars and pot holes. We spent the day swimming under the afternoon sun, so that when we got home our mom asked us what was darker, the floor or us? She feigned a stern posture, her hands on her hips and her mouth puckered. We played along. Looking down, Debbie and I said in unison, "Us."

That evening at dinner we all sat down in our bathing suits to eat our beans, laughing and chewing loudly. Our mom was in a good mood, so I took a risk and asked her if sometime we could have turtle soup. A few days before I had watched a television program in which a Polynesian tribe killed a large turtle, gutted it, and then stewed it over an open fire. The turtle, basted in a sugary sauce, looked delicious as I ate an afternoon bowl of cereal, but my sister, who was watching the program with a glass of Kool-Aid between her knees, said, "Caca."

My mother looked at me in bewilderment. "Boy, are you a crazy Mexican. Where did you get the idea that people eat turtles?"

"On television," I said, explaining the program. Then I took it a step 15 further. "Mom, do you think we could get dressed up for dinner one of these days? David King does."

"Ay, Dios," my mother laughed. She started collecting the dinner plates, but my brother wouldn't let go of his. He was still drawing a picture in the bean sauce. Giggling, he said it was me, but I didn't want to listen because I wanted an answer from Mom. This was the summer when I spent the mornings in front of the television that showed the comfortable lives of white kids. There were no beatings, no rifts in the family. They wore bright clothes; toys tumbled from their closets. They hopped into bed with kisses and woke to glasses of fresh orange juice, and to a father sitting before his morning coffee while the mother buttered his toast. They hurried through the day making friends and gobs of money, returning home to a warmly lit living room, and then dinner. *Leave It to Beaver* was the program I replayed in my mind:

"May I have the mashed potatoes?" asks Beaver with a smile.

"Sure, Beav," replies Wally as he taps the corners of his mouth with a starched napkin.

The father looks on in his suit. The mother, decked out in earrings and a pearl necklace, cuts into her steak and blushes. Their conversation is politely clipped.

"Swell," says Beaver, his cheeks puffed with food.   20

Our own talk at dinner was loud with belly laughs and marked by our pointing forks at one another. The subjects were commonplace.

"Gary, let's go to the ditch tomorrow," my brother suggests. He explains that he has made a life preserver out of four empty detergent bottles strung together with twine and that he will make me one if I can find more bottles. "No way are we going to drown."

"Yeah, then we could have a dirt clod fight," I reply, so happy to be alive.

Whereas the Beaver's family enjoyed dessert in dishes at the table, our mom sent us outside, and more often than not I went into the alley to peek over the neighbor's fences and spy out fruit, apricots or peaches.

I had asked my mom and again she laughed that I was a crazy   25
chavalo[3] as she stood in front of the sink, her arms rising and falling with suds, face glistening from the heat. She sent me outside where my brother and sister were sitting in the shade that the fence threw out like a blanket. They were talking about me when I plopped down next to them. They looked at one another and then Debbie, my eight-year-old sister, started in.

"What's this crap about getting dressed up?"

She had entered her *profanity* stage. A year later she would give up such words and slip into her Catholic uniform, and into squealing on my brother and me when we "cussed this" and "cussed that."

I tried to convince them that if we improved the way we looked we might get along better in life. White people would like us more. They might invite us to places, like their homes or front yards. They might not hate us so much.

My sister called me a "craphead," and got up to leave with a stalk of grass dangling from her mouth. "They'll never like us."

My brother's mood lightened as he talked about the ditch—the   30
white water, the broken pieces of glass, and the rusted car fenders that awaited our knees. There would be toads, and rocks to smash them.

[3]*chavalo:* Kid.

David King, the only person we knew who resembled the middle class, called from over the fence. David was Catholic, of Armenian and French descent, and his closet was filled with toys. A bear-shaped cookie jar, like the ones on television, sat on the kitchen counter. His mother was remarkably kind while she put up with the racket we made on the street. Evenings, she often watered the front yard and it must have upset her to see us—my brother and I and others—jump from trees laughing, the unkillable kids of the very poor, who got up unshaken, brushed off, and climbed into another one to try again.

David called again. Rick got up and slapped grass from his pants. When I asked if I could come along he said no. David said no. They were two years older so their affairs were different from mine. They greeted one another with foul names and took off down the alley to look for trouble.

I went inside the house, turned on the television, and was about to sit down with a glass of Kool-Aid when Mom shooed me outside.

"It's still light," she said. "Later you'll bug me to let you stay out longer. So go on."

I downed my Kool-Aid and went outside to the front yard. No one was around. The day had cooled and a breeze rustled the trees. Mr. Jackson, the plumber, was watering his lawn and when he saw me he turned away to wash off his front steps. There was more than an hour of light left, so I took advantage of it and decided to look for work. I felt suddenly alive as I skipped down the block in search of an overgrown flower bed and the dime that would end the day right. 35

ENGAGING THE TEXT

1. Why is the narrator attracted to the kind of family life depicted on TV? What, if anything, does he think is wrong with his life? Why do his desires apparently have so little impact on his family?

2. Why does the narrator first go looking for work? How has the meaning of work changed by the end of the story, when he goes out again "in search of an overgrown flower bed and the dime that would end the day right"? Explain.

3. As Soto looks back on his nine-year-old self, he has a different perspective on things than he had as a child. How would you characterize the mature Soto's thoughts about his childhood family life? (Was it "a good family"? What was wrong with Soto's thinking as a nine-year-old?) Back up your remarks with specific references to the narrative.

4. Review the story to find each mention of food or drink. Explain the role these references play.

5. Review the cast of "supporting characters" in this narrative—the mother, sister, brother, friends, and neighbors. What does each contribute to the story and in particular to the meaning of family within the story?

EXPLORING CONNECTIONS

6. Read Roger Jack's "An Indian Story" in the Chapter 1 e-Pages for this text (see bedfordstmartins.com/rereading/epages). Compare Soto's family to the one Roger Jack describes. In particular, consider gender roles, the household atmosphere, and the expectations placed on children and parents.

7. Compare and contrast the relationship of school and family in this narrative to that described by Mike Rose (p. 151), Richard Rodriguez (see bedford stmartins.com/rereading/epages), or Inés Hernández-Ávila (p. 198).

EXTENDING THE CRITICAL CONTEXT

8. Write a journal entry about a time when you wished your family were somehow different. What caused your dissatisfaction? What did you want your family to be like? Was your dissatisfaction ever resolved?

9. "Looking for Work" is essentially the story of a single day. Write a narrative of one day when you were eight or nine or ten; use details as Soto does to give the events of the day broader significance.

WHAT WE REALLY MISS ABOUT THE 1950s
STEPHANIE COONTZ

Popular myth has it that the 1950s were the ideal decade for the American family. In this example of academic writing at its best, Stephanie Coontz provides a clear, well-documented, and insightful analysis of what was really going on and suggests that our nostalgia for the 1950s could mislead us today. Stephanie Coontz teaches family studies and history at the Evergreen State College in Olympia, Washington. An award-winning writer and internationally recognized expert on the family, she has testified before a House Select Committee on families, appeared in several television documentaries, and published extensively for both general and scholarly audiences. Her latest book is *A Strange Stirring: The Feminine Mystique and American Women at the Dawn of the 1960s* (2011); the selection below is excerpted from her earlier study *The Way We Really Are: Coming to Terms with America's Changing Families* (1997).

IN A 1996 POLL BY THE KNIGHT-RIDDER NEWS AGENCY, more Americans chose the 1950s than any other single decade as the best time for children to grow up.[1] And despite the research I've done on the underside of 1950s families, I don't think it's crazy for people to feel nostalgic about the period. For one thing, it's easy to see why people might look back fondly to a decade when real wages grew more in any single year than in the entire ten years of the 1980s combined, a time when the average 30-year-old man could buy a median-priced home on only 15–18 percent of his salary.[2]

But it's more than just a financial issue. When I talk with modern parents, even ones who grew up in unhappy families, they associate the 1950s with a yearning they feel for a time when there were fewer complicated choices for kids or parents to grapple with, when there was more predictability in how people formed and maintained families, and when there was a coherent "moral order" in their community to serve as a reference point for family norms. Even people who found that moral order grossly unfair or repressive often say that its presence provided them with something concrete to push against.

I can sympathize entirely. One of my most empowering moments occurred the summer I turned 12, when my mother marched down to the library with me to confront a librarian who'd curtly refused to let me check out a book that was "not appropriate" for my age. "Don't you *ever* tell my daughter what she can and can't read," fumed my mom. "She's a mature young lady and she can make her own choices." In recent years I've often thought back to the gratitude I felt toward my mother for that act of trust in me. I wish I had some way of earning similar points from my own son. But much as I've always respected his values, I certainly wouldn't have walked into my local video store when he was 12 and demanded that he be allowed to check out absolutely anything he wanted!

Still, I have no illusions that I'd actually like to go back to the 1950s, and neither do most people who express such occasional nostalgia. For example, although the 1950s got more votes than any other decade in the Knight-Ridder poll, it did not win an outright majority: 38 percent of respondents picked the 1950s; 27 percent picked the 1960s or the 1970s. Voters between the ages of 50 and 64 were most likely to choose the 1950s, the decade in which they themselves came of age, as the best time for kids; voters under 30 were more likely to choose the 1970s. African Americans differed over whether the 1960s, 1970s, or 1980s were best, but all age groups of blacks agreed that later decades were definitely preferable to the 1950s.

[1]Steven Thomma, "Nostalgia for '50s Surfaces," *Philadelphia Inquirer*, Feb. 4, 1996. [All notes are Coontz's.]

[2]Frank Levy, *Dollars and Dreams: The Changing American Income Distribution* (New York: Russell Sage, 1987), p. 6; Frank Levy, "Incomes and Income Inequality," in Reynolds Farley, ed., *State of the Union: America in the 1990s*, vol. 1 (New York: Russell Sage, 1995), pp. 1–57; Richard May and Kathryn Porter, "Poverty and Income Trends, 1994," Washington, D.C.: Center on Budget and Policy Priorities, March 1996; Rob Nelson and Jon Cowan, "Buster Power," *USA Weekend*, October 14–16, 1994, p. 10.

Nostalgia for the 1950s is real and deserves to be taken seriously, but it usually shouldn't be taken literally. Even people who *do* pick the 1950s as the best decade generally end up saying, once they start discussing their feelings in depth, that it's not the family arrangements in and of themselves that they want to revive. They don't miss the way women used to be treated, they sure wouldn't want to live with most of the fathers they knew in their neighborhoods, and "come to think of it"—I don't know how many times I've recorded these exact words—"I communicate with my kids *much* better than my parents or grandparents did." When Judith Wallerstein recently interviewed 100 spouses in "happy" marriages, she found that only five "wanted a marriage like their parents'." The husbands "consciously rejected the role models provided by their fathers. The women said they could never be happy living as their mothers did."[3]

People today understandably feel that their lives are out of balance, but they yearn for something totally *new*—a more equal distribution of work, family, and community time for both men and women, children and adults. If the 1990s are lopsided in one direction, the 1950s were equally lopsided in the opposite direction.

What most people really feel nostalgic about has little to do with the internal structure of 1950s families. It is the belief that the 1950s provided a more family-friendly economic and social environment, an easier climate in which to keep kids on the straight and narrow, and above all, a greater feeling of hope for a family's long-term future, especially for its young. The contrast between the perceived hopefulness of the fifties and our own misgivings about the future is key to contemporary nostalgia for the period. Greater optimism *did* exist then, even among many individuals and groups who were in terrible circumstances. But if we are to take people's sense of loss seriously, rather than merely to capitalize on it for a hidden political agenda, we need to develop a historical perspective on where that hope came from.

Part of it came from families comparing their prospects in the 1950s to their unstable, often grindingly uncomfortable pasts, especially the two horrible decades just before. In the 1920s, after two centuries of child labor and income insecurity, and for the first time in American history, a bare majority of children had come to live in a family with a male breadwinner, a female homemaker, and a chance at a high school education. Yet no sooner did the ideals associated with such a family begin to blossom than they were buried by the stock market crash of 1929 and the Great Depression of the 1930s. During the 1930s domestic violence soared; divorce rates fell, but informal separations jumped; fertility plummeted. Murder rates were higher in 1933 than they were in the 1980s. Families were uprooted or torn apart.

[3]Judith Wallerstein and Sandra Blakeslee, *The Good Marriage: How and Why Love Lasts* (Boston: Houghton Mifflin, 1995), p. 15.

Thousands of young people left home to seek work, often riding the rails across the country.[4]

World War II brought the beginning of economic recovery, and people's renewed interest in forming families resulted in a marriage and childbearing boom, but stability was still beyond most people's grasp. Postwar communities were rocked by racial tensions, labor strife, and a right-wing backlash against the radical union movement of the 1930s. Many women resented being fired from wartime jobs they had grown to enjoy. Veterans often came home to find that they had to elbow their way back into their families, with wives and children resisting their attempts to reassert domestic authority. In one recent study of fathers who returned from the war, four times as many reported painful, even traumatic, reunions as remembered happy ones.[5]

By 1946 one in every three marriages was ending in divorce. Even couples who stayed together went through rough times, as an acute housing shortage forced families to double up with relatives or friends. Tempers frayed and generational relations grew strained. "No home is big enough to house two families, particularly two of different generations, with opposite theories on child training," warned a 1948 film on the problems of modern marriage.[6]

So after the widespread domestic strife, family disruptions, and violence of the 1930s and the instability of the World War II period, people were ready to try something new. The postwar economic boom gave them the chance. The 1950s was the first time that a majority of Americans could even *dream* of creating a secure oasis in their immediate nuclear families. There they could focus their emotional and financial investments, reduce obligations to others that might keep them from seizing their own chance at a new start, and escape the interference of an older generation of neighbors or relatives who tried to tell them how to run their lives and raise their kids. Oral histories of the postwar period resound with the theme of escaping from in-laws, maiden aunts, older parents, even needy siblings.

The private family also provided a refuge from the anxieties of the new nuclear age and the cold war, as well as a place to get away from the political witch hunts led by Senator Joe McCarthy and his allies. When having the wrong friends at the wrong time or belonging to any "suspicious" organization could ruin your career and reputation, it was safer to pull out of groups you might have joined earlier and to focus on your family. On a more positive note, the nuclear family was where

10

---

[4]Donald Hernandez, *America's Children: Resources from Family, Government and the Economy* (New York: Russell Sage, 1993), pp. 99, 102; James Morone, "The Corrosive Politics of Virtue," *American Prospect* 26 (May–June 1996), p. 37; "Study Finds U.S. No. 1 in Violence," *Olympian,* November 13, 1992. See also Stephen Mintz and Susan Kellogg, *Domestic Revolutions: A Social History of American Family Life* (New York: The Free Press, 1988).

[5]William Tuttle, Jr., *"Daddy's Gone to War": The Second World War in the Lives of America's Children* (New York: Oxford University Press, 1993).

[6]"Marriage and Divorce," *March of Time,* film series 14 (1948).

people could try to satisfy their long-pent-up desires for a more stable marriage, a decent home, and the chance to really enjoy their children.

The 1950s Family Experiment

The key to understanding the successes, failures, and comparatively short life of 1950s family forms and values is to understand the period as one of *experimentation* with the possibilities of a new kind of family, not as the expression of some longstanding tradition. At the end of the 1940s, the divorce rate, which had been rising steadily since the 1890s, dropped sharply; the age of marriage fell to a 100-year low; and the birth rate soared. Women who had worked during the Depression or World War II quit their jobs as soon as they became pregnant, which meant quite a few women were specializing in child raising; fewer women remained childless during the 1950s than in any decade since the late nineteenth century. The timing and spacing of childbearing became far more compressed, so that young mothers were likely to have two or more children in diapers at once, with no older sibling to help in their care. At the same time, again for the first time in 100 years, the educational gap between young middle-class women and men increased, while job segregation for working men and women seems to have peaked. These demographic changes increased the dependence of women on marriage, in contrast to gradual trends in the opposite direction since the early twentieth century.[7]

The result was that family life and gender roles became much more predictable, orderly, and settled in the 1950s than they were either twenty years earlier or would be twenty years later. Only slightly more than one in four marriages ended in divorce during the 1950s. Very few young people spent any extended period of time in a nonfamily setting: They moved from their parents' family into their own family, after just a brief experience with independent living, and they started having children soon after marriage. Whereas two-thirds of women aged 20 to 24 were not yet married in 1990, only 28 percent of women this age were still single in 1960.[8]

Ninety percent of all the households in the country were families 15 in the 1950s, in comparison with only 71 percent by 1990. Eighty-six percent of all children lived in two-parent homes in 1950, as opposed to just 72 percent in 1990. And the percentage living with both biological parents—rather than, say, a parent and stepparent—was

---

[7]Arlene Skolnick and Stacey Rosencrantz, "The New Crusade for the Old Family," *American Prospect,* Summer 1994, p. 65; Hernandez, *America's Children,* pp. 128–32; Andrew Cherlin, "Changing Family and Household: Contemporary Lessons from Historical Research," *Annual Review of Sociology* 9 (1983), pp. 54–58; Sam Roberts, *Who We Are: A Portrait of America Based on the Latest Census* (New York: Times Books, 1995), p. 45.

[8]Levy, "Incomes and Income Inequality," p. 20; Arthur Norton and Louisa Miller, *Marriage, Divorce, and Remarriage in the 1990s,* Current Population Reports Series P23-180 (Washington, D.C.: Bureau of the Census, October 1992); Roberts, *Who We Are* (1995 ed.), pp. 50–53.

dramatically higher than it had been at the turn of the century or is today: seventy percent in 1950, compared with only 50 percent in 1990. Nearly 60 percent of kids—an all-time high—were born into male breadwinner–female homemaker families; only a minority of the rest had mothers who worked in the paid labor force.[9]

If the organization and uniformity of family life in the 1950s were new, so were the values, especially the emphasis on putting all one's emotional and financial eggs in the small basket of the immediate nuclear family. Right up through the 1940s, ties of work, friendship, neighborhood, ethnicity, extended kin, and voluntary organizations were as important a source of identity for most Americans, and sometimes a *more* important source of obligation, than marriage and the nuclear family. All this changed in the postwar era. The spread of suburbs and automobiles, combined with the destruction of older ethnic neighborhoods in many cities, led to the decline of the neighborhood social club. Young couples moved away from parents and kin, cutting ties with traditional extrafamilial networks that might compete for their attention. A critical factor in this trend was the emergence of a group of family sociologists and marriage counselors who followed Talcott Parsons in claiming that the nuclear family, built on a sharp division of labor between husband and wife, was the cornerstone of modern society.

The new family experts tended to advocate views such as those first raised in a 1946 book, *Their Mothers' Sons,* by psychiatrist Edward Strecker. Strecker and his followers argued that American boys were infantilized and emasculated by women who were old-fashioned "moms" instead of modern "mothers." One sign that you might be that dreaded "mom," Strecker warned women, was if you felt you should take your aging parents into your own home, rather than putting them in "a good institution . . . where they will receive adequate care and comfort." Modern "mothers" placed their parents in nursing homes and poured all their energies into their nuclear family. They were discouraged from diluting their wifely and maternal commitments by maintaining "competing" interests in friends, jobs, or extended family networks, yet they were also supposed to cheerfully grant early independence to their (male) children—an emotional double bind that may explain why so many women who took this advice to heart ended up abusing alcohol or tranquilizers over the course of the decade.[10]

[9]Dennis Hogan and Daniel Lichter, "Children and Youth: Living Arrangements and Welfare," in Farley, ed., *State of the Union,* vol. 2, p. 99; Richard Gelles, *Contemporary Families: A Sociological View* (Thousand Oaks, Calif.: Sage, 1995), p. 115; Hernandez, *America's Children,* p. 102. The fact that only a small percentage of children had mothers in the paid labor force, though a full 40 percent did not live in male breadwinner–female homemaker families, was because some children had mothers who worked, unpaid, in farms or family businesses, or fathers who were unemployed, or the children were not living with both parents.

[10]Edward Strecker, *Their Mothers' Sons: The Psychiatrist Examines an American Problem* (Philadelphia: J. B. Lippincott, 1946), p. 209.

The call for young couples to break from their parents and youth-ful friends was a consistent theme in 1950s popular culture. In *Marty,* one of the most highly praised TV plays and movies of the 1950s, the hero almost loses his chance at love by listening to the carping of his mother and aunt and letting himself be influenced by old friends who resent the time he spends with his new girlfriend. In the end, he turns his back on mother, aunt, and friends to get his new marriage and a little business of his own off to a good start. Other movies, novels, and popular psychology tracts portrayed the dreadful things that happened when women became more interested in careers than marriage or men resisted domestic conformity.

Yet many people felt guilty about moving away from older parents and relatives; "modern mothers" worried that fostering independence in their kids could lead to defiance or even juvenile delinquency (the re-curring nightmare of the age); there was considerable confusion about how men and women could maintain clear breadwinner-homemaker distinctions in a period of expanding education, job openings, and con-sumer aspirations. People clamored for advice. They got it from the new family education specialists and marriage counselors, from columns in women's magazines, from government pamphlets, and above all from television. While 1950s TV melodramas warned against letting any-thing dilute the commitment to getting married and having kids, the new family sitcoms gave people nightly lessons on how to make their marriage or rapidly expanding family work—or, in the case of *I Love Lucy,* probably the most popular show of the era, how *not* to make their marriage and family work. Lucy and Ricky gave weekly comic remind-ers of how much trouble a woman could get into by wanting a career or hatching some hare-brained scheme behind her husband's back.

At the time, everyone knew that shows such as *Donna Reed, Ozzie* [20] *and Harriet, Leave It to Beaver,* and *Father Knows Best* were not the way families really were. People didn't watch those shows to see their own lives reflected back at them. They watched them to see how fami-lies were *supposed* to live—and also to get a little reassurance that they were headed in the right direction. The sitcoms were simultaneously advertisements, etiquette manuals, and how-to lessons for a new way of organizing marriage and child raising. I have studied the scripts of these shows for years, since I often use them in my classes on family history, but it wasn't until I became a parent that I felt their extraordi-nary pull. The secret of their appeal, I suddenly realized, was that they offered 1950s viewers, wracked with the same feelings of parental inad-equacy as was I, the promise that there were easy answers and surefire techniques for raising kids.

Ever since, I have found it useful to think of the sitcoms as the 1950s equivalent of today's beer ads. As most people know, beer ads are con-sciously aimed at men who *aren't* as strong and sexy as the models in the commercials, guys who are uneasily aware of the gap between the ideal masculine pursuits and their own achievements. The promise is that if the viewers on the couch will just drink brand X, they too will be able to run 10 miles without gasping for breath. Their bodies will firm up, their complexions will clear up, and maybe the Swedish bikini team will come over and hang out at their place.

Similarly, the 1950s sitcoms were aimed at young couples who had married in haste, women who had tasted new freedoms during World War II and given up their jobs with regret, veterans whose children resented their attempts to reassert paternal authority, and individuals disturbed by the changing racial and ethnic mix of postwar America. The message was clear: Buy these ranch houses, Hotpoint appliances, and child-raising ideals; relate to your spouse like this; get a new car to wash with your kids on Sunday afternoons; organize your dinners like that—and you too can escape from the conflicts of race, class, and political witch hunts into harmonious families where father knows best, mothers are never bored or irritated, and teenagers rush to the dinner table each night, eager to get their latest dose of parental wisdom.

Many families found it possible to put together a good imitation of this way of living during the 1950s and 1960s. Couples were often able to construct marriages that were much more harmonious than those in which they had grown up, and to devote far more time to their children. Even when marriages were deeply unhappy, as many were, the new stability, economic security, and educational advantages parents were able to offer their kids counted for a lot in people's assessment of their life satisfaction. And in some matters, ignorance could be bliss: The lack of media coverage of problems such as abuse or incest was terribly hard on the casualties, but it protected more fortunate families from knowledge and fear of many social ills.[11]

There was tremendous hostility to people who could be defined as "others": Jews, African Americans, Puerto Ricans, the poor, gays or lesbians, and "the red menace." Yet on a day-to-day basis, the civility that prevailed in homogeneous neighborhoods allowed people to ignore larger patterns of racial and political repression. Racial clashes were ever-present in the 1950s, sometimes escalating into full-scale antiblack riots, but individual homicide rates fell to almost half the levels of the 1930s. As nuclear families moved into the suburbs, they retreated from social activism but entered voluntary relationships with people who had children the same age; they became involved in PTAs together, joined bridge clubs, went bowling. There does seem to have been a stronger sense of neighborly commonalities than many of us feel today. Even though this local community was often the product of exclusion or repression, it sometimes looks attractive to modern Americans whose

[11]For discussion of the discontents, and often searing misery, that were considered normal in a "good-enough" marriage in the 1950s and 1960s, see Lillian Rubin, *Worlds of Pain: Life in the Working-Class Family* (New York: Basic Books, 1976); Mirra Komarovsky, *Blue Collar Marriage* (New Haven, Conn.: Vintage, 1962); Elaine Tyler May, *Homeward Bound: American Families in the Cold War Era* (New York: Basic Books, 1988).

commutes are getting longer and whose family or work patterns give them little in common with their neighbors.[12]

The optimism that allowed many families to rise above their internal difficulties and to put limits on their individualistic values during the 1950s came from the sense that America was on a dramatically different trajectory than it had been in the past, an upward and expansionary path that had already taken people to better places than they had ever seen before and would certainly take their children even further. This confidence that almost everyone could look forward to a better future stands in sharp contrast to how most contemporary Americans feel, and it explains why a period in which many people were much worse off than today sometimes still looks like a better period for families than our own.

Throughout the 1950s, poverty was higher than it is today, but it was less concentrated in pockets of blight existing side-by-side with extremes of wealth, and, unlike today, it was falling rather than rising. At the end of the 1930s, almost two-thirds of the population had incomes below the poverty standards of the day, while only one in eight had a middle-class income (defined as two to five times the poverty line). By 1960, a majority of the population had climbed into the middle-income range.[13]

Unmarried people were hardly sexually abstinent in the 1950s, but the age of first intercourse was somewhat higher than it is now, and despite a tripling of nonmarital birth rates between 1940 and 1958, more than 70 percent of nonmarital pregnancies led to weddings before the child was born. Teenage birth rates were almost twice as high in 1957 as in the 1990s, but most teen births were to married couples, and the effect of teen pregnancy in reducing further schooling for young people did not hurt their life prospects the way it does today. High school graduation rates were lower in the 1950s than they are today, and minority students had far worse test scores, but there were jobs for people who dropped out of high school or graduated without good reading skills—jobs that actually had a future. People entering the job market

[12]See Robert Putnam, "The Strange Disappearance of Civic America," *American Prospect,* Winter 1996. For a glowing if somewhat lopsided picture of 1950s community solidarities, see Alan Ehrenhalt, *The Lost City: Discovering the Forgotten Virtues of Community in the Chicago of the 1950s* (New York: Basic Books, 1995). For a chilling account of communities uniting against perceived outsiders, in the same city, see Arnold Hirsch, *Making the Second Ghetto: Race and Housing in Chicago, 1940–1960* (Cambridge, Mass.: Harvard University Press, 1983). On homicide rates, see "Study Finds United States No. 1 in Violence," *Olympian,* November 13, 1992; *New York Times,* November 13, 1992, p. A9; and Douglas Lee Eckberg, "Estimates of Early Twentieth-Century U.S. Homicide Rates: An Econometric Forecasting Approach," *Demography* 32 (1995), p. 14. On lengthening commutes, see "It's Taking Longer to Get to Work," *Olympian,* December 6, 1995.

[13]The figures in this and the following paragraph come from Levy, "Incomes and Income Inequality," pp. 1–57; May and Porter, "Poverty and Income Trends, 1994"; Reynolds Farley, *The New American Reality: Who We Are, How We Got Here, Where We Are Going* (New York: Russell Sage, 1996), pp. 83–85; Gelles, *Contemporary Families,* p. 115; David Grissmer, Sheila Nataraj Kirby, Mark Bender, and Stephanie Williamson, *Student Achievement and the Changing American Family,* Rand Institute on Education and Training (Santa Monica, Calif.: Rand, 1994), p. 106.

in the 1950s had no way of knowing that they would be the last generation to have a good shot at reaching middle-class status without the benefit of postsecondary schooling.

Millions of men from impoverished, rural, unemployed, or poorly educated family backgrounds found steady jobs in the steel, auto, appliance, construction, and shipping industries. Lower-middle-class men went further on in college during the 1950s than they would have been able to expect in earlier decades, enabling them to make the transition to secure white-collar work. The experience of shared sacrifices in the Depression and war, reinforced by a New Deal–inspired belief in the ability of government to make life better, gave people a sense of hope for the future. Confidence in government, business, education, and other institutions was on the rise. This general optimism affected people's experience and assessment of family life. It is no wonder modern Americans yearn for a similar sense of hope.

But before we sign on to any attempts to turn the family clock back to the 1950s we should note that the family successes and community solidarities of the 1950s rested on a totally different set of political and economic conditions than we have today. Contrary to widespread belief, the 1950s was not an age of laissez-faire government and free market competition. A major cause of the social mobility of young families in the 1950s was that federal assistance programs were much more generous and widespread than they are today.

In the most ambitious and successful affirmative action program 30 ever adopted in America, 40 percent of young men were eligible for veterans' benefits, and these benefits were far more extensive than those available to Vietnam-era vets. Financed in part by a federal income tax on the rich that went up to 87 percent and a corporate tax rate of 52 percent, such benefits provided quite a jump start for a generation of young families. The GI bill paid most tuition costs for vets who attended college, doubling the percentage of college students from prewar levels. At the other end of the life span, Social Security began to build up a significant safety net for the elderly, formerly the poorest segment of the population. Starting in 1950, the federal government regularly mandated raises in the minimum wage to keep pace with inflation. The minimum wage may have been only $1.40 as late as 1968, but a person who worked for that amount full-time, year-round, earned 118 percent of the poverty figure for a family of three. By 1995, a full-time minimum-wage worker could earn only 72 percent of the poverty level.[14]

[14]William Chafe, *The Unfinished Journey: America Since World War II* (New York: Oxford University Press, 1986), pp. 113, 143; Marc Linder, "Eisenhower-Era Marxist-Confiscatory Taxation: Requiem for the Rhetoric of Rate Reduction for the Rich," *Tulane Law Review* 70 (1996), p. 917; Barry Bluestone and Teresa Ghilarducci, "Rewarding Work: Feasible Antipoverty Policy," *American Prospect* 28 (1996), p. 42; Theda Skocpol, "Delivering for Young Families," *American Prospect* 28 (1996), p. 67.

An important source of the economic expansion of the 1950s was that public works spending at all levels of government comprised nearly 20 percent of total expenditures in 1950, as compared to less than 7 percent in 1984. Between 1950 and 1960, nonmilitary, nonresidential public construction rose by 58 percent. Construction expenditures for new schools (in dollar amounts adjusted for inflation) rose by 72 percent; funding on sewers and waterworks rose by 46 percent. Government paid 90 percent of the costs of building the new Interstate Highway System. These programs opened up suburbia to growing numbers of middle-class Americans and created secure, well-paying jobs for blue-collar workers.[15]

Government also reorganized home financing, underwriting low down payments and long-term mortgages that had been rejected as bad business by private industry. To do this, government put public assets behind housing lending programs, created two new national financial institutions to facilitate home loans, allowed veterans to put down payments as low as a dollar on a house, and offered tax breaks to people who bought homes. The National Education Defense Act funded the

[15]Joel Tarr, "The Evolution of the Urban Infrastructure in the Nineteenth and Twentieth Centuries," in Royce Hanson, ed., *Perspectives on Urban Infrastructure* (Washington, D.C.: National Academy Press, 1984); Mark Aldrich, *A History of Public Works Investment in the United States,* report prepared by the CPNSAD Research Corporation for the U.S. Department of Commerce, April 1980.

socioeconomic mobility of thousands of young men who trained them-selves for well-paying jobs in such fields as engineering.[16]

Unlike contemporary welfare programs, government investment in 1950s families was not just for immediate subsistence but encouraged long-term asset development, rewarding people for increasing their in-vestment in homes and education. Thus it was far less likely that such families or individuals would ever fall back to where they started, even after a string of bad luck. Subsidies for higher education were greater the longer people stayed in school and the more expensive the school they selected. Mortgage deductions got bigger as people traded up to better houses.[17]

These social and political support systems magnified the impact of the postwar economic boom. "In the years between 1947 and 1973," reports economist Robert Kuttner, "the median paycheck more than doubled, and the bottom 20 percent enjoyed the greatest gains." High rates of unionization meant that blue-collar workers were making much more financial progress than most of their counterparts today. In 1952, when eager home buyers flocked to the opening of Levittown, Pennsylvania, the largest planned community yet constructed, "it took a factory worker one day to earn enough money to pay the closing costs on a new Levittown house, then selling for $10,000." By 1991, such a home was selling for $100,000 or more, and it took a factory worker *eighteen weeks* to earn enough money for just the closing costs.[18]

The legacy of the union struggle of the 1930s and 1940s, combined with government support for raising people's living standards, set limits on corporations that have disappeared in recent decades. Corporations paid 23 percent of federal income taxes in the 1950s, as compared to just 9.2 percent in 1991. Big companies earned higher profit margins than smaller firms, partly due to their dominance of the market, partly to America's postwar economic advantage. They chose (or were forced) to share these extra earnings, which economists call "rents," with em-ployees. Economists at the Brookings Institution and Harvard University estimate that 70 percent of such corporate rents were passed on to workers at all levels of the firm, benefiting secretaries and janitors as well as CEOs. Corporations routinely retained workers even in slack periods, as a way of ensuring workplace stability. Although they often received more generous tax breaks from communities than they gave back in investment, at least they kept their plants and employment of-fices in the same place. AT&T, for example, received much of the tech-

35

---

[16]For more information on this government financing, see Kenneth Jackson, *Crabgrass Frontier: The Suburbanization of the United States* (New York: Oxford University Press, 1985); and *The Way We Never Were*, chapter 4.

[17]John Cook and Laura Sherman, "Economic Security Among America's Poor: The Impact of State Welfare Waivers on Asset Accumulation," Center on Hunger, Poverty, and Nutrition Policy, Tufts University, May 1996.

[18]Robert Kuttner, "The Incredible Shrinking American Paycheck," *Washington Post National Weekly Edition*, November 6–12, 1995, p. 23; Donald Bartlett and James Steele, *America: What Went Wrong?* (Kansas City: Andrews McMeel, 1992), p. 20.

nology it used to finance its postwar expansion from publicly funded communications research conducted as part of the war effort, and, as current AT&T Chairman Robert Allen puts it, there "used to be a life-long commitment on the employee's part and on our part." Today, how-ever, he admits, "the contract doesn't exist anymore."[19]

Television trivia experts still argue over exactly what the fathers in many 1950s sitcoms did for a living. Whatever it was, though, they ob-viously didn't have to worry about downsizing. If most married people stayed in long-term relationships during the 1950s, so did most corpora-tions, sticking with the communities they grew up in and the employ-ees they originally hired. Corporations were not constantly relocating in search of cheap labor during the 1950s; unlike today, increases in worker productivity usually led to increases in wages. The number of workers covered by corporate pension plans and health benefits in-creased steadily. So did limits on the work week. There is good reason that people look back to the 1950s as a less hurried age: The average American was working a shorter workday in the 1950s than his or her counterpart today, when a quarter of the workforce puts in 49 or more hours a week.[20]

So politicians are practicing quite a double standard when they tell us to return to the family forms of the 1950s while they do nothing to restore the job programs and family subsidies of that era, the limits on corporate relocation and financial wheeling-dealing, the much higher share of taxes paid by corporations then, the availability of union jobs for noncollege youth, and the subsidies for higher education such as the National Defense Education Act loans. Furthermore, they're not telling the whole story when they claim that the 1950s was the most prosper-ous time for families and the most secure decade for children. Instead, playing to our understandable nostalgia for a time when things seemed to be getting better, not worse, they engage in a tricky chronological shell game with their figures, diverting our attention from two impor-tant points. First, many individuals, families, and groups were excluded from the economic prosperity, family optimism, and social civility of the 1950s. Second, the all-time high point of child well-being and fam-ily economic security came not during the 1950s but *at the end of the 1960s.*

[19]Richard Barnet, "Lords of the Global Economy," *Nation,* December 19, 1994, p. 756; Clay Chandler, "U.S. Corporations: Good Citizens or Bad?" *Washington Post National Weekly Edition,* May 20–26, 1996, p. 16; Steven Pearlstein, "No More Mr. Nice Guy: Corporate America Has Done an About-Face in How It Pays and Treats Employees," *Washington Post National Weekly Edition,* December 18–24, 1995, p. 10; Robert Kuttner, "Ducking Class Warfare," *Washington Post National Weekly Edition,* March 11–17, 1996, p. 5; Henry Allen, "Ha! So Much for Loyalty," *Washington Post National Weekly Edition,* March 4–10, 1996, p. 11.

[20]Ehrenhalt, *The Lost City,* pp. 11–12; Jeremy Rifken, *The End of Work: The Decline of the Global Labor Force and the Dawn of the Post-Market Era* (New York: G. P. Putnam's Sons, 1995), pp. 169, 170, 231; Juliet Schorr, *The Overworked American: The Unexpected Decline of Leisure* (New York: Basic Books, 1991).

We now know that 1950s family culture was not only nontraditional; it was also not idyllic. In important ways, the stability of family and community life during the 1950s rested on pervasive discrimination against women, gays, political dissidents, non-Christians, and racial or ethnic minorities, as well as on a systematic cover-up of the underside of many families. Families that were harmonious and fair of their own free will may have been able to function more easily in the fifties, but few alternatives existed for members of discordant or oppressive families. Victims of child abuse, incest, alcoholism, spousal rape, and wife battering had no recourse, no place to go, until well into the 1960s.[21]

At the end of the 1950s, despite ten years of economic growth, 27.3 percent of the nation's children were poor, including those in white "underclass" communities such as Appalachia. Almost 50 percent of married-couple African American families were impoverished—a figure far higher than today. It's no wonder African Americans are not likely to pick the 1950s as a golden age, even in comparison with the setbacks they experienced in the 1980s. When blacks moved north to find jobs in the postwar urban manufacturing boom they met vicious harassment and violence, first to prevent them from moving out of the central cities, then to exclude them from public space such as parks or beaches.

In Philadelphia, for example, the City of Brotherly Love, there were more than 200 racial incidents over housing in the first six months of 1955 alone. The Federal Housing Authority, such a boon to white working-class families, refused to insure homes in all-black or in racially mixed neighborhoods. Two-thirds of the city dwellers evicted by the urban renewal projects of the decade were African Americans and Latinos; government did almost nothing to help such displaced families find substitute housing.[22]

Women were unable to take out loans or even credit cards in their own names. They were excluded from juries in many states. A lack of options outside marriage led some women to remain in desperately unhappy unions that were often not in the best interests of their children or themselves. Even women in happy marriages often felt humiliated by the constant messages they received that their whole lives had to revolve around a man. "You are not ready when he calls—miss one turn," was a rule in the Barbie game marketed to 1950s girls; "he criticizes your hairdo—go to the beauty shop." Episodes of *Father Knows Best* advised young women: "The worst thing you can do is to try to

---

[21]For documentation that these problems existed, see chapter 2 of *The Way We Never Were*.

[22]The poverty figures come from census data collected in *The State of America's Children Yearbook, 1996* (Washington, D.C.: Children's Defense Fund, 1996), p. 77. See also Hirsch, *Making the Second Ghetto*; Raymond Mohl, "Making the Second Ghetto in Metropolitan Miami, 1940–1960," *Journal of Urban History* 25 (1995), p. 396; Micaela di Leonardo, "Boys on the Hood," *Nation*, August 17–24, 1992, p. 180; Jackson, *Crabgrass Frontier*, pp. 226–227.

beat a man at his own game. You just beat the women at theirs." One character on the show told women to always ask themselves, "Are you after a job or a man? You can't have both."[23]

The Fifties Experiment Comes to an End

The social stability of the 1950s, then, was a response to the stick of racism, sexism, and repression as well as to the carrot of economic opportunity and government aid. Because social protest mounted in the 1960s and unsettling challenges were posed to the gender roles and sexual mores of the previous decade, many people forget that families continued to make gains throughout the 1960s and into the first few years of the 1970s. By 1969, child poverty was down to 14 percent, its lowest level ever; it hovered just above that marker until 1975, when it began its steady climb up to contemporary figures (22 percent in 1993; 21.2 percent in 1994). The high point of health and nutrition for poor children was reached in the early 1970s.[24]

So commentators are being misleading when they claim that the 1950s was the golden age of American families. They are disregarding the number of people who were excluded during that decade and ignoring the socioeconomic gains that continued to be made through the 1960s. But they are quite right to note that the improvements of the 1950s and 1960s came to an end at some point in the 1970s (though not for the elderly, who continued to make progress).

Ironically, it was the children of those stable, enduring, supposedly idyllic 1950s families, the recipients of so much maternal time and attention, that pioneered the sharp break with their parents' family forms and gender roles in the 1970s. This was not because they were led astray by some youthful Murphy Brown in her student rebel days or inadvertently spoiled by parents who read too many of Dr. Spock's child-raising manuals.

Partly, the departure from 1950s family arrangements was a logical extension of trends and beliefs pioneered in the 1950s, or of inherent contradictions in those patterns. For example, early and close-spaced childbearing freed more wives up to join the labor force, and married women began to flock to work. By 1960, more than 40 percent of women over the age of 16 held a job, and working mothers were the fastest growing component of the labor force. The educational aspirations and opportunities that opened up for kids of the baby boom could not be confined to males, and many tight-knit, male-breadwinner,

45

[23]Susan Douglas, *Where the Girls Are: Growing Up Female with the Mass Media* (New York: Times Books, 1994), pp. 25, 37.
[24]*The State of America's Children Yearbook, 1966*, p. 77; May and Porter, "Poverty and Income Trends: 1994," p. 23; Sara McLanahan et al., *Losing Ground: A Critique*, University of Wisconsin Institute for Research on Poverty, Special Report No. 38, 1985.

nuclear families in the 1950s instilled in their daughters the ambition to be something other than a homemaker.[25]

Another part of the transformation was a shift in values. Most people would probably agree that some changes in values were urgently needed: the extension of civil rights to racial minorities and to women; a rejection of property rights in children by parents and in women by husbands; a reaction against the political intolerance and the wasteful materialism of 1950s culture. Other changes in values remain more controversial: opposition to American intervention abroad; repudiation of the traditional sexual double standard; rebellion against what many young people saw as the hypocrisy of parents who preached sexual morality but ignored social immorality such as racism and militarism.

Still other developments, such as the growth of me-first individualism, are widely regarded as problematic by people on all points along the political spectrum. It's worth noting, though, that the origins of antisocial individualism and self-indulgent consumerism lay at least as much in the family values of the 1950s as in the youth rebellion of the 1960s. The marketing experts who never allowed the kids in *Ozzie and Harriet* sitcoms to be shown drinking milk, for fear of offending soft-drink companies that might sponsor the show in syndication, were ultimately the same people who slightly later invested billions of dollars to channel sexual rebelliousness and a depoliticized individualism into mainstream culture.

There were big cultural changes brewing by the beginning of the 1970s, and tremendous upheavals in social, sexual, and family values. And yes, there were sometimes reckless or simply laughable excesses in some of the early experiments with new gender roles, family forms, and personal expression. But the excesses of 1950s gender roles and family forms were every bit as repellent and stupid as the excesses of the sixties: Just watch a dating etiquette film of the time period, or recall that therapists of the day often told victims of incest that they were merely having unconscious oedipal fantasies.

Ultimately, though, changes in values were not what brought the 1950s family experiment to an end. The postwar family compacts between husbands and wives, parents and children, young and old, were based on the postwar social compact between government, corporations, and workers. While there was some discontent with those family bargains among women and youth, the old relations did not really start to unravel until people began to face the erosion of the corporate wage bargain and government broke its tacit societal bargain that it would continue to invest in jobs and education for the younger generation.

---

[25]For studies of how both middle-class and working-class women in the 1950s quickly departed from, or never quite accepted, the predominant image of women, see Joanne Meyerowitz, ed., *Not June Cleaver: Women and Gender in Postwar America, 1945–1960* (Philadelphia: Temple University Press, 1994).

In the 1970s, new economic trends began to clash with all the social expectations that 1950s families had instilled in their children. That clash, not the willful abandonment of responsibility and commitment, has been the primary cause of both family rearrangements and the growing social problems that are usually attributed to such family changes, but in fact have *separate* origins.

ENGAGING THE TEXT

1. According to Coontz, what do we really miss about the 1950s? In addition, what *don't* we miss?

2. In Coontz's view, what was the role of the government in making the 1950s in America what they were? What part did broader historical forces or other circumstances play?

3. Although she concentrates on the 1950s, Coontz also describes the other decades from the 1920s to the 1990s, when she wrote this piece. Use her information to create a brief chart naming the key characteristics of each decade. Then consider your own family history and see how well it fits the pattern Coontz outlines. Discuss the results with classmates or write a journal entry reflecting on what you learn.

4. Consider the most recent ten years of American history. What events or trends (for example, same-sex marriage legislation, financial crises, the Obama presidency) do you think a sociologist or cultural historian might consider important for understanding our current mythologies of family? How do you think our ideas about family have changed in this decade?

EXPLORING CONNECTIONS

5. Study the photo from *The Donna Reed Show* (p. 17) and the Norman Rockwell painting *Freedom from Want* (p. 58), comparing these iconic images to the account Coontz provides. How does Coontz help us understand such images in a cultural context? If the images seem like quaint artifacts, do you think the values they project still appeal to Americans?

6. Review "Looking for Work" by Gary Soto (p. 22). How does this narrative evoke nostalgia for a simpler, better era for families? Does it reveal any of the problems with the 1950s that Coontz describes?

EXTENDING THE CRITICAL CONTEXT

7. Coontz suggests that an uninformed nostalgia for the 1950s could promote harmful political agendas. (See, for example, paras. 7 and 37.) Do you see any evidence in contemporary media of nostalgia for the 1950s? Do you agree with Coontz that such nostalgia can be dangerous? Why or why not?

8. Watch an episode of a 1950s sitcom such as *Father Knows Best*, *The Donna Reed Show*, *Leave It to Beaver*, or *I Love Lucy*. Analyze the extent to which

it reveals both positive and negative aspects of the 1950s that Coontz discusses (for example, an authoritarian father figure, limited roles for wives, economic prosperity, or a sense of a secure community).

AUNT IDA PIECES A QUILT
MELVIN DIXON

This is an extraordinary poem about AIDS, love, and family life. Its author, Melvin Dixon (1950–1992), received his Ph.D. from Brown University; in addition to teaching English at Queens College in New York, he published poetry, literary criticism, translations, and two novels. "Aunt Ida" appeared in *Brother to Brother: New Writings by Black Gay Men* (1991). Dixon died of complications from AIDS in 1992.

You are right, but your patch isn't big enough.—JESSE JACKSON

When a cure is found and the last panel is sewn into place, the Quilt will be displayed in a permanent home as a national monument to the individual, irreplaceable people lost to AIDS—and the people who knew and loved them most.
—CLEVE JONES, *founder*, THE NAMES PROJECT

They brought me some of his clothes. The hospital gown,
those too-tight dungarees, his blue choir robe
with the gold sash. How that boy could sing!
His favorite color in a necktie. A Sunday shirt.
What I'm gonna do with all this stuff?   5
I can remember Junie without this business.
My niece Francine say they quilting all over the country.
So many good boys like her boy, gone.

At my age I ain't studying no needle and thread.
My eyes ain't so good now and my fingers lock in a fist,   10
they so eaten up with arthritis. This old back
don't take kindly to bending over a frame no more.
Francine say ain't I a mess carrying on like this.
I could make two quilts the time I spend running my mouth.

Just cut his name out the cloths, stitch something nice   15
about him. Something to bring him back. You can do it,
Francine say. Best sewing our family ever had.

Quilting ain't that easy, I say. Never was easy.
Y'all got to help me remember him good.

Most of my quilts was made down South. My mama   20
And my mama's mama taught me. Popped me on the tail
if I missed a stitch or threw the pattern out of line.
I did "Bright Star" and "Lonesome Square" and "Rally Round,"
what many folks don't bother with nowadays. Then Elmo and me
married and came North where the cold in Connecticut   25
cuts you like a knife. We was warm, though.
We had sackcloth and calico and cotton, 100% pure.
What they got now but polyester rayon. Factory made.

Let me tell you something. In all my quilts there's a secret
nobody knows. Every last one of them got my name Ida   30
stitched on the back side in red thread.
That's where Junie got his flair. Don't let nobody fool you.
When he got the Youth Choir standing up and singing
the whole church would rock. He'd throw up his hands
from them wide blue sleeves and the church would hush   35
right down to the funeral parlor fans whisking the air.
He'd toss his head back and holler and we'd all cry holy.

And nevermind his too-tight dungarees.
I caught him switching down the street one Saturday night,
and I seen him more than once. I said, Junie,   40
you ain't got to let the world know all your business.
Who cared where he went when he wanted to have fun.
He'd be singing his heart out come Sunday morning.

When Francine say she gonna hang this quilt in the church
I like to fall out. A quilt ain't no showpiece,   45
it's to keep you warm. Francine say it can do both.
Now I ain't so old-fashioned I can't change,
but I made Francine come over and bring her daughter
Belinda. We cut and tacked his name, *JUNIE.*
Just plain and simple, *"JUNIE, our boy."*   50
Cut the *J* in blue, the *U* in gold. *N* in dungarees
just as tight as you please. The *I* from the hospital gown
and the white shirt he wore First Sunday. Belinda
put the necktie in *E* in the cross stitch I showed her.

Wouldn't you know we got to talking about Junie.   55
We could smell him in the cloth.
Underarm. Afro Sheen pomade.[1] Gravy stains.
I forgot all about my arthritis.

---

[1] *Afro Sheen pomade:* Hair-care product for African Americans. [Eds.]

When Francine left me to finish up, I swear
I heard Junie giggling right along with me   60
as I stitched Ida on the back side in red thread.

Francine say she gonna send this quilt to Washington
like folks doing from all 'cross the country,
so many good people gone. Babies, mothers, fathers
and boys like our Junie. Francine say   65
they gonna piece this quilt to another one,
another name and another patch
all in a larger quilt getting larger and larger.

Maybe we all like that, patches waiting to be pieced.
Well, I don't know about Washington.   70
We need Junie here with us. And Maxine,
she cousin May's husband's sister's people,
she having a baby and here comes winter already.
The cold cutting like knives. Now where did I put that needle?

ENGAGING THE TEXT

1. Identify all of the characters and their relationships in the poem. Then retell the story of the poem in your own words.

2. Discuss the movement of Aunt Ida's mind and her emotions as we move from stanza to stanza. What happens to Aunt Ida in the poem? What is the dominant feeling at the end of the poem?

3. Junie's clothes take on symbolic weight in the quilt and, of course, in the poem as well. What do the hospital gown, the dungarees, the choir robe, and the white shirt and necktie represent?

4. What is Aunt Ida about to make at the end of the poem, and what is its significance?

EXPLORING CONNECTIONS

5. Look at the images in this chapter's Visual Portfolio (p. 57). Discuss how you might tell the story of "Aunt Ida Pieces a Quilt" visually instead of ver-bally—for example, as a painting, a mural, a photograph, or a photo essay. Sketch or draw an image based on the poem and share it with classmates.

6. What roles do women play in "Aunt Ida Pieces a Quilt"? Compare these roles to those played by women in Gary Soto's "Looking for Work" (p. 22), and "What We Really Miss About the 1950s" by Stephanie Coontz (p. 27). Based on these examples, would it be fair to conclude that Americans see "the family" as predominantly a woman's responsibility?

EXTENDING THE CRITICAL CONTEXT

7. Write a screenplay or dramatic script to "translate" the story of "Aunt Ida Pieces a Quilt" into dramatic form. Time permitting, organize a group to read or perform the piece for the class.

8. Watch the documentary *Common Threads: Stories from the Quilt* and write a poem based on the life of one of the people profiled in this film.

THE COLOR OF FAMILY TIES: RACE, CLASS, GENDER, AND EXTENDED FAMILY INVOLVEMENT

NAOMI GERSTEL AND NATALIA SARKISIAN

The myth of the nuclear family is not just a harmless cliché; rather, it can lock us into fundamental misunderstandings of how American families live, misunderstandings that can divide groups and promote simplistic public policy. In this study, sociologists Naomi Gerstel and Natalia Sarkisian examine data on black, white, and Latino / Latina families to challenge the popular notion that minority families have weaker ties and are more fragmented than white families. They find that social class is more important than ethnicity; moreover, while differences between ethnic groups do exist, each group has developed ways to cope with the practical, emotional, and financial challenges they face and to maintain family solidarity. Gerstel and Sarkisian are professors of sociology, Gerstel at the University of Massachusetts, Amherst, and Sarkisian at Boston College. Their coauthored article on gender, employment, and help given to parents (in *Journal of Marriage and the Family*, 2004) won the 2005 Rosabeth Moss Kanter International Award for Research Excellence in Families and Work. "The Color of Family Ties" appeared in *American Families: A Multicultural Reader*, edited by Stephanie Coontz (see p. 27) with Maya Parson and Gabrielle Raley (2008).

WHEN TALKING ABOUT FAMILY OBLIGATIONS and solidarities, politicians and social commentators typically focus on the ties between married couples and their children. We often hear that Black and Latino/a, especially Puerto Rican, families are more disorganized than White families, and that their family ties are weaker, because rates of non-marriage and single parenthood are higher among these minority

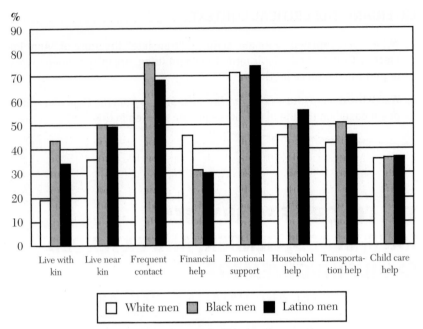

Figure 1. Ethnicity and extended kin involvement among men.
Source: National Survey of Families and Households, 1992–94.

groups. But this focus on the nuclear family ignores extended family solidarities and caregiving activities. Here we examine these often overlooked extended kinship ties.[1]

Taking this broader perspective on family relations refutes the myth that Blacks and Latinos/as lack strong families. Minority individuals are more likely to live in extended family homes than Whites and in many ways more likely to help out their aging parents, grandparents, adult children, brothers, sisters, cousins, aunts, uncles, and other kin.

[1]For the extensive analysis underlying this discussion, see: (1) Natalia Sarkisian, Mariana Gerena, and Naomi Gerstel, "Extended Family Integration among Mexican and Euro Americans: Ethnicity, Gender, and Class," *Journal of Marriage and Family*, 69 (2007), 1 (February), 40–54. (2) Natalia Sarkisian, Mariana Gerena, and Naomi Gerstel, "Extended Family Ties among Mexicans, Puerto Ricans and Whites: Superintegration or Disintegration?," *Family Relations*, 55 (2006), 3 (July), 331–344. (3) Natalia Sarkisian and Naomi Gerstel, "Kin Support Among Blacks and Whites: Race and Family Organization," *American Sociological Review*, 69 (2004), 4 (December), 812–837. (4) Amy Armenia and Naomi Gerstel, "Family Leaves, The FMLA, and Gender Neutrality: The Intersection of Race and Gender," *Social Science Research*, 35 (2006), 871–891. (5) Naomi Gerstel and Natalia Sarkisian, "A Sociological Perspective on Families and Work: The Import of Gender, Class, and Race," in Marcie Pitt Catsouphes, Ellen Kossek, and Steven Sweet (eds.), *The Work and Family Handbook: Multi-disciplinary Perspectives, Methods, and Approaches* (Mahwah, NJ: Lawrence Erlbaum, 2006), pp. 237–266. (6) Naomi Gerstel and Natalia Sarkisian, "Marriage: The Good, the Bad, and the Greedy," *Contexts*, 5 (2006) 4 (November), 16–21. (7) Naomi Gerstel and Natalia Sarkisian, "Intergenerational Care and the Greediness of Adult Children's Marriages," in J. Suitor and T. Owens (eds.), *Interpersonal Relations across the Life Course. Advances in the Life Course Research*, Volume 12 (Greenwich, CT: Elsevier/JAI Press, 2007). [Gerstel and Sarkisian's note.]

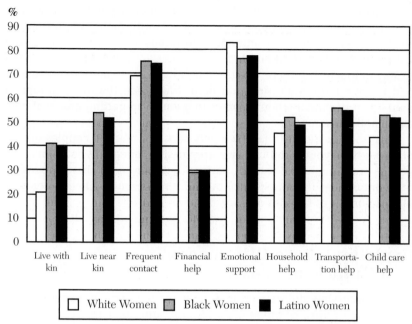

Figure 2.   Ethnicity and extended kin involvement among women.
Source: National Survey of Families and Households, 1992–94.

According to our research using the second wave of the National Survey of Families and Households, as Figures 1 and 2 show, Blacks and Latinos/as, both women and men, are much more likely than Whites to share a home with extended kin: 42 percent of Blacks and 37 percent of Latinos/as, but only 20 percent of Whites, live with relatives. Similar patterns exist for living near relatives: 54 percent of Blacks and 51 percent of Latinos/as, but only 37 percent of Whites, live within two miles of kin. Blacks and Latinos/as are also more likely than Whites to frequently visit kin. For example, 76 percent of Blacks, 71 percent of Latinos/as, but just 63 percent of Whites see their relatives once a week or more.

Even if they don't live together, Blacks and Latinos/as are as likely as Whites—and in some ways more likely—to be supportive family members. But there are important racial and ethnic differences in the type of support family members give each other. Whites are more likely than ethnic minorities to give and receive large sums of money, and White women are more likely than minority women to give and receive emotional support, such as discussing personal problems and giving each other advice. When it comes to help with practical tasks, however, we find that Black and Latino/a relatives are more likely than Whites to be supportive: they are more likely to give each other help with household work and child care, as well as with providing rides and running errands. These differences are especially pronounced among women.

This is not to say that Black and Latino men are not involved with kin, as is implied in popular images of minority men hanging out on street corners rather than attending to family ties. In fact, Black and Latino men are more likely than White men to live near relatives and to stay in touch with them. White men, however, are more likely to give and receive large-scale financial help. Moreover, the three groups of men are very similar when it comes to giving and getting practical help and emotional support.

These data suggest that if we only consider married couples or parents and their young children, we are missing much of what families in general and families of color in particular do for each other. A focus on nuclear families in discussions of race differences in family life creates a biased portrait of families of color.

Explaining Race Differences: Is It Culture or Class?

When discussing differences in family experiences of various racial and ethnic groups, commentators often assume that these differences can be traced to cultural differences or competing "family values." Sometimes these are expressed in a positive way, as in the stereotype that Latino families have more extended ties because of their historical traditions and religious values. Other times these are expressed in a negative way, as when Blacks are said to lack family values because of the cultural legacy of slavery and subsequent years of oppression. Either way, differences in family behaviors are often explained by differences in cultural heritage.

In contrast, in our research, we find that social class rather than culture is the key to understanding the differences in extended family ties and behaviors between Whites and ethnic minorities. To be sure, differences in cultural values do exist. Blacks and Latinos/as are more likely than Whites to say they believe that extended family is important; both groups are also more likely to attend religious services. Blacks tend to hold more egalitarian beliefs about gender than Whites, while Latinos/as, especially Mexican Americans, tend to hold more "traditional" views. But these differences in values do not explain racial differences in actual involvement with relatives. It is, instead, social class that matters most in explaining these differences.

It is widely known (and confirmed by U.S. Census data presented in Table 1) that Blacks and Latinos/as tend to have far less income and education than Whites. Families of color are also much more likely than White families to be below the official poverty line. In our research, we find that the differences in extended family ties and behaviors between Whites and ethnic minorities are primarily the result of these social class disparities.

Simply put, White, Black, and Latino/a individuals with the same amount of income and education have similar patterns of involvement

TABLE 1 **Education, Income, and Poverty Rates by Race**

	WHITES	BLACKS	LATINOS/AS
Median household income	$50,784	$30,858	$35,967
Percentage below poverty line	8.4%	24.7%	22.0%
Education:			
Less than high school	14.5%	27.6%	47.6%
High school graduate	58.5%	58.1%	42.0%
Bachelor's degree or higher	27.0%	14.3%	10.4%

Source: U.S. Census Bureau, 2005.

with their extended families. Just like poor minorities, impoverished Whites are more likely to exchange practical aid and visit with extended kin than are their wealthier counterparts. Just like middle-class Whites, middle-class Blacks and Latinos/as are more likely to talk about their personal concerns or share money with relatives than are their poorer counterparts.

More specifically, it is because Whites tend to have more income than Blacks and Latinos/as that they are more likely to give money to their relatives or get it from them. And the higher levels of emotional support among White women can be at least in part traced to their higher levels of education, perhaps because schooling encourages women to talk out their problems and makes them more likely to give (and get) advice.

Conversely, we find that the relative economic deprivation of racial/ethnic minorities leads in many ways to higher levels of extended family involvement. Individuals' lack of economic resources increases their need for help from kin and boosts their willingness to give help in return. Because Blacks and Latinos/as typically have less income and education than Whites, they come to rely more on their relatives for daily needs such as child care, household tasks, or rides. The tendency of Blacks and Latinos/as to live with or near kin may also reflect their greater need for kin cooperation, as well as their decreased opportunities and pressures to move away, including moving for college.

Social Class and Familial Trade-Offs

How do our findings on race, social class, and familial involvement challenge common understandings of minority families? They show that poor minority families do not necessarily lead lives of social isolation or lack strong family solidarities. The lower rates of marriage among impoverished groups may reflect not a rejection of family values but a realistic assessment of how little a woman (and her children) may be able to depend upon marriage. Sociologists Kathryn Edin and Maria Kefalas

(2007) recently found that because disadvantaged men are often unable to offer women the kind of economic security that advantaged men provide, poor women are less likely to marry. Instead, these women create support networks beyond the nuclear family, regularly turning to extended kin for practical support.

Reliance on extended kin and lack of marital ties are linked. In another analysis of the National Survey of Families and Households, we found that, contrary to much rhetoric about marriage as a key source of adult social ties, marriage actually diminishes ties to kin. Married people—women as well as men—are less involved with their parents and siblings than those never married or previously married. These findings indicate a trade-off between commitments to nuclear and extended family ties. Marriage, we have found, is a "greedy" institution: it has a tendency to consume the bulk of people's energies and emotions and to dilute their commitments beyond the nuclear family.

On the one hand, then, support given to spouses and intimate partners sometimes comes at the expense of broader kin and community ties. Indeed, married adult children take care of elderly parents less often than their unmarried siblings. Marriage can also cut people off from networks of mutual aid. Married mothers, for example, whether Black, Latina, or White, are often unable to obtain help from kin in the way that their single counterparts can. Although the "greedy" nature of marriage may pose a problem across social class, it is especially problematic for those less well off economically, as these individuals most need to cultivate wider circles of obligation, mutual aid, and reciprocity. 15

On the other hand, support to relatives sometimes comes at the expense of care for partners, and can interfere with nuclear family formation or stability. Indeed, individuals who are deeply immersed in relationships with extended families may be less likely to get married or, if they marry, may be less likely to put the marital ties first in their loyalties. Several decades ago in her observations of a poor Black community, anthropologist Carol Stack (1974) found that the reciprocal patterns of sharing with kin and "fictive kin" forged in order to survive hardship often made it difficult for poor Blacks either to move up economically or to marry. To prevent the dilution of their social support networks, some extended families may even discourage their members from getting married, or unconsciously sabotage relationships that threaten to pull someone out of the family orbit. As sociologists Domínguez and Watkins (2003) argue, the ties of mutual aid that help impoverished individuals survive on a day-to-day basis may also prevent them from saying "no" to requests that sap their ability to get ahead or pursue individual opportunities.

Overall, we should avoid either denigrating or glorifying the survival strategies of the poor. Although social class disparities are key to understanding racial and ethnic variation in familial involvement, it is too simple to say that class differences create "more" involvement with relatives in one group and "less" in another. In some ways economic

MORE NONTRADITIONAL FAMILY UNITS

Guy, Chair, Three-Way Lamp

A Woman, Her Daughter, Forty-four My Little Ponies

The Troy Triplets and Their Personal Trainer

Two Guys, Two Gals, Two Phones, a Fax, and a Blender

R. Chast

deprivation increases ties to kin (e.g., in terms of living nearby or exchanging practical help) and in other ways it reduces them (e.g., in terms of financial help or emotional support). These findings remind us that love and family connections are expressed both through talk and action. Equally important, focusing solely on the positive or on the negative aspects of either minority or White families is problematic.

Instead, we need to think in terms of trade-offs—among different kinds of care and between the bonds of kinship and the bonds of marriage. Both trade-offs are linked to social class.

Why Do These Differences in Family Life Matter?

Commentators often emphasize the disorganization and dysfunction of Black and Latino/a family life. They suggest that if we could "fix" family values in minority communities and get them to form married-couple households, all their problems would be solved. This argument misunderstands causal connections by focusing on the family as the source of problems. Specifically, it ignores the link between race and class and attributes racial or ethnic differences to cultural values. Instead, we argue, it is important to understand that family strategies and behaviors often emerge in response to the challenges of living in economic deprivation or constant economic insecurity. Therefore, social policies should not focus on changing family behaviors, but rather aim to support a range of existing family arrangements and improve economic conditions for the poor.

Social policies that overlook extended family obligations may introduce, reproduce, or even increase ethnic inequalities. For example, the relatives of Blacks and Latinos/as are more likely than those of Whites to provide various kinds of support that policymakers tend to assume is only provided by husbands and wives. Such relatives may need the rights and support systems that we usually reserve for spouses. For instance, the Family and Medical Leave Act is an important social policy, but it only guarantees unpaid leave from jobs to provide care to spouses, children, or elderly parents requiring medical attention. Our findings suggest that, if we really want to support families, such policies must be broadened to include adult children, needy grown-up brothers and sisters, cousins, aunts and uncles. Similarly, Medicaid regulations that only pay for non-familial care of ill, injured, or disabled individuals implicitly discriminate against Blacks and Latinos/as who provide significant amounts of care to extended kin. "Pro-marriage" policies that give special incentives to impoverished women for getting married may penalize other women who turn down marriage to a risky mate and rely instead on grandparents or other relatives to help raise their children.

Extended family obligations should be recognized and accommodated where possible. But they should not be counted on as a substitute for antipoverty measures, nor should marriage promotion be used in this way. Policymakers must recognize that support from family—whether extended or nuclear—cannot fully compensate for the disadvantages of being poor, or minority, or both. Neither marital ties nor extended family ties can substitute for educational opportunities, jobs with decent wages, health insurance, and affordable child care.

Instead of hoping that poor families pull themselves out of poverty by their own bootstraps, social policy should explicitly aim to rectify economic disadvantages. In turn, improvements in economic opportunities and resources will likely shape families.

References

Domínguez, Silvia, and Celeste Watkins. "Creating Networks for Survival and Mobility: Examining Social Capital Amongst Low-Income African-American and Latin-American Mothers." *Social Problems*, 50 (2003), 1 (February), 111–135.

Edin, Kathryn, and Kefalas, Maria. *Promises I Can Keep: Why Poor Women Put Motherhood Before Marriage.* (Berkeley, CA: University of California Press, 2007).

Stack, Carol B. *All Our Kin: Strategies for Survival in a Black Community.* (New York: Harper and Row, 1974).

ENGAGING THE TEXT

1. In paragraph 1, what might politicians and social commentators mean when they describe black and Latino / Latina families as "more disorganized" than white families? How accurate is this label in Gerstel and Sarkisian's view? Why might a politician find the term "disorganized" useful?

2. What evidence do Gerstel and Sarkisian give that social class is even more important than ethnicity in understanding differences between families? Why is this a critical distinction to the authors?

3. What examples of "extended family solidarities and caretaking activities" (para. 1) do the authors provide? How common or uncommon are these in your own family or community? Do your personal experiences and those of your classmates tend to support, refute, or complicate Gerstel and Sarkisian's analysis?

4. Explain why you agree or disagree with the claim that "social policy should explicitly aim to rectify economic disadvantages" (para. 20). What would this abstract language mean in practice?

EXPLORING CONNECTIONS

5. Review the selections listed below. To what extent could these families be described as "disorganized" (para. 1) and to what extent do they exhibit "extended family solidarities and caretaking activities" (para. 1)?

   Gary Soto, "Looking for Work" (p. 22)

   Roger Jack, "An Indian Story" (see bedfordstmartins.com/rereading/epages)

   Melvin Dixon, "Aunt Ida Pieces a Quilt" (p. 44)

6. Carefully study the frontispiece to Chapter Three on page 241. What symbols of affluence does the photograph contain? How might Gerstel and Sarkisian read the importance of family background in the man's level of economic achievement?

7. How might Gerstel and Sarkisian read the cartoon on page 53?

EXTENDING THE CRITICAL CONTEXT

8. In this article, Gerstel and Sarkisian focus on just three groups — blacks, Latinos, and whites. What do you think the data would look like for other groups such as Asian Americans, Pacific Islanders, Native Americans, or recent immigrants? Find data to support or refute your guesses.

9. Study the footnote on page 48, which lists seven articles by Gerstel, Sarkisian, and others. Based on the journal and article titles in the footnote, what can you say about the scope, purpose, and methodologies of Gerstel and Sarkisian's research? To extend the assignment, read one of the articles and report its key findings to the class.

VISUAL PORTFOLIO

READING IMAGES OF AMERICAN FAMILIES

Freedom from Want, by Norman Rockwell.

VISUAL PORTFOLIO

READING IMAGES OF AMERICAN FAMILIES

1. The photograph of Thomas Jefferson's descendants (p. 57) is clearly posed. Explain in detail why you think photographer Erica Burger organized the image as she did. What events in American history can you link to specific details in this photo, and what does the image say to you about the next century of American history?

2. What ideas about family does Rockwell promote in his painting *Freedom from Want* (p. 58)? How are social class, gender roles, and ethnicity portrayed here? Based on this painting and other examples of Rockwell's work in this anthology (pp. 180, 181, and 617), do you agree with the common criticism that his vision of America was overly optimistic?

3. The image on page 59, featuring the cast of the television series *Modern Family*, closely mirrors *Freedom from Want*, the iconic painting by Norman Rockwell on the facing page. Begin by listing all the similarities and any differences you can see. Then explain how you read the relationship between the two images. For example, is *Modern Family* making fun of Rockwell's art, or perhaps paying tribute to it? If you are familiar with the television series, explain to what extent it embraces or rejects the traditional values that Rockwell's painting captures. Do you think the kind of family life pictured on these pages appeals to most twenty-first-century Americans?

4. The photograph on page 60 shows a family posing for a group portrait. What do you think might be the occasion? Who do you think the people are, and what are their relationships? What impression do you get about them from their facial expressions, their clothing, and the room and its furnishings? In terms of its messages about family, how closely does this resemble the images on the preceding two pages?

5. What is the emotional impact of the photograph of a woman bathing her child in a washtub in the kitchen (p. 61)? Why does the photographer consider this moment worthy of our attention? How might sociologists Gerstel and Sarkisian (p. 47) interpret the image?

6. The photograph on page 62 shows Phyllis Siegel kissing her wife Connie Kopelov just after their marriage on July 24, 2011, the day New York's Marriage Equality Act went into effect. What emotions do you imagine Siegel, Kopelov, and the people clapping in the background are experiencing? How do individual lives, law, politics, and media intersect in the image? Discuss whether a similar photo of thirty-year-olds would have a significantly different meaning.

7. The women's signs on p. 63 read "Thanks for evolving on same sex marriage." For whom was their message intended, and what was the occasion? How would you describe the tone of the photograph, and how do the details of the image help shape your response? Why, in our era of instant global communication,

would the women use such old-fashioned materials as balloons and sandwich boards? Finally, how would you assess the balance of personal expression and political activism in the photo?

8. The custom bicycle on page 64 is being prepared to make a delivery. Who is delivering what to whom? What does the photo say about the contemporary American family?

PROPOSITION 8: THE CALIFORNIA MARRIAGE PROTECTION ACT

The movement to secure equal marriage rights for gay and lesbian citizens, which has been gaining momentum for many years, has now moved same-sex marriage to the foreground in American political, legal, and cultural debate. Marriage laws currently differ by state: while nine states and Washington, D.C., permit same-sex marriage, many states have adopted, or are pursuing, Proposition 8-style restrictions of marriage to "a man and a woman." Here are some key moments in Proposition 8's tangled legal history:

- In May 2008, a state supreme court ruling made same-sex marriages legal in California under the state Constitution as it then existed.

- Opponents of same-sex marriage gathered enough signatures to put Proposition 8 on the ballot, and in November 2008 voters passed the measure, thereby changing the state Constitution and making same-sex marriage invalid.

- In May 2009, the state supreme court upheld the constitutionality of Proposition 8, but also held that some 18,000 marriages performed between May 2008 and the passage of Proposition 8 were valid.

- Also in May 2009, attorneys Theodore Olson and David Boies (see p. 75) filed *Perry v. Schwarzenegger* on behalf of two same-sex couples in California who had been denied marriage licenses. In August 2010, ruling in the *Perry* case, Judge Vaughn R. Walker of the U.S. District Court for the Northern District of California struck down Proposition 8 as a violation of due process and equal protection rights under the U.S. Constitution. The decision was immediately appealed.

- In February 2012, the federal Court of Appeals for the Ninth Circuit upheld Walker's lower court ruling. California's same-sex marriage ban remained in effect, however, pending U.S. Supreme Court action.

- In December 2012, the U.S. Supreme Court announced that it would hear the Proposition 8 case.

In a different same-sex marriage case at the federal level, the First Circuit Court of Appeals ruled, by a 3–0 vote in May 2012, that the 1996 Defense of Marriage Act (DOMA) is unconstitutional because it denies federal recognition of same-sex marriages in states that allow such marriages.

THIS INITIATIVE MEASURE IS SUBMITTED to the people in accordance with the provisions of Article II, Section 8, of the California Constitution.

This initiative measure expressly amends the California Constitution by adding a section thereto; therefore, new provisions proposed to be added are printed in *italic type* to indicate that they are new.

SECTION 1.   Title

This measure shall be known and may be cited as the "California Marriage Protection Act."

SECTION 2.   Section 7.5 is added to Article I of the California Constitution, to read:

SEC. 7.5.   Only marriage between a man and a woman is valid or recognized in California.

ENGAGING THE TEXT

1. The title of the ballot initiative measure is the "California Marriage Protection Act." What is the title's intended rhetorical impact? How might Prop 8 opponents critique this title, and what titles might they suggest for Prop 8?

2. The heart of Prop 8 is one apparently simple sentence — "Only marriage between a man and a woman is valid or recognized in California." Closely consider each key word here — marriage, man, woman, valid, recognized, California — and discuss whether there is any chance of ambiguity, interpretation, or disagreement in the meanings of these terms or of the sentence as a whole.

3. To what extent would the word "marriage" remain significant if lesbian and gay couples everywhere could live together, raise children, file joint tax returns, and so on, under the protection of a different term, such as "joint partnership" or "civil union"?

4. Founding Father and fourth president James Madison warned in *Federalist Paper No. 10* that "measures are too often decided, not according to the rules of justice and the rights of the minor party, but by the superior force of an interested and overbearing majority." What, if anything, limits the power of a majority in a case like Prop 8? Can Prop 8 reasonably be seen as the "tyranny of the majority"?

5. Write a one- or two-sentence proposition which would have the opposite effect of Proposition 8 — that is, to guarantee equal marriage rights to same-sex partners. Share with classmates and discuss how each proposition is worded. To extend the assignment, compare your efforts with Section 1 of the Fourteenth Amendment to the U.S. Constitution.

EXPLORING CONNECTIONS

6. Consider the couple pictured on page 62 just after their marriage in New York. If Siegel and Kopelov moved to your state, would they still be married in the eyes of your state? If they were to divorce in New York, could they remarry in

your state? Do you think they can file a federal tax return as a married couple? Why or why not? What does this exercise suggest about the relationship of personal experience to the law?

7. Look at Norman Rockwell's *Freedom from Want* (p. 58) and *Freedom of Speech* (p. 617). Then design a "Freedom to Marry" poster, or sketch out ideas for a low-budget "Freedom to Marry" video.

EXTENDING THE CRITICAL CONTEXT

8. Establish small teams to research current marriage / domestic partnership law in your state and several others. (Also pay attention to any pending legislation, ballot initiatives, or court cases.) How substantially do the laws vary from state to state? What scenarios can you imagine in which crossing a border might cause legal problems or ambiguities? You may want to begin your search at a marriage-equality Web site such as www.freedomtomarry.org or www.marriageequality.org.

9. Prop 8 is an example of "direct democracy" in the sense that voters established the law themselves, without the legislature, governor, or courts. Research the procedures for direct democracy in your state (for example, ballot initiatives, referendums, recalls), the kinds of issues they have been used to address, and the advantages and disadvantages of your state's system. Do you think direct democracy is working well in your state, or do you think that state legislators would usually make better decisions than the voters?

PROP 8 HURT MY FAMILY — ASK ME HOW
MARRIAGE EQUALITY USA

Marriage Equality USA is a national organization whose mission is "to secure legally recognized civil marriage equality for all, at the federal and state level, without regard to gender identity or sexual orientation." The 2009 report excerpted here documents the physical and emotional toll that anti same-sex amendments take on lesbian, gay, bisexual, transgender, and intersex (LGBTI) individuals and their allies. Problems include vandalism, name-calling, threats, bullying of children, and more. We reprint here the report's introduction and first section, which together offer a broad overview of the problem and several short accounts of harassment.

Introduction

In January 2009, the American Psychological Association (APA) released three separate studies that described the psychological distress associated with anti same-sex marriage amendments. One study using national survey responses of LGBTI[1] individuals found that those who live in states that have passed marriage amendments experienced increased psychological stress not due to other pre-existing conditions but as "a direct result of the negative images and messages associated with the ballot campaign and the passage of the amendment." Furthermore, participants reported feeling "alienated from their community, fearful they would lose their children, and concerned they would become victims of anti-gay violence." These studies also reported that this harm extends to Lesbian, Gay, Bisexual, Transgender, and Intersex (LGBTI) family members and straight allies who experience a form of "secondary minority stress." Finally, "although many participants displayed resiliency and effective coping with this stress, some experienced strong negative consequences to their mental and physical health."

Marriage Equality USA, through a series of town halls held across California and a national on-line survey of over 3,100 respondents, collected community input regarding the homophobia and other harm experienced through initiative campaigns, like Proposition 8,[2] and received personal stories that mirror these APA findings. In our report "Prop 8 Hurt My Family—Ask Me How," we collected almost 1,200 individual experiences which illustrate how:

- LGBTI people experience increased verbal abuse, homophobia, physical harm, and other discrimination associated with or resulting from the Prop 8 campaign;

- Children of same-sex couples express fear due to direct exposure to homophobia and hate and concerns that the passage of Prop 8 means they could be taken from their families and targeted for further violence;

- LGBTI youth and their supporters experience increased bullying at schools as Prop 8's passage fosters a supportive environment for homophobic acts of physical and emotional violence;

- Straight allies experience the impact of homophobia firsthand and express shock and fear for their LGBTI family members and friends and the danger they may experience if they were perceived as gay or an ally;

- Families are torn apart as relatives divide on Prop 8; and

- Communities are destroyed from the aftermath of abusive behavior toward them during local street demonstrations, neighborhood

---

[1]*LGBTI:* Lesbian, gay, bisexual, transsexual, intersex. "Intersex" refers to a number of medical conditions in which an individual's sex anatomy is not considered standard. Like "hermaphrodite," the term is problematic; a 2006 "Consensus Statement on Intersex Disorders" published by the American Academy of Pediatrics recommended instead the term Disorders of Sex Development (DSD) to refer to "congenital conditions in which development of chromosomal, gonadal, or anatomic sex is atypical."

[2]*Proposition 8:* See "Proposition 8: The California Marriage Protection Act" (p. 67).

divisions, and the impact of "knowing your neighbor" voted against your family.

Despite the harm and discrimination that opponents of Prop 8 experienced, LGBTI people, their families and friends, and supportive community members stated that they are more resolved and determined to fight until every family receives the same dignity and protection that only marriage can provide. But the report also documents the inherent unfairness and strife that comes from putting the fundamental rights of some of the community up for a popular vote and points out the lasting harm and fear that is generated from these campaigns.

We conclude this report with stories that describe why some believe it is important for the California Supreme Court to overturn Prop 8. Our hope in sharing these stories is that all Californians, including those who voted Yes on 8, can reflect on the harm that has resulted from this initiative campaign and come to the conclusion that we don't want to repeat this experience. We hope California lives up to our ideals and that our Constitution remains intact and continues to serve its role in protecting the minority from the tyranny of the majority. In the words of President and Chief Justice William Howard Taft, "Constitutions are checks upon the hasty action of the majority. They are self-imposed restraints of a whole people upon a majority of them to secure sober action and a respect for the rights of the minority."

PROP 8 HURT REAL PEOPLE

I think the LGBTI community has been under constant stress for the last eight years. We have been used as a political punching bag. The anxiety affects all of us and most of us just want to live our lives quietly with the same rights and responsibilities as everyone else. We are a tiny minority, but our well-being is at the mercy of a still homophobic majority.

—CONTRA COSTA COUNTY

Not only did LGBTI people lose their right to marry, but they were verbally assaulted, had property vandalized and destroyed, received death threats, and several people reported being terminated from their jobs because they were gay and/or due to their opposition to Prop 8.

Anti-gay initiative campaigns promote an environment that fosters discrimination, rejection, and homophobia. Marriage Equality USA's on-line survey found that over 40 percent of all respondents, the majority being LGBTI individuals, indicated they faced homophobia, hate speech, violence, or threats resulting from California's Prop 8 campaign. Many town hall participants and survey respondents described the whole ballot initiative process as homophobic, starting with the failed effort to encourage Californians to decline to sign the proposed initiative followed by being forced to endure Yes on 8 advertisements, media coverage and letters to the editor that reinforced negative stereotypes, prejudice and discrimination, and finally suffering the brutal realization that California voters would not support their right to be treated as equal citizens.

LGBTI community members expressed pride and felt empowered through participating in rallies, phone banking, wearing No on 8 buttons or having No on 8 bumper stickers or lawn signs; however this involvement also increased their exposure to glares, obscenities, harassment, threats, and violence as demonstrated by the following examples:

- "One day, I was called a faggot four times in Oakland while wearing my No on 8 button." — Alameda County

- "We put up a No on 8 lawn sign and people would drive by our house just to give us dirty looks and flip us off, even in front of our daughter." — Fresno County

- "While in my car at a red light, four men came up to my window and started yelling threats because of my No on 8 bumper sticker. One man yelled, 'I will kill you bitch. I will follow you home.' I had to call the police and they escorted me home." — Sacramento County

- "Every rally included a day long barrage of classic slurs being shouted from passing cars. One man drove by several times with four boys in the car shouting 'fuck you faggots' and flashing their middle fingers. It was like the adult was modeling, teaching, and celebrating gay bashing behavior." — San Diego County

- "My employer received anonymous threats about me and implying personal risk for the children I teach. I was suspended with pay while the school district assessed the threat. My home was vandalized with anti-gay slogans and slurs. Our car was destroyed when someone put sugar in the tank. All this because of an article about our marriage." — San Bernardino County

Prop 8 was not a school bond or redistricting initiative, it was an effort to eliminate the fundamental right of marriage for same-sex couples. As one San Luis Obispo respondent described, "Marriage never was hugely important to me, so it came as quite a shock when I read the [California Supreme Court marriage decision] and started to sob. Someone had finally said I was a decent human being and deserved equal protection under the laws." Marriage matters and for those personally affected, Prop 8 was a personal attack on our lives and families. Living through this campaign exerted a high toll on the sense of well-being and connection within the larger community that affected everyone. As one Santa Clara County respondent stated, "It is frustrating and exhausting to go through the course of each day feeling like we somehow have to defend our marriage. It weighs on a person and on a couple." Another resident from San Francisco described, "The psychological trauma of having my civil rights debated by people who do not even know me has been astounding. I didn't realize the effect this vote would have on me until after it happened."

For same-sex couples who were unable to marry before November 4th, they expressed despair over the passage of Prop 8. As one Alameda County respondent described, "I don't want to wait until I have gray hair to marry my girlfriend. I deeply regret not having the money to do it while I had the chance. I never thought Prop 8 would pass." Many same-sex couples who were married also expressed concerns their marriages were at risk, and their fears were validated when Prop 8 proponents filed papers to have their marriage licenses take away.

For other LGBTI community members, the passage of Prop 8 has resulted in increased anxiety and fear. As one Sonoma County resident described, "There's a quiet rift between my friends, family, and I now—gay and straight. This is painful. I wonder who hates me. Am I in danger in this situation? How about this one? Who voted against my rights?" Another Santa Clara County resident shared, "Since Prop 8 passed, my wife had developed significant anxiety. She feels like at any moment we will be hate-crime victims. When she heard about the lesbian in Richmond who was gang raped, it was as if they were coming for us next. I think a lot of the LGBTI community feels that way." And a Sonoma County resident summed up, "Every time an anti-gay measure passes, it makes the LGBTI community more vulnerable. I have been physically threatened before because I am gay, and that fear is always in the back of my mind, particularly when there is a general feeling that the majority of the people in my state (or country) are systematically stripping us of rights."

Despite all the homophobia and hate that LGBTI community members faced, we received many comments that demonstrate the courage and resolve to continue our fight for marriage equality, including this one from San Joaquin County, "This election has been very emotional and hurtful for me. Although at the same time, it has made me stronger to fight for what I believe in."

ENGAGING THE TEXT

1. The Marriage Equality USA report cites three recent studies by the American Psychological Association and presents findings from Marriage Equality USA's own town hall meetings and national online survey. Does this body of evidence fully persuade you that the campaigns for anti-same-sex marriage amendments have caused real and serious harm to many Americans? Explain why or why not.

2. How persuasive or instructive do you find the embedded personal comments and stories? How many of the people quoted in the report would you say have been victims of criminal acts?

3. Most readers of the Marriage Equality USA report are probably already in favor of the full legality of same-sex marriage. What might be the purpose of a report like this if it is not to persuade such readers?

EXPLORING CONNECTIONS

4. Watch "Speaking Out," the e-Page video selection for Chapter Four, "True Women and Real Men: Myths of Gender." Compare the harassment described in "Prop 8 Hurt My Family" to Kevin's experience of going to a movie with his boyfriend. To what extent was homophobia tolerated or resisted in schools you attended?

5. Look at the "Thanks for Evolving" photo on page 63 in this chapter's Visual Portfolio. If the women pictured carried their signs in your community or on your campus, how safe would they be from the types of harassment documented by the Marriage Equality USA report?

EXTENDING THE CRITICAL CONTEXT

6. Consult the full report at www.marriageequalityusa.org. Summarize the findings of one or more of the other sections (e.g. "Prop 8 Promoted Bullying in Schools") and report to the class.

7. Find one of the 2009 American Psychological Association studies mentioned in paragraph 1 of the report and summarize its methods and conclusions for the class.

THE CONSERVATIVE CASE FOR GAY MARRIAGE
Why Same-sex Marriage Is an American Value

THEODORE B. OLSON

This essay concludes a trio of readings about same-sex marriage, which together offer a clear example of how complex issues often carry us beyond simple pro/con positions: whereas California's Proposition 8 (p. 67) offers a conservative defense of traditional marriage and "Prop 8 Hurt My Family" (p. 69) offers an impassioned liberal rebuttal, Olson offers the surprising argument that same-sex marriage is completely in line with a conservative view of liberty and law. Olson's view matters, not only because he is a leading American conservative—*Time* magazine named him one of the 100 most influential people in the world in 2010, but because he has helped bring Proposition 8 before the U.S. Supreme Court. Theodore Olson (b. 1940) has had a distinguished career, primarily as a practicing attorney in Los Angeles and Washington, D.C. He also worked for the U.S. Department of Justice during the Reagan presidency and served as U.S. Solicitor General from 2001 to 2004. He has argued before the U.S. Supreme Court in fifty-eight cases, including the two *Bush v. Gore* cases that helped George W. Bush reach the White House after the contested presidential election of 2000. This article appeared in *Newsweek* on January 8, 2012. To see Olson and his colleague David Boies[1] being interviewed by Bill Moyers, go to www.pbs.org/moyers /journal/02262010/watch.html.

TOGETHER WITH MY GOOD FRIEND and occasional courtroom adversary David Boies, I am attempting to persuade a federal court to invalidate California's Proposition 8—the voter-approved measure that overturned California's constitutional right to marry a person of the same sex.

My involvement in this case has generated a certain degree of consternation among conservatives. How could a politically active, lifelong Republican, a veteran of the Ronald Reagan and George W. Bush administrations, challenge the "traditional" definition of marriage and press for an "activist" interpretation of the Constitution to create another "new" constitutional right?

My answer to this seeming conundrum rests on a lifetime of exposure to persons of different backgrounds, histories, viewpoints, and

---

[1]*David Boies*: Prominent American attorney; Olson's co-counsel in the *Perry* case that challenges Proposition 8, but his former adversary in *Bush v. Gore*. [All notes are the editors'.]

intrinsic characteristics, and on my rejection of what I see as super-ficially appealing but ultimately false perceptions about our Constitution and its protection of equality and fundamental rights.

Many of my fellow conservatives have an almost knee-jerk hostil-ity toward gay marriage. This does not make sense, because same-sex unions promote the values conservatives prize. Marriage is one of the basic building blocks of our neighborhoods and our nation. At its best, it is a stable bond between two individuals who work to create a lov-ing household and a social and economic partnership. We encourage couples to marry because the commitments they make to one another provide benefits not only to themselves but also to their families and communities. Marriage requires thinking beyond one's own needs. It transforms two individuals into a union based on shared aspirations, and in doing so establishes a formal investment in the well-being of society. The fact that individuals who happen to be gay want to share in this vital social institution is evidence that conservative ideals enjoy widespread acceptance. Conservatives should celebrate this, rather than lament it.

Legalizing same-sex marriage would also be a recognition of basic   5 American principles, and would represent the culmination of our na-tion's commitment to equal rights. It is, some have said, the last major civil-rights milestone yet to be surpassed in our two-century struggle to attain the goals we set for this nation at its formation.

This bedrock American principle of equality is central to the political and legal convictions of Republicans, Democrats, liberals, and conserva-tives alike. The dream that became America began with the revolutionary concept expressed in the Declaration of Independence in words that are among the most noble and elegant ever written: "We hold these truths to be self-evident, that all men are created equal, that they are endowed by their Creator with certain unalienable Rights, that among these are Life, Liberty and the pursuit of Happiness."

Sadly, our nation has taken a long time to live up to the promise of equality. In 1857, the Supreme Court held that an African-American could not be a citizen.[2] During the ensuing Civil War, Abraham Lincoln eloquently reminded the nation of its founding principle: "our fathers brought forth on this continent, a new nation, conceived in liberty and dedicated to the proposition that all men are created equal."

At the end of the Civil War, to make the elusive promise of equality a reality, the 14th Amendment to the Constitution added the command that "no State ... shall deprive any person of life, liberty or property, without due process of law; nor deny to any person...the equal protec-tion of the laws."

---

[2]*an African-American could not be a citizen:* A reference to the infamous Dred Scott decision, in which the Supreme Court ruled that Scott, a slave who brought suit to win his freedom after he had been taken to free territory, was a resident neither of Missouri nor of the United States and thus had no rights under U.S. law.

Subsequent laws and court decisions have made clear that equality under the law extends to persons of all races, religions, and places of origin. What better way to make this national aspiration complete than to apply the same protection to men and women who differ from others only on the basis of their sexual orientation? I cannot think of a single reason—and have not heard one since I undertook this venture—for continued discrimination against decent, hardworking members of our society on that basis.

Various federal and state laws have accorded certain rights and privileges to gay and lesbian couples, but these protections vary dramatically at the state level, and nearly universally deny true equality to gays and lesbians who wish to marry. The very idea of marriage is basic to recognition as equals in our society; any status short of that is inferior, unjust, and unconstitutional.

The United States Supreme Court has repeatedly held that marriage is one of the most fundamental rights that we have as Americans under our Constitution. It is an expression of our desire to create a social partnership, to live and share life's joys and burdens with the person we love, and to form a lasting bond and a social identity. The Supreme Court has said that marriage is a part of the Constitution's protections of liberty, privacy, freedom of association, and spiritual identification. In short, the right to marry helps us to define ourselves and our place in a community. Without it, there can be no true equality under the law.

It is true that marriage in this nation traditionally has been regarded as a relationship exclusively between a man and a woman, and many of our nation's multiple religions define marriage in precisely those terms. But while the Supreme Court has always previously considered marriage in that context, the underlying rights and liberties that marriage embodies are not in any way confined to heterosexuals.

Marriage is a civil bond in this country as well as, in some (but hardly all) cases, a religious sacrament. It is a relationship recognized by governments as providing a privileged and respected status, entitled to the state's support and benefits. The California Supreme Court described marriage as a "union unreservedly approved and favored by the community." Where the state has accorded official sanction to a relationship and provided special benefits to those who enter into that relationship, our courts have insisted that withholding that status requires powerful justifications and may not be arbitrarily denied.

What, then, are the justifications for California's decision in Proposition 8 to withdraw access to the institution of marriage for some of its citizens on the basis of their sexual orientation? The reasons I have heard are not very persuasive.

The explanation mentioned most often is tradition. But simply because something has always been done a certain way does not mean that it must always remain that way. Otherwise we would still have segregated schools and debtors' prisons. Gays and lesbians have always been among us, forming a part of our society, and they have lived as couples in our neighborhoods and communities. For a long time, they have experienced discrimination and even persecution; but we, as a society, are starting to become more tolerant, accepting, and understanding. California and many other states have allowed gays and lesbians to form domestic partnerships (or civil unions) with most of the rights of married heterosexuals. Thus, gay and lesbian individuals are now permitted to live together in state-sanctioned relationships. It therefore seems anomalous to cite "tradition" as a justification for withholding the status of marriage and thus to continue to label those relationships as less worthy, less sanctioned, or less legitimate.

The second argument I often hear is that traditional marriage furthers the state's interest in procreation—and that opening marriage to same-sex couples would dilute, diminish, and devalue this goal. But that is plainly not the case. Preventing lesbians and gays from marrying does not cause more heterosexuals to marry and conceive more children. Likewise, allowing gays and lesbians to marry someone of the same sex will not discourage heterosexuals from marrying a person of the opposite sex. How, then, would allowing same-sex marriages reduce the number of children that heterosexual couples conceive?

This procreation argument cannot be taken seriously. We do not inquire whether heterosexual couples intend to bear children, or have the capacity to have children, before we allow them to marry. We permit marriage by the elderly, by prison inmates, and by persons who have no intention of having children. What's more, it is pernicious to think marriage should be limited to heterosexuals because of the state's desire to promote procreation. We would surely not accept as constitutional a ban on marriage if a state were to decide, as China has done, to discourage procreation.

Another argument, vaguer and even less persuasive, is that gay marriage somehow does harm to heterosexual marriage. I have yet to meet anyone who can explain to me what this means. In what way would allowing same-sex partners to marry diminish the marriages of heterosexual couples? Tellingly, when the judge in our case asked our opponent to identify the ways in which same-sex marriage would harm heterosexual marriage, to his credit he answered honestly: he could not think of any.

The simple fact is that there is no good reason why we should deny marriage to same-sex partners. On the other hand, there are many reasons why we should formally recognize these relationships and embrace the rights of gays and lesbians to marry and become full and equal members of our society.

No matter what you think of homosexuality, it is a fact that gays [20] and lesbians are members of our families, clubs, and workplaces. They are our doctors, our teachers, our soldiers (whether we admit it or not), and our friends. They yearn for acceptance, stable relationships, and success in their lives, just like the rest of us.

Conservatives and liberals alike need to come together on principles that surely unite us. Certainly, we can agree on the value of strong families, lasting domestic relationships, and communities populated by persons with recognized and sanctioned bonds to one another. Confining some of our neighbors and friends who share these same values to an outlaw or second-class status undermines their sense of belonging and weakens their ties with the rest of us and what should be our common aspirations. Even those whose religious convictions preclude endorsement of what they may perceive as an unacceptable "lifestyle" should recognize that disapproval should not warrant stigmatization and unequal treatment.

When we refuse to accord this status to gays and lesbians, we discourage them from forming the same relationships we encourage for others. And we are also telling them, those who love them, and society as a whole that their relationships are less worthy, less legitimate, less permanent, and less valued. We demean their relationships and we demean them as individuals. I cannot imagine how we benefit as a society by doing so.

I understand, but reject, certain religious teachings that denounce homosexuality as morally wrong, illegitimate, or unnatural; and I take strong exception to those who argue that same-sex relationships should be discouraged by society and law. Science has taught us, even if history has not, that gays and lesbians do not choose to be homosexual any more than the rest of us choose to be heterosexual. To a very large extent, these characteristics are immutable, like being left-handed. And, while our Constitution guarantees the freedom to exercise our individual religious convictions, it equally prohibits us from forcing our beliefs on others. I do not believe that our society can ever live up to the promise of equality, and the fundamental rights to life, liberty, and the pursuit of happiness, until we stop invidious discrimination on the basis of sexual orientation.

If we are born heterosexual, it is not unusual for us to perceive those who are born homosexual as aberrational and threatening. Many religions and much of our social culture have reinforced those impulses. Too often, that has led to prejudice, hostility, and discrimination. The antidote is understanding, and reason. We once tolerated laws throughout this nation that prohibited marriage between persons of different races. California's Supreme Court was the first to find that discrimination unconstitutional. The U.S. Supreme Court unanimously agreed 20 years later, in 1967, in a case called *Loving v. Virginia*. It seems inconceivable today that only 40 years ago there were places in this country where a black woman could not legally marry a white man. And it was only 50 years ago that 17 states mandated segregated public education—until the Supreme Court unanimously struck down that practice in *Brown v. Board of Education*. Most Americans are proud of these decisions and the fact that the discriminatory state laws that spawned them have been discredited. I am convinced that Americans will be equally proud when we no longer discriminate against gays and lesbians and welcome them into our society.

Reactions to our lawsuit have reinforced for me these essential truths. I have certainly heard anger, resentment, and hostility, and words like "betrayal" and other pointedly graphic criticism. But mostly I have been overwhelmed by expressions of gratitude and good will from persons in all walks of life, including, I might add, from many conservatives and libertarians whose names might surprise. I have been particularly moved by many personal renditions of how lonely and personally destructive it is to be treated as an outcast and how meaningful it will be to be respected by our laws and civil institutions as an American, entitled to equality and dignity. I have no doubt that we are on the right side of this battle, the right side of the law, and the right side of history.

Some have suggested that we have brought this case too soon, and that neither the country nor the courts are "ready" to tackle this issue and remove this stigma. We disagree. We represent real clients—two wonderful couples in California who have longtime relationships. Our lesbian clients are raising four fine children who could not ask for better parents. Our clients wish to be married. They believe that they have that constitutional right. They wish to be represented in court to seek vindication of that right by mounting a challenge under the United States Constitution to the validity of Proposition 8 under the equal-protection and due-process clauses of the 14th Amendment. In fact, the California attorney general has conceded the unconstitutionality of Proposition 8, and the city of San Francisco has joined our case to defend the rights of gays and lesbians to be married. We do not tell persons who have a legitimate claim to wait until the time is "right" and the populace is "ready" to recognize their equality and equal dignity under the law.

Citizens who have been denied equality are invariably told to "wait their turn" and to "be patient." Yet veterans of past civil-rights battles found that it was the act of insisting on equal rights that ultimately sped acceptance of those rights. As to whether the courts are "ready" for this case, just a few years ago, in *Romer v. Evans*, the United States Supreme Court struck down a popularly adopted Colorado constitutional amendment that withdrew the rights of gays and lesbians in that state to the protection of anti-discrimination laws. And seven years ago, in *Lawrence v. Texas*, the Supreme Court struck down, as lacking any rational basis, Texas laws prohibiting private, intimate sexual practices between persons of the same sex, overruling a contrary decision just 20 years earlier.

These decisions have generated controversy, of course, but they are decisions of the nation's highest court on which our clients are entitled to rely. If all citizens have a constitutional right to marry, if state laws that withdraw legal protections of gays and lesbians as a class are unconstitutional, and if private, intimate sexual conduct between persons of the same sex is protected by the Constitution, there is very little left on which opponents of same-sex marriage can rely. As Justice Antonin Scalia, who dissented in the *Lawrence* case, pointed out, "[W]hat [remaining] justification could there possibly be for denying the benefits of marriage to homosexual couples exercising '[t]he liberty protected by the Constitution'?" He is right, of course. One might agree or not with these decisions, but even Justice Scalia has acknowledged that they lead in only one direction.

California's Proposition 8 is particularly vulnerable to constitutional challenge, because that state has now enacted a crazy-quilt of marriage regulation that makes no sense to anyone. California recognizes marriage between men and women, including persons on death row, child abusers, and wife beaters. At the same time, California prohibits marriage by loving, caring, stable partners of the same sex, but tries to make up for it by giving them the alternative of "domestic partnerships" with virtually all of the rights of married persons except the official, state-approved status of marriage. Finally, California recognizes 18,000 same-sex marriages that took place in the months between the state Supreme Court's ruling that upheld gay-marriage rights and the decision of California's citizens to withdraw those rights by enacting Proposition 8.

So there are now three classes of Californians: heterosexual cou- 30
ples who can get married, divorced, and remarried, if they wish; same-sex couples who cannot get married but can live together in domestic

"Do you have any California wines that support same-sex marriage?"

partnerships; and same-sex couples who are now married but who, if they divorce, cannot remarry. This is an irrational system, it is discriminatory, and it cannot stand.

Americans who believe in the words of the Declaration of Independence, in Lincoln's Gettysburg Address, in the 14th Amendment, and in the Constitution's guarantees of equal protection and equal dignity before the law cannot sit by while this wrong continues. This is not a conservative or liberal issue; it is an American one, and it is time that we, as Americans, embraced it.

ENGAGING THE TEXT

1. As Olson notes in his opening paragraph, his case for same-sex marriage runs counter to what most people expect from a "conservative" thinker. How does this essay challenge your assumptions about conservative perspectives on marriage equality? How does Olson define or redefine conservative values, and how closely do his ideas mirror your own views of what it means to be "conservative"?

2. Create a reverse outline of Olson's essay: sketch its main points and organization in rough outline form; then analyze the essay's scope and coherence. Can you find any gaps, inconsistencies, or unwarranted assumptions?

3. Do you agree that religious and civic marriages can reasonably be separated? Why is this issue critically important to Olson, and how does he handle it, both logically and rhetorically?

EXPLORING CONNECTIONS

4. See the Declaration of Independence (p. 625) and the First Amendment to the Constitution (p. 628) in Chapter Six. Do you think the First Amendment means that religious belief must not shape public policy or state law concerning marriage? Does the Declaration of Independence imply that same-sex marriage is a fundamental human right? By what logic can Olson use these documents to support an idea that Thomas Jefferson, James Madison, and their fellow revolutionaries may never have imagined, much less espoused?

5. Compare Olson's essay to "Prop 8 Hurt My Family" on page 69 in terms of audience, purpose, and strategies of argumentation. Whose approach do you find more powerful, and why?

6. The image on page 62 in this chapter's Visual Portfolio shows the just-wed couple Phyllis Siegel and Connie Kopelov. Based on your reading of "The Conservative Case for Gay Marriage," how do you think Olson might interpret this event and this specific visual image?

7. Look ahead to Katherine Mangu-Ward's "The War on Negative Liberty" in Chapter Six (p. 659) and her discussion of positive liberty ("freedom to fulfill your potential") and negative liberty ("freedom from"). How might

Mangu-Ward apply these concepts to the issue of marriage equality? Explain why you think Olson's argument addresses marriage equality as a positive liberty, a negative liberty, or a combination of the two.

EXTENDING THE CRITICAL CONTEXT

8. The status of same-sex marriage can change overnight due to new legislation, ballot initiatives, and court decisions. Research the current laws and recent developments in a state of your choice (or Washington, D.C.) and report to the class. (Eight states with particularly interesting histories are California, Hawaii, Minnesota, New Jersey, North Carolina, Ohio, Rhode Island, and Washington.) What do you think Olson might say about the information you find? To what extent does your research support or undermine the case for marriage equality?

9. Olson focuses on American history, law, social customs, and religion. Discuss how his arguments might change if his scope were global — that is, if he chose to assert that same-sex partnerships, equal in law and status to heterosexual marriage, are a universal, fundamental human right.

THE ACCORDION FAMILY: BOOMERANG KIDS, ANXIOUS PARENTS, AND THE PRIVATE TOLL OF GLOBAL COMPETITION
KATHERINE S. NEWMAN

The "Accordion Family" of Newman's title describes households in which adult children live with their parents, thus "stretching" the nuclear-family model. In recent years such families have become increasingly common — and increasingly controversial — and this trend has profound consequences for family life and even for what it means to be an adult. In addition to analyzing empirical data, Newman and her colleagues listened to the stories of dozens of members of accordion families, some of whom are profiled below. Although *The Accordion Family* (2012) is based on interviews spanning six countries, the excerpt here focuses on multigenerational families in the U.S. — specifically in Newton, Massachusetts, an affluent city just west of Boston. Author of eleven books, Katherine S. Newman is one of America's leading sociologists, with particular expertise in class mobility and the working poor. Currently Dean of the Krieger School of Arts and Sciences at Johns Hopkins University, she has also held teaching or administrative positions at Columbia University, Princeton, Harvard, and the University of California, Berkeley.

Private Safety Nets

In the United States, we have seen a 50-percent increase since the 1970s in the proportion of people age thirty to thirty-four who live with their parents. As the recession of 2008–2009 continued to deepen, this trend became even more entrenched. Kids who cannot find jobs after finishing college, divorced mothers who can't afford to provide a home for their children, unemployed people at their wits' end, the ranks of the foreclosed—all of these people are beating a path back to their parents' homes to take shelter underneath the only reliable roof available.

To some degree, this has always been the way of the private safety net. Families double up when misfortune derails their members, and the generations that have been lucky enough to buy into an affordable housing market, that enjoyed stable jobs for decades, find they must open their arms (and houses) to receive these economic refugees back into the fold. Blue-collar working-class families and the poor have never known anything different: their kids have no choice but to stay home while they try to outrun a labor market that has become increasingly inhospitable. Their parents have had it hard as well, as layoffs have spread through the factories of the Midwest and the South; pooling income across the generations is often the only sensible survival strategy, even if the climate becomes testy. Those who remember the 1970s sitcom *All in the Family* will recall Archie and Edith Bunker's daughter, Gloria, and errant son-in-law, "Meathead," who lived with her parents because they could not make ends meet otherwise. This was the comic version of the accordion family, working-class style.

Until relatively recently, the middle class in most prosperous countries did not need to act as an economic shock absorber for such a prolonged period in the lives of their adult children. Their households might expand to take in a wayward divorcee or support a child who had taken a non-paying internship, but the norm for most white-collar parents was to send young people out into the world and look on in satisfaction as they took their places in the corporate world or the professions, found their life mates, and established their own nests.

What is newsworthy about current trends is less the return of the unfortunate to the parental fold but the growth in the numbers of young adults in their late twenties and thirties who have never been independent in the first place. Why, in the world's most affluent societies, are young (and not so young) adults unable to stand on their own two feet? And what kind of fallout is this "failure to launch" producing?

The media around the world picked up on these issues early in the 1990s, when a raft of headlines lamented the emergence of a generation of slackers. In Japan, the cover stories pointed at the young and called them out as "parasite singles," kids who mooched off their parents and refused to accept the strictures of adulthood....[I]t appeared that Japanese youth were somehow defective. They seemed happy to accept part-time jobs and live at home, where their parents picked up the tab for daily expenses, freeing them to go out and party. In a country with famously rigid norms of appropriate behavior, the debut of this slacker generation was a social calamity capable of stopping the presses and flooding the TV talk shows. How could such a serious problem have festered beneath their notice? How had the orderly transition from youth to adulthood suddenly run off the rails?

Americans are generally more tolerant of social change, but here, too, the broadcast media and the daily newspapers began to fill with articles about boys in their mid-twenties sitting in darkened basements, whiling away their time on video games rather than buckling down to pursue adult goals. Psychiatrists diagnosed the problem as a kind of retreat from reality and hinted that indulgent parents were suffering from some kind of "'60s infection." Baby boomers, caricatured as being unable to say no, were accused of alternately cocooning their kids and indulging themselves. "Helicopter parents," who hovered over their progeny, following them off to college to help choose their courses, tending to their every need, were said to lack the backbone to let their children grow up by learning from their failures. If everything has to be perfect, boomers were admonished, your kids are going to be basket cases when they actually try to stand on their own two feet. No wonder Jack and Jill were coming home to live out their twenties: their parents were ready to wrap them in swaddling clothes all over again. Pathetic!

Structural Barriers to Independence

These complaints were largely off the mark. For the most part, young people the world over are still keen on establishing their independence. Twenty-six-year-olds who enjoy the comforts of home still look forward to the day they establish their own hearth. Yet, there are many reasons why that deadline is receding to more distant horizons. The contours of the household are stretching—creating accordion families—because there are few other choices, particularly in societies with weak welfare states (like Japan, Spain, or Italy) and because the advantages to delayed departure are significant compared to launching an independent life with insufficient resources in societies like our own.

Globalization has insured that the economic conditions that underwrote the earlier, more traditional, road to adulthood no longer hold. International competition is greater than it once was, and many countries, fearful of losing markets for their goods and services, are responding by restructuring the labor market to cut the wage bill. Countries that regulated jobs to insure they were full-time, well-paid, and protected from layoffs, now permit part-time, poorly-paid jobs and let employers fire without restriction. That may serve the interests of firms—a debatable low-road strategy—but it has destroyed the options for millions of new entrants to the labor market throughout the advanced postindustrial societies....

In America, we deploy a familiar cultural arsenal in crafting meaning: the work ethic and the hope of upward mobility. If Joe lives at home because it will help him get somewhere in the long run, that's fine. If he's hiding in the basement playing video games, it's not fine. The accordion family has to be in the service of larger goals or it smacks of deviance.

All of these adaptations are responses to central structural forces 10 beyond the control of any of us. Global competition is taking us into uncharted waters, reshaping the life course in ways that would have been scarcely visible only thirty years ago. It's a brave new world, and the accordion family is absorbing the blows as best it can....

Destigmatizing Delayed Adulthood

From one perspective, adulthood is still defined by a clear set of responsibilities; it simply takes longer to get to the point where a young person can reasonably assume them. When that goal becomes so distant, when it stretches into the thirties, parents may look for ways to destigmatize the condition. In the U.S. and elsewhere we see the invention of new kinds of benchmarks that shift the emphasis to a psychological concept of maturity, unhinged from traditional manifestations of adulthood. Jane Azarian, a Newton (Mass.) mother who has long been an activist in feminist circles, sees her daughter's world in these terms. She doesn't completely discount financial independence as a marker of adulthood, but other qualities are more important in her mind:

> I think that being able to support yourself is important. [But it is also important] that you are an attendant to the world, you're not just an adult that is buried in the movies and parties and isn't paying attention to the world. You have to be plugged into the world beyond your family and your next-door neighbors, and that to me is a sign of an adult. And not just aware but figuring out some little thing you can do to be part of making the world a better place.
>
> I also think that being in respectful, caring relationships, not necessarily being married and not necessarily having children but caring about the people in your community and doing something that is one-on-one. If personal meets the political in the things that you do that help an individual, and there are things that you do that help lots of individuals, not necessarily the ones that you see. And I believe that it's important that you do both kinds of things. And do I see it as a sign of being an adult? Yes, I do. That's my definition.

Larry Keegan grew up working class in Brooklyn. He jumped these developmental hurdles "on time" because no one was going to catch him and provide the support that would enable him to slow down and discover himself at a more leisurely pace. He might be the kind of person inclined to be judgmental about the differences between generations, but he is instead fairly even tempered about them. Fate—in the form of the economy—has intervened, he says, to create a different set of conditions for his kids:

"My fellow-graduates, today we leave behind the trappings of youth, step boldly onto the road of life, and move back in with our parents."

The milestones are still the same. It is just a lot harder to achieve. Which is probably what is causing young adults today to figure new solutions to how to do it. A young adult is someone who is willing to take full responsibility for their actions. Someone who is financially independent. Somebody who has a plan of where they are trying to go. And in trying to achieve where they are trying to go, I would say the obstacles are much greater.

In a recent article, Robin Henig, a writer for the *New York Times Magazine*, helped to destigmatize delayed adulthood in ways that underline the psychological theory emerging in the minds of people like Jane. Henig recounts research that claims the brain is still plastic, still growing, still forming new connections well into the twenties. In "What Is It About 20-Somethings?" she reviewed research promoted by Jeffrey Jensen Arnett, a psychology professor at Clark University, that suggested a physiological reason for the spread of delayed departure: the brain just isn't ready yet. Arnett suggests that "emerging adulthood" is no "social construction" but rather a stage of development through which everyone must pass before their bodies are ready for full independence. If the brain is the culprit, it cannot be a source of embarrassment to be living with Mom and Dad. It's just natural.

It is difficult to square this account with the variations we have seen in the space of less than forty years in patterns of adulthood. The gene pool doesn't mutate that fast. If leading-edge boomers were dying to be out on their own, ready to put up with cheap digs, fraying blue jeans, and a diet of pasta in order to maintain their independence, while their younger siblings stuck close to home to preserve a higher standard of living, it is hard to imagine that brain development could explain this divergence. Instead, social conditions are promoting a new way of thinking about developmental pathways. This shift in perspective is not apparent only in the United States but in other countries where social and economic changes have promoted a similarly elastic definition of adulthood....

American parents are...forgiving and...malleable in their expec- 15 tations, particularly if they believe their own choices in life were more constrained than they would have liked. If their own affluence can buy their children more discretion, more time to reach the right landing spot, so much the better. William Rollo from Newton thinks it's just fine for his son, John, to travel and become a cosmopolitan. He wants John to have advantages he didn't have, including the freedom to sample alternative futures so that he is truly content with the choices he makes. That, after all, is what William says he has worked for, to give John options:

> A lot of what he is doing is [trying] to understand what he would like to do for a living. I spent a lot of time doing what I have been doing for the last twenty-five years, and I probably would have liked to have done what I originally went to school for, and it didn't work out, so I would like for him to find out for himself what he would like to do now and go ahead and do it.
>
> That's kind of why I am willing to let him go by not being as strict about paying his share. I continue to do what [I do for a living] in a large part because we wanted to live in a nice place for them to go to school and to help pay for their college education for both of [our sons]. I did that willingly; no one forced me to do it. When it comes down to the end, I think my biggest accomplishment was the kids I produced. I'm feeling that if they turned out OK, and I think they have, and I say that honestly.

Though William is a successful podiatrist, he came up from less elevated circumstances. He wasn't poor, but he didn't grow up in the kind of privilege he has conveyed to his kids. Giving them a boost, making sure that they will benefit from his hard work, is half the reason for being a parent in the first place. If that means protecting them from the pressures of the market through their twenties, then so be it. "My generation, whose parents grew up in the Depression and World War II," William explains, "didn't want to see their children having to live like [they did]." He adds:

> I grew up in a little apartment, and I shared a room with my sister until I was like sixteen, and my sister was six years younger than me and we didn't really have a bedroom. It's nice that I give my kids more than what I had as a kid. At least in this society, every generation that comes

after doesn't want to work as hard as the generation before. Just like the generation before didn't want to work as hard as the parents before them had to work.

Of course, not all middle-class parents can ensure their children want to follow in their footsteps. Some have to redefine what constitutes a respectable career to incorporate different pathways. Gary Mack went to law school and works as a computer network consultant. His son dropped out of the University of Massachusetts and wants to be a blacksmith. Gary explains:

> I suppose there could be [a stigma] if people thought that a child living at home was living at home because they are just good-for-nothing leeches. Then there would be that, but there are plenty of other reasons why kids would live at home. If I knew of somebody whose kid was living with them at home, I would not at all think of it as stigmatizing. If I knew more about the family situation and I knew that the kid was a lazy, good-for-nothing leech then, yeah, but I wouldn't have concluded that simply because they were living at home.

Gary's son wants to live a solid life as a skilled blue-collar worker. And that's just fine with Gary, even if it's hard to explain to his neighbors. But a hard-working, gainfully employed man who can take care of his family—that's a success story in his book. He is willing to support his son to underwrite that future.[1]

To be sure, not all Newton families find these arrangements easy to swallow. Teddy Yoo lives with his parents because he cannot afford the alternatives, but he is not happy about it. Teddy worked in a financial services firm as a customer service representative but lost that job. Perhaps because his living situation is forced by financial limitations, he casts his situation as a form of humiliation:

> [Living at home] is a good thing monetarily but a bad thing spiritually. Because you are living in your parents' household, and it's their rules, and they have those silent and unspoken expectations of you.

Teddy's distress is amplified by his complex relations with his immigrant parents. Tension between immigrants and their more assimilated children is common no matter what the national origin, but Teddy sees it as a rift specific to Asian parents, with their high expectations 20

---

[1]See Jim Cullen, *The American Dream: A Short History of an Idea That Shaped a Nation* (New York: Oxford University Press, 2003); Katherine S. Newman, *Declining Fortunes: The Withering of the American Dream* (New York: Basic Books, 1993). In his 1931 book *The Epic of America*, James Truslow Adams characterized the American Dream as a "better, richer, and happier life for all our citizens of every rank." For many years, society seemed to focus on "richer" as the fulfillment of the dream. However, economic changes have made financial advancement harder to obtain, leading to the inability of young people to achieve even their parents' level of success, much less surpass it. An increased emphasis on personal happiness in all aspects of life may be replacing the emphasis on wealth with the dream of personal fulfillment. [All notes are Newman's.]

and strong sense of self-sacrifice on behalf of the next generation.[2] He explains:

> Living here is very spiritually deadening because my parents are your typical Asian parents. They support you financially but not emotionally. They say the right things, but they always had this expectation of me when I was a kid that I would be a doctor or a lawyer and you're going to go to Harvard. And Asian parents are like that. Some Asian males say it's the white mom. The white mom is someone that says: "Oh so what if you stole your boss's car from work and totaled it? I still love you, and you are a great boy." This is an exaggeration, [but it means that] the white mom will always be supportive no matter what and give you money no matter what.

Second-generation immigrants—those born in the United States of foreign-born parents—do not always experience the kind of conflict brewing in the Yoo household.[3] Some are nostalgic for the close-knit, multigenerational household that was common in their parents' lives in the old country, wherever it was to be found. When their own children boomerang back into the natal home, it feels like a throwback to an earlier era in their family history. Take Esther Goodman, a divorced mother living in Newton whose parents emigrated from Yugoslavia. With a son, daughter, and the daughter's child living at home, she says:

[2]See Amy Chua, *Battle Hymn of the Tiger Mother* (New York: Penguin, 2011). When an excerpt from Yale law professor Chua's book appeared in the *Wall Street Journal* under the headline "Why Chinese Mothers Are Superior," it set off a firestorm of debate. Chua, who was raised by Chinese immigrant parents, details her own childrearing methods, which included not allowing sleepovers or playdates, forcing one of her daughters in elementary school to do two thousand math problems per night until she surpassed her Korean competitor, and refusing the gift of her four-year-old's handmade birthday card that she deemed inadequate in effort. Interestingly, the long subtitle of Chua's book is "This is a story about a mother, two daughters, and two dogs. This was *supposed* to be a story of how Chinese parents are better at raising kids than Western ones. But instead, it's about a bitter clash of cultures, a fleeting taste of glory, and how I was humbled by a thirteen-year-old." Certainly Chua's version of events lends credence to Teddy's assessment of Asian immigrant parents and to the culture clash that such parental expectations can engender for children raised in Western society.

[3]Richard Alba and Victor Nee, *Remaking the American Mainstream: Assimilation and the New Immigration* (Cambridge, MA: Harvard University Press, 2003); H. J. Gans, "Comment: Ethnic Invention and Acculturation: A Bumpy-Line Approach," *Journal of American Ethnic History* 11 (1992): 42–52; Milton M. Gordon, *Assimilation in American Life: The Role of Race, Religion, and National Origins* (New York: Oxford University Press, 1964); A. Portes and M. Zhou, "The New Second Generation: Segmented Assimilation and Its Variants," *Annals of the American Academy of Political and Social Science* 530 (1993): 74–96. There are many theories of assimilation, and patterns outlined may better apply to some immigrant groups than others. Straight-line assimilation theory, long the predominant theory in immigration literature, assumes that over generations of living in the United States, everyone will eventually assume the same norms and values (see Gordon), but contemporary theorists have questioned this model. Alba and Nee propose that assimilation is a two-way street, with immigrants, native residents, and institutions gradually adapting to one another. Gans posits that assimilation can take a long time and that immigrants might assimilate in some areas long before others, a process he terms "bumpy assimilation." Portes and Zhou propose that some immigrants will not assimilate to the dominant values of the overall society but to the dominant norms of the neighborhoods in which they settle. Some immigrants might thus experience downward assimilation, a process Portes and Zhou posit will affect non-white immigrants in particular. Of course, the fact that there are large pockets throughout the United States filled with people who have not assimilated to dominant values and norms also indicates that straight-line assimilation has not occurred consistently and that alternate norms and values have long prevailed among subgroups.

I grew up in an extended family myself, so I am repeating that pattern in a way. It was my grandparents, parents, myself, and my sister living in a single-family home together. Despite the fact that after college I never considered returning home, the fact that my daughter and granddaughter are here is quite natural given the home that I grew up in. I was very close with my grandfather as a child, and I am having that sense with my granddaughter. There is that same availability of grandparents. That is part of the experience.

My granddaughter even said one day when she came home from kindergarten, "I really like living with you" or something like that. It had to do with other children in her class going on some long trip to visit a grandparent and how they didn't get to see them that much and regretting that. She said, "I am really lucky that you live right here." It's a nice experience to watch her grow. I get a lot of pleasure watching my daughter and granddaughter together. I enjoy seeing them together and seeing that sweet interaction.

Elaine Mark is a Newton mother who grew up in Zimbabwe, where her Jewish family settled after World War II. Like Esther, she has fond feelings about accordion households. It feels to Elaine like part of the natural order of things:

I always went home when I was at a certain point and needing to make a decision for my next point in my own family. So I would go home, so I assumed that this was what everybody does. In Europe, for example, a lot of people never left home to go to college or university and assumed that is where you go and maybe get married and you go somewhere else. Here I think it is very strange that everybody goes away to live in a dorm at the university in the same city. That's strange.

If adulthood was once a station in life, marked by cultural conventions of marriage, parenthood, and a "real job," it has become something else in the globalized world we inhabit now. Adult children are migrating home or refraining from leaving in the first place, and there they stay for many years longer than was the case in most countries for decades. It is disruptive to our sense of social order to think of these stay-at-home thirty-year-olds as perpetual adolescents. And indeed, that is not how they describe their state of mind. They see themselves jumping over psychological barriers, feeling that they are taking greater responsibility for their actions than they did in those dreaded teen years. When a twentysomething claims to "feel like an adult," we credit this as a meaningful assertion because they have captured something real: a sense of responsibility and increased mastery, a capacity to imagine a more defined future and plan for it, at least to a greater degree than was common in earlier stages of life.

Adults who came of age in an earlier era are not likely to think this is an adequate substitute for the real thing. But they are coconspirators in the effort to develop this psychological side. All too aware of how much harder it is to afford education and residential autonomy than it was back in the day, American parents recognize that life is simply more costly today, the job market is problematic, and all that combines to limit the capacity of their kids to do what they did in the distant past.

Yet even in countries where cost isn't the question—as is largely the case in Scandinavia—the spread of a "psychological theory" of adulthood is unmistakable. A secular trend is underway that removes the imperatives to leap status hurdles to get to the holy grail of adult respect. Instead, thinking more like a grown-up makes everyone feel like one, and that seems to be the consequence of the spread of accordion families.

The economic conditions that have made it so difficult for today's young people to find a footing in the labor market, coupled with the emergence (and then collapse) of housing bubbles throughout the developed world, have conspired to make it financially difficult to be independent and all the more important for families to band together to pool their resources. Accordion families are, then, a natural response to economic insecurity. 25

ENGAGING THE TEXT

1. How common are "accordion families" in your community or among your friends? If you know adults who are living in their parents' households, is their motivation exclusively economic, or might there be other reasons, such as caring for elders or siblings?

2. Do you think "boomerang kids" or their parents are stigmatized? If so, how is this stigma expressed?

3. Newman briefly profiles several Newton residents: Jane Azarian, Larry Keegan, William Rollo, Gary Mack, Teddy Yoo, Esther Goodman, and Elaine Mark. What does each profile contribute to her composite picture? How comfortable or uncomfortable does each of these people seem in a multigenerational household? Pick one of these residents and write a paragraph predicting what his or her life will be like ten years in the future; share these with classmates to find areas of consensus and disagreement.

4. Analyze the phrases listed below. What assumptions do they make about family life and parent-child relationships? What metaphors do you find, and why have these particular metaphors entered our conversations about families? To what extent do these phrases stigmatize parents or young adults who share a household?

accordion family	failure to launch
boomerang kids	'60s infection
parasite singles	delayed departure
helicopter parents	cocooning

5. Role-play a scenario in which a college graduate talks to his or her parents about moving back in.

EXPLORING CONNECTIONS

6. Discuss the cartoon by David Sipress on page 87. Do you find it funny? Does it mock graduates who will move back in with their parents?

7. Chapter Three of *Rereading America* ("Money and Success: The Myth of Individual Opportunity") is about the "American Dream." What does Newman's analysis tell us about money and success? Do accordion families signal that the American Dream is fading or that downward mobility is now the norm?

8. Read the excerpt from Horatio Alger's *Ragged Dick* on page 246 in Chapter Three. Then write a letter from Ragged Dick to William Rollo, Gary Mack, or Teddy Yoo. Trade letters with a classmate and write responses from the contemporary point of view.

EXTENDING THE CRITICAL CONTEXT

9. Interview one or two seniors majoring in a field that interests you. Have they considered living with their parents after college, and would their parents be open to that idea? Under what circumstances would this be the best option — or the only choice? How similar are your respondents to the people Newman profiles above?

10. In paragraph 13 Newman mentions psychologist Jeffrey Jensen Arnett. Read and report on Arnett's brief article "Oh, Grow Up! Generational Grumbling and the New Life Stage of Emerging Adulthood—Commentary on Trzesniewski & Donnellan" (*Perspectives on Psychological Science* 5(1): 89–92). How does Arnett characterize young adults? To what extent do you agree with his claim that a new life stage has emerged?

QUALITY TIME, REDEFINED

ALEX WILLIAMS

Americans consume an astonishing array of media products — games, videos, blogs, tunes, podcasts, maps — using a host of high-tech devices like laptops, tablets, nanos, and of course increasingly smart smartphones. How is this proliferation of gadgets affecting family life? Are we increasingly isolated from our family members as we text and Tweet and surf, or might the technologies be harmless or even beneficial to family unity and communication? This article from the *New York Times* (April 29, 2011) explores these issues, drawing on opinions from ordinary parents and from experts in psychology, pop culture, and technology studies. Alex Williams is a reporter for the *New York Times* and a contributing editor of *New York Magazine*.

IT WAS A VISION OF FAMILY TOGETHERNESS out of a Norman Rockwell painting, if Rockwell had worked in the era of WiFi. After a taco dinner one Wednesday in March, Dianne Vavra and her family

retreated to the living room of their Cape Cod-style house in Huntington, N.Y., where they curled up on the spacious beige sofa amid hand-stitched quilts as an icy rain pelted the windows.

Ms. Vavra, a cosmetics industry executive in Manhattan, looked up from her iPad, where she was catching up on the latest spring looks at Refinery29.com, and noticed that her husband, Michael Combs, was transfixed, streaming the N.C.A.A. men's basketball tournament on his laptop. Their son, Tom, 8, was absorbed by the Wii game Mario Kart on the widescreen television. Their daughter, Eve, 10, was fiddling with a game app called the Love Calculator on an iPod Touch. "The family was in the same room, but not *together*," Ms. Vavra recalled.

One family. One room. Four screens. Four realities, basically. While it may look like some domestic version of "The Matrix"—families sharing a common space, but plugged into entirely separate planes of existence through technology—a scene like this has become an increasingly familiar evening ritual. As a result, the American living room in 2011 can often seem less like an oasis for shared activity, even if that just means watching television together, than an entangled intersection of data traffic—everyone huddled in a cyber-cocoon.

Call it what you will, it is a wholly different form of quality time.

The culture of home-based iDistraction has already become a pop- 5 culture trope, and no wonder: Never has there been so much to consume, on so many devices. On a recent episode of ABC's "Modern Family," the character Claire Dunphy explodes when she tries to serve the family breakfast, only to be ignored by a husband adjusting his fantasy football roster on his iPad, a son playing video games on his Nintendo DS and two daughters e-mailing each other from across the table. "O.K., now that's it, everybody, gadgets down, now!" she declares. "You're all so involved in your little gizmos, nobody is even talking. Families are supposed to talk!"

Haley, the eldest daughter, writes to her sister, Alex, "Mom's insane," as everyone returns to their screens.

Billy Crystal, in an interview with Jon Stewart on "The Daily Show," joked that couples these days have no qualms about texting someone else during sex — "Oh, is that you!" "Yes!" "LOL!"

CERTAINLY, people have been hyper-wired as long as there have been laptops, and the tendency became more pronounced with the advent of wireless Internet. Nearly 60 percent of American families with children own two or more computers, and more than 60 percent of those have either a wired or wireless network to connect to the Internet, according to studies by the Pew Research Center's Internet and American Life Project. A third of all Americans log on from home multiple times a day, nearly twice the number that did so in 2004.

On top of that, iPads have inundated homes since they were introduced a year ago, as have fast-downloading smartphones. Media companies are jumping on board to make sure their content is available at any time, on any device. In the last six months, Netflix has added thousands of movies available for instant streaming, via its Watch Instantly option. In March, Time Warner Cable made selected channels available on an iPad app. Subscribers to MLB.TV can stream major league baseball games any day of the week through a $14.99 iPhone app. And Amazon recently announced a plan to make e-books from 11,000 public libraries available on its Kindle this year.

That amounts to more screen time in homes where everyone already seems glued to their BlackBerrys or sucked in by Facebook, Twitter, blogs — or work. ¹⁰

It's a profound shift, and one that is not lost on cultural theorists who study the online habits of Americans.

"The transformation of the American living room into a multiscreen communication and entertainment hub" promises to "change our domestic sphere," said Lutz Koepnick, a media professor at Washington University in St. Louis who studies digital culture. "Individual family members might find themselves contently connected to parallel worlds almost all the time."

Indeed, Brad Kahn, an environmental consultant in Seattle, said he often communicates with his wife, Erin, by e-mail even when they are seated a few feet apart on the sofa with their laptops. He will cut her off if she starts instructing him orally about what he calls his "honey-do" list of weekend chores, he said, and ask her to send it electronically.

To Mr. Kahn, 40, it's simply more efficient. "If I misunderstood any directions, having a written record can be very useful in maintaining marital bliss," he said.

Such behavior is not limited to the sofa. Evan Gotlib, who runs advertising sales at blip.tv, an Internet company in Manhattan, recalled ¹⁵

"Me? I thought you were raising them."

sitting in bed recently with his wife, Lindsey Pollak, as both were using iPads. He was playing an online version of Scrabble against his sister, Val, remotely, and at one point said, "Val just got a 46-point word!"

"Ugh," his wife said, "she just hit a 32-pointer against me." At that moment, Mr. Gotlib realized his wife was also playing her own game against his sister.

Typically, at their home in Manhattan, Polly Blitzer Wolkstein and her husband, Mark Wolkstein, settle into the sofa around 7 p.m., perch their respective laptops on opposite armrests, place their BlackBerrys between them and surrender to their multiplicity of screens, often until midnight.

If they're not catching up on work—he is a partner at financial research firm, she runs the Beauty Blitz Web site—Mr. Wolkstein, 38, might be half-watching one show on Hulu on his laptop, another movie on Netflix on his iPad and carrying on a game of Angry Birds. Ms. Blitzer Wolkstein, 35, will be right there beside him, tapping out texts on her BlackBerry while she chases down bonus footage of reality shows on the network Web sites.

Even efforts to have a date night, when they watch the same movie at the same time, go nowhere.

"We gradually migrate to polar ends of the couch, where we bal- 20 ance our laptops and iPads on the arm of the couch, then cyber-indulge during the entire movie, and have to rinse-and-repeat the next night because we missed the entire thing," Ms. Blitzer Wolkstein said in an e-mail. "We've been meaning to watch a documentary about ventriloquists called 'Dumbstruck,' and tonight is supposed to be our 4th attempt."

Sometimes they hold hands while looking at their screens. But failing that, the couple has developed a form of physical shorthand, an "'I'm still here' signal" in which "one of us will tap the other one a couple of times with an index finger."

It's not hard to interpret such moments as evidence that technology has become an alien, and alienating, force in the contemporary home. That view has no shortage of proponents.

Prominent among them is Sherry Turkle, a professor of social studies of science and technology at the Massachusetts Institute of Technology, and the author of "Alone Together: Why We Expect More From Technology and Less From Each Other." The book argues that people's reliance on technology to establish emotional intimacy—whether by "friending" strangers on Facebook or nuzzling robotic Furby pets—can actually increase our sense of feeling inundated and empty. "The new technologies allow us to 'dial down' human contact, to titrate its nature and extent," she writes.

It's a concern shared by Ben Schippers, who runs a software development company in Brooklyn and spends many evenings with his wife, immersed in virtual worlds of their own.

Such evenings, he admits, are rare these days. His wife, Hedda 25 Burnett, is attending veterinary school at Iowa State University, so they manage to see each other in person only every few weeks and otherwise keep in touch over Skype. Mr. Schippers finds evenings oddly similar, whether his wife is in Ames, Iowa, or in New York beside him. Either way, "She's on her LCD, I'm on my LCD," he said.

He wondered about a cost in emotional intimacy in American homes, as more households adopt a similar evening ritual. "What does a television in the bedroom do to someone's sex life?" he asked. Now screens are popping up between people throughout the house.

James Gleick, the author of the new book "The Information: A History, a Theory, a Flood," said he has been known to spend evenings at home with his wife, each tapped into their own iPad, white cords dangling from their ears. In the near future, he said jokingly, "A new skill that will be taught by relationship counselors will be knowing when and how to interrupt one's loved ones: Is a particular joke you've just read on Twitter worth her yanking out her earbuds?"

Joanne Cantor, a professor emerita and a director of the Center for Communication Research at the University of Wisconsin, suggests it's almost as if adults and older children are reverting to a form of "parallel play," the developmental stage when toddlers sit beside each other in silence, playing with toys of their own. Even in the very recent past, when family members would be watching TV together, she said, "We all had conversations during the commercials, even if it was just to say, 'Wasn't that stupid?'"

THEN again, this is not the first time that the appearance of home media has caused an outcry—perhaps needlessly, in hindsight.

"If you go back 200 years, there were similar complaints about technological devices, but it was books at that time," Dr. Koepnick said. "The family room filled with different people reading books created a lot of concerns and anxiety, particularly regarding women, because all of a sudden they were on their own, their minds were drifting into areas that could no longer be controlled." 30

Likewise, the emergence of television led to decades of hand-wringing over the specter of American families transformed into sitcom-addicted zombies. Dr. Koepnick also points out that those evenings of family television usually involved a struggle over the channel knob, or later, the remote.

In that light, iPads and laptops can be a tool of democratization, if not détente. Now, he said, "everyone has their own device, streams their own films, their own media, so there's no longer a struggle or challenge within the family over what is it we want to see."

Even before iPads, there was evidence that Web-centric home life might not, in fact, be eating away at family unity. Barry Wellman, a professor of sociology at the University of Toronto who studies the effect of technology on social communities, said that his research supports the findings of studies like a 2009 survey of 4,000 people by a Canadian market research company indicating that people believe technology is bringing the family together, not pulling it apart, by a substantial margin.

This might be even truer in households nowadays, when the proliferation of devices and media options makes it easier for family members to pursue their interests online while seated in the same room, Dr. Wellman said.

Behavior inside a cyber-cocoon can be surprisingly interactive. "There's a lot of, 'Hey, look at this!' 'Let's plan our trip to Vegas!'" he said. "People get up from their laptops, come together on one screen: 'Hey, look what I just found, isn't this weird?' It isn't the image of one person huddled in isolation with their screen." 35

Robert Rosenthal, who runs a marketing company in Manhattan, also recalls his youth, when his mother had to call around to friends' houses in the evening to find him. "When everyone is doing their digital thing out in the open," he said, "the total death of privacy is a parental advantage." Now, he usually just needs to check the far corners of his living room. There's Ariana, 15, doing her homework online or poking friends on Facebook. There's Veronica, 11, iChatting with friends, next to his wife, Carolyn Kremins, who might be shoe shopping on Gilt .com on her MacBook, while Mr. Rosenthal, himself, catches up on work e-mail.

Mr. Gotlib, of Manhattan, said that new online hardware and media options allow him and his wife to "to experience new levels of closeness." In recent weeks, they sat next to each other in the evening; he was wearing headphones and watching an entire season of "The Wire" that he'd downloaded off iTunes on his iPad, while she read "The Art of Immersion" by Frank Rose on hers.

"Three or four years ago, I would have been downstairs watching TV, and she would have been upstairs reading," Mr. Gotlib said. "I guarantee that we spend 80 percent more time together because of the iPad."

Rather than a sign of a dysfunctional relationship, such behavior can actually be interpreted as the sign of health, said Ronald Levant, a professor of psychology at the University of Akron. "People who think every minute we're together we have to connect are going to drive each other crazy, because we all need some alone time, no matter how compatible a couple might be," Dr. Levant said. "At a certain point in your relationship," he added, "your task to keeping the relationship vital and refreshed is managed togetherness and separateness. Technology could be used as a tool to assist that."

In the end, that was the conclusion that Ms. Vavra, the cosmetics 40 executive, reached after a series of nights like the one after taco night. Even though she and her husband were moved to declare "tech-free Sundays" so they could pursue outdoor activities, far from the clutter of devices, she has learned to appreciate the interchange that comes from nights when everyone is peering up from screens of their own.

"There's a lot of crossover," she said. "My daughter will be doing something on the iTouch, and say 'Mommy, look at this!' I'll be doing something on my iPad, and she's interested in what I'm doing. And my son is excited because he 'un-locked' something on Mario Kart. I don't know exactly what that means, but we're all there to witness the unlocking."

Arguably, she said, an evening like that can bring more closeness than a night spent huddling over a board game back in the days of analog.

"'Together time' in the past was sometimes an effort, and a forced moment, where we would schedule it — 'O.K., after dinner every night at 7 we're going to watch this or play this,' and the kids would say, 'But Mom, I wanted to do this,'" Ms. Vavra recalled. "Now, it's not forced at all. It just organically happens. Everyone gets to do their own thing, rather than, 'Do we have to play Clue again?'"

ENGAGING THE TEXT

1. Working from direct observation or from memory, list the technological devices your family members use to access media. Roughly how much time do they spend engaged with digital media? If Williams visited your home, would he find your family living in a "cyber-cocoon"?

2. In your experience, does the presence of four screens in a room suggest that people are living in four largely separate realities? Do you see any evidence that "technology has become an alien, and alienating, force in the

contemporary home" (para. 22)? Do you find the families profiled in the article extreme in their media consumption, or fairly typical?

3. Ms. Vavra's executive job, the family's "Cape Cod-style" house, the "hand-stitched quilts" and "spacious beige sofa"—all these suggest a certain level of affluence. Discuss how technologies like smartphones and WiFi are affecting middle-class family life. What about working-class family life?

4. In small groups, work through "Quality Time, Redefined" and list what each female mentioned is doing with her technology and what each male is doing with his. Is there a clear gender divide in media consumption, and if so, what implications does this hold for family life and raising children? To extend the assignment, analyze generational differences suggested by the article—how parents and kids may use technologies differently.

EXPLORING CONNECTIONS

5. Williams begins his article by referring to Norman Rockwell's paintings of American family life. One of these iconic images, *Freedom from Want*, appears in this chapter's Visual Portfolio (p. 58). Compare and contrast Rockwell's image with the photo by Yana Paskova (p. 94), paying attention to the people in the images, the physical environment, the objects, and especially the messages you think the images communicate.

6. "Looking for Work" by Gary Soto (p. 22) and "An Indian Story" by Roger Jack (see bedfordstmartins.com/rereading/epages) describe growing up in environments where media options were less diverse and arguably less pervasive. Does "quality time" in those environments seem any healthier for kids or families than the redefined quality time Williams describes in this article?

EXTENDING THE CRITICAL CONTEXT

7. Spend thirty minutes with classmates, friends, or family playing an old-fashioned board game like Monopoly or Clue in a gadget-free zone—no phones, iPods, TV, Internet, and so on. Describe and reflect on the experience in class discussion or a journal entry. Where did you find a non-digital game? Was the half hour excruciatingly boring or kind of fun? Did you begin to suffer cell-phone withdrawal? Do you see any evidence that taking an occasional break from technology might enhance interactions with friends or family?

8. Use the first "Engaging the Text" question above as the foundation of a class survey of media consumption: after recording how often your own family uses various media, pool your data with that of classmates and construct a table, bar graph, or pie chart of media use. Which media are most popular or consume the greatest amount of time and attention? Which promote family interaction, and which might tend to isolate family members? Does the media use you observe suggest any fundamental change in how families work, or simply an expanding range of convenient or entertaining technologies?

FURTHER CONNECTIONS

1. Family relationships are a frequent subject for novels and films, perhaps because these extended forms can take the time to explore the complexities of family dynamics. Keeping in mind the issues raised in this chapter, write an essay analyzing the portrayal of family in a single contemporary novel or film.

2. Writers and analysts routinely use data from the U.S. Census Bureau to get a "snapshot" of the American population as a whole or to track national trends over time. However, the bureau also provides a wealth of information at the state and county levels. Choose two counties in your state that you think are substantially different demographically; explore the Census Bureau Web site (www.census.gov) and gather statistical data on items like size of households, their median income, the number of households headed by women, and so on. Report your findings to the class, or collaborate with classmates to build an overview of your state.

3. Tolstoy wrote that all happy families are alike, but that each unhappy family is unhappy in its own way. Taking into account your own experience and the readings in this chapter, write a journal entry or an essay articulating your views of what makes families happy or unhappy, and assessing your own experiences of family up to this point in your life.

4. **Connecting to the e-Pages.** Choose a single aspect of family life that has been important in your own family's history—for example, religious faith, working mothers, home schooling, family vacations, or divorce and remarriage. Focusing on your selected topic and using the e-Pages video *Just a Family* as inspiration, create a short video or podcast exploring the experiences and opinions of at least two generations of your family. What has changed through the years, and what common threads link the generations?

LEARNING POWER
The Myth of Education and Empowerment

FAST FACTS

1. In 2010, the mean annual earnings of U.S. workers by educational level were:

Without a high school diploma	$20, 241
With a high school diploma	$30,627
With a bachelor's degree	$56,665
With a master's degree	$73,738
With a professional degree	$127,803

2. As of May 2012, the nationwide unemployment rates for U.S. citizens over the age of 25 by educational level were:

Without a high school diploma	13%
With a high school diploma	8.1%
With a bachelor's degree or higher	3.9%

3. According to a 2007 Gates Foundation report, 71% of U.S. students earn a high school diploma, with fewer than six in ten minority students graduating with their peers. Of those who drop out, 48% say their classes weren't interesting, 38% say they had too much freedom and not enough rules, and 32% say that they had to get a job.

4. Today, the average white U.S. student attends a school with 77% white enrollment; black and Latino students attend schools where two-thirds of the total enrollment is made up of blacks and Latinos. In these "intensely segregated" schools, 75% of the students live near or below the poverty line.

5. Average tuition and fees at public 4-year colleges in the United States increased at a rate of 6.5% a year from $8,600 in 2001 to $15,100 in 2010. If this trend continues, the annual cost of a public college education will go up to more than $22,000 by 2016.

6. In 2012, two-thirds of all bachelor's degree recipients took out loans to attend college, with the average student debt exceeding $25,000; at $1 trillion, total U.S. student loan debt now exceeds total U.S. credit card debt.

Sources: (1) U.S. Census Bureau; (2) U.S. Bureau of Labor Statistics; (3) The Bill and Melinda Gates Foundation; (4) The UCLA Civil Rights Project, *Historic Reversals, Accelerating Resegregation, and the Need for Integration Strategies*; (5) U.S. Department of Education.

Broke out of Chester gaol,[1] last night, one James Rockett, a very short well set fellow, pretends to be a schoolmaster, of a fair complexion, and smooth fac'd; Had on when he went away, a light colored camblet coat, a blue cloth jacket, without sleeves, a check shirt, a pair of old dy'd leather breaches, gray worsted stockings, a pair of half worn pumps, and an almost new beaver hat; his hair is cut off, and wears a cap; he is a great taker of snuff, and very apt to get drunk; he has with him two certificates, one from some inhabitants in Burlington county, Jersey, which he will no doubt produce as a pass. Who ever takes up and secures said Rockett in any gaol, shall have two Pistoles reward, paid by October 27, 1756. —SAMUEL SMITH, Gaoler*

—ADVERTISEMENT FOR A "RUNAWAY SCHOOLMASTER"
PENNSYLVANIA GAZETTE, NOVEMBER 25, 1756

AMERICANS HAVE ALWAYS HAD mixed feelings about schooling. Today, most Americans tend to see education as something intrinsically valuable or important. After all, education is the engine that drives the American Dream. The chance to learn, better oneself, and gain the skills that pay off in upward mobility has sustained the hope of millions of Americans. As a nation we look up to figures like Abraham Lincoln and Frederick Douglass, who learned to see beyond poverty and slavery by learning to read. Education tells us that the American Dream can work for everyone. It reassures us that we are, in fact, "created equal" and that the path to achievement lies through individual effort and hard work, not blind luck or birth.

But as the advertisement quoted above suggests, American attitudes toward teachers and teaching haven't always been overwhelmingly positive. The Puritans who established the Massachusetts Bay Colony viewed education with respectful skepticism. Schooling in Puritan society was a force for spiritual rather than worldly advancement. Lessons were designed to reinforce moral and religious training and to teach children to read the Bible for themselves. Education was important to the Puritan "Divines" because it was a source of order, control, and discipline. But when education aimed at more worldly goals or was undertaken for self-improvement, it was seen as a menacing, sinful luxury. Little wonder, then, that the Puritans often viewed teaching as something less than an ennobling profession. In fact, teachers in the early colonies were commonly treated as menial employees by the families and communities they served. The following list of the "Duties of a Schoolmaster" gives you some idea of the status of American educators in the year 1661:

1. Act as court-messenger
2. Serve summonses
3. Conduct certain ceremonial church services
4. Lead Sunday choir

[1] *gaol:* Jail.

5. Ring bell for public worship
6. Dig graves
7. Take charge of school
8. Perform other occasional duties

Colonial American teachers were frequently indentured servants who had sold themselves for five to ten years, often for the price of passage to the New World. Once here, they drilled their masters' children in spiritual exercises until they earned their freedom — or escaped.

The reputation of education in America began to improve with the onset of the Revolutionary War. Following the overthrow of British rule, leaders sought to create a spirit of nationalism that would unify the former colonies. Differences were to be set aside, for, as George Washington pointed out, "the more homogeneous our citizens can be made...the greater will be our prospect of permanent union." The goal of schooling became the creation of uniformly loyal, patriotic Americans. In the words of Benjamin Rush, one of the signers of the Declaration of Independence, "Our schools of learning, by producing one general and uniform system of education, will render the mass of people more homogeneous and thereby fit them more easily for uniform and peaceable government."

Thomas Jefferson saw school as a training ground for citizenship and democratic leadership. Recognizing that an illiterate and ill-informed population would be unable to assume the responsibilities of self-government, Jefferson laid out a comprehensive plan in 1781 for public education in the state of Virginia. According to Jefferson's blueprint, all children would be eligible for three years of free public instruction. Of those who could not afford further schooling, one promising "genius" from each school was to be "raked from the rubbish" and given six more years of free education. At the end of that time, ten boys would be selected to attend college at public expense. Jeffersonian Virginia may have been the first place in the United States where education so clearly offered the penniless boy a path to self-improvement. However, this path was open to very few, and Jefferson, like Washington and Rush, was more concerned with benefiting the state than serving the individual student: "We hope to avail the state of those talents which nature has sown as liberally among the poor as the rich, but which perish without use, if not sought for and cultivated." For leaders of the American Revolution, education was seen as a tool for nation-building, not personal development.

Perhaps that's why Native American leaders remained lukewarm to the idea of formal education despite its growing popularity with their colonial neighbors. When, according to Ben Franklin's report, the government of Virginia offered to provide six American Indian youths with the best college education it could afford in 1744, the tribal leaders of the Six Nations politely declined, pointing out that

> our ideas of this kind of education happen not to be the same with yours. We have had some experience of it; several of our young people were formerly brought up at the colleges of the northern provinces; they were instructed in all your sciences; but when they came back to us, they were bad runners; ignorant of every means of living in the woods; unable to bear either cold or hunger; knew neither how to build a cabin, take a deer, or kill an enemy; spoke our language imperfectly; were therefore neither fit for hunters, warriors, or counselors: they were totally good for nothing.

It's not surprising that these tribal leaders saw American education as useless. Education works to socialize young people — to teach them the values, beliefs, and skills central to their society; the same schooling that prepared students for life in Anglo-American culture made them singularly unfit for tribal life. As people who stood outside the dominant society, Native Americans were quick to realize education's potential as a tool for enforcing cultural conformity. But despite their resistance, by the 1880s the U.S. government had established special "Indian schools" dedicated to assimilating Indian children into Anglo-American culture and destroying tribal knowledge and tribal ways.

In the nineteenth century two great historical forces — industrialization and immigration — combined to exert even greater pressure for the "homogenization" of young Americans. Massive immigration from Ireland and Eastern and Central Europe led to fears that "non-native" peoples would undermine the cultural identity of the United States. Many saw school as the first line of defense against this perceived threat, a place where the children of "foreigners" could become Americanized. In a meeting of educators in 1836, one college professor stated the problem as bluntly as possible:

> Let us now be reminded, that unless we educate our immigrants, they will be our ruin. It is no longer a mere question of benevolence, of duty, or of enlightened self-interest, but the intellectual and religious training of our foreign population has become essential to our own safety; we are prompted to it by the instinct of self-preservation.

Industrialization gave rise to another kind of uniformity in nineteenth-century public education. Factory work didn't require the kind of educational preparation needed to transform a child into a craftsman or merchant. So, for the first time in American history, school systems began to categorize students into different educational "tracks" that offered qualitatively different kinds of education to different groups. Some — typically students from well-to-do homes — were prepared for professional and managerial positions. But most were consigned to education for life "on the line." Increasing demand for factory workers put a premium on young people who were obedient and able to work in large groups according to fixed schedules. As a result, leading educators in 1874 proposed a system of schooling that would meet the needs of the "modern industrial community" by stressing "punctuality, regularity, attention, and silence, as habits necessary through life." History complicates the myth of education as a source of personal empowerment. School can bind as effectively as it can liberate; it can enforce conformity and limit life chances as well as foster individual talent.

But history also supplies examples of education serving the idealistic goals of democracy, equality, and self-improvement. Nineteenth-century educator and reformer Horace Mann worked to expand educational opportunity to all Americans. Mann believed that genuine democratic self-government would become a reality only if every citizen were sufficiently educated to make reasoned judgments about even the thorniest public issues. "Education," according to Mann, "must prepare our citizens to become municipal officers, intelligent jurors, honest witnesses, legislators, or competent judges of legislation — in fine, to fill all the manifold relations of life." In Mann's conception, the "common school," offering educational opportunity to anyone with the will to learn, would make good on the central promise of American democracy; it would become "the great equalizer of the conditions of men."

At the turn of the century, philosopher and educational theorist John Dewey made even greater claims for educational empowerment. A fierce opponent of the kind of "tracking" associated with industrial education, Dewey proposed that schools should strive to produce thinking citizens rather than obedient workers. As members of a democracy, all men and women, according to Dewey, are entitled to an education that helps them make the best of their natural talents and enables them to participate as fully as possible in the life of their community: "only by being true to the full growth of the individuals who make it up, can society by any chance be true to itself." Most of our current myths of education echo the optimism of Mann and Dewey. Guided by their ideas, most Americans still believe that education leads to self-improvement and can help us empower ourselves — and perhaps even transform our society.

Does education empower us? Or does it stifle personal growth by squeezing us into prefabricated cultural molds? This chapter takes a critical look at American education: what it can do and how it shapes or enhances our identities. The first set of readings provides a starting point for exploring the myth of educational empowerment. We begin with a classic statement of the goals of American education — Horace Mann's 1848 "Report of the Massachusetts Board of Education." Mann's optimistic view of education as a means of social mobility in a democratic state provides a clear statement of the myth of personal empowerment through education. For a quick update on where we stand a century and a half later, we turn to documentary filmmaker Michael Moore's scathing assessment of the current state of American education in "Idiot Nation."

Next, in "Against School," veteran teacher and libertarian John Taylor Gatto offers his own provocative analysis of how public education "cripples our kids." In "'I Just Wanna Be Average,'" Mike Rose provides a moving personal account of the dream of educational success and pays tribute to an inner-city teacher who never loses sight of what can be achieved in a classroom. An excerpt from Jean Anyon's "Social Class and the Hidden Curriculum of Work" rounds off the section by suggesting that schools virtually program students for success or failure according to their socioeconomic status.

Following these initial readings, the chapter's Visual Portfolio features two paintings by Norman Rockwell that represent some of America's most hallowed cultural memories of the classroom experience. Rockwell's "The Graduate" and his famous civil-rights-era portrait of Ruby Bridges invite you to reflect on the place of education in America's cultural mythology. Additional images of contemporary classrooms raise questions about the current state of education in America.

The next group of readings offers you the chance to explore the complex interaction of education, race, and power in American society. In "Learning to Read," Malcolm X describes how his own self-education in prison liberated him from the "whitened" account of history he learned in school. Next, in her poem "Para Teresa," Inés Hernández-Ávila asks whether academic success requires cultural self-betrayal or whether it can also be an act of rebellion against racism and social oppression. Educational activist Jonathan Kozol follows with "Still

Separate, Still Unequal," his examination of the resegregation of America's urban schools and the negative impact of the education reform movement.

The chapter concludes with two selections focusing on issues in higher education. In "College at Risk," Andrew Delbanco reflects on the meaning of liberal education and on the social, economic, and technological forces that threaten its future. "Underground Undergrads," the final selection in the chapter, presents the voices of two "undocumented" college students who make the case for passage of the DREAM Act and with it the opportunity to follow their own dreams of educational success.

The e-Pages for *Rereading America* offer more opportunities for continuing your exploration of education and empowerment. In *The Achievement of Desire*, Richard Rodriguez describes what it means to be a "scholarship boy" and to feel torn between family, home culture, and school. Next, the video *The Commercial Campus* highlights a potentially disturbing trend in higher education: the use of students by corporations to sell products directly to their unsuspecting peers. See bedfordstmartins.com/rereading/epages for these two selections.

Sources

Best, John Hardin, and Robert T. Sidwell, eds. *The American Legacy of Learning: Readings in the History of Education*. Philadelphia: J. B. Lippincott Co., 1966. Print.

Cohen, Sol, ed. *Education in the United States: A Documentary History*. 5 vols. New York: Random House, 1974. Print.

Dewey, John. "The School and Society" (1899) and "My Pedagogic Creed" (1897). *John Dewey on Education*. New York: Modern Library, 1964. Print.

Franklin, Benjamin. "Remarks Concerning the Savages of North America." *The Works of Dr. Benjamin Franklin*. Hartford: S. Andrus and Son, 1849. Print.

Jefferson, Thomas. *Notes on the State of Virginia*. Chapel Hill: University of North Carolina Press, 1955. Print.

Pangle, Lorraine Smith and Thomas L. *The Learning of Liberty: The Educational Ideas of the American Founders*. Lawrence: University Press of Kansas, 1993. Print.

Pitt, Leonard. *We Americans*. 3rd ed. Vol. 2. Dubuque: Kendall/Hunt, 1987. Print.

Stevens, Edward, and George H. Wood. *Justice, Ideology, and Education: An Introduction to the Social Foundations of Education*. New York: Random House, 1987. Print.

Vallance, Elizabeth. "Hiding the Hidden Curriculum: An Interpretation of the Language of Justification in Nineteenth-Century Educational Reform." *Curriculum Theory Network*, Vol. 4. No. 1. Toronto: Ontario Institute for Studies in Education, 1973–1974. 5–21. Print.

Westbrook, Robert B. "Public Schooling and American Democracy." *Democracy, Education, and the Schools*. Ed. Roger Soder. San Francisco: Jossey-Bass Publishers, 1996. Print.

BEFORE READING

- Freewrite for fifteen or twenty minutes about your best and worst educational experiences. Then, working in groups, compare notes to see if you can find recurring themes or ideas in what you've written. What aspects of school seem to stand out most clearly in your memories? Do the best experiences have anything in common? How about the worst? What aspects of your school experience didn't show up in the freewriting?

- Work in small groups to draw a collective picture that expresses your experience of high school or college. Don't worry about your drawing skill—just load the page with imagery, feelings, and ideas. Then show your work to other class members and let them try to interpret it.

- Write a journal entry from the point of view of the girl pictured on the title page of this chapter (p. 103). Try to capture the thoughts that are going through her head. What has her day in school been like? What is she looking forward to? What is she dreading? Share your entries with your classmates and discuss your responses.

FROM REPORT OF THE MASSACHUSETTS BOARD OF EDUCATION, 1848

HORACE MANN

If you check a list of schools in your home state, you'll probably discover at least a few dedicated to the memory of Horace Mann. We memorialize Mann today in school systems across the country because he may have done more than any other American to codify the myth of empowerment through education. Born on a farm in Franklin, Massachusetts, in 1796, Mann raised himself out of rural poverty to a position of national eminence through hard work and study. His first personal educational experiences, however, were far from pleasurable: the ill-trained and often brutal school-masters he first encountered in rural Massachusetts made rote memorization and the power of the rod the focus of their educational approach. After graduating from Brown University in 1819, Mann pursued a career in law and politics and eventually served as president of the Massachusetts State Senate. Discouraged by the condition of the state's public schools, Mann abandoned his political career to become secretary of the Massachusetts Board of Education in 1837. Mann's vision of "the common school," the centerpiece of his approach to democratic education, grew out of research he conducted on the Prussian school system during his tour of Europe in 1843. Presented originally as an address to the Massachusetts State Legislature, the report of 1848 has had a lasting impact on the goals and content of American education.

WITHOUT UNDERVALUING ANY OTHER HUMAN AGENCY, IT MAY BE safely affirmed that the common school, improved and ener-gized as it can easily be, may become the most effective and benignant of all the forces of civilization. Two reasons sustain this position. In the first place, there is a universality in its operation, which can be affirmed of no other institution whatever. If administered in the spirit of justice and conciliation, all the rising generation may be brought within the circle of its reformatory and elevating influences. And, in the second place, the materials upon which it operates are so pliant and ductile as to be susceptible of assuming a greater variety of forms than any other earthly work of the Creator. The inflexibility and ruggedness of the oak, when compared with the lithe sapling or the tender germ, are but feeble emblems to typify the docility of childhood when contrasted with the obduracy and intractableness of man. It is these inherent advantages of the common school, which, in our own State, have produced results so striking, from a system so imperfect, and an administration so feeble. In teaching the blind and the deaf and dumb, in kindling the latent spark of intelligence that lurks in an idiot's mind, and in the more holy work of reforming abandoned and outcast children, education has proved what it can do by glorious experiments. These wonders it has done in its infancy, and with the lights of a limited experience; but when its faculties shall be fully developed, when it shall be trained to wield its mighty energies for the protection of society against the giant vices which now invade and torment it,—against intemperance, avarice, war, slavery, bigotry, the woes of want, and the wickedness of waste,—then there will not be a height to which these enemies of the race can escape which it will not scale, nor a Titan among them all whom it will not slay.

I proceed, then, in endeavoring to show how the true business of the schoolroom connects itself, and becomes identical, with the great interests of society. The former is the infant, immature state of those interests; the latter their developed, adult state. As "the child is father to the man," so may the training of the schoolroom expand into the institutions and fortunes of the State.

Physical Education

In the worldly prosperity of mankind, health and strength are indispensable ingredients....

Leaving out, then, for the present purpose, all consideration of the pains of sickness and the anguish of bereavement, the momentous truth still remains, that sickness and premature death are positive evils for the statesman and political economist to cope with. The earth, as a hospital for the diseased, would soon wear out the love of life; and, if but the half of mankind were sick, famine, from non-production, would speedily threaten the whole.

Now, modern science has made nothing more certain than that both good and ill health are the direct result of causes mainly within our own control. In other words, the health of the race is dependent upon the conduct of the race. The health of the individual is determined primarily by his parents, secondarily by himself. The vigorous growth of the body, its strength and its activity, its powers of endurance, and its length of life, on the one hand; and dwarfishness, sluggishness, infirmity, and premature death on the other,—are all the subjects of unchangeable laws. These laws are ordained of God; but the knowledge of them is left to our diligence, and the observance of them to our free agency....

My general conclusion, then, under this head, is, that it is the duty of all the governing minds in society—whether in office or out of it—to diffuse a knowledge of these beautiful and beneficent laws of health and life throughout the length and breadth of the State; to popularize them; to make them, in the first place, the common acquisition of all, and, through education and custom, the common inheritance of all, so that the healthful habits naturally growing out of their observance shall be inbred in the people, exemplified in the personal regimen of each individual, incorporated into the economy of every household, observable in all private dwellings, and in all public edifices, especially in those buildings which are erected by capitalists for the residence of their work-people, or for renting to the poorer classes; obeyed, by supplying cities with pure water; by providing public baths, public walks, and public squares; by rural cemeteries; by the drainage and sewerage of populous towns, and by whatever else may promote the general salubrity of the atmosphere: in fine, by a religious observance of all those sanitary regulations with which modern science has blessed the world.

For this thorough diffusion of sanitary intelligence, the common school is the only agency. It is, however, an adequate agency....

Intellectual Education as a Means of Removing Poverty, and Securing Abundance

...According to the European theory, men are divided into classes,— some to toil and earn, others to seize and enjoy. According to the Massachusetts theory, all are to have an equal chance for earning, and equal security in the enjoyment of what they earn. The latter tends to equality of condition; the former, to the grossest inequalities....

But is it not true that Massachusetts, in some respects, instead of adhering more and more closely to her own theory, is becoming emulous of the baneful examples of Europe? The distance between the two extremes of society is lengthening, instead of being abridged. With every generation, fortunes increase on the one hand, and some new privation is added to poverty on the other. We are verging towards those extremes of opulence and of penury, each of which unhumanizes the human mind. A perpetual struggle for the bare necessaries of life, without the ability to obtain them, makes men wolfish. Avarice, on the other hand, sees, in all the victims of misery around it, not objects for pity and succor, but only crude materials to be worked up into more money.

I suppose it to be the universal sentiment of all those who mingle any 10 ingredient of benevolence with their notions on political economy, that vast and overshadowing private fortunes are among the greatest dangers to which the happiness of the people in a republic can be subjected. Such fortunes would create a feudalism of a new kind, but one more oppressive and unrelenting than that of the middle ages. The feudal lords in England and on the Continent never held their retainers in a more abject condition of servitude than the great majority of foreign manufacturers and capitalists hold their operatives and laborers at the present day. The means employed are different; but the similarity in results is striking. What force did then, money does now. The villein of the middle ages had no spot of earth on which he could live, unless one were granted to him by his lord. The operative or laborer of the present day has no employment, and therefore no bread, unless the capitalist will accept his services. The vassal had no shelter but such as his master provided for him. Not one in five thousand of English operatives or farm-laborers is able to build or own even a hovel; and therefore they must accept such shelter as capital offers them. The baron prescribed his own terms to his retainers: those terms were peremptory, and the serf must submit or perish. The British manufacturer or farmer prescribes the rate of wages he will give to his work-people; he reduces these wages under whatever pretext he pleases; and they, too, have no alternative but submission or starvation. In some respects, indeed, the condition of the modern dependant is more forlorn than that of the corresponding serf class in former times. Some attributes of the patriarchal relation did spring up between the lord and his lieges to soften the harsh relations subsisting between them. Hence came some oversight of the condition of children, some relief in sickness, some protection and support in the decrepitude of age. But only in instances comparatively few have kindly offices smoothed the rugged relation between British capital and British labor. The children of the work-people are abandoned to their fate; and notwithstanding the privations they suffer, and the dangers they threaten, no power in the realm has yet been able to secure them an education; and when the adult laborer is prostrated by sickness, or eventually worn out by toil and age, the poorhouse, which has all along been his destination, becomes his destiny....

Now, surely nothing but universal education can counterwork this tendency to the domination of capital and servility of labor. If one class possesses all the wealth and the education, while the residue of society is ignorant and poor, it matters not by what name the relation between them may be called: the latter, in fact and in truth, will be the servile dependants and subjects of the former. But, if education be equably diffused, it will draw property after it by the strongest of all attractions, for such a thing never did happen, and never can happen, as that an intelligent and practical body of men should be permanently poor. Property and labor in different classes are essentially antagonistic; but property and labor in the same class are essentially fraternal. The people of Massachusetts have, in some degree, appreciated the truth, that the unexampled prosperity of the State—its comfort, its competence, its general intelligence and virtue—is attributable to the education, more or less perfect, which all its people have received: but are they sensible of a fact equally important; namely, that it is to this same education that two-thirds of the people are indebted for not being today the vassals of as severe a tyranny, in the form of capital, as the lower classes of Europe are bound to in the form of brute force?

Education, then, beyond all other devices of human origin, is the great equalizer of the conditions of men,—the balance-wheel of the social machinery. I do not here mean that it so elevates the moral nature as to make men disdain and abhor the oppression of their fellow-men. This idea pertains to another of its attributes. But I mean that it gives each man the independence and the means by which he can resist the selfishness of other men. It does better than to disarm the poor of their hostility towards the rich: it prevents being poor. Agrarianism is the revenge of poverty against wealth. The wanton destruction of the property of others—the burning of hay-ricks and corn-ricks, the demolition of machinery because it supersedes hand-labor, the sprinkling of vitriol on rich dresses—is only agrarianism run mad. Education prevents both the revenge and the madness. On the other hand, a fellow-feeling for one's class or caste is the common instinct of hearts not wholly sunk in selfish regards for person or for family. The spread of education, by enlarging the cultivated class or caste, will open a wider area over which the social feelings will expand; and, if this education should be universal and complete, it would do more than all things else to obliterate factitious distinctions in society....

For the creation of wealth, then,—for the existence of a wealthy people and a wealthy nation,—intelligence is the grand condition. The number of improvers will increase as the intellectual constituency, if I may call it, increases. In former times, and in most parts of the world even at the present day, not one man in a million has ever had such a development of mind as made it possible for him to become a contributor to art or science. Let this development precede, and contributions, numberless, and of inestimable value, will be sure to follow. That political economy, therefore, which busies itself about capital and labor, supply and demand, interest and rents, favorable and unfavorable balances of trade, but leaves out of account the element of a widespread mental development, is nought but stupendous folly. The greatest of all the arts in political economy is to change a consumer into a producer; and the next greatest is to increase the producer's producing power,—an end to be directly attained by increasing his intelligence. For mere delving, an ignorant man is but little better than a swine, whom he so much resembles in his appetites, and surpasses in his powers of mischief....

Political Education

The necessity of general intelligence,—that is, of education (for I use the terms as substantially synonymous, because general intelligence can never exist without general education, and general education will be sure to produce general intelligence),—the necessity of general intelligence under a republican form of government, like most other very important truths, has become a very trite one. It is so trite, indeed, as to have lost much of its force by its familiarity. Almost all the champions of education seize upon this argument first of all, because it is so simple as to be understood by the ignorant, and so strong as to convince the sceptical. Nothing would be easier than to follow in the train of so many writers, and to demonstrate by logic, by history, and by the nature of the case, that a republican form of government, without intelligence in the people, must be, on a vast scale, what a madhouse, without superintendent or keepers, would be on a small one,—the despotism of a few succeeded by universal anarchy, and anarchy by despotism, with no change but from bad to worse....

However elevated the moral character of a constituency may be, however well informed in matters of general science or history, yet they must, if citizens of a republic, understand something of the true nature and functions of the government under which they live. That any one, who is to participate in the government of a country when he becomes a man, should receive no instruction respecting the nature and functions of the government he is afterwards to administer, is a political solecism. In all nations, hardly excepting the most rude and barbarous, the future sovereign receives some training which is supposed to fit him for the exercise of the powers and duties of his anticipated station. Where, by force of law, the government devolves upon the heir while yet in a state of legal infancy, some regency, or other substitute, is appointed to act in his stead until his arrival at mature age; and, in the mean time, he is subjected to such a course of study and discipline as will tend to prepare him, according to the political theory of the time and the place, to assume the reins of authority at the appointed age. If in England, or in the most enlightened European monarchies, it would be a proof of restored barbarism to permit the future sovereign to grow up without any knowledge of his duties,—and who can doubt that it would be such a proof?—then, surely, it would be not less a proof of restored or of never-removed barbarism amongst us to empower any individual to use the elective franchise without preparing him for so momentous a trust. Hence the Constitution of the United States, and of our own State, should be made a study in our public schools. The partition of the powers of government into the three co-ordinate branches,—legislative, judicial, and executive—with the duties appropriately devolving upon each; the mode of electing or of appointing all officers, with the reasons on which it was founded; and, especially, the duty of every citizen, in a government of laws, to appeal to the courts for redress in all cases of alleged wrong, instead of undertaking to vindicate his own rights by his own arm; and, in a government where the people are the acknowledged sources of power, the duty of changing laws and rulers by an appeal to the ballot, and not by rebellion,—should be taught to all the children until they are fully understood.

Had the obligations of the future citizen been sedulously inculcated upon all the children of this Republic, would the patriot have had to mourn over so many instances where the voter, not being able to accomplish his purpose by voting, has proceeded to accomplish it by violence; where, agreeing with his fellow-citizens to use the machinery of the ballot, he makes a tacit reservation, that, if that machinery does not move according to his pleasure, he will wrest or break it? If the responsibleness and value of the elective franchise were duly appreciated, the day of our state and national elections would be among the most solemn and religious days in the calendar. Men would approach them, not only with preparation and solicitude, but with the sobriety and solemnity with which discreet and religious-minded men meet the great crises of life. No man would throw away his vote through caprice or wantonness, any more than he would throw away his estate, or sell his family into bondage. No man would cast his vote through malice or revenge, any more than a good surgeon would amputate a limb, or a good navigator sail through perilous straits, under the same criminal passions.

But perhaps it will be objected, that the Constitution is subject to different readings, or that the policy of different administrations has become the subject of party strife; and, therefore, if any thing of constitutional or political law is introduced into our schools, there is danger that teachers will be chosen on account of their affinities to this or that political party, or that teachers will feign affinities which they do not feel in order that they may be chosen; and so each schoolroom will at length become a miniature political club-room, exploding with political resolves, or flaming out with political addresses, prepared by beardless boys in scarcely legible hand-writing and in worse grammar.

With the most limited exercise of discretion, all apprehensions of this kind are wholly groundless. There are different readings of the Constitution, it is true; and there are partisan topics which agitate the country from side to side: but the controverted points, compared with those about which there is no dispute, do not bear the proportion of one to a hundred. And, what is more, no man is qualified, or can be qualified, to discuss the disputable questions, unless previously and thoroughly versed in those questions about which there is no dispute. In the terms and principles common to all, and recognized by all, is to be found the only common medium of language and of idea by which the parties can become intelligible to each other; and there, too, is the only common ground whence the arguments of the disputants can be drawn....

...Thus may all the children of the Commonwealth receive instruction in all the great essentials of political knowledge,—in those elementary ideas without which they will never be able to investigate more recondite and debatable questions; thus will the only practicable method be adopted for discovering new truths, and for discarding, instead of perpetuating, old errors; and thus, too, will that pernicious race of intolerant zealots, whose whole faith may be summed up in two articles,—that they themselves are always infallibly right, and that all dissenters are certainly wrong,—be extinguished,—extinguished, not by violence, nor by proscription, but by the more copious inflowing of the light of truth.

Moral Education

Moral education is a primal necessity of social existence. The unre- 20 strained passions of men are not only homicidal, but suicidal; and a community without a conscience would soon extinguish itself. Even with a natural conscience, how often has evil triumphed over good! From the beginning of time, wrong has followed right, as the shadow the substance....

But to all doubters, disbelievers, or despairers in human progress, it may still be said, there is one experiment which has never yet been tried. It is an experiment, which, even before its inception, offers the highest authority for its ultimate success. Its formula is intelligible to all; and it is as legible as though written in starry letters on an azure sky. It is expressed in these few and simple words: *"Train up a child in the way he should go; and, when he is old, he will not depart from it."* This declaration is positive. If the conditions are complied with, it makes no provision for a failure. Though pertaining to morals, yet, if the terms of the direction are observed, there is no more reason to doubt the result than there would be in an optical or a chemical experiment.

But this experiment has never yet been tried. Education has never yet been brought to bear with one-hundredth part of its potential force upon the natures of children, and, through them, upon the character of men and of the race. In all the attempts to reform mankind which have hitherto been made, whether by changing the frame of government, by aggravating or softening the severity of the penal code, or by substituting a government-created for a God-created religion,—in all these attempts, the infantile and youthful mind, its amenability to influences, and the enduring and self-operating character of the influences it receives, have been almost wholly unrecognized. Here, then, is a new agency, whose powers are but just beginning to be understood, and whose mighty energies hitherto have been but feebly invoked; and yet, from our experience, limited and imperfect as it is, we do know, that, far beyond any other earthly instrumentality, it is comprehensive and decisive....

...So far as human instrumentalities are concerned, we have abundant means for surrounding every child in the State with preservative and moral influences as extensive and as efficient as those under which the present industrious, worthy, and virtuous members of the community were reared. And as to all those things in regard to which we are directly dependent upon the divine favor, have we not the promise, explicit and unconditional, that the men SHALL NOT depart from the way in which they should go, if the children are trained up in it? It has been overlooked that this promise is not restricted to parents, but seems to be addressed indiscriminately to all, whether parents, communities, states, or mankind....

Religious Education

But it will be said that this grand result in practical morals is a consummation of blessedness that can never be attained without religion, and that no community will ever be religious without a religious education. Both these propositions I regard as eternal and immutable truths. Devoid of religious principles and religious affections, the race can never fall so low but that it may sink still lower; animated and sanctified by them, it can never rise so high but that it may ascend still higher. And is it not at least as presumptuous to expect that mankind will attain to the knowledge of truth, without being instructed in truth, and without that general expansion and development of faculty which will enable them to recognize and comprehend truth in any other department of human interest as in the department of religion?...

...That our public schools are not theological seminaries, is admit- 25 ted. That they are debarred by law from inculcating the peculiar and distinctive doctrines of any one religious denomination amongst us, is claimed; and that they are also prohibited from ever teaching that what they do teach is the whole of religion, or all that is essential to religion or to salvation, is equally certain. But our system earnestly inculcates all Christian morals; it founds its morals on the basis of religion; it welcomes the religion of the Bible; and, in receiving the Bible, it allows it to do what it is allowed to do in no other system, — *to speak for itself.* But here it stops, not because it claims to have compassed all truth, but because it disclaims to act as an umpire between hostile religious opinions.

The very terms "public school" and "common school" bear upon their face that they are schools which the children of the entire community may attend. Every man not on the pauper-list is taxed for their support; but he is not taxed to support them as special religious institutions: if he were, it would satisfy at once the largest definition of a religious establishment. But he is taxed to support them as a *preventive* means against dishonesty, against fraud, and against violence, on the same principle that he is taxed to support criminal courts as a *punitive* means against the same offences. He is taxed to support schools, on the same principle that he is taxed to support paupers, — because a child without education is poorer and more wretched than a man without bread. He is taxed to support schools, on the same principle that he would be taxed to defend the nation against foreign invasion, or against rapine committed by a foreign foe, — because the general prevalence of ignorance, superstition, and vice, will breed Goth and Vandal at home more fatal to the public well-being than any Goth or Vandal from abroad. And, finally, he is taxed to support schools, because they are the most effective means of developing and training those powers and faculties in a child, by which, when he becomes a man, he may understand what his highest interests and his highest duties are, and may be in fact, and not in name only, a free agent. The elements of a political education are not bestowed upon any school child for the purpose of making him vote with this or that political party when he becomes of age, but for the purpose of enabling him to choose for himself with which party he will vote. So the religious education which a child receives at school is not imparted to him for the purpose of making him join this or that denomination when he arrives at years of discretion, but for the purpose of enabling him to judge for himself, according to the dictates of his own reason and conscience, what his religious obligations are, and whither they lead....

Such, then, in a religious point of view, is the Massachusetts system of common schools. Reverently it recognizes and affirms the sovereign rights of the Creator, sedulously and sacredly it guards the religious rights of the creature; while it seeks to remove all hinderances, and to supply all furtherances, to a filial and paternal communion between man and his Maker. In a social and political sense, it is a *free* school-system. It knows no distinction of rich and poor, of bond and free, or between those, who, in the imperfect light of this world, are seeking, through different avenues, to reach the gate of heaven. Without money and without price, it throws open its doors, and spreads the table of its bounty, for all the children of the State. Like the sun, it shines not only upon the good, but upon the evil, that they may become good; and, like the rain, its blessings descend not only upon the just, but upon the unjust, that their injustice may depart from them, and be known no more.

ENGAGING THE TEXT

1. What is Mann's view of the powers of education? What does he see as education's role in society? To what extent would you agree that education successfully carries out these functions today?

2. What does Mann mean by "sanitary intelligence" (para. 7)? Why did he feel that the development of this kind of intelligence was such an important aspect of schooling? In what ways has your own education stressed the development of sanitary intelligence? How valuable has this nonacademic instruction been?

3. How does Mann view the role of education in relation to wealth and poverty? How do you think such views would be received today if advocated by a school-board candidate or contender for the presidency? In your estimation, how effective has education been in addressing economic differences in American society?

4. Mann suggests that education plays a special role in preparing citizens to become active participants in a republican form of government. In what ways has your education prepared you to participate in democratic decision making? How

effective has this preparation been? What could be done to improve the way that schools currently prepare students for their role as citizens?

5. What, according to Mann, is the proper relationship of public education to issues of morality and religion? What specific moral or ethical principles should public schools attempt to teach?

EXPLORING CONNECTIONS

6. Read "Class in America — 2009" by Gregory Mantsios (p. 281), and "Stephen Cruz" by Studs Terkel (see bedfordstmartins.com/rereading/epages), and write an essay in which you discuss how class differences in American society complicate the educational program outlined by Mann.

7. Review the cartoon "If All the 'Education Reforms' Happened at Once," which appears below. As a class, debate whether or not American education is trying to do too much today.

IF ALL THE "EDUCATION REFORMS" HAPPENED AT ONCE,

EXTENDING THE CRITICAL CONTEXT

8. Research recent court decisions and legislative initiatives on the issue of prayer in school. How do prevailing views of the separation of church and state compare with the ideas presented in Mann's assessment of the goals of public education in 1848? Then, as a class, debate the proper role of moral and religious instruction in public education.

9. Working in small groups, draft a list of what you think the proper goals of public education in a democracy should be. Exchange these lists, then compare and discuss your results. How does your class's view of the powers of education differ from that offered by Mann?

IDIOT NATION

MICHAEL MOORE

When Michael Moore (b. 1954) held up his Oscar for best documentary during the 2002 Academy Awards show and shouted "Shame on you, Mr. Bush" to a chorus of boos from the audience, no one who knew his work would have been shocked. A social gadfly and cinematic activist without equal for the past two decades, Moore isn't the type to shy away from telling the president what he thinks of him on national TV; nor is he the type to disguise his contempt for the general level of idiocy he sees in American society. In this selection from *Stupid White Men . . . and Other Sorry Excuses for the State of the Nation!*, his best-selling 2001 diatribe against our collective cluelessness, Moore zeroes in on the sorry state of American education. Serving up generous examples from his own less-than-stellar educational career, Moore takes us on a tour of the failings of America's schoolrooms — from libraries without books to commanders in chief who can't distinguish between countries and continents. Along the way, he touches on topics like the cultural illiteracy of television talk show hosts, the growing movement for educational "accountability," and the corporate takeover of America's classrooms. He even offers a list of things every student can do to fight back against educational subservience. Before winning the Oscar in 2002 for his *Bowling for Columbine*, Moore directed *Roger and Me* (1989), which chronicled his attempts to question then-General Motors-chairman Roger Smith about a series of factory closures that devastated the economy of Flint, Michigan, Moore's hometown. His films include *Fahrenheit 9/11* (2005), a documentary exploring the Bush administration's response to the 9/11 terrorist attacks, and *Sicko*, an indictment of the American healthcare system, which was nominated for an

Academy Award in 2007. Moore published his autobiography, *Here Comes Trouble: Stories from My Life*, in 2011.

DO YOU FEEL LIKE YOU LIVE in a nation of idiots?

I used to console myself about the state of stupidity in this country by repeating this to myself: *Even if there are two hundred million stone-cold idiots in this country, that leaves at least eighty million who'll get what I'm saying—and that's still more than the populations of the United Kingdom and Iceland combined!*

Then came the day I found myself sharing an office with the ESPN game show *Two-Minute Drill*. This is the show that tests your knowledge of not only who plays what position for which team, but who hit what where in a 1925 game between Boston and New York, who was rookie of the year in 1965 in the old American Basketball Association, and what Jake Wood had for breakfast the morning of May 12, 1967.

I don't know the answer to any of those questions—but for some reason I do remember Jake Wood's uniform number: 2. Why on earth am I retaining that useless fact?

I don't know, but after watching scores of guys waiting to audition for that ESPN show, I think I do know something about intelligence and the American mind. Hordes of these jocks and lunkheads hang out in our hallway awaiting their big moment, going over hundreds of facts and statistics in their heads and challenging each other with questions I can't see why anyone would be able to answer other than God Almighty Himself. To look at these testosterone-loaded bruisers you would guess that they were a bunch of illiterates who would be lucky if they could read the label on a Bud.

In fact, they are geniuses. They can answer all thirty obscure trivia questions in less than 120 seconds. That's four seconds a question—including the time used by the slow-reading celebrity athletes who ask the questions.

I once heard the linguist and political writer Noam Chomsky say that if you want proof the American people aren't stupid, just turn on any sports talk radio show and listen to the incredible retention of facts. It is amazing—and it's proof that the American mind is alive and well. It just isn't challenged with anything interesting or exciting. *Our* challenge, Chomsky said, was to find a way to make politics as gripping and engaging as sports. When we do that, watch how Americans will do nothing but talk about who did what to whom at the WTO.[1]

But first, they have to be able to read the letters *WTO*.

There are forty-four million Americans who cannot read and write above a fourth-grade level—in other words, who are functional illiterates.

5

---

[1]*WTO:* World Trade Organization. [All notes are the editors'.]

How did I learn this statistic? Well, I *read* it. And now you've read it. So we've already eaten into the mere 99 hours a *year* an average American adult spends reading a book—compared with 1,460 hours watching television.

I've also read that only 11 percent of the American public bothers to *read* a daily newspaper, beyond the funny pages or the used car ads.

So if you live in a country where forty-four million can't read—and perhaps close to another two hundred million can read but usually don't—well, friends, you and I are living in one very scary place. A nation that not only churns out illiterate students BUT GOES OUT OF ITS WAY TO REMAIN IGNORANT AND STUPID is a nation that should not be running the world—at least not until a majority of its citizens can locate Kosovo[2] (or any other country it has bombed) on the map.

It comes as no surprise to foreigners that Americans, who love to revel in their stupidity, would "elect" a president who rarely reads *any-thing*—including his own briefing papers—and thinks Africa is a nation, not a continent. An idiot leader of an idiot nation. In our glorious land of plenty, less is always more when it comes to taxing any lobe of the brain with the intake of facts and numbers, critical thinking, or the comprehension of anything that isn't...well, sports.

Our Idiot-in-Chief does nothing to hide his ignorance—he even brags about it. During his commencement address to the Yale Class of 2001, George W. Bush spoke proudly of having been a mediocre student at Yale. "And to the C students, I say you, too, can be President of the United States!" The part where you also need an ex-President father, a brother as governor of a state with missing ballots, and a Supreme Court full of your dad's buddies must have been too complicated to bother with in a short speech.

As Americans, we have quite a proud tradition of being represented by ignorant high-ranking officials. In 1956 President Dwight D. Eisenhower's nominee as ambassador to Ceylon (now Sri Lanka) was unable to identify either the country's prime minister or its capital during his Senate confirmation hearing. Not a problem—Maxwell Gluck was confirmed anyway. In 1981 President Ronald Reagan's nominee for deputy secretary of state, William Clark, admitted to a wide-ranging lack of knowledge about foreign affairs at his confirmation hearing. Clark had no idea how our allies in Western Europe felt about having American nuclear missiles based there, and didn't know the names of the prime ministers of South Africa or Zimbabwe. Not to worry—he was confirmed, too. All this just paved the way for Baby Bush, who hadn't quite absorbed the names of the leaders of India or Pakistan, two of the seven nations that possess the atomic bomb.

And Bush went to Yale *and* Harvard.

[2]*Kosovo:* Province that precipitated the 1999 NATO invasion of Serbia after it demanded increased autonomy.

Recently a group of 556 seniors at fifty-five prestigious American universities (e.g., Harvard, Yale, Stanford) were given a multiple-choice test consisting of questions that were described as "high school level." Thirty-four questions were asked. These top students could only answer 53 percent of them correctly. And only one student got them all right.

A whopping 40 percent of these students did not know when the Civil War took place—even when given a wide range of choices: A. 1750–1800; B. 1800–1850; C. 1850–1900; D. 1900–1950; or E. after 1950. *(The answer is C, guys.)* The two questions the college seniors scored highest on were (1) Who is Snoop Doggy Dog? (98 percent got that one right), and (2) Who are Beavis and Butt-head? (99 percent knew). For my money, Beavis and Butt-head represented some of the best American satire of the nineties, and Snoop and his fellow rappers have much to say about America's social ills, so I'm not going down the road of blaming MTV.

What I *am* concerned with is why politicians like Senators Joe Lieberman of Connecticut and Herbert Kohl of Wisconsin want to go after MTV when *they* are the ones responsible for the massive failure of American education. Walk into any public school, and the odds are good that you'll find overflowing classrooms, leaking ceilings, and demoralized teachers. In one out of four schools, you'll find students "learning" from textbooks published in the 1980s—or earlier.

Why is this? Because the political leaders—and the people who vote for them—have decided it's a bigger priority to build another bomber than to educate our children. They would rather hold hearings about the depravity of a television show called *Jackass* than about their own depravity in neglecting our schools and children and maintaining our title as Dumbest Country on Earth.

I hate writing these words. I *love* this big lug of a country and the crazy people in it. But when I can travel to some backwater village in Central America, as I did back in the eighties, and listen to a bunch of twelve-year-olds tell me their concerns about the World Bank, I get the feeling that *something* is lacking in the United States of America.

Our problem isn't just that our kids don't know nothin' but that the adults who pay their tuition are no better. I wonder what would happen if we tested the U.S. Congress to see just how much our representatives know. What if we were to give a pop quiz to the commentators who cram our TVs and radios with all their nonstop nonsense? How many would *they* get right?

A while back, I decided to find out. It was one of those Sunday mornings when the choice on TV was the *Parade of Homes* real estate show or *The McLaughlin Group*. If you like the sound of hyenas on Dexedrine, of course, you go with *McLaughlin*. On this particular Sunday morning, perhaps as my punishment for not being at Mass, I was forced to listen to magazine columnist Fred Barnes (now an editor at the right-wing *Weekly Standard* and co-host of the Fox News show *The Beltway Boys*) whine on and on about the sorry state of American education, blaming the teachers and their evil union for why students are doing so poorly.

"These kids don't even know what *The Iliad* and *The Odyssey* are!" he bellowed, as the other panelists nodded in admiration at Fred's noble lament.

The next morning I called Fred Barnes at his Washington office. "Fred," I said, "tell me what *The Iliad* and *The Odyssey* are."

He started hemming and hawing. "Well, they're ... uh ... you know ... uh ... okay, fine, you got me — I don't know what they're about. Happy now?"

No, not really. You're one of the top TV pundits in America, seen every week on your own show and plenty of others. You gladly hawk your "wisdom" to hundreds of thousands of unsuspecting citizens, gleefully scorning others for their ignorance. Yet you and your guests know little or nothing yourselves. Grow up, get some books, and go to your room.

Yale and Harvard. Princeton and Dartmouth. Stanford and Berkeley. Get a degree from one of those universities, and you're set for life. So what if, on that test of the college seniors I previously mentioned, 70 percent of the students at those fine schools had never heard of the Voting Rights Act[3] or President Lyndon Johnson's Great Society initiatives?[4] Who needs to know stuff like that as you sit in your Tuscan villa watching the sunset and checking how well your portfolio did today?

So what if *not one* of these top universities that the ignorant students attend requires that they take even one course in American history to graduate? Who needs history when you are going to be tomorrow's master of the universe?

Who cares if 70 percent of those who graduate from America's colleges are not required to learn a foreign language? Isn't the rest of the world speaking English now? And if they aren't, hadn't all those damn foreigners better GET WITH THE PROGRAM?

And who gives a rat's ass if, out of the seventy English Literature programs at seventy major American universities, only twenty-three now require English majors to take a course in Shakespeare? Can somebody please explain to me what Shakespeare and English have to do with each other? What good are some moldy old plays going to be in the business world, anyway?

Maybe I'm just jealous because I don't have a college degree. Yes, I, Michael Moore, am a college dropout.

Well, I never *officially* dropped out. One day in my sophomore year, I drove around and around the various parking lots of our commuter

[3] *Voting Rights Act:* 1965 legislation that guaranteed equal voting rights for African Americans.
[4] *Lyndon Johnson's Great Society initiatives:* 1964–65 program of economic and social welfare legislation designed by Lyndon Johnson, thirty-sixth president of the United States, to eradicate poverty.

campus in Flint, searching desperately for a parking space. There simply was no place to park—every spot was full, and no one was leaving. After a frustrating hour spent circling around in my '69 Chevy Impala, I shouted out the window, "That's it, I'm dropping out!" I drove home and told my parents I was no longer in college.

"Why?" they asked.

"Couldn't find a parking spot," I replied, grabbing a Redpop and 35 moving on with the rest of my life. I haven't sat at a school desk since.

My dislike of school started somewhere around the second month of first grade. My parents—and God Bless Them Forever for doing this—had taught me to read and write by the time I was four. So when I entered St. John's Elementary School, I had to sit and feign interest while the other kids, like robots, sang, "A-B-C-D-E-F-G... Now I know my ABCs, tell me what you think of me!" Every time I heard that line, I wanted to scream out, "Here's what I think of you—quit singing that damn song! Somebody get me a Twinkie!"

I was bored beyond belief. The nuns, to their credit, recognized this, and one day Sister John Catherine took me aside and said that they had decided to skip me up to second grade, effective immediately. I was thrilled. When I got home I excitedly announced to my parents that I had already advanced a grade in my first month of school. They seemed underwhelmed by this new evidence of my genius. Instead they let out a "WHAT THE—," then went into the kitchen and closed the door. I could hear my mother on the phone explaining to the Mother Superior that there was *no way* her little Michael was going to be attending class with kids bigger and older than him, so please, Sister, put him back in first grade.

I was crushed. My mother explained to me that if I skipped first grade I'd always be the youngest and littlest kid in class all through my school years (well, inertia and fast food eventually proved her wrong on that count). There would be no appeals to my father, who left most education decisions to my mother, the valedictorian of her high school class. I tried to explain that if I was sent back to first grade it would appear that I'd *flunked* second grade on my first day—putting myself at risk of having the crap beaten out of me by the first graders I'd left behind with a rousing "See ya, suckers!" But Mom wasn't falling for it; it was then I learned that the only person with higher authority than Mother Superior was Mother Moore.

The next day I decided to ignore all instructions from my parents to go back to first grade. In the morning, before the opening bell, all the students had to line up outside the school with their classmates and then march into the building in single file. Quietly, but defiantly, I went and stood in the second graders' line, praying that God would strike the nuns blind so they wouldn't see which line I was in. The bell rang—and no one had spotted me! The second grade line started to move, and I went with it. *Yes!* I thought. *If I can pull this off, if I can just get into that second grade classroom and take my seat, then nobody will be able to get me out of there.* Just as I was about to enter the door of the school, I felt a hand grab me by the collar of my coat. It was Sister John Catherine.

"I think you're in the wrong line, Michael," she said firmly. "You are now in first grade again." I began to protest: my parents had it "all wrong," or "those weren't *really* my parents," or...

For the next twelve years I sat in class, did my work, and remained constantly preoccupied, looking for ways to bust out. I started an underground school paper in fourth grade. It was shut down. I started it again in sixth. It was shut down. In eighth grade I not only started the paper again, I convinced the good sisters to let me write a play for our class to perform at the Christmas pageant. The play had something to do with how many rats occupied the parish hall and how all the rats in the country had descended on St. John's Parish Hall to have their annual "rat convention." The priest put a stop to that one—and shut down the paper again. Instead, my friends and I were told to go up on stage and sing three Christmas carols and then leave the stage without uttering a word. I organized half the class to go up there and utter nothing. So we stood there and refused to sing the carols, our silent protest against censorship. By the second song, intimidated by the stern looks from their parents in the audience, most of the protesters joined in on the singing—and by the third song, I too, had capitulated, joining in on "O Holy Night," and promising myself to live to fight another day.

High school, as we all know, is some sort of sick, sadistic punishment of kids by adults seeking vengeance because they can no longer lead the responsibility-free, screwing-around-24/7 lives young people enjoy. What other explanation could there be for those four brutal years of degrading comments, physical abuse, and the belief that you're the only one not having sex?

As soon as I entered high school—and the public school system—all the grousing I'd done about the repression of the Sisters of St. Joseph was forgotten; suddenly they all looked like scholars and saints. I was now walking the halls of a two-thousand-plus-inmate holding pen. Where the nuns had devoted their lives to teaching for no earthly reward, those running the public high school had one simple mission: "Hunt these little pricks down like dogs, then cage them until we can either break their will or ship them off to the glue factory!" Do this, don't do that, tuck your shirt in, wipe that smile off your face, where's your hall pass, THAT'S THE WRONG PASS! *YOU—DETENTION!!*

One day I came home from school and picked up the paper. The headline read: "26th Amendment Passes—Voting Age Lowered to 18." Below that was another headline: "School Board President to Retire, Seat Up for Election."

Hmm. I called the county clerk.

"Uh, I'm gonna be eighteen in a few weeks. If I can vote, does that mean I can also run for office?"

"Let me see," the lady replied. "That's a new question!"

She ruffled through some papers and came back on the phone. "Yes," she said, "you can run. All you need to do is gather twenty signatures to place your name on the ballot."

Twenty signatures? That's it? I had no idea running for elective office required so little work. I got the twenty signatures, submitted my petition, and started campaigning. My platform? "Fire the high school principal and the assistant principal!"

Alarmed at the idea that a high school student might actually find a legal means to remove the very administrators he was being paddled by, five local "adults" took out petitions and got themselves added to the ballot, too.

Of course, they ended up splitting the older adult vote five ways— and I won, getting the vote of every single stoner between the ages of eighteen and twenty-five (who, though many would probably never vote again, relished the thought of sending their high school wardens to the gallows).

The day after I won, I was walking down the hall at school (I had one more week to serve out as a student), and I passed the assistant principal, my shirt tail proudly untucked.

"Good morning, Mr. Moore," he said tersely. The day before, my name had been "Hey-You!" Now I was his boss.

Within nine months after I took my seat on the school board, the principal and assistant principal had submitted their "letters of resignation," a face-saving device employed when one is "asked" to step down. A couple of years later the principal suffered a heart attack and died.

I had known this man, the principal, for many years. When I was eight years old, he used to let me and my friends skate and play hockey on this little pond beside his house. He was kind and generous, and always left the door to his house open in case any of us needed to change into our skates or if we got cold and just wanted to get warm. Years later, I was asked to play bass in a band that was forming, but I didn't own a bass. He let me borrow his son's.

I offer this to remind myself that all people are actually good at their core, and to remember that someone with whom I grew to have serious disputes was also someone with a free cup of hot chocolate for us shivering little brats from the neighborhood.

Teachers are now the politicians' favorite punching bag. To listen to the likes of Chester Finn, a former assistant secretary of education in Bush the Elder's administration, you'd think all that has crumbled in our society can be traced back to lax, lazy, and incompetent teachers. "If you put out a Ten-Most-Wanted list of who's killing American education, I'm not sure who you would have higher on the list: the teachers' union or the education school faculties," Finn said.

Sure, there are a lot of teachers who suck, and they'd be better suited to making telemarketing calls for Amway. But the vast majority are dedicated educators who have chosen a profession that pays them less than what some of their students earn selling Ecstasy, and for that sacrifice we seek to punish them. I don't know about you, but I want the people who have the direct attention of my child more hours a day than I do treated with tender loving care. Those are my kids they're "preparing" for this world, so why on earth would I want to piss them off?

You would think society's attitude would be something like this:

> *Teachers, thank you so much for devoting your life to my child. Is there ANYTHING I can do to help you? Is there ANYTHING you need? I am here for you. Why? Because you are helping my child—MY BABY—learn and grow. Not only will you be largely responsible for her ability to make a living, but your influence will greatly affect how she views the world, what she knows about other people in this world, and how she will feel about herself. I want her to believe she can attempt anything—that no doors are closed and that no dreams are too distant. I am entrusting the most valuable person in my life to you for seven hours each day. You are thus one of the most important people in my life! Thank you.*

No, instead, this is what teachers hear:

60

- "You've got to wonder about teachers who claim to put the interests of children first—and then look to milk the system dry through wage hikes." (*New York Post*, 12/26/00)

- "Estimates of the number of bad teachers range from 5 percent to 18 percent of the 2.6 million total." (Michael Chapman, *Investor's Business Daily*, 9/21/98)

- "Most education professionals belong to a closed community of devotees...who follow popular philosophies rather than research on what works." (Douglas Carminen, quoted in the *Montreal Gazette*, 1/6/01)

- "Teachers unions have gone to bat for felons and teachers who have had sex with students, as well as those who simply couldn't teach." (Peter Schweizen, *National Review*, 8/17/98)

What kind of priority do we place on education in America? Oh, it's on the funding list—somewhere down between OSHA[5] and meat inspectors. The person who cares for our child every day receives an average of $41,351 annually. A Congressman who cares only about which tobacco lobbyist is taking him to dinner tonight receives $145,100.

Considering the face-slapping society gives our teachers on a daily basis, is it any wonder so few choose the profession? The national teacher shortage is so big that some school systems are recruiting teachers outside the United States. Chicago recently recruited and hired teachers from twenty-eight foreign countries, including China, France, and Hungary. By the time the new term begins in New York City, seven

---

[5]*OSHA:* Occupational Safety and Health Administration.

thousand veteran teachers will have retired—and 60 percent of the new teachers hired to replace them are uncertified.

But here's the kicker for me: 163 New York City schools opened the 2000–2001 school year *without a principal!* You heard right—school, with *no one in charge.* Apparently the mayor and the school board are experimenting with chaos theory—throw five hundred poor kids into a crumbling building, and watch nature take its course! In the city from which most of the wealth in the world is controlled, where there are more millionaires per square foot than there is gum on the sidewalk, we somehow can't find the money to pay a starting teacher more than $31,900 a year. And we act surprised when we can't get results.

And it's not just teachers who have been neglected—American schools are *literally* falling apart. In 1999 one-quarter of U.S. public schools reported that the condition of at least one of their buildings was inadequate. In 1997 the entire Washington, D.C., school system had to delay the start of school for three weeks because nearly *one-third* of the schools were found to be unsafe.

Almost 10 percent of U.S. public schools have enrollments that are more than 25 percent greater than the capacity of their permanent buildings. Classes have to be held in the hallways, outdoors, in the gym, in the cafeteria; one school I visited even held classes in a janitor's closet. It's not as if the janitor's closets are being used for anything related to cleaning, anyway—in New York almost 15 percent of the eleven hundred public schools are without full-time custodians, forcing teachers to mop their own floors and students to do without toilet paper. We already send our kids out into the street to hawk candy bars so their schools can buy band instruments—what's next? Car washes to raise money for toilet paper?

Further proof of just how special our little offspring are is the number of public and even school libraries that have been shut down or had their hours cut back. The last thing we need is a bunch of kids hanging out around a bunch of books!

Apparently "President" Bush agrees: in his first budget he proposed cutting federal spending on libraries by $39 million, down to $168 million—a nearly 19 percent reduction. Just the week before, his wife, former school librarian Laura Bush, kicked off a national campaign for America's libraries, calling them "community treasure chests, loaded with a wealth of information available to everyone, equally." The President's mother, Barbara Bush, heads the Foundation for Family Literacy. Well, there's nothing like having firsthand experience with illiteracy in the family to motivate one into acts of charity.

For kids who are exposed to books at home, the loss of a library is sad. But for kids who come from environments where people don't read, the loss of a library is a tragedy that might keep them from ever discovering the joys of reading—or from gathering the kind of information that will decide their lot in life. Jonathan Kozol, for decades an advocate for disadvantaged children, has observed that school libraries "remain the clearest window to a world of noncommercial satisfactions and enticements that most children in poor neighborhoods will ever know."

Kids deprived of access to good libraries are also being kept from developing the information skills they need to keep up in workplaces that are increasingly dependent on rapidly changing information. The ability to conduct research is "probably the most essential skill [today's students] can have," says Julie Walker, executive director of the American Association of School Librarians. "The knowledge [students] acquire in school is not going to serve them throughout their lifetimes. Many of them will have four to five careers in a lifetime. It will be their ability to navigate information that will matter."

Who's to blame for the decline in libraries? Well, when it comes to school libraries, you can start by pointing the finger (yes, *that* finger) at Richard Nixon. From the 1960s until 1974, school libraries received specific funding from the government. But in 1974 the Nixon administration changed the rules, stipulating that federal education money be doled out in "block grants" to be spent by states however they chose. Few states chose to spend the money on libraries, and the downslide began. This is one reason that materials in many school libraries today date from the 1960s and early 1970s, before funding was diverted. ("No, Sally, the Soviet Union isn't our enemy. The Soviet Union has been kaput for ten years....")

This 1999 account by an *Education Week* reporter about the "library" at a Philadelphia elementary school could apply to any number of similarly neglected schools:

> Even the best books in the library at T. M. Pierce Elementary School are dated, tattered, and discolored. The worst—many in a latter state of disintegration—are dirty and fetid and leave a moldy residue on hands and clothing. Chairs and tables are old, mismatched, or broken. There isn't a computer in sight....Outdated facts and theories and offensive stereotypes leap from the authoritative pages of encyclopedias and biographies, fiction and nonfiction tomes. Among the volumes on these shelves a student would find it all but impossible to locate accurate information on AIDS or other contemporary diseases, explorations of the moon and Mars, or the past five U.S. presidents.

The ultimate irony in all of this is that the very politicians who refuse to fund education in America adequately are the same ones who go ballistic over how our kids have fallen behind the Germans, the Japanese, and just about every other country with running water and an economy not based on the sale of Chiclets. Suddenly they want "accountability." They want the teachers held responsible and to be tested. And they want the kids to be tested—over and over and over.

There's nothing terribly wrong with the concept of using standardized testing to determine whether kids are learning to read and write and do math. But too many politicians and education bureaucrats have created a national obsession with testing, as if everything that's wrong with the educational system in this country would be magically fixed if we could just raise those scores.

The people who really should be tested (besides the yammering pundits) are the so-called political leaders. Next time you see your state representative or congressman, give him this pop quiz—and remind him that any future pay raises will be based on how well he scores:

1. What is the annual pay of your average constituent?

2. What percent of welfare recipients are children?

3. How many known species of plants and animals are on the brink of extinction?

4. How big is the hole in the ozone layer?

5. Which African countries have a lower infant mortality rate than Detroit?

6. How many American cities still have two competing newspapers?

7. How many ounces in a gallon?

8. Which do I stand a greater chance of being killed by: a gun shot in school or a bolt of lightning?

9. What's the only state capital without a McDonald's?

10. Describe the story of either *The Iliad* or *The Odyssey*.

Answers

1. $28,548

2. 67 percent

3. 11,046

4. 10.5 million square miles

5. Libya, Mauritius, Seychelles

6. 34

7. 128 ounces

8. You're twice as likely to be killed by lightning as by a gun shot in school.

9. Montpelier, Vermont

10. *The Iliad* is an ancient Greek epic poem by Homer about the Trojan War. *The Odyssey* is another epic poem by Homer recounting the ten-year journey home from the Trojan War made by Odysseus, the king of Ithaca.

Chances are, the genius representing you in the legislature won't score 50 percent on the above test. The good news is that you get to flunk him within a year or two.

There is one group in the country that isn't just sitting around carping about all them lamebrain teachers—a group that cares deeply about what kinds of students will enter the adult world. You could say they have a vested interest in this captive audience of millions of young people...or in the billions of dollars they spend each year. (Teenagers alone spent more than $150 billion last year.) Yes, it's Corporate America, whose generosity to our nation's schools is just one more example of their continuing patriotic service.

Just how committed are these companies to our children's schools?

According to numbers collected by the Center for the Analysis of Commercialism in Education (CACE), their selfless charity has seen a tremendous boom since 1990. Over the past ten years, school programs and activities have seen corporate sponsorship increase by 248 percent. In exchange for this sponsorship, schools allow the corporation to associate its name with the events.

For example, Eddie Bauer sponsors the final round of the National Geography Bee. Book covers featuring Calvin Klein and Nike ads are distributed to students. Nike and other shoemakers, looking for early access to tomorrow's stars, sponsor inner-city high school basketball teams.

Pizza Hut set up its "Book-It!" program to encourage children to read. When students meet the monthly reading goal, they are rewarded with a certificate for a Pizza Hut personal pan pizza. At the restaurant, the store manager personally congratulates the children and gives them each a sticker and a certificate. Pizza Hut suggests school principals place a "Pizza Hut Book-It!" honor roll list in the school for everyone to see. 80

General Mills and Campbell's Soup thought up a better plan. Instead of giving free rewards, they both have programs rewarding schools for getting parents to buy their products. Under General Mills's "Box Tops for Education" program, schools get ten cents for each box top logo they send in, and can earn up to $10,000 a year. That's 100,000 General Mills products sold. Campbell's Soup's "Labels for Education" program is no better. It touts itself as "Providing America's children with FREE school equipment!" Schools can earn one "free" Apple iMac computer for only 94,950 soup labels. Campbell's suggests setting a goal of a label a day from each student. With Campbell's conservative estimate of five labels per week per child, all you need is a school of 528 kids to get that free computer.

It's not just this kind of sponsorship that brings these schools and corporations together. The 1990s saw a phenomenal 1,384 percent increase in exclusive agreements between schools and soft-drink bottlers. Two hundred and forty school districts in thirty-one states have sold exclusive rights to one of the big three soda companies (Coca-Cola, Pepsi, Dr. Pepper) to push their products in schools. Anybody wonder why there are more overweight kids than ever before? Or more young women with calcium deficiencies because they're drinking less milk?

And even though federal law prohibits the sale of soft drinks in schools until lunch periods begin, in some overcrowded schools "lunch" begins in midmorning. Artificially flavored carbonated sugar water—the breakfast of champions! (In March 2001 Coke responded to public pressure, announcing that it would add water, juice, and other sugar-free, caffeine-free, and calcium-rich alternatives to soda to its school vending machines.)

I guess they can afford such concessions when you consider their deal with the Colorado Springs school district. Colorado has been a trailblazer when it comes to tie-ins between the schools and soft drink companies. In Colorado Springs, the district will receive $8.4 million over ten years from its deal with Coca-Cola—and more if it exceeds its "requirement" of selling seventy thousand cases of Coke products a year. To ensure the levels are met, school district officials urged principals to allow students unlimited access to Coke machines and allow students to drink Coke in the classroom.

But Coke isn't alone. In the Jefferson County, Colorado, school district (home of Columbine High School), Pepsi contributed $1.5 million to help build a new sports stadium. Some county schools tested a science course, developed in part by Pepsi, called "The Carbonated Beverage Company." Students taste-tested colas, analyzed cola samples, watched a video tour of a Pepsi bottling plant, and visited a local plant.

The school district in Wylie, Texas, signed a deal in 1996 that shared 85 the rights to sell soft drinks in the schools between Coke and Dr. Pepper. Each company paid $31,000 a year. Then, in 1998, the county changed its mind and signed a deal with Coke worth $1.2 million over fifteen years. Dr. Pepper sued the county for breach of contract. The school district bought out Dr. Pepper's contract, costing them $160,000—plus another $20,000 in legal fees.

It's not just the companies that sometimes get sent packing. Students who lack the proper corporate school spirit do so at considerable risk. When Mike Cameron wore a Pepsi shirt on "Coke Day" at Greenbrier High School in Evans, Georgia, he was suspended for a day. "Coke Day" was part of the school's entry in a national "Team Up With Coca-Cola" contest, which awards $10,000 to the high school that comes up with the best plan for distributing Coke discount cards. Greenbrier school officials said Cameron was suspended for "being disruptive and trying to destroy the school picture" when he removed an outer shirt and revealed the Pepsi shirt as a photograph was being taken of students posed to spell out the word *Coke*. Cameron said the shirt was visible all day, but he didn't get in trouble until posing for the picture. No slouch in the marketing department, Pepsi quickly sent the high school senior a box of Pepsi shirts and hats.

If turning the students into billboards isn't enough, schools and corporations sometimes turn the school itself into one giant neon sign for corporate America. Appropriation of school space, including scoreboards, rooftops, walls, and textbooks, for corporate logos and advertising is up 539 percent.

Colorado Springs, not satisfied to sell its soul only to Coca-Cola, has plastered its school buses with advertisements for Burger King, Wendy's, and other big companies. Free book covers and school planners with ads for Kellogg's Pop-Tarts and pictures of FOX TV personalities were also handed out to the students.

After members of the Grapevine-Colleyville Independent School District in Texas decided they didn't want advertisements in the classrooms, they allowed Dr. Pepper and 7-Up logos to be painted on the rooftops of two high schools. The two high schools, not coincidentally, lie under the Dallas airport flight path.

The schools aren't just looking for ways to advertise; they're also 90 concerned with the students' perceptions of various products. That's why, in some schools, companies conduct market research in classrooms during school hours. Education Market Resources of Kansas reports that "children respond openly and easily to questions and stimuli" in the classroom setting. (Of course, that's what they're *supposed* to be doing in a classroom—but for their own benefit, not that of some corporate pollsters.) Filling out marketing surveys instead of learning, however, is probably *not* what they should be doing.

Companies have also learned they can reach this confined audience by "sponsoring" educational materials. This practice, like the others, has exploded as well, increasing 1,875 percent since 1990.

Teachers have shown a Shell Oil video that teaches students that the way to experience nature is by driving there—after filling your Jeep's gas tank at a Shell station. ExxonMobil prepared lesson plans about the flourishing wildlife in Prince William Sound, site of the ecological disaster caused by the oil spill from the Exxon *Valdez*. A third-grade math book features exercises involving counting Tootsie Rolls. A Hershey's-sponsored curriculum used in many schools features "The Chocolate Dream Machine," including lessons in math, science, geography—and nutrition.

In a number of high schools, the economics course is supplied by General Motors. GM writes and provides the textbooks and the course outline. Students learn from GM's example the benefits of capitalism and how to operate a company—like GM.

And what better way to imprint a corporate logo on the country's children than through television and the Internet beamed directly into the classroom. Electronic marketing, where a company provides programming or equipment to schools for the right to advertise to their students, is up 139 percent.

One example is the ZapMe! Corporation, which provides schools 95 with a free computer lab and access to pre-selected Web sites. In return, schools must promise that the lab will be in use at least four hours a day. The catch? The ZapMe! Web browser has constantly scrolling advertisements—and the company gets to collect information on students' browsing habits, information they can then sell to other companies.

Perhaps the worst of the electronic marketers is Channel One Television. Eight million students in 12,000 classrooms watch Channel

One, an in-school news *and advertising* program, every day. (That's right: EVERY day.) Kids are spending the equivalent of six full school days a year watching Channel One in almost 40 percent of U.S. middle and high schools. Instructional time lost to the ads alone? One entire day per year. That translates into an annual cost to taxpayers of more than $1.8 billion.

Sure, doctors and educators agree that our kids can never watch enough TV. And there's probably a place in school for some television programs—I have fond memories of watching astronauts blasting off on the television rolled into my grade school auditorium. But out of the daily twelve-minute Channel One broadcasts, only 20 percent of the airtime is devoted to stories about politics, the economy, and cultural and social issues. That leaves a whopping 80 percent for advertising, sports, weather, features, and Channel One promotions.

Channel One is disproportionately shown in schools in low income communities with large minority populations, where the least money is available for education, and where the least amount is spent on textbooks and other academic materials. Once these districts receive corporate handouts, government's failure to provide adequate school funding tends to remain unaddressed.

For most of us, the only time we enter an American high school is to vote at our local precinct. (There's an irony if there ever was one—going to participate in democracy's sacred ritual while two thousand students in the same building live under some sort of totalitarian dictatorship.) The halls are packed with burned-out teenagers shuffling from class to class, dazed and confused, wondering what the hell they're doing there. They learn how to regurgitate answers the state wants them to give, and any attempt to be an individual is now grounds for being suspected to be a member of the trench coat mafia.[6] I visited a school recently, and some students asked me if I noticed that they and the other students in the school were all wearing white or some neutral color. Nobody dares wear black, or anything else wild and distinct. That's a sure ticket to the principal's office—where the school psychologist will be waiting to ascertain whether that Limp Bizkit shirt you have on means that you intend to shoot up Miss Nelson's fourth hour geometry class.

So the kids learn to submerge any personal expression. They learn 100 that it's better to go along so that you get along. They learn that to rock the boat could get them rocked right out of the school. Don't question authority. Do as you're told. Don't think, just do as I say.

Oh, and have a good and productive life as an active, well-adjusted participant in our thriving democracy!

---

[6]*trench coat mafia:* Name of a self-styled group of students that included Columbine High School shooters Eric Harris and Dylan Klebold; hence, any potentially violent group of students.

ARE YOU A POTENTIAL SCHOOL SHOOTER?

The following is a list of traits the FBI has identified as "risk factors" among students who may commit violent acts. Stay away from any student showing signs of:

- Poor coping skills

- Access to weapons

- Depression

- Drug and alcohol abuse

- Alienation

- Narcissism

- Inappropriate humor

- Unlimited, unmonitored television and Internet use

Since this includes all of you, drop out of school immediately. Home schooling is not a viable option, because you must also stay away from yourself.

How to Be a Student Subversive Instead of a Student Subservient

There are many ways you can fight back at your high school—and have fun while doing it. The key thing is to learn what all the rules are, and what your rights are by law and by school district policy. This will help to prevent you getting in the kinds of trouble you don't need.

It may also get you some cool perks. David Schankula, a college student who has helped me on this book, recalls that when he was in high school in Kentucky, he and his buddies found some obscure state law that said any student who requests a day off to go to the state fair must be given the day off. The state legislature probably passed this law years ago to help some farm kid take his prize hog to the fair without being penalized at school. But the law was still on the books, and it gave any student the right to request the state fair day off—regardless of the reason. So you can imagine the look on the principal's face when David and his city friends submitted their request for their free day off from school—and there was nothing the principal could do.

Here's a few more things you can do:

1. Mock the Vote.

Student council and class elections are the biggest smokescreen the 105
school throws up, fostering the illusion that you actually have any say
in the running of the school. Most students who run for these offices either take the charade too seriously—or they just think it'll look good on
their college applications.

So why not run yourself? Run just to ridicule the whole ridiculous
exercise. Form your own party, with its own stupid name. Campaign on
wild promises: *If elected, I'll change the school mascot to an amoeba*,
or *If elected, I'll insist that the principal must first eat the school lunch
each day before it is fed to the students.* Put up banners with cool slogans: "Vote for me—a real loser!"

If you get elected, you can devote your energies to accomplishing
things that will drive the administration crazy, but help out your fellow
students (demands for free condoms, student evaluations of teachers,
less homework so you can get to bed by midnight, etc).

2. Start a School Club.

You have a right to do this. Find a sympathetic teacher to sponsor it.
The Pro-Choice Club. The Free Speech Club. The Integrate Our Town
Club. Make every member a "president" of the club, so they all can
claim it on their college applications. One student I know tried to start
a Feminist Club, but the principal wouldn't allow it because then they'd
be obliged to give equal time to a Male Chauvinist Club. That's the kind
of idiot thinking you'll encounter, but don't give up. (Heck, if you find
yourself in that situation, just say *fine*—and suggest that the principal
could sponsor the Chauvinist Club.)

3. Launch Your Own Newspaper or Webzine.

You have a constitutionally protected right to do this. If you take
care not to be obscene, or libelous, or give them any reason to shut you
down, this can be a great way to get the truth out about what's happening at your school. Use humor. The students will love it.

4. Get Involved in the Community.

Go to the school board meetings and inform them what's going on 110
in the school. Petition them to change things. They will try to ignore
you or make you sit through a long, boring meeting before they let you
speak, but they have to let you speak. Write letters to the editor of your
local paper. Adults don't have a clue about what goes on in your high
school. Fill them in. More than likely you'll find someone there who'll
support you.

Any or all of this will raise quite a ruckus, but there's help out there
if you need it. Contact the local American Civil Liberties Union if the
school retaliates. Threaten lawsuits—school administrators HATE to

hear that word. Just remember: there's no greater satisfaction than seeing the look on your principal's face when you have the upper hand. Use it.

And Never Forget This:

There Is No Permanent Record!

ENGAGING THE TEXT

1. What evidence does Moore offer to support his contention that America is a nation of idiots? To what extent would you agree with this blunt assessment of American intelligence? Why? What limitations, if any, do you see in the "question/answer" approach that Moore takes to gauging intelligence?

2. Moore shares a number of personal experiences in this selection to dramatize his disgust with formal education. How do your own elementary and high school memories compare with Moore's school experiences? Overall, how would you characterize his attitude toward schools and schooling? To what extent would you agree with him?

3. How accurate is the grim picture of American schools that Moore offers in this selection? Would you agree with his assessment of the typical class room, the quality of the average school library, and the general ability of American teachers and of the staff who support them?

4. Who, in Moore's view, is responsible for the sorry state of America's schools? To what extent would you agree? What reforms do you think Moore would like to see, and what changes, if any, would you recommend?

5. How does Moore feel about corporate involvement in public education? Why? What possible conflicts of interest or ethical questions do you see arising in relation to the following kinds of corporate/school collaboration:

   • Sponsorship of sports teams and clubs

   • Exclusive contracts for soda and snack vending machines

   • Fast-food franchise "food courts"

   • Sponsorship of libraries, computer labs, etc.

   • Commercial instruction via cable TV

   • Free books with inserted advertising

   • Free courses on history or economics with business or corporate content

   • Volunteer "teachers" and tutors from corporate ranks

   What role, if any, do you think corporations should play in support of American public schools? Why?

6. What does Moore suggest that individual students do to "fight back" against the deadening effects of the educational system? What did you do when you were in elementary and secondary school to make your own experience more meaningful? Now that you're in college, what can you do to be a "student subversive instead of a student subservient"?

EXPLORING CONNECTIONS

7. How does Moore's portrayal of the current state of American education com-pare with the image of the American school as described by Horace Mann (p. 110)? What seems to be the mission or goal of public schooling, according to Moore? How would you expect him to react to the goals that Mann envisions for the school? Why? Would you agree with Moore?

8. To what extent does Moore's depiction of the idiocy of schools support or challenge John Taylor Gatto's critique of American public education in "Against School" (below)? Do you think that Moore would agree with Gatto's claim that mandatory public schooling has turned us into a nation of children?

EXTENDING THE CRITICAL CONTEXT

9. Test Moore's central thesis about the idiocy of the average American by working in groups to devise and administer your own general information test. You can borrow questions from the many bits of information that Moore offers through-out this selection, or simply pool your own knowledge supplemented with ad-ditional library research. Administer your questionnaire to groups of fellow stu-dents, professors, family, friends, or members of the community at large. Then compare your results to see if Americans really are as uninformed as Moore suggests.

10. As Moore suggests, even some top American universities no longer require students to take basic courses in subjects like history or foreign language. How comprehensive are the general education requirements at your college? Do you think that they provide the average student with a well-rounded education? What additional courses or requirements, if any, would you include? Why?

AGAINST SCHOOL

JOHN TAYLOR GATTO

The official mission statements of most American schools brim with good intentions. On paper, schools exist to help students realize their full potential, to equip them with the skills they'll need to achieve success and contribute to society, or to foster the development of independence, critical thinking, and strong ethical values. But as John Taylor Gatto (b. 1935) sees it, public schools actually exist to fulfill six covert functions meant to "cripple our kids." The frightening thing is that Gatto might know what he's talking about. An award-winning educator and ardent libertarian, Gatto has taught in New York public schools for more than two decades. In 1989, 1990, and 1991, he was named New York City Teacher of the Year, and in 1991 he was also honored as New York State Teacher of the Year. His publications include *Dumbing Us Down: The Hidden Curriculum of Compulsory Schooling* (1992), *A Different Kind of Teacher* (2000), *The Underground History of American Education* (2001), and *Weapons of Mass Instruction: A Schoolteacher's Journey through the Dark World of Compulsory Schooling* (2008). This selection originally appeared in *Harper's* magazine in 2003.

I TAUGHT FOR THIRTY YEARS in some of the worst schools in Manhattan, and in some of the best, and during that time I became an expert in boredom. Boredom was everywhere in my world, and if you asked the kids, as I often did, *why* they felt so bored, they always gave the same answers: They said the work was stupid, that it made no sense, that they already knew it. They said they wanted to be doing something real, not just sitting around. They said teachers didn't seem to know much about their subjects and clearly weren't interested in learning more. And the kids were right: their teachers were every bit as bored as they were.

Boredom is the common condition of schoolteachers, and anyone who has spent time in a teachers' lounge can vouch for the low energy, the whining, the dispirited attitudes, to be found there. When asked why *they* feel bored, the teachers tend to blame the kids, as you might expect. Who wouldn't get bored reaching students who are rude and interested only in grades? If even that. Of course, teachers are themselves products of the same twelve-year compulsory school programs that so thoroughly bore their students, and as school personnel they are trapped inside structures even more rigid than those imposed upon the children. Who, then, is to blame?

We all are. My grandfather taught me that. One afternoon when I was seven I complained to him of boredom, and he batted me hard on the head. He told me that I was never to use that term in his presence again, that if I was bored it was my fault and no one else's. The obligation to amuse and instruct myself was entirely my own, and people who didn't know that were childish people, to be avoided if possible. Certainly not to be trusted. That episode cured me of boredom forever, and here and there over the years I was able to pass on the lesson to some remarkable student. For the most part, however, I found it futile to challenge the official notion that boredom and childishness were the natural state of affairs in the classroom. Often I had to defy custom, and even bend the law, to help kids break out of this trap.

The empire struck back, of course; childish adults regularly conflate opposition with disloyalty. I once returned from a medical leave to discover that all evidence of my having been granted the leave had been purposely destroyed, that my job had been terminated, and that I no longer possessed even a teaching license. After nine months of tormented effort I was able to retrieve the license when a school secretary testified to witnessing the plot unfold. In the meantime my family suffered more than I care to remember. By the time I finally retired in 1991, I had more than enough reason to think of our schools—with their long-term, cell-block-style, forced confinement of both students and teachers—as virtual factories of childishness. Yet I honestly could not see *why* they had to be that way. My own experience had revealed to me what many other teachers must learn along the way, too, yet keep to themselves for fear of reprisal: if we wanted to we could easily and inexpensively jettison the old, stupid structures and help kids *take* an education rather than merely *receive* a schooling. We could encourage the best qualities of youthfulness—curiosity, adventure, resilience, the capacity for surprising insight—simply by being more flexible about time, texts, and tests, by introducing kids to truly competent adults, and by giving each student what autonomy he or she needs in order to take a risk every now and then.

But we don't do that. And the more I asked why not, and persisted in thinking about the "problem" of schooling as an engineer might, the more I missed the point: What if there is no "problem" with our schools? What if they are the way they are, so expensively flying in the face of common sense and long experience in how children learn things, not because they are doing something wrong but because they are doing something right? Is it possible that George W. Bush accidentally spoke the truth when he said we would "leave no child behind"? Could it be that our schools are designed to make sure not one of them ever really grows up? 5

Do we really need school? I don't mean education, just forced schooling: six classes a day, five days a week, nine months a year, for twelve years. Is this deadly routine really necessary? And if so, for what? Don't hide behind reading, writing, and arithmetic as a rationale, because 2 million happy homeschoolers have surely put that banal justification to rest. Even if they hadn't, a considerable number of well-known Americans never went through the twelve-year wringer our kids currently go through, and they turned out all right. George Washington, Benjamin Franklin, Thomas Jefferson, Abraham Lincoln? Someone taught them, to be sure, but they were not products of a school *system*, and not one of them was ever "graduated" from a secondary school. Throughout most of American history, kids generally didn't go to high school, yet the unschooled rose to be admirals, like Farragut;[1] inventors, like Edison; captains of industry, like Carnegie[2] and Rockefeller;[3]

[1] *Farragut:* Admiral David Glasgow Farragut (1801–1870), American naval officer who won several important victories for the North in the Civil War, including the capture of the port of New Orleans in 1862. [All notes are the editors'.]
[2] *Carnegie:* Andrew Carnegie (1835–1919), American businessman and philanthropist who made his enormous fortune in the steel industry.
[3] *Rockefeller:* John D. Rockefeller (1839–1937), American industrialist who founded Standard Oil and who was for a time the richest man in the world.

writers, like Melville and Twain and Conrad;[4] and even scholars, like Margaret Mead.[5] In fact, until pretty recently people who reached the age of thirteen weren't looked upon as children at all. Ariel Durant, who cowrote an enormous, and very good, multivolume history of the world with her husband, Will, was happily married at fifteen, and who could reasonably claim that Ariel Durant[6] was an uneducated person? Unschooled, perhaps, but not uneducated.

We have been taught (that is, schooled) in this country to think of "success" as synonymous with, or at least dependent upon, "schooling," but historically that isn't true in either an intellectual or a financial sense. And plenty of people throughout the world today find a way to educate themselves without resorting to a system of compulsory secondary schools that all too often resemble prisons. Why, then, do Americans confuse education with just such a system? What exactly is the purpose of our public schools?

Mass schooling of a compulsory nature really got its teeth into the United States between 1905 and 1915, though it was conceived of much earlier and pushed for throughout most of the nineteenth century. The reason given for this enormous upheaval of family life and cultural traditions was, roughly speaking, threefold:

1. To make good people.

2. To make good citizens.

3. To make each person his or her personal best.

These goals are still trotted out today on a regular basis, and most of us accept them in one form or another as a decent definition of public education's mission, however short schools actually fall in achieving them. But we are dead wrong. Compounding our error is the fact that the national literature holds numerous and surprisingly consistent statements of compulsory schooling's true purpose. We have, for example, the great H. L. Mencken,[7] who wrote in *The American Mercury* for April 1924 that the aim of public education is not

> to fill the young of the species with knowledge and awaken their intelligence.... Nothing could be further from the truth. The aim...is simply to reduce as many individuals as possible to the same safe level, to breed and train a standardized citizenry, to put down dissent

---

[4]*Melville and Twain and Conrad:* Herman Melville (1819–1891), American novelist best known as the author of *Moby-Dick* (1851); Mark Twain, the pen name of American writer Samuel Langhorne Clemens (1835–1910), author of *Adventures of Huckleberry Finn* (1884); and Polish-born writer Joseph Conrad (1857–1924), best known for the novella "Heart of Darkness" (1899).

[5]*Margaret Mead:* American anthropologist (1901–1978) and author of the groundbreaking book *Coming of Age in Samoa* (1928).

[6]*Ariel Durant:* With husband Will (1885–1981), Ariel (1898–1981) won the Pulitzer Prize for literature for volume ten of their eleven-volume *The Story of Civilization*, published from 1935 to 1975.

[7]*H. L. Mencken:* American social critic and commentator known for his satiric wit (1880–1956).

and originality. That is its aim in the United States...and that is its aim everywhere else.

Because of Mencken's reputation as a satirist, we might be tempted to dismiss this passage as a bit of hyperbolic sarcasm. His article, however, goes on to trace the template for our own educational system back to the now vanished, though never to be forgotten, military state of Prussia. And although he was certainly aware of the irony that we had recently been at war with Germany, the heir to Prussian thought and culture, Mencken was being perfectly serious here. Our educational system really is Prussian in origin, and that really is cause for concern.

The odd fact of a Prussian provenance for our schools pops up again 10 and again once you know to look for it. William James[8] alluded to it many times at the turn of the century. Orestes Brownson,[9] the hero of Christopher Lasch's[10] 1991 book, *The True and Only Heaven*, was publicly denouncing the Prussianization of American schools back in the 1840s. Horace Mann's[11] "Seventh Annual Report" to the Massachusetts State Board of Education in 1843 is essentially a paean to the land of Frederick the Great[12] and a call for its schooling to be brought here. That Prussian culture loomed large in America is hardly surprising given our early association with that utopian state. A Prussian served as Washington's aide during the Revolutionary War, and so many German-speaking people had settled here by 1795 that Congress considered publishing a German-language edition of the federal laws. But what shocks is that we should so eagerly have adopted one of the very worst aspects of Prussian culture: an educational system deliberately designed to produce mediocre intellects, to hamstring the inner life, to deny students appreciable leadership skills, and to ensure docile and incomplete citizens—all in order to render the populace "manageable."

It was from James Bryant Conant—president of Harvard for twenty years, World War I poison-gas specialist, World War II executive on the atomic-bomb project, high commissioner of the American zone in Germany after World War II, and truly one of the most influential figures of the twentieth century—that I first got wind of the real purposes of American schooling. Without Conant, we would probably not have the same style and degree of standardized testing that we enjoy today, nor would we be blessed with gargantuan high schools that warehouse 2,000 to 4,000 students at a time, like the famous Columbine High[13] in

[8]*William James:* American psychologist and philosopher (1842–1910).

[9]*Orestes Brownson:* American philosopher and essayist (1803–1876).

[10]*Christopher Lasch:* American historian and social critic (1932–1994), probably best known for *The Culture of Narcissism: American Life in an Age of Diminished Expectations* (1979) and *The Revolt of the Elites: And the Betrayal of Democracy* (1994).

[11]*Horace Mann:* Secretary of the State Board of Education in Massachusetts. See the excerpt from *Report of the Massachusetts Board of Education*, 1848 (p. 116).

[12]*Frederick the Great:* King of Prussia (now part of present-day Germany), who reigned from 1740 to 1786.

[13]*Columbine High:* Site of April 20, 1999, massacre by students Eric Harris and Dylan Klebold, who killed twelve and wounded twenty-four others before killing themselves.

Littleton, Colorado. Shortly after I retired from teaching I picked up Conant's 1959 book-length essay, *The Child, the Parent, and the State*, and was more than a little intrigued to see him mention in passing that the modern schools we attend were the result of a "revolution" engineered between 1905 and 1930. A revolution? He declines to elaborate, but he does direct the curious and the uninformed to Alexander Inglis's 1918 book, *Principles of Secondary Education*, in which "one saw this revolution through the eyes of a revolutionary."

Inglis, for whom a lecture in education at Harvard is named, makes it perfectly clear that compulsory schooling on this continent was intended to be just what it had been for Prussia in the 1820s: a fifth column[14] into the burgeoning democratic movement that threatened to give the peasants and the proletarians a voice at the bargaining table. Modern, industrialized, compulsory schooling was to make a sort of surgical incision into the prospective unity of these underclasses. Divide children by subject, by age-grading, by constant rankings on tests, and by many other more subtle means, and it was unlikely that the ignorant mass of mankind, separated in childhood, would ever re-integrate into a dangerous whole.

Inglis breaks down the purpose—the *actual* purpose—of modern schooling into six basic functions, any one of which is enough to curl the hair of those innocent enough to believe the three traditional goals listed earlier:

1. The *adjustive* or *adaptive* function. Schools are to establish fixed habits of reaction to authority. This, of course, precludes critical judgment completely. It also pretty much destroys the idea that useful or interesting material should be taught, because you can't test for *reflexive* obedience until you know whether you can make kids learn, and do, foolish and boring things.

2. The *integrating* function. This might well be called "the conformity function," because its intention is to make children as alike as possible. People who conform are predictable, and this is of great use to those who wish to harness and manipulate a large labor force.

3. The *diagnostic and directive* function. School is meant to determine each student's proper social role. This is done by logging evidence mathematically and anecdotally on cumulative records. As in "your permanent record." Yes, you do have one.

4. The *differentiating* function. Once their social role has been "diagnosed," children are to be sorted by role and trained only so far as their destination in the social machine merits—and not one step further. So much for making kids their personal best.

---

[14] *a fifth column:* Secret group of infiltrators who undermine a nation's defenses.

5. The *selective* function. This refers not to human choice at all but to Darwin's theory of natural selection as applied to what he called "the favored races." In short, the idea is to help things along by consciously attempting to improve the breeding stock. Schools are meant to tag the unfit—with poor grades, remedial placement, and other punishments—clearly enough that their peers will accept them as inferior and effectively bar them from the reproductive sweepstakes. That's what all those little humiliations from first grade onward were intended to do: wash the dirt down the drain.

6. The *propaedeutic* function. The societal system implied by these rules will require an elite group of caretakers. To that end, a small fraction of the kids will quietly be taught how to manage this continuing project, how to watch over and control a population deliberately dumbed down and declawed in order that government might proceed unchallenged and corporations might never want for obedient labor.

That, unfortunately, is the purpose of mandatory public education in this country. And lest you take Inglis for an isolated crank with a rather too cynical take on the educational enterprise, you should know that he was hardly alone in championing these ideas. Conant himself, building on the ideas of Horace Mann and others, campaigned tirelessly for an American school system designed along the same lines. Men like George Peabody, who funded the cause of mandatory schooling throughout the South, surely understood that the Prussian system was useful in creating not only a harmless electorate and a servile labor force but also a virtual herd of mindless consumers. In time a great number of industrial titans came to recognize the enormous profits to be had by cultivating and tending just such a herd via public education, among them Andrew Carnegie and John D. Rockefeller.

There you have it. Now you know. We don't need Karl Marx's conception of a grand warfare between the classes to see that it is in the interest of complex management, economic or political, to dumb people down, to demoralize them, to divide them from one another, and to discard them if they don't conform. Class may frame the proposition, as when Woodrow Wilson, then president of Princeton University, said the following to the New York City School Teachers Association in 1909: "We want one class of persons to have a liberal education, and we want another class of persons, a very much larger class, of necessity, in every society, to forgo the privileges of a liberal education and fit themselves to perform specific difficult manual tasks." But the motives behind the disgusting decisions that bring about these ends need not be class-based at all. They can stem purely from fear, or from the by now familiar belief that "efficiency" is the paramount virtue, rather than love, liberty, laughter, or hope. Above all, they can stem from simple greed.

There were vast fortunes to be made, after all, in an economy based on mass production and organized to favor the large corporation rather than the small business or the family farm. But mass production required mass consumption, and at the turn of the twentieth century most Americans considered it both unnatural and unwise to buy things they didn't actually need. Mandatory schooling was a godsend on that count. School didn't have to train kids in any direct sense to think they should consume nonstop, because it did something even better: it encouraged them not to think at all. And that left them sitting ducks for another great invention of the modern era—marketing.

Now, you needn't have studied marketing to know that there are two groups of people who can always be convinced to consume more than they need to: addicts and children. School has done a pretty good job of turning our children into addicts, but it has done a spectacular job of turning our children into children. Again, this is no accident. Theorists from Plato to Rousseau[15] to our own Dr. Inglis knew that if children could be cloistered with other children, stripped of responsibility and independence, encouraged to develop only the trivializing emotions of greed, envy, jealousy, and fear, they would grow older but never truly grow up. In the 1934 edition of his once well-known book *Public Education in the United States,* Ellwood P. Cubberley detailed and praised the way the strategy of successive school enlargements had extended childhood by two to six years, and forced schooling was at that point still quite new. This same Cubberley—who was dean of Stanford's School of Education, a textbook editor at Houghton Mifflin, and Conant's friend and correspondent at Harvard—had written the following in the 1922 edition of his book *Public School Administration:* "Our schools are...factories in which the raw products (children) are to be shaped and fashioned.... And it is the business of the school to build its pupils according to the specifications laid down."

It's perfectly obvious from our society today what those specifications were. Maturity has by now been banished from nearly every aspect of our lives. Easy divorce laws have removed the need to work at relationships; easy credit has removed the need for fiscal self-control; easy entertainment has removed the need to learn to entertain oneself; easy answers have removed the need to ask questions. We have become a nation of children, happy to surrender our judgments and our wills to political exhortations and commercial blandishments that would insult actual adults. We buy televisions, and then we buy the things we see on the television. We buy computers, and then we buy the things we see on the computer. We buy $150 sneakers whether we need them or not, and when they fall apart too soon we buy another pair. We drive SUVs and believe the lie that they constitute a kind of life insurance, even when we're upside-down in them. And, worst of all, we don't bat an eye when Ari Fleischer[16] tells us to "be careful what you say," even if we remember having been told somewhere

---

[15]*Plato to Rousseau:* Plato (c. 427–c. 347 B.C.E.), extraordinarily influential Greek philosopher. Jean-Jacques Rousseau, Swiss philosopher and writer (1712–1778).

[16]*Ari Fleischer:* Press secretary for George W. Bush from 2001 to 2003 (b. 1960).

back in school that America is the land of the free. We simply buy that one too. Our schooling, as intended, has seen to it.

Now for the good news. Once you understand the logic behind modern schooling, its tricks and traps are fairly easy to avoid. School trains children to be employees and consumers; teach your own to be leaders and adventurers. School trains children to obey reflexively; teach your own to think critically and independently. Well-schooled kids have a low threshold for boredom; help your own to develop an inner life so that they'll never be bored. Urge them to take on the serious material, the *grown-up* material, in history, literature, philosophy, music, art, economics, theology—all the stuff schoolteachers know well enough to avoid. Challenge your kids with plenty of solitude so that they can learn to enjoy their own company, to conduct inner dialogues. Well-schooled people are conditioned to dread being alone, and they seek constant companionship through the TV, the computer, the cell phone, and through shallow friendships quickly acquired and quickly abandoned. Your children should have a more meaningful life, and they can.

First, though, we must wake up to what our schools really are: laboratories of experimentation on young minds, drill centers for the habits and attitudes that corporate society demands. Mandatory education serves children only incidentally; its real purpose is to turn them into servants. Don't let your own have their childhoods extended, not even for a day. If David Farragut could take command of a captured British warship as a preteen, if Thomas Edison could publish a broadsheet at the age of twelve, if Ben Franklin could apprentice himself to a printer at the same age (then put himself through a course of study that would choke a Yale senior today), there's no telling what your own kids could do. After a long life, and thirty years in the public school trenches, I've concluded that genius is as common as dirt. We suppress our genius only because we haven't yet figured out how to manage a population of educated men and women. The solution, I think, is simple and glorious. Let them manage themselves.

ENGAGING THE TEXT

1. Why does Gatto think that school is boring and childish? How does Gatto's depiction of school compare with your own elementary and secondary school experience?

2. What, according to Gatto, are the six unstated purposes of public schooling? To what extent does your own prior educational experience support this bleak view of American education?

3. To what extent would you agree that we really don't need to go to school? Given the current state of technology and a globalizing economy, do you think most people would gain the abilities they need to survive and thrive through homeschooling?

From *Love Is Hell.* Copyright © 1986 Matt Groening. All rights reserved. Reprinted by permission of Pantheon Books, a division of Random House, Inc., New York. Courtesy of Acme Features Syndicate.

4. How would you go about teaching your own children to be "leaders and adventurers," to think "critically and independently," and to "develop an inner life so that they'll never be bored"? How many parents, in your estimation, have the time, experience, and resources to make Gatto's ideal education a reality?

EXPLORING CONNECTIONS

5. Compare Horace Mann's view of the purpose of public education (p. 110) with Gatto's analysis of the hidden purposes of compulsory schooling. Which of these depictions of public education does your own experience of schooling support?

6. Look ahead to Jean Anyon's excerpt from *Social Class and the Hidden Curriculum of Work* (p. 163) and compare Anyon's analysis of the real agenda of American public education with that described by Gatto. To what extent does Anyon's class-based analysis of education in America support Gatto's description of the unspoken purposes of public schooling?

EXTENDING THE CRITICAL CONTEXT

7. Working in groups, write a proposal for a school that wouldn't be boring or childish and that would create the kind of independent, critical, active thinkers that Gatto prizes. What would a day in such a school be like? What would the students do? What would they learn? Who would teach them?

8. Research the state of Prussia and Frederick the Great to learn more about Prussian history and culture. How might your findings change your response to Gatto's argument? Would you agree that the Prussian influence on American schooling is really a "cause for concern"? Why? What other nineteenth-century nation might have offered a better model?

"I JUST WANNA BE AVERAGE"
MIKE ROSE

Mike Rose is anything but average: he has published poetry, scholarly research, a textbook, and several widely praised books on education in America. A professor in the School of Education at UCLA, Rose (b. 1944) has won awards from the National Academy of Education, the National Council of Teachers of English, and the John Simon Guggenheim Memorial Foundation. Below you'll read the story of how this highly successful teacher and writer started high school in the vocational education track, learning dead-end skills from teachers who were often underprepared or incompetent. Rose shows that students whom the system has written off can have tremendous unrealized potential, and his critique of the school system specifies several reasons for the failure of students who go through high school belligerent, fearful, stoned, frustrated, or just plain bored. This selection comes from *Lives on the Boundary* (1989), Rose's exploration of America's educationally underprivileged. His publications also include *Possible Lives* (1996), an explanation of nationwide educational innovation; *The Mind at Work* (2006), a study of the complex thinking involved in common labor; and, *Back to School: Why Everyone Deserves a Second Chance at Education* (2012). Rose is currently a professor at the UCLA Graduate School of Education and Information Studies.

IT TOOK TWO BUSES TO GET TO Our Lady of Mercy. The first started deep in South Los Angeles and caught me at midpoint. The second drifted through neighborhoods with trees, parks, big lawns, and lots of flowers. The rides were long but were livened up by a group of South L.A. veterans whose parents also thought that Hope had set up shop in the west end of the county. There was Christy Biggars, who, at sixteen, was dealing and was, according to rumor, a pimp as well. There were Bill Cobb and Johnny Gonzales, grease-pencil artists extraordinaire, who left Nembutal-enhanced[1] swirls of "Cobb" and "Johnny" on the corrugated walls of the bus. And then there was Tyrrell Wilson. Tyrrell was the coolest kid I knew. He ran the dozens[2] like a metric halfback, laid down a rap that outrhymed and outpointed Cobb, whose rap was good but not great—the curse of a moderately soulful kid trapped in white skin. But it was Cobb who would sneak a radio onto the bus, and thus underwrote his patter with Little Richard, Fats Domino, Chuck Berry, the Coasters, and Ernie K. Doe's[3] mother-in-law, an awful woman who was "sent from down below." And so it was that Christy and Cobb and Johnny G. and Tyrrell and I and assorted others picked up along the way passed our days in the back of the bus, a funny mix brought together by geography and parental desire.

Entrance to school brings with it forms and releases and assessments. Mercy relied on a series of tests, mostly the Stanford-Binet,[4] for placement, and somehow the results of my tests got confused with those of another student named Rose. The other Rose apparently didn't do very well, for I was placed in the vocational track, a euphemism for the bottom level. Neither I nor my parents realized what this meant. We had no sense that Business Math, Typing, and English-Level D were dead ends. The current spate of reports on the schools criticizes parents for not involving themselves in the education of their children. But how would someone like Tommy Rose, with his two years of Italian schooling, know what to ask? And what sort of pressure could an exhausted waitress apply? The error went undetected, and I remained in the vocational track for two years. What a place.

My homeroom was supervised by Brother Dill, a troubled and unstable man who also taught freshman English. When his class drifted away from him, which was often, his voice would rise in paranoid accusations, and occasionally he would lose control and shake or smack us. I hadn't been there two months when one of his brisk, face-turning slaps had my glasses sliding down the aisle. Physical education was also pretty harsh. Our teacher was a stubby ex-lineman who had played old-time pro ball in the Midwest. He routinely had us grabbing our ankles

---

[1] *Nembutal:* Trade name for pentobarbital, a sedative drug. [All notes are the editors'.]
[2] *the dozens:* A verbal game of African origin in which competitors try to top each other's insults.
[3] *Little Richard, Fats Domino, Chuck Berry, the Coasters, and Ernie K. Doe:* Popular black musicians of the 1950s.
[4] *Stanford-Binet:* An IQ test.

to receive his stinging paddle across our butts. He did that, he said, to make men of us. "Rose," he bellowed on our first encounter; me standing geeky in line in my baggy shorts. " 'Rose'? What the hell kind of name is that?"

"Italian, sir," I squeaked.

"Italian! Ho. Rose, do you know the sound a bag of shit makes 5 when it hits the wall?"

"No, sir."

"Wop!"[5]

Sophomore English was taught by Mr. Mitropetros. He was a large, bejeweled man who managed the parking lot at the Shrine Auditorium. He would crow and preen and list for us the stars he'd brushed against. We'd ask questions and glance knowingly and snicker, and all that fueled the poor guy to brag some more. Parking cars was his night job. He had little training in English, so his lesson plan for his day work had us reading the district's required text, *Julius Caesar,* aloud for the semester. We'd finished the play way before the twenty weeks was up, so he'd have us switch parts again and again and start again: Dave Snyder, the fastest guy at Mercy, muscling through Caesar to the breathless squeals of Calpurnia, as interpreted by Steve Fusco, a surfer who owned the school's most envied paneled wagon. Week ten and Dave and Steve would take on new roles, as would we all, and render a water-logged Cassius and a Brutus that are beyond my powers of description.

Spanish I—taken in the second year—fell into the hands of a new recruit. Mr. Montez was a tiny man, slight, five foot six at the most, soft-spoken and delicate. Spanish was a particularly rowdy class, and Mr. Montez was as prepared for it as a doily maker at a hammer throw. He would tap his pencil to a room in which Steve Fusco was propelling spitballs from his heavy lips, in which Mike Dweetz was taunting Billy Hawk, a half-Indian, half-Spanish, reed-thin, quietly explosive boy. The vocational track at Our Lady of Mercy mixed kids traveling in from South L.A. with South Bay surfers and a few Slavs and Chicanos from the harbors of San Pedro. This was a dangerous miscellany: surfers and hodads[6] and South-Central blacks all ablaze to the metronomic tapping of Hector Montez's pencil.

One day Billy lost it. Out of the corner of my eye I saw him strike 10 out with his right arm and catch Dweetz across the neck. Quick as a spasm, Dweetz was out of his seat, scattering desks, cracking Billy on the side of the head, right behind the eye. Snyder and Fusco and others broke it up, but the room felt hot and close and naked. Mr. Montez's tenuous authority was finally ripped to shreds, and I think everyone felt a little strange about that. The charade was over, and when it came down to it, I don't think any of the kids really wanted it to end this way.

---

[5] *Wop:* Derogatory term for Italian.
[6] *hodads:* Nonsurfers.

They had pushed and pushed and bullied their way into a freedom that both scared and embarrassed them.

Students will float to the mark you set. I and the others in the vocational classes were bobbing in pretty shallow water. Vocational education has aimed at increasing the economic opportunities of students who do not do well in our schools. Some serious programs succeed in doing that, and through exceptional teachers—like Mr. Gross in *Horace's Compromise*[7]—students learn to develop hypotheses and troubleshoot, reason through a problem, and communicate effectively—the true job skills. The vocational track, however, is most often a place for those who are just not making it, a dumping ground for the disaffected. There were a few teachers who worked hard at education; young Brother Slattery, for example, combined a stern voice with weekly quizzes to try to pass along to us a skeletal outline of world history. But mostly the teachers had no idea of how to engage the imaginations of us kids who were scuttling along at the bottom of the pond.

And the teachers would have needed some inventiveness, for none of us was groomed for the classroom. It wasn't just that I didn't know things—didn't know how to simplify algebraic fractions, couldn't identify different kinds of clauses, bungled Spanish translations—but that I had developed various faulty and inadequate ways of doing algebra and making sense of Spanish. Worse yet, the years of defensive tuning out in elementary school had given me a way to escape quickly while seeming at least half alert. During my time in Voc. Ed., I developed further into a mediocre student and a somnambulant problem solver, and that affected the subjects I did have the wherewithal to handle: I detested Shakespeare; I got bored with history. My attention flitted here and there. I fooled around in class and read my books indifferently—the intellectual equivalent of playing with your food. I did what I had to do to get by, and I did it with half a mind.

But I did learn things about people and eventually came into my own socially. I liked the guys in Voc. Ed. Growing up where I did, I understood and admired physical prowess, and there was an abundance of muscle here. There was Dave Snyder, a sprinter and halfback of true quality. Dave's ability and his quick wit gave him a natural appeal, and he was welcome in any clique, though he always kept a little independent. He enjoyed acting the fool and could care less about studies, but he possessed a certain maturity and never caused the faculty much trouble. It was a testament to his independence that he included me among his friends—I eventually went out for track, but I was no jock. Owing to the Latin alphabet and a dearth of *R*s and *S*s, Snyder sat behind Rose, and we started exchanging one-liners and became friends.

There was Ted Richard, a much-touted Little League pitcher. He was chunky and had a baby face and came to Our Lady of Mercy as a seasoned street fighter. Ted was quick to laugh and he had a loud, jolly

[7] *Horace's Compromise:* A 1984 book on American education by Theodore Sizer.

laugh, but when he got angry he'd smile a little smile, the kind that simply raises the corner of the mouth a quarter of an inch. For those who knew, it was an eerie signal. Those who didn't found themselves in big trouble, for Ted was very quick. He loved to carry on what we would come to call philosophical discussions: What is courage? Does God exist? He also loved words, enjoyed picking up big ones like *salubrious* and *equivocal* and using them in our conversations—laughing at himself as the word hit a chuckhole rolling off his tongue. Ted didn't do all that well in school—baseball and parties and testing the courage he'd speculated about took up his time. His textbooks were *Argosy* and *Field and Stream,* whatever newspapers he'd find on the bus stop—from the *Daily Worker* to pornography—conversations with uncles or hobos or businessmen he'd meet in a coffee shop, *The Old Man and the Sea.* With hindsight, I can see that Ted was developing into one of those rough-hewn intellectuals whose sources are a mix of the learned and the apocryphal, whose discussions are both assured and sad.

And then there was Ken Harvey. Ken was good-looking in a puffy   15
way and had a full and oily ducktail and was a car enthusiast...a hodad. One day in religion class, he said the sentence that turned out to be one of the most memorable of the hundreds of thousands I heard in those Voc. Ed. years. We were talking about the parable of the talents, about achievement, working hard, doing the best you can do, blah-blah-blah, when the teacher called on the restive Ken Harvey for an opinion. Ken thought about it, but just for a second, and said (with studied, minimal affect), "I just wanna be average." That woke me up. Average? Who wants to be average? Then the athletes chimed in with the clichés that make you want to laryngectomize them, and the exchange became a platitudinous melee. At the time, I thought Ken's assertion was stupid, and I wrote him off. But his sentence has stayed with me all these years, and I think I am finally coming to understand it.

Ken Harvey was gasping for air. School can be a tremendously disorienting place. No matter how bad the school, you're going to encounter notions that don't fit with the assumptions and beliefs that you grew up with—maybe you'll hear these dissonant notions from teachers, maybe from the other students, and maybe you'll read them. You'll also be thrown in with all kinds of kids from all kinds of backgrounds, and that can be unsettling—this is especially true in places of rich ethnic and linguistic mix, like the L.A. basin. You'll see a handful of students far excel you in courses that sound exotic and that are only in the curriculum of the elite: French, physics, trigonometry. And all this is happening while you're trying to shape an identity, your body is changing, and your emotions are running wild. If you're a working-class kid in the vocational track, the options you'll have to deal with this will be constrained in certain ways: you're defined by your school as "slow"; you're placed in a curriculum that isn't designed to liberate you but to occupy you, or, if you're lucky, train you, though the training is for work the society does not esteem; other students are picking up the cues from your school and your curriculum and interacting with you in particular ways. If you're a kid like Ted Richard, you turn your back on all this and let your mind roam where it may. But youngsters like Ted are rare. What Ken and so many others do is protect themselves from such suffocating madness by taking on with a vengeance the identity implied in the vocational track. Reject the confusion and frustration by openly defining yourself as the Common Joe. Champion the average. Rely on your own good sense. Fuck this bullshit. Bullshit, of course, is everything you—and the others—fear is beyond you: books, essays, tests, academic scrambling, complexity, scientific reasoning, philosophical inquiry.

The tragedy is that you have to twist the knife in your own gray matter to make this defense work. You'll have to shut down, have to reject intellectual stimuli or diffuse them with sarcasm, have to cultivate stupidity, have to convert boredom from a malady into a way of confronting the world. Keep your vocabulary simple, act stoned when you're not or act more stoned than you are, flaunt ignorance, materialize your dreams. It is a powerful and effective defense—it neutralizes the insult and the frustration of being a vocational kid and, when perfected, it drives teachers up the wall, a delightful secondary effect. But like all strong magic, it exacts a price.

My own deliverance from the Voc. Ed. world began with sophomore biology. Every student, college prep to vocational, had to take biology, and unlike the other courses, the same person taught all sections. When teaching the vocational group, Brother Clint probably slowed down a bit or omitted a little of the fundamental biochemistry, but he used the same book and more or less the same syllabus across the board. If one class got tough, he could get tougher. He was young and powerful and very handsome, and looks and physical strength were high currency. No one gave him any trouble.

I was pretty bad at the dissecting table, but the lectures and the textbook were interesting: plastic overlays that, with each turned page, peeled away skin, then veins and muscle, then organs, down to the very bones that Brother Clint, pointer in hand, would tap out on our hanging skeleton. Dave Snyder was in big trouble, for the study of life—versus the living of it—was sticking in his craw. We worked out a code for our multiple-choice exams. He'd poke me in the back: once for the answer under *A*, twice for *B*, and so on; and when he'd hit the right one, I'd look up to the ceiling as though I were lost in thought. Poke: cytoplasm. Poke, poke: methane. Poke, poke, poke: William Harvey. Poke, poke, poke, poke: islets of Langerhans. This didn't work out perfectly, but Dave passed the course, and I mastered the dreamy look of a guy on a record jacket. And something else happened. Brother Clint puzzled over this Voc. Ed. kid who was racking up 98s and 99s on his tests. He checked the school's records and discovered the error. He recommended that I begin my junior year in the College Prep program. According to all I've read since, such a shift, as one report put it, is virtually impossible. Kids at that level rarely cross tracks. The telling thing is how chancy both my placement into and exit from Voc. Ed. was; neither I nor my parents had anything to do with it. I lived in one world during spring semester, and when I came back to school in the fall, I was living in another.

Switching to College Prep was a mixed blessing. I was an erratic student. I was undisciplined. And I hadn't caught onto the rules of the game: why work hard in a class that didn't grab my fancy? I was also hopelessly behind in math. Chemistry was hard; toying with my chemistry set years before hadn't prepared me for the chemist's equations. Fortunately, the priest who taught both chemistry and second-year algebra was also the school's athletic director. Membership on the track team covered me; I knew I wouldn't get lower than a C. U.S. history was taught pretty well, and I did okay. But civics was taken over by a football coach who had trouble reading the textbook aloud—and reading aloud was the centerpiece of his pedagogy. College Prep at Mercy was certainly an improvement over the vocational program—at least it carried some status—but the social science curriculum was weak, and the mathematics and physical sciences were simply beyond me. I had a miserable quantitative background and ended up copying some assignments and finessing the rest as best I could. Let me try to explain how it feels to see again and again material you should once have learned but didn't.

You are given a problem. It requires you to simplify algebraic fractions or to multiply expressions containing square roots. You know this is pretty basic material because you've seen it for years. Once a teacher took some time with you, and you learned how to carry out these operations. Simple versions, anyway. But that was a year or two or more in the past, and these are more complex versions, and now you're not sure. And this, you keep telling yourself, is ninth- or even eighth-grade stuff.

Next it's a word problem. This is also old hat. The basic elements are as familiar as story characters: trains speeding so many miles per hour or shadows of buildings angling so many degrees. Maybe you know enough, have sat through enough explanations, to be able to begin setting up the problem: "If one train is going this fast..." or "This shadow is really one line of a triangle..." Then: "Let's see..." "How did Jones do this?" "Hmmmm." "No." "No, that won't work." Your attention wavers. You wonder about other things: a football game, a dance, that cute new checker at the market. You try to focus on the problem again. You scribble on paper for a while, but the tension wins out and your attention flits elsewhere. You crumple the paper and begin daydreaming to ease the frustration.

The particulars will vary, but in essence this is what a number of students go through, especially those in so-called remedial classes. They open their textbooks and see once again the familiar and impenetrable formulas and diagrams and terms that have stumped them for years. There is no excitement here. *No* excitement. Regardless of what the teacher says, this is not a new challenge. There is, rather, embarrassment and frustration and, not surprisingly, some anger in being reminded once again of long-standing inadequacies. No wonder so many students finally attribute their difficulties to something inborn, organic: "That part of my brain just doesn't work." Given the troubling histories many of these students have, it's miraculous that any of them can lift the shroud of hopelessness sufficiently to make deliverance from these classes possible.

Through this entire period, my father's health was deteriorating with cruel momentum. His arteriosclerosis progressed to the point where a simple nick on his shin wouldn't heal. Eventually it ulcerated and widened. Lou Minton would come by daily to change the dressing. We tried renting an oscillating bed—which we placed in the front room—to force blood through the constricted arteries in my father's legs. The bed hummed through the night, moving in place to ward off the inevitable. The ulcer continued to spread, and the doctors finally had to amputate. My grandfather had lost his leg in a stockyard accident. Now my father too was crippled. His convalescence was slow but steady, and the doctors placed him in the Santa Monica Rehabilitation Center, a sunbleached building that opened out onto the warm spray of the Pacific. The place gave him some strength and some color and some training in walking with an artificial leg. He did pretty well for a year or so until he slipped and broke his hip. He was confined to a wheelchair after that, and the confinement contributed to the diminishing of his body and spirit.

I am holding a picture of him. He is sitting in his wheelchair and 25 smiling at the camera. The smile appears forced, unsteady, seems to quaver, though it is frozen in silver nitrate. He is in his mid-sixties and looks eighty. Late in my junior year, he had a stroke and never came out of the resulting coma. After that, I would see him only in dreams, and to this day that is how I join him. Sometimes the dreams are sad and grisly and primal: my father lying in a bed soaked with his suppuration,[8] holding me, rocking me. But sometimes the dreams bring him back to me healthy: him talking to me on an empty street, or buying some pictures to decorate our old house, or transformed somehow into someone strong and adept with tools and the physical.

Jack MacFarland couldn't have come into my life at a better time. My father was dead, and I had logged up too many years of scholastic indifference. Mr. MacFarland had a master's degree from Columbia and decided, at twenty-six, to find a little school and teach his heart out. He never took any credentialing courses, couldn't bear to, he said, so he had to find employment in a private system. He ended up at Our Lady of Mercy teaching five sections of senior English. He was a beatnik who was born too late. His teeth were stained, he tucked his sorry tie

---

[8]*suppuration:* Discharge from wounds.

in between the third and fourth buttons of his shirt, and his pants were chronically wrinkled. At first, we couldn't believe this guy, thought he slept in his car. But within no time, he had us so startled with work that we didn't much worry about where he slept or if he slept at all. We wrote three or four essays a month. We read a book every two to three weeks, starting with the *Iliad* and ending up with Hemingway. He gave us a quiz on the reading every other day. He brought a prep school curriculum to Mercy High.

MacFarland's lectures were crafted, and as he delivered them he would pace the room jiggling a piece of chalk in his cupped hand, using it to scribble on the board the names of all the writers and philosophers and plays and novels he was weaving into his discussion. He asked questions often, raised everything from Zeno's paradox to the repeated last line of Frost's "Stopping by Woods on a Snowy Evening." He slowly and carefully built up our knowledge of Western intellectual history — with facts, with connections, with speculations. We learned about Greek philosophy, about Dante, the Elizabethan world view, the Age of Reason, existentialism. He analyzed poems with us, had us reading sections from John Ciardi's *How Does a Poem Mean?*, making a potentially difficult book accessible with his own explanations. We gave oral reports on poems Ciardi didn't cover. We imitated the styles of Conrad, Hemingway, and *Time* magazine. We wrote and talked, wrote and talked. The man immersed us in language.

Even MacFarland's barbs were literary. If Jim Fitzsimmons, hung over and irritable, tried to smart-ass him, he'd rejoin with a flourish that would spark the indomitable Skip Madison — who'd lost his front teeth in a hapless tackle — to flick his tongue through the gap and opine, "good chop," drawing out the single "o" in stinging indictment. Jack MacFarland, this tobacco-stained intellectual, brandished linguistic weapons of a kind I hadn't encountered before. Here was this *egghead,* for God's sake, keeping some pretty difficult people in line. And from what I heard, Mike Dweetz and Steve Fusco and all the notorious Voc. Ed. crowd settled down as well when MacFarland took the podium. Though a lot of guys groused in the schoolyard, it just seemed that giving trouble to this particular teacher was a silly thing to do. Tomfoolery, not to mention assault, had no place in the world he was trying to create for us, and instinctively everyone knew that. If nothing else, we all recognized MacFarland's considerable intelligence and respected the hours he put into his work. It came to this: the troublemaker would look foolish rather than daring. Even Jim Fitzsimmons was reading *On the Road* and turning his incipient alcoholism to literary ends.

There were some lives that were already beyond Jack MacFarland's ministrations, but mine was not. I started reading again as I hadn't since elementary school. I would go into our gloomy little bedroom or sit at the dinner table while, on the television, Danny McShane was paralyzing Mr. Moto with the atomic drop, and work slowly back through *Heart of Darkness,* trying to catch the words in Conrad's sentences. I certainly was not MacFarland's best student; most of the other guys in College Prep, even my fellow slackers, had better backgrounds than I did. But I worked very hard, for MacFarland had hooked me. He tapped my old interest in reading and creating stories. He gave me a way to feel special by using my mind. And he provided a role model that wasn't shaped on physical prowess alone, and something inside me that I wasn't quite aware of responded to that. Jack MacFarland established a literacy club, to borrow a phrase of Frank Smith's, and invited me—invited all of us—to join.

There's been a good deal of research and speculation suggest- 30 ing that the acknowledgment of school performance with extrinsic rewards—smiling faces, stars, numbers, grades—diminishes the intrinsic satisfaction children experience by engaging in reading or writing or problem solving. While it's certainly true that we've created an educational system that encourages our best and brightest to become cynical grade collectors and, in general, have developed an obsession with evaluation and assessment, I must tell you that venal though it may have been, I loved getting good grades from MacFarland. I now know how subjective grades can be, but then they came tucked in the back of essays like bits of scientific data, some sort of spectroscopic readout that said, objectively and publicly, that I had made something of value. I suppose I'd been mediocre for too long and enjoyed a public redefinition. And I suppose the workings of my mind, such as they were, had been private for too long. My linguistic play moved into the world;...these papers with their circled, red B-pluses and A-minuses linked my mind to something outside it. I carried them around like a club emblem.

One day in the December of my senior year, Mr. MacFarland asked me where I was going to go to college. I hadn't thought much about it. Many of the students I teach today spent their last year in high school with a physics text in one hand and the Stanford catalog in the other, but I wasn't even aware of what "entrance requirements" were. My folks would say that they wanted me to go to college and be a doctor, but I don't know how seriously I ever took that; it seemed a sweet thing to say, a bit of supportive family chatter, like telling a gangly daughter she's graceful. The reality of higher education wasn't in my scheme of things: no one in the family had gone to college; only two of my uncles had completed high school. I figured I'd get a night job and go to the local junior college because I knew that Snyder and Company were going there to play ball. But I hadn't even prepared for that. When I finally said, "I don't know," MacFarland looked down at me—I was seated in his office—and said, "Listen, you can write."

My grades stank. I had A's in biology and a handful of B's in a few English and social science classes. All the rest were C's—or worse. MacFarland said I would do well in his class and laid down the law about doing well in the others. Still, the record for my first three years wouldn't have been acceptable to any four-year school. To nobody's surprise, I was turned down flat by USC and UCLA. But Jack MacFarland was on the case. He had received his bachelor's degree from Loyola University, so he made calls to old professors and talked to somebody in admissions and wrote me a strong letter. Loyola finally accepted me as a probationary student. I would be on trial for the first year, and if I did okay, I would be granted regular status. MacFarland also intervened to get me a loan, for I could never have afforded a private college without it. Four more years of religion classes and four more years of boys at one school, girls at another. But at least I was going to college. Amazing.

In my last semester of high school, I elected a special English course fashioned by Mr. MacFarland, and it was through this elective that there arose at Mercy a fledgling literati. Art Mitz, the editor of the school newspaper and a very smart guy, was the kingpin. He was joined by me and by Mark Dever, a quiet boy who wrote beautifully and who would die before he was forty. MacFarland occasionally invited us to his apartment, and those visits became the high point of our apprenticeship: we'd clamp on our training wheels and drive to his salon.

He lived in a cramped and cluttered place near the airport, tucked away in the kind of building that architectural critic Reyner Banham calls a *dingbat.* Books were all over: stacked, piled, tossed, and crated, underlined and dog eared, well worn and new. Cigarette ashes crusted with coffee in saucers or spilling over the sides of motel ashtrays. The little bedroom had, along two of its walls, bricks and boards loaded with notes, magazines, and oversized books. The kitchen joined the living room, and there was a stack of German newspapers under the sink. I had never seen anything like it: a great flophouse of language furnished by City Lights and Café le Metro. I read every title. I flipped through paperbacks and scanned jackets and memorized names: Gogol, *Finnegans Wake,* Djuna Barnes, Jackson Pollock, *A Coney Island of the Mind,* F. O. Matthiessen's *American Renaissance,* all sorts of Freud, *Troubled Sleep,* Man Ray, *The Education of Henry Adams,* Richard Wright, *Film as Art,* William Butler Yeats, Marguerite Duras, *Redburn, A Season in Hell, Kapital.* On the cover of Alain-Fournier's *The Wanderer* was an Edward Gorey drawing of a young man on a road winding into dark trees. By the hotplate sat a strange Kafka novel called *Amerika,* in which an adolescent hero crosses the Atlantic to find the Nature Theater of Oklahoma. Art and Mark would be talking about a movie or the school newspaper, and I would be consuming my English teacher's library. It was heady stuff. I felt like a Pop Warner[9] athlete on steroids.

Art, Mark, and I would buy stogies and triangulate from MacFarland's 35 apartment to the Cinema, which now shows X-rated films but was then L.A.'s premier art theater, and then to the musty Cherokee Bookstore in Hollywood to hobnob with beatnik homosexuals—smoking, drinking bourbon and coffee, and trying out awkward phrases we'd gleaned from our mentor's bookshelves. I was happy and precocious and a little scared

[9]*Pop Warner:* A nationwide youth athletics organization.

as well, for Hollywood Boulevard was thick with a kind of decadence that was foreign to the South Side. After the Cherokee, we would head back to the security of MacFarland's apartment, slaphappy with hipness.

Let me be the first to admit that there was a good deal of adolescent passion in this embrace of the avant-garde: self-absorption, sexually charged pedantry, an elevation of the odd and abandoned. Still it was a time during which I absorbed an awful lot of information: long lists of titles, images from expressionist paintings, new wave shibboleths,[10] snippets of philosophy, and names that read like Steve Fusco's misspellings—Goethe, Nietzsche, Kierkegaard. Now this is hardly the stuff of deep understanding. But it was an introduction, a phrase book, a Baedeker[11] to a vocabulary of ideas, and it felt good at the time to know all these words. With hindsight I realize how layered and important that knowledge was.

It enabled me to do things in the world. I could browse bohemian bookstores in far-off, mysterious Hollywood; I could go to the Cinema and see events through the lenses of European directors; and, most of all, I could share an evening, talk that talk, with Jack MacFarland, the man I most admired at the time. Knowledge was becoming a bonding agent. Within a year or two, the persona of the disaffected hipster would prove too cynical, too alienated to last. But for a time it was new and exciting: it provided a critical perspective on society, and it allowed me to act as though I were living beyond the limiting boundaries of South Vermont.[12]

ENGAGING THE TEXT

1. Describe Rose's life in Voc. Ed. What were his teachers like? Have you ever had experience with teachers like these?

2. What did Voc. Ed. do to Rose and his fellow students? How did it affect them intellectually, emotionally, and socially? Why was it subsequently so hard for Rose to catch up in math?

3. Why is high school so disorienting to students like Ken Harvey? How does he cope with it? What other strategies do students use to cope with the pressures and judgments they encounter in school?

4. What does Jack MacFarland offer Rose that finally helps him learn? Do you think it was inevitable that someone with Rose's intelligence would eventually succeed?

EXPLORING CONNECTIONS

5. To what extent do Rose's experiences challenge or confirm John Taylor Gatto's critique of public education in "Against School" (p. 141)? How might Gatto account for the existence of truly remarkable teachers like Rose's Jack MacFarland?

---

[10]*new wave shibboleths:* Trendy phrases or jargon.
[11]*Baedeker:* Travel guide.
[12]*South Vermont:* A street in an economically depressed area of Los Angeles.

6. How does Michael Moore's assessment of the general state of intelligence in America in "Idiot Nation" (p. 121) help to explain the attitudes of Rose's friends toward education? How would you account for the fact that many American teens seem to feel it's OK to be "average" intellectually even as they strive for other kinds of excellence?

7. Draw a Groening-style cartoon (see pp. 140 and 150) or comic strip of Rose in the vocational track, or of Rose before and after his liberation from Voc. Ed.

8. Read Gregory Mantsios's "Class in America — 2009" (p. 281) and write an imaginary dialogue between Rose and Mantsios about why some students, like Rose, seem to be able to break through social class barriers and others, like Dave Snyder, Ted Richard, and Ken Harvey, do not.

EXTENDING THE CRITICAL CONTEXT

9. Rose explains that high school can be a "tremendously disorienting place" (para. 16). What, if anything, do you find disorienting about college? What steps can students at your school take to lessen feelings of disorientation? What could the college do to help them?

10. Review one or more of Rose's descriptions of his high school classmates; then write a description of one of your own high school classmates, trying to capture in a nutshell how that person coped or failed to cope with the educational system.

11. Watch any one of the many films that have been made about charismatic teachers (for example, *Dangerous Minds, Renaissance Man, Stand and Deliver*, or *Dead Poets Society*) and compare Hollywood's depiction of a dynamic teacher to Rose's portrayal of Jack MacFarland. What do such charismatic teachers offer their students personally and intellectually? Do you see any disadvantages to classes taught by teachers like these?

FROM SOCIAL CLASS AND THE HIDDEN CURRICULUM OF WORK

JEAN ANYON

It's no surprise that schools in wealthy communities are better than those in poor communities, or that they better prepare their students for desirable jobs. It may be shocking, however, to learn how vast the differences in schools are — not so much in resources as in teaching methods and philosophies of education. Jean Anyon observed five elementary schools over the course of a full school year and concluded that fifth graders of different economic backgrounds are already being prepared to occupy particular rungs on the social ladder. In a sense, some whole schools are on the vocational education track, while others are geared to produce future doctors, lawyers, and business leaders. Anyon's main audience is professional educators, so you may find her style and vocabulary challenging, but, once you've read her descriptions of specific classroom activities, the more analytic parts of the essay should prove easier to understand. Anyon is professor of educational policy in the Graduate Center of the City University of New York. Her publications include *Radical Possibilities: Public Policy, Urban Education and a New Social Movement* (2005) and *Theory and Educational Research: Toward Critical Social Explanation* (2009). This essay first appeared in the *Journal of Education* in 1980.

SCHOLARS IN POLITICAL ECONOMY and the sociology of knowledge have recently argued that public schools in complex industrial societies like our own make available different types of educational experience and curriculum knowledge to students in different social classes. Bowles and Gintis,[1] for example, have argued that students in different social-class backgrounds are rewarded for classroom behaviors that correspond to personality traits allegedly rewarded in the different occupational strata — the working classes for docility and obedience, the managerial classes for initiative and personal assertiveness. Basil Bernstein, Pierre Bourdieu, and Michael W. Apple,[2] focusing on school knowledge, have argued that knowledge and skills leading to social power and regard (medical, legal, managerial) are made available to the advantaged social groups but are withheld from the working classes, to whom a more "practical" curriculum is offered (manual skills, clerical knowledge). While there has been considerable argumentation of these points regarding education in England, France, and North America, there has been little or no attempt to investigate these ideas empirically in elementary or secondary schools and classrooms in this country.[3]

This article offers tentative empirical support (and qualification) of the above arguments by providing illustrative examples of differences in student *work* in classrooms in contrasting social-class communities. The examples were gathered as part of an ethnographical[4] study of curricular, pedagogical, and pupil evaluation practices in five elementary

[1]S. Bowles and H. Gintis, *Schooling in Capitalist America: Educational Reform and the Contradictions of Economic Life* (New York: Basic Books, 1976). [All notes are Anyon's, except 4 and 11.]

[2]B. Bernstein, *Class, Codes and Control,* Vol. 3. *Towards a Theory of Educational Transmission,* 2d ed. (London: Routledge & Kegan Paul, 1977); P. Bourdieu and J. Passeron, *Reproduction in Education, Society and Culture* (Beverly Hills, Calif.: Sage, 1977); M. W. Apple, *Ideology and Curriculum* (Boston: Routledge & Kegan Paul, 1979).

[3]But see, in a related vein, M. W. Apple and N. King, "What Do Schools Teach?" *Curriculum Inquiry* 6 (1977): 341–58; R. C. Rist, *The Urban School: A Factory for Failure* (Cambridge, MA: MIT Press, 1973).

[4]*ethnographical:* Based on an anthropological study of cultures or subcultures — the "cultures" in this case being the five schools observed. [Eds.]

schools. The article attempts a theoretical contribution as well and assesses student work in the light of a theoretical approach to social-class analysis....It will be suggested that there is a "hidden curriculum" in schoolwork that has profound implications for the theory—and consequence—of everyday activity in education....

The Sample of Schools

...The social-class designation of each of the five schools will be identified, and the income, occupation, and other relevant available social characteristics of the students and their parents will be described. The first three schools are in a medium-sized city district in northern New Jersey, and the other two are in a nearby New Jersey suburb.

The first two schools I will call *working-class schools.* Most of the parents have blue-collar jobs. Less than a third of the fathers are skilled, while the majority are in unskilled or semiskilled jobs. During the period of the study (1978–1979), approximately 15 percent of the fathers were unemployed. The large majority (85 percent) of the families are white. The following occupations are typical: platform, storeroom, and stockroom workers; foundrymen, pipe welders, and boilermakers; semiskilled and unskilled assemblyline operatives; gas station attendants, auto mechanics, maintenance workers, and security guards. Less than 30 percent of the women work, some part-time and some full-time, on assembly lines, in storerooms and stockrooms, as waitresses, barmaids, or sales clerks. Of the fifth-grade parents, none of the wives of the skilled workers had jobs. Approximately 15 percent of the families in each school are at or below the federal "poverty" level;[5] most of the rest of the family incomes are at or below $12,000, except some of the skilled workers whose incomes are higher. The incomes of the majority of the families in these two schools (at or below $12,000) are typical of 38.6 percent of the families in the United States.[6]

The third school is called the *middle-class school,* although because of neighborhood residence patterns, the population is a mixture of several social classes. The parents' occupations can be divided into three groups: a small group of blue-collar "rich," who are skilled, well-paid workers such as printers, carpenters, plumbers, and construction workers. The second group is composed of parents in working-class and middle-class white-collar jobs: women in office jobs, technicians, supervisors in industry, and parents employed by the city (such as firemen, policemen, and several of the school's teachers). The third group is

5

[5]The U.S. Bureau of the Census defines *poverty* for a nonfarm family of four as a yearly income of $6,191 a year or less. U.S. Bureau of the Census, *Statistical Abstract of the United States: 1978* (Washington, DC: U.S. Government Printing Office, 1978), 465, table 754.

[6]U.S. Bureau of the Census, "Money Income in 1977 of Families and Persons in the United States," *Current Population Reports* Series P-60, no. 118 (Washington, DC: U.S. Government Printing Office, 1979), p. 2, table A.

composed of occupations such as personnel directors in local firms, accountants, "middle management," and a few small capitalists (owners of shops in the area). The children of several local doctors attend this school. Most family incomes are between $13,000 and $25,000, with a few higher. This income range is typical of 38.9 percent of the families in the United States.[7]

The fourth school has a parent population that is at the upper income level of the upper middle class and is predominantly professional. This school will be called the *affluent professional school.* Typical jobs are: cardiologist, interior designer, corporate lawyer or engineer, executive in advertising or television. There are some families who are not as affluent as the majority (the family of the superintendent of the district's schools, and the one or two families in which the fathers are skilled workers). In addition, a few of the families are more affluent than the majority and can be classified in the capitalist class (a partner in a prestigious Wall Street stock brokerage firm). Approximately 90 percent of the children in this school are white. Most family incomes are between $40,000 and $80,000. This income span represents approximately 7 percent of the families in the United States.[8]

In the fifth school the majority of the families belong to the capitalist class. This school will be called the *executive elite school* because most of the fathers are top executives (for example, presidents and vice-presidents) in major United States–based multinational corporations—for example, AT&T, RCA, Citibank, American Express, U.S. Steel. A sizable group of fathers are top executives in financial firms on Wall Street. There are also a number of fathers who list their occupations as "general counsel" to a particular corporation, and these corporations are also among the large multinationals. Many of the mothers do volunteer work in the Junior League, Junior Fortnightly, or other service groups; some are intricately involved in town politics; and some are themselves in well-paid occupations. There are no minority children in the school. Almost all the family incomes are over $100,000, with some in the $500,000 range. The incomes in this school represent less than 1 percent of the families in the United States.[9]

Since each of the five schools is only one instance of elementary education in a particular social-class context, I will not generalize beyond the sample. However, the examples of schoolwork which follow will suggest characteristics of education in each social setting that appear to have theoretical and social significance and to be worth investigation in a larger number of schools....

---

[7]Ibid.

[8]This figure is an estimate. According to the Bureau of the Census, only 2.6 percent of families in the United States have money income of $50,000 or over. U.S. Bureau of the Census, *Current Population Reports* Series P-60. For figures on income at these higher levels, see J. D. Smith and S. Franklin, "The Concentration of Personal Wealth, 1922–1969," *American Economic Review* 64 (1974): 162–67.

[9]Smith and Franklin, "The Concentration of Personal Wealth."

The Working-Class Schools

In the two working-class schools, work is following the steps of a procedure. The procedure is usually mechanical, involving rote behavior and very little decision making or choice. The teachers rarely explain why the work is being assigned, how it might connect to other assignments, or what the idea is that lies behind the procedure or gives it coherence and perhaps meaning or significance. Available textbooks are not always used, and the teachers often prepare their own dittos or put work examples on the board. Most of the rules regarding work are designations of what the children are to do; the rules are steps to follow. These steps are told to the children by the teachers and are often written on the board. The children are usually told to copy the steps as notes. These notes are to be studied. Work is often evaluated not according to whether it is right or wrong but according to whether the children followed the right steps.

The following examples illustrate these points. In math, when two-digit division was introduced, the teacher in one school gave a four-minute lecture on what the terms are called (which number is the divisor, dividend, quotient, and remainder). The children were told to copy these names in their notebooks. Then the teacher told them the steps to follow to do the problems, saying, "This is how you do them." The teacher listed the steps on the board, and they appeared several days later as a chart hung in the middle of the front wall: "Divide, Multiply, Subtract, Bring Down." The children often did examples of two-digit division. When the teacher went over the examples with them, he told them what the procedure was for each problem, rarely asking them to conceptualize or explain it themselves: "Three into twenty-two is seven; do your subtraction and one is left over." During the week that two-digit division was introduced (or at any other time), the investigator did not observe any discussion of the idea of grouping involved in division, any use of manipulables, or any attempt to relate two-digit division to any other mathematical process. Nor was there any attempt to relate the steps to an actual or possible thought process of the children. The observer did not hear the terms *dividend, quotient,* and so on, used again. The math teacher in the other working-class school followed similar procedures regarding two-digit division and at one point her class seemed confused. She said, "You're confusing yourselves. You're tensing up. Remember, when you do this, it's the same steps over and over again—and that's the way division always is." Several weeks later, after a test, a group of her children "still didn't get it," and she made no attempt to explain the concept of dividing things into groups or to give them manipulables for their own investigation. Rather, she went over the steps with them again and told them that they "needed more practice."

In other areas of math, work is also carrying out often unexplained fragmented procedures. For example, one of the teachers led the children through a series of steps to make a 1-inch grid on their paper *without* telling them that they were making a 1-inch grid or that it would be used to study scale. She said, "Take your ruler. Put it across the top. Make a mark at every number. Then move your ruler down to the bottom. No, put it across the bottom. Now make a mark on top of every number. Now draw a line from..." At this point a girl said that she had a faster way to do it and the teacher said, "No, you don't; you don't even know what I'm making yet. Do it this way or it's wrong." After they had made the lines up and down and across, the teacher told them she wanted them to make a figure by connecting some dots and to measure that, using the scale of 1 inch equals 1 mile. Then they were to cut it out. She said, "Don't cut it until I check it."

In both working-class schools, work in language arts is mechanics of punctuation (commas, periods, question marks, exclamation points), capitalization, and the four kinds of sentences. One teacher explained to me, "Simple punctuation is all they'll ever use." Regarding punctuation, either a teacher or a ditto stated the rules for where, for example, to put commas. The investigator heard no classroom discussion of the aural context of punctuation (which, of course, is what gives each mark its meaning). Nor did the investigator hear any statement or inference that placing a punctuation mark could be a decision-making process, depending, for example, on one's intended meaning. Rather, the children were told to follow the rules. Language arts did not involve creative writing. There were several writing assignments throughout the year, but in each instance the children were given a ditto, and they wrote answers to questions on the sheet. For example, they wrote their "autobiography" by answering such questions as "Where were you born?" "What is your favorite animal?" on a sheet entitled "All About Me."

In one of the working-class schools, the class had a science period several times a week. On the three occasions observed, the children were not called upon to set up experiments or to give explanations for facts or concepts. Rather, on each occasion the teacher told them in his own words what the book said. The children copied the teacher's sentences from the board. Each day that preceded the day they were to do a science experiment, the teacher told them to copy the directions from the book for the procedure they would carry out the next day and to study the list at home that night. The day after each experiment, the teacher went over what they had "found" (they did the experiments as a class, and each was actually a class demonstration led by the teacher). Then the teacher wrote what they "found" on the board, and the children copied that in their notebooks. Once or twice a year there are science projects. The project is chosen and assigned by the teacher from a box of 3-by-5-inch cards. On the card the teacher has written the question to be answered, the books to use, and how much to write. Explaining the cards to the observer, the teacher said, "It tells them exactly what to do, or they couldn't do it."

Social studies in the working-class schools is also largely mechanical, rote work that was given little explanation or connection to larger contexts. In one school, for example, although there was a book available, social studies work was to copy the teacher's notes from the board. Several times a week for a period of several months the children copied these notes. The fifth grades in the district were to study United States history. The teacher used a booklet she had purchased called "The Fabulous Fifty States." Each day she put information from the booklet in outline form on the board and the children copied it. The type of information did not vary: the name of the state, its abbreviation, state capital, nickname of the state, its main products, main business, and a "Fabulous Fact" ("Idaho grew twenty-seven billion potatoes in one year. That's enough potatoes for each man, woman, and..."). As the children finished copying the sentences, the teacher erased them and wrote more. Children would occasionally go to the front to pull down the wall map in order to locate the states they were copying, and the teacher did not dissuade them. But the observer never saw her refer to the map; nor did the observer ever hear her make other than perfunctory remarks concerning the information the children were copying. Occasionally the children colored in a ditto and cut it out to make a stand-up figure (representing, for example, a man roping a cow in the Southwest). These were referred to by the teacher as their social studies "projects."

Rote behavior was often called for in classroom work. When going 15 over math and language arts skills sheets, for example, as the teacher asked for the answer to each problem, he fired the questions rapidly, staccato, and the scene reminded the observer of a sergeant drilling recruits: above all, the questions demanded that you stay at attention: "The next one? What do I put here?...Here? Give us the next." Or "How many commas in this sentence? Where do I put them...The next one?"

The four fifth-grade teachers observed in the working-class schools attempted to control classroom time and space by making decisions without consulting the children and without explaining the basis for their decisions. The teacher's control thus often seemed capricious. Teachers, for instance, very often ignored the bells to switch classes—deciding among themselves to keep the children after the period was officially over to continue with the work or for disciplinary reasons or so they (the teachers) could stand in the hall and talk. There were no clocks in the rooms in either school, and the children often asked, "What period is this?" "When do we go to gym?" The children had no access to materials. These were handed out by teachers and closely guarded. Things in the room "belonged" to the teacher: "Bob, bring me my garbage can." The teachers continually gave the children orders. Only three times did the investigator hear a teacher in either working-class school preface a directive with an unsarcastic "please," or "let's," or "would you." Instead, the teachers said, "Shut up," "Shut your mouth," "Open your books," "Throw your gum away—if you want to rot your teeth, do it on your own time." Teachers made every effort to control the movement of the children, and often shouted, "Why are you out of your seat??!!" If the children got permission to leave the room, they had to take a written pass with the date and time....

Middle-Class School

In the middle-class school, work is getting the right answer. If one accumulates enough right answers, one gets a good grade. One must follow the directions in order to get the right answers, but the directions often call for some figuring, some choice, some decision making. For example, the children must often figure out by themselves what the directions ask them to do and how to get the answer: what do you do first, second, and perhaps third? Answers are usually found in books or by listening to the teacher. Answers are usually words, sentences, numbers, or facts and dates; one writes them on paper, and one should be neat. Answers must be given in the right order, and one cannot make them up.

The following activities are illustrative. Math involves some choice: one may do two-digit division the long way or the short way, and there are some math problems that can be done "in your head." When the teacher explains how to do two-digit division, there is recognition that a cognitive process is involved; she gives you several ways and says, "I want to make sure you understand what you're doing—so you get it right"; and, when they go over the homework, she asks the *children* to tell how they did the problem and what answer they got.

In social studies the daily work is to read the assigned pages in the textbook and to answer the teacher's questions. The questions are almost always designed to check on whether the students have read the assignment and understood it: who did so-and-so; what happened after that; when did it happen, where, and sometimes, why did it happen? The answers are in the book and in one's understanding of the book; the teacher's hints when one doesn't know the answers are to "read it again" or to look at the picture or at the rest of the paragraph. One is to search for the answer in the "context," in what is given.

Language arts is "simple grammar, what they need for everyday 20 life." The language arts teacher says, "They should learn to speak properly, to write business letters and thank-you letters, and to understand what nouns and verbs and simple subjects are." Here, as well, actual work is to choose the right answers, to understand what is given. The teacher often says, "Please read the next sentence and then I'll question you about it." One teacher said in some exasperation to a boy who was fooling around in class, "If you don't know the answers to the questions I ask, then you can't stay in this *class!* [pause] You *never* know the answers to the questions I ask, and it's not fair to me—and certainly not to you!"

Most lessons are based on the textbook. This does not involve a critical perspective on what is given there. For example, a critical perspective in social studies is perceived as dangerous by these teachers because it may lead to controversial topics; the parents might complain.

The children, however, are often curious, especially in social studies. Their questions are tolerated and usually answered perfunctorily. But after a few minutes the teacher will say, "All right, we're not going any farther. Please open your social studies workbook." While the teachers spend a lot of time explaining and expanding on what the textbooks say, there is little attempt to analyze how or why things happen, or to give thought to how pieces of a culture, or, say, a system of numbers or elements of a language fit together or can be analyzed. What has happened in the past and what exists now may not be equitable or fair, but (shrug) that is the way things are and one does not confront such matters in school. For example, in social studies after a child is called on to read a passage about the pilgrims, the teacher summarizes the paragraph and then says, "So you can see how strict they were about everything." A child asks, "Why?" "Well, because they felt that if you weren't busy you'd get into trouble." Another child asks, "Is it true that they burned women at the stake?" The teacher says, "Yes, if a woman did anything strange, they hanged them. [*sic*] What would a woman do, do you think, to make them burn them? [*sic*] See if you can come up with better answers than my other [social studies] class." Several children offer suggestions, to which the teacher nods but does not comment. Then she says, "Okay, good," and calls on the next child to read.

Work tasks do not usually request creativity. Serious attention is rarely given in school work on *how* the children develop or express their own feelings and ideas, either linguistically or in graphic form. On the occasions when creativity or self-expression is requested, it is peripheral to the main activity or it is "enrichment" or "for fun." During a lesson on what similes are, for example, the teacher explains what they are, puts several on the board, gives some other examples herself, and then asks the children if they can "make some up." She calls on three children who give similes, two of which are actually in the book they have open before them. The teacher does not comment on this and then asks several others to choose similes from the list of phrases in the book. Several do so correctly, and she says, "Oh good! You're picking them out! See how good we are?" Their homework is to pick out the rest of the similes from the list.

Creativity is not often requested in social studies and science projects, either. Social studies projects, for example, are given with directions to "find information on your topic" and write it up. The children are not supposed to copy but to "put it in your own words." Although a number of the projects subsequently went beyond the teacher's direction to find information and had quite expressive covers and inside illustrations, the teacher's evaluative comments had to do with the amount of information, whether they had "copied," and if their work was neat.

The style of control of the three fifth-grade teachers observed in this school varied from somewhat easygoing to strict, but in contrast to the working-class schools, the teachers' decisions were usually based on external rules and regulations—for example, on criteria that were known or available to the children. Thus, the teachers always honor the bells for changing classes, and they usually evaluate children's work by what is in the textbooks and answer booklets.

There is little excitement in schoolwork for the children, and the assignments are perceived as having little to do with their interests and feelings. As one child said, what you do is "store facts up in your head like cold storage—until you need it later for a test or your job." Thus, doing well is important because there are thought to be *other*, likely rewards: a good job or college.[10]

Affluent Professional School

In the affluent professional school, work is creative activity carried out independently. The students are continually asked to express and apply ideas and concepts. Work involves individual thought and expressiveness, expansion and illustration of ideas, and choice of appropriate method and material. (The class is not considered an open classroom, and the principal explained that because of the large number of discipline problems in the fifth grade this year they did not departmentalize. The teacher who agreed to take part in the study said she is "more structured" this year than she usually is.) The products of work in this class are often written stories, editorials and essays, or representations of ideas in mural, graph, or craft form. The products of work should not be like everybody else's and should show individuality. They should exhibit good design, and (this is important) they must also fit empirical reality. Moreover, one's work should attempt to interpret or "make sense" of reality. The relatively few rules to be followed regarding work are usually criteria for, or limits on, individual activity. One's product is usually evaluated for the quality of its expression and for the appropriateness of its conception to the task. In many cases, one's own satisfaction with the product is an important criterion for its evaluation. When right answers are called for, as in commercial materials like SRA (Science Research Associates) and math, it is important that the children decide on an answer as a result of thinking about the idea involved in what they're being asked to do. Teacher's hints are to "think about it some more."

The following activities are illustrative. The class takes home a sheet requesting each child's parents to fill in the number of cars they have, the number of television sets, refrigerators, games, or rooms in the house, and so on. Each child is to figure the average number of a type of possession owned by the fifth grade. Each child must compile the "data" from all the sheets. A calculator is available in the classroom to do the mechanics of finding the average. Some children decide to send sheets to the

---

[10]A dominant feeling, expressed directly and indirectly by teachers in this school, was boredom with their work. They did, however, in contrast to the working-class schools, almost always carry out lessons during class times.

fourth-grade families for comparison. Their work should be "verified" by a classmate before it is handed in.

Each child and his or her family has made a geoboard. The teacher asks the class to get their geoboards from the side cabinet, to take a handful of rubber bands, and then to listen to what she would like them to do. She says, "I would like you to design a figure and then find the perimeter and area. When you have it, check with your neighbor. After you've done that, please transfer it to graph paper and tomorrow I'll ask you to make up a question about it for someone. When you hand it in, please let me know whose it is and who verified it. Then I have something else for you to do that's really fun. [pause] Find the average number of chocolate chips in three cookies. I'll give you three cookies, and you'll have to *eat* your way through, I'm afraid!" Then she goes around the room and gives help, suggestions, praise, and admonitions that they are getting noisy. They work sitting, or standing up at their desks, at benches in the back, or on the floor. A child hands the teacher his paper and she comments, "I'm not accepting this paper. Do a better design." To another child she says, "That's fantastic! But you'll never find the area. Why don't you draw a figure inside [the big one] and subtract to get the area?"

The school district requires the fifth grade to study ancient civilization (in particular, Egypt, Athens, and Sumer). In this classroom, the emphasis is on illustrating and re-creating the culture of the people of ancient times. The following are typical activities: the children made an 8mm film on Egypt, which one of the parents edited. A girl in the class wrote the script, and the class acted it out. They put the sound on themselves. They read stories of those days. They wrote essays and stories depicting the lives of the people and the societal and occupational divisions. They chose from a list of projects, all of which involved graphic representations of ideas: for example, "Make a mural depicting the division of labor in Egyptian society."

Each child wrote and exchanged a letter in hieroglyphics with a fifth 30 grader in another class, and they also exchanged stories they wrote in cuneiform. They made a scroll and singed the edges so it looked authentic. They each chose an occupation and made an Egyptian plaque representing that occupation, simulating the appropriate Egyptian design. They carved their design on a cylinder of wax, pressed the wax into clay, and then baked the clay. Although one girl did not choose an occupation but carved instead a series of gods and slaves, the teacher said, "That's all right, Amber, it's beautiful." As they were working the teacher said, "Don't cut into your clay until you're satisfied with your design."

Social studies also involves almost daily presentation by the children of some event from the news. The teacher's questions ask the children to expand what they say, to give more details, and to be more specific. Occasionally she adds some remarks to help them see connections between events.

The emphasis on expressing and illustrating ideas in social studies is accompanied in language arts by an emphasis on creative writing. Each child wrote a rebus story for a first grader whom they had interviewed to see what kind of story the child liked best. They wrote editorials on pending decisions by the school board and radio plays, some of which were read over the school intercom from the office and one of which was performed in the auditorium. There is no language arts textbook because, the teacher said, "The principal wants us to be creative." There is not much grammar, but there is punctuation. One morning when the observer arrived, the class was doing a punctuation ditto. The teacher later apologized for using the ditto. "It's just for review," she said. "I don't teach punctuation that way. We use their language." The ditto had three unambiguous rules for where to put commas in a sentence. As the teacher was going around to help the children with the ditto, she repeated several times, "Where you put commas depends on how you say the sentence; it depends on the situation and what you want to say." Several weeks later the observer saw another punctuation activity. The teacher had printed a five-paragraph story on an oak tag and then cut it into phrases. She read the whole story to the class from the book, then passed out the phrases. The group had to decide how the phrases could best be put together again. (They arranged the phrases on the floor.) The point was not to replicate the story, although that was not irrelevant, but to "decide what you think the best way is." Punctuation marks on cardboard pieces were then handed out, and the children discussed and then decided what mark was best at each place they thought one was needed. At the end of each paragraph the teacher asked, "Are you satisfied with the way the paragraphs are now? Read it to yourself and see how it sounds." Then she read the original story again, and they compared the two.

Describing her goals in science to the investigator, the teacher said, "We use ESS (Elementary Science Study). It's very good because it gives a hands-on experience—so they can make *sense* out of it. It doesn't matter whether it [what they find] is right or wrong. I bring them together and there's value in discussing their ideas."

The products of work in this class are often highly valued by the children and the teacher. In fact, this was the only school in which the investigator was not allowed to take original pieces of the children's work for her files. If the work was small enough, however, and was on paper, the investigator could duplicate it on the copying machine in the office.

The teacher's attempt to control the class involves constant negotiation. She does not give direct orders unless she is angry because the children have been too noisy. Normally, she tries to get them to foresee the consequences of their actions and to decide accordingly. For example, lining them up to go see a play written by the sixth graders, she says, "I presume you're lined up by someone with whom you want to sit. I hope you're lined up by someone you won't get in trouble with." ...

One of the few rules governing the children's movement is that no more than three children may be out of the room at once. There is a school rule that anyone can go to the library at any time to get a book. In the fifth grade I observed, they sign their name on the chalkboard and leave. There are no passes. Finally, the children have a fair amount of officially sanctioned say over what happens in the class. For example, they often negotiate what work is to be done. If the teacher wants to move on to the next subject, but the children say they are not ready, they want to work on their present projects some more, she very often lets them do it.

Executive Elite School

In the executive elite school, work is developing one's analytical intellectual powers. Children are continually asked to reason through a problem, to produce intellectual products that are both logically sound and of top academic quality. A primary goal of thought is to conceptualize rules by which elements may fit together in systems and then to apply these rules in solving a problem. Schoolwork helps one to achieve, to excel, to prepare for life.

The following are illustrative. The math teacher teaches area and perimeter by having the children derive formulas for each. First she helps them, through discussion at the board, to arrive at $A = W \times L$ as a formula (not *the* formula) for area. After discussing several, she says, "Can anyone make up a formula for perimeter? Can you figure that out yourselves? [pause] Knowing what we know, can we think of a formula?" She works out three children's suggestions at the board, saying to two, "Yes, that's a good one," and then asks the class if they can think of any more. No one volunteers. To prod them, she says, "If you use rules and good reasoning, you get many ways. Chris, can you think up a formula?"

She discusses two-digit division with the children as a decision-making process. Presenting a new type of problem to them, she asks, "What's the *first* decision you'd make if presented with this kind of example? What is the first thing you'd *think*? Craig?" Craig says, "To find my first partial quotient." She responds, "Yes, that would be your first decision. How would you do that?" Craig explains, and then the teacher says, "OK, we'll see how that works for you." The class tries his way. Subsequently, she comments on the merits and shortcomings of several other children's decisions. Later, she tells the investigator that her goals in math are to develop their reasoning and mathematical thinking and that, unfortunately, "there's no *time* for manipulables."

While right answers are important in math, they are not "given" 40 by the book or by the teacher but may be challenged by the children. Going over some problems in late September the teacher says, "Raise your hand if you do not agree." A child says, "I don't agree with sixty-four." The teacher responds, "OK, there's a question about sixty-four. [to class] Please check it. Owen, they're disagreeing with you. Kristen, they're checking yours." The teacher emphasized this repeatedly during September and October with statements like "Don't be afraid to say you disagree. In the last [math] class, somebody disagreed, and they were right. Before you disagree, check yours, and if you still think we're wrong, then we'll check it out." By Thanksgiving, the children did not often speak in terms of right and wrong math problems but of whether they agreed with the answer that had been given.

There are complicated math mimeos with many word problems. Whenever they go over the examples, they discuss how each child has set up the problem. The children must explain it precisely. On one occasion the teacher said, "I'm more—just as interested in *how* you set up the problem as in what answer you find. If you set up a problem in a good way, the answer is *easy* to find."

Social studies work is most often reading and discussion of concepts and independent research. There are only occasional artistic, expressive, or illustrative projects. Ancient Athens and Sumer are, rather, societies to analyze. The following questions are typical of those that guide the children's independent research. "What mistakes did Pericles make after the war?" "What mistakes did the citizens of Athens make?" "What are the elements of a civilization?" "How did Greece build an economic empire?" "Compare the way Athens chose its leaders with the way we choose ours." Occasionally the children are asked to make up sample questions for their social studies tests. On an occasion when the investigator was present, the social studies teacher rejected a child's question by saying, "That's just fact. If I asked you that question on a test, you'd complain it was just memory! Good questions ask for concepts."

In social studies—but also in reading, science, and health—the teachers initiate classroom discussions of current social issues and problems. These discussions occurred on every one of the investigator's visits, and a teacher told me, "These children's opinions are important—it's important that they learn to reason things through." The classroom discussions always struck the observer as quite realistic and analytical, dealing with concrete social issues like the following: "Why do workers strike?" "Is that right or wrong?" "Why do we have inflation, and what can be done to stop it?" "Why do companies put chemicals in food when the natural ingredients are available?" and so on. Usually the children did not have to be prodded to give their opinions. In fact, their statements and the interchanges between them struck the observer as quite sophisticated conceptually and verbally, and well-informed. Occasionally the teachers would prod with statements such as, "Even if you don't know [the answers], if you think logically about it, you can figure it out." And "I'm asking you [these] questions to help you think this through."

Language arts emphasizes language as a complex system, one that should be mastered. The children are asked to diagram sentences of complex grammatical construction, to memorize irregular verb conjugations (he lay, he has lain, and so on...), and to use the proper participles, conjunctions, and interjections in their speech. The teacher (the same one who teaches social studies) told them, "It is not enough to get these right on tests; you must use what you learn [in grammar classes] in your written and oral work. I will grade you on that."

Most writing assignments are either research reports and essays for social studies or experiment analyses and write-ups for science. There is only an occasional story or other "creative writing" assignment. On the occasion observed by the investigator (the writing of a Halloween story), the points the teacher stressed in preparing the children to write involved the structural aspects of a story rather than the expression of feelings or other ideas. The teacher showed them a filmstrip, "The Seven Parts of a Story," and lectured them on plot development, mood setting, character development, consistency, and the use of a logical or appropriate ending. The stories they subsequently wrote were, in fact, well-structured, but many were also personal and expressive. The teacher's evaluative comments, however, did not refer to the expressiveness or artistry but were all directed toward whether they had "developed" the story well.

Language arts work also involved a large amount of practice in presentation of the self and in managing situations where the child was expected to be in charge. For example, there was a series of assignments in which each child had to be a "student teacher." The child had to plan a lesson in grammar, outlining, punctuation, or other language arts topic and explain the concept to the class. Each child was to prepare a worksheet or game and a homework assignment as well. After each presentation, the teacher and other children gave a critical appraisal of the "student teacher's" performance. Their criteria were: whether the student spoke clearly, whether the lesson was interesting, whether the student made any mistakes, and whether he or she kept control of the class. On an occasion when a child did not maintain control, the teacher said, "When you're up there, you have authority and you have to use it. I'll back you up." ...

The executive elite school is the only school where bells do not demarcate the periods of time. The two fifth-grade teachers were very strict about changing classes on schedule, however, as specific plans for each session had been made. The teachers attempted to keep tight control over the children during lessons, and the children were sometimes flippant, boisterous, and occasionally rude. However, the children may be brought into line by reminding them that "It is up to you," "You must control yourself," "You are responsible for your work," you must "set your own priorities." One teacher told a child, "You are the only driver of your car—and only you can regulate your speed." A new teacher complained to the observer that she had thought "these children" would have more control.

While strict attention to the lesson at hand is required, the teachers make relatively little attempt to regulate the movement of the children at other times. For example, except for the kindergartners the children in this school do not have to wait for the bell to ring in the morning; they may go to their classroom when they arrive at school. Fifth graders often came early to read, to finish work, or to catch up. After the first two months of school, the fifth-grade teachers did not line the children up to change classes or to go to gym, and so on, but, when the children

were ready and quiet, they were told they could go — sometimes without the teachers.

In the classroom, the children could get materials when they
needed them and took what they needed from closets and from the
teacher's desk. They were in charge of the office at lunchtime. During
class they did not have to sign out or ask permission to leave the room;
they just got up and left. Because of the pressure to get work done,
however, they did not leave the room very often. The teachers were
very polite to the children, and the investigator heard no sarcasm, no
nasty remarks, and few direct orders. The teachers never called the
children "honey" or "dear" but always called them by name. The
teachers were expected to be available before school, after school, and
for part of their lunchtime to provide extra help if needed....

The foregoing analysis of differences in schoolwork in contrasting   50
social-class contexts suggests the following conclusion: the "hidden
curriculum" of schoolwork is tacit preparation for relating to the process
of production in a particular way. Differing curricular, pedagogical, and
pupil evaluation practices emphasize different cognitive and behavioral
skills in each social setting and thus contribute to the development in
the children of certain potential relationships to physical and symbolic
capital,[11] to authority, and to the process of work. School experience,
in the sample of schools discussed here, differed qualitatively by social class. These differences may not only contribute to the development in the children in each social class of certain types of economically
significant relationships and not others but would thereby help to *reproduce* this system of relations in society. In the contribution to the reproduction of unequal social relations lies a theoretical meaning and social
consequence of classroom practice.

The identification of different emphases in classrooms in a sample
of contrasting social-class contexts implies that further research should
be conducted in a large number of schools to investigate the types of
work tasks and interactions in each to see if they differ in the ways discussed here and to see if similar potential relationships are uncovered.
Such research could have as a product the further elucidation of complex but not readily apparent connections between everyday activity in
schools and classrooms and the unequal structure of economic relationships in which we work and live.

ENGAGING THE TEXT

1. Examine the ways any single subject is taught in the four types of schools Anyon
   describes. What differences in teaching methods and in the student-teacher relationship do they reflect? What other differences do you note in the schools? What

---

   [11]*physical and symbolic capital:* Elsewhere Anyon defines *capital* as "property that
is used to produce profit, interest, or rent"; she defines *symbolic capital* as the knowledge
and skills that "may yield social and cultural power." [Eds.]

schools in your geographic region would closely approximate the working-class, middle-class, affluent professional, and executive elite schools of her article?

2. What attitudes toward knowledge and work are the four types of schools teaching their students? What kinds of jobs are students being prepared to do? Do you see any evidence that the schools in your community are producing particular kinds of workers?

3. What is the "hidden curriculum" of Anyon's title? How is this curriculum taught, and what social, cultural, or political purposes does it serve?

EXPLORING CONNECTIONS

4. Which of the four types of schools that Anyon describes do you think Michael Moore attended, given the experiences he offers from his own education in "Idiot Nation" (p. 121)? Why? Do you think his attitude toward the state of schooling in America would be different if he had attended a different kind of school?

5. How might Anyon explain the boredom, absurdity, and childishness that John Taylor Gatto (p. 141) associates with compulsory public education? To what extent do Anyon and Gatto seem to agree about the relationship between school and social class?

6. Draw a Groening-like (see pp. 140 and 150) cartoon or comic strip about a classroom situation in a working-class, middle-class, professional, or elite school (but do not identify the type of school explicitly). Pool all the cartoons from the class. In small groups, sort the comics according to the type of school they represent.

7. Analyze the teaching styles that Mike Rose encounters at Our Lady of Mercy (p. 151). Which of Anyon's categories would they fit best? Do Rose's experiences at his high school tend to confirm or complicate Anyon's analysis?

EXTENDING THE CRITICAL CONTEXT

8. Should all schools be run like professional or elite schools? What would be the advantages of making these schools models for all social classes? Do you see any possible disadvantages?

9. Choose a common elementary school task or skill that Anyon does not mention. Outline four ways it might be taught in the four types of schools.

VISUAL PORTFOLIO

READING IMAGES OF EDUCATION
AND EMPOWERMENT

The Graduate (1959), by Norman Rockwell.

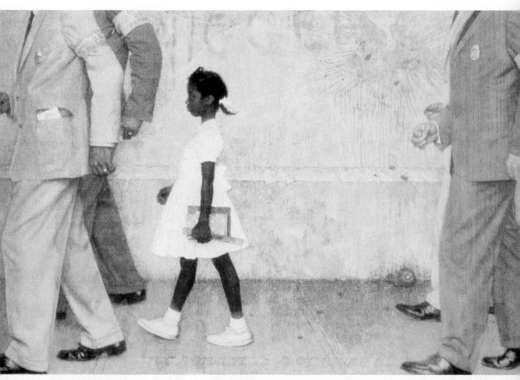

The Problem We All Live With (1964), by Norman Rockwell.

"Unemployed Superhero, Master of Degrees, Shackled with Debts," Occupy Wall Street, New York, October 2011. Photo: Jacquelyn Martin. © AP.

VISUAL PORTFOLIO

READING IMAGES OF EDUCATION AND EMPOWERMENT

1. In *The Graduate* (p. 180), why has Rockwell chosen to place his subject in front of a newspaper? To what extent are the headlines of the paper relevant? What is Rockwell suggesting through the young man's posture and attitude?

2. Plan an updated version of the portrait on page 180, featuring a twenty-first-century graduate and a more contemporary background.

3. What is the setting of *The Problem We All Live With* (p. 181)? What event does it commemorate? How do you interpret the painting's title?

4. What does Rockwell suggest about the relationship of education, society, power, and violence through the visual details included in this painting? What significance do you see, for example, in the absence of the men's faces, the position of their hands and arms, the rhythm of their strides, the smallness of the girl, her attitude, the materials she carries, and so forth?

5. What, do you imagine, is the Native American high school student in the photo on page 182 thinking as she leafs through a brochure during a Harvard University college day at her reservation high school? Why might she want to go to Harvard? What challenges do you think she might face there as an undergrad? Overall, what are images like this, taken from Harvard's online newsletter, designed to suggest about educational opportunity and personal empowerment in America?

6. How would you describe the preparatory school classroom in the photo on page 183? What can you tell about the socioeconomic status of the students? What do you think their parents do for a living? What kinds of neighborhoods do they live in? What do they do during the summer? What will they do after graduation? Overall, what do you think their experience of school is like? Would you want to be a student in this school? Why or why not?

7. What does the sign on page 184 suggest about the real priorities of the North Georgia Falcons? How might John Taylor Gatto (p. 141) and Michael Moore (p. 121) assess the sign and interpret what it says about contemporary American secondary education? Make a similar sign stating the priorities of the high school you attended. Share these in class and discuss what they reveal.

8. How many of the students in the college pictured on page 185, in your view, are actually taking notes? What do you think the rest of the students are doing? How common are laptops and cell phones in the classes at your college or university? In general, do you think they enhance or disrupt the classroom experience? Should colleges prohibit or limit their use? Why or why not?

9. What does the photo of an Occupy Wall Street protester on page 186 suggest about the myth of personal empowerment through educational success? Why do

you think he calls himself a "superhero"? Go online to learn more about recent increases in college tuition and the debt accrued by college students as the result of student loans. How much debt would you be willing to assume to get your degree? How might being "shackled by debt" affect the values, attitudes, and choices of future American college grads? Would students and society benefit if public colleges were tuition-free for all qualified students?

LEARNING TO READ

MALCOLM X

Born Malcolm Little on May 19, 1925, Malcolm X was one of the most articulate and powerful leaders of black America during the 1960s. A street hustler convicted of robbery in 1946, he spent seven years in prison, where he educated himself and became a disciple of Elijah Muhammad, founder of the Nation of Islam. In the days of the civil rights movement, Malcolm X emerged as the leading spokesman for black separatism, a philosophy that urged black Americans to cut political, social, and economic ties with the white community. After a pilgrimage to Mecca, the capital of the Muslim world, in 1964, he became an orthodox Muslim, adopted the Muslim name El Hajj Malik El-Shabazz, and distanced himself from the teachings of the black Muslims. He was assassinated in 1965. In the following excerpt from his autobiography, coauthored with Alex Haley and published the year of his death, Malcolm X describes his self-education.

IT WAS BECAUSE OF MY LETTERS that I happened to stumble upon starting to acquire some kind of a homemade education.

I became increasingly frustrated at not being able to express what I wanted to convey in letters that I wrote, especially those to Mr. Elijah Muhammad.[1] In the street, I had been the most articulate hustler out there—I had commanded attention when I said something. But now, trying to write simple English, I not only wasn't articulate, I wasn't even functional. How would I sound writing in slang, the way I would *say* it, something such as, "Look, daddy, let me pull your coat about a cat, Elijah Muhammad—"

Many who today hear me somewhere in person, or on television, or those who read something I've said, will think I went to school far beyond the eighth grade. This impression is due entirely to my prison studies.

It had really begun back in the Charlestown Prison, when Bimbi[2] first made me feel envy of his stock of knowledge. Bimbi had always taken charge of any conversations he was in, and I had tried to emulate him. But every book I picked up had few sentences which didn't contain anywhere from one to nearly all of the words that might as well have been in Chinese. When I just skipped those words, of course, I really ended up with little idea of what the book said. So I had come to the Norfolk Prison Colony still going through only book-reading motions.

---

[1]*Elijah Muhammad:* American clergyman (1897–1975); leader of the Nation of Islam, 1935–1975. [All notes are the editors'.]

[2]*Bimbi:* A fellow inmate whose encyclopedic learning and verbal facility greatly impressed Malcolm X.

Pretty soon, I would have quit even these motions, unless I had received the motivation that I did.

I saw that the best thing I could do was get hold of a dictionary—to study, to learn some words. I was lucky enough to reason also that I should try to improve my penmanship. It was sad. I couldn't even write in a straight line. It was both ideas together that moved me to request a dictionary along with some tablets and pencils from the Norfolk Prison Colony school.

I spent two days just riffling uncertainly through the dictionary's pages. I'd never realized so many words existed! I didn't know *which* words I needed to learn. Finally, just to start some kind of action, I began copying.

In my slow, painstaking, ragged handwriting, I copied into my tablet everything printed on that first page, down to the punctuation marks.

I believe it took me a day. Then, aloud, I read back, to myself, everything I'd written on the tablet. Over and over, aloud, to myself, I read my own handwriting.

I woke up the next morning, thinking about those words—immensely proud to realize that not only had I written so much at one time, but I'd written words that I never knew were in the world. Moreover, with a little effort, I also could remember what many of these words meant. I reviewed the words whose meanings I didn't remember. Funny thing, from the dictionary first page right now, that "aardvark" springs to my mind. The dictionary had a picture of it, a long-tailed, long-eared, burrowing African mammal, which lives off termites caught by sticking out its tongue as an anteater does for ants.

I was so fascinated that I went on—I copied the dictionary's next page. And the same experience came when I studied that. With every succeeding page, I also learned of people and places and events from history. Actually the dictionary is like a miniature encyclopedia. Finally the dictionary's A section had filled a whole tablet—and I went on into the B's. That was the way I started copying what eventually became the entire dictionary. It went a lot faster after so much practice helped me to pick up handwriting speed. Between what I wrote in my tablet, and writing letters, during the rest of my time in prison I would guess I wrote a million words.

I suppose it was inevitable that as my word-base broadened, I could for the first time pick up a book and read and now begin to understand what the book was saying. Anyone who has read a great deal can imagine the new world that opened. Let me tell you something: from then until I left that prison, in every free moment I had, if I was not reading in the library, I was reading on my bunk. You couldn't have gotten me out of books with a wedge. Between Mr. Muhammad's teachings, my correspondence, my visitors,…and my reading of books, months passed without my even thinking about being imprisoned. In fact, up to then, I never had been so truly free in my life.

The Norfolk Prison Colony's library was in the school building. A variety of classes was taught there by instructors who came from such places as Harvard and Boston universities. The weekly debates between inmate teams were also held in the school building. You would be astonished to know how worked up convict debaters and audiences would get over subjects like "Should Babies Be Fed Milk?"

Available on the prison library's shelves were books on just about every general subject. Much of the big private collection that Parkhurst[3] had willed to the prison was still in crates and boxes in the back of the library—thousands of old books. Some of them looked ancient: covers faded, old-time parchment-looking binding. Parkhurst...seemed to have been principally interested in history and religion. He had the money and the special interest to have a lot of books that you wouldn't have in a general circulation. Any college library would have been lucky to get that collection.

As you can imagine, especially in a prison where there was heavy emphasis on rehabilitation, an inmate was smiled upon if he demonstrated an unusually intense interest in books. There was a sizable number of well-read inmates, especially the popular debaters. Some were said by many to be practically walking encyclopedias. They were almost celebrities. No university would ask any student to devour literature as I did when this new world opened to me, of being able to read and *understand.*

I read more in my room than in the library itself. An inmate who 15 was known to read a lot could check out more than the permitted maximum number of books. I preferred reading in the total isolation of my own room.

When I had progressed to really serious reading, every night at about ten P.M. I would be outraged with the "lights out." It always seemed to catch me right in the middle of something engrossing.

Fortunately, right outside my door was a corridor light that cast a glow into my room. The glow was enough to read by, once my eyes adjusted to it. So when "lights out" came, I would sit on the floor where I could continue reading in that glow.

At one-hour intervals at night guards paced past every room. Each time I heard the approaching footsteps, I jumped into bed and feigned sleep. And as soon as the guard passed, I got back out of bed onto the floor area of that light-glow, where I would read for another fifty-eight minutes until the guard approached again. That went on until three or four every morning. Three or four hours of sleep a night was enough for me. Often in the years in the streets I had slept less than that.

The teachings of Mr. Muhammad stressed how history had been "whitened"—when white men had written history books, the black man simply had been left out. Mr. Muhammad couldn't have said anything that would have struck me much harder. I had never forgotten how when my class, me and all of those whites, had studied seventh-grade

[3]*Parkhurst:* Charles Henry Parkhurst (1842–1933); American clergyman, reformer, and president of the Society for the Prevention of Crime.

United States history back in Mason, the history of the Negro had been covered in one paragraph, and the teacher had gotten a big laugh with his joke, "Negroes' feet are so big that when they walk, they leave a hole in the ground."

This is one reason why Mr. Muhammad's teachings spread so 20 swiftly all over the United States, among *all* Negroes, whether or not they became followers of Mr. Muhammad. The teachings ring true—to every Negro. You can hardly show me a black adult in America—or a white one, for that matter—who knows from the history books anything like the truth about the black man's role. In my own case, once I heard of the "glorious history of the black man," I took special pains to hunt in the library for books that would inform me on details about black history.

I can remember accurately the very first set of books that really impressed me. I have since bought that set of books and I have it at home for my children to read as they grow up. It's called *Wonders of the World*. It's full of pictures of archeological finds, statues that depict, usually, non-European people.

I found books like Will Durant's[4] *Story of Civilization*. I read H. G. Wells'[5] *Outline of History*. *Souls of Black Folk* by W. E. B. Du Bois[6] gave me a glimpse into the black people's history before they came to this country. Carter G. Woodson's[7] *Negro History* opened my eyes about black empires before the black slave was brought to the United States, and the early Negro struggles for freedom.

J. A. Rogers'[8] three volumes of *Sex and Race* told about race-mixing before Christ's time; and Aesop being a black man who told fables; about Egypt's Pharaohs; about the great Coptic Christian Empire;[9] about Ethiopia, the earth's oldest continuous black civilization, as China is the oldest continuous civilization.

Mr. Muhammad's teaching about how the white man had been created led me to *Findings in Genetics,* by Gregor Mendel.[10] (The dictionary's G section was where I had learned what "genetics" meant.) I really studied this book by the Austrian monk. Reading it over and over, especially certain sections, helped me to understand that if you started with a black man, a white man could be produced; but starting with a

[4] *Will Durant:* American author and historian (1885–1981). Durant, with his wife Ariel (1898–1981), won the Pulitzer Prize for literature for volume ten of their eleven-volume *The Story of Civilization*, published from 1935 to 1975.

[5] *H. G. Wells:* English novelist and historian (1866–1946).

[6] *W. E. B. Du Bois:* William Edward Burghardt Du Bois, distinguished black scholar, author, and activist (1868–1963). Du Bois was the first director of the NAACP and was an important figure in the Harlem Renaissance; his best-known book is *The Souls of Black Folk.*

[7] *Carter G. Woodson:* Distinguished African American historian (1875–1950); considered the father of black history.

[8] *J. A. Rogers:* African American historian and journalist (1883–1965).

[9] *Coptic Christian Empire:* The domain of the Coptic Church, a native Egyptian Christian church that retains elements of its African origins.

[10] *Gregor Mendel:* Austrian monk, botanist, and pioneer in genetic research (1822–1884).

white man, you never could produce a black man—because the white chromosome is recessive. And since no one disputes that there was but one Original Man, the conclusion is clear.

During the last year or so, in the *New York Times,* Arnold Toynbee[11] used the word "bleached" in describing the white man. His words were: "White (i.e., bleached) human beings of North European origin...." Toynbee also referred to the European geographic area as only a peninsula of Asia. He said there was no such thing as Europe. And if you look at the globe, you will see for yourself that America is only an extension of Asia. (But at the same time Toynbee is among those who have helped to bleach history. He has written that Africa was the only continent that produced no history. He won't write that again. Every day now, the truth is coming to light.)

I never will forget how shocked I was when I began reading about slavery's total horror. It made such an impact upon me that it later became one of my favorite subjects when I became a minister of Mr. Muhammad's. The world's most monstrous crime, the sin and the blood on the white man's hands, are almost impossible to believe. Books like the one by Frederick Olmsted[12] opened my eyes to the horrors suffered when the slave was landed in the United States. The European woman, Fanny Kemble,[13] who had married a Southern white slaveowner, described how human beings were degraded. Of course I read *Uncle Tom's Cabin.*[14] In fact, I believe that's the only novel I have ever read since I started serious reading.

Parkhurst's collection also contained some bound pamphlets of the Abolitionist[15] Anti-Slavery Society of New England. I read descriptions of atrocities, saw those illustrations of black slave women tied up and flogged with whips; of black mothers watching their babies being dragged off, never to be seen by their mothers again; of dogs after slaves, and of the fugitive slave catchers, evil white men with whips and clubs and chains and guns. I read about the slave preacher Nat Turner, who put the fear of God into the white slavemaster. Nat Turner wasn't going around preaching pie-in-the-sky and "non-violent" freedom for the black man. There in Virginia one night in 1831, Nat and seven other slaves started out at his master's home and through the night they went from one plantation "big house" to the next, killing, until by the next morning 57 white people were dead and Nat had about 70 slaves following him. White people, terrified for their lives, fled from their homes, locked themselves up in public buildings, hid in the woods, and some even left the state. A small army of soldiers took two months to catch

---

[11]*Arnold Toynbee:* English historian (1889–1975).

[12]*Frederick Olmsted:* Frederick Law Olmsted (1822–1903), American landscape architect, city planner, and opponent of slavery.

[13]*Fanny Kemble:* Frances Anne Kemble, English actress and author (1809–1893); best known for her autobiographical *Journal of a Residence on a Georgia Plantation,* published in 1863 to win support in Britain for the abolitionist cause.

[14]*Uncle Tom's Cabin:* Harriet Beecher Stowe's 1852 antislavery novel.

[15]*Abolitionist:* Advocating the prohibition of slavery.

and hang Nat Turner. Somewhere I have read where Nat Turner's example is said to have inspired John Brown[16] to invade Virginia and attack Harpers Ferry nearly thirty years later, with thirteen white men and five Negroes.

I read Herodotus,[17] "the father of History," or, rather, I read about him. And I read the histories of various nations, which opened my eyes gradually, then wider and wider, to how the whole world's white men had indeed acted like devils, pillaging and raping and bleeding and draining the whole world's non-white people. I remember, for instance, books such as Will Durant's *The Story of Oriental Civilization*, and Mahatma Gandhi's[18] accounts of the struggle to drive the British out of India.

Book after book showed me how the white man had brought upon the world's black, brown, red, and yellow peoples every variety of the suffering of exploitation. I saw how since the sixteenth century, the so-called "Christian trader" white man began to ply the seas in his lust for Asian and African empires, and plunder, and power. I read, I saw, how the white man never has gone among the non-white peoples bearing the Cross in the true manner and spirit of Christ's teachings—meek, humble, and Christlike.

I perceived, as I read, how the collective white man had been actually nothing but a piratical opportunist who used Faustian machinations[19] to make his own Christianity his initial wedge in criminal conquests. First, always "religiously," he branded "heathen" and "pagan" labels upon ancient non-white cultures and civilizations. The stage thus set, he then turned upon his non-white victims his weapons of war. 30

I read how, entering India—half a *billion* deeply religious brown people—the British white man, by 1759, through promises, trickery, and manipulations, controlled much of India through Great Britain's East India Company. The parasitical British administration kept tentacling out to half of the sub-continent. In 1857, some of the desperate people of India finally mutinied—and, excepting the African slave trade, nowhere has history recorded any more unnecessary bestial and ruthless human carnage than the British suppression of the non-white Indian people.

Over 115 million African blacks—close to the 1930s population of the United States—were murdered or enslaved during the slave trade. And I read how when the slave market was glutted, the cannibalistic white powers of Europe next carved up, as their colonies, the richest areas of the black continent. And Europe's chancelleries for the next

---

[16]*John Brown:* American abolitionist (1800–1859); leader of an attack on Harpers Ferry, West Virginia, in 1859.

[17]*Herodotus:* Early Greek historian (484?–425? B.C.E.).

[18]*Mahatma Gandhi:* Hindu religious leader, social reformer, and advocate of nonviolence (1869–1948).

[19]*Faustian machinations:* Evil plots or schemes. Faust was a legendary character who sold his soul to the devil for knowledge and power.

century played a chess game of naked exploitation and power from Cape Horn to Cairo.

Ten guards and the warden couldn't have torn me out of those books. Not even Elijah Muhammad could have been more eloquent than those books were in providing indisputable proof that the collective white man had acted like a devil in virtually every contact he had with the world's collective non-white man. I listen today to the radio, and watch television, and read the headlines about the collective white man's fear and tension concerning China. When the white man professes ignorance about why the Chinese hate him so, my mind can't help flashing back to what I read, there in prison, about how the blood forebears of this same white man raped China at a time when China was trusting and helpless. Those original white "Christian traders" sent into China millions of pounds of opium. By 1839, so many of the Chinese were addicts that China's desperate government destroyed twenty thousand chests of opium. The first Opium War[20] was promptly declared by the white man. Imagine! Declaring *war* upon someone who objects to being narcotized! The Chinese were severely beaten, with Chinese-invented gunpowder.

The Treaty of Nanking made China pay the British white man for the destroyed opium; forced open China's major ports to British trade; forced China to abandon Hong Kong; fixed China's import tariffs so low that cheap British articles soon flooded in, maiming China's industrial development.

After a second Opium War, the Tientsin Treaties legalized the ravaging opium trade, legalized a British-French-American control of China's customs. China tried delaying that Treaty's ratification; Peking was looted and burned. 35

"Kill the foreign white devils!" was the 1901 Chinese war cry in the Boxer Rebellion.[21] Losing again, this time the Chinese were driven from Peking's choicest areas. The vicious, arrogant white man put up the famous signs, "Chinese and dogs not allowed."

Red China after World War II closed its doors to the Western white world. Massive Chinese agricultural, scientific, and industrial efforts are described in a book that *Life* magazine recently published. Some observers inside Red China have reported that the world never has known such a hate-white campaign as is now going on in this non-white country where, present birth-rates continuing, in fifty more years Chinese will be half the earth's population. And it seems that some Chinese chickens will soon come home to roost, with China's recent successful nuclear tests.

---

[20]*Opium War:* 1839–1842 war between Britain and China that ended with China's cession of Hong Kong to British rule.

[21]*Boxer Rebellion:* The 1898–1900 uprising by members of a secret Chinese society who opposed foreign influence in Chinese affairs.

Let us face reality. We can see in the United Nations a new world order being shaped, along color lines—an alliance among the non-white nations. America's U.N. Ambassador Adlai Stevenson[22] complained not long ago that in the United Nations "a skin game"[23] was being played. He was right. He was facing reality. A "skin game" *is* being played. But Ambassador Stevenson sounded like Jesse James accusing the marshal of carrying a gun. Because who in the world's history ever has played a worse "skin game" than the white man?

Mr. Muhammad, to whom I was writing daily, had no idea of what a new world had opened up to me through my efforts to document his teachings in books.

When I discovered philosophy, I tried to touch all the landmarks 40 of philosophical development. Gradually, I read most of the old philosophers, Occidental and Oriental. The Oriental philosophers were the ones I came to prefer; finally, my impression was that most Occidental philosophy had largely been borrowed from the Oriental thinkers. Socrates, for instance, traveled in Egypt. Some sources even say that Socrates was initiated into some of the Egyptian mysteries. Obviously Socrates got some of his wisdom among the East's wise men.

I have often reflected upon the new vistas that reading opened to me. I knew right there in prison that reading had changed forever the course of my life. As I see it today, the ability to read awoke inside me some long dormant craving to be mentally alive. I certainly wasn't seeking any degree, the way a college confers a status symbol upon its students. My homemade education gave me, with every additional book that I read, a little bit more sensitivity to the deafness, dumbness, and blindness that was afflicting the black race in America. Not long ago, an English writer telephoned me from London, asking questions. One was, "What's your alma mater?" I told him, "Books." You will never catch me with a free fifteen minutes in which I'm not studying something I feel might be able to help the black man.

Yesterday I spoke in London, and both ways on the plane across the Atlantic I was studying a document about how the United Nations proposes to insure the human rights of the oppressed minorities of the world. The American black man is the world's most shameful case of minority oppression. What makes the black man think of himself as only an internal United States issue is just a catch-phrase, two words, "civil rights." How is the black man going to get "civil rights" before first he wins his *human* rights? If the American black man will start thinking about his *human* rights, and then start thinking of himself as part of one of the world's great peoples, he will see he has a case for the United Nations.

[22]*Adlai Stevenson:* American politician (1900–1965); Democratic candidate for the presidency in 1952 and 1956.
[23]*skin game:* A dishonest or fraudulent scheme, business operation, or trick, with the added reference in this instance to skin color.

I can't think of a better case! Four hundred years of black blood and sweat invested here in America, and the white man still has the black man begging for what every immigrant fresh off the ship can take for granted the minute he walks down the gangplank.

But I'm digressing. I told the Englishman that my alma mater was books, a good library. Every time I catch a plane, I have with me a book that I want to read—and that's a lot of books these days. If I weren't out here every day battling the white man, I could spend the rest of my life reading, just satisfying my curiosity—because you can hardly mention anything I'm not curious about. I don't think anybody ever got more out of going to prison than I did. In fact, prison enabled me to study far more intensively than I would have if my life had gone differently and I had attended some college. I imagine that one of the biggest troubles with colleges is there are too many distractions, too much panty-raiding, fraternities, and boola-boola and all of that. Where else but in a prison could I have attacked my ignorance by being able to study intensely sometimes as much as fifteen hours a day?

ENGAGING THE TEXT

1. What motivated Malcolm X to educate himself?

2. What kind of knowledge did Malcolm X gain by learning to read? How did this knowledge free or empower him?

3. Would it be possible for public schools to empower students in the way that Malcolm X's self-education empowered him? If so, how? If not, why not?

4. Some readers are offended by the strength of Malcolm X's accusations and by his grouping of all members of a given race into "collectives." Given the history of racial injustice he recounts here, do you feel he is justified in taking such a position?

EXPLORING CONNECTIONS

5. Visit the Bedford e-Pages for this chapter and read Richard Rodriguez's "The Achievement of Desire" (bedfordstmartins.com/rereading/epages). Then compare

THE BOONDOCKS   **by AARON MCGRUDER**

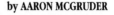

and contrast Malcolm X's views on the meaning and purpose of education—or on the value and nature of reading—with those of Richard Rodriguez (p. 000). How can you account for the differences in their attitudes?

6. Imagine that John Taylor Gatto (p. 141), Mike Rose (p. 151), Richard Rodriguez (See bedfordstmartins.com/rereading/epages), and Malcolm X have been appointed to redesign American education. Working in groups, role-play a meeting in which the committee attempts to reach consensus on its recommendations. Report to the class the results of the committee's deliberations and discuss them.

7. What does the *Boondocks* cartoon (p. 197) suggest about the possibility of teaching and learning "revolutionary" ideas within the setting of a public school system?

EXTENDING THE CRITICAL CONTEXT

8. Survey some typical elementary or secondary school textbooks to test the currency of Malcolm X's charge that the educational establishment presents a "whitened" view of America. What view of America is presently being projected in public school history and social science texts?

9. Go to the library and read one page of a dictionary chosen at random. Study the meanings of any unfamiliar words and follow up on the information on your page by consulting encyclopedias, books, or articles. Let yourself be guided by chance and by your interests. After you've tried this experiment, discuss in class the benefits and drawbacks of an unsystematic self-education like Malcolm X's.

PARA TERESA[1]

INÉS HERNÁNDEZ-ÁVILA

This poem explores and attempts to resolve an old conflict between its speaker and her schoolmate, two Chicanas at "Alamo which-had-to-be-its-name" Elementary School who have radically different ideas about what education means and does. Inés Hernández-Ávila (b. 1947) is director of the Chicana/Latina Research Center at the University of California, Davis. This poem appeared in her collection *Con Razón, Corazón* (1987).

A tí-Teresa
Te dedico las palabras estás
que explotan de mi corazón[2]

[1] *Para Teresa:* For Teresa. [All notes are Hernández-Ávila's.]
[2] *A...corazón:* To you, Teresa, I dedicate these words that explode from my heart.

That day during lunch hour
at Alamo which-had-to-be-its-name
Elementary
my dear raza
That day in the bathroom
Door guarded
Myself cornered
I was accused by you, Teresa
Tú y las demás de tus amigas
Pachucas todas
Eran Uds. cinco.[3]

Me gritaban que porque me creía tan grande[4]
What was I trying to do, you growled
Show you up?
Make the teachers like me, pet me,
Tell me what a credit to my people I was?
I was playing right into their hands, you challenged
And you would have none of it.
I was to stop.

I was to be like you
I was to play your game of deadly defiance
Arrogance, refusal to submit.
The game in which the winner takes nothing
Asks for nothing
Never lets his weaknesses show.

But I didn't understand.
My fear salted with confusion
Charged me to explain to you
I did nothing *for the teachers.*
I studied for my parents and for my grandparents
Who cut out honor roll lists
Whenever their nietos'[5] names appeared
For my shy mother who mastered her terror
to demand her place in mother's clubs
For my carpenter-father who helped me patiently with my math.
For my abuelos que me regalaron lápices en la Navidad[6]
And for myself.

Porque reconocí en aquel entonces
una verdad tremenda
que me hizo a mi un rebelde

---

[3]*Tú...cinco:* You and the rest of your friends, all Pachucas, there were five of you.
[4]*Me...grande:* You were screaming at me, asking me why I thought I was so hot.
[5]*nietos':* Grandchildren's.
[6]*abuelos...Navidad:* Grandparents who gave me gifts of pencils at Christmas.

Aunque tú no te habías dadocuenta[7]
We were not inferior   45
You and I, y las demás de tus amigas
Y los demás de nuestra gente[8]
I knew it the way I knew I was alive
We were good, honorable, brave
Genuine, loyal, strong   50
And smart.
Mine was a deadly game of defiance, also.
My contest was to prove
beyond any doubt
that we were not only equal but superior to them.   55
That was why I studied.
If I could do it, we all could.

You let me go then.
Your friends unblocked the way
I who-did-not-know-how-to-fight   60
was not made to engage with you-who-grew-up-fighting
Tu y yo,[9] Teresa
We went in different directions
Pero fuimos juntas.[10]

In sixth grade we did not understand   65
Uds. with the teased, dyed-black-but-reddening hair,
Full petticoats, red lipsticks
and sweaters with the sleeves
pushed up
Y yo conformándome con lo que deseaba mi mamá[11]   70
Certainly never allowed to dye, to tease, to paint myself
I did not accept your way of anger,
Your judgements
You did not accept mine.

But now in 1975, when I am twenty-eight   75
Teresa
I remember you.
Y sabes—
Te comprendo,
Es más, te respeto.   80
Y si me permites,
Te nombro— "hermana."[12]

---

[7]*Porque...dadocuenta:* Because I recognized a great truth then that made me a rebel, even though you didn't realize it.

[8]*Y...gente:* And the rest of your friends / And the rest of our people.

[9]*Tu y yo:* You and I.

[10]*Pero fuimos juntas:* But we were together.

[11]*Y...mamá:* And I conforming to my mother's wishes.

[12]*Y sabes... "hermana":* And do you know what, I understand you. Even more, I respect you. And, if you permit me, I name you my sister.

ENGAGING THE TEXT

1. The speaker says that she didn't understand Teresa at the time of the incident she describes. What didn't she understand, and why? How have her views of Teresa and of herself changed since then? What seems to have brought about this change?

2. What attitudes toward school and the majority culture do Teresa and the speaker represent? What about the speaker's family? In what way are both girls playing a game of "deadly defiance"? What arguments can you make for each form of rebellion?

3. Why do you think Hernández-Ávila wrote this poem in both Spanish and English? What does doing so say about the speaker's life? About her change of attitude toward Teresa?

EXPLORING CONNECTIONS

4. Visit the Bedford e-Pages for this chapter of *Rereading America* (bedfordstmartins .com/rereading/epages) and read Richard Rodriguez's "The Achievement of Desire." Then compare Rodriguez's attitude toward school and family with the speaker's attitudes in this poem. What motivates each of them? What tensions do they feel between their home and school selves?

5. Write a dialogue between the speaker of this poem, who wants to excel, and Ken Harvey, the boy whom Mike Rose said just wanted to be average (p. 151). Explore the uncertainties, pressures, and desires that these students felt. In what ways are these two apparently contrasting students actually similar?

EXTENDING THE CRITICAL CONTEXT

6. Was there a person or group you disliked, feared, or fought with in elementary school? Has your understanding of your adversary or of your own motives changed since then? If so, what brought about this change?

STILL SEPARATE, STILL UNEQUAL
JONATHAN KOZOL

In *Brown v. Board of Education* (1954), the U.S. Supreme Court overturned its ruling in *Plessy v. Ferguson* (1896), which had sanctioned "separate but equal" facilities for blacks and whites throughout the South for more than half a century. The Court's decision in *Brown* ended the deliberate segregation of U.S. schools and promised to usher in a new era of equality in American education. But according to longtime educational critic Jonathan Kozol, American schools today may be more segregated than at any time since 1954. And the "educational apartheid" that Kozol sees in U.S. schools isn't just about color. Kozol associates the "resegregation" of public education with a deterioration of classroom conditions and teaching practices that threatens an entire generation of Americans.

After graduating from Harvard with a degree in literature and studying as a Rhodes Scholar at Oxford University, Kozol (b. 1936) took his first job teaching in an inner-city elementary school near Boston. His account of that experience, *Death at an Early Age: The Destruction of the Hearts and Minds of Negro Children in the Boston Public Schools* (1967) won national acclaim and established him as one of the country's foremost educational activists and social reformers. Since then, his work with poor children and their families has resulted in a dozen books, including *Free Schools* (1972), *Illiterate America* (1980), *On Being a Teacher* (1981), *Rachael and Her Children: Homeless Families in America* (1988), *Savage Inequalities* (1991), and *The Shame of the Nation: The Restoration of Apartheid Schooling in America* (2005), the source of this selection. His most recent book is *Letters to a Young Teacher* (2007).

MANY AMERICANS who live far from our major cities and who have no firsthand knowledge of the realities to be found in urban public schools seem to have the rather vague and general impression that the great extremes of racial isolation that were matters of grave national significance some thirty-five or forty years ago have gradually but steadily diminished in more recent years. The truth, unhappily, is that the trend, for well over a decade now, has been precisely the reverse. Schools that were already deeply segregated twenty-five or thirty years ago are no less segregated now, while thousands of other schools around the country that had been integrated either voluntarily or by the force of law have since been rapidly resegregating.

In Chicago, by the academic year 2002–2003, 87 percent of public-school enrollment was black or Hispanic; less than 10 percent of children in the schools were white. In Washington, D.C., 94 percent of children were black or Hispanic; less than 5 percent were white. In St. Louis, 82 percent of the student population were black or Hispanic; in Philadelphia and Cleveland, 79 percent; in Los Angeles, 84 percent, in Detroit, 96 percent; in Baltimore, 89 percent. In New York City, nearly three quarters of the students were black or Hispanic.

Even these statistics, as stark as they are, cannot begin to convey how deeply isolated children in the poorest and most segregated sections of these cities have become. In the typically colossal high schools of the Bronx, for instance, more than 90 percent of students (in most cases, more than 95 percent) are black or Hispanic. At John F. Kennedy High School in 2003, 93 percent of the enrollment of more than 4,000 students were black and Hispanic; only 3.5 percent of students at the school were white. At Harry S. Truman High School, black and

Hispanic students represented 96 percent of the enrollment of 2,700 students; 2 percent were white. At Adlai Stevenson High School, which enrolls 3,400 students, blacks and Hispanics made up 97 percent of the student population; a mere eight-tenths of one percent were white.

A teacher at P.S. 65 in the South Bronx once pointed out to me one of the two white children I had ever seen there. His presence in her class was something of a wonderment to the teacher and to the other pupils. I asked how many white kids she had taught in the South Bronx in her career. "I've been at this school for eighteen years," she said. "This is the first white student I have ever taught."

One of the most disheartening experiences for those who grew up in the years when Martin Luther King Jr. and Thurgood Marshall[1] were alive is to visit public schools today that bear their names, or names of other honored leaders of the integration struggles that produced the temporary progress that took place in the three decades after *Brown v. Board of Education,*[2] and to find out how many of these schools are bastions of contemporary segregation. It is even more disheartening when schools like these are not in deeply segregated inner-city neighborhoods but in racially mixed areas where the integration of a public school would seem to be most natural, and where, indeed, it takes a conscious effort on the part of parents or school officials in these districts to avoid the integration option that is often right at their front door.

In a Seattle neighborhood that I visited in 2002, for instance, where approximately half the families were Caucasian, 95 percent of students at the Thurgood Marshall Elementary School were black, Hispanic, Native American, or of Asian origin. An African American teacher at the school told me—not with bitterness but wistfully—of seeing clusters of white parents and their children each morning on the corner of a street close to the school, waiting for a bus that took the children to a predominantly white school.

"At Thurgood Marshall," according to a big wall poster in the school's lobby, "the dream is alive." But school-assignment practices and federal court decisions that have countermanded long-established policies that previously fostered integration in Seattle's schools make the realization of the dream identified with Justice Marshall all but unattainable today. In San Diego there is a school that bears the name of Rosa Parks in which 86 percent of students are black and Hispanic and only some 2 percent are white. In Los Angeles there is a school that bears the name of Dr. King that is 99 percent black and Hispanic, and another in Milwaukee in which black and Hispanic children also make up 99 percent of the enrollment. There is a high school in Cleveland that is named for Dr. King

---

[1]*Thurgood Marshall:* First African American justice on the Supreme Court (1908–1993). [All notes are the editors', except 3, 6, and 8.]

[2]*Brown v. Board of Education:* 1954 Supreme Court case outlawing public school segregation. The court ruled, "Separate educational facilities are inherently unequal."

in which black students make up 97 percent of the student body, and the graduation rate is only 35 percent. In Philadelphia, 98 percent of children at a high school named for Dr. King are black. At a middle school named for Dr. King in Boston, black and Hispanic children make up 98 percent of the enrollment....

There is a well-known high school named for Martin Luther King Jr. in New York City too. This school, which I've visited repeatedly in recent years, is located in an upper-middle-class white neighborhood, where it was built in the belief—or hope—that it would draw large numbers of white students by permitting them to walk to school, while only their black and Hispanic classmates would be asked to ride the bus or come by train. When the school was opened in 1975, less than a block from Lincoln Center in Manhattan, "it was seen," according to the *New York Times,* "as a promising effort to integrate white, black and Hispanic students in a thriving neighborhood that held one of the city's cultural gems." Even from the start, however, parents in the neighborhood showed great reluctance to permit their children to enroll at Martin Luther King, and, despite "its prime location and its name, which itself creates the highest of expectations," notes the *Times,* the school before long came to be a destination for black and Hispanic students who could not obtain admission into more successful schools. It stands today as one of the nation's most visible and problematic symbols of an expectation rapidly receding and a legacy substantially betrayed.

Perhaps most damaging to any serious effort to address racial segregation openly is the refusal of most of the major arbiters of culture in our northern cities to confront or even clearly name an obvious reality they would have castigated with a passionate determination in another section of the nation fifty years before—and which, moreover, they still castigate today in retrospective writings that assign it to a comfortably distant and allegedly concluded era of the past. There is, indeed, a seemingly agreed-upon convention in much of the media today not even to use an accurate descriptor like "racial segregation" in a narrative description of a segregated school. Linguistic sweeteners, semantic somersaults, and surrogate vocabularies are repeatedly employed. Schools in which as few as 3 or 4 percent of students may be white or Southeast Asian or of Middle Eastern origin, for instance—and where *every other child* in the building is black or Hispanic—are referred to as "diverse." Visitors to schools like these discover quickly the eviscerated meaning of the word, which is no longer a proper adjective but a euphemism for a plainer word that has apparently become unspeakable.

School systems themselves repeatedly employ this euphemism in describing the composition of their student populations. In a school I visited in the fall of 2004 in Kansas City, Missouri, for example, a document distributed to visitors reports that the school's curriculum "addresses the needs of children from diverse backgrounds." But as I went from class to class, I did not encounter any children who were white or Asian—or 10

Hispanic, for that matter—and when I was later provided with precise statistics for the demographics of the school, I learned that 99.6 percent of students there were African American. In a similar document, the school board of another district, this one in New York State, referred to "the diversity" of its student population and "the rich variations of ethnic backgrounds." But when I looked at the racial numbers that the district had reported to the state, I learned that there were 2,800 black and Hispanic children in the system, 1 Asian child, and 3 whites. Words, in these cases, cease to have real meaning; or, rather, they mean the opposite of what they say.

High school students whom I talk with in deeply segregated neighborhoods and public schools seem far less circumspect than their elders and far more open in their willingness to confront these issues. "It's more like being hidden," said a fifteen-year-old girl named Isabel[3] I met some years ago in Harlem, in attempting to explain to me the ways in which she and her classmates understood the racial segregation of their neighborhoods and schools. "It's as if you have been put in a garage where, if they don't have room for something but aren't sure if they should throw it out, they put it there where they don't need to think of it again."

I asked her if she thought America truly did not "have room" for her or other children of her race. "Think of it this way," said a sixteen-year-old girl sitting beside her. "If people in New York woke up one day and learned that we were gone, that we had simply died or left for somewhere else, how would they feel?"

"How do you think they'd feel?" I asked.

"I think they'd be relieved," this very solemn girl replied.

Many educators make the argument today that given the demo- 15
graphics of large cities like New York and their suburban areas, our only realistic goal should be the nurturing of strong, empowered, and well-funded schools in segregated neighborhoods. Black school officials in these situations have sometimes conveyed to me a bitter and clear-sighted recognition that they're being asked, essentially, to mediate and render functional an uncontested separation between children of their race and children of white people living sometimes in a distant section of their town and sometimes in almost their own immediate communities. Implicit in this mediation is a willingness to set aside the promises of *Brown* and—though never stating this or even thinking of it clearly in these terms—to settle for the promise made more than a century ago in *Plessy v. Ferguson,* the 1896 Supreme Court ruling in which "separate but equal" was accepted as a tolerable rationale for the perpetuation of a dual system in American society.

---

[3]The names of children mentioned in this article have been changed to protect their privacy. [Kozol's note]

Equality itself—equality alone—is now, it seems, the article of faith to which most of the principals of inner-city public schools subscribe. And some who are perhaps most realistic do not even dare to ask for, or expect, complete equality, which seems beyond the realm of probability for many years to come, but look instead for only a sufficiency of means—"adequacy" is the legal term most often used today—by which to win those practical and finite victories that appear to be within their reach. Higher standards, higher expectations, are repeatedly demanded of these urban principals, and of the teachers and students in their schools, but far lower standards—certainly in ethical respects—appear to be expected of the dominant society that isolates these children in unequal institutions.

"Dear Mr. Kozol," wrote the eight-year-old, "we do not have the things you have. You have Clean things. We do not have. You have a clean bathroom. We do not have that. You have Parks and we do not have Parks. You have all the thing and we do not have all the thing. Can you help us?"

The letter, from a child named Alliyah, came in a fat envelope of twenty-seven letters from a class of third-grade children in the Bronx. Other letters that the students in Alliyah's classroom sent me registered some of the same complaints. "We don't have no gardens," "no Music or Art," and "no fun places to play," one child said. "Is there a way to fix this Problem?" Another noted a concern one hears from many children in such overcrowded schools: "We have a gym but it is for lining up. I think it is not fair." Yet another of Alliyah's classmates asked me, with a sweet misspelling, if I knew the way to make her school into a "good" school—"like the other kings have"—and ended with the hope that I would do my best to make it possible for "all the kings" to have good schools.

The letter that affected me the most, however, had been written by a child named Elizabeth. "It is not fair that other kids have a garden and new things. But we don't have that," said Elizabeth. "I wish that this school was the most beautiful school in the whole why world."

"The whole why world" stayed in my thoughts for days. When I 20 later met Elizabeth, I brought her letter with me, thinking I might see whether, in reading it aloud, she'd change the "why" to "wide" or leave it as it was. My visit to her class, however, proved to be so pleasant, and the children seemed so eager to bombard me with their questions about where I lived, and why I lived there rather than in New York, and who I lived with, and how many dogs I had, and other interesting questions of that sort, that I decided not to interrupt the nice reception they had given me with questions about usages and spelling. I left "the whole why world" to float around unedited and unrevised in my mind. The letter itself soon found a resting place on the wall above my desk.

In the years before I met Elizabeth, I had visited many other schools in the South Bronx and in one northern district of the Bronx as well.

I had made repeated visits to a high school where a stream of water flowed down one of the main stairwells on a rainy afternoon and where green fungus molds were growing in the office where the students went for counseling. A large blue barrel was positioned to collect rainwater coming through the ceiling. In one makeshift elementary school housed in a former skating rink next to a funeral establishment in yet another nearly all-black-and-Hispanic section of the Bronx, class size rose to thirty-four and more; four kindergarten classes and a sixth-grade class were packed into a single room that had no windows. The air was stifling in many rooms, and the children had no place for recess because there was no outdoor playground and no indoor gym.

In another elementary school, which had been built to hold 1,000 children but was packed to bursting with some 1,500, the principal poured out his feelings to me in a room in which a plastic garbage bag had been attached somehow to cover part of the collapsing ceiling. "This," he told me, pointing to the garbage bag, then gesturing around him at the other indications of decay and disrepair one sees in ghetto schools much like it elsewhere, "would not happen to white children."

Libraries, once one of the glories of the New York City school system, were either nonexistent or, at best, vestigial in large numbers of the elementary schools. Art and music programs had also for the most part disappeared. "When I began to teach in 1969," the principal of an elementary school in the South Bronx reported to me, "every school had a full-time licensed art and music teacher and librarian." During the subsequent decades, he recalled, "I saw all of that destroyed."

School physicians also were removed from elementary schools during these years. In 1970, when substantial numbers of white children still attended New York City's public schools, 400 doctors had been present to address the health needs of the children. By 1993 the number of doctors had been cut to 23, most of them part-time—a cutback that affected most severely children in the city's poorest neighborhoods, where medical facilities were most deficient and health problems faced by children most extreme. Teachers told me of asthmatic children who came into class with chronic wheezing and who at any moment of the day might undergo more serious attacks, but in the schools I visited there were no doctors to attend to them.

In explaining these steep declines in services, political leaders in 25 New York tended to point to shifting economic factors, like a serious budget crisis in the middle 1970s, rather than to the changing racial demographics of the student population. But the fact of economic ups and downs from year to year, or from one decade to the next, could not convincingly explain the permanent shortchanging of the city's students, which took place routinely in good economic times and bad. The bad times were seized upon politically to justify the cuts, and the money was never restored once the crisis years were past.

"If you close your eyes to the changing racial composition of the schools and look only at budget actions and political events," says

Noreen Connell, the director of the nonprofit Educational Priorities Panel in New York, "you're missing the assumptions that are underlying these decisions." When minority parents ask for something better for their kids, she says, "the assumption is that these are parents who can be discounted. These are kids who just don't count—children we don't value."

This, then, is the accusation that Alliyah and her classmates send our way: "You have...We do not have." Are they right or are they wrong? Is this a case of naive and simplistic juvenile exaggeration? What does a third-grader know about these big-time questions of fairness and justice? Physical appearances apart, how in any case do you begin to measure something so diffuse and vast and seemingly abstract as having more, or having less, or not having at all?

Around the time I met Alliyah in the school year 1997–1998, New York's Board of Education spent about $8,000 yearly on the education of a third-grade child in a New York City public school. If you could have scooped Alliyah up out of the neighborhood where she was born and plunked her down in a fairly typical white suburb of New York, she would have received a public education worth about $12,000 a year. If you were to lift her up once more and set her down in one of the wealthiest white suburbs of New York, she would have received as much as $18,000 worth of public education every year and would likely have had a third-grade teacher paid approximately $30,000 more than her teacher in the Bronx was paid.

The dollars on both sides of the equation have increased since then, but the discrepancies between them have remained. The present per-pupil spending level in the New York City schools is $11,700, which may be compared with a per-pupil spending level in excess of $22,000 in the well-to-do suburban district of Manhasset, Long Island. The present New York City level is, indeed, almost exactly what Manhasset spent per pupil eighteen years ago, in 1987, when that sum of money bought a great deal more in services and salaries than it can buy today. In dollars adjusted for inflation, New York City has not yet caught up to where its wealthiest suburbs were a quarter-century ago....

As racial isolation deepens and the inequalities of education finance remain unabated and take on new and more innovative forms, the principals of many inner-city schools are making choices that few principals in public schools that serve white children in the mainstream of the nation ever need to contemplate. Many have been dedicating vast amounts of time and effort to create an architecture of adaptive strategies that promise incremental gains within the limits inequality allows.

New vocabularies of stentorian determination, new systems of incentive, and new modes of castigation, which are termed "rewards and sanctions," have emerged. Curriculum materials that are alleged to be aligned with governmentally established goals and standards and particularly suited to what are regarded as "the special needs and learning styles" of low-income urban children have been introduced. Relentless emphasis on raising test scores, rigid policies of nonpromotion and non-graduation, a new empiricism and the imposition of unusually detailed lists of named and numbered "outcomes" for each isolated parcel of instruction, an oftentimes fanatical insistence upon uniformity of teachers in their management of time, an openly conceded emulation of the rigorous approaches of the military and a frequent use of terminology that comes out of the world of industry and commerce—these are just a few of the familiar aspects of these new adaptive strategies.

Although generically described as "school reform," most of these practices and policies are targeted primarily at poor children of color; and although most educators speak of these agendas in broad language that sounds applicable to all, it is understood that they are valued chiefly as responses to perceived catastrophe in deeply segregated and unequal schools.

"If you do what I tell you to do, how I tell you to do it, when I tell you to do it, you'll get it right," said a determined South Bronx principal observed by a reporter for the *New York Times.* She was laying out a memorizing rule for math to an assembly of her students. "If you don't, you'll get it wrong." This is the voice, this is the tone, this is the rhythm and didactic certitude one hears today in inner-city schools that have embraced a pedagogy of direct command and absolute control. "Taking their inspiration from the ideas of B. F. Skinner[4]..." says the *Times,* proponents of scripted rote-and-drill curricula articulate their aim as the establishment of "faultless communication" between "the teacher, who is the stimulus," and "the students, who respond."

The introduction of Skinnerian approaches (which are commonly employed in penal institutions and drug-rehabilitation programs), as a way of altering the attitudes and learning styles of black and Hispanic children, is provocative, and it has stirred some outcries from respected scholars. To actually go into a school where you know some of the children very, very well and see the way that these approaches can affect their daily lives and thinking processes is even more provocative.

On a chilly November day four years ago in the South Bronx, I entered P.S. 65, a school I had been visiting since 1993. There had been major changes since I'd been there last. Silent lunches had been instituted in the cafeteria, and on days when children misbehaved, silent recess had been introduced as well. On those days the students were obliged to sit in rows and maintain perfect silence on the floor of a small indoor room instead of going out to play. The words SUCCESS FOR ALL, the brand name of a scripted curriculum—better known by its acronym, SFA—were prominently posted at the top of the main stairway and, as I would later find, in almost every room. Also frequently displayed within the halls and classrooms were a number of administrative memos that

[4]*B. F. Skinner:* American psychologist (1904–1990) known for his theories on stimulus and response.

were worded with unusual didactic absoluteness. "Authentic Writing," read a document called "Principles of Learning" that was posted in the corridor close to the principal's office, "is driven by curriculum and instruction." I didn't know what this expression meant. Like many other undefined and arbitrary phrases posted in the school, it seemed to be a dictum that invited no interrogation.

I entered the fourth grade of a teacher I will call Mr. Endicott, a man in his mid-thirties who had arrived here without training as a teacher, one of about a dozen teachers in the building who were sent into this school after a single summer of short-order preparation. Now in his second year, he had developed a considerable sense of confidence and held the class under a tight control.

As I found a place to sit in a far corner of the room, the teacher and his young assistant, who was in her first year as a teacher, were beginning a math lesson about building airport runways, a lesson that provided children with an opportunity for measuring perimeters. On the wall behind the teacher, in large letters, was written: "Portfolio Protocols: 1. You are responsible for the selection of [your] work that enters your portfolio. 2. As your skills become more sophisticated this year, you will want to revise, amend, supplement, and possibly replace items in your portfolio to reflect your intellectual growth." On the left side of the room: "Performance Standards Mathematics Curriculum: M-5 Problem Solving and Reasoning. M-6 Mathematical Skills and Tools..."

My attention was distracted by some whispering among the children sitting to the right of me. The teacher's response to this distraction was immediate: his arm shot out and up in a diagonal in front of him, his hand straight up, his fingers flat. The young co-teacher did this, too. When they saw their teachers do this, all the children in the classroom did it, too.

"Zero noise," the teacher said, but this instruction proved to be unneeded. The strange salute the class and teachers gave each other, which turned out to be one of a number of such silent signals teachers in the school were trained to use, and children to obey, had done the job of silencing the class.

"Active listening!" said Mr. Endicott. "Heads up! Tractor beams!" 40 which meant, "Every eye on me."

On the front wall of the classroom, in handwritten words that must have taken Mr. Endicott long hours to transcribe, was a list of terms that could be used to praise or criticize a student's work in mathematics. At Level Four, the highest of four levels of success, a child's "problem-solving strategies" could be described, according to this list, as "systematic, complete, efficient, and possibly elegant," while the student's capability to draw conclusions from the work she had completed could be termed "insightful" or "comprehensive." At Level Two, the child's capability to draw conclusions was to be described as "logically unsound"; at Level One, "not present." Approximately 50 separate categories of proficiency, or lack of such, were detailed in this wall-sized tabulation.

A well-educated man, Mr. Endicott later spoke to me about the form of classroom management that he was using as an adaptation from a model of industrial efficiency. "It's a kind of 'Taylorism'[5] in the classroom," he explained, referring to a set of theories about the management of factory employees introduced by Frederick Taylor in the early 1900s. "Primitive utilitarianism" is another term he used when we met some months later to discuss these management techniques with other teachers from the school. His reservations were, however, not apparent in the classroom. Within the terms of what he had been asked to do, he had, indeed, become a master of control. It is one of the few classrooms I had visited up to that time in which almost nothing even hinting at spontaneous emotion in the children or the teacher surfaced while I was there.

The teacher gave the "zero noise" salute again when someone whispered to another child at his table. "In two minutes you will have a chance to talk and share this with your partner." Communication between children in the class was not prohibited but was afforded time slots and, remarkably enough, was formalized in an expression that I found included in a memo that was posted on the wall beside the door. "An opportunity...to engage in Accountable Talk."

Even the teacher's words of praise were framed in terms consistent with the lists that had been posted on the wall. "That's a Level Four suggestion," said the teacher when a child made an observation other teachers might have praised as simply "pretty good" or "interesting" or "mature."

There was, it seemed, a formal name for every cognitive event within this school: "Authentic Writing," "Active Listening," "Accountable Talk." The ardor to assign all items of instruction or behavior a specific name was unsettling me. The adjectives had the odd effect of hyping every item of endeavor. "Authentic Writing" was, it seemed, a more important act than what the children in a writing class in any ordinary school might try to do. "Accountable Talk" was something more self-conscious and significant than merely useful conversation. 45

Since that day at P.S. 65, I have visited nine other schools in six different cities where the same Skinnerian curriculum is used. The signs on the walls, the silent signals, the curious salute, the same insistent naming of all cognitive particulars, became familiar as I went from one school to the next.

"Meaningful Sentences," began one of the many listings of proficiencies expected of the children in the fourth grade of an inner-city elementary school in Hartford (90 percent black, 10 percent Hispanic) that I visited a short time later. "Noteworthy Questions," "Active Listening," and other designations like these had been posted elsewhere in the

---

[5]*Taylorism:* Approach to management named after American engineer and business school professor Frederick Taylor. His *Principles of Scientific Management* (1911) sought to increase efficiency and productivity.

room. Here, too, the teacher gave the kids her outstretched arm, with hand held up, to reestablish order when they grew a little noisy, but I noticed that she tried to soften the effect of this by opening her fingers and bending her elbow slightly so it did not look quite as forbidding as the gesture Mr. Endicott had used. A warm and interesting woman, she later told me she disliked the regimen intensely.

Over her desk, I read a "Mission Statement," which established the priorities and values for the school. Among the missions of the school, according to the printed statement, which was posted also in some other classrooms of the school, was "to develop productive citizens" who have the skills that will be needed "for successful global competition," a message that was reinforced by other posters in the room. Over the heads of a group of children at their desks, a sign anointed them BEST WORKERS OF 2002.

Another signal now was given by the teacher, this one not for silence but in order to achieve some other form of class behavior, which I could not quite identify. The students gave exactly the same signal in response. Whatever the function of this signal, it was done as I had seen it done in the South Bronx and would see it done in other schools in months to come. Suddenly, with a seeming surge of restlessness and irritation—with herself, as it appeared, and with her own effective use of all the tricks that she had learned—she turned to me and said, "I can do this with my dog." ...

In some inner-city districts, even the most pleasant and old- 50 fashioned class activities of elementary schools have now been overtaken by these ordering requirements. A student teacher in California, for example, wanted to bring a pumpkin to her class on Halloween but knew it had no ascertainable connection to the California standards. She therefore had developed what she called "The Multi-Modal Pumpkin Unit" to teach science (seeds), arithmetic (the size and shape of pumpkins, I believe—this detail wasn't clear), and certain items she adapted out of language arts, in order to position "pumpkins" in a frame of state proficiencies. Even with her multi-modal pumpkin, as her faculty adviser told me, she was still afraid she would be criticized because she knew the pumpkin would not really help her children to achieve expected goals on state exams.

Why, I asked a group of educators at a seminar in Sacramento, was a teacher being placed in a position where she'd need to do preposterous curricular gymnastics to enjoy a bit of seasonal amusement with her kids on Halloween? How much injury to state-determined "purpose" would it do to let the children of poor people have a pumpkin party once a year for no other reason than because it's something fun that other children get to do on autumn days in public schools across most of America?

"Forcing an absurdity on teachers does teach something," said an African-American professor. "It teaches acquiescence. It breaks down the will to thumb your nose at pointless protocols—to call absurdity 'absurd.'" Writing out the standards with the proper numbers on the chalkboard has a similar effect, he said; and doing this is "terribly important" to the principals in many of these schools. "You *have* to post the standards, and the way you know the children know the standards is by asking them to *state* the standards. And they *do* it—and you want to be quite certain that they do it if you want to keep on working at that school."

In speaking of the drill-based program in effect at P.S. 65, Mr. Endicott told me he tended to be sympathetic to the school administrators, more so at least than the other teachers I had talked with seemed to be. He said he believed his principal had little choice about the implementation of this program, which had been mandated for all elementary schools in New York City that had had rock-bottom academic records over a long period of time. "This puts me into a dilemma," he went on, "because I love the kids at P.S. 65." And even while, he said, "I know that my teaching SFA is a charade...if I don't do it I won't be permitted to teach these children."

Mr. Endicott, like all but two of the new recruits at P.S. 65—there were about fifteen in all—was a white person, as were the principal and most of the administrators at the school. As a result, most of these neophyte instructors had had little or no prior contact with the children of an inner-city neighborhood; but, like the others I met, and despite the distancing between the children and their teachers that resulted from the scripted method of instruction, he had developed close attachments to his students and did not want to abandon them. At the same time, the class- and race-specific implementation of this program obviously troubled him. "There's an expression now," he said. "'The rich get richer, and the poor get SFA.'" He said he was still trying to figure out his "professional ethics" on the problem that this posed for him.

White children made up "only about one percent" of students in 55 the New York City schools in which this scripted teaching system was imposed,[6] according to the *New York Times,* which also said that "the prepackaged lessons" were intended "to ensure that all teachers—even novices or the most inept"—would be able to teach reading. As seemingly pragmatic and hardheaded as such arguments may be, they are desperation strategies that come out of the acceptance of inequity. If we did not have a deeply segregated system in which more experienced instructors teach the children of the privileged and the least experienced are sent to teach the children of minorities, these practices would not be needed and could not be so convincingly defended. They are confections of apartheid,[7] and no matter by what arguments

[6]SFA has since been discontinued in the New York City public schools, though it is still being used in 1,300 U.S. schools, serving as many as 650,000 children. Similar scripted systems are used in schools (overwhelmingly minority in population) serving several million children. [Kozol's note]

[7]*Apartheid:* Literally "apartness," the policy of racial segregation and discrimination in South Africa, restricting the rights of nonwhites, which ended in 1990.

of urgency or practicality they have been justified, they cannot fail to further deepen the divisions of society.

There is no misery index for the children of apartheid education. There ought to be; we measure almost everything else that happens to them in their schools. Do kids who go to schools like these enjoy the days they spend in them? Is school, for most of them, a happy place to be? You do not find the answers to these questions in reports about achievement levels, scientific methods of accountability, or structural revisions in the modes of governance. Documents like these don't speak of happiness. You have to go back to the schools themselves to find an answer to these questions. You have to sit down in the little chairs in first and second grade, or on the reading rug with kindergarten kids, and listen to the things they actually say to one another and the dialogue between them and their teachers. You have to go down to the basement with the children when it's time for lunch and to the playground with them, if they have a playground, when it's time for recess, if they still have recess at their school. You have to walk into the children's bathrooms in these buildings. You have to do what children do and breathe the air the children breathe. I don't think that there is any other way to find out what the lives that children lead in school are really like.

High school students, when I first meet them, are often more reluctant than the younger children to open up and express their personal concerns; but hesitation on the part of students did not prove to be a problem when I visited a tenth-grade class at Fremont High School in Los Angeles. The students were told that I was a writer, and they took no time in getting down to matters that were on their minds.

"Can we talk about the bathrooms?" asked a soft-spoken student named Mireya.

In almost any classroom there are certain students who, by the force of their directness or the unusual sophistication of their way of speaking, tend to capture your attention from the start. Mireya later spoke insightfully about some of the serious academic problems that were common in the school, but her observations on the physical and personal embarrassments she and her schoolmates had to undergo cut to the heart of questions of essential dignity that kids in squalid schools like this one have to deal with all over the nation.

Fremont High School, as court papers filed in a lawsuit against the 60 state of California document, has fifteen fewer bathrooms than the law requires. Of the limited number of bathrooms that are working in the school, "only one or two... are open and unlocked for girls to use." Long lines of girls are "waiting to use the bathrooms," which are generally "unclean" and "lack basic supplies," including toilet paper. Some of the classrooms, as court papers also document, "do not have air conditioning," so that students, who attend school on a three-track schedule that runs year-round, "become red-faced and unable to concentrate" during "the extreme heat of summer." The school's maintenance records report that rats were found in eleven classrooms. Rat droppings were found "in the bins and drawers" of the high school's kitchen, and school records note that "hamburger buns" were being "eaten off [the] bread-delivery rack."

No matter how many tawdry details like these I've read in legal briefs or depositions through the years, I'm always shocked again to learn how often these unsanitary physical conditions are permitted to continue in the schools that serve our poorest students—even after they have been vividly described in the media. But hearing of these conditions in Mireya's words was even more unsettling, in part because this student seemed so fragile and because the need even to speak of these indignities in front of me and all the other students was an additional indignity.

"The problem is this," she carefully explained. "You're not allowed to use the bathroom during lunch, which is a thirty-minute period. The only time that you're allowed to use it is between your classes." But "this is a huge building," she went on. "It has long corridors. If you have one class at one end of the building and your next class happens to be way down at the other end, you don't have time to use the bathroom and still get to class before it starts. So you go to your class and then you ask permission from your teacher to go to the bathroom and the teacher tells you, 'No. You had your chance between the periods...'

"I feel embarrassed when I have to stand there and explain it to a teacher."

"This is the question," said a wiry-looking boy named Edward, leaning forward in his chair. "Students are not animals, but even animals need to relieve themselves sometimes. We're here for eight hours. What do they think we're supposed to do?"

"It humiliates you," said Mireya, who went on to make the inter- 65 esting statement that "the school provides solutions that don't actually work," and this idea was taken up by several other students in describing course requirements within the school. A tall black student, for example, told me that she hoped to be a social worker or a doctor but was programmed into "Sewing Class" this year. She also had to take another course, called "Life Skills," which she told me was a very basic course— "a retarded class," to use her words—that "teaches things like the six continents," which she said she'd learned in elementary school.

When I asked her why she had to take these courses, she replied that she'd been told they were required, which as I later learned was not exactly so. What was required was that high school students take two courses in an area of study called "The Technical Arts," and which the Los Angeles Board of Education terms "Applied Technology." At schools that served the middle class or upper-middle class, this requirement was likely to be met by courses that had academic substance and, perhaps, some relevance to college preparation. At Beverly Hills High School, for example, the technical-arts requirement could be fulfilled by taking subjects like residential architecture, the designing of commercial struc- tures, broadcast journalism, advanced computer graphics, a sophisticated course in furniture design, carving and sculpture, or an honors course in engineering research and design. At Fremont High, in contrast, this re- quirement was far more often met by courses that were basically voca- tional and also obviously keyed to low-paying levels of employment.

Mireya, for example, who had plans to go to college, told me that she had to take a sewing class last year and now was told she'd been assigned to take a class in hairdressing as well. When I asked her teacher why Mireya could not skip these subjects and enroll in classes that would help her to pursue her college aspirations, she replied, "It isn't a question of what students want. It's what the school may have available. If all the other elective classes that a student wants to take are full, she has to take one of these classes if she wants to graduate."

A very small girl named Obie, who had big blue-tinted glasses tilted up across her hair, interrupted then to tell me with a kind of wild gusto that she'd taken hairdressing *twice*! When I expressed surprise that this was possible, she said there were two levels of hairdressing offered here at Fremont High. "One is in hairstyling," she said. "The other is in braiding."

Mireya stared hard at this student for a moment and then suddenly began to cry. "I don't *want* to take hairdressing. I did not need sewing either. I knew how to sew. My mother is a seamstress in a factory. I'm trying to go to college. I don't need to sew to go to college. My mother sews. I hoped for something else."

"What would you rather take?" I asked.   70

"I wanted to take an AP class," she answered.

Mireya's sudden tears elicited a strong reaction from one of the boys who had been silent up till now: a thin, dark-eyed student named Fortino, who had long hair down to his shoulders. He suddenly turned directly to Mireya and spoke into the silence that followed her last words.

"Listen to me," he said. "The owners of the sewing factories need laborers. Correct?"

"I guess they do," Mireya said.

"It's not going to be their own kids. Right?"   75

"Why not?" another student said.

"So they can grow beyond themselves," Mireya answered quietly. "But we remain the same."

"You're ghetto," said Fortino, "so we send you to the factory." He sat low in his desk chair, leaning on one elbow, his voice and dark eyes loaded with a cynical intelligence. "You're ghetto—so you sew!"

"There are higher positions than these," said a student named Samantha.

"You're ghetto," said Fortino unrelentingly, "So sew!"   80

Admittedly, the economic needs of a society are bound to be re- flected to some rational degree within the policies and purposes of pub- lic schools. But, even so, there must be *something* more to life as it is lived by six-year-olds or ten-year-olds, or by teenagers, for that matter, than concerns about "successful global competition." Childhood is not merely basic training for utilitarian adulthood. It should have some claims upon our mercy, not for its future value to the economic interests of competitive societies but for its present value as a perishable piece of life itself.

Very few people who are not involved with inner-city schools have any real idea of the extremes to which the mercantile distortion of the purposes and character of education have been taken or how unabashedly proponents of these practices are willing to defend them. The head of a Chicago school, for instance, who was criticized by some for emphasizing rote instruction that, his critics said, was turning children into "robots," found no reason to dispute the charge. "Did you ever stop to think that these robots will never burglarize your home?" he asked, and "will never snatch your pocketbooks.... These robots are going to be producing taxes."

Corporate leaders, when they speak of education, sometimes pay lip-service to the notion of "good critical and analytic skills," but it is reasonable to ask whether they have in mind the critical analysis of *their* priorities. In principle, perhaps some do; but, if so, this is not a principle that seems to have been honored widely in the schools I have been visiting. In all the various business-driven inner-city classrooms I have observed in the past five years, plastered as they are with corporation brand names and managerial vocabularies, I have yet to see the two words "labor unions." Is this an oversight? How is that possible? Teachers and principals themselves, who are almost always members of

US Schools Plan on Letting 300,000 Teachers Go

a union, seem to be so beaten down that they rarely even question this omission.

It is not at all unusual these days to come into an urban school in which the principal prefers to call himself or herself "building CEO" or "building manager." In some of the same schools teachers are described as "classroom managers."[8] I have never been in a suburban district in which principals were asked to view themselves or teachers in this way. These terminologies remind us of how wide the distance has become between two very separate worlds of education....

ENGAGING THE TEXT

1. Compare notes in class on your own elementary and secondary school experiences. How do the schools you attended compare with the public schools Kozol describes, both in terms of physical condition and teaching approach?

2. What evidence have you seen of reluctance on the part of politicians, educators, and the media to talk about the segregated state of America's public schools? Would you agree that the current state of public education in the United States amounts to "resegregation" and is, in fact, evidence of "apartheid" in American society?

3. Who is to blame for the current resegregation of American public schools, according to Kozol? Whom — or what — would you blame? To what extent would you agree that the state of inner-city schools represents a "moral failure" in America? Why might it be so important to Kozol to see this issue in moral — and not simply in political or social — terms?

EXPLORING CONNECTIONS

4. Compare Mike Rose's account of his own school experience during the 1950s and 1960s (p. 151) with the contemporary urban classrooms described by Kozol in this selection. How might Rose assess the teaching methods that dominate the

---

[8]A school I visited three years ago in Columbus, Ohio, was littered with "Help Wanted" signs. Starting in kindergarten, children in the school were being asked to think about the jobs that they might choose when they grew up. In one classroom there was a poster that displayed the names of several retail stores: J. C. Penney, Wal-Mart, Kmart, Sears, and a few others. "It's like working in a store," a classroom aide explained. "The children are learning to pretend they're cashiers." At another school in the same district, children were encouraged to apply for jobs in their classrooms. Among the job positions open to the children in this school, there was an "Absence Manager" and a "Behavior Chart Manager," a "Form Collector Manager," a "Paper Passer Outer Manager," a "Paper Collecting Manager," a "Paper Returning Manager," an "Exit Ticket Manager," even a "Learning Manager," a "Reading Corner Manager," and a "Score Keeper Manager." I asked the principal if there was a special reason why those two words "management" and "manager" kept popping up throughout the school. "We want every child to be working as a manager while he or she is in this school," the principal explained. "We want to make them understand that, in this country, companies will give you opportunities to work, to prove yourself, no matter what you've done." I wasn't sure what she meant by "no matter what you've done," and asked her if she could explain it. "Even if you have a felony arrest," she said, "we want you to understand that you can be a manager someday." [Kozol's note]

school reforms Kozol describes? Do you think a Jack MacFarland would succeed in today's inner-city schools? Why or why not?

5. Compare what Kozol, Michael Moore (p. 121), and John Taylor Gatto (p. 141) have to say about the impact of corporate America on U.S. schools. To what extent does your own prior educational experience suggest that corporate influence is undermining American education?

6. How well do the schools that Kozol describes fit any of the four categories of schools presented by Jean Anyon (p. 163)? To what extent do you think it would be possible to adapt the approaches and methods used in Anyon's professional or elite schools more broadly?

EXTENDING THE CRITICAL CONTEXT

7. Working in groups, sample news and magazine stories published in the last year to determine if Kozol is correct when he says that the media are reluctant to discuss the "segregation" of American public education. How many of the articles you identify address the idea of segregation? Of the inequalities of public education?

8. Learn more about the "No Child Left Behind Act" and other aspects of the accountability reform movement in education. What kinds of accountability reforms have been implemented in your area? What evidence do you find that these measures have worked? To what extent would you agree that accountability reforms have turned children into robots and reduced teaching to mechanical drill?

9. Over the past few years, a number of states have begun requiring high school students to take standardized "exit exams" to guarantee that they meet minimum academic standards before graduation. Research this educational reform to find out more about its impact on students, and then debate its merits in class. Would you support recent proposals that would require a similar nationwide test for college students before they receive their degrees? Why or why not?

COLLEGE AT RISK

ANDREW DELBANCO

What should a college education do? Many of us enter college without thinking much about the aims of higher learning. We go to college to "finish" our education, to get a good job, to meet interesting people, to explore new ideas. For Andrew Delbanco, however, the American college has a special purpose, one he associates with the tradition of "liberal education." Unfortunately, as he sees it, today that ideal is threatened by a world undergoing radical social, technological, and economic changes. The director of the American Studies program at Columbia University, Delbanco (b. 1952) has served there as the Julian Clarence Levi Professor in the Humanities since 1995. His many books include *Required Reading: Why Our American Classics Matter Now* (1997), *Melville: His World and Work* (2005), and *College: What It Was, Is, and Should Be* (2012).

IF THERE'S ONE THING about which Americans agree these days, it's that we can't agree. Gridlock is the name of our game. We have no common ground.

There seems, however, to be at least one area of cordial consensus— and I don't mean bipartisan approval of the killing of Osama bin Laden or admiration for former Rep. Gabrielle Giffords's courage and grace.

I mean the public discourse on education. On that subject, Republicans and Democrats speak the same language—and so, with striking uniformity, do more and more college and university leaders. "Education is how to make sure we've got a work force that's productive and competitive," said President Bush in 2004. "Countries that outteach us today," as President Obama put it in 2009, "will outcompete us tomorrow."

What those statements have in common—and there is truth in both—is an instrumental view of education. Such a view has urgent pertinence today as the global "knowledge economy" demands marketable skills that even the best secondary schools no longer adequately provide. Recent books, such as *Academically Adrift: Limited Learning on College Campuses*, by Richard Arum and Josipa Roksa, and *We're Losing Our Minds: Rethinking American Higher Education*, by Richard P. Keeling and Richard H.H. Hersh, marshal disturbing evidence that our colleges and universities are not providing those skills, either—at least not well or widely enough. But that view of teaching and learning as an economic driver is also a limited one, which puts at risk America's most distinctive contribution to the history and, we should hope, to the future of higher education. That distinctiveness is embodied, above all, in the American college, whose mission goes far beyond creating a competent work force through training brains for this or that functional task.

College, of course, is hardly an American invention. In ancient 5 Greece and Rome, young men attended lectures that resembled our notion of a college course, and gatherings of students instructed by settled teachers took on some of the attributes we associate with modern colleges (libraries, fraternities, organized sports). By the Middle Ages, efforts were under way to regulate the right to teach by issuing licenses, presaging the modern idea of a faculty with exclusive authority to grant degrees. In that broad sense, college as a place where young people encounter ideas and ideals from teachers, and debate them with peers, has a history that exceeds two millennia.

But in several important respects, the American college is a unique institution. In most of the world, students who continue their education beyond secondary school are expected to choose their field of specialization before they arrive at university. In America there has been an impulse to slow things down, to extend the time for second chances and defer the day when determinative choices must be made. When, in 1851, Herman Melville wrote in his great American novel *Moby-Dick* that "a whaleship was my Yale College and my Harvard," he used the word "college" as a metaphor for the place where, as we would say today, he "found himself." In our own time, a former president of Amherst College writes of a young man experiencing in college the "stirring and shaping, perhaps for the first time in his life, [of] actual convictions—not just gut feelings—among his friends and, more important, further down, in his own soul."

In principle, if not always in practice, this transformative ideal has entailed the hope of reaching as many citizens as possible. In ancient Greece and Rome, where women were considered inferior and slavery was an accepted feature of society, the study of artes liberates was reserved for free men with leisure and means. Conserved by medieval scholastics, renewed in the scholarly resurgence we call the Renaissance and again in the Enlightenment, the tradition of liberal learning survived in the Old World but remained largely the possession of ruling elites.

But in the New World, beginning in the Colonial era with church-sponsored scholarships for promising schoolboys, the story of higher education has been one of increasing inclusion. That story continued in the early national period through the founding of state colleges, and later through the land-grant[1] colleges created by the federal government during the Civil War. In the 20th century, it accelerated with the GI Bill,[2] the "California plan" (a tiered system designed to provide virtually universal postsecondary education), the inclusion of women and minorities in previously all-male or all-white institutions, the growth of community colleges, and the adoption of "need-based" financial-aid policies. American higher education has been built on the premise that human capital is widely distributed among social classes and does not correlate with conditions of birth or social status.

Seen in that long view, the distinctive contribution of the United States to the history of liberal education has been to deploy it on behalf of the cardinal American principle that all persons have the right to pursue happiness, and that "getting to know," in Matthew Arnold's[3]

[1]*land-grant colleges:* Land-grant colleges and universities were created under the auspices of the Morrill Acts of 1862 and 1890, which provided federal land for the creation of institutions dedicated primarily to the teaching of agriculture, science, and engineering. [All notes are the editors'.]

[2]*GI Bill:* The Servicemen's Readjustment Act of 1944 provided a range of benefits to veterans returning from World War II, including educational grants that allowed more than two million Americans to go to college.

[3]*Matthew Arnold's much-quoted phrase:* British poet and cultural critic (1822–1888).

much-quoted phrase, "the best which has been thought and said in the world" is helpful to that pursuit. That understanding of what it means to be educated is sometimes caricatured as elite or effete, but in fact it is neither, as Arnold makes clear by the (seldom-quoted) phrase with which he completes his point: "and through this knowledge, turning a stream of fresh and free thought upon our stock notions and habits." Knowledge of the past, in other words, helps citizens develop the capacity to think critically about the present—an indispensable attribute of a healthy democracy.

THESE IDEALS AND ACHIEVEMENTS are among the glories of 10 our civilization, and all Americans should be alarmed as they come to be regarded as luxuries unaffordable for all but the wealthy few. A former director of the for-profit University of Phoenix put it this way in an interview on Frontline:[4] "I'm happy that there are places in the world where people sit down and think. We need that. But that's very expensive. And not everybody can do that." Meanwhile, too many selective nonprofit colleges are failing to enroll significant numbers of students from low-income families, and those colleges are thereby reinforcing rather than ameliorating the discrepancies of wealth and opportunity in American society. Yet even at selective nonprofit colleges, where students come overwhelmingly from affluent families and are still invited to "sit down and think," they are more and more likely to choose fields of study for their preprofessional utility—on the assumption that immersing themselves in learning for the sheer joy of it, with the aim of deepening their understanding of culture, nature, and, ultimately, themselves, is a vain indulgence.

One of the difficulties in making the case for liberal education against the rising tide of skepticism is that it is almost impossible to persuade doubters who have not experienced it for themselves. The Puritan founders of our oldest colleges would have called it "such a mystery as none can read but they that know it."

Testimony by converts can help. One student, born and educated in China, who came to the United States recently to attend Bowdoin College, encountered the modern version of the Puritan principle that no communicants should "take any ancient doctrine for truth till they have examined it" for themselves. "Coming from a culture in which a 'standard answer' is provided for every question, I did not argue with others even when I disagreed. However, Bowdoin forced me to reconsider 'the answer' and reach beyond my comfort zone. In my first-year seminar, 'East Asian Politics,' I was required to debate with others and develop a habit of class engagement," he said in an interview with the Web site Inside Higher Ed about a book he and two other Chinese students wrote for an audience in China, about their liberal-arts educations in America.

---

[4]Frontline: A Public Broadcasting System news series.

"One day we debated what roles Confucianism[5] played in the development of Chinese democracy. Of the 16 students in the classroom, 15 agreed that Confucianism impeded China's development; but I disagreed. I challenged my classmates. Bowdoin made me consistently question the 'prescribed answer.'"

That kind of education does not lack for eloquent exponents. A current roster would include, among many others, Martha C. Nussbaum (in her books *Not For Profit: Why Democracy Needs the Humanities,* 2010, and *Cultivating Humanity: A Classical Defense of Reform in Liberal Education,* 1997, as well as in an essay in *The Chronicle,* "The Liberal Arts Are Not Elitist"), Anthony T. Kronman (*Education's End: Why Our Colleges and Universities Have Given Up on the Meaning of Life,* 2007), Mark William Roche (*Why Choose the Liberal Arts,* 2010), and, most recently, in *The Chronicle,* Nannerl O. Keohane, "The Liberal Arts as Guideposts in the 21st Century." But in our time of economic retrenchment, defenders of the faith are sounding beleaguered. Everyone who is honest about academe knows that colleges and universities tend to be wasteful and plagued by expensive redundancies. The demand for greater efficiency is reasonable and, in some respects, belated. The cost of college must be reined in, and its "productivity"—in the multiple senses of student proficiency, graduation rates, and job attainment—must be improved. The trouble is that many reforms, and most efficiencies, whether achieved through rational planning or imposed by the ineluctable process of technological change, are at odds with practices that are essential if liberal education is to survive and thrive.

High on the list of such practices is the small-class experience that 15 opened the mind of the Chinese student at Bowdoin. One of the distinctive features of the American college has always been the idea that students have something to learn not only from their teachers but also from each other. That idea of lateral learning originates from the Puritan conception of the gathered church, in which the criterion for membership was the candidate's "aptness to edifie another." The idea persists to this day in the question that every admissions officer in every selective college is supposed to ask of every applicant: "What would this candidate bring to the class?" It underlies the opinion by Justice Lewis Powell in the landmark case of *Regents of the University of California v. Bakke* (1978), in which the Supreme Court ruled that considering a candidate's race is constitutional for the purpose of ensuring "the interplay of ideas and the exchange of views" among students from different backgrounds. Those are modern reformulations of the ancient (by American standards) view that a college, no less than a church, exists fundamentally as what one scholar of Puritanism calls the "interaction of consciences."

[5]*Confucianism:* Philosophical and ethical system inspired by the Chinese philosopher Confucius (551–479 B.C.E.).

A well-managed discussion among peers of diverse interests and talents can help students learn the difference between informed insights and mere opinionating. It can provide the pleasurable chastisement of discovering that others see the world differently, and that their experience is not replicable by, or even reconcilable with, one's own. It is a rehearsal for deliberative democracy.

Unfortunately, at many colleges, as fiscal imperatives overwhelm educational values, this kind of experience is becoming the exception more than the rule. The educational imperative is clear: A class should be small enough to permit every student to participate in the give-and-take of discussion under the guidance of an informed, skilled, and engaged teacher. But the economic imperative is also clear: The lower the ratio between students and faculty, the higher the cost. One obvious way to mitigate the cost is to put fewer full-time tenured or tenure-track faculty in the classroom, and to replace them with underpaid, overworked part-timers—something that is happening at a frightening pace across the nation.

An even more promising strategy for cost containment is to install one or another technological "delivery system" in place of the cumbersome old system of teachers mentoring students. On that matter, the academic community is divided among true believers, diehard opponents, and those trying to find some middle ground in the form of "hybrid" or "blended" learning, whereby students are instructed and assessed through electronic means but do not entirely lose face-to-face human contact with their teachers and with one another.

Those of us who have trouble imagining how technology can advance liberal learning are liable to be charged with mindless obedience to what the English classicist F.M. Cornford famously called the first law of academe: "Nothing should ever be done for the first time." No doubt there is some truth to that charge. But as a more recent English scholar, Alison Wolf, puts it in her book *Does Education Matter? Myths About Education and Economic Growth*, "We have not found any low-cost, high-technology alternatives to expert human teachers." At least not yet.

Meanwhile, American academic leaders, long accustomed to as- 20 suming that their institutions are without peer abroad, are looking nervously over their collective shoulder at the rising universities of Asia, as well as at "the Bologna process" in Europe—the movement to make degree requirements compatible across national borders, so that, for example, a baccalaureate in chemistry earned in a French university will qualify the holder for further study or skilled employment in, say, Belgium. They are watching, too, those countries—notably China and Germany—that have a long tradition of standardized national examinations by which students are evaluated quite apart from whatever academic credentials they hold.

The standardized-testing regime (along with the mania for institutional rankings) is spreading throughout the world and making inroads in the historically decentralized education system of the United States. With it arises the specter that our colleges will be subject to some version of what, in our elementary and secondary schools, has come to be known as the No Child Left Behind (NCLB)[6] assessment program. There is no reason to doubt President Bush's good intentions when, on behalf of minority children in weak schools, he called for the imposition of enforceable standards to put an end to "the soft bigotry of low expectations." But there is mounting evidence that the law has had little positive effect, while driving "soft" subjects such as art and music to the margins or out of the curriculum altogether.

There is also no reason to doubt President Obama's deep understanding—as anyone will recognize who has read his prepresidential writings—of the immense and immeasurable value of a liberal education. But as the distinguished psychologist Robert J. Sternberg, provost of Oklahoma State University, wrote recently in an open letter to the president published in *Inside Higher Ed*, there is reason to worry that blunt "metrics for progress" of the NCLB type would "undermine liberal education in this country." So far President Obama's plans are not yet sharply defined. His initial emphasis has been on the cost of education, the promise of technology, and the establishment of standards for the transition from school to college. As a strategy emerges in more detail for holding colleges accountable for cost and quality, we need to keep in mind that standardized tests—at least those that exist today—are simply incapable of measuring the qualities that should be the fruits of a true liberal education: creativity, wisdom, humility, and insight into ethical as well as empirical questions.

As we proceed into the future, fantasies of retrieving an irretrievable past won't help. College is our American pastoral. We imagine it as a verdant world where the harshest sounds are the reciprocal thump of tennis balls or the clatter of cleats as young bodies trot up and down the field-house steps. Perhaps our brains are programmed to edit out the failures and disappointments—the botched exams, missed free throws, unrequited loves—that can make college a difficult time for young people struggling to grow up.

In fact, most college students today have nothing like the experience preserved in myth and selective memory. For a relatively few, college remains the sort of place that Kronman, a former dean of Yale Law School, recalls from his days at Williams College, where his favorite class took place at the home of a philosophy professor whose two golden retrievers slept on either side of the fireplace "like bookends beside the hearth" while the sunset lit the Berkshire hills "in scarlet and gold." But for many more students, college means the anxious pursuit of marketable skills in overcrowded, underresourced institutions, where

---

[6]*No Child Left Behind:* The No Child Left Behind Act is a 2001 federal educational reform law that mandates periodic standardized assessment of K–12 students as the condition of continued federal funding.

little attention is paid to that elusive entity sometimes called the "whole person." For still others, it means traveling by night to a fluorescent-lit office building or to a classroom that exists only in cyberspace.

It is a pipe dream to imagine that every student can have the sort of [25] experience that our richest colleges, at their best, still provide. But it is a nightmare society that affords the chance to learn and grow only to the wealthy, brilliant, or lucky few. Many remarkable teachers in America's community colleges, unsung private colleges, and underfinanced public colleges live this truth every day, working to keep the ideal of liberal education for all citizens alive.

It seems beyond doubt that the American college is going through a period of truly radical, perhaps unprecedented, change. It is buffeted by forces—globalization; economic instability; the continuing revolution in information technology; the increasingly evident inadequacy of elementary and secondary education; the elongation of adolescence; the breakdown of faculty tenure[7] as an academic norm; and, perhaps most important, the collapse of consensus about what students should know—that make its task more difficult and contentious than ever before.

Moreover, students tend to arrive in college already largely formed in their habits and attitudes, or, in the case of the increasing number of "nontraditional" (that is, older) students, preoccupied with the struggles of adulthood: finding or keeping a job, making or saving a marriage, doing right by their children. Many college women, who now outnumber men, are already mothers, often single. And regardless of age or gender or social class, students experience college—in the limited sense of attending lectures, writing papers, taking exams—as a smaller part of daily life than did my generation, which came of age in the 1960s and 70s. They live in an ocean of digital noise, logged on, online, booted up, as the phrase goes, 24/7, linked to one another through an arsenal of gadgets that are never powered down.

As we try to meet those challenges, it would be folly to dismiss as naïveté or nostalgia an abiding attachment to the college ideal—however much or little it ever conforms to reality. The power of this ideal is evident at every college commencement in the eyes of parents who watch their children advance into life. What parents want for their children is not just prosperity but happiness. And though it is foolish to deny the linkage between the two, they are not the same thing.

As the literary scholar Norman Foerster once put it, the American college has always sought to prepare students for more than "pecuniary advantage over the unprepared." To succeed in sustaining college as a place where liberal learning still takes place will be very costly. But in the long run, it will be much more costly if we fail.

---

[7]*faculty tenure:* The guarantee that professors may keep their positions for life unless terminated for "just cause," tenure is meant to promote academic freedom by protecting college faculty from administrative or political punishment when they express dissenting or controversial ideas.

A few years ago, when I was beginning to work on my book about the American college, I came across a manuscript diary kept in the early 1850s by a student at a small Methodist college in southwest Virginia. One spring evening, after attending a sermon by the college president that left him troubled and apprehensive, he made the following entry: "Oh that the Lord would show me how to think and how to choose." That sentence, poised somewhere between a wish and a plea, sounds archaic today. But even if the religious note is dissonant to some of us, it seems hard to come up with a better formulation of what a college should strive to be: an aid to reflection, a place and process whereby young people take stock of their talents and passions and begin to sort out their lives in a way that is true to themselves and responsible to others. "Show me how to think and how to choose."

Candorville

ENGAGING THE TEXT

1. Make a list of the many attributes Delbanco associates with a liberal education. What, in his view, should students gain from the experience of college? What should a college education do for—or to—you?

2. What's wrong, according to Delbanco, with the notion that college should prepare students for economic success? Is Delbanco a nostalgic elitist, or is he right when he says that education should be about more than the pursuit of marketable skills?

3. What is "lateral learning" (para. 15), and why does Delbanco feel it is essential for life in a "deliberative democracy"? How important is lateral learning at your college?

4. What social, technological, and economic developments does Delbanco identify as threatening the ideal of liberal education? How, for example, might standardized degree requirements, enforced learning standards, virtual classrooms, and the end of tenure undermine the goals of liberal education?

5. According to Delbanco, the experience of school has become "a smaller part of daily life" for many contemporary college students. How big a role does college play in your daily life? What distractions, demands, and responsibilities compete

for your attention? What could be done to make your college experience more like Delbanco's ideal of liberal education?

EXPLORING CONNECTIONS

6. How would you expect Michael Moore (p. 121) and John Taylor Gatto (p. 141) to react to Delbanco's ideal of liberal education? Would they be likely to embrace the notion of education as a form of self-discovery and transformation? Why or why not?

7. How do the educational experiences of Mike Rose (p. 151) and Malcolm X (p. 189) compare with the kind of liberal college education that Delbanco describes? To what extent do their experiences support or challenge Delbanco's liberal ideal?

8. Which of the schools that Jean Anyon describes (p. 163) best prepares students for the kind of liberal education that Delbanco describes? How well did your own elementary and secondary educations prepare you for the kind of critical thinking demanded by the most challenging college work?

9. Drawing on Jonathan Kozol's analysis of K–12 school reforms (p. 201) and Delbanco's evaluation of the threats to higher education, write a journal entry, blog, or brief essay on the notion of apartheid in American education. Is the nation developing two different types of educational systems — with different aims, expectations, and methods — for students from differing backgrounds? And if so, should we be concerned?

EXTENDING THE CRITICAL CONTEXT

10. Survey students outside your class to learn more about why they want a college education. How many see economic advancement as their primary goal? How many expect college to provoke them to rethink their ideas and values — or to transform them in some way? Compare the results of your surveys in class and discuss what they suggest about the future of liberal education in America.

11. Research the rising cost of college since the 1960s. How much has the annual cost of attending college gone up over the past fifty years? How might the increasing costs of college be changing our view of the purpose of a college education? What would happen, in your view, if colleges were tuition-free?

12. Visit the Bedford e-Pages for this chapter of *Rereading America* (bedfordstmartins .com/rereading/epages) and view *The Commercial Campus*. Then break into groups and discuss whether or not you think it's appropriate for corporations like Target or American Eagle to hire college students to sell products to their younger peers. What evidence do you see at your college of the commercialization of higher education and student life?

FROM UNDERGROUND UNDERGRADS
UCLA CENTER FOR LABOR STUDIES AND EDUCATION

Who are the new American Dreamers? With more than 14 million undocumented immigrants in the United States, it is estimated that some 50,000 high school students graduate each year without legal immigrant status. Assured of access to a free public education by the U.S. Supreme Court in 1982, these students often do all the right things: they work hard, get good grades, take AP classes, and devote themselves to extracurricular activities. And yet, after receiving their diplomas, most find the door to further opportunity firmly shut. In many states, undocumented immigrants can't apply for admission to public colleges. In others, they are expected to pay full out-of-state tuition without the help of financial aid. And even those who do complete a degree find that federal immigration law blocks their chances of ever getting a decent job.

Over the past decade, legislators have proposed a number of state and federal laws to help these students. The most ambitious of these efforts, the federal Dream Act, was designed to offer a pathway to citizenship for any undocumented immigrant who enters the United States under the age of sixteen, finishes high school in the United States, and completes a minimum of two years of study at a college or university or serves for at least two years in the military. Originally proposed in 2001, the Dream Act has never been put to a vote in Congress. But as the following selection suggests, students like Veronica Valdez and Antonio Alvarez continue to believe in the dream of educational opportunity, despite the challenges they face as undocumented immigrants. Veronica and Antonio published their stories in *Underground Undergrads: UCLA Undocumented Students Immigrant Students Speak Out* (2008), which grew out of the first Immigrant Rights, Labor, and Higher Education course offered at the University of California, Los Angeles in 2007. The course and the book were made possible by Dr. Kent Wong, Director of UCLA's Center for Labor Studies and Education.

WALKING ACROSS THE STAGE

VERONICA VALDEZ

I BOUGHT MY GRADUATION ROBE three weeks before I graduated from UCLA. As I paid for my robe, I reminisced about how far I had come in my endeavors to succeed. Yet I could focus only on the fact that my life was now more uncertain than ever. My undocumented status has left me in a marginalized state where, even as a college graduate, the direction of my life is in limbo. I have achieved one component of the American dream: a great education. Nevertheless, I am left without opportunities for jobs in which I can use my degree—a degree that took all my perseverance to achieve, following a path that began over eighteen years ago.

My parents' decision to come to the United States in the late 1980s forever changed their lives as well as mine. From the point of our arrival as undocumented immigrants—my mother as a twenty-one-year-old and me as a four-year-old—our lives have been full of struggle and uncertainty.

It was an early Thursday morning when my mother and I got on the road to leave Mexico for the United States. My mother took only what she believed was necessary. We were headed to the border, specifically to Tijuana, where we would meet a friend of my father's who would get us across the U.S.-Mexico border. When we finally arrived in Los Angeles, my mother was relieved to finally be with my father. I do not remember reuniting with my father or crossing the border, but my mother said that I was very happy. I had cried a lot when my father first left.

My mother gave birth to my younger sister in 1991 and with a new child in the home, the need for more money became a pressing issue. My mother did not have a lot of work experience in Mexico; she worked only one job before coming to America. At the age of thirteen, her parents took her out of school and put her to work so that she could contribute to her family's household income. She worked in a restaurant until she was sixteen, and then she left her job after she met my father. She was married and had a child by the age of seventeen.

It was very complicated for my mother to find a job in the United States because of her undocumented status, which prevented her from just applying at any business with a "Help Wanted" sign. Additionally she did not know English and was unsure of where to go to learn English. She found her first jobs through friends in our apartment building and at the parent center at my elementary school. My mother's first jobs were in sales—from Mary Kay to Avon and then to Tupperware—my mom sold it all. Eventually she met a woman who worked with an agency that places workers in factories. Since 1997 my mother has worked in factories, ranging from clothing factories to packaging factories. In her current job, she packs beauty products into boxes. My mother wakes up every morning at 5:30 to go to her job in the packaging factory. Since she cannot legally get a license in the state of California, my mother takes the bus. She is too scared of being pulled over and possibly going to jail or even being deported, to drive.

For my mother, the concept of working has always been something you have to do, as opposed to an opportunity to make a difference in the world or to find fulfillment. Every day my mother comes home from work exhausted, wondering whether she will have her job the next day. She has no health benefits. Being undocumented has definitely made her position in the workforce an uncertain, frightening place to be. She has changed jobs several times because the factories have closed down, and she was advised at certain locations not to come in to work or to leave early because immigration services were going to come. Seeing my mother go through these experiences and feeling her fear of the workplace has been a major push for me to attain my college degree.

My history in the United States began at the age of four when I was brought across the border. It has been full of both difficulties and joy. Throughout my childhood and now as an adult, I have considered the United States my home. My K–12 education was in the Los Angeles public schools. Despite the fact that I have lived in this country almost all my life, legalization has not been possible because of the complete lack of immigration legislation that addresses the needs of people like myself.

Growing up I did not have any friends who were undocumented, and I was unaware of my immigration status until I was fifteen. When I was fifteen, I decided it was time to get a job because my parents did not have a lot of money, and I wanted to buy things for myself. It was at this time that my parents notified me that I could not get a job because I had not been born in this country. From that point on, my view of what my life would be like completely changed. This knowledge made it very difficult for me to face the real world. My work experiences have varied, but most have been "under the table." I got my first job in a bakery when I was eighteen. It was the worst job I ever had. They paid me below the minimum wage, and I did not have any benefits. The work at the bakery was very hard. Being the cashier was the least of my worries; I also washed dishes, mopped the floor, cleaned the bathroom, baked the bread. I worked long hours. I had to wake up every morning before sunrise to work, and then I attended class late at night, only to come home to do class assignments. I worked very hard in school and earned good grades, but I felt humiliated. I had always had aspirations of becoming a professor, not mopping floors for low wages. I only worked at the bakery for a month before I quit. It was very hard to realize that even though I felt like a young American and had been educated entirely in this nation, my immigration status limited my options and ultimately how I could live my life.

My second job was as a waitress in a Mexican restaurant, where I worked for almost two years. At that restaurant I earned the money I needed to pay my college tuition. I worked full-time, six days a week, and simultaneously maintained my status as a full-time student. As my college education progressed, it became too difficult to hold a full-time job and maintain high grades, so I left my job. From that moment on, I have been earning money from jobs such as babysitting, washing dogs, and transcribing. I grew up seeing how hard my parents worked for the few things they have, and I wanted a better life for me and for them.

My immigration status has been a huge factor in my life in the 10 United States. It has brought many challenges, including the inability to obtain financial aid, grants, or scholarships, to receive a valid state-issued ID or license, or to have job opportunities that match my educational level. These obstacles have contributed to my family's life of poverty. The feeling of constant uncertainty has affected me, yet I have overcome almost all the obstacles that have come my way. I learned the English language, and I have helped my family. I have paid for my college tuition, and I am obtaining the education I always desired at the university of my dreams, UCLA.

My mother has also overcome many of the challenges she has faced in the United States. She attended English classes that were offered in the middle school I attended, and she bought tapes and videos to improve her English language skills. She found a job that has provided steady income for the last ten years. My mother has matured and given her children the motivation and advice necessary for them to succeed.

We have not been able to change our undocumented status even though we arrived in this country almost eighteen years ago. The Dream Act would allow me to change my undocumented status, opening up a path that would lead to citizenship. As beneficial as the Dream Act would be for undocumented students, we need comprehensive immigration reform that will change the legal status of millions of U.S. residents.

When I asked my mother if she would have done anything differently in terms of coming to America, she said, "Yes, I would have tried to enter the country legally, to try to find the opportunity to come legally." When I asked why she did not try to enter the country legally from the beginning, she said, "Because when the people go from here to over there, they tell you that here you earn a lot of money, that it is very easy, and they tell you of a country that is very pretty and different than what it really is. And because I did not think. I was young and did not have the maturity. I did not even know what to expect. Simply, I followed your father." I believe my mother's experience mirrors the experiences of many immigrants who have come to the United States, led by the fairy tales that exist about the country. Unfortunately many immigrants have realized that these stories are only fantasies.

My mother has not seen her mother or much of the rest of her family in almost eighteen years. With no legal way of leaving and then reentering the country, traveling to Mexico has been out of the question for years. My mother never thought she would live and raise her children in California. Yet going to live once more in Mexico is not a possibility. She feels her home is where her children are, and her children consider the United States their home. My mother and I, and many other undocumented immigrants, have faced challenges every day in our attempt to create a better life for our families.

I consider myself American. My friends, boyfriend, family, hopes, and dreams are in this country. Thus, I work in every way I can, in every movement I can, to be recognized by the nation I have lived in for so long. 15

OUT OF MY HANDS

ANTONIO ALVAREZ

AS I RAN DOWNSTAIRS from the third floor, I looked forward to playing with the other children living in our apartment building. Some of my friends were playing with *trompos* (a top spun with yarn, like a dreidel), others with marbles, and some of the girls were jumping rope. I noticed that one of the children had a water gun very similar to mine. I approached the boy, took a closer look at the toy, and realized that it actually was mine. I asked the boy why he had taken my water gun and told him that he needed to return it. He said, "No, your mother sold it to me because you guys are leaving. You guys are moving away, somewhere else." This was when I first knew that I was going to the United States. I was four years old.

My father, Antonio, said that he decided to go to the United States "to be able to have a better life, a better future, in being able to realize our dreams, the American dream." Similarly my mother, Alida, "did not see a future for us in Mexico" and viewed the United States as the answer to our problems. During the 1980s, Mexico underwent a major economic crisis, leaving my father without a stable job to support our family. The instinct to survive led both of my parents to view immigration as their only option. My father left in mid-1988, and the rest of the family—me, my mother, two-year-old brother Isai, and eight-month-old sister Alida—left in late December 1989.

The plan was for my father to work in the United States and send money back home to support us and hopefully to accumulate enough to start up our own business. My mother grew impatient in Mexico when my father did not return however. She believed he needed to see his children. She decided to migrate with the entire family to the United States without giving prior notice to my father. To finance our trip north, my mother resorted to selling our belongings; thus, my toy gun contributed toward the trip.

From what I remember of the trip, it started at a motel in Tijuana, where we stayed for two nights before crossing the border early in the morning. I remember my mother making a phone call from Tijuana to my father, telling him that we were on our way to Los Angeles. There were about fifteen or twenty people crossing that day. The coyotes—the men we paid to help us cross the border—were extremely scared to take us, telling my mother, "Lady, we have never crossed children before. You know this is very risky." My mom told them that she knew and acknowledged the risk factor but said we were going to cross. I just thought it was the way everyone went to the United States: walking and running for hours as quietly as possible through rough terrain.

We started the actual walking part of the trip at a dump yard and   5 continued on until the dump yard ended and turned into scrubby hills. From that point on, we ran, jogged, and walked for hours. I remember at one point, my shoes became dirty from stepping in the mud, and I said, "Oh no, my shoes are dirty," and everyone in the group loudly said "shhhhh" for fear of detection. The border patrol agents were inside vehicles that gave them an elevated view of the area and allowed them to more easily spot any immigrants. From that moment on, I realized that I had to stay as quiet as possible throughout the trip. Some moments my mother vividly remembers from the trip include crossing the I-5 freeway, and the other migrants telling my mother, "Come on, lady, run, run! Come on, run," and me telling her, "Come on, mami, run! Run so you don't get left behind, run, hurry, hurry mami!" She also remembers how I held my little brother's hand for part of the trip to help him along the way and how a young immigrant couple helped my mother by carrying my baby sister for most of the trip.

After traveling for several hours on foot, we arrived at a cabin in the hills with other crossing immigrants. At this point, I was extremely hungry. Inside the cabin, as my family rested, I spotted three or four over-toasted, cold tortillas—hard, like tostadas—that someone had left. I ate one and took another one for my little brother. Though they did not taste good, my brother and I finished them out of hunger. We left the cabin and got inside a car that the coyote had obtained. With about three other immigrants in the car, the coyote drove us to Los Angeles, where my father was waiting at a bus stop. My mother was the first to see him standing on the street. As I looked at him for the first time in over a year, all I wanted was to run up and hug him. We arrived in Los Angeles a few days before Christmas.

My parents' plan was not to permanently settle in the United States; however, as time passed, they decided to stay. One of our goals became, and continues to be, to adjust our residential status from undocumented to documented permanent residents. My father filled out numerous applications to adjust his residential status, and the process was long and arduous. He began in 1992, but due to a mistake of addresses when we changed residences, and a long waiting list, it took my father about fourteen years to adjust his status. He obtained a work permit in 2003 and finally his permanent residency in 2006. Now he has petitioned for permanent residency for me, my siblings, and my mother, but the waiting list is so long—a lifetime for us.

Along with our residential status, anti-immigrant laws have shaped our lives in the United States. My parents said that the laws that have affected us most severely include California's Proposition 187,[1] which was approved by voters in 1994. My mother believed it was not fair to keep children out of public schools and to keep them from receiving medical treatment. We were surprised at how much support the proposition gained and that an overwhelming majority of Californians voted for it. My mother told me that I would probably not be able to attend school any more if my undocumented status was reported by anyone on the school staff. Though the proposition passed, it was struck down as unconstitutional by the courts, and I continued to attend school.

I remember the 1996 driver's license legislation's passing and going into effect, because my dad was worried to death by it. He was mortified because at that time and up until 2006, he had been working two jobs—one of them as a pizza delivery worker for different pizza chains, which required a valid driver's license. It was hard watching how much stress he had because he knew renewing his driver's license would be impossible, since the new law prohibited undocumented immigrants from receiving licenses or renewing them. By the time my father had to renew his license, however, he had received his work permit. It allowed him to renew his driver's license without any legal trouble.

Though I remember these laws as severe obstacles for our family's livelihood, legislation affecting higher education opportunities for undocumented students stand out in my memory most prominently. I realized that I was an immigrant and that something was not right during the Proposition 187 campaign but until I reached high school, I did not understand that my future would be seriously limited. During my freshman year, I discovered that I could not obtain a license because I was undocumented, and during my junior year, I realized the hardships I would face upon entering college. I had achieved almost a 4.0 grade point average up until my sophomore year, but when I learned that I could not receive any federal or state financing to attend a four-year university, I became demoralized, and my grades suffered from it. I thought there was no point to continuing to work so hard in high school if attending a community college—where my high school grades would be irrelevant—was my only option.

My outlook changed a few months before high school graduation. I talked to one of my teachers who was once an undocumented immigrant student but is now a permanent resident. He told me about AB 540 and explained that it would allow me to pay in-state tuition at

10

---

[1]*California's Proposition 187:* A ballot initiative that would have denied education, non-emergency health care, and other social services to all undocumented immigrants, overturned by the Supreme Court in 1995. [All notes are the editors'.]

UC, CSU, and community college. Though I was accepted to CSU Los Angeles and CSU Fullerton, he recommended I first attend a community college for its affordability, complete my first two years there, save money, and then transfer to a four-year university.

I took his advice and enrolled at East Los Angeles College (ELAC) in the summer of 2003 and quickly followed this by searching for a job. As a result of my undocumented status, I could not work anywhere I wanted and was limited to low-wage jobs that did not require identification or background checks. I was hired at a market, where I worked over thirty hours a week. I now had a goal. My plan at ELAC was to work and go to school and then to transfer to a CSU because the UCs and private schools were too expensive and required longer commutes. Though it was a good plan, it saddened me because my ideal dream from years before—ever since I had visited the UCLA campus during an elementary school field trip—had been to attend a top university.

I enjoyed the schooling I received at ELAC, and I flourished. I took sociology classes and fell in love with the subject. It was then that I realized that I wanted a career in helping others, specifically individuals whose voices were muted in society. Impressed by my work, both my sociology and English professors told me I needed to include a UC in my future. When I finally did apply to transfer, I was accepted to every university I applied to: USC, UC San Diego, UC Berkeley, and UCLA. I decided to attend UCLA, where I struggle for the thousands of dollars to finance my education. I will graduate with a degree in sociology and Chicana/o studies.

Being undocumented has been a way of life for me, my family, and millions of others. When I apply for jobs that I know I am overqualified for but that do not include background checks, I experience strong feelings of detachment and frustration, followed by hints of helplessness. I work these jobs to pay for a college experience that does not include semesters abroad and living in a dorm and other experiences that "normal" students have. I hope that by sharing some of my family's history and experiences—as undocumented immigrants, undocumented workers, undocumented students, undocumented people, and second-class human beings—I can help produce an emphatic and humanistic approach to immigration that vigorously rejects the notion that a human can be illegal.

TEA PARTYERS ARE GATHERING SIGNATURES TO TRY TO REPEAL THE CALIFORNIA DREAM ACT, WHICH ALLOWS CHILDREN OF ILLEGAL IMMIGRANTS TO APPLY FOR COLLEGE FINANCIAL AID. LET'S GET FAMILIAR WITH THE

ENGAGING THE TEXT

1. What challenges have Veronica and Antonio faced in school because of their status as undocumented immigrants? How has being undocumented shaped their college experiences? How might your own educational story be different if you had been an undocumented immigrant?

2. How has the American Dream influenced the lives of Veronica and Antonio and their families? What traditional American values or qualities do they embody?

3. What's the difference between calling students like Veronica and Antonio "illegal" or "undocumented" immigrants? Should they be considered criminals? Why or why not?

4. What contradictions do you see in the educational and immigration policies of the United States? Does it make sense, for example, to provide free public education to nondocumented children and then deny them access to college and financial aid after they graduate from high school? Would it be better to deny them an education in the first place? Why or why not?

EXPLORING CONNECTIONS

5. How might the vision of the common school provided by Horace Mann (p. 110) support the case for extending free public education to all children in the United States, regardless of immigration status?

6. Given his belief in liberal education, would you expect Andrew Delbanco (p. 219), to support or oppose the notion of allowing undocumented students the chance to attend college and receive financial aid? Why or why not?

EXTENDING THE CRITICAL CONTEXT

7. Research the history of Dream Act legislation in your state. Can undocumented students enroll in public colleges and universities in your community? Are they eligible for financial aid? How many of the students at your college do you think are undocumented?

8. Do additional research on the history and provisions of the federal Dream Act, and then debate the case for passing the act in class. What social, economic, and ethical issues are involved in arguments for and against the Dream Act? What has been the impact of President Obama's 2012 executive order allowing Dreamers to stay in the United States on a limited basis? What do you think should happen to the undocumented immigrant students it would apply to and why?

9. Go online and view *Undocumented Americans: Inside the Immigration Debate* at: www.time.com/time/video/player/0,32068,1688176871001_2117188,00 .html. Then read "My Life as an Undocumented Immigrant" by Jose Antonio Vargas, which is also available online at: www.nytimes.com/2011/06/26/magazine /my-life-as-an-undocumented-immigrant.html?pagewanted=all. What do the voices and stories of the students featured in the video add to the debate on the Dream Act? Why does Vargas believe he should qualify for citizen status? Do you think Vargas was right to "come out" about his undocumented status? Do you think other Dreamers should join him?

FURTHER CONNECTIONS

1. In the United States, the notion of schooling as the road to success has always been balanced by a pervasive distrust of education. This phenomenon, known as "American anti-intellectualism" grew out of the first settlers' suspicion of anything that reminded them of the "corrupting" influences of European sophistication. American anti-intellectualism often shows up most vividly in pop-cultural portrayals of school, students, and educators. Working in groups, survey recent treatments of school on television, in films, and on Internet blogs and Web sites. How is schooling treated in the mass media and by popular bloggers on the left and the right? Overall, how powerful does anti-intellectualism seem to be in American culture today?

2. Over the past few years, educational critics across the political spectrum have voiced concern about declining success rates for males in America's schools and colleges. During the last decade, for example, the number of women in America's colleges and universities has steadily increased until, today, women outnumber men in almost every academic field outside the so-called hard sciences. Research this issue to learn more about how males are faring in America's schools. Do you think, as some critics claim, that school in America has become a "feminized" institution that is particularly hostile to boys? What other reasons might explain declines in male educational achievement over the past two decades?

3. In his book on the impact of globalization, *The World Is Flat: A Brief History of the 21st Century* (2005), journalist and social commentator Thomas Friedman argues that America's schools are failing to equip students with the essential math, science, and language skills they'll need to compete in a global world economy. Compare notes with your classmates about how well you feel your own school experiences have prepared you for competition in the global marketplace. How much math and science did you study in high school? How would you rate your own ability in math and science? How much did you learn about other cultures and languages? In general, do you feel that America's schools today are preparing most students to compete successfully in a globalizing world?

4. Working in groups, research the educational systems in other countries to see how they compare with secondary education in the United States. For example, how is secondary school education handled in countries like England, France, Germany, Denmark, Japan, China, Cuba, and Russia? What role do testing and the rote memorization of facts play in the educational system you selected to study? To what

extent does this system emphasize creativity, personal expression, and critical thinking? Overall, how effective is this nation's educational system in terms of preparing students for a productive and successful life? What, if anything, might we as a nation learn from this approach to secondary education?

5. Educational researchers estimate that 25 percent to 60 percent of the ninth graders in America's urban public schools will drop out before graduation. Do additional research on the "dropout crisis" to learn more about the scope and causes of this problem. Why are so many Americans opting out of school today? Which groups are most in danger of leaving school before graduation? What can be done to encourage young Americans to stay in school?

6. Under the principle of affirmative action, American colleges and universities were permitted to consider the racial background of applicants in admissions decisionmaking. As a result, the percentage of minority students in America's colleges and universities increased steadily from 1965 until the late 1990s when several states reversed or seriously weakened earlier affirmative action admissions policies. Since then, the diversity of many college campuses across the country has declined significantly. Research the history of the college systems in your state. How has the decline of affirmative action affected college enrollments? What are the arguments for and against the consideration of race as an element of college admissions?

7. **Connecting to the e-Pages.** Read Richard Rodriguez's "The Achievement of Desire" (see bedfordstmartins.com/rereading/epages). Then write a three-way dialogue between him, the speaker of Inéz Hernández Ávila's poem "Para Teresa" (p. 198), and Mike Rose (p. 151) on education as a process of self-transformation. How does the experience of school change their understanding of home, their aspirations, and their views of themselves. How has school changed you?

MONEY AND SUCCESS
The Myth of Individual Opportunity

FAST FACTS

1. Roughly 27 percent of blacks and Hispanics, 12 percent of Asians, 10 percent of whites, and 20 percent of foreign-born residents are below the official poverty line.

2. White Americans have roughly 22 times more wealth on average than black Americans; in 2010, median household net worth was $110,729 for white households and $4,955 for black households.

3. Full-time female workers in the U.S. earn about 78 cents for every dollar earned by their male counterparts. Fifty years ago it was 61 cents.

4. According to a *New York Times* story, retail workers in Apple stores earned $11.91 per hour while bringing in an average of $473,000 each in annual revenue for their stores. Apple CEO Timothy Cook's 2011 compensation (base salary, bonus, and stock awards) totaled more than $377,000,000.

5. The 400 wealthiest Americans have a combined net worth greater than the bottom 150,000,000 Americans.

6. Economic mobility is more limited in the United States than in Canada, Germany, France, Denmark, Sweden, Norway, or Finland. Roughly 65 percent of Americans born in the bottom fifth stay in the bottom two-fifths, while 62 percent raised in the top fifth of incomes stay in the top two-fifths.

7. More than 600,000 Americans are homeless on a given night, with more than a third of those in unsheltered locations. Although homelessness among veterans declined in 2011, more than 67,000 were homeless on a single night in January.

Sources: (1, 2, and 3) U.S. Census Bureau; (4) *New York Times*, June 24, 2012 and June 17, 2012; (5) *New York Times*, October 16, 2011; (6) Economic Mobility Project of the Pew Charitable Trusts. *New York Times*, January 4, 2012; (7) U.S. Department of Housing and Urban Development.

AMERICANS CHERISH THE NOTION THAT THE UNITED STATES is a land of unequaled opportunity, where hard work and smart choices yield big rewards, where no one is stuck on the lower rungs of the economic ladder. Yet statistically speaking, upward mobility is no easier here than in England and France, and it is harder here than in Canada and some Scandinavian countries. Moreover, it is extraordinarily difficult to escape poverty if you've "chosen" the wrong parents: 95 percent of children born to poor parents will themselves be poor all their lives. Even for more fortunate Americans, the recession that battered world economies in 2008 made maintaining the comfortable lifestyle of the middle class seem increasingly dependent not on hard work but on global economic forces like the price of crude oil and the migration of American jobs overseas.

Despite the profound effects of money, or the lack thereof, on our daily lives, most Americans dislike talking about social class. For example, both our rich and our poor shun those terms. When we do talk about money and success, most of us favor a "meritocracy," a fair competition for success that's not rigged according to race, gender, or family history. A wealth of data relating success to education, ethnicity, gender, and inheritance, however, suggests that our reality falls short of our ideals; no individual is guaranteed success or doomed to failure, but the odds are stacked against women, people of color, and those born into poverty.

Our current cultural myths about success have deep roots and a long history. Indeed, the dream of individual opportunity has been at home in America since Europeans discovered a "new world" in the Western hemisphere. Early immigrants like J. Hector St. John de Crèvecoeur extolled the freedom and opportunity to be found in this new land. His glowing descriptions of a classless society where anyone could attain success through honesty and hard work fired the imaginations of many European readers: in *Letters from an American Farmer* (1782) he wrote, "We are all animated with the spirit of an industry which is unfettered and unrestrained, because each person works for himself. . . . We have no princes, for whom we toil, starve, and bleed: we are the most perfect society now existing in the world." The promise of a land where "the rewards of [a man's] industry follow with equal steps the progress of his labor" drew poor immigrants from Europe and fueled national expansion into the western territories.

Our national mythology abounds with illustrations of the American success story. There's Benjamin Franklin, the very model of the self-educated, self-made man, who rose from modest origins to become a renowned scientist, philosopher, and statesman. In the nineteenth century, Horatio Alger, a writer of pulp fiction for young boys — fiction that you will get to sample below — became America's best-selling author with rags-to-riches tales like *Struggling Upward* (1886) and *Bound to Rise* (1873). The notion of success haunts us: we spend millions every year reading about the rich and famous, learning how to "make a fortune in real estate with no money down," and "dressing for success." The myth of success has even invaded our personal relationships: today it's as important to be "successful" in marriage or parenthood as it is to come out on top in business.

But dreams easily turn into nightmares. Every American who hopes to "make it" also knows the fear of failure, because the myth of success inevitably implies comparison between the haves and the have-nots, the achievers and the drones, the stars and the anonymous crowd. Under pressure of the myth, we become engrossed in status symbols: we try to live in the "right" neighborhoods, wear the "right" clothes, eat the "right" foods. These emblems of distinction assure us and others that we are different, that we stand out from the crowd. It is one of the great paradoxes of our culture that we believe passionately in the fundamental equality of all yet strive as hard as we can to separate ourselves from our fellow citizens. This separation is particularly true of our wealthiest citizens, who have increasingly isolated themselves from everyone else with gated communities, exclusive schools, and private jets.

Steeped in a Puritan theology that vigorously preached the individual's responsibility to the larger community, colonial America balanced the drive for individual gain with concern for the common good. To Franklin, the way to wealth lay in practicing the virtues of honesty, hard work, and thrift: "Without industry and frugality nothing will do, and with them every thing. He that gets all he can honestly, and saves all he gets . . . will certainly become RICH" ("Advice to a Young Tradesman," 1748). And Alger's heroes were as concerned with moral rectitude as they were with financial gain: a benefactor advises Ragged Dick, "If you'll try to be somebody, and grow up into a respectable member of society, you will. You may not become rich, — it isn't everybody that becomes rich, you know, — but you can obtain a good position and be respected." But in the twentieth century the mood of the myth changed.

In the 1970s, Robert Ringer's enormously popular *Looking Out for Number One* urged readers to "forget foundationless traditions, forget the 'moral' standards others may have tried to cram down your throat . . . and, most important, think of yourself — Number One. . . . You and you alone will be responsible for your success or failure." The myth of success may have been responsible for making the United States what it is today, but it also seems to be pulling us apart. Can we exist as a living community if our greatest value can be summed up by the slogan "Me first"?

The chapter opens with a pair of strongly contrasting narratives about young people learning about money and opportunity. The first, an excerpt from Horatio Alger's classic rags-to-riches novel *Ragged Dick,* unambiguously promotes the myth of individual success. The second, Toni Cade Bambara's "The Lesson," dramatizes economic inequality through the eyes of a group of Harlem kids who travel uptown to see how the rich live and spend. Next, in "Horatio Alger," Harlon L. Dalton examines the cultural meanings of such storytelling and finds the myth Alger popularized not just misleading but "socially destructive."

The three subsequent readings offer a wealth of information about social class from very different perspectives. Barbara Ehrenreich's "Serving in Florida" investigates the daily grind of working-class life by recounting her personal experience of struggling to make ends meet on waitressing wages. Next, "Class in America — 2009" by Gregory Mantsios examines class from a broader and more theoretical perspective; citing compelling statistics, Mantsios presents a stark portrayal of a social and economic system that serves the powerful and wealthy. Focusing on young workers and recent college graduates, Don Peck's "Generation R: The Changing Fortunes of America's Youth" explains how young people who enter the workforce during a recession may suffer economic and psychological harm that can last a lifetime.

Midway through the chapter you will find visual and media selections on money and success. The Visual Portfolio, "Reading Images of Individual Opportunity," explores dreams of success, the cost of failure, public protests against economic inequality, and the relationship of opportunity to race, gender, and education. The chapter's media selection — Diana Kendall's "Framing Class, Vicarious Living, and Conspicuous Consumption" — studies how TV tends to distort our view of economic inequalities, for example by treating poverty as individual misfortune rather than systematic oppression.

The chapter concludes with four probing assessments of how social class operates in the United States today and where we seem to be headed as a nation. First, Adam Davidson's "Making It in America" profiles a young American factory worker who finds herself competing not only with cheaper workers overseas, but also with machines that could someday take her job. Next, in an excerpt from *America's New Working Class*, political scientist Kathleen R. Arnold makes the provocative argument that government programs usually thought to aid poor Americans are in fact systems designed to punish, control, and monitor them. The chapter ends with contrasting interpretations of one of the most striking trends of recent years — the quickly expanding gap between the rich and everyone else. In the chapter's conservative selection, "The New American Divide," Charles Murray argues that the most fundamental issues are cultural rather than economic and can be fixed "one family at a time" through a return to values like solid marriages, a strong work ethic, and religion. The chapter concludes with an excerpt from Timothy Noah's book *The Great Divergence*, in which the prize-winning journalist describes how Wall Street "ate the economy" and calls on the nation to change direction before it's too late.

The e-Pages for *Rereading America* extend the range of genres and perspectives found throughout this chapter. "Stephen Cruz," an oral history by Studs Terkel, describes a man who has moved beyond pursuing money to a way of life he finds more rewarding; in the video *The High Price of Materialism*, Tim Kasser details the numerous ways in which pursuing material wealth harms both individuals and the planet. See bedfordstmartins.com/rereading/epages for these two selections.

Sources

Baida, Peter. *Poor Richard's Legacy: American Business Values from Benjamin Franklin to Donald Trump*. New York: William Morrow, 1990. Print.

Correspondents of the New York Times. *Class Matters*. New York: Times Books/Henry Holt, 2005. Print.

McNamee, Stephen J. and Robert K. Miller Jr. *The Meritocracy Myth*. New York: Rowman & Littlefield, 2004. Print.

St. John de Crèvecoeur, J. Hector. *Letters from an American Farmer*. New York: Dolphin Books, 1961. First published in London, 1782. Print.

BEFORE READING

- Working alone or in groups, make a list of people who best represent your idea of success. (You may want to consider public and political figures, leaders in government, entertainment, sports, education, or other fields.) List the specific qualities or accomplishments that make these people successful. Compare notes with your classmates, then freewrite about the meaning of success: What does it mean to you? To the class as a whole? Keep your list and your definition. As you work through this chapter, reread and reflect on what you've written, comparing your ideas with those of the authors included here.

- Write an imaginative profile of the man pictured in the frontispiece for this chapter (p. 241). For example, where was he born, what do you imagine his parents did for a living, and where was he educated? What do his clothes, his posture, his facial expression, and the limousine say about him today? Where does he live, what is his current job or profession, and how much money does he make? Compare your profile with those of classmates to see shared or divergent ideas about some of the issues explored throughout *Rereading America* — the "American Dream," certainly, but also cultural myths of family, education, gender, and ethnicity.

- Write down the job and salary you expect to have in the next 10–15 years. Share with classmates and keep the guesstimate in mind as you read this chapter, adjusting up or down as you gain new information.

FROM *RAGGED DICK*

HORATIO ALGER

The choice of Horatio Alger to exemplify the myth of individual opportunity is almost automatic. Alger's rags-to-riches stories have become synonymous with the notion that anyone can succeed — even to generations of Americans who have never read one of the books that were best-sellers a century ago. The excerpt below is typical of Alger's work in that it focuses on a young man's progress from a poor background toward "fame and fortune." Alger (1832–1899) published over a hundred such stories; most observers agree that their popularity depended less on their literary accomplishments than on the promises they made about opportunity in America and the rewards of hard work.

DICK NOW BEGAN TO LOOK ABOUT for a position in a store or counting-room. Until he should obtain one he determined to devote half the day to blacking boots, not being willing to break in upon his small capital. He found that he could earn enough in half a day to pay all his necessary expenses, including the entire rent of the room. Fosdick desired to pay his half; but Dick steadily refused, insisting upon paying so much as compensation for his friend's services as instructor.

It should be added that Dick's peculiar way of speaking and use of slang terms had been somewhat modified by his education and his intimacy with Henry Fosdick. Still he continued to indulge in them to some extent, especially when he felt like joking, and it was natural to Dick to joke, as my readers have probably found out by this time. Still his manners were considerably improved, so that he was more likely to obtain a situation than when first introduced to our notice.

Just now, however, business was very dull, and merchants, instead of hiring new assistants, were disposed to part with those already in their employ. After making several ineffectual applications, Dick began to think he should be obliged to stick to his profession until the next season. But about this time something occurred which considerably improved his chances of preferment.

This is the way it happened.

As Dick, with a balance of more than a hundred dollars in the savings bank, might fairly consider himself a young man of property, he thought himself justified in occasionally taking a half holiday from business, and going on an excursion. On Wednesday afternoon Henry Fosdick was sent by his employer on an errand to that part of Brooklyn near Greenwood Cemetery. Dick hastily dressed himself in his best, and determined to accompany him.

The two boys walked down to the South Ferry, and, paying their two cents each, entered the ferry-boat. They remained at the stern, and stood by the railing, watching the great city, with its crowded wharves, receding from view. Beside them was a gentleman with two children, — a girl of eight and a little boy of six. The children were talking gayly to their father. While he was pointing out some object of interest to the little girl, the boy managed to creep, unobserved, beneath the chain that extends across the boat, for the protection of passengers, and, stepping incautiously to the edge of the boat, fell over into the foaming water.

At the child's scream, the father looked up, and, with a cry of horror, sprang to the edge of the boat. He would have plunged in, but, being unable to swim, would only have endangered his own life, without being able to save his child.

"My child!" he exclaimed in anguish, — "who will save my child? A thousand — ten thousand dollars to any one who will save him!"

There chanced to be but few passengers on board at the time, and nearly all these were either in the cabins or standing forward. Among the few who saw the child fall was our hero.

Now Dick was an expert swimmer. It was an accomplishment which he had possessed for years, and he no sooner saw the boy fall than he resolved to rescue him. His determination was formed before he heard the liberal offer made by the boy's father. Indeed, I must do Dick the justice to say that, in the excitement of the moment, he did not hear it at all, nor would it have stimulated the alacrity with which he sprang to the rescue of the little boy.

Little Johnny had already risen once, and gone under for the second time, when our hero plunged in. He was obliged to strike out for the boy, and this took time. He reached him none too soon. Just as he was sinking for the third and last time, he caught him by the jacket. Dick was stout and strong, but Johnny clung to him so tightly, that it was with great difficulty he was able to sustain himself.

"Put your arms round my neck," said Dick.

The little boy mechanically obeyed, and clung with a grasp strengthened by his terror. In this position Dick could bear his weight better. But the ferry-boat was receding fast. It was quite impossible to reach it. The father, his face pale with terror and anguish, and his hands clasped in suspense, saw the brave boy's struggles, and prayed with agonizing fervor that he might be successful. But it is probable, for they were now midway of the river, that both Dick and the little boy whom he had bravely undertaken to rescue would have been drowned, had not a row-boat been fortunately near. The two men who were in it witnessed the accident, and hastened to the rescue of our hero.

"Keep up a little longer," they shouted, bending to their oars, "and we will save you."

Dick heard the shout, and it put fresh strength into him. He battled 15 manfully with the treacherous sea, his eyes fixed longingly upon the approaching boat.

"Hold on tight, little boy," he said. "There's a boat coming."

The little boy did not see the boat. His eyes were closed to shut out the fearful water, but he clung the closer to his young preserver. Six long, steady strokes, and the boat dashed along side. Strong hands seized Dick and his youthful burden, and drew them into the boat, both dripping with water.

"God be thanked!" exclaimed the father, as from the steamer he saw the child's rescue. "That brave boy shall be rewarded, if I sacrifice my whole fortune to compass it."

"You've had a pretty narrow escape, young chap," said one of the boatmen to Dick. "It was a pretty tough job you undertook."

"Yes," said Dick. "That's what I thought when I was in the water. If 20 it hadn't been for you, I don't know what would have 'come of us."

"Anyhow you're a plucky boy, or you wouldn't have dared to jump into the water after this little chap. It was a risky thing to do."

"I'm used to the water," said Dick, modestly. "I didn't stop to think of the danger, but I wasn't going to see that little fellow drown without tryin' to save him."

The boat at once headed for the ferry wharf on the Brooklyn side. The captain of the ferry-boat, seeing the rescue, did not think it necessary to stop his boat, but kept on his way. The whole occurrence took place in less time than I have occupied in telling it.

The father was waiting on the wharf to receive his little boy, with what feeling of gratitude and joy can be easily understood. With a burst of happy tears he clasped him to his arms. Dick was about to withdraw modestly, but the gentleman perceived the movement, and, putting down the child, came forward, and, clasping his hand, said with emotion, "My brave boy, I owe you a debt I can never repay. But for your timely service I should now be plunged into an anguish which I cannot think of without a shudder."

Our hero was ready enough to speak on most occasions, but always 25 felt awkward when he was praised.

"It wasn't any trouble," he said, modestly. "I can swim like a top."

"But not many boys would have risked their lives for a stranger," said the gentleman. "But," he added with a sudden thought, as his glance rested on Dick's dripping garments, "both you and my little boy will take cold in wet clothes. Fortunately I have a friend living close at hand, at whose house you will have an opportunity of taking off your clothes, and having them dried."

Dick protested that he never took cold; but Fosdick, who had now joined them, and who, it is needless to say, had been greatly alarmed at Dick's danger, joined in urging compliance with the gentleman's proposal, and in the end our hero had to yield. His new friend secured a hack, the driver of which agreed for extra recompense to receive the dripping boys into his carriage, and they were whirled rapidly to a pleasant house in a side street, where matters were quickly explained, and both boys were put to bed.

"I aint used to goin' to bed quite so early," thought Dick. "This is the queerest excursion I ever took."

Like most active boys Dick did not enjoy the prospect of spending half 30 a day in bed; but his confinement did not last as long as he anticipated.

In about an hour the door of his chamber was opened, and a servant appeared, bringing a new and handsome suit of clothes throughout.

"You are to put on these," said the servant to Dick; "but you needn't get up till you feel like it."

"Whose clothes are they?" asked Dick.

"They are yours."

"Mine! Where did they come from?" 35

"Mr. Rockwell sent out and bought them for you. They are the same size as your wet ones."

"Is he here now?"

"No. He bought another suit for the little boy, and has gone back to New York. Here's a note he asked me to give you."

Dick opened the paper, and read as follows, —

"Please accept this outfit of clothes as the first instalment of a debt 40 which I can never repay. I have asked to have your wet suit dried, when you can reclaim it. Will you oblige me by calling to-morrow at my counting room, No. —, Pearl Street.

"Your friend,
"James Rockwell."

When Dick was dressed in his new suit, he surveyed his figure with pardonable complacency. It was the best he had ever worn, and fitted him as well as if it had been made expressly for him.

"He's done the handsome thing," said Dick to himself; "but there wasn't no 'casion for his givin' me these clothes. My lucky stars are shinin' pretty bright now. Jumpin' into the water pays better than shinin' boots; but I don't think I'd like to try it more'n once a week."

About eleven o'clock the next morning Dick repaired to Mr. Rockwell's counting-room on Pearl Street. He found himself in front of a large and handsome warehouse. The counting-room was on the lower floor. Our hero entered, and found Mr. Rockwell sitting at a desk. No sooner did that gentleman see him than he arose, and, advancing, shook Dick by the hand in the most friendly manner.

"My young friend," he said, "you have done me so great a service that I wish to be of some service to you in return. Tell me about yourself, and what plans or wishes you have formed for the future."

Dick frankly related his past history, and told Mr. Rockwell of his desire to get into a store or counting-room, and of the failure of all his applications thus far. The merchant listened attentively to Dick's statement, and, when he had finished, placed a sheet of paper before him, and, handing him a pen, said, "Will you write your name on this piece of paper?"

Dick wrote, in a free, bold hand, the name Richard Hunter. He had very much improved his penmanship, as has already been mentioned, and now had no cause to be ashamed of it.

Mr. Rockwell surveyed it approvingly.

"How would you like to enter my counting-room as clerk, Richard?" he asked.

Dick was about to say "Bully," when he recollected himself, and answered, "Very much."

"I suppose you know something of arithmetic, do you not?"

"Yes, sir."

"Then you may consider yourself engaged at a salary of ten dollars a week. You may come next Monday morning."

"Ten dollars!" repeated Dick, thinking he must have misunderstood.

"Yes; will that be sufficient?"

"It's more than I can earn," said Dick, honestly.

"Perhaps it is at first," said Mr. Rockwell, smiling; "but I am willing to pay you that. I will besides advance you as fast as your progress will justify it."

Dick was so elated that he hardly restrained himself from some demonstration which would have astonished the merchant; but he exercised self-control, and only said, "I'll try to serve you so faithfully, sir, that you won't repent having taken me into your service."

"And I think you will succeed," said Mr. Rockwell, encouragingly. "I will not detain you any longer, for I have some important business to attend to. I shall expect to see you on Monday morning."

Dick left the counting-room, hardly knowing whether he stood on his head or his heels, so overjoyed was he at the sudden change in his fortunes. Ten dollars a week was to him a fortune, and three times as much as he had expected to obtain at first. Indeed he would have been glad, only the day before, to get a place at three dollars a week. He reflected that with the stock of clothes which he had now on hand, he could save up at least half of it, and even then live better than he had been accustomed to do; so that his little fund in the savings bank, instead of being diminished, would be steadily increasing. Then he was to be advanced if he deserved it. It was indeed a bright prospect for a boy who, only a year before, could neither read nor write, and depended for a night's lodging upon the chance hospitality of an alley-way or old wagon. Dick's great ambition to "grow up 'spectable" seemed likely to be accomplished after all.

"I wish Fosdick was as well off as I am," he thought generously. But 60 he determined to help his less fortunate friend, and assist him up the ladder as he advanced himself.

When Dick entered his room on Mott Street, he discovered that some one else had been there before him, and two articles of wearing apparel had disappeared.

"By gracious!" he exclaimed; "somebody's stole my Washington coat and Napoleon pants. Maybe it's an agent of Barnum's, who expects to make a fortun' by exhibitin' the valooable wardrobe of a gentleman of fashion."

Dick did not shed many tears over his loss, as, in his present circumstances, he never expected to have any further use for the well-worn garments. It may be stated that he afterwards saw them adorning the figure of Micky Maguire; but whether that estimable young man stole them himself, he never ascertained. As to the loss, Dick was rather pleased that it had occurred. It seemed to cut him off from the old vagabond life which he hoped never to resume. Henceforward he meant to press onward, and rise as high as possible.

Although it was yet only noon, Dick did not go out again with his brush. He felt that it was time to retire from business. He would leave his share of the public patronage to other boys less fortunate than himself. That evening Dick and Fosdick had a long conversation. Fosdick rejoiced heartily in his friend's success, and on his side had the pleasant news to communicate that his pay had been advanced to six dollars a week.

"I think we can afford to leave Mott Street now," he continued. 65 "This house isn't as neat as it might be, and I should like to live in a nicer quarter of the city."

"All right," said Dick. "We'll hunt up a new room tomorrow. I shall have plenty of time, having retired from business. I'll try to get my reg'lar customers to take Johnny Nolan in my place. That boy hasn't any enterprise. He needs somebody to look out for him."

"You might give him your box and brush, too, Dick."

"No," said Dick; "I'll give him some new ones, but mine I want to keep, to remind me of the hard times I've had, when I was an ignorant boot-black, and never expected to be anything better."

"When, in short, you were 'Ragged Dick.' You must drop that name, and think of yourself now as" —

"Richard Hunter, Esq.," said our hero, smiling.   70

"A young gentleman on the way to fame and fortune," added Fosdick.

ENGAGING THE TEXT

1. List the values, characteristics, and actions that help Ragged Dick succeed. How valuable do you consider these today? How important is virtue compared to good luck—in the story and in your own experience?

2. Skim the Alger selection to find as many mentions of money as you can. How frequent are they? What seem to be Alger's ideas about money, wealth, salaries, and other financial issues?

3. By the time we reach the end of this story, quite a few things have changed from the time Dick "was an ignorant boot-black, and never expected to be anything better" (para. 68). Working in small groups, list as many changes as you can. What seems to be Alger's attitude toward them?

4. Why is Alger careful to note that Dick does not hear Mr. Rockwell's offer of $10,000 to whoever would save Little Johnny? Is Dick being short-changed by getting a job and clothes but not a $10,000 reward?

EXPLORING CONNECTIONS

5. Look ahead to "Horatio Alger" by Harlon L. Dalton later in this chapter (p. 260). How does Dalton's analysis of the Alger myth change your understanding of this excerpt? What elements in this story might Dalton cite to support his claims?

6. Review "Looking for Work" by Gary Soto in Chaper One (p. 22). Compare and contrast Alger's ideas about work, money, and aspiration to those found in Soto's narrative.

EXTENDING THE CRITICAL CONTEXT

7. Dick considers himself a "young man of property" when he has $100 in the bank. Talk to classmates and see if you can reach any consensus about what it would take today to be a "young man or woman of property." Similarly, see if you can agree on what a good starting salary would be for a recent college graduate, or on what levels of wealth and income define the poor, the middle class, and the upper class in the United States today. Write a journal entry summarizing your conclusions and keep it for reference as you read the rest of this chapter.

8. If you did the first "Before Reading" assignment on page 245, compare and contrast the qualities that made the people on your list successful with the qualities Alger gives to Ragged Dick.

THE LESSON

TONI CADE BAMBARA

"The Lesson" looks at wealth through the eyes of a poor black girl whose education includes a field trip to one of the world's premier toy stores. The story speaks to serious social issues with a comic, energetic, and utterly engaging voice. Toni Cade Bambara (1939–1995) grew up in the Harlem and Bedford-Stuyvesant areas of New York City. Trained at Queens College and City College of New York in dance, drama, and literature, she is best known for her collections of stories, *Gorilla, My Love* (1972) and *The Seabirds Are Still Alive and Other Stories* (1977), and for her novels, *If Blessing Comes* (1987) and *The Salt Eaters* (1980), winner of the American Book Award. Her novel *Those Bones Are Not My Child*, edited by Toni Morrison, was published posthumously in 1999. "The Lesson" is taken from *Gorilla, My Love*.

BACK IN THE DAYS when everyone was old and stupid or young and foolish and me and Sugar were the only ones just right, this lady moved on our block with nappy hair and proper speech and no makeup. And quite naturally we laughed at her, laughed the way we did at the junk man who went about his business like he was some big-time president and his sorry-ass horse his secretary. And we kinda hated her too, hated the way we did the winos who cluttered up our parks and pissed on our handball walls and stank up our hallways and stairs so you couldn't halfway play hide-and-seek without a goddamn gas mask. Miss Moore was her name. The only woman on the block with no first name. And she was black as hell, cept for her feet, which were fish-white and spooky. And she was always planning these boring-ass things for us to do, us being my cousin, mostly, who lived on the block cause we all moved North the same time and to the same apartment then spread out gradual to breathe. And our parents would yank our heads into some kinda shape and crisp up our clothes so we'd be presentable for travel with Miss Moore, who always looked like she was going to church, though she never did. Which is just one of the things the grownups talked about when they talked behind her back like a dog. But when she came calling with some sachet[1] she'd sewed up or some ginger-bread she'd made or some book, why then they'd all be too embarrassed to turn her down and we'd get handed out all spruced up. She'd been to college and said it only right that she should take responsibility for the young ones' education, and she not even related by marriage or blood. So they'd go for it. Specially Aunt Gretchen. She was the main gofer in the family. You got some ole dumb shit foolishness you want

---

[1]*sachet:* A small bag filled with a sweet-smelling substance. Sachets are often placed in drawers to scent clothes.

somebody to go for, you send for Aunt Gretchen. She been screwed into the go-along for so long, it's a blood-deep natural thing with her. Which is how she got saddled with me and Sugar and Junior in the first place while our mothers were in a la-de-da apartment up the block having a good ole time.

So this one day Miss Moore rounds us all up at the mailbox and it's puredee hot and she's knockin herself out about arithmetic. And school suppose to let up in summer I heard, but she don't never let up. And the starch in my pinafore scratching the shit outta me and I'm really hating this nappy-head bitch and her goddamn college degree. I'd much rather go to the pool or to the show where it's cool. So me and Sugar leaning on the mailbox being surly, which is a Miss Moore word. And Flyboy checking out what everybody brought for lunch. And Fat Butt already wasting his peanut-butter-and-jelly sandwich like the pig he is. And Junebug punchin on Q.T.'s arm for potato chips. And Rosie Giraffe shifting from one hip to the other waiting for somebody to step on her foot or ask her if she from Georgia so she can kick ass, preferably Mercedes'. And Miss Moore asking us do we know what money is, like we a bunch of retards. I mean real money, she say, like it's only poker chips or monopoly papers we lay on the grocer. So right away I'm tired of this and say so. And would much rather snatch Sugar and go to the Sunset and terrorize the West Indian kids and take their hair ribbons and their money too. And Miss Moore files that remark away for next week's lesson on brotherhood, I can tell. And finally I say we oughta get to the subway cause it's cooler and besides we might meet some cute boys. Sugar done swiped her mama's lipstick, so we ready.

So we heading down the street and she's boring us silly about what things cost and what our parents make and how much goes for rent and how money ain't divided up right in this country. And then she gets to the part about we all poor and live in the slums, which I don't feature. And I'm ready to speak on that, but she steps out in the street and hails two cabs just like that. Then she hustles half the crew in with her and hands me a five-dollar bill and tells me to calculate 10 percent tip for the driver. And we're off. Me and Sugar and Junebug and Flyboy hangin out the window and hollering to everybody, putting lipstick on each other cause Flyboy a faggot anyway, and making farts with our sweaty armpits. But I'm mostly trying to figure how to spend this money. But they all fascinated with the meter ticking and Junebug starts laying bets as to how much it'll read when Flyboy can't hold his breath no more. Then Sugar lays bets as to how much it'll be when we get there. So I'm stuck. Don't nobody want to go for my plan, which is to jump out at the next light and run off to the first bar-b-que we can find. Then the driver tells us to get the hell out cause we are there already. And the meter reads eighty-five cents. And I'm stalling to figure out the tip and Sugar say give him a dime. And I decide he don't need it bad as I do, so later for him. But then he tries to take off with Junebug foot still in the door so we talk about his mama something ferocious. Then we check out that we on Fifth Avenue[2] and everybody dressed up in stockings. One lady in a fur coat, hot as it is. White folks crazy.

"This is the place," Miss Moore say, presenting it to us in the voice she uses at the museum. "Let's look in the windows before we go in."

"Can we steal?" Sugar asks very serious like she's getting the ground rules square away before she plays. "I beg your pardon," say Miss Moore, and we fall out. So she leads us around the windows of the toy store and me and Sugar screamin, "This is mine, that's mine, I gotta have that, that was made for me, I was born for that," till Big Butt drowns us out.

"Hey, I'm goin to buy that there."

"That there? You don't even know what it is, stupid."

"I do so," he say punchin on Rosie Giraffe. "It's a microscope."

"Whatcha gonna do with a microscope, fool?"

"Look at things."

"Like what, Ronald?" ask Miss Moore. And Big Butt ain't got the first notion. So here go Miss Moore gabbing about the thousands of bacteria in a drop of water and the somethinorother in a speck of blood and the million and one living things in the air around us is invisible to the naked eye. And what she say that for? Junebug go to town on that "naked" and we rolling. Then Miss Moore ask what it cost. So we all jam into the window smudgin it up and the price tag say $300. So then she ask how long'd take for Big Butt and Junebug to save up their allowances. "Too long," I say. "Yeh," adds Sugar, "outgrown it by that time." And Miss Moore say no, you never outgrow learning instruments. "Why, even medical students and interns and," blah, blah, blah. And we ready to choke Big Butt for bringing it up in the first damn place.

"This here costs four hundred eighty dollars," say Rosie Giraffe. So we pile up all over her to see what she pointin out. My eyes tell me it's a chunk of glass cracked with something heavy, and different-color inks dripped into the splits, then the whole thing put into a oven or something. But for $480 it don't make sense.

"That's a paperweight made of semi-precious stones fused together under tremendous pressure," she explains slowly, with her hands doing the mining and all the factory work.

"So what's a paperweight?" asks Rosie Giraffe.

"To weigh paper with, dumbbell," say Flyboy, the wise man from the East.

"Not exactly," say Miss Moore, which is what she say when you warm or way off too. "It's to weigh paper down so it won't scatter and make your desk untidy." So right away me and Sugar curtsy to each other and then to Mercedes who is more the tidy type.

"We don't keep paper on top of the desk in my class," say Junebug, figuring Miss Moore crazy or lyin one.

---

[2]*Fifth Avenue:* The street in New York most famous for its expensive stores.

"At home, then," she say. "Don't you have a calendar and a pencil case and a blotter and a letter-opener on your desk at home where you do your homework?" And she know damn well what our homes look like cause she nosys around in them every chance she gets.

"I don't even have a desk," say Junebug. "Do we?"

"No. And I don't get no homework neither," say Big Butt.   20

"And I don't even have a home," say Flyboy like he do at school to keep the white folks off his back and sorry for him. Send this poor kid to camp posters, is his speciality.

"I do," say Mercedes. "I have a box of stationery on my desk and a picture of my cat. My godmother bought the stationery and the desk. There's a big rose on each sheet and the envelopes smell like roses."

"Who want to know about your smelly-ass stationery," say Rosie Giraffe fore I can get my two cents in.

"It's important to have a work area all your own so that..."

"Will you look at this sailboat, please," say Flyboy, cuttin her off   25 and pointin to the thing like it was his. So once again we tumble all over each other to gaze at this magnificent thing in the toy store which is just big enough to maybe sail two kittens across the pond if you strap them to the posts tight. We all start reciting the price tag like we in assembly. "Handcrafted sailboat of fiberglass at one thousand one hundred ninety-five dollars."

"Unbelievable," I hear myself say and am really stunned. I read it again for myself just in case the group recitation put me in a trance. Same thing. For some reason this pisses me off. We look at Miss Moore and she lookin at us, waiting for I dunno what.

"Who'd pay all that when you can buy a sailboat set for a quarter at Pop's, a tube of glue for a dime, and a ball of string for eight cents? It must have a motor and a whole lot else besides," I say. "My sailboat cost me about fifty cents."

"But will it take water?" say Mercedes with her smart ass.

"Took mine to Alley Pond Park once," say Flyboy. "String broke. Lost it. Pity."

"Sailed mine in Central Park and it keeled over and sank. Had to   30 ask my father for another dollar."

"And you got the strap," laugh Big Butt. "The jerk didn't even have a string on it. My old man wailed on his behind."

Little Q.T. was staring hard at the sailboat and you could see he wanted it bad. But he too little and somebody'd just take it from him. So what the hell. "This boat for kids, Miss Moore?"

"Parents silly to buy something like that just to get all broke up," say Rosie Giraffe.

"That much money it should last forever," I figure.

"My father'd buy it for me if I wanted it."   35

"Your father, my ass," say Rosie Giraffe getting a chance to finally push Mercedes.

"Must be rich people shop here," say Q.T.

"You are a very bright boy," say Flyboy. "What was your first clue?" And he rap him on the head with the back of his knuckles, since Q.T. the only one he could get away with. Though Q.T. liable to come up behind you years later and get his licks in when you half expect it.

"What I want to know is," I says to Miss Moore though I never talk to her, I wouldn't give the bitch that satisfaction, "is how much a real boat costs? I figure a thousand'd get you a yacht any day."

"Why don't you check that out," she says, "and report back to the 40 group?" Which really pains my ass. If you gonna mess up a perfectly good swim day least you could do is have some answers. "Let's go in," she say like she got something up her sleeve. Only she don't lead the way. So me and Sugar turn the corner to where the entrance is, but when we get there I kinda hang back. Not that I'm scared, what's there to be afraid of, just a toy store. But I feel funny, shame. But what I got to be shamed about? Got as much right to go in as anybody. But somehow I can't seem to get hold on the door, so I step away for Sugar to lead. But she hangs back too. And I look at her and she looks at me and this is ridiculous. I mean, damn, I have never ever been shy about doing nothing or going nowhere. But then Mercedes steps up and then Rosie Giraffe and Big Butt crowd in behind and shove, and next thing we all stuffed into the doorway with only Mercedes squeezing past us, smoothing out her jumper and walking right down the aisle. Then the rest of us tumble in like a glued-together jigsaw done all wrong. And people lookin at us. And it's like the time me and Sugar crashed into the Catholic church on a dare. But once we got in there and everything so hushed and holy and the candles and the bowin and the handkerchiefs on all the drooping heads, I just couldn't go through with the plan. Which was for me to run up to the altar and do a tap dance while Sugar played the nose flute and messed around in the holy water. And Sugar kept givin me the elbow. Then later teased me so bad I tied her up in the shower and turned it on and locked her in. And she'd be there till this day if Aunt Gretchen hadn't finally figured I was lying about the boarder takin a shower.

Same thing in the store. We all walkin on tiptoe and hardly touchin the games and puzzles and things. And I watched Miss Moore who is steady watchin us like she waitin for a sign. Like Mama Drewery watches the sky and sniffs the air and takes note of just how much slant is in the bird formation. Then me and Sugar bump smack into each other, so busy gazing at the toys, 'specially the sailboat. But we don't laugh and go into our fat-lady bump-stomach routine. We just stare at that price tag. Then Sugar run a finger over the whole boat. And I'm jealous and want to hit her. Maybe not her, but I sure want to punch somebody in the mouth.

"Watcha bring us here for, Miss Moore?"

"You sound angry, Sylvia. Are you mad about something?" Give me one of them grins like she tellin a grown-up joke that never turns out to be funny. And she's lookin very closely at me like maybe she plannin to do my portrait from memory. I'm mad, but I won't give her that satisfaction. So I slouch around the store bein very bored and say, "Let's go."

Me and Sugar at the back of the train watchin' the tracks whizzin by large then small then gettin gobbled up in the dark. I'm thinkin about this tricky toy I saw in the store. A clown that somersaults on a bar then does chin-ups just cause you yank lightly at his leg. Cost $35. I could see me askin my mother for a $35 birthday clown. "You wanna who that costs what?" she'd say, cockin her head to the side to get a better view of the hole in my head. Thirty-five dollars could buy new bunk beds for Junior and Gretchen's boy. Thirty-five dollars and the whole household could go visit Granddaddy Nelson in the country. Thirty-five dollars would pay for the rent and the piano bill too. Who are these people that spend that much for performing clowns and $1,000 for toy sailboats? What kinda work they do and how they live and how come we ain't in on it? Where we are is who we are, Miss Moore always pointin out. But it don't necessarily have to be that way, she always adds then waits for somebody to say that poor people have to wake up and demand their share of the pie and don't none of us know what kind of pie she talkin about in the first damn place. But she ain't so smart cause I still got her four dollars from the taxi and she sure ain't gettin it. Messin up my day with this shit. Sugar nudges me in my pocket and winks.

Miss Moore lines us up in front of the mailbox where we started 45
from, seem like years ago, and I got a headache for thinkin so hard. And we lean all over each other so we can hold up under the draggy-ass lecture she always finishes us off with at the end before we thank her for borin us to tears. But she just looks at us like she readin tea leaves. Finally she say, "Well, what did you think of F.A.O. Schwarz?"[3]

Rosie Giraffe mumbles, "White folks crazy."

"I'd like to go in there again when I get my birthday money," says Mercedes, and we shove her out the pack so she has to lean on the mailbox by herself.

"I'd like a shower. Tiring day," say Flyboy.

Then Sugar surprises me by saying, "You know, Miss Moore, I don't think all of us here put together eat in a year what that sailboat costs." And Miss Moore lights up like somebody goosed her. "And?" she say, urging Sugar on. Only I'm standin on her foot so she don't continue.

"Imagine for a minute what kind of society it is in which some people 50
can spend on a toy what it would cost to feed a family of six or seven. What do you think?"

"I think," say Sugar pushing me off her feet like she never done before, cause I whip her ass in a minute, "that this is not much of a democracy if you ask me. Equal chance to pursue happiness means an equal crack at the dough, don't it?" Miss Moore is besides herself and I am disgusted with Sugar's treachery. So I stand on her foot one more time to see if she'll shove me. She shuts up, and Miss Moore looks at

---

[3]*F.A.O. Schwarz:* The name and the toy store are real. The store, in fact, has become a tourist attraction.

me, sorrowfully I'm thinkin. And somethin weird is going on, I can feel it in my chest.

"Anybody else learn anything today?" lookin dead at me. I walk away and Sugar has to run to catch up and don't even seem to notice when I shrug her arm off my shoulder.

"Well, we got four dollars anyway," she says.

"Uh hunh."

"We could go to Hascombs and get half a chocolate layer and then 55 go to the Sunset and still have plenty money for potato chips and ice-cream sodas."

"Uh hunh."

"Race you to Hascombs," she say.

We start down the block and she gets ahead which is O.K. by me cause I'm goin to the West End and then over to the Drive to think this day through. She can run if she want to and even run faster. But ain't nobody gonna beat me at nuthin.

LA CUCARACHA By Lalo Alcarez

ENGAGING THE TEXT

1. What lesson is Miss Moore trying to teach in this story? How well is it received by Mercedes, Sugar, and the narrator, Sylvia? Why does the narrator react differently from Sugar, and what is the meaning of her last line in the story, "But ain't nobody gonna beat me at nuthin"?

2. Why did Bambara write the story from Sylvia's point of view? How would the story change if told from Miss Moore's perspective? From Sugar's? How would it change if the setting were a contemporary American city?

3. The story mentions several expensive items: a fur coat, a microscope, a paperweight, a sailboat, and a toy clown. Why do you think the author chose each of these details? If the story were set in the present instead of circa 1970, what items might serve the same purposes?

4. In paragraph 44 Sylvia says, "Where we are is who we are, Miss Moore always pointin out. But it don't necessarily have to be that way." What does Miss Moore mean by this? Do you agree? What does Miss Moore expect the children to do to change the situation?

EXPLORING CONNECTIONS

5. Both Sylvia and Ragged Dick (p. 246) can be seen as trying to find their place in the world of money and social status. Compare their situations and their attitudes about class and upward mobility. How do Bambara's ideas about money and opportunity differ from Alger's?

6. "The Lesson" describes education outside of the schoolroom. How might John Taylor Gatto (p. 141) or Jean Anyon (p. 163) assess the effectiveness of Miss Moore's teaching? Do you think Miss Moore's lessons directly challenge the children's classroom learning? Explain.

7. Compare Sylvia and Sugar's relationship here with that of Teresa and the speaker of the poem in "Para Teresa" (p. 198). Which girls stand the better chance of achieving success? Why?

EXTENDING THE CRITICAL CONTEXT

8. For the next class meeting, browse the Web or magazines, newspapers, and catalogs to find the most overpriced, unnecessary item you can. Spend a few minutes swapping examples, then discuss the information you've gathered: Are there any lessons to be learned here about wealth, success, and status?

9. The opening lines of "The Lesson" suggest that Sylvia is now a mature woman looking back on her youth. Working in groups, write a brief biography explaining what has happened to Sylvia since the day of "The Lesson." What has she done? Who has she become? Read your profiles aloud to the class and explain your vision of Sylvia's development.

HORATIO ALGER

HARLON L. DALTON

The first reading in this chapter dramatized the American Dream coming true in an uncomplicated if rather contrived way: the ambitious young Ragged Dick determines to improve himself, works hard, seizes his opportunity, and quickly makes his way to "fame and fortune." The essay below by Harlon L. Dalton repudiates that myth, calling it not only false, but worse — "socially destructive." Using Alger as his prime example, Dalton systematically explains how the rags-to-riches myth can conceal important social realities like race and class. Harlon L. Dalton is Emeritus Professor at Yale Law School; his areas of special expertise include critical race theory and the relationship of law to theology and psychology. He has served on the board of directors for the American Civil Liberties Union and was a member of the National Commission on AIDS. "Horatio Alger" is taken from his book *Racial Healing: Confronting the Fear Between Blacks and Whites* (1995).

AH, HORATIO ALGER, whose name more than any other is associated with the classic American hero. A writer of mediocre fiction, Alger had a formula for commercial success that was simple and straightforward: his lead characters, young boys born into poverty, invariably managed to transcend their station in life by dint of hard work, persistence, initiative, and daring.[1] Nice story line. There is just one problem—it is a myth. Not just in the sense that it is fictional, but more fundamentally because the lesson Alger conveys is a false one. To be sure, many myths are perfectly benign, and more than a few are salutary, but on balance Alger's myth is socially destructive.

The Horatio Alger myth conveys three basic messages: (1) each of us is judged solely on her or his own merits; (2) we each have a fair opportunity to develop those merits; and (3) ultimately, merit will out. Each of them is, to be charitable, problematic. The first message is a variant on the rugged individualism ethos....In this form, it suggests that success in life has nothing to do with pedigree, race, class background, gender, national origin, sexual orientation—in short, with anything beyond our individual control. Those variables may exist, but they play no appreciable role in how our actions are appraised.

This simply flies in the face of reality. There are doubtless circumstances—the hiring of a letter carrier in a large metropolitan post office, for example—where none of this may matter, but that is the exception rather than the rule. Black folk certainly know what it is like to be favored, disfavored, scrutinized, and ignored all on the basis of our race. Sometimes we are judged on a different scale altogether. Stephen Carter has written movingly about what he calls "the best black syndrome," the tendency of White folk to judge successful Black people only in relation to each other rather than against all comers. Thus, when Carter earned the second-highest score in his high school on the National Merit Scholarship qualifying test, he was readily recognized as "the best Black" around, but somehow not seen as one of the best students, period.[2]

Although I would like to think that things are much different now, I know better. Not long ago a student sought my advice regarding how to deal with the fact that a liberal colleague of mine (and of Stephen Carter's) had written a judicial clerkship recommendation for her in which he described her as the best Black student to have ever taken his class. Apparently the letter caused a mild stir among current law clerks in several courthouses, one of whom saw fit to inform the student.

[1] Edwin P. Hoyt, *Horatio's Boys: The Life and Works of Horatio Alger, Jr.* (Radnor, Penn.: Chilton Book Company, 1974). [All notes are Dalton's.]
[2] Stephen L. Carter, *Reflections of an Affirmative Action Baby* (New York: Basic Books, 1991), 47–49.

"What was the professor [whom she declined to name] thinking of?" she wondered aloud. "What does his comment mean? What is a judge supposed to make of it? 'If for some reason you think you have to hire one of them, then she's the way to go'? I could understand if he said I was one of the top ten students or even the top thousand, but what does the 'best Black' mean?"

Black folk also know what it is like to be underestimated because 5 of the color of their skin. For example, those of us who communicate in standard English are often praised unduly for how well we speak. This is, I might add, an experience all too familiar to Asian-Americans, including those born and bred in the U.S.A. And we know what it is like to be feared, pitied, admired, and scorned on account of our race, before we even have a chance to say boo! We, in turn, view White people through the prism of our own race-based expectations. I honestly am surprised every time I see a White man who can play basketball above the rim, just as Puerto Ricans and Cubans tend to be surprised to discover "Americans" who salsa truly well. All of which is to say that the notion that every individual is judged solely on personal merit, without regard for sociological wrapping, is mythical at best.

The second message conveyed by Horatio Alger is that we all have a shot at reaching our true potential. To be fair, neither Alger nor the myth he underwrote suggests that we start out equal. Nor does the myth necessarily require that we be given an equal opportunity to succeed. Rather, Alger's point is that each of us has the power to create our own opportunities. That turns out to be a difficult proposition to completely disprove, for no matter what evidence is offered up to show that a particular group of people have not fared well, it can always be argued that they did not try hard enough, or that they spent too much time wallowing in their predicament and not enough figuring out how to rise above it. Besides, there are always up-by-the-bootstraps examples to point to, like Colin Powell, whose name has so frequently been linked with that of Horatio Alger's that he must think they are related.[3] Nevertheless, it is by now generally agreed that there is a large category of Americans — some have called it the underclass — for whom upward mobility is practically impossible without massive changes in the structure of the economy and in the allocation of public resources.

As for the notion that merit will out, it assumes not only a commitment to merit-based decision making but also the existence of standards

[3]Sandy Grady, "Will He or Won't He?: Win or Lose, Presidential Pursuit by Colin Powell Would Do America a Necessary Service," *Kansas City Star,* 24 April 1995; Thomas B. Edsall, "For Powell, Timing Could be Crucial: As Gulf War Hero Hints at 1996 Bid, Associates Look into Details," *Washington Post,* 6 April 1995; J. F. O. McAllister, "The Candidate of Dreams," *Time,* 13 March 1995; Deroy Murdock, "Colin Powell: Many Things to Many People," *Washington Times,* 16 January 1995; Doug Fischer, "U.S. Politics: War Hero Well-Placed to Become First Black President," *Ottawa Citizen,* 8 October 1994; "General Nice Guy: Profile Colin Powell," *Sunday Telegraph,* 25 September 1994; Otto Kreisher, "As a Civilian, Powell's Options Are Enviable," *San Diego Union-Tribune,* 26 September 1993.

THE BOONDOCKS   by AARON MCGRUDER

for measuring merit that do not unfairly favor one individual over another. Such standards, of course, must come from somewhere. They must be decided upon by somebody. And that somebody is rarely without a point of view. Ask a devotee of West Coast basketball what skills you should look for in recruiting talent and near the top of his list will be the ability to "get out on the break," to "be creative in the open court," and "to finish the play." On the other hand, ask someone who prefers East Coast basketball and her list will rank highly the ability "to d-up [play defense]," "to board [rebound]," and "to maintain focus and intensity."

Or, to take another example, what makes a great Supreme Court justice? Brains to spare? Common sense? Proper judicial temperament? Political savvy? Extensive lawyering experience? A well-developed ability to abstract? Vision? Well-honed rhetorical skills? A reverence for our rich legal heritage? The capacity to adapt to changing times? Even if one is tempted to say "all of the above," how should these (or any other set of characteristics) be ranked? Measured? Evaluated?

The answers depend in part on whom you ask. Practicing lawyers, for example, are probably likely to rank extensive lawyering experience more highly than, say, brains. They are also likely to pay close attention to judicial temperament, which for them means whether the prospective justice would be inclined to treat them with respect during a court appearance. Sitting judges are also likely to rank judicial temperament highly, meaning whether the prospective justice would be a good colleague. In choosing among the other characteristics, they might each favor the ones that they happen to possess in abundance. Politicians might well see more merit in political savvy than would, say, academics, who could be expected to favor brains, the ability to abstract, and perhaps rhetorical skills.

All of these relevant actors might be honestly trying to come up with appropriate standards for measuring merit, but they would arrive at markedly different results. And any given result would screen out people who would succeed under another, equally plausible set of standards. Thus, if there is a genuine commitment to merit-based decision making it is possible that merit will out, but only for those who have the right kind of merit.

10

Which brings us to the prior question: is merit all we care about in deciding who gets what share of life's goodies? Clearly not. Does anyone, for example, honestly believe that any Supreme Court justice in recent memory was nominated solely on the basis of merit (however defined)? Any President? Any member of Congress? Does anyone believe that America's health-care resources are distributed solely on merit? That tax breaks are distributed solely on merit? That baseball club owners are selected solely on merit?

As I suggested earlier, the mere fact that a myth is based on false premises or conveys a false image of the world does not necessarily make it undesirable. Indeed, I place great stock in the idea that some illusions are, or at least can be, positive. As social psychologist Shelley Taylor has observed, "[normal] people who are confronted with the normal rebuffs of everyday life seem to construe their experience [so] as to develop and maintain an exaggeratedly positive view of their own attributes, an unrealistic optimism about the future, and a distorted faith in their ability to control what goes on around them."[4] Taylor's research suggests that, up to a point, such self-aggrandizement actually improves one's chances of worldly success.[5]

This may well explain the deep appeal of the Horatio Alger myth. True or not, it can help to pull people in the direction they want to go. After all, in order to succeed in life, especially when the odds are stacked against you, it is often necessary to first convince yourself that there is a reason to get up in the morning. So what is my beef? Where is the harm?

In a nutshell, my objection to the Alger myth is that it serves to maintain the racial pecking order. It does so by mentally bypassing the role of race in American society. And it does so by fostering beliefs that themselves serve to trivialize, if not erase, the social meaning of race. The Alger myth encourages people to blink at the many barriers to racial equality (historical, structural, and institutional) that litter the social landscape. Yes, slavery was built on the notion that Africans were property and not persons; yes, even after that "peculiar institution" collapsed, it continued to shape the life prospects of those who previously were enslaved; yes, the enforced illiteracy and cultural disruption of slavery, together with the collapse of Reconstruction, virtually assured that the vast majority of "freedmen" and "freedwomen" would not be successfully integrated into society; yes, Jim Crow laws, segregation, and a separate and unequal social reality severely undermined the prospects for Black achievement; yes, these and other features of our national life created a racial caste system that persists to this day; yes, the short-lived civil rights era of the 1950s and 1960s was undone by a broad and sustained White backlash; yes, the majority of Black people in America are mired in poverty; yes, economic mobility is not what it

---

[4]Shelley E. Taylor, *Positive Illusions: Creative Self-Deception and the Healthy Mind* (New York: Basic Books, 1989), xi.
[5]Ibid., xi, 7, 228–46.

used to be, given the decline in our manufacturing and industrial base; yes, the siting of the illicit drug industry in our inner cities has had pernicious effects on Black and Latino neighborhoods; yes, yes, yes, BUT (drumroll) "all it takes to make it in America is initiative, hard work, persistence, and pluck." After all, just look at Colin Powell!

There is a fundamental tension between the promise of opportunity enshrined in the Alger myth and the realities of a racial caste system. The main point of such a system is to promote and maintain inequality. The main point of the Alger myth is to proclaim that everyone can rise above her station in life. Despite this tension, it is possible for the myth to coexist with social reality. To quote Shelley Taylor once again:

> [T]he normal human mind is oriented toward mental health and...at every turn it construes events in a manner that promotes benign fictions about the self, the world, and the future. The mind is, with some significant exceptions, intrinsically adaptive, oriented toward overcoming rather than succumbing to the adverse events of life....At one level, it constructs beneficent interpretations of threatening events that raise self-esteem and promote motivation; yet at another level, it recognizes the threat or challenge that is posed by these events.[6]

Not surprisingly, then, there are lots of Black folk who subscribe to the Alger myth and at the same time understand it to be deeply false. They live with the dissonance between myth and reality because both are helpful and healthful in dealing with "the adverse events of life." Many Whites, however, have a strong interest in resolving the dissonance in favor of the myth. Far from needing to be on guard against racial "threat[s] or challenge[s]," they would just as soon put the ugliness of racism out of mind. For them, the Horatio Alger myth provides them the opportunity to do just that.[7]

Quite apart from the general way in which the myth works to submerge the social realities of race, each of the messages it projects is also incompatible with the idea of race-based advantage or disadvantage. If, as the myth suggests, we are judged solely on our individual merits, then caste has little practical meaning. If we all can acquire the tools needed to reach our full potential, then how important can the disadvantage of race be? If merit will eventually carry the day, then shouldn't we be directing our energies toward encouraging Black initiative and follow-through rather than worrying about questions of power and privilege?

By interring the myth of Horatio Alger, or at least forcing it to coexist with social reality, we can accomplish two important goals. First, we can give the lie to the idea that Black people can simply lift themselves up by their own bootstraps. With that pesky idea out of the way, it is easier to see why White folk need to take joint ownership of the nation's race

[6]Ibid., xi.

[7] Robert T. Carter, et al., "White Racial Identity Development and Work Values," *Journal of Vocational Behavior, Special Issue: Racial Identity and Vocational Behavior* 44, no. 2 (April 1994): 185–97.

problem. Second, the realization that hard work and individual merit, while certainly critical, are not guarantors of success should lead at least some White people to reflect on whether their own achievements have been helped along by their preferred social position.

Finally, quite apart from race, it is in our national interest to give the Horatio Alger myth a rest, for it broadcasts a fourth message no less false than the first three—that we live in a land of unlimited potential. Although that belief may have served us well in the past, we live today in an era of diminished possibilities. We need to make a series of hard choices, followed by yet more hard choices regarding how to live with the promise of less. Confronting that reality is made that much harder by a mythology that assures us we can have it all.

ENGAGING THE TEXT

1. The first message communicated by the Alger myth, according to Dalton, is that "each of us is judged solely on her or his own merits" (para. 2). What does this message mean to Dalton, and why does he object to it? How does he make his case against it, and what kind of evidence does he provide? Explain why you agree or disagree with his claim that this first message "simply flies in the face of reality" (para. 3).

2. Dalton says it is "generally agreed," but do *you* agree that "there is a large category of Americans...for whom upward mobility is practically impossible" (para. 6)? Why or why not?

3. How persuasive do you find Dalton's claims that American society is far from operating as a strictly merit-based system?

4. Why does Dalton believe that the Alger myth is destructive? Do you think the power of the American Dream to inspire or motivate people is outweighed by the negative effects Dalton cites, or vice versa? Write a journal entry explaining your position.

EXPLORING CONNECTIONS

5. Test Dalton's claims against the actual excerpt from Horatio Alger's *Ragged Dick* beginning on page 246. For example, does the novel seem to match the formula Dalton summarizes in his first paragraph? Similarly, can you find any examples of the three messages Dalton identifies in his second paragraph? On balance, does the excerpt from Alger seem to promote ideas that you consider socially destructive? Why or why not?

6. How do you think Dalton would assess the chances for success of Sylvia and her friends in "The Lesson" (p. 253)? Explain why you think he would praise or critique Miss Moore's attempts to educate the children about social class and money.

7. What ideas and attitudes about success are expressed in the cartoon by Aaron McGruder on page 263? How do they compare with those of Ragged

Dick (p. 246) and the children in "The Lesson" (p. 253)? How might Harlon Dalton explain the humor of the cartoon?

EXTENDING THE CRITICAL CONTEXT

8. Pick several contemporary cultural icons such as Barack Obama, Oprah Winfrey, Sonia Sotomayor, Alex Rodriguez, Venus Williams, Yo-Yo Ma, LeBron James, Salma Hayek, Jay-Z (Shawn Corey Carter), J. Lo (Jennifer Lopez), Jet Li (Li Lian-jie), Beyoncé Knowles-Carter, and Henry Louis Gates Jr. Conduct a minipoll about what their success means to race relations in the United States. Do the responses you get support Dalton's contention that such figures encourage people "to blink at the many barriers to racial equality" (para. 14)?

9. Dalton argues that the Alger myth should be "interred." Supposing for the moment that you agree, how could that be accomplished? How is a cultural myth challenged, revised, or robbed of its mythic power?

SERVING IN FLORIDA

BARBARA EHRENREICH

What's it like to live on minimum wage? As a journalist preparing to write about working-class life, Barbara Ehrenreich decided to take a series of unglamorous jobs—waitressing, housecleaning, retail sales—and to live on the meager wages these jobs paid. In this narrative, Ehrenreich describes trying to make ends meet by adding a second waitressing job (at "Jerry's") to her eight-hour shift at "The Hearthside," having discovered that $2.43 an hour plus tips doesn't add up as fast as her rent and other bills. The full account of Ehrenreich's "plunge into poverty" may be found in the *New York Times* bestseller *Nickel and Dimed: On (Not) Getting By in America* (2001). Ehrenreich has published articles in many of America's leading magazines and newspapers and has authored more than a dozen books. Recent works include *Dancing in the Streets: A History of Collective Joy* (2006), *This Land Is Their Land: Reports from a Divided Nation* (2008), and *Bright-Sided: How Positive Thinking Is Undermining America* (2009).

PICTURE A FAT PERSON'S HELL, and I don't mean a place with no food. Instead there is everything you might eat if eating had no bodily consequences—the cheese fries, the chicken-fried steaks, the fudge-laden desserts—only here every bite must be paid for, one way or another, in human discomfort. The kitchen is a cavern, a stomach leading to the lower intestine that is the garbage and dishwashing area, from which issue bizarre smells combining the edible and the offal: creamy carrion, pizza barf, and that unique and enigmatic Jerry's[1] scent, citrus fart. The floor is slick with spills, forcing us to walk through the kitchen with tiny steps, like Susan McDougal in leg irons.[2] Sinks everywhere are clogged with scraps of lettuce, decomposing lemon wedges, water-logged toast crusts. Put your hand down on any counter and you risk being stuck to it by the film of ancient syrup spills, and this is unfortunate because hands are utensils here, used for scooping up lettuce onto the salad plates, lifting out pie slices, and even moving hash browns from one plate to another. The regulation poster in the single unisex rest room admonishes us to wash our hands thoroughly, and even offers instructions for doing so, but there is always some vital substance missing—soap, paper towels, toilet paper—and I never found all three at once. You learn to stuff your pockets with napkins before going in there, and too bad about the customers, who must eat, although they don't realize it, almost literally out of our hands.

The break room summarizes the whole situation: there is none, because there are no breaks at Jerry's. For six to eight hours in a row, you never sit except to pee. Actually, there are three folding chairs at a table immediately adjacent to the bathroom, but hardly anyone ever sits in this, the very rectum of the gastroarchitectural system. Rather, the function of the peri-toilet area is to house the ashtrays in which servers and dishwashers leave their cigarettes burning at all times, like votive candles, so they don't have to waste time lighting up again when they dash back here for a puff. Almost everyone smokes as if their pulmonary well-being depended on it—the multinational mélange of cooks; the dishwashers, who are all Czechs here; the servers, who are American natives—creating an atmosphere in which oxygen is only an occasional pollutant. My first morning at Jerry's, when the hypoglycemic shakes set in, I complain to one of my fellow servers that I don't understand how she can go so long without food. "Well, I don't understand how *you* can go so long without a cigarette," she responds in a tone of reproach. Because work is what you do for others; smoking is what you do for yourself. I don't know why the antismoking crusaders have never grasped the element of defiant self-nurturance that makes the habit so endearing to its victims—as if, in the American workplace, the only thing people have to call their own is the tumors they are nourishing and the spare moments they devote to feeding them.

Now, the Industrial Revolution is not an easy transition, especially, in my experience, when you have to zip through it in just a couple of days. I have gone from craft work straight into the factory, from the

---

[1]*Jerry's:* Not the real name of the restaurant where Ehrenreich worked; the restaurant was part of a "well-known national chain." [All notes are the editors', except 8, 11, and 12.]

[2]*Susan McDougal in leg irons:* McDougal refused to testify against President Bill Clinton and Hillary Clinton before the Whitewater grand jury in 1996; she spent almost twenty-two months in various prisons and eventually received a presidential pardon in 2001.

air-conditioned morgue of the Hearthside[3] directly into the flames. Customers arrive in human waves, sometimes disgorged fifty at a time from their tour buses, puckish and whiny. Instead of two "girls" on the floor at once, there can be as many as six of us running around in our brilliant pink-and-orange Hawaiian shirts. Conversations, either with customers or with fellow employees, seldom last more than twenty seconds at a time. On my first day, in fact, I am hurt by my sister servers' coldness. My mentor for the day is a supremely competent, emotionally uninflected twenty-three-year-old, and the others, who gossip a little among themselves about the real reason someone is out sick today and the size of the bail bond someone else has had to pay, ignore me completely. On my second day, I find out why. "Well, it's good to see *you* again," one of them says in greeting. "Hardly anyone comes back after the first day." I feel powerfully vindicated—a survivor—but it would take a long time, probably months, before I could hope to be accepted into this sorority.

I start out with the beautiful, heroic idea of handling the two jobs at once, and for two days I almost do it: working the breakfast/lunch shift at Jerry's from 8:00 till 2:00, arriving at the Hearthside a few minutes late, at 2:10, and attempting to hold out until 10:00. In the few minutes I have between jobs, I pick up a spicy chicken sandwich at the Wendy's drive-through window, gobble it down in the car, and change from khaki slacks to black, from Hawaiian to rust-colored polo. There is a problem, though. When, during the 3:00–4:00 o'clock dead time, I finally sit down to wrap silver, my flesh seems to bond to the seat. I try to refuel with a purloined cup of clam chowder, as I've seen Gail and Joan do dozens of times, but Stu[4] catches me and hisses "No *eating!*" although there's not a customer around to be offended by the sight of food making contact with a server's lips. So I tell Gail I'm going to quit, and she hugs me and says she might just follow me to Jerry's herself.

But the chances of this are minuscule. She has left the flophouse and her annoying roommate and is back to living in her truck. But, guess what, she reports to me excitedly later that evening, Phillip has given her permission to park overnight in the hotel parking lot, as long as she keeps out of sight, and the parking lot should be totally safe since it's patrolled by a hotel security guard! With the Hearthside offering benefits like that, how could anyone think of leaving? This must be Phillip's theory, anyway. He accepts my resignation with a shrug, his main concern being that I return my two polo shirts and aprons.

Gail would have triumphed at Jerry's, I'm sure, but for me it's a crash course in exhaustion management. Years ago, the kindly fry cook who trained me to waitress at a Los Angeles truck stop used to say: Never make an unnecessary trip; if you don't have to walk fast, walk

---

[3]*Hearthside:* The other restaurant where Ehrenreich worked.

[4]*Gail, Joan, Stu:* Waitress, hostess, and assistant manager at the Hearthside restaurant. Phillip, mentioned in the subsequent paragraph, is the top manager.

slow; if you don't have to walk, stand. But at Jerry's the effort of distinguishing necessary from unnecessary and urgent from whenever would itself be too much of an energy drain. The only thing to do is to treat each shift as a one-time-only emergency: you've got fifty starving people out there, lying scattered on the battlefield, so get out there and feed them! Forget that you will have to do this again tomorrow, forget that you will have to be alert enough to dodge the drunks on the drive home tonight—just burn, burn, burn! Ideally, at some point you enter what servers call a "rhythm" and psychologists term a "flow state," where signals pass from the sense organs directly to the muscles, bypassing the cerebral cortex, and a Zen-like emptiness sets in. I'm on a 2:00–10:00 p.m. shift now, and a male server from the morning shift tells me about the time he "pulled a triple"—three shifts in a row, all the way around the clock—and then got off and had a drink and met this girl, and maybe he shouldn't tell me this, but they had sex right then and there and it was like *beautiful.*

But there's another capacity of the neuromuscular system, which is pain. I start tossing back drugstore-brand ibuprofens as if they were vitamin C, four before each shift, because an old mouse-related repetitive-stress injury in my upper back has come back to full-spasm strength, thanks to the tray carrying. In my ordinary life, this level of disability might justify a day of ice packs and stretching. Here I comfort myself with the Aleve commercial where the cute blue-collar guy asks: If you quit after working four hours, what would your boss say? And the not-so-cute blue-collar guy, who's lugging a metal beam on his back, answers: He'd fire me, that's what. But fortunately, the commercial tells us, we workers can exert the same kind of authority over our painkillers that our bosses exert over us. If Tylenol doesn't want to work for more than four hours, you just fire its ass and switch to Aleve.

True, I take occasional breaks from this life, going home now and then to catch up on e-mail and for conjugal visits (though I am careful to "pay" for everything I eat here, at $5 for a dinner, which I put in a jar), seeing *The Truman Show*[5] with friends and letting them buy my ticket. And I still have those what-am-I-doing-here moments at work, when I get so homesick for the printed word that I obsessively reread the six-page menu. But as the days go by, my old life is beginning to look exceedingly strange. The e-mails and phone messages addressed to my former self come from a distant race of people with exotic concerns and far too much time on their hands. The neighborly market I used to cruise for produce now looks forbiddingly like a Manhattan yuppie emporium. And when I sit down one morning in my real home to pay bills from my past life, I am dazzled by the two- and three-figure sums owed to outfits like Club Body Tech and Amazon.com.

---

[5]*The Truman Show:* 1998 film (directed by Peter Weir and starring Jim Carrey) about a man who discovers his whole life is actually a TV show.

Management at Jerry's is generally calmer and more "professional" than at the Hearthside, with two exceptions. One is Joy, a plump, blowsy woman in her early thirties who once kindly devoted several minutes of her time to instructing me in the correct one-handed method of tray carrying but whose moods change disconcertingly from shift to shift and even within one. The other is B.J., aka B.J. the Bitch, whose contribution is to stand by the kitchen counter and yell, "Nita, your order's up, move it!" or "Barbara, didn't you see you've got another table out there? Come *on*, girl!" Among other things, she is hated for having replaced the whipped cream squirt cans with big plastic whipped-cream-filled baggies that have to be squeezed with both hands—because, reportedly, she saw or thought she saw employees trying to inhale the propellant gas from the squirt cans, in the hope that it might be nitrous oxide. On my third night, she pulls me aside abruptly and brings her face so close that it looks like she's planning to butt me with her forehead. But instead of saying "You're fired," she says, "You're doing fine." The only trouble is I'm spending time chatting with customers: "That's how they're getting you." Furthermore I am letting them "run me," which means harassment by sequential demands: you bring the catsup and they decide they want extra Thousand Island; you bring that and they announce they now need a side of fries, and so on into distraction. Finally she tells me not to take her wrong. She tries to say things in a nice way, but "you get into a mode, you know, because everything has to move so fast."[6]

I mumble thanks for the advice, feeling like I've just been stripped   10 naked by the crazed enforcer of some ancient sumptuary law:[7] No chatting for *you*, girl. No fancy service ethic allowed for the serfs. Chatting with customers is for the good-looking young college-educated servers in the downtown carpaccio and ceviche joints, the kids who can make $70–$100 a night. What had I been thinking? My job is to move orders from tables to kitchen and then trays from kitchen to tables. Customers are in fact the major obstacle to the smooth transformation of information into food and food into money—they are, in short, the enemy. And the painful thing is that I'm beginning to see it this way myself. There are the traditional asshole types—frat boys who down multiple Buds and then make a fuss because the steaks are so emaciated and the fries so sparse—as well as the variously impaired—due to age, diabetes, or literacy issues—who require patient nutritional counseling. The worst, for some reason, are the Visible Christians—like the ten-person table, all jolly and sanctified after Sunday night service, who run

[6]In *Workers in a Lean World: Unions in the International Economy* (Verso, 1997), Kim Moody cites studies finding an increase in stress-related workplace injuries and illness between the mid-1980s and the early 1990s. He argues that rising stress levels reflect a new system of "management by stress" in which workers in a variety of industries are being squeezed to extract maximum productivity, to the detriment of their health. [Ehrenreich's note.]

[7]*sumptuary laws:* Laws which regulate personal behavior on moral or religious grounds.

me mercilessly and then leave me $1 on a $92 bill. Or the guy with the crucifixion T-shirt (someone to look up to) who complains that his baked potato is too hard and his iced tea too icy (I cheerfully fix both) and leaves no tip at all. As a general rule, people wearing crosses or WWJD? ("What Would Jesus Do?") buttons look at us disapprovingly no matter what we do, as if they were confusing waitressing with Mary Magdalene's original profession.

I make friends, over time, with the other "girls" who work my shift: Nita, the tattooed twenty-something who taunts us by going around saying brightly, "Have we started making money yet?" Ellen, whose teenage son cooks on the graveyard shift and who once managed a restaurant in Massachusetts but won't try out for management here because she prefers being a "common worker" and not "ordering people around." Easygoing fiftyish Lucy, with the raucous laugh, who limps toward the end of the shift because of something that has gone wrong with her leg, the exact nature of which cannot be determined without health insurance. We talk about the usual girl things—men, children, and the sinister allure of Jerry's chocolate peanut-butter cream pie—though no one, I notice, ever brings up anything potentially expensive, like shopping or movies. As at the Hearthside, the only recreation ever referred to is partying, which requires little more than some beer, a joint, and a few close friends. Still, no one is homeless, or cops to it anyway, thanks usually to a working husband or boyfriend. All in all, we form a reliable mutual-support group: if one of us is feeling sick or overwhelmed, another one will "bev" a table or even carry trays for her. If one of us is off sneaking a cigarette or a pee, the others will do their best to conceal her absence from the enforcers of corporate rationality.[8]

But my saving human connection—my oxytocin receptor, as it were—is George, the nineteen-year-old Czech dishwasher who has been in this country exactly one week. We get talking when he asks me, tortuously, how much cigarettes cost at Jerry's. I do my best to explain that they cost over a dollar more here than at a regular store and suggest that he just take one from the half-filled packs that are always lying around on the break table. But that would be unthinkable. Except for the one tiny earring signaling his allegiance to some vaguely alternative point of view, George is a perfect straight arrow—crew-cut, hardworking, and hungry for eye contact. "Czech Republic," I ask, "or

[8]Until April 1998, there was no federally mandated right to bathroom breaks. According to Marc Linder and Ingrid Nygaard, authors of *Void Where Prohibited: Rest Breaks and the Right to Urinate on Company Time* (Cornell University Press, 1997), "The right to rest and void at work is not high on the list of social or political causes supported by professional or executive employees, who enjoy personal workplace liberties that millions of factory workers can only dream about.... While we were dismayed to discover that workers lacked an acknowledged right to void at work, [the workers] were amazed by outsiders' naïve belief that their employers would permit them to perform this basic bodily function when necessary.... A factory worker, not allowed a break for six-hour stretches, voided into pads worn inside her uniform; and a kindergarten teacher in a school without aides had to take all twenty children with her to the bathroom and line them up outside the stall door while she voided." [Ehrenreich's note.]

Slovakia?" and he seems delighted that I know the difference. "Vaclav Havel," I try, "Velvet Revolution, Frank Zappa?" "Yes, yes, 1989," he says, and I realize that for him this is already history.

My project is to teach George English. "How are you today, George?" I say at the start of each shift. "I am good, and how are you today, Barbara?" I learn that he is not paid by Jerry's but by the "agent" who shipped him over—$5 an hour, with the agent getting the dollar or so difference between that and what Jerry's pays dishwashers. I learn also that he shares an apartment with a crowd of other Czech "dishers," as he calls them, and that he cannot sleep until one of them goes off for his shift, leaving a vacant bed. We are having one of our ESL sessions late one afternoon when B.J. catches us at it and orders "Joseph" to take up the rubber mats on the floor near the dishwashing sinks and mop underneath. "I thought your name was George," I say loud enough for B.J. to hear as she strides off back to the counter. Is she embarrassed? Maybe a little, because she greets me back at the counter with "George, Joseph—there are so many of them!" I say nothing, neither nodding nor smiling, and for this I am punished later, when I think I am ready to go and she announces that I need to roll fifty more sets of silverware, and isn't it time I mixed up a fresh four-gallon batch of blue-cheese dressing? May you grow old in this place, B.J., is the curse I beam out at her when I am finally permitted to leave. May the syrup spills glue your feet to the floor.

I make the decision to move closer to Key West. First, because of the drive. Second and third, also because of the drive: gas is eating up $4–$5 a day, and although Jerry's is as high-volume as you can get, the tips average only 10 percent, and not just for a newbie like me. Between the base pay of $2.15 an hour and the obligation to share tips with the busboys and dishwashers, we're averaging only about $7.50 an hour. Then there is the $30 I had to spend on the regulation tan slacks worn by Jerry's servers—a setback it could take weeks to absorb. (I had combed the town's two downscale department stores hoping for something cheaper but decided in the end that these marked-down Dockers, originally $49, were more likely to survive a daily washing.) Of my fellow servers, everyone who lacks a working husband or boyfriend seems to have a second job: Nita does something at a computer eight hours a day; another welds. Without the forty-five-minute commute, I can picture myself working two jobs and still having the time to shower between them.

So I take the $500 deposit I have coming from my landlord, the $400   15
I have earned toward the next month's rent, plus the $200 reserved for emergencies, and use the $1,100 to pay the rent and deposit on trailer number 46 in the Overseas Trailer Park, a mile from the cluster of budget hotels that constitute Key West's version of an industrial park. Number 46 is about eight feet in width and shaped like a barbell inside, with a narrow region—because of the sink and the stove—separating the bedroom from what might optimistically be called the "living" area, with its two-person table and half-sized couch. The bathroom is so small my knees rub against the shower stall when I sit on the toilet, and you can't just leap out of the bed, you have to climb down to the foot of it in order to find a patch of floor space to stand on. Outside, I am within a few yards of a liquor store, a bar that advertises "free beer tomorrow," a convenience store, and a Burger King—but no supermarket or, alas, Laundromat. By reputation, the Overseas park is a nest of crime and crack, and I am hoping at least for some vibrant multicultural street life. But desolation rules night and day, except for a thin stream of pedestrians heading for their jobs at the Sheraton or the 7-Eleven. There are not exactly people here but what amounts to canned labor, being preserved between shifts from the heat.

In line with my reduced living conditions, a new form of ugliness arises at Jerry's. First we are confronted—via an announcement on the computers through which we input orders—with the new rule that the hotel bar, the Driftwood, is henceforth off-limits to restaurant employees. The culprit, I learn through the grapevine, is the ultraefficient twenty-three-year-old who trained me—another trailer home dweller and a mother of three. Something had set her off one morning, so she slipped out for a nip and returned to the floor impaired. The restriction mostly hurts Ellen, whose habit it is to free her hair from its rubber band and drop by the Driftwood for a couple of Zins[9] before heading home at the end of her shift, but all of us feel the chill. Then the next day, when I go for straws, I find the dry-storage room locked. It's never been locked before; we go in and out of it all day—for napkins, jelly containers, Styrofoam cups for takeout. Vic, the portly assistant manager

---

[9]*Zins:* Glasses of zinfandel wine.

who opens it for me, explains that he caught one of the dishwashers attempting to steal something and, unfortunately, the miscreant will be with us until a replacement can be found—hence the locked door. I neglect to ask what he had been trying to steal but Vic tells me who he is—the kid with the buzz cut and the earring, you know, he's back there right now.

I wish I could say I rushed back and confronted George to get his side of the story. I wish I could say I stood up to Vic and insisted that George be given a translator and allowed to defend himself or announced that I'd find a lawyer who'd handle the case pro bono.[10] At the very least I should have testified as to the kid's honesty. The mystery to me is that there's not much worth stealing in the dry-storage room, at least not in any fenceable quantity: "Is Gyorgi here, and am having 200—maybe 250—catsup packets. What do you say?" My guess is that he had taken—if he had taken anything at all—some Saltines or a can of cherry pie mix and that the motive for taking it was hunger.

So why didn't I intervene? Certainly not because I was held back by the kind of moral paralysis that can mask as journalistic objectivity. On the contrary, something new—something loathsome and servile—had infected me, along with the kitchen odors that I could still sniff on my bra when I finally undressed at night. In real life I am moderately brave, but plenty of brave people shed their courage in POW camps, and maybe something similar goes on in the infinitely more congenial milieu of the low-wage American workplace. Maybe, in a month or two more at Jerry's, I might have regained my crusading spirit. Then again, in a month or two I might have turned into a different person altogether—say, the kind of person who would have turned George in.

But this is not something I was slated to find out. When my month-long plunge into poverty was almost over, I finally landed my dream job—housekeeping. I did this by walking into the personnel office of the only place I figured I might have some credibility, the hotel attached to Jerry's, and confiding urgently that I had to have a second job if I was to pay my rent and, no, it couldn't be front-desk clerk. "All *right*," the personnel lady fairly spits, "so it's *housekeeping*," and marches me back to meet Millie, the housekeeping manager, a tiny, frenetic Hispanic woman who greets me as "babe" and hands me a pamphlet emphasizing the need for a positive attitude. The pay is $6.10 an hour and the hours are nine in the morning till "whenever," which I am hoping can be defined as a little before two. I don't have to ask about health insurance once I meet Carlotta, the middle-aged African American woman who will be training me. Carlie, as she tells me to call her, is missing all of her top front teeth.

On that first day of housekeeping and last day—although I don't 20 yet know it's the last—of my life as a low-wage worker in Key West,

---

[10]*pro bono:* Free of charge.

Carlie is in a foul mood. We have been given nineteen rooms to clean, most of them "checkouts," as opposed to "stay-overs," and requiring the whole enchilada of bed stripping, vacuuming, and bathroom scrubbing. When one of the rooms that had been listed as a stay-over turns out to be a checkout, she calls Millie to complain, but of course to no avail. "So make up the motherfucker," she orders me, and I do the beds while she sloshes around the bathroom. For four hours without a break I strip and remake beds, taking about four and a half minutes per queen-sized bed, which I could get down to three if there were any reason to. We try to avoid vacuuming by picking up the larger specks by hand, but often there is nothing to do but drag the monstrous vacuum cleaner—it weighs about thirty pounds—off our cart and try to wrestle it around the floor. Sometimes Carlie hands me the squirt bottle of "Bam" (an acronym for something that begins, ominously, with "butyric"—the rest of it has been worn off the label) and lets me do the bathrooms. No service ethic challenges me here to new heights of performance. I just concentrate on removing the pubic hairs from the bathtubs, or at least the dark ones that I can see.

I had looked forward to the breaking-and-entering aspect of cleaning the stay-overs, the chance to examine the secret physical existence of strangers. But the contents of the rooms are always banal and surprisingly neat—zipped-up shaving kits, shoes lined up against the wall (there are no closets), flyers for snorkeling trips, maybe an empty wine bottle or two. It is the TV that keeps us going, from Jerry to Sally to *Hawaii Five-O* and then on to the soaps. If there's something especially arresting, like "Won't Take No for an Answer" on Jerry, we sit down on the edge of a bed and giggle for a moment, as if this were a pajama party instead of a terminally dead-end job. The soaps are the best, and Carlie turns the volume up full blast so she won't miss anything from the bathroom or while the vacuum is on. In Room 503, Marcia confronts Jeff about Lauren. In 505, Lauren taunts poor cheated-on Marcia. In 511, Helen offers Amanda $10,000 to stop seeing Eric, prompting Carlie to emerge from the bathroom to study Amanda's troubled face. "You take it, girl," she advises. "I would for sure."

The tourists' rooms that we clean and, beyond them, the far more expensively appointed interiors in the soaps begin after a while to merge. We have entered a better world—a world of comfort where every day is a day off, waiting to be filled with sexual intrigue. We are only gate-crashers in this fantasy, however, forced to pay for our presence with backaches and perpetual thirst. The mirrors, and there are far too many of them in hotel rooms, contain the kind of person you would normally find pushing a shopping cart down a city street—bedraggled, dressed in a damp hotel polo shirt two sizes too large, and with sweat dribbling down her chin like drool. I am enormously relieved when Carlie announces a half-hour meal break, but my appetite fades when I see that the bag of hot dog rolls she has been carrying around on our cart is not trash salvaged from a checkout but what she has brought for her lunch.

Between the TV and the fact that I'm in no position, as a first dayer, to launch new topics of conversation, I don't learn much about Carlie except that she hurts, and in more than one way. She moves slowly about her work, muttering something about joint pain, and this is probably going to doom her, since the young immigrant housekeepers— Polish and Salvadoran—like to polish off their rooms by two in the afternoon, while she drags the work out till six. It doesn't make any sense to hurry, she observes, when you're being paid by the hour. Already, management has brought in a woman to do what sounds like time-motion studies and there's talk about switching to paying by the room.[11] She broods, too, about all the little evidences of disrespect that come her way, and not only from management. "They don't care about us," she tells me of the hotel guests; in fact, they don't notice us at all unless something gets stolen from a room—"then they're all over you." We're eating our lunch side by side in the break room when a white guy in a maintenance uniform walks by and Carlie calls out, "Hey you," in a friendly way, "what's your name?"

"Peter Pan," he says, his back already to us.

"That wasn't funny," Carlie says, turning to me. "That was no kind of answer. Why did he have to be funny like that?" I venture that he has an attitude, and she nods as if that were an acute diagnosis. "Yeah, he got a attitude all right."

"Maybe he's having a bad day," I elaborate, not because I feel any obligation to defend the white race but because her face is so twisted with hurt.

When I request permission to leave at about 3:30, another housekeeper warns me that no one has so far succeeded in combining housekeeping with serving at Jerry's: "Some kid did it once for five days, and you're no kid." With that helpful information in mind, I rush back to number 46, down four Advils (the name brand this time), shower, stooping to fit into the stall, and attempt to compose myself for the oncoming shift. So much for what Marx termed the "reproduction of labor power," meaning the things a worker has to do just so she'll be ready to labor again. The only unforeseen obstacle to the smooth transition from job to job is that my tan Jerry's slacks, which had looked reasonably clean by 40-watt bulb last night when I hand washed my Hawaiian shirt, prove by daylight to be mottled with catsup and ranch-dressing stains. I spend most of my hour-long break between jobs attempting to remove the edible portions of the slacks with a sponge and then drying them over the hood of my car in the sun.

I can do this two-job thing, is my theory, if I can drink enough caffeine and avoid getting distracted by George's ever more obvious

[11]A few weeks after I left, I heard ads on the radio for housekeeping jobs at this hotel at the amazing rate of "up to $9 an hour." When I inquired, I found out that the hotel had indeed started paying by the room, and I suspect that Carlie, if she lasted, was still making the equivalent of $6 an hour or quite a bit less. [Ehrenreich's note]

suffering.[12] The first few days after the alleged theft, he seemed not to understand the trouble he was in, and our chirpy little conversations had continued. But the last couple of shifts he's been listless and un-shaven, and tonight he looks like the ghost we all know him to be, with dark half-moons hanging from his eyes. At one point, when I am briefly immobilized by the task of filling little paper cups with sour cream for baked potatoes, he comes over and looks as if he'd like to explore the limits of our shared vocabulary, but I am called to the floor for a table. I resolve to give him all my tips that night, and to hell with the experi-ment in low-wage money management. At eight, Ellen and I grab a snack together standing at the mephitic end of the kitchen counter, but I can only manage two or three mozzarella sticks, and lunch had been a mere handful of McNuggets. I am not tired at all, I assure myself, though it may be that there is simply no more "I" left to do the tiredness monitoring. What I would see if I were more alert to the situation is that the forces of destruction are already massing against me. There is only one cook on duty, a young man named Jesus ("Hay-Sue," that is), and he is new to the job. And there is Joy, who shows up to take over in the middle of the shift dressed in high heels and a long, clingy white dress and fuming as if she'd just been stood up in some cocktail bar.

Then it comes, the perfect storm. Four of my tables fill up at once. Four tables is nothing for me now, but only so long as they are oblig-ingly staggered. As I bev table 27, tables 25, 28, and 24 are watching enviously. As I bev 25, 24 glowers because their bevs haven't even been ordered. Twenty-eight is four yuppyish types, meaning every-thing on the side and agonizing instructions as to the chicken Caesars. Twenty-five is a middle-aged black couple who complain, with some justice, that the iced tea isn't fresh and the tabletop is sticky. But table 24 is the meteorological event of the century: ten British tourists who seem to have made the decision to absorb the American experience entirely by mouth. Here everyone has at least two drinks—iced tea *and* milk shake, Michelob *and* water (with lemon slice in the water, please)—and a huge, promiscuous orgy of breakfast specials, mozz sticks, chicken strips, quesadillas, burgers with cheese and without, sides of hash browns with cheddar, with onions, with gravy, seasoned fries, plain fries, banana splits. Poor Jesus! Poor me! Because when I arrive with their first tray of food—after three prior trips just to refill bevs—Princess Di refuses to eat her chicken strips with her pancake and sausage special since, as she now reveals, the strips were meant to be an appetizer. Maybe the others would have accepted their meals, but Di, who is deep into her third Michelob, insists that everything else

[12]In 1996 the number of persons holding two or more jobs averaged 7.8 million, or 6.2 percent of the workforce. It was about the same rate for men and for women (6.1 versus 6.2). About two-thirds of multiple jobholders work one job full-time and the other part-time. Only a heroic minority—4 percent of men and 2 percent of women—work two full-time jobs simultaneously (John F. Stinson Jr., "New Data on Multiple Jobholding Available from the CPS," *Monthly Labor Review*, March 1997). [Ehrenreich's note]

go back while they work on their starters. Meanwhile, the yuppies are waving me down for more decaf and the black couple looks ready to summon the NAACP.

Much of what happens next is lost in the fog of war. Jesus starts going under. The little printer in front of him is spewing out orders faster than he can rip them off, much less produce the meals. A menacing restlessness rises from the tables, all of which are full. Even the invincible Ellen is ashen from stress. I take table 24 their reheated main courses, which they immediately reject as either too cold or fossilized by the microwave. When I return to the kitchen with their trays (three trays in three trips) Joy confronts me with arms akimbo: "What *is* this?" She means the food—the plates of rejected pancakes, hash browns in assorted flavors, toasts, burgers, sausages, eggs. "Uh, scrambled with cheddar," I try, "and that's—" "*No*," she screams in my face, "is it a traditional, a super-scramble, an eye-opener?" I pretend to study my check for a clue, but entropy has been up to its tricks, not only on the plates but in my head, and I have to admit that the original order is beyond reconstruction. "You don't know an eye-opener from a traditional?" she demands in outrage. All I know, in fact, is that my legs have lost interest in the current venture and have announced their intention to fold. I am saved by a yuppie (mercifully not one of mine) who chooses this moment to charge into the kitchen to bellow that his food is twenty-five minutes late. Joy screams at him to get the hell out of her kitchen, *please*, and then turns on Jesus in a fury, hurling an empty tray across the room for emphasis.

I leave. I don't walk out, I just leave. I don't finish my side work or pick up my credit card tips, if any, at the cash register or, of course, ask Joy's permission to go. And the surprising thing is that you *can* walk out without permission, that the door opens, that the thick tropical night air parts to let me pass, that my car is still parked where I left it. There is no vindication in this exit, no fuck-you surge of relief, just an overwhelming dank sense of failure pressing down on me and the entire parking lot. I had gone into this venture in the spirit of science, to test a mathematical proposition, but somewhere along the line, in the tunnel vision imposed by long shifts and relentless concentration, it became a test of myself, and clearly I have failed. Not only had I flamed out as a housekeeper/server, I had forgotten to give George my tips, and, for reasons perhaps best known to hardworking, generous people like Gail and Ellen, this hurts. I don't cry, but I am in a position to realize, for the first time in many years, that the tear ducts are still there and still capable of doing their job.

When I moved out of the trailer park, I gave the key to number 46 to Gail and arranged for my deposit to be transferred to her. She told me that Joan was still living in her van and that Stu had been fired from the Hearthside. According to the most up-to-date rumors, the drug he ordered from the restaurant was crack and he was caught dipping into the cash register to pay for it. I never found out what happened to George.

ENGAGING THE TEXT

1. What's the point of Ehrenreich's experiment? What do you think she was hoping to learn by stepping down the economic ladder, and what can you learn as her reader? Explain why you find her approach more or less effective than one that provides economic data and analysis.

2. Throughout this selection Ehrenreich seeks not merely to narrate facts but to elicit emotional responses from her readers. Explain how you react to one or more of the passages listed below and identify specific details in the text that help shape your responses:

   the opening description of Jerry's (paras. 1–2)

   the description of customers (para. 10)

   George's story (paras. 12–13, 16–18)

   the description of trailer number 46 (para. 15)

   the footnotes throughout the narrative

3. Ehrenreich ordinarily lives much more comfortably than she did as a waitress, and of course she had an escape hatch from her experiment — she would not serve food or clean rooms forever and could have gone back to her usual life if necessary at any time. Explain the effect her status as a "tourist" in working-class culture has on you as a reader.

4. Write a journal entry about your worst job. How did your experience of being "nickeled and dimed" compare with Ehrenreich's? What was the worst aspect of this work experience for you? What, if anything, did you learn from this job — about work, about success, and about yourself?

EXPLORING CONNECTIONS

5. What, if anything, do you think Gail, Ellen, and George could do to substantially improve their material and economic well-being? What are the greatest barriers they face? What advice might Horatio Alger (p. 246) give them, and how do you think it would be received?

6. Using Gail, Ellen, or George as a rough model for your central character, write a detailed plot summary for a novel that would be the anti-*Ragged Dick*, a story in which someone pursues the American Dream and fails. How plausible is your story line compared to the one Horatio Alger created for Ragged Dick (p. 246)?

7. Look ahead to "Making It in America" by Adam Davidson (p. 333). How does Maddie Parlier's work compare to Ehrenreich's? Why do you think Maddie seems relatively happy with her job while Ehrenreich seems miserable?

EXTENDING THE CRITICAL CONTEXT

8. Ehrenreich made $6.10 per hour as a housekeeper. Working in groups, sketch out a monthly budget based on this salary for (a) an individual, (b) a single parent with a preteen child, and (c) a family of four in which one adult is ill or has been laid off. Be sure to include money for basics like rent, utilities, food, clothing, transportation, and medical care.

9. Research the *least* promising job prospects in your community. Talk to potential employers and learn as much as you can about such issues as wages, working conditions, hours, drug screening, and healthcare, retirement, or other benefits.

10. Order a meal at whichever restaurant in your community is most like "Jerry's." Study the working conditions in the restaurant, paying special attention to the kinds of problems Ehrenreich faced on her shifts. Write up an informal journal entry from the imagined point of view of a server at the restaurant.

CLASS IN AMERICA — 2009

GREGORY MANTSIOS

Which of these gifts might a high school graduate in your family receive — a corsage, a $500 savings bond, or a BMW? The answer hints at your social class, a key factor in American lives that runs counter to the more comfortable notion that the U.S. is essentially a middle-class nation. The selection below makes it hard to deny class distinctions and their nearly universal influence on our lives. The essay juxtaposes myths and realities as Mantsios outlines four widely held beliefs about class in the United States and then systematically refutes them with statistical evidence. Even if you already recognize the importance of social class, some of the numbers the author cites are likely to surprise you. Mantsios is director of the Joseph S. Murphy Institute for Worker Education and Labor Studies at Queens College of the City University of New York; he is editor of *A New Labor Movement for the New Century* (1998). The essay reprinted below appeared in *Race, Class, and Gender in the United States: An Integrated Study*, edited by Paula S. Rothenberg (2010).

PEOPLE IN THE UNITED STATES don't like to talk about class. Or so it would seem. We don't speak about class privileges, or class oppression, or the class nature of society. These terms are not part of our everyday

The author wishes to thank Mark Major for his assistance in updating this article.
From Gregory Mantsios, *Class in America: Myths and Realities.* Copyright © Gregory Mantsios, 2006. Reprinted by permission of the author.

vocabulary, and in most circles they are associated with the language of the rhetorical fringe. Unlike people in most other parts of the world, we shrink from using words that classify along economic lines or that point to class distinctions: phrases like "working class," "upper class," and "ruling class" are rarely uttered by Americans.

For the most part, avoidance of class-laden vocabulary crosses class boundaries. There are few among the poor who speak of themselves as lower class; instead, they refer to their race, ethnic group, or geographic location. Workers are more likely to identify with their employer, industry, or occupational group than with other workers, or with the working class.[1]

Neither are those at the other end of the economic spectrum likely to use the word "class." In her study of thirty-eight wealthy and socially prominent women, Susan Ostrander asked participants if they considered themselves members of the upper class. One participant responded, "I hate to use the word 'class.' We are responsible, fortunate people, old families, the people who have something."

Another said, "I hate [the term] upper class. It is so non-upper class to use it. I just call it 'all of us,' those who are wellborn.[2]

It is not that Americans, rich or poor, aren't keenly aware of class   5 differences—those quoted above obviously are; it is that class is not in the domain of public discourse. Class is not discussed or debated in public because class identity has been stripped from popular culture. The institutions that shape mass culture and define the parameters of public debate have avoided class issues. In politics, in primary and secondary education, and in the mass media, formulating issues in terms of class is unacceptable, perhaps even un-American. See my paper, "Media Magic: Making Class Invisible," Selection 7 in Part VIII of this volume.

There are, however, two notable exceptions to this phenomenon. First, it is acceptable in the United States to talk about "the middle class." Interestingly enough, such references appear to be acceptable precisely because they mute class differences. References to the middle class by politicians, for example, are designed to encompass and attract the broadest possible constituency. Not only do references to the

[1]See Jay MacLead, *Ain't No Makin' It: Aspirations and Attainment in a Lower-Income Neighborhood* (Boulder, CO: Westview Press, 1995); Benjamin DeMott, *The Imperial Middle* (New York: Morrow, 1990); Ira Katznelson, *City Trenches: Urban Politics and Patterning of Class in the United States* (New York: Pantheon Books, 1981); Charles W. Tucker, "A Comparative Analysis of Subjective Social Class: 1945–1963," *Social Forces*, no. 46, June 1968, pp. 508-514; Robert Nisbet, "The Decline and Fall of Social Class," *Pacific Sociological Review*, vol. 2, Spring 1959, pp. 11–17; and Oscar Glantz, "Class Consciousness and Political Solidarity," *American Sociological Review*, vol. 23, August 1958, pp. 375–382. [All notes are Mantsios'.]

[2]Susan Ostander, "Upper-Class Women: Class Consciousness as Conduct and Meaning," in G. William Domhoff, *Power Structure Research* (Beverly Hills, CA: Sage Publications, 1980), pp. 78–79. Also see Stephen Birmingham, *America's Secret Aristocracy* (Boston: Little Brown, 1987).

middle class gloss over differences, but these references also avoid any suggestion of conflict or injustice.

This leads us to the second exception to the class-avoidance phenomenon. We are, on occasion, presented with glimpses of the upper class and the lower class (the language used is "the wealthy" and "the poor"). In the media, these presentations are designed to satisfy some real or imagined voyeuristic need of "the ordinary person." As curiosities, the ground-level view of street life and the inside look at the rich and the famous serve as unique models, one to avoid and one to aspire to. In either case, the two models are presented without causal relation to each other: one is not rich because the other is poor.

Similarly, when social commentators or liberal politicians draw attention to the plight of the poor, they do so in a manner that obscures the class structure and denies any sense of exploitation. Wealth and poverty are viewed as one of several natural and inevitable states of being: differences are only differences. One may even say differences are the American way, a reflection of American social diversity.

We are left with one of two possibilities: either talking about class and recognizing class distinctions are not relevant to U.S. society, or we mistakenly hold a set of beliefs that obscure the reality of class differences and their impact on people's lives.

Let us look at four common, albeit contradictory, beliefs about the United States. 10

Myth 1: The United States is fundamentally a classless society. Class distinctions are largely irrelevant today, and whatever differences do exist in economic standing, they are—for the most part—insignificant. Rich or poor, we are all equal in the eyes of the law, and such basic needs as health care and education are provided to all regardless of economic standing.

Myth 2: We are, essentially, a middle-class nation. Despite some variations in economic status, most Americans have achieved relative affluence in what is widely recognized as a consumer society.

Myth 3: We are all getting richer. The American public as a whole is steadily moving up the economic ladder, and each generation propels itself to greater economic well-being. Despite some fluctuations, the U.S. position in the global economy has brought previously unknown prosperity to most, if not all, Americans.

Myth 4: Everyone has an equal chance to succeed. Success in the United States requires no more than hard work, sacrifice, and perseverance: "In America, anyone can become a millionaire; it's just a matter of being in the right place at the right time."

In trying to assess the legitimacy of these beliefs, we want to ask 15 several important questions. Are there significant class differences among Americans? If these differences do exist, are they getting bigger or smaller, and do these differences have a significant impact on the way we live? Finally, does everyone in the United States really have an equal opportunity to succeed?

The Economic Spectrum

Let's begin by looking at difference. An examination of available data reveals that variations in economic well-being are, in fact, immense. Consider the following:

- The wealthiest 1 percent of the American population holds 34 percent of the total national wealth. That is, they own over one-third of all the consumer durables (such as houses, cars, and stereos) and financial assets (such as stocks, bonds, property, and savings accounts). The richest 20 percent of Americans hold nearly 85 percent of the total household wealth in the country.[3]

- Approximately 338,761 Americans, or approximately eight-tenths of 1 percent of the adult population, earn more than $1 million **annually**.[4] There are nearly 400 billionaires in the U.S today, more than three dozen of them worth more than $10 billion each. It would take the typical (median) American (earning $49,568 and spending absolutely nothing at all) a total of 20,174 years (or approximately 298 lifetimes) to earn just $1 billion.

Affluence and prosperity are clearly alive and well in certain segments of the U.S. population. However, this abundance is in contrast to the poverty and despair that is also prevalent in the United States. At the other end of the spectrum:

- Approximately 13 percent of the American population—that is, nearly one of every eight people in this country—live below the official poverty line (calculated in 2007 at $10,590 for an individual and $21,203 for a family of four).[5] An estimated 3.5 million people—of whom nearly 1.4 million are children—experience homelessness in any given year.[6]

The contrast between rich and poor is sharp, and with nearly one-third of the American population living at one extreme or the other, it

---

[3]Lawrence Mishel, Jared Bernstein, and Sylvia Allegretto, *State of Working America: 2006/2007* (Ithaca, NY: Cornell University Press, 2007), pp. 251, 253.

[4]The number of individuals filing tax returns showing a gross adjusted income of $1 million or more in 2006 was 355,204 (Tax Stats at a Glance, Internal Revenue Service, U.S. Treasury Department, available at http://www.irs.gov/taxstats/article/0„id= 102886,00.html).

[5]Carmen DeNavas-Walt, Bernadette D. Proctor, and Jessica C. Smith, U.S. Census Bureau, Current Population Reports, P60–235, *Income, Poverty, and Health Insurance Coverage in the United States: 2007* (Washington, DC: U.S. Government Printing Office, 2008), pp. 12–19, available at http://pubdb3.census.gov/macro/032008/pov/new01_100_01 .htm.

[6]National Coalition for the Homeless, "How Many People Experience Homelessness?" NCH Fact Sheet #2 (June 2008), available at http://www.nationalhomeless.org/publications /facts/How_Many.html. Also see National Coalition for the Homeless, "How Many People Experience Homelessness?" NCH Fact Sheet #2 (June 2006), citing a 2004 National Law Center on Homelessness and Poverty study, available at http://www.nationalhomeless.org /publications/facts/How_Many.pdf; U.S. Conference of Mayors, *Hunger and Homelessness Survey, 2008: A Survey Report on Homelessness and Hunger in American Cities* (Washington, DC: U.S. Conference of Mayors, 2008), pp. 13–23; Martha Burt, *What Will it Take to End Homelessness?* (Washington, DC: Urban Institute, September 2001); Martha Burt, "Chronic Homelessness: Emergence of a Public Policy," *Fordham Urban Law Journal, 30*, no. 3 (2003), pp. 1267–1279; and Kim Hopper, *Reckoning with Homelessness* (Ithaca, NY: Cornell University Press, 2002).

is difficult to argue that we live in a classless society. Big-payoff reality shows, celebrity salaries, and multi-million dollar lotteries notwithstanding, evidence suggests that the level of inequality in the United States is getting higher. Census data show the gap between the rich and the poor to be the widest since the government began collecting information in 1947[7] and that this gap is continuing to grow. In one year alone, from 2003 to 2004, the average after-tax income of the top 1 percent increased by 20 percent to $145,500 per year. This is the largest one-year increase going to the top 1 percent in fifteen years. On average the income of the bottom 80 percent increased only 2.7 percent.[8]

Nor is such a gap between rich and poor representative of the rest of the industrialized world. In fact, the United States has by far the most unequal distribution of household income.[9] The income gap between rich and poor in the United States (measured as the percentage of total income held by the wealthiest 10 percent of the population as compared to the poorest 10 percent) is approximately 5.4 to 1, the highest ratio in the industrialized world.[10]

Reality 1: There are enormous differences in the economic standing of American citizens. A sizable proportion of the U.S. population occupies opposite ends of the economic spectrum. In the middle range of the economic spectrum:

- Sixty percent of the American population holds less than 4 percent of the nation's wealth.[11]

- While the real income of the top 1 percent of U.S. families more than doubled (111 percent) between 1979 and 2003, the income of the middle fifth of the population grew only slightly (9 percent over that same 24-year period) and its share of income (15 percent of the total compared to 48 percent of the total for the wealthiest fifth) actually declined during this period.[12]

- Regressive changes in governmental tax policies and the weakening of labor unions over the last quarter century have led to a significant rise in the level of inequality between the rich and the middle class. Between 1979 and 2005, the gap in household income between the top fifth and middle fifth of the population rose by almost 40 percent.[13] From 1962 to 2004, the wealth held by most Americans (80 percent of the total population) increased from $40,000 to $82,000 (not adjusted for inflation). During that same period, the average wealth of the top 1 percent increased from $5.6 million to $14.8

[7]Mishel et al., op. cit., p. 253.

[8]Arloc Sherman and Aviva Aron-Dine, "New CBO Data Show Income Inequality Continues to Widen" (Washington, DC: Center on Budget and Policy Priorities, January 2007), p. 3.

[9]Based on a comparison of 19 industrialized states: Mishel et al., op. cit., pp. 344–349.

[10]Mishel et al., op. cit., p. 345.

[11]Derived from Mishel et al., p. 255, Table 5.3.

[12]Mishel et al., op. cit., p. 64.

[13]Ibid., p. 59.

million.[14] One prominent economist described economic growth in the United States as a "spectator sport for the majority of American families."[15] Economic decline, on the other hand, is much more "inclusive," with layoffs impacting hardest on middle- and lower-income families—those with fewer resources to fall back on.

The level of inequality is sometimes difficult to comprehend fully by looking at dollar figures and percentages. To help his students visualize the distribution of income, the well-known economist Paul Samuelson asked them to picture an income pyramid made of children's blocks, with each layer of blocks representing $1,000. If we were to construct Samuelson's pyramid today, the peak of the pyramid would be much higher than the Eiffel Tower, yet almost all of us would be within six feet of the ground.[16] In other words, the distribution of income is heavily skewed; a small minority of families take the lion's share of national income, and the remaining income is distributed among the vast majority of middle-income and low-income families. Keep in mind that Samuelson's pyramid represents the distribution of income, not wealth. The distribution of wealth is skewed even further.

Reality 2: The middle class in the United States holds a very small share of the nation's wealth and that share is declining steadily. The gap between rich and poor and between rich and the middle class is larger than it has ever been.

American Life-Styles

At last count, nearly 37 million Americans across the nation lived in unrelenting poverty.[17] Yet, as political scientist Michael Harrington once commented, "America has the best dressed poverty the world has ever known."[18] Clothing disguises much of the poverty in the United States, and this may explain, in part, its middle-class image. With increased mass marketing of "designer" clothing and with shifts in the nation's economy from blue-collar (and often better-paying) manufacturing jobs to white-collar and pink-collar jobs in the service sector, it is becoming increasingly difficult to distinguish class differences based on appearance.[19] The dress-down environment prevalent in the high-tech industry (what one author refers to as the "no-collars movement") has reduced superficial distinctions even further.[20]

Beneath the surface, there is another reality. Let's look at some "typical" and not-so-typical life-styles.

[14]Ibid., p. 255.

[15]Alan Blinder, quoted by Paul Krugman, in "Disparity and Despair," *U.S. News and World Report*, March 23, 1992, p. 54.

[16]Paul Samuelson, *Economics*, 10th ed. (New York: McGraw-Hill, 1976), p. 84.

[17]DeNavas-Walt et al., op. cit., p. 12.

[18]Michael Harrington, *The Other America* (New York: Macmillan, 1962), pp. 12–13.

[19]Stuart Ewen and Elizabeth Ewen, *Channels of Desire: Mass images and the Shaping of American Consciousness* (New York: McGraw-Hill, 1982).

[20]Andrew Ross, *No-Collar: The Humane Work Place and Its Hidden Costs* (New York: Basic Books, 2002).

American Profile

Name:	Harold S. Browning
Father:	manufacturer, industrialist
Mother:	prominent social figure in the community
Principal child-rearer:	governess
Primary education:	an exclusive private school on Manhattan's Upper East Side

Note: a small, well-respected primary school where teachers and administrators have a reputation for nurturing student creativity and for providing the finest educational preparation

Ambition: "to become President"

Supplemental tutoring:	tutors in French and mathematics
Summer camp:	sleep-away camp in northern Connecticut

Note: camp provides instruction in the creative arts, athletics, and the natural sciences

Secondary education: a prestigious preparatory school in Westchester County

Note: classmates included the sons of ambassadors, doctors, attorneys, television personalities, and well-known business leaders

Supplemental education: private SAT tutor

After-school activities: private riding lessons

Ambition: "to take over my father's business"

High-school graduation gift: BMW

Family activities: theater, recitals, museums, summer vacations in Europe, occasional winter trips to the Caribbean

Note: as members of and donors to the local art museum, the Brownings and their children attend private receptions and exhibit openings at the invitation of the museum director

Higher education:	an Ivy League liberal arts college in Massachusetts *Major:* economics and political science *After-class activities:* debating club, college newspaper, swim team *Ambition:* "to become a leader in business"
First full-time job (age 23):	assistant manager of operations, Browning Tool and Die, Inc. (family enterprise)
Subsequent employment:	*3 years*—executive assistant to the president, Browning Tool and Die *Responsibilities included:* purchasing (materials and equipment), personnel, and distribution networks *4 years*—advertising manager, Lackheed Manufacturing (home appliances) *3 years*—director of marketing and sales, Comerex, Inc. (business machines)
Present employment (age 38):	executive vice president, SmithBond and Co. (digital instruments) *Typical daily activities:* review financial reports and computer printouts, dictate memoranda, lunch with clients, initiate conference calls, meet with assistants, plan business trips, meet with associates *Transportation to and from work:* chauffeured company limousine *Annual salary:* $324,000 *Ambition:* "to become chief executive officer of the firm, or one like it, within the next five to ten years"
Present residence:	eighteenth-floor condominium on Manhattan's Upper West Side, eleven rooms, including five spacious bedrooms and terrace overlooking river *Interior:* professionally decorated and accented with elegant furnishings, valuable antiques, and expensive artwork *Note:* building management provides doorman and elevator attendant; family employs au pair for children and maid for other domestic chores

Second residence:	farm in northwestern Connecticut, used for weekend retreats and for horse breeding (investment/hobby)
	Note: to maintain the farm and cater to the family when they are there, the Brownings employ a part-time maid, groundskeeper, and horse breeder

Harold Browning was born into a world of nurses, maids, and governesses. His world today is one of airplanes and limousines, five-star restaurants, and luxurious living accommodations. The life and life-style of Harold Browning is in sharp contrast to that of Bob Farrell.

American Profile

Name:	Bob Farrell
Father:	machinist
Mother:	retail clerk
Principal child-rearer:	mother and sitter
Primary education:	a medium-size public school in Queens, New York, characterized by large class size, outmoded physical facilities, and an educational philosophy emphasizing basic skills and student discipline
	Ambition: "to become President"
Supplemental tutoring:	none
Summer camp:	YMCA day camp
	Note: emphasis on team sports, arts and crafts
Secondary education:	large regional high school in Queens
	Note: classmates included the sons and daughters of carpenters, postal clerks, teachers, nurses, shopkeepers, mechanics, bus drivers, police officers, salespersons
	Supplemental education: SAT prep course offered by national chain
	After-school activities: basketball and handball in school park
	Ambition: "to make it through college"
	High-school graduation gift: $500 savings bond

Family activities:	family gatherings around television set, softball, an occasional trip to the movie theater, summer Sundays at the public beach
Higher education:	a two-year community college with a technical orientation *Major:* electrical technology *After-school activities:* employed as a part-time bagger in local supermarket *Ambition:* "to become an electrical engineer"
First full-time job (age 19):	service-station attendant *Note:* continued to take college classes in the evening
Subsequent employment:	mail clerk at large insurance firm; manager trainee, large retail chain
Present employment (age 38):	assistant sales manager, building supply firm *Typical daily activities:* demonstrate products, write up product orders, handle customer complaints, check inventory *Transportation to and from work:* city subway
Annual salary:	$45,261 *Ambition:* "to open up my own business" *Additional income:* $6,100 in commissions from evening and weekend work as salesman in local men's clothing store
Present residence:	the Farrells own their own home in a working-class neighborhood in Queens, New York

Bob Farrell and Harold Browning live very differently: the life-style of one is privileged; that of the other is not so privileged. The differences are class differences, and these differences have a profound impact on the way they live. They are differences between playing a game of handball in the park and taking riding lessons at a private stable; watching a movie on television and going to the theater; and taking the subway to work and being driven in a limousine. More important, the difference in class determines where they live, who their friends are, how well they are educated, what they do for a living, and what they come to expect from life.

Yet, as dissimilar as their life-styles are, Harold Browning and Bob Farrell have some things in common; they live in the same city, they work long hours, and they are highly motivated. More important, they are both white males.

Let's look at someone else who works long and hard and is highly motivated. This person, however, is black and female.

American Profile	
Name:	Cheryl Mitchell
Father:	janitor
Mother:	waitress
Principal child-rearer:	grandmother
Primary education:	large public school in Ocean Hill-Brownsville, Brooklyn, New York *Note:* rote teaching of basic skills and emphasis on conveying the importance of good attendance, good manners, and good work habits; school patrolled by security guards *Ambition:* "to be a teacher"
Supplemental tutoring:	none
Summer camp:	none
Secondary education:	large public school in Ocean Hill-Brownsville *Note:* classmates included sons and daughters of hairdressers, groundskeepers, painters, dressmakers, dishwashers, domestics *Supplemental education:* none *After-school activities:* domestic chores, part-time employment as babysitter and housekeeper *Ambition:* "to be a social worker" *High-school graduation gift:* corsage
Family activities:	church-sponsored socials
Higher education:	one semester of local community college *Note:* dropped out of school for financial reasons
First full-time job (age 17):	counter clerk, local bakery
Subsequent employment:	file clerk with temporary-service agency, supermarket checker

Present employment (age 38):	nurse's aide at a municipal hospital *Typical daily activities:* make up hospital beds, clean out bedpans, weigh patients and assist them to the bathroom, take temperature readings, pass out and collect food trays, feed patients who need help, bathe patients, and change dressings *Annual salary:* $16,850 *Ambition:* "to get out of the ghetto"
Present residence:	three-room apartment in the South Bronx, needs painting, has poor ventilation, is in a high-crime area *Note:* Cheryl Mitchell lives with her four-year-old son and her elderly mother

When we look at the lives of Cheryl Mitchell, Bob Farrell, and Harold Browning, we see life-styles that are very different. We are not looking, however, at economic extremes. Cheryl Mitchell's income as a nurse's aide puts her above the government's official poverty line.[21] Below her on the income pyramid are 37 million poverty-stricken Americans. Far from being poor, Bob Farrell has an annual income as an assistant sales manager that puts him well above the median income level—that is, more than 50 percent of the U.S. population earns less money than Bob Farrell.[22] And while Harold Browning's income puts him in a high-income bracket, he stands only a fraction of the way up Samuelson's income pyramid. Well above him are the 338,761 individuals whose annual salary exceeds $1 million. Yet Harold Browning spends more money on his horses than Cheryl Mitchell earns in a year.

Reality 3: Even ignoring the extreme poles of the economic spectrum, we find enormous class differences in the life-styles among the haves, the have-nots, and the have-littles.

Class affects more than life-style and material well-being. It has a significant impact on our physical and mental well-being as well.

Researchers have found an inverse relationship between social class and health. Lower-class standing is correlated to higher rates of infant mortality, eye and ear disease, arthritis, physical disability, diabetes, nutritional deficiency, respiratory disease, mental illness, and

---

[21]Based on a poverty threshold for a three-person household in 2007 of $16,650. DeNavas-Walt et al., op. cit., p. 1.

[22]The median income in 2007 was $45,113 for men working full time, year round; $35,102 for women; and $50,233 for households. DeNavas-Walt et al., op. cit., p. 6.

heart disease.[23] In all areas of health, poor people do not share the same life chances as those in the social class above them. Furthermore, lower-class standing is correlated with a lower quality of treatment for illness and disease. The results of poor health and poor treatment are borne out in the life expectancy rates within each class. Researchers have found that the higher your class standing, the higher your life expectancy. Conversely, they have also found that within each age group, the lower one's class standing, the higher the death rate; in some age groups, the figures are as much as two and three times as high.[24]

Reality 4: From cradle to grave, class standing has a significant impact on our chances for survival.

The lower one's class standing, the more difficult it is to secure appropriate housing, the more time is spent on the routine tasks of everyday life, the greater is the percentage of income that goes to pay for food and other basic necessities, and the greater is the likelihood of crime victimization.[25] Class can accurately predict chances for both survival and success.

Class and Educational Attainment

School performance (grades and test scores) and educational attainment (level of schooling completed) also correlate strongly with economic class. Furthermore, despite some efforts to make testing fairer and schooling more accessible, current data suggest that the level of inequity is staying the same or getting worse.

In his study for the Carnegie Council on Children in 1978, Richard De Lone examined the test scores of over half a million students who

[23]U.S. Government Accountability Office, *Poverty in America: Economic Research Shows Adverse Impacts on Health Status and Other Social Conditions* (Washington, DC: U. S. Government Accountability Office, 2007), pp. 9–16. Also see E. Pamuk, D. Makuc, K. Heck, C. Reuben, and K. Lochner, *Socioeconomic Status and Health Chartbcok, Health, United States, 1998* (Hyattsville, MD: National Center for Health Statistics, 1998), pp. 145–159; Vincente Navarro, "Class, Race, and Health Care in the United States," in Bersh Berberoglu, *Critical Perspectives in Sociology*, 2nd ed. (Dubuque, IA: Kendall/Hunt, 1993), pp. 148–156; Melvin Krasner, *Poverty and Health in New York City* (New York: United Hospital Fund of New York, 1989); U.S. Department of Health and Human Services, *Health Status of Minorities and Low Income Groups, 1985*; and Dan Hughes, Kay Johnson, Sara Rosenbaum, Elizabeth Butler, and Janet Simons, *The Health of America's Children* (The Children's Defense Fund, 1988).

[24]E. Pamuk et al., op. cit.; Kenneth Neubeck and Davita Glassberg, *Sociology; A Critical Approach* (New York: McGraw-Hill, 1996), pp. 436–438; Aaron Antonovsky, "Social Class, Life Expectancy, and Overall Mortality," in *The Impact of Social Class* (New York: Thomas Crowell, 1972), pp. 467–491. See also Harriet Duleep, "Measuring the Effect of Income on Adult Mortality Using Longitudinal Administrative Record Data," *Journal of Human Resources*, vol. 21, no. 2, Spring 1986. See also Paul Farmer, *Pathologies of Power: Health, Human Rights, and the New War on the Poor* (Berkeley: University of California Press, 2005).

[25]E. Pamuk et al., op. cit., fig. 20; Dennis W. Roncek, "Dangerous Places: Crime and Residential Environment," *Social Forces*, vol. 60, no. 1, September 1981, pp. 74–96. Also see Steven D. Levitt, "The Changing Relationship between Income and Crime Victimization," *Economic Policy Review*, 5, No. 3, September 1999.

took the College Board exams (SATs). His findings were consistent with earlier studies that showed a relationship between class and scores on standardized tests; his conclusion: "the higher the student's social status, the higher the probability that he or she will get higher grades."[26] Today, more than thirty years after the release of the Carnegie report, College Board surveys reveal data that are no different: test scores still correlate strongly with family income.

Average Combined Scores by Income (400 to 1600 scale)[27]

FAMILY INCOME	MEDIAN SCORE
More than $100,000	1113
$80,000 to $100,000	1057
$70,000 to $80,000	1032
$60,000 to $70,000	1020
$50,000 to $60,000	1009
$40,000 to $50,000	994
$30,000 to $40,000	966
$20,000 to $30,000	936
$10,000 to $20,000	910
less than $10,000	886

These figures are based on the test results of 1,465,744 SAT takers in 2006.

In another study conducted thirty years ago, researcher William Sewell showed a positive correlation between class and overall educational achievement. In comparing the top quartile (25 percent) of his sample to the bottom quartile, he found that students from upper-class families were twice as likely to obtain training beyond high school and four times as likely to attain a postgraduate degree. Sewell concluded: "Socioeconomic background...operates independently of academic ability at every stage in the process of educational attainment."[28]

Today, the pattern persists. There are, however, two significant changes. On the one hand, the odds of getting into college have improved for the bottom quartile of the population, although they still remain relatively low compared to the top. On the other hand, the chances of completing a college degree have deteriorated markedly for the bottom quartile. Researchers estimate the chances of completing a

[26]Richard De Lone, *Small Futures* (New York: Harcourt Brace Jovanovich, 1978), pp. 14–19.
[27]Derived from Viji Sathy, Sandra Barbuti, and Krista Mattern, "The New SAT and Trends in Test Performance," *College Board*, 2006, pp. 18–20.
[28]William H. Sewell, "Inequality of Opportunity for Higher Education," *American Sociological Review*, vol. 36, no. 5, 1971, pp. 793–809.

four-year college degree (by age 24) to be nineteen times as great for the top 25 percent of the population as it is for the bottom 25 percent.[29]

Reality 5: Class standing has a significant impact on chances for educational achievement.

Class standing, and consequently life chances, are largely determined at birth. Although examples of individuals who have gone from rags to riches abound in the mass media, statistics on class mobility show these leaps to be extremely rare. In fact, dramatic advances in class standing are relatively infrequent. One study showed that fewer than one in five men surpass the economic status of their fathers.[30] For those whose annual income is in six figures, economic success is due in large part to the wealth and privileges bestowed on them at birth. Over 66 percent of the consumer units with incomes of $100,000 or more have inherited assets. Of these units, over 86 percent reported that inheritances constituted a substantial portion of their total assets.[31]

Economist Harold Wachtel likens inheritance to a series of Monopoly games in which the winner of the first game refuses to relinquish his or her cash and commercial property for the second game. "After all," argues the winner, "I accumulated my wealth and income by my own wits." With such an arrangement, it is not difficult to predict the outcome of subsequent games.[32]

Reality 6: All Americans do not have an equal opportunity to succeed. Inheritance laws ensure a greater likelihood of success for the offspring of the wealthy.

Spheres of Power and Oppression

When we look at society and try to determine what it is that keeps most people down—what holds them back from realizing their potential as healthy, creative, productive individuals—we find institutional forces that are largely beyond individual control. Class domination is one of these forces. People do not choose to be poor or working class; instead,

[29]The Mortenson Report on Public Policy Analysis of Opportunity for Postsecondary Education, "Postsecondary Education Opportunity" (Iowa City, IA: September 1993, no. 16).

[30]De Lone, op. cit., pp. 14–19. Also see Daniel McMurrer, Mask Condon, and Isabel Sawhili, "Intergenerational Mobility in the United States" (Washington, DC: Urban Institute, 1997), available at http://www.Urbaninstitute.org/url.cfm?ID=406796; and Bhashkar Mazumder, "Earnings Mobility in the US: A New Look at Intergenerational Inequality" (March 21, 2001), FRB Chicago Working Paper No. 2001–18, available at SSRN: http://ssrn .com/abstract=295559, or DOI: 10.2139/ssrn.295559.

[31]Howard Tuchman, *Economics of the Rich* (New York: Random House, 1973), p. 15. Also see Greg Duncan, Ariel Kalil, Susan Mayer, Robin Tepper, and Monique Payne, "The Apple Does not Fall Far from the Tree," in Samuel Bowles, Herbert Gintis, and Melissa Groves, *Unequal Chances: Family Background and Economic Success* (Princeton, NJ: Princeton University Press, 2008), pp. 23–79; Bhashkar Mazumder, "The Apple Falls Even Closer to the Tree than We Thought," in Bowles et al., pp. 80–99. For more information on inheritance, see Sam Bowles and Herbert Gintis, "The Inheritance of Inequality," *The Journal of Economic Perspectives*, 16, no. 3 (Summer 2002), pp. 2–30; and Tom Hertz, *Understanding Mobility in America*, Center for American Progress, available at http:// www.americanprogress.org/kf/hertz_mobility_analysis.pdf.

[32]Howard Wachtel, *Labor and the Economy* (Orlando, FL: Academic Press, 1984), pp. 161–162.

they are limited and confined by the opportunities afforded or denied them by a social and economic system. The class structure in the United States is a function of its economic system: capitalism, a system that is based on private rather than public ownership and control of commercial enterprises. Under capitalism, these enterprises are governed by the need to produce a profit for the owners, rather than to fulfill societal needs. Class divisions arise from the differences between those who own and control corporate enterprise and those who do not.

Racial and gender domination are other forces that hold people down. Although there are significant differences in the way capitalism, racism, and sexism affect our lives, there are also a multitude of parallels. And although class, race, and gender act independently of each other, they are at the same time very much interrelated.

On the one hand, issues of race and gender cut across class lines. Women experience the effects of sexism whether they are well-paid professionals or poorly paid clerks. As women, they are not only subjected to catcalls and stereotyping, but face discrimination and are denied opportunities and privileges that men have. Similarly, a wealthy black man faces racial oppression, is subjected to racial slurs, and is denied opportunities because of his color. Regardless of their class standing, women and members of minority races are constantly dealing with institutional forces that are holding them down precisely because of their gender, the color of their skin, or both.

On the other hand, the experiences of women and minorities are differentiated along class lines. Although they are in subordinate positions vis-à-vis white men, the particular issues that confront women and people of color may be quite different depending on their position in the class structure.

Power is incremental, and class privileges can accrue to individual women and to individual members of a racial minority. While power is incremental, oppression is cumulative, and those who are poor, black, and female are often subject to all of the forces of class, race, and gender discrimination simultaneously. This cumulative situation is what is meant by the double and triple jeopardy of women and minorities.

Furthermore, oppression in one sphere is related to the likelihood of oppression in another. If you are black and female, for example, you

Chances of Being Poor in America[33]

WHITE MALE/ FEMALE	WHITE FEMALE HEAD*	HISPANIC MALE/ FEMALE	HISPANIC FEMALE HEAD*	BLACK MALE/ FEMALE	BLACK FEMALE HEAD*
1 in 12	1 in 5	1 in 5	1 in 3	1 in 4	1 in 3

*Persons in families with female householder, no husband present.

[33]Derived from U.S. Census Bureau, *Current Population Survey*, Tables POV01 and POV2, available at http://pubdb3.census.gov/macro/032008/pov/toc.htm.

are much more likely to be poor or working class than you would be as a white male. Census figures show that the incidence of poverty varies greatly by race and gender.

In other words, being female and being nonwhite are attributes in our society that increase the chances of poverty and of lower-class standing.

Reality 7: Racism and sexism significantly compound the effects of class in society. 50

None of this makes for a very pretty picture of our country. Despite what we like to think about ourselves as a nation, the truth is that opportunity for success and life itself are highly circumscribed by our race, our gender, and the class we are born into. As individuals, we feel hurt and anger when someone is treating us unfairly; yet as a society we tolerate unconscionable injustice. A more just society will require a radical redistribution of wealth and power. We can start by reversing the current trends that further polarize us as a people and adapt policies and practices that narrow the gaps in income, wealth, and privilege.

I CAN HAVE A HUGE FAMILY, A HUGE HOUSE, A HUGE AMOUNT OF STUFF, A HUGE CAR... WITHOUT ANY HUGE CONSEQUENCES!

Me, Too!

SELF-DELUSION: AMERICA'S RENEWABLE RESOURCE

ENGAGING THE TEXT

1. Re-examine the four myths Mantsios identifies (paras. 10–14). What does he say is wrong about each myth, and what evidence does he provide to critique each? How persuasive do you find his evidence and reasoning?

2. Does the essay make a case that the wealthy are exploiting the poor? Does it simply assume this? Are there other possible interpretations of

the data Mantsios provides? Explain your position, taking into account the information in "Class in America — 2009."

3. Work out a rough budget for a family of three with an annual income of $19,090, the poverty guideline for 2012. Be sure to include costs for food, clothing, housing, transportation, healthcare, and other unavoidable expenses. Do you think this is a reasonable "poverty line," or is it too high or too low?

4. Imagine that you are Harold S. Browning, Bob Farrell, or Cheryl Mitchell. Write an entry for this person's journal after a tough day on the job. Compare and contrast your entry with those written by other students.

5. In this essay, Mantsios does not address solutions to the problems he cites. What changes do you imagine Mantsios would like to see? What changes, if any, would you recommend?

EXPLORING CONNECTIONS

6. Working in small groups, discuss which class each of the following would belong to and how this class affiliation would shape the life chances of each:

    Gary Soto in "Looking for Work" (p. 22)

    Sylvia in "The Lesson" (p. 253)

    Mike Rose (p. 151)

    George in "Serving in Florida" (p. 267)

    The narrator of "An Indian Story" (See bedfordstmartins.com/rereading /epages.)

    Richard Rodriguez (See bedfordstmartins.com/rereading/epages.)

    Stephen Cruz (See bedfordstmartins.com/rereading/epages.)

7. Both Mantsios and Harlon Dalton (p. 260) look beyond myths of success to underlying realities. Compare the ways these two writers challenge the American mythology of success. Do the two readings complement one another, or do you see fundamental disagreements between them? Whose approach do you find more persuasive, insightful, or informative, and why?

8. Read "Making It in America" by Adam Davidson (p. 333) and write an "American Profile" for Maddie Parlier following the template Mantsios provides in "Class in America — 2009."

EXTENDING THE CRITICAL CONTEXT

9. Mantsios points out, "Inheritance laws ensure a greater likelihood of success for the offspring of the wealthy" (para. 48). Explain why you think this is or is not a serious problem. Keeping in mind the difference between wealth and income, discuss how society might attempt to remedy this problem and what policies you would endorse.

10. Skim through a few recent issues of a financial magazine like *Forbes* or *Money*. Who is the audience for these publications? What kind of advice is offered? What kinds of products and services are advertised? What levels of income and investment are discussed?

11. Study the employment listings at an online source such as Monster.com. Roughly what percentage of the openings would you consider upper class, middle class, and lower class? On what basis do you make your distinctions? What do the available jobs suggest about the current levels of affluence in your area?

GENERATION R: THE CHANGING FORTUNES OF AMERICA'S YOUTH

DON PECK

The "R" in Generation R stands for "Recession" — clearly not the label you want to describe your age group. In the reading below journalist Don Peck delivers some unwelcome but thought-provoking news. Graduating during an economic slump, for example, could cost you $100,000 over the course of your lifetime — *if* you get a job, that is. If you experience long-term unemployment, you may be at increased risk of depression, substance abuse, and even early death. Don Peck is a features editor at the *Atlantic*; the selection below is excerpted from his book *Pinched: How the Great Recession Has Narrowed Our Futures and What We Can Do About It* (2011).

I'M DEFINITELY SEEING[1] a lot of the older generation saying, 'Oh, this [recession] is so awful,'" Robert Sherman, a 2009 graduate of Syracuse University, told the *New York Times* in July 2009. "But my generation isn't getting as depressed and uptight." Sherman had recently turned down a $50,000-a-year job at a consulting firm, after careful deliberation with his parents, because he hadn't connected well with his potential bosses. Instead, he was doing odd jobs and trying to get a couple of tech companies off the ground. "The economy will rebound," he said.

Over the past two generations, particularly among many college grads, the twenties have become a sort of netherworld between adolescence and adulthood. Job-switching is common, and with it, periods of voluntary, transitional unemployment. And as marriage and parenthood have receded farther into the future, the first years after college have

---

[1] "*I'm definitely seeing*": Steve Friess, "In Recession, Optimistic College Grads Turn Down Jobs," *New York Times*, July 24, 2009. [All notes are Peck's except 2 and 7.]

become, arguably, more carefree. Early in this recession, the term *fun-employment* gained some currency among single twentysomethings, prompting a small raft of youth-culture stories in the *Los Angeles Times* and *San Francisco Weekly*, on Gawker,[2] and in other venues.

Most of the people interviewed in these stories seem merely to be trying to stay positive and make the best of a bad situation. They note that it's a good time to reevaluate career choices; that since joblessness is now so common among their peers, it has lost much of its stigma; and that since they don't have mortgages or kids, they have flexibility, and in this respect, they are lucky. All of this sounds sensible enough—it is intuitive to think that youth will be spared the worst of the recession's scars.

But in fact a whole generation of young adults is likely to see its life chances permanently diminished by this recession. Lisa Kahn, an economist at Yale, has studied the impact of recessions on the lifetime earnings of young workers. In one recent study,[3] she followed the career paths of white men who graduated from college between 1979 and 1989. She found that, all else equal, for every one-percentage-point increase in the national unemployment rate, the starting income of new graduates fell by as much as 7 percent; the unluckiest graduates of the decade, who emerged into the teeth of the 1981–82 recession, made roughly 25 percent less in their first year than graduates who stepped into boom times.

What's truly remarkable is the persistence of the earnings gap. 5 Five, ten, fifteen years after graduation, after untold promotions and career changes spanning booms and busts, the unlucky graduates never closed the gap. Seventeen years after graduation, those who had entered the workforce during inhospitable times were still earning 10 percent less on average than those who had emerged into a more bountiful climate. When you add up all the earnings losses over the years, Kahn says, it's as if the lucky graduates had been given a gift of about $100,000, adjusted for inflation, immediately upon graduation—or, alternatively, as if the unlucky ones had been saddled with a debt of the same size.

When Kahn looked more closely at the unlucky graduates at mid-career, she found some surprising characteristics. They were significantly less likely to work in professional occupations or other prestigious spheres. And they clung more tightly to their jobs: average job tenure was unusually long. People who entered the workforce during the recession "didn't switch jobs as much, and particularly for young workers, that's how you increase wages," Kahn told me. This behavior may have resulted from a lingering risk aversion, born of a tough start. But a lack of opportunities may have played a larger role, she said:

---

[2]*Gawker*: gawker.com, an online site for news and gossip.
[3]*In one recent study:* Lisa B. Kahn, "The Long-Term Labor Market Consequences of Graduating from College in a Bad Economy" (paper, Yale School of Management, 2009); Lisa Kahn, conversation with author, 2009.

when you're forced to start work in a particularly low-level job or un-sexy career, it's easy for other employers to dismiss you as having low potential. Moving up, or moving on to something different and better, becomes more difficult.

"Graduates' first jobs[4] have an inordinate impact on their career path and [lifetime earnings]," wrote Austan Goolsbee, now a member of President Obama's Council of Economic Advisers, in 2006. "People essentially cannot close the wage gap by working their way up the company hierarchy. While they may work their way up, the people who started above them do, too. They don't catch up." Recent research suggests that as much as two-thirds of real lifetime wage growth typically occurs in the first ten years of a career. After that, as people start families and their career paths lengthen and solidify, jumping the tracks becomes harder.

This job environment[5] is not one in which fast-track jobs are plentiful, to say the least. According to the National Association of Colleges and Employers, job offers to graduating seniors declined 21 percent in 2009. They rebounded by 5 percent in 2010 and are expected to rise again in 2011, but not by nearly as much as they've fallen. In the San Francisco Bay Area, an organization called JobNob has been holding networking happy hours since the recession began to try to match college graduates with start-up companies looking primarily for unpaid labor. Julie Greenberg, a cofounder of JobNob, says that at the first event she expected perhaps 30 people, but 300 showed up. New graduates didn't have much of a chance; most of the people there had several years of work experience—quite a lot were thirtysomethings—and some had more than one degree. JobNob has since held events for alumni of Stanford, Berkeley, and Harvard; all have been well attended (at the Harvard event, Greenberg tried to restrict attendance to seventy-five people, but about a hundred managed to get in), and all have been dominated by people with significant work experience.

When experienced workers holding prestigious degrees are taking unpaid internships, not much is left for newly minted B.A.s. Yet if those same B.A.s don't find purchase in the job market, they'll soon have to compete with a fresh class of graduates—ones without white space on their résumé to explain. This is a tough squeeze to escape, and it only gets tighter over time.

Strong evidence suggests[6] that people who don't find solid roots   10
in the job market within a year or two have a particularly hard time

---

[4] *"Graduates' first jobs":*   Austan Goolsbee, "Hello Young Workers: One Way to Reach the Top Is to Start There," *New York Times,* May 25, 2006.

[5] *This job environment:*   National Association of Colleges and Employers, "Job Outlook 2011," 2011, http://www.naceweb.org/Research/Job_Outlook/Job_Outlook.aspx?referal= research&menuID=377.

[6] *Strong evidence suggests:*   Krysia Mossakowski, "The Influence of Past Unemployment Duration on Symptoms of Depression Among Young Women and Men in the United States," *American Journal of Public Health* 99: 1826–32; Krysia Mossakowski, conversation with author, 2009.

righting themselves. In part, that's because many of them become dif- ferent—and damaged—people. Krysia Mossakowski, a sociologist at the University of Miami, has found that in young adults, long bouts of unemployment provoke long-lasting changes in behavior and mental health. "Some people say, 'Oh, well, they're young, they're in and out of the workforce, so unemployment shouldn't matter much psychologi- cally,'" Mossakowski told me. "But that isn't true."

Examining national longitudinal data,[7] Mossakowski has found that people who were unemployed for long periods in their teens or early twenties are far more likely to develop a habit of heavy drinking (five or more drinks in one sitting) by the time they approach middle age. They are also more likely to develop depressive symptoms. Prior drinking be- havior and psychological history do not explain these problems—they result from unemployment itself. And the problems are not limited to those who never find steady work; they show up quite strongly as well in people who are later working regularly.

As we've seen, young men who suffered hardship during the Depression carried scars for the rest of their lives; even forty years later, unlike peers who had been largely spared in the 1930s, they gener- ally displayed a lack of ambition, direction, and confidence in them- selves—a belief that they were powerless before the fates. Today in Japan,[8] according to the Japan Productivity Center for Socio-Economic Development, workers who began their careers during the "lost de- cade" of the 1990s and are now in their thirties make up six out of every ten cases of depression, stress, and work-related mental disabilities re- ported by employers.

A large and long-standing body of research shows that physical health tends to deteriorate during unemployment, most likely through a combination of fewer financial resources and a higher stress level. The most-recent research suggests that poor health is prevalent[9] among the young, and endures for a lifetime. Till Von Wachter, an economist at Columbia University, and Daniel Sullivan, of the Federal Reserve Bank of Chicago, recently looked at the mortality rates of men who had lost their jobs in Pennsylvania in the 1970s and '80s. They found that par- ticularly among men in their forties or fifties, mortality rates rose mark- edly soon after a layoff. But regardless of age, all men were left with an elevated risk of dying in each year following their episode of unem- ployment, for the rest of their lives. And so, the younger the worker, the more pronounced the effect on his lifespan: the lives of workers who had lost their job at thirty, Von Wachter and Sullivan found, were

[7]*longitudinal data*: data from a long-term study, often a decade or more.

[8]*Today in Japan:*   Kenji Hall and Ian Rowley, "Japan's Lost Generation," *BusinessWeek*, May 28, 2007; additional data from the Productivity Center for Socio-Economic Devel- opment provided to author by Kenji Hall.

[9]*poor health is prevalent:*   Till Von Wachter and Daniel Sullivan, "Job Displacement and Mortality: An Analysis Using Administrative Data," *Quarterly Journal of Economics* 124, no. 3 (August 2009): 1265–1306; Till Von Wachter, conversation with author, 2009.

shorter than those of workers who had lost their job at fifty or fifty-five—and more than a year and a half shorter than the lives of workers who'd never lost their job at all.

Journalists and academics have thrown various labels[10] at today's young adults,[11] hoping one might stick—Generation Y, Generation Next, the Net Generation, the Millennials, the Echo Boomers. Recently, the *New York Times* reporter Steven Greenhouse has aptly suggested Generation Recession, or simply Generation R. All of these efforts contain an unavoidable element of folly; the diversity of character within a generation is always infinitely larger than the gap between generations. Still, the cultural and economic environment in which each generation is incubated clearly matters. It is no coincidence that the members of Generation X—painted as cynical, apathetic slackers—first emerged into the workforce in the weak job market of the early to mid-1980s. Nor is it a coincidence that the early members of Generation Y—labeled as optimistic, rule-following achievers—came of age during the Internet boom of the late 1990s.

Many of today's young adults seem temperamentally unprepared 15 for the circumstances in which they now find themselves. Jean Twenge, an associate professor of psychology at San Diego State University, has carefully compared the attitudes of today's young adults with those of previous generations when they were the same age. Using national survey data, she's found that to an unprecedented degree, people who graduated from high school in the aughts dislike the idea of work for work's sake, and expect jobs and career to be tailored to their interests and lifestyle. Yet they also have much higher material expectations than previous generations, and believe financial success is extremely important. "There's this idea that, 'Yeah, I don't want to work, but I'm still going to get all the stuff I want,'" Twenge told me. "It's a generation in which every kid has been told, 'You can be anything you want. You're special.'"

In her 2006 book,[12] *Generation Me,* Twenge notes that self-esteem in children began rising sharply around 1980, and hasn't stopped since. By 1999, according to one survey, 91 percent of teens described themselves as responsible, 74 percent as physically attractive, and 79 percent as very intelligent. (More than 40 percent of teens also expected that they would be earning $75,000 a year or more by age thirty; the median salary made by a thirty-year-old was $27,000 that year.) Twenge attributes the shift to broad changes in parenting styles and teaching methods, in response to the growing belief that children should always feel good about themselves, no matter what. As the years have

[10]*various labels:* Steven Greenhouse, "As Plants Close, Teenagers Focus More on College," *New York Times*, June 25, 2009.
[11]*today's young adults:* Jean Twenge, *Generation Me* (New York: Free Press, 2006); Jean Twenge, conversation with author, 2009.
[12]*In her 2006 book:* Twenge, *Generation Me.*

passed, efforts to boost self-esteem—and to decouple it from performance—have become widespread.

These efforts have succeeded in making today's youth more confident and individualistic. But that may not benefit them in adulthood, particularly in this economic environment. Twenge writes that "self-esteem without basis encourages laziness rather than hard work," and that "the ability to persevere and keep going" is "a much better predictor of life outcomes than self-esteem." She worries that many young people might be inclined to simply give up in this job market. "You'd think if people are more individualistic, they'd be more independent," she told me. "But it's not really true. There's an element of entitlement—they expect people to figure things out for them."

Ron Alsop, a former reporter[13] for the *Wall Street Journal* and the author of *The Trophy Kids Grow Up: How the Millennial Generation Is Shaking Up the Workplace*, says a combination of entitlement and highly structured childhood has resulted in a lack of independence and entrepreneurialism in many twentysomethings. They're used to checklists, he says, and "don't excel at leadership or independent problem solving." Alsop interviewed dozens of employers for his book, and concluded that unlike previous generations, Millennials, as a group, "need almost constant direction" in the workplace. "Many flounder without precise guidelines but thrive in structured situations that provide clearly defined rules."

All of these characteristics are troubling, given a harsh economic environment that requires perseverance, adaptability, humility, and entrepreneurialism. Perhaps most worrisome, though, is the fatalism and lack of agency that both Twenge and Alsop discern in today's young adults. Trained throughout childhood to disconnect performance from reward, and told repeatedly that they are destined for great things, many are quick to place blame elsewhere when something goes wrong, and inclined to believe that bad situations will sort themselves out—or will be sorted out by parents or other helpers.

In his 2009 commencement[14] remarks, as the *New York Times* re- 20
ported, University of Connecticut president Michael Hogan addressed the phenomenon of students' turning down jobs, with no alternatives, because they didn't feel the jobs were good enough. "My first word of advice is this," he told the graduates. "Say yes. In fact, say yes as often as you can. Saying yes begins things. Saying yes is how things grow. Saying yes leads to new experiences, and new experiences will lead to knowledge and wisdom. *Yes* is for young people, and an attitude of yes is how you will be able to go forward in these uncertain times."

Larry Druckenbrod, the university's assistant director of career services, told me, "This is a group that's done résumé building since

---

[13]*Ron Alsop, a former reporter:* Ron Alsop, "The 'Trophy Kids' Go to Work," *Wall Street Journal*, October 21, 2008; Ron Alsop, conversation with author, 2009.
[14]*In his 2009 commencement:* Steve Friess, "In Recession, Optimistic."

middle school. They've been told they've been preparing to go out and do great things after college. And now they've been dealt a 180." For many, that's led to "immobilization." Druckenbrod said that about a third of the seniors he talked to were seriously looking for work; another third were planning to go to grad school. The final third, he said, were "not even engaging with the job market—these are the ones whose parents have already said, 'Just come home and live with us.'"

According to a recent Pew survey,[15] 10 percent of adults younger than thirty-five have moved back in with their parents as a result of the recession. But that's merely an acceleration of a trend that has been under way for a generation or more. By the middle of the aughts, for instance, the percentage of twenty-six-year-olds living with their parents reached 20 percent, nearly double what it was in 1970. Well before the recession began, this generation of young adults was less likely to work, or at least work steadily, than other recent generations. Since 2000, the percentage of people ages sixteen to twenty-four participating in the labor force has been declining (from 66 percent to 56 percent across the decade). Increased college attendance explains only part of the shift; the rest is a puzzle. Lingering weakness in the job market since 2001 may be one cause. Twenge believes the propensity of this generation to pursue "dream" careers that are, for most people, unlikely to work out may also be partly responsible. (In 2004, a national survey found that about one out of eighteen college freshmen expected to make a living as an actor, musician, or artist.)

Whatever the reason, the fact that so many young adults weren't firmly rooted in the workforce even before the crash is deeply worrying. It means that a very large number of young adults entered the recession already vulnerable to all the ills that joblessness produces over time. It means that for a sizable proportion of twenty- and thirtysomethings, the next few years will likely be toxic.

ENGAGING THE TEXT

1. Draft the resumé you would like to have in hand when you graduate. Include your expected degree, GPA, work experience, special skills, internships, and community or volunteer service. What kinds of jobs do you think you will be able to land with this resumé, and at what salary? What obstacles might you have to overcome to build a strong resumé?

2. Make a list of the claims and assumptions about Generation R made by Peck or the authors he quotes such as Jean Twenge and Ron Alsop. Then debate the accuracy of Peck's characterization of "Generation R."

3. Drawing on information from some of the experts Peck cites—Lisa Kahn, Krysia Mossakowski, Jean Twenge, and Ron Alsop—write a one-page

---

[15]*According to a recent Pew survey:* Sam Roberts, "Economy Is Forcing Young Adults Back Home in Big Numbers, Survey Finds," *New York Times*, November 24, 2009.

summary of the psychological dimensions of job hunting, career struggles, or unemployment in a tough economy.

4. A portion of Lisa Kahn's research, described in paragraphs 4–6, covers the decade 1979 to 1989. Does this research remain relevant today? Explain why or why not.

5. Write a journal entry on where you see yourself five years after graduation. What kind of job do you expect to have, and at what salary? Where will you be living? How much money will you have in the bank, and what major expenses might you have to deal with — for example, credit card payments, student loans, child care, or medical bills? Compare notes with classmates and discuss whose plans seem realistic given the current job market and financial climate.

EXPLORING CONNECTIONS

6. Review the excerpt from *The Accordion Family* by Katherine Newman (p. 83), which examines the trend of young adults moving back in with their parents after graduation. Based on your reading of "Generation R," do you think Peck would see this strategy as a good way of weathering a recession, or might it hurt one's chances in the job market?

7. Imagine what would happen to one or more of the individuals listed below during a prolonged recession of seven or eight years. Write a brief description of how they would fare and discuss your ideas with classmates.

   "Ragged Dick," page 246

   Sylvia in "The Lesson," page 253

   Harold Browning, Bob Farrell, or Cheryl Mitchell from "Class in America — 2009," page 281

   Maddie Parlier, from "Making It in America," page 333

   the narrator of "An Indian Story" (See bedfordstmartins.com/rereading /epages.)

EXTENDING THE CRITICAL CONTEXT

8. In paragraph 8 Peck cites data from the National Association of Colleges and Employers. Visit the NACE Web site to research and report on job and internship information for college graduates. (Some NACE resources are by subscription only, but many are free.)

9. Go online to the "We Are the 99 Percent" pages at http://wearethe99percent .tumblr.com and read several statements from "Generation R" members who are struggling in the current economy. Which stories and images do you find most moving, and why? Do the experiences of these young men and women support or challenge Peck's view of "Generation R"? What story or image would you post?

VISUAL PORTFOLIO

READING IMAGES OF INDIVIDUAL OPPORTUNITY

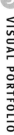

VISUAL PORTFOLIO

READING IMAGES OF INDIVIDUAL OPPORTUNITY

1. In the photograph of a man repairing novelty items during vocational training (p. 307), what else is going on? What is the man thinking? What is his relationship to his work, to the toys, and to his coworkers? What do you make of the slogan on his T-shirt, "Freedom by any means necessary"?

2. Who are the men waiting for work on page 308, and what life histories do you imagine have brought them to this place? What kinds of work are they are hoping for? Could you find a scene like this in or near your community, and if so, what kind of wages would such workers earn? Which worker do you think is most likely to get hired, and why?

3. What are the police officers doing in front of the JPMorgan Chase & Co. building on page 309? What is happening outside the building, inside the building, and at the entryway? Analyze specific elements of the photo including the company name, the street address, the people on the second floor looking out, and the facial expressions and body language of the officers.

4. What has happened to the house with boarded-up windows (p. 310)? What do you imagine has happened to its owners? Who do you think wrote the graffiti, and what might it mean?

5. What narrative would you construct to explain the image on page 311? Who are the adults, and what are they doing? What are they wearing, and what are the tools of their trades? What items might they be removing from the cubbyholes? What is the significance of the large television and its image from an animated film? Finally, explain the impact of including the child in the photo. What is happening from the child's point of view?

6. The man pictured on page 312 is protesting corporate greed. What message is he sending by taping a dollar bill over his mouth? What effects do his age, his facial expression, and his clothing have on your reading of the image? Compare this photograph to the one on page 309, taken at 270 Park Avenue in New York.

FRAMING CLASS, VICARIOUS LIVING, AND CONSPICUOUS CONSUMPTION

DIANA KENDALL

Diana Kendall, a professor of sociology at Baylor University, has performed an extensive study of how newspapers and TV have portrayed social class in the last half-century. She concludes that the media shape public opinions about the upper, middle, working, and poverty classes by "framing" their stories and their programming in a relatively small number of patterned, predictable, and misleading ways. For example, "the media glorify the upper classes, even when they are accused of wrongdoing." In this excerpt from her award-winning book *Framing Class: Media Representations of Wealth and Poverty in America* (2005), Kendall analyzes how several common media frames communicate cultural messages about social class. Her most recent books include *Members Only: Elite Clubs and the Process of Exclusion* (2008), and *Sociology in Our Times: The Essentials* (2009).

> *"The Simple Life 2"—the second season of the reality show, on which the celebutante Paris Hilton and her Best Friend Forever, the professional pop-star-daughter Nicole Richie, are set on a cross-country road trip—once again takes the heaviest of topics and makes them as weightless as a social X-ray.*[1]

THIS STATEMENT BY TELEVISION CRITIC CHOIRE SICHA, in her review of FOX TV's reality-based entertainment show *The Simple Life*, sums up a recurring theme of *Framing Class:* The media typically take "the heaviest of topics," such as class and social inequality, and trivialize it. Rather than providing a meaningful analysis of inequality and showing realistic portrayals of life in various social classes, the media either play class differences for laughs or sweep the issue of class under the rug so that important distinctions are rendered invisible. By ignoring class or trivializing it, the media involve themselves in a social construction of reality that rewards the affluent and penalizes the working class and the poor. In real life, Paris Hilton and Nicole Richie are among the richest young women in the world; however, in the world of *The Simple Life*, they can routinely show up somewhere in the city or the country, pretend they are needy, and rely on the kindness of strangers who have few economic resources.

---

[1]Choire Sicha, "They'll Always Have Paris," *New York Times*, June 13, 2004, AR31 [emphasis added]. [All notes are Kendall's unless otherwise indicated.]

The Simple Life is only one example of many that demonstrate how class is minimized or played for laughs by the media. [Below] I have provided many examples of how class is framed in the media and what messages those framing devices might convey to audiences. In this chapter, I will look at the sociological implications of how framing contributes to our understanding of class and how it leads to vicarious living and excessive consumerism by many people. I will also discuss reasons why prospects for change in how journalists and television writers portray the various classes are limited. First, we look at two questions: How do media audiences understand and act upon popular culture images or frames? Is class understood differently today because of these frames?

Media Framing and the Performance of Class in Everyday Life

In a mass-mediated culture such as ours, the media do not simply mirror society; rather, they help to shape it and to create cultural perceptions.[2] The blurring between what is real and what is not real encourages people to emulate the upper classes and shun the working class and

²Tim Delaney and Allene Wilcox, "Sports and the Role of the Media," in *Values, Society and Evolution*, ed. Harry Birx and Tim Delaney, 199–215 (Auburn, N.Y.: Legend, 2002).

the poor. Television shows, magazines, and newspapers sell the idea that the only way to get ahead is to identify with the rich and power- ful and to live vicariously through them. From sitcoms to reality shows, the media encourage ordinary people to believe that they may rise to fame and fortune; they too can be the next American Idol. Constantly bombarded by stories about the lifestyles of the rich and famous, view- ers feel a sense of intimacy with elites, with whom they have little or no contact in their daily lives.[3] According to the social critic bell hooks, we overidentify with the wealthy, because the media socialize us to believe that people in the upper classes are better than we are. The media also suggest that we need have no allegiance to people in our own class or to those who are less fortunate.[4]

Vicarious living—watching how other individuals live rather than experiencing life for ourselves—through media representations of wealth and success is reflected in many people's reading and viewing habits and in their patterns of consumption. According to hooks, televi- sion promotes hedonistic consumerism:

> Largely through marketing and advertising, television promoted the myth of the classless society, offering on one hand images of an American dream fulfilled wherein any and everyone can become rich and on the other suggesting that the lived experience of this lack of class hierarchy was expressed by our *equal right to purchase anything we could afford.*[5]

As hooks suggests, equality does not exist in contemporary society,   5 but media audiences are encouraged to view themselves as having an "equal right" to purchase items that somehow will make them equal to people above them in the social class hierarchy. However, the catch is that we must actually be able to afford these purchases. Manufacturers and the media have dealt with this problem by offering relatively cheap products marketed by wealthy celebrities. Paris Hilton, an heir to the Hilton Hotel fortune, has made millions of dollars by marketing products that give her fans a small "slice" of the good life she enjoys. Middle- and working-class people can purchase jewelry from the Paris Hilton Collection—sterling silver and Swarovski crystal jewelry rang- ing in price from fifteen to a hundred dollars—and have something that is "like Paris wears." For less than twenty dollars per item, admir- ers can purchase the Paris Hilton Wall Calendar; a "Paris the Heiress" Paper Doll Book; Hilton's autobiography, *Confessions of an Heiress;* and even her dog's story, *The Tinkerbell Hilton Diaries: My Life Tailing Paris Hilton.* But Hilton is only one of thousands of celebrities who make money by encouraging unnecessary consumerism among people who are inspired by media portrayals of the luxurious and supposedly happy lives of rich celebrities. The title of Hilton's television show, *The Simple*

---

[3]bell hooks [Gloria Watkins], *Where We Stand: Class Matters* (New York: Routledge, 2000), 73.

[4]hooks, *Where We Stand,* 77.

[5]hooks, *Where We Stand,* 71 [emphasis added].

Life, appropriates the image of simple people, such as the working class and poor, who might live happy, meaningful lives, and transfers this image to women whose lives are anything but simple as they flaunt designer clothing and spend collectively millions of dollars on entertainment, travel, and luxuries that can be afforded only by the very wealthy.[6]

How the media frame stories about class *does* make a difference in what we think about other people and how we spend our money. Media frames constitute a mental shortcut (schema) that helps us formulate our thoughts.

The Upper Classes: Affluence and Consumerism for All

Although some media frames show the rich and famous in a negative manner, they still glorify the material possessions and lifestyles of the upper classes. Research has found that people who extensively watch television have exaggerated views of how wealthy most Americans are and what material possessions they own. Studies have also found that extensive television viewing leads to higher rates of spending and to lower savings, presumably because television stimulates consumer desires.[7]

For many years, most media framing of stories about the upper classes has been positive, ranging from *consensus framing* that depicts members of the upper class as being like everyone else, to *admiration framing* that portrays them as generous, caring individuals. The frame most closely associated with rampant consumerism is *emulation framing*, which suggests that people in all classes should reward themselves with a few of the perks of the wealthy, such as buying a piece of Paris's line of jewelry. The writers of television shows such as ABC's *Life of Luxury*, E!'s *It's Good to Be*...[a wealthy celebrity, such as Nicole Kidman], and VH1's *The Fabulous Life* rely heavily on admiration and price-tag framing, by which the worth of a person is measured by what he or she owns and how many assistants constantly cater to that person's whims. On programs like FOX's *The O.C.* and *North Shore* and NBC's *Las Vegas,* the people with the most expensive limousines, yachts, and jet aircraft are declared the winners in life. Reality shows like *American Idol, The Billionaire, For Love or Money,* and *The Apprentice* suggest that anyone can move up the class ladder and live like the rich if he or she displays the best looks, greatest talent, or sharpest entrepreneurial skills. It is no wonder that the economist Juliet B. Schor finds that the overriding goal of children age ten to thirteen is to get rich. In response to the statement "I want to make a lot of money when I grow up," 63 percent of the children in Schor's study agreed, whereas only 7 percent disagreed.[8]

---

[6]hooks, *Where We Stand,* 72.

[7]Juliet B. Schor, *Born to Buy: The Commercialized Child and the New Consumer Culture* (New York: Scribner, 2004).

[8]Schor, *Born to Buy.*

Many adults who hope to live the good life simply plunge farther into debt. Many reports show that middle- and working-class American consumers are incurring massive consumer debts as they purchase larger houses, more expensive vehicles, and many other items that are beyond their means. According to one analyst, media portrayals of excessive consumer spending and a bombardment of advertisements by credit-card companies encourage people to load up on debt.[9] With the average U.S. household now spending 13 percent of its after-tax income to *service* debts (not pay off the principal!), people with average incomes who continue to aspire to lives of luxury like those of the upper classes instead may find themselves spending their way into the "poor house" with members of the poverty class.

The Poor and Homeless: "Not Me!" — Negative Role Models in the Media

The sharpest contrasts in media portrayals are between depictions of people in the upper classes and depictions of people at the bottom of the class structure. At best, the poor and homeless are portrayed as deserving of our sympathy on holidays or when disaster strikes. In these situations, those in the bottom classes are depicted as being temporarily down on their luck or as working hard to get out of their current situation but in need of public assistance. At worst, however, the poor are blamed for their own problems; stereotypes of the homeless as bums, alcoholics, and drug addicts, caught in a hopeless downward spiral because of their *individual* pathological behavior, are omnipresent in the media.

For the most part, people at the bottom of the class structure remain out of sight and out of mind for most media audiences. *Thematic framing* depicts the poor and homeless as "faceless" statistics in reports on poverty. *Episodic framing* highlights some problems of the poor but typically does not link their personal situations [and] concerns to such larger societal problems as limited educational opportunities, high rates of unemployment, and jobs that pay depressingly low wages.

The poor do not fare well on television entertainment shows, where writers typically represent them with one-dimensional, bedraggled characters standing on a street corner holding cardboard signs that read "Need money for food." When television writers tackle the issue of homelessness, they often portray the lead characters (who usually are white and relatively affluent) as helpful people, while the poor and homeless are depicted as deviants who might harm themselves or others. Hospital and crime dramas like *E.R., C.S.I.,* and *Law & Order* frequently portray the poor and homeless as "crazy," inebriated in public, or incompetent to provide key information to officials. Television reality shows like *Cops* go so far as to advertise that they provide "footage

[9]Joseph Nocera, *A Piece of the Action: How the Middle Class Joined the Money Class* (New York: Simon and Schuster, 1994).

of debris from the bottom tiers of the urban social order."[10] Statements such as this say a lot about the extent to which television producers, directors, and writers view (or would have us view) the lower classes.

From a sociological perspective, framing of stories about the poor and homeless stands in stark contrast to framing of stories about those in the upper classes, and it suggests that we should distance ourselves from "those people." We are encouraged to view the poor and homeless as the *Other*, the outsider; in the media we find little commonality between our lives and the experiences of people at the bottom of the class hierarchy. As a result, it is easy for us to buy into the dominant ideological construction that views poverty as a problem of individuals, not of the society as a whole, and we may feel justified in our rejection of such people.[11]

The Working Class: Historical Relics and Jokes

The working class and the working poor do not fare much better than the poor and homeless in media representations. The working class is described as "labor," and people in this class are usually nothing more than faces in a crowd on television shows. The media portray people who *produce* goods and services as much less interesting than those who *excessively consume* them, and this problem can only grow worse as more of the workers who produce the products are thousands of miles away from us, in nations like China, very remote from the typical American consumer.[12]

Contemporary media coverage carries little information about the working class or its problems. Low wages, lack of benefits, and hazardous working conditions are considered boring and uninteresting topics, except on the public broadcasting networks or an occasional television "news show" such as *60 Minutes* or *20/20*, when some major case of worker abuse has recently been revealed. The most popular portrayal of the working class is *caricature framing*, which depicts people in negative ways, such as being dumb, white trash, buffoons, bigots, or slobs. Many television shows featuring working-class characters play on the idea that the clothing, manners, and speech patterns of the working class are not as good as those of the middle or upper classes. For example, working-class characters (such as Roseanne, the animated Homer Simpson,

[10]Karen De Coster and Brad Edmonds, "TV Nation: The Killing of American Brain Cells," Lewrockwell.com, 2004, www.lewrockwell.com/decoster/decoster78.html (accessed July 7, 2004).

[11]Judith Butler ("Performative Acts and Gender Constitution: An Essay in Phenomenology and Feminist Theory," in *Performing Feminisms: Feminist Critical Theory and Theatre*, ed. Sue-Ellen Case [Baltimore: Johns Hopkins University Press, 1990], 270) has described gender identity as performative, noting that social reality is not a given but is continually created as an illusion "through language, gesture, and all manner of symbolic social sign." In this sense, class might also be seen as performative, in that people act out their perceived class location not only in terms of their own class-related identity but in regard to how they treat other people, based on their perceived class position.

[12]See Thomas Ginsberg, "Union Hopes to Win Over Starbucks Shop Workers," *Austin American-Statesman*, July 2, 2004, D6.

and *The King of Queens'* Doug) may compare themselves to the middle and upper classes by saying that they are not as "fancy as the rich people." Situation comedy writers have perpetuated working-class stereotypes, and now a number of reality shows, such as *The Swan* and *Extreme Makeover,* try to take "ordinary" working-class people and "improve" them through cosmetic surgery, new clothing, and different hairstyles.

Like their upper-class celebrity counterparts, so-called working-class comedians like Jeff Foxworthy have ridiculed the blue-collar lifestyle. They also have marketed products that make fun of the working class. Foxworthy's website, for example, includes figurines ("little statues for *inside* the house"), redneck cookbooks, Games Rednecks Play, and calendars that make fun of the working class generally. Although some people see these items as humorous ("where's yore sense of humor?"), the real message is that people in the lower classes lack good taste, socially acceptable manners, and above all, middle-class values. If you purchase "redneck" merchandise, you too can make fun of the working class and clearly distance yourself from it.

Middle-Class Framing and Kiddy-Consumerism

Media framing of stories about the middle class tells us that this economic group is the value center and backbone of the nation. *Middleclass values framing* focuses on the values of this class and suggests that they hold the nation together. Early television writers were aware that their shows needed to appeal to middle-class audiences, who were the targeted consumers for the advertisers' products, and middle-class values of honesty, integrity, and hard work were integral ingredients of early sitcoms. However, some contemporary television writers spoof the middle class and poke fun at values supposedly associated with people in this category. The writers of FOX's *Malcolm in the Middle* and *Arrested Development,* for example, focus on the dysfunctions in a fictional middle-class family, including conflicts between husband and wife, between parents and children, and between members of the family and outsiders.

Why do these shows make fun of the middle class? Because corporations that pay for the advertisements want to capture the attention of males between ages eighteen and thirty-nine, and individuals in this category are believed to enjoy laughing at the uptight customs of conventional middle-class families. In other shows, as well, advertisers realize the influence that their programs have on families. That is why they are happy to spend billions of dollars on product placements (such as a Diet Coke can sitting on a person's desk) in the shows and on ads during commercial breaks. In recent research, Schor examined why very young children buy into the consumerism culture and concluded that extensive media exposure to products was a key reason. According to Schor, "More children [in the United States] than anywhere else believe that their clothes and brands describe who they are and define their social status. American kids display more brand affinity than their counterparts anywhere else in the world; indeed, experts describe them as increasingly 'bonded to brands.'"[13]

Part of this bonding occurs through constant television watching and Internet use, as a steady stream of ads targets children and young people. Schor concludes that we face a greater problem than just excessive consumerism. A child's well-being is undermined by the consumer culture: "High consumer involvement is a significant cause of depression, anxiety, low self-esteem, and psychosomatic complaints."[14] Although no similar studies have been conducted to determine the effects of the media's emphasis on wealth and excessive consumerism among adults, it is likely that today's children will take these values with them into adulthood if our society does not first reach the breaking point with respect to consumer debt.

The issue of class in the United States is portrayed in the media not through a realistic assessment of wealth, poverty, or inequality but instead through its patterns of rampant consumerism. The general message remains, one article stated, "We pledge allegiance to the mall."[15]

Media Framing and Our Distorted View of Inequality

Class clearly permeates media culture and influences our thinking on social inequality. How the media frame stories involving class constitutes a *socially constructed reality* that is not necessarily an accurate reflection of the United States. Because of their pervasive nature, the media have the symbolic capacity to define the world for other people. In turn, readers and viewers gain information from the media that they use to construct a picture of class and inequality—a picture that becomes, at least to them, a realistic representation of where they stand in the class structure, what they should (or should not) aspire to achieve, and whether and why they should view other people as superior, equal, or inferior to themselves.

Because of the media's power to socially construct reality, we must make an effort to find out about the objective nature of class and evaluate social inequality on our own terms. Although postmodern thinkers believe that it is impossible to distinguish between real life and the fictionalized version of reality that is presented by the media, some sociologists argue that we can learn the difference between media images of reality and the actual facts pertaining to wealth, poverty, and inequality. The more we become aware that we are not receiving "raw"

[13]Schor, *Born to Buy*, 13.
[14]Schor, *Born to Buy*, 167.
[15]Louis Uchitelle, "We Pledge Allegiance to the Mall," *New York Times*, December 6, 2004, C12.

information or "just" entertainment from the media, the more we are capable of rationally thinking about how we are represented in media portrayals and what we are being encouraged to do (engage in hedonistic consumerism, for example) by these depictions. The print and electronic media have become extremely adept at framing issues of class in a certain manner, but we still have the ability to develop alternative frames that better explain who we are and what our nation is truly like in regard to class divisions.

The Realities of Class

What are the realities of inequality? The truth is that the rich are getting richer and that the gulf between the rich and the poor continues to widen in the United States. Since the 1990s, the poor have been more likely to stay poor, and the affluent have been more likely to stay affluent. How do we know this? Between 1991 and 2001, the income of the top one-fifth of U.S. families increased by 31 percent; during the same period, the income of the bottom one-fifth of families increased by only 10 percent.[16] The chasm is even wider across racial and ethnic categories; African Americans and Latinos/Latinas are overrepresented among those in the bottom income levels. Over one-half of African American and Latino/Latina households fall within the lowest income categories.

Wealth inequality is even more pronounced. The super-rich (the top 0.5 percent of U.S. households) own 35 percent of the nation's wealth, with net assets averaging almost nine million dollars. The very rich (the next 0.5 percent of households) own about 7 percent of the nation's wealth, with net assets ranging from $1.4 million to $2.5 million. The rich (9 percent of households) own 30 percent of the wealth, with net assets of a little over four hundred thousand dollars. Meanwhile, everybody else (the bottom 90 percent of households) owns only 28 percent of the nation's wealth. Like income, wealth disparities are greatest across racial and ethnic categories. According to the Census Bureau, the net worth of the average white household in 2000 was more than ten times that of the average African American household and more than eight times that of the average Latino/Latina household. Moreover, in 2002, almost thirty-five million people lived below the official government poverty level of $18,556 for a family of four, an increase of more than one million people in poverty since 2001.[17]

The Realities of Hedonistic Consumerism

Consumerism is a normal part of life; we purchase the things that we need to live. However, hedonistic consumerism goes beyond all

25

---

[16]Carmen DeNavas-Walt and Robert W. Cleveland, "Income in the United States: 2002," *U.S. Census Bureau: Current Population Reports*, P60–221 (Washington, DC: U.S. Government Printing Office, 2003).

[17]Bernadette D. Proctor and Joseph Dalaker, "Poverty in the United States: 2002," *U.S. Census Bureau: Current Population Reports*, P60–222 (Washington, DC: U.S. Government Printing Office, 2003).

necessary and meaningful boundaries. As the word *hedonism* suggests, some people are so caught up in consumerism that this becomes the main reason for their existence, the primary thing that brings them happiness. Such people engage in the self-indulgent pursuit of happiness through what they buy. An example of this extreme was recently reported in the media. When Antoinette Millard was sued by American Express for an allegedly past-due account, she filed a counterclaim against American Express for having provided her with a big-spender's credit card that allowed her to run up bills of nearly a million dollars in luxury stores in New York.[18] Using the "victim defense," Millard claimed that, based on her income, the company should not have solicited her to sign up for the card. Although this appears to be a far-fetched defense (especially in light of some of the facts),[19] it may be characteristic of the lopsided thinking of many people who spend much more money than they can hope to earn. Recent studies have shown that the average American household is carrying more than eight thousand dollars in credit-card debt and that (statistically speaking) every fifteen seconds a person in the United States goes bankrupt.[20] Although fixed costs (such as housing, food, and gasoline) have gone up for most families over the past thirty years, these debt-and-bankruptcy statistics in fact result from more people buying items that are beyond their means and cannot properly use anyway. Our consumer expectations for ourselves and our children have risen as the media have continued to attractively portray the "good life" and to bombard us with ads for something else that we *must* have.

Are we Americans actually interested in learning about class and inequality? Do we want to know where we really stand in the U.S. class structure? Although some people may prefer to operate in a climate of denial, media critics believe that more people are finally awakening to biases in the media, particularly when they see vast inconsistencies between media portrayals of class and their everyday lives. According to the sociologists Robert Perrucci and Earl Wysong, "It is apparent that increasing experiences with and knowledge about class-based inequalities among the nonprivileged is fostering a growing awareness of and concerns about the nature and extent of superclass interests, motives,

---

[18]Antoinette Millard, also known as Lisa Walker, allegedly was so caught up in hedonistic consumerism that she created a series of false identities (ranging from being a Saudi princess to being a lawyer, a model, and a wealthy divorcee) and engaged in illegal behavior (such as trying to steal $250,000 from an insurance company by reporting that certain jewelry had been stolen, when she actually had sold it). See Vanessa Grigoriadis, "Her Royal Lie-ness: The So-Called Saudi Princess Was Only One of the Many Identities Lisa Walker Tried On Like Jewelry," *New York Metro*, www.newyorkmetro.com/nymetro/news/people /columns/intelligencer/n_10418 (accessed December 18, 2004); Samuel Maull, "Antoinette Millard Countersues American Express for $2 Million for Allowing Her to Charge $951,000," creditsuit.org/credit.php/blog/comments/antoinette_millard_countersues_american_express _for_2_million_for_allowing (accessed December 18, 2004).

[19]Steve Lohr, "Maybe It's Not All Your Fault," *New York Times*, December 5, 2004, WR1.
[20]Lohr, "Maybe It's Not All Your Fault."

and power in the economic and political arenas."[21] Some individuals are becoming aware of the effect that media biases can have on what they read, see, and hear. A recent Pew Research Center poll, for example, reflects that people in the working class do not unquestioningly accept media information and commentary that preponderantly support the status quo.[22]

Similarly, Perrucci and Wysong note that television can have a paradoxical effect on viewers: It can serve both as a pacifier and as a source of heightened class consciousness. Programs that focus on how much money the very wealthy have may be a source of entertainment for nonelites, but they may also produce antagonism among people who work hard and earn comparatively little, when they see people being paid so much for doing so little work (e.g., the actress who earns seventeen million dollars per film or the sports star who signs a hundred-million-dollar multiyear contract). Even more egregious are individuals who do not work at all but are born into the "right family" and inherit billions of dollars.

Although affluent audiences might prefer that the media industry work to "reinforce and disguise privileged-class interests,"[23] there is a good chance that the United States will become more class conscious and that people will demand more accurate assessments of the problems we face if more middle- and working-class families see their lifestyles continue to deteriorate in the twenty-first century.

Is Change Likely? Media Realities Support the Status Quo

Will journalists and entertainment writers become more cognizant of class-related issues in news and in television shows? Will they more accurately portray those issues in the future? It is possible that the media will become more aware of class as an important subject to address, but several trends do not bode well for more accurate stories and portrayals of class. Among these are the issues of media ownership and control.

Media Ownership and Senior Management

Media ownership has become increasingly concentrated in recent decades. Massive mergers and acquisitions involving the three major television networks (ABC, CBS, and NBC) have created three media "behemoths"—Viacom, Disney, and General Electric—and the news and entertainment divisions of these networks now constitute only small elements of much larger, more highly diversified corporate structures. Today, these media giants control most of that industry, and a television 30

[21]Robert Perrucci and Earl Wysong, *The New Class Society*, 2nd ed. (Lanham, Md.: Rowman & Littlefield, 2003), 199.

[22]Perrucci and Wysong, *The New Class Society*.

[23]Perrucci and Wysong, *The New Class Society*, 284.

network is viewed as "just another contributor to the bottom line."[24] As the media scholar Shirley Biagi states, "The central force driving the media business in America is the desire to make money. American media are businesses, vast businesses. The products of these businesses are information and entertainment....But American media are, above all, profit-centered."[25]

Concentration of media ownership through chains, broadcast networks, cross-media ownership, conglomerates, and vertical integration (when one company controls several related aspects of the same business) are major limitations to change in how class is represented in the news and entertainment industry. Social analysts like Greg Mantsios[26] are pessimistic about the prospects for change, because of the upper-class-based loyalties of media corporate elites:

> It is no wonder Americans cannot think straight about class. The mass media is neither objective, balanced, independent, nor neutral. Those who own and direct the mass media are themselves part of the upper class, and neither they nor the ruling class in general have to conspire to manipulate public opinion. Their interest is in preserving the status quo, and their view of society as fair and equitable comes naturally to them. But their ideology dominates our society and justifies what is in reality a perverse social order—one that perpetuates unprecedented elite privilege and power on the one hand and widespread deprivation on the other.[27]

According to Mantsios, wealthy media shareholders, corporate executives, and political leaders have a vested interest in obscuring class relations not only because these elites are primarily concerned about profits but because—being among the "haves" themselves—they do not see any reason to stir up class-related animosities. Why should they call attention to the real causes of poverty and inequality and risk the possibility of causing friction among the classes?

Media executives do not particularly care if the general public criticizes the *content* of popular culture as long as audiences do not begin to question the superstructure of media ownership and the benefits these corporations derive from corporate-friendly public policies. According to the sociologist Karen Sternheimer,

> Media conglomerates have a lot to gain by keeping us focused on the popular culture "problem," lest we decide to close some of the corporate tax loopholes to fund more social programs....In short, the news media promote media phobia because it doesn't threaten the bottom line. Calling for social programs to reduce inequality and poverty would.[28]

[24]Committee of Concerned Journalists, "The State of the News Media 2004," www.journalism.org (accessed June 17, 2004).

[25]Shirley Biagi, *Media Impact: An Introduction to Mass Media* (Belmont, Calif.: Wadsworth, 2003), 21.

[26]*Mantsios:* See "Class in America—2006" (p. 304). [Editors' note]

[27]Gregory Mantsios, "Media Magic: Making Class Invisible," in *Privilege: A Reader,* ed. Michael S. Kimmel and Abby L. Ferber, 99–109 (Boulder, Colo.: Westview, 2003), 108.

[28]Karen Sternheimer, *It's Not the Media: The Truth about Pop Culture's Influence on Children* (Boulder, Colo.: Westview, 2003), 211.

Although the corporate culture of the media industry may be set by shareholders and individuals in the top corporate ranks, day-to-day decisions often rest in the hands of the editor-in-chief (or a person in a similar role) at a newspaper or a television executive at a local station. Typically, the goals of these individuals reflect the profit-driven missions of their parent companies and the continual need to generate the right audiences (often young males between eighteen and thirty-five years of age) for advertisers. Television commentator Jeff Greenfield acknowledges this reality: "The most common misconception most people have about television concerns its product. To the viewer, the product is the programming. To the television executive, the product is the audience."[29] The profits of television networks and stations come from selling advertising, not from producing programs that are accurate reflections of social life.

Recent trends in the media industry—including concentration of ownership, a focus on increasing profits, and a move toward less regulation of the media by the federal government—do not offer reassurance that media representations of class (along with race, gender, age, and sexual orientation) will be of much concern to corporate shareholders or executives at the top media giants—unless, of course, this issue becomes related to the bottom line or there is public demand for change, neither of which seems likely. However, it does appear that there is a possibility for change among some journalists and entertainment writers.

Journalists: Constraints and Opportunities

Some analysts divide journalists into the "big time" players—reporters and journalists who are rich, having earned media salaries in the millions and by writing best-selling books (e.g., ABC's Peter Jennings)—and the "everyday" players, who are primarily known in their local or regional media markets.[30] Elite journalists in the first category typically are employed by major television networks (ABC, CBS, and NBC), popular cable news channels (such as CNN and FOX News), or major national newspapers such as the *Wall Street Journal, New York Times,* or *USA Today.* These journalists may be influential in national media agenda-setting, whereas the everyday media players, beat reporters, journalists, and middle- to upper-level managers at local newspapers or television stations at best can influence local markets.

Some of these individuals—at either level—are deeply concerned about the state of journalism in this country, as one recent Pew Research

35

[29]Quoted in Biagi, *Media Impact*, 170.

[30]One study identified the "typical journalist" as "a white Protestant male who has a bachelor's degree from a public college, is married, 36 years old, earns about $31,000 a year, has worked in journalism for about 12 years, does not belong to a journalism association, and works for a medium-sized (42 journalists), group-owned daily newspaper" (Weaver and Wilhoit 1996). Of course, many journalists today are white women, people of color, non-Protestants, and individuals who are between the ages of 45 and 54 (Committee of Concerned Journalists, "The State of the News Media 2004").

Center for the People and the Press study of 547 national and local reporters, editors, and executives found.[31] One of the major concerns among these journalists was that the economic behavior of their companies was eroding the quality of journalism in the United States. By way of example, some journalists believe that business pressures in the media industry are making the news "thinner and shallower."[32] Journalists are also concerned that the news media pay "too little attention...to complex issues."[33] However, a disturbing finding in the Pew study was that some journalists believe that news content is becoming more shallow because that is what the public *wants*. This cynical view may become a self-fulfilling prophecy that leads journalists to produce a shallower product, based on the mistaken belief that the public cannot handle anything else.[34]

Despite all this, some opportunities do exist in the local and national news for *civic journalism*—"a belief that journalism has an obligation to public life—an obligation that goes beyond just telling the news or unloading lots of facts."[35] Civic journalism is rooted in the assumption that journalism has the ability either to empower a community or to help disable it. Based on a civic journalism perspective, a news reporter gathering information for a story has an opportunity to introduce other voices beyond those of the typical mainstream spokesperson called upon to discuss a specific issue such as the loss of jobs in a community or the growing problem of homelessness. Just as more journalists have become aware of the importance of fair and accurate representations of people based on race, gender, age, disability, and sexual orientation, it may be possible to improve media representations of class. Rather than pitting the middle class against the working class and the poor, for example, the media might frame stories in such a way as to increase people's awareness of their shared concerns in a nation where the upper class typically is portrayed as more important and more deserving than the average citizen.

The process of civic journalism encourages journalists to rethink their use of frames. Choosing a specific frame for a story is "the most powerful decision a journalist will make."[36] As journalists become more aware that the media are more than neutral storytelling devices, perhaps more of them will develop alternative frames that look deeply into a community of interest (which might include the class-based realities of neighborhoods) to see "how the community interacts with, interrelates

[31]Pew Center for Civic Journalism, "Finding Third Places: Other Voices, Different Stories," 2004, www.pewcenter.org/doingcj/videos/thirdplaces.html (accessed July 6, 2004).

[32]Bill Kovach, Tom Rosenstiel, and Amy Mitchell, "A Crisis of Confidence: A Commentary on the Findings," Pew Research Center for the People and the Press, 2004, www.stateofthenewsmedia.org/prc.pdf (accessed July 6, 2004), 27.

[33]Kovach, Rosenstiel, and Mitchell, "A Crisis of Confidence," 29.

[34]Kovach, Rosenstiel, and Mitchell, "A Crisis of Confidence."

[35]Pew Center for Civic Journalism, "Finding Third Places."

[36]Steve Smith, "Developing New Reflexes in Framing Stories," Pew Center for Civic Journalism, 1997, www.pewcenter.org/doingcj/civiccat/displayCivcat.php?id=97 (accessed July 3, 2004).

to, and potentially solves a pressing community problem." By asking "What is the essence of this story?" rather than "What is the conflict value of this story?" journalists might be less intent, for example, on pitting the indigenous U.S. working class against more recent immigrants or confronting unionized workers with their nonunionized counterparts. Stories that stress conflict have winners and losers, victors and villains; they suggest that people must compete, rather than cooperate, across class lines.[37] An exploration of other types of framing devices might produce better results in showing how social mobility does or does not work in the U.S. stratification system—highlighting, for example, what an individual's real chances are for moving up the class ladder (as is promised in much of the jargon about the rich and famous).

Advocates of civic journalism suggest that two practices might help journalists do a better job of framing in the public interest: *public listening* and *civic mapping*. Public listening refers to "the ability of journalists to listen with open minds and open ears; to understand what people are really saying."[38] Journalists engaged in public listening would be less interested in getting "superficial quotes or sound bites" and instead would move more deeply into the conversations that are actually taking place. Journalists would use open-ended questions in their interviews, by which they could look more deeply into people's hopes, fears, and values, rather than asking closed-ended questions to which the only allowable response choices are "yes/no" or "agree/disagree"—answers that in effect quickly (and superficially) gauge an individual's opinion on a topic. When journalists use civic mapping, they seek out underlying community concerns through discussions with people. They attempt to look beneath the surface of current public discourse on an issue. Mapping helps journalists learn about the ideas, attitudes, and opinions that really exist among diverse groups of people, not just "public opinion" or politicians' views of what is happening.

By seeking out *third places* where they can find "other voices" and hear "different stories," journalists may learn more about people from diverse backgrounds and find out what they are actually thinking and experiencing.[39] A "third place" is a location where people gather and often end up talking about things that are important to them. According to the sociologist Ray Oldenburg, the third place is "a great variety of public places that host the regular, voluntary, informal, and happily anticipated gatherings of individuals beyond the realms of home and work."[40] If the first place is the home, and the second place is the work setting, then the third place includes such locations as churches, community centers, cafes, coffee shops, bookstores, bars, and other places

40

---

[37]Richard Harwood, "Framing a Story: What's It Really About?" Pew Center for Civic Journalism, 2004, www.pewcenter.org/doingcj/videos/framing.html (accessed July 3, 2004).

[38]Smith, "Developing New Reflexes in Framing Stories."

[39]Pew Center for Civic Journalism, "Finding Third Places."

[40]Ray Oldenburg, *The Great Good Place: Cafés, Coffee Shops, Bookstores, Bars, Hair Salons and Other Hangouts at the Heart of a Community* (New York: Marlowe, 1999), 16.

where people informally gather. As journalists join in the conversation, they can learn what everyday people are thinking about a social issue such as tax cuts for the wealthy. They can also find out what concerns people have and what they think contributes to such problems as neighborhood deterioration.

In addition to listening to other voices and seeking out different stories in third places, journalists might look more systematically at how changes in public policies—such as in tax laws, welfare initiatives, or policies that affect publicly funded child care or public housing—might affect people in various class locations. What are the political and business pressures behind key policy decisions like these? How do policies affect the middle class? The working class? Others? For example, what part does class play in perceptions about local law enforcement agencies? How are police officers viewed in small, affluent incorporated cities that have their own police departments, as compared to low-income neighborhoods of the bigger cities? While wealthy residents in the smaller cities may view police officers as "employees" who do their bidding (such as prohibiting the "wrong kind of people" from entering their city limits at night), in some low-income sectors of larger cities the police may be viewed as "oppressors" or as "racists" who contribute to, rather than reduce, problems of lawlessness and crime in the community. Journalists who practice civic journalism might look beyond typical framing devices to tell a more compelling story about how the intersections of race *and* class produce a unique chemistry between citizens and law enforcement officials. In this way, journalists would not be using taken-for-granted framing devices that have previously been employed to "explain" what is happening in these communities.

Given current constraints on the media, including the fact that much of the new investment in journalism today is being spent on disseminating the news rather than on collecting it,[41] there is room for only cautious optimism that some journalists will break out of the standard reflexive mode to explore the microscopic realities of class at the level where people live, and at the macroscopic level of society, where corporate and governmental elites make important decisions that affect everyone else.

Some media analysts believe that greater awareness of class-related realities in the media would strengthen the democratic process in the United States. According to Mantsios, "A mass media that did not have its own class interests in preserving the status quo would acknowledge that inordinate wealth and power undermine democracy and that a 'free market' economy can ravage a people and their communities."[42] It remains to be seen, however, whether organizations like the Project for Excellence in Journalism and the Committee of Concerned Journalists will be successful in their efforts to encourage journalists to move beyond

[41]Committee of Concerned Journalists, "The State of the News Media 2004."
[42]Mantsios, "Media Magic," 108.

the standard reflexive mode so that they will use new frames that more accurately reflect class-based realities.

Like journalists, many television entertainment writers could look for better ways to frame stories. However, these writers are also beleaguered by changes in the media environment, including new threats to their economic security from reality shows that typically do not employ in-house or freelance writers like continuing series do. As a result, it has become increasingly difficult for entertainment writers to stay gainfully employed, let alone bring new ideas into television entertainment.[43]

We cannot assume that most journalists and television writers are in 45 a position to change media portrayals of class and inequality; however, in the final analysis, the responsibility rests with each of us to evaluate the media and to treat it as only one, limited, source of information and entertainment in our lives. For the sake of our children and grandchildren, we must balance the perspectives we gain from the media with our own lived experiences and use a wider sociological lens to look at what is going on around us in everyday life. Some analysts believe that the media amuse and lull audiences rather than stimulating them to think, but we must not become complacent, thinking that everything is all right as our society and world become increasingly divided between the "haves" and the "have nots."[44] If the media industry persists in retaining the same old frames for class, it will behoove each of us as readers and viewers to break out of those frames and more thoroughly explore these issues on our own.

Bibliography

Biagi, Shirley. *Media Impact: An Introduction to Mass Media*, Belmont, Calif.: Wadsworth, 2003.

Butler, Judith. "Performative Acts and Gender Constitution: An Essay in Phenomenology and Feminist Theory." In *Performing Feminisms: Feminist Critical Theory and Theatre*. Edited by Sue-Ellen Case. Baltimore: Johns Hopkins University Press, 1990.

Committee of Concerned Journalists. "The State of the News Media 2004." www.journalism.org (accessed June 17, 2004).

De Coster, Karen, and Brad Edmonds. Lewrockwell.com, 2003. "TV Nation: The Killing of American Brain Cells." www.lewrockwell.com/decoster/decoster78 .html (accessed July 7, 2004).

Delaney, Tim, and Allene Wilcox. "Sports and the Role of the Media." In *Values, Society and Evolution*, edited by Harry Birx and Tim Delaney, 199–215. Auburn, N.Y. Legend, 2002.

DeNavas-Walt, Carmen, and Robert W. Cleveland. "Income in the United States: 2002." *U.S. Census Bureau: Current Population Reports*, P60–221. Washington, DC: U.S. Government Printing Office, 2003.

Ginsberg, Thomas. "Union Hopes to Win Over Starbucks Shop Workers." *Austin American-Statesman*, July 2, 2004, D6.

---

[43] "So You Wanna Be a Sitcom Writer?" soyouwanna.com, 2004, www.soyouwanna.com /site/syws/sitcom/sitcom.html (accessed July 7, 2004).

[44] Sternheimer, *It's Not the Media*.

Grigoriadis, Vanessa. "Her Royal Lie-ness: The So-Called Saudi Princess Was Only One of the Many Identities Lisa Walker Tried On Like Jewelry." *New York Metro.* www.newyorkmetro.com/nymetro/news/people/columns/intelligencer /n_10418 (accessed December 18, 2004).

Harwood, Richard. "Framing a Story: What's It Really About?" Pew Center for Civic Journalism, 2004. www.pewcenter.org/doingcj/videos/framing.html (accessed July 3, 2004).

hooks, bell [Gloria Watkins]. *Where We Stand: Class Matters.* New York: Routledge, 2000.

Kovach, Bill, Tom Rosenstiel, and Amy Mitchell. "A Crisis of Confidence: A Commentary on the Findings." Pew Research Center for the People and the Press, 2004. www.stateofthenewsmedia.org/prc.pdf (accessed July 6, 2004).

Mantsios, Gregory. "Media Magic: Making Class Invisible." In *Privilege: A Reader,* edited by Michael S. Kimmel and Abby L. Ferber, 99–109. Boulder, Colo.: Westview, 2003.

Maull, Samuel. "Antoinette Millard Countersues American Express for $2 Million for Allowing Her to Charge $951,000." creditsuit.org/credit.php/blog /comments/antoinette_millard_countersues_american_express_for_2_million _for_allowing (accessed December 18, 2004).

Nocera, Joseph. *A Piece of the Action: How the Middle Class Joined the Money Class.* New York: Simon and Schuster, 1994.

Oldenburg, Ray. *The Great Good Place: Cafés, Coffee Shops, Bookstores, Bars Hair Salons and Other Hangouts at the Heart of a Community.* New York: Marlowe, 1999.

Perrucci, Robert, and Earl Wysong. *The New Class Society.* 2nd edition. Lanham, Md.: Rowman & Littlefield, 2003.

Pew Center for Civic Journalism. 2004, "Finding Third Places: Other Voices, Different Stories." www.pewcenter.org/doingcj/videos/thirdplaces.html (accessed July 6, 2004).

Proctor, Bernadette D., and Joseph Dalaker. "Poverty in the United States: 2002." *U.S. Census Bureau: Current Population Reports,* P60–22. Washington, DC: U.S. Government Printing Office, 2003.

Schor, Juliet B. *Born to Buy: The Commercialized Child and the New Consumer Culture.* New York: Scribner, 2004.

Sicha, Choire. "They'll Always Have Paris." *New York Times,* June 13, 2004, AR31, AR41.

Smith, Steve. "Developing New Reflexes in Framing Stories." Pew Center for Civic Journalism, 1997. www.pewcenter.org/doingcj/civiccat/displayCivcat .php?id=97 (accessed July 3, 2004).

"So You Wanna Be a Sitcom Writer?" soyouwanna.com, 2004. www.soyouwanna .com/site/syws/sitcom/sitcom.html (accessed July 7, 2004).

Sternheimer, Karen. *It's Not the Media: The Truth about Pop Culture's Influence on Children.* Boulder, Colo.: Westview, 2003.

Uchitelle, Louis. "We Pledge Allegiance to the Mall." *New York Times,* December 6, 2004, C12.

Weaver, David H., and G. Cleveland Wilhoit. *The American Journalist in the 1990s.* Mahwah, N.J.: Lawrence Erlbaum, 1996.

ENGAGING THE TEXT

1. Debate Kendall's assertion that "the media do not simply mirror society; rather, they help to shape it and to create cultural perceptions" (para. 3). Do you agree with Kendall's claim that the media distort our perceptions of

social inequality? Do you think that watching TV inclines Americans to run up credit card debt?

2. Review Kendall's explanation of why middle- and working-class people sometimes buy items beyond their means, particularly items associated with wealthy celebrities. Do you agree that this behavior is best understood as "vicarious living" and "unnecessary consumerism"? In small groups, brainstorm lists of purchases you think exemplify hedonistic or unnecessary consumerism. How does hedonistic consumerism appear in a college setting?

3. Kendall says the media use "thematic framing" and "episodic framing" in portraying poor Americans. Define these terms in your own words and discuss whether the media typically portray the poor as "deviant" or "Other."

4. According to Kendall, how do media representations of the working class and the middle class differ? Do you see evidence of this difference in the shows she mentions or in others you are familiar with?

5. What does Kendall mean by "civic journalism" (para. 37)? Why is she pessimistic about the future of civic journalism in national news organizations? Do you see any evidence of such journalism in your local news outlets?

EXPLORING CONNECTIONS

6. Imagine what "Looking for Work" (p. 22) or "The Lesson" (p. 253) might look like if it were turned into a TV episode. Keeping Kendall's observations in mind, how do you think TV might frame these stories about social class?

7. Re-examine the images in the Visual Portfolio (p. 307). Discuss how they "frame" issues of social class and how each image supports or challenges conventional media frames.

EXTENDING THE CRITICAL CONTEXT

8. Review Kendall's definitions of consensus framing, admiration framing, emulation framing, and price-tag framing. Then watch one of the TV shows she mentions in paragraph 8 or a similar current show and look for evidence of these framing devices. Discuss with classmates how prominent these frames seem to be in contemporary TV programs.

MAKING IT IN AMERICA
ADAM DAVIDSON

> In this profile of a factory worker in South Carolina, journalist Adam Davidson introduces a young woman who embodies the insecurity of living near the edge of the economy. "Maddie" has overcome some serious setbacks and managed to find a steady job that she likes, but despite her hard work and intelligence she is more likely to lose her job to a robot than to advance to a well-paid career. Davidson specializes in explaining complex economic issues to the general public—though he has also covered stories as diverse as the U.S. occupation of Baghdad, the aftermath of Hurricane Katrina, and the youth riots in Paris in 2005. A winner of every major award in broadcast journalism, he is cofounder and cohost of *Planet Money*, produced by National Public Radio, and *This American Life*. "Making It in America," the source of this excerpt, originally appeared in the *Atlantic*, January/February 2012.

I FIRST MET MADELYN "Maddie" Parlier in the "clean room" of Standard Motor Products' fuel-injector assembly line in Greenville, South Carolina. Like everyone else, she was wearing a blue lab coat and a hairnet. She's so small that she seemed swallowed up by all the protective gear.

Tony Scalzitti, the plant manager, was giving me the grand tour, explaining how bits of metal move through a series of machines to become precision fuel injectors. Maddie, hunched forward and moving quickly from one machine to another, almost bumped into us, then shifted left and darted away. Tony, in passing, said, "She's new. She's one of our most promising Level 1s."

Later, I sat down with Maddie in a quiet factory office where nobody needs to wear protective gear. Without the hairnet and lab coat, she is a pretty, intense woman, 22 years old, with bright blue eyes that seemed to bore into me as she talked, as fast as she could, about her life. She told me how much she likes her job, because she hates to sit still and there's always something going on in the factory. She enjoys learning, she said, and she's learned how to run a lot of the different machines. At one point, she looked around the office and said she'd really like to work there one day, helping to design parts rather than stamping them out. She said she's noticed that robotic arms and other machines seem to keep replacing people on the factory floor, and she's worried that this could happen to her. She told me she wants to go back to school — as her parents and grandparents keep telling her to do — but she is a single mother, and she can't leave her two kids alone at night while she takes classes.

I had come to Greenville to better understand what, exactly, is happening to manufacturing in the United States, and what the future holds for people like Maddie — people who still make physical things for a living and, more broadly, people (as many as 40 million adults in the U.S.) who lack higher education, but are striving for a middle-class life. We do still make things here, even though many people don't believe me when I tell them that. Depending on which stats you believe, the United States is either the No. 1 or No. 2 manufacturer in the world (China may have surpassed us in the past year or two). Whatever the country's current rank, its manufacturing output continues to grow strongly; in the past decade alone, output from American factories, adjusted for inflation, has risen by a third.

Yet the success of American manufacturers has come at a cost. Factories have replaced millions of workers with machines. Even if you know the rough outline of this story, looking at the Bureau of Labor Statistics data is still shocking. A historical chart of U.S. manufacturing employment shows steady growth from the end of the Depression until the early 1980s, when the number of jobs drops a little. Then things stay largely flat until about 1999. After that, the numbers simply collapse. In the 10 years ending in 2009, factories shed workers so fast that they erased almost all the gains of the previous 70 years; roughly one out of every three manufacturing jobs — about 6 million in total — disappeared. About as many people work in manufacturing now as did at the end of the Depression, even though the American population is more than twice as large today.

I came here to find answers to questions that arise from the data. How, exactly, have some American manufacturers continued to survive, and even thrive, as global competition has intensified? What, if anything, should be done to halt the collapse of manufacturing employment? And what does the disappearance of factory work mean for the rest of us?

Across America, many factory floors look radically different than they did 20 years ago: far fewer people, far more high-tech machines, and entirely different demands on the workers who remain. The still-unfolding story of manufacturing's transformation is, in many respects, that of our economic age. It's a story with much good news for the nation as a whole. But it's also one that is decidedly less inclusive than the story of the 20th century, with a less certain role for people like Maddie Parlier, who struggle or are unlucky early in life.

The Life and Times of Maddie Parlier

The Greenville Standard Motor Products plant sits just off I-85, about 100 miles southwest of Charlotte, North Carolina. It's a sprawling beige one-story building, surrounded by a huge tended lawn. Nearby are dozens of other similarly boxy factory buildings. Neighbors include a big Michelin tire plant, a nutrition-products factory, and, down the road, BMW's only car plant on American soil. Greenville is at the center of the 20-year-old manufacturing boom that's still taking place throughout the "New South." Nearby, I visited a Japanese-owned fiber-optic-material manufacturer, and a company that makes specialized metal parts for intercontinental ballistic missiles.

Standard makes and distributes replacement auto parts, known in the industry as "aftermarket" parts. Companies like Standard directly compete with Chinese firms for shelf space in auto-parts retail stores. This competition has intensified the pressure on all parts makers—American, Chinese, European. And of course it means that Maddie is, effectively, competing directly with workers in China who are willing to do similar work for much less money.

When Maddie says something important, something she wants you 10 to really hear, she repeats it. She'll say it one time in a flat, matter-of-fact voice, and then again with a lot of upstate South Carolina twang.

"I'm a redneck," she'll say. "I'm a *reeeeeedneck*."

"I'm smart," she told me the first time we met. "There's no other way to say it. I am *smaaaart*. I am."

Maddie flips back and forth between being a stereotypical redneck and being awfully smart. She will say, openly, that she doesn't know all that much about the world outside of Easley, South Carolina, where she's spent her whole life. Since her childhood, she's seen Easley transform from a quiet country town to a busy suburb of Greenville. (It's now a largely charmless place, thick with chain restaurants and shopping centers.) Maddie was the third child born to her young mother, Heather. Her father left when Maddie was young, never visited again, and died after he drove drunk into a car carrying a family of four, killing all of them as well.

Until her senior year of high school, Maddie seemed to be headed for the American dream—a college degree and a job with a middle-class wage. She got good grades, and never drank or did drugs or hung out with the bad kids. For the most part, she didn't hang out with any-body outside her family; she went to school, went home, went to church on Sundays. When she was 17, she met a boy who told her she should make friends with other kids at school. He had an easy way with people and he would take Maddie to Applebee's and cookouts and other places where the cool kids hung out. He taught her how to fit in, and he told her she was pretty.

Maddie's senior year started hopefully. She had finished most of   15
her high-school requirements and was taking a few classes at nearby Tri-County Technical College. She planned to go to a four-year col-lege after graduation, major in criminal justice, and become an animal-control officer. Around Christmas, she found out she was pregnant. She did finish school and, she's proud to say, graduated with honors. "On my graduation, I was six months pregnant," she says. "*Six months.*" The father and Maddie didn't stay together after the birth, and Maddie couldn't afford to pay for day care while she went to college, so she gave up on school and eventually got the best sort of job available to high-school graduates in the Greenville area: factory work.

If Maddie had been born in upstate South Carolina earlier in the 20th century, her working life would have been far more secure. Her 22 years overlap the final collapse of most of the area's once-dominant cotton mills and the birth of an advanced manufacturing economy. Hundreds of mills here once spun raw cotton into thread and then wove and knit the thread into clothes and textiles. For about 100 years, right through the 1980s and into the 1990s, mills in the Greenville area had plenty of work for people willing to put in a full day, no matter how little education they had. But around the time Maddie was born, two si-multaneous transformations hit these workers. After NAFTA[1] and, later, the opening of China to global trade, mills in Mexico and China were able to produce and ship clothing and textiles at much lower cost, and mill after mill in South Carolina shut down. At the same time, the mills that continued to operate were able to replace their workers with a new generation of nearly autonomous, computer-run machines. (There's a joke in cotton country that a modern textile mill employs only a man and a dog. The man is there to feed the dog, and the dog is there to keep the man away from the machines.)

Other parts of the textile South have never recovered from these two blows, but upstate South Carolina—thanks to its proximity to I-85, and to foresighted actions by community leaders—attracted manufac-turers of products far more complicated than shirts and textiles. These new plants have been a godsend for the local economy, but they have not provided the sort of wide-open job opportunities that the textile mills once did. Some workers, especially those with advanced manu-facturing skills, now earn higher wages and have more opportunity, but

---

[1]*NAFTA:* The controversial 1994 North American Free Trade Agreement, which re-moved many trade barriers between Mexico, Canada, and the United States. [Eds.]

there are not enough jobs for many others who, like Maddie, don't have training past high school.

Maddie got her job at Standard through both luck and hard work. She was temping for a local agency and was sent to Standard for a three-day job washing walls in early 2011. "People came up to me and said, 'You have to hire that girl—she is working so hard,'" Tony Scalzitti, the plant manager, told me. Maddie was hired back and assigned to the fuel-injector clean room, where she continued to impress people by working hard, learning quickly, and displaying a good attitude. But, as we'll see, this may be about as far as hustle and personality can take her. In fact, they may not be enough even to keep her where she is....

The Remnant Workforce

Tony Scalzitti, the factory manager, guides me through the logic of Maddie's employment. He's bookish and thoughtful—nothing like my mental image of a big, hulking factory manager. Trained as an engineer, he is constantly drawing charts and making lists as he talks, in order to explain modern American manufacturing. Sitting at a table in his office in the administrative area off the factory floor, Tony takes out a pen and writes down the definitions.

"Unskilled worker," he narrates, "can train in a short amount of time. The machine controls the quality of the part." 20

"High-skill worker," on the other hand, "can set up machines and make a variety of small adjustments; they use their judgment to assure product quality." ...

[Maddie] runs the laser welding machine, which sounds difficult and dangerous, but is neither. The laser welder is tiny, more like a cigarette lighter than like something you might aim at a Klingon. Maddie receives a tray of sealed injector interiors, and her job is to weld on a cap. The machine looks a little like a microscope; she puts the injector body in a hole in the base, and the cap in a clamp where the microscope lens would be. The entire machine—like most machines in the clean room—sits inside a large metal-and-plexiglass box with sensors to make sure that Maddie removes her hands from the machine before it runs. Once Maddie inserts the two parts and removes her hands, a protective screen comes down, and a computer program tells the machine to bring the cap and body together, fire its tiny beam, and rotate the part to create a perfect seal. The process takes a few seconds. Maddie then retrieves the part and puts it into another simple machine, which runs a test to make sure the weld created a full seal. If Maddie sees a green light, the part is sent on to the next station; if she sees a red or yellow light, the part failed and Maddie calls one of the skilled techs, who will troubleshoot and, if necessary, fix the welding machine.

The last time I visited the factory, Maddie was training a new worker. Teaching her to operate the machine took just under two minutes. Maddie then spent about 25 minutes showing her the various instructions Standard engineers have prepared to make certain that the machine operator doesn't need to use her own judgment. "Always check your sheets," Maddie says.

By the end of the day, the trainee will be as proficient at the laser welder as Maddie. This is why all assembly workers have roughly the same pay grade—known as Level 1—and are seen by management as largely interchangeable and fairly easy to replace. A Level 1 worker makes about $13 an hour, which is a little more than the average wage in this part of the country. The next category, Level 2, is defined by Standard as a worker who knows the machines well enough to set up the equipment and adjust it when things go wrong. The skilled machinists...are Level 2s, and make about 50 percent more than Maddie does.

For Maddie to achieve her dreams—to own her own home, to take her family on vacation to the coast, to have enough saved up so her children can go to college—she'd need to become one of the advanced Level 2s. A decade ago, a smart, hard-working Level 1 might have persuaded management to provide on-the-job training in Level-2 skills. But these days, the gap between a Level 1 and a 2 is so wide that it doesn't make financial sense for Standard to spend years training someone who might not be able to pick up the skills or might take that training to a competing factory.

It feels cruel to point out all the Level-2 concepts Maddie doesn't 25 know, although Maddie is quite open about these shortcomings. She doesn't know the computer-programming language that runs the machines she operates; in fact, she was surprised to learn they are run by a specialized computer language. She doesn't know trigonometry or calculus, and she's never studied the properties of cutting tools or metals. She doesn't know how to maintain a tolerance of 0.25 microns, or what *tolerance* means in this context, or what a micron is.

Tony explains that Maddie has a job for two reasons. First, when it comes to making fuel injectors, the company saves money and minimizes product damage by having both the precision and non-precision work done in the same place. Even if Mexican or Chinese workers could do Maddie's job more cheaply, shipping fragile, half-finished parts to another country for processing would make no sense. Second, Maddie is cheaper than a machine. It would be easy to buy a robotic arm that could take injector bodies and caps from a tray and place them precisely in a laser welder. Yet Standard would have to invest about $100,000 on the arm and a conveyance machine to bring parts to the welder and send them on to the next station. As is common in factories, Standard invests only in machinery that will earn back its cost within two years. For Tony, it's simple: Maddie makes less in two years than the machine would cost, so her job is safe—for now. If the robotic machines become a little cheaper, or if demand for fuel injectors goes up and Standard starts running three shifts, then investing in those robots might make sense.

"What worries people in factories is electronics, robots," she tells me. "If you don't know jack about computers and electronics, then you don't have anything in this life anymore. One day, they're not going to need people; the machines will take over. People like me, we're not going to be around forever." ...

Workers' Paradise?

... Is there a crisis in manufacturing in America? Looking just at the dollar value of manufacturing output, the answer seems to be an emphatic no. Domestic manufacturers make and sell more goods than ever before. Their success has been grounded in incredible increases in productivity, which is a positive way of saying that factories produce more with fewer workers.

Productivity, in and of itself, is a remarkably good thing. Only through productivity growth can the average quality of human life improve. Because of higher agricultural productivity, we don't all have to work in the fields to make enough food to eat. Because of higher industrial productivity, few of us need to work in factories to make the products we use. In theory, productivity growth should help nearly everyone in a society. When one person can grow as much food or make as many car parts as 100 used to, prices should fall, which gives everyone in that society more purchasing power; we all become a little richer. In the economic models, the benefits of productivity growth should not go just to the rich owners of capital. As workers become more productive, they should be able to demand higher salaries.

Throughout much of the 20th century, simultaneous technological 30 improvements in both agriculture and industry happened to create conditions that were favorable for people with less skill. The development of mass production allowed low-skilled farmers to move to the city, get a job in a factory, and produce remarkably high output. Typically, these workers made more money than they ever had on the farm, and eventually, some of their children were able to get enough education to find less-dreary work. In that period of dramatic change, it was the highly skilled craftsperson who was more likely to suffer a permanent loss of wealth. Economists speak of the middle part of the 20th century as the "Great Compression," the time when the income of the unskilled came closest to the income of the skilled.

The double shock we're experiencing now—globalization and computer-aided industrial productivity—happens to have the opposite impact: income inequality is growing, as the rewards for being skilled grow and the opportunities for unskilled Americans diminish.

I went to South Carolina, and spent so much time with Maddie, precisely because these issues are so large and so overwhelming. I wanted to see how this shift affected regular people's lives. I didn't come away with a handy list of policies that would solve all the problems of unskilled workers, but I did note some principles that seem important to improving their situation.

It's hard to imagine what set of circumstances would reverse recent trends and bring large numbers of jobs for unskilled laborers back to the U.S. Our efforts might be more fruitfully focused on getting Maddie the education she needs for a better shot at a decent living in the years to come. Subsidized job-training programs tend to be fairly popular among Democrats and Republicans, and certainly benefit some people. But these programs suffer from all the ills in our education system; opportunities go, disproportionately, to those who already have initiative, intelligence, and—not least—family support.

I never heard Maddie blame others for her situation; she talked, often, about the bad choices she made as a teenager and how those have limited her future. I came to realize, though, that Maddie represents a large population: people who, for whatever reason, are not going to be able to leave the workforce long enough to get the skills they need....Those with the right ability and circumstances will, most likely, make the right adjustments, get the right skills, and eventually thrive. But I fear that those who are challenged now will only fall further behind. To solve all the problems that keep people from acquiring skills would require tackling the toughest issues our country faces: a broken educational system, teen pregnancy, drug use, racial discrimination, a fractured political culture.

This may be the worst impact of the disappearance of manufacturing work. In older factories and, before them, on the farm, there were opportunities for almost everybody: the bright and the slow, the sociable and the awkward, the people with children and those without. All came to work unskilled, at first, and then slowly learned things, on the job, that made them more valuable. Especially in the mid-20th century, as manufacturing employment was rocketing toward its zenith, mistakes and disadvantages in childhood and adolescence did not foreclose adult opportunity.

For most of U.S. history, most people had a slow and steady wind at their back, a combination of economic forces that didn't make life easy but gave many of us little pushes forward that allowed us to earn a bit more every year. Over a lifetime, it all added up to a better sort of life than the one we were born into. That wind seems to be dying for a lot of Americans. What the country will be like without it is not quite clear.

ENGAGING THE TEXT

1. Explain the double meaning of the title "Making It in America."

2. Why does Davidson choose to write about Maddie Parlier? What elements of her biography, her personality, and her circumstances make her story interesting and illuminating? How does Davidson use the experience of one young woman in South Carolina to shed light on national and international issues?

3. At $13 an hour, how long would it take Maddie to make what the average chief executive officer at a major company makes in one year ($20 million)? Is this fair? Do the salaries of low-skilled workers say anything about their value as human beings?

4. What can be done to help workers like Maddie? Discuss what you think schools, businesses, government, or community organizations should do to improve opportunities for low-skilled workers.

5. Davidson is clearly sympathetic toward Maddie. How do you read his perspective on plant manager Tony Scalzitti? How does "Making It in America" support or challenge the familiar idea of labor locked in a struggle against management or owners?

6. Some of the material in Davidson's story is factual—for example, he provides economic data, records conversations, summarizes Maddie's past, and explains how a laser welding machine works. But he also reflects on what he sees, sharing his reactions and opinions with the reader. Roughly how much of the reading selection is expository, and how much is reflective or analytical? To what extent do you think Davidson makes an argument, explicit or implied, about Maddie or the American economy?

EXPLORING CONNECTIONS

7. Review "Serving in Florida" by Barbara Ehrenreich (p. 267), noting her descriptions of waitressing and housekeeping jobs. Imagine that Ehrenreich's next "undercover" job were at the Standard Motor Products factory. Write notes from Ehrenreich's point of view about being trained by Maddie to operate the laser welding machine and working her first week on the assembly line.

8. Maddie has not achieved the kind of life to which she once aspired, but according to Davidson she blames herself for the poor choices she made as a teenager. How does Davidson complicate this view of her restricted options, and how might one or more of the following writers view Maddie, her history, and her prospects: Gregory Mantsios (p. 281), Timothy Noah (p. 356), Mike Rose (p. 151), Jean Anyon (p. 163), Martha Nussbaum (p. 669)? To what extent do you think Maddie's life is a result of her free choices, and to what degree has it been shaped by circumstances or forces beyond her control?

9. Review the last section of Diana Kendall's "Framing Class, Vicarious Living, and Conspicuous Consumption" (paras. 35–45 on pp. 326–330). Explain why you think Kendall would or would not consider "Making It in America" an example of "civic journalism."

10. Review the excerpt from *The Accordion Family* by Katherine S. Newman (p. 83). Discuss whether it would be a good idea for Maddie and her two kids to share a household with her parents or grandparents so that she could attend evening courses and earn a college diploma.

EXTENDING THE CRITICAL CONTEXT

11. The economy where you live may differ significantly from upstate South Carolina's. Working in small groups, list the industries and the economic trends that you consider most important to your region. Then think about

what kinds of local work and workers a journalist like Davidson would most like to learn about: where might he find an individual who symbolizes the economic opportunities or challenges of your area? If possible, arrange an interview with such a representative worker and then report to the class or write up a short journalistic profile.

12. Listen to the radio version of this story, where you can hear Adam Davidson talking to Maddie Parlier and Larry Sills, the third-generation CEO of family-owned Standard Motor Products. (The story, "The Transformation of American Factory Jobs, in One Company" is archived at National Public Radio: www.npr.org/blogs/money/2012/01/13/145039131/the-transformation -of-american-factory-jobs-in-one-company). The radio segment contains material you have not read above, so you may want to take notes. Discuss how and why hearing the story differs from reading it.

FROM AMERICA'S NEW WORKING CLASS
KATHLEEN R. ARNOLD

Most Americans would probably agree that the purpose of federal welfare programs is to provide economic assistance such as food stamps to people who need it, who can't quite make ends meet. Such a view regards welfare as an essentially humanitarian endeavor. In the reading below, political theorist Kathleen R. Arnold proposes a rather more sinister alternative—that the real purpose of welfare programs is to maintain a supply of cheap labor while disciplining and closely monitoring welfare recipients. Arnold teaches political science at the University of Texas, San Antonio. She is the editor of *Anti-Immigration in the United States: A Historical Encyclopedia* (2011) and author of *America's New Working Class: Race, Gender, and Ethnicity in a Biopolitical Age* (2007), from which this selection is excerpted.

[WELFARE AND "WORKFARE"][1] should be viewed in the same terms as parole—the recipient is not merely a client, an individual whose transaction with a bureaucracy has a beginning and end. Rather, like parole, welfare entails strict adherence to rules (including the monitoring of one's sexual activities and limits to the number of children one can have), close scrutiny of what are normally considered private details, and harsh penalties for noncompliance. For parolees, the threat is a return to prison; for noncompliant welfare or workfare recipients, the threats involve one's very existence: homelessness, malnourishment,

---

[1]*welfare, workfare:* Welfare programs provide economic support to persons in need; workfare programs require aid recipients to work to receive social assistance. [Eds.]

and a deeper descent into poverty.[2] As Sheldon Wolin states: "The state is, therefore, allowed to deal arbitrarily with all welfare recipients, not by lynching them but by redefining the conditions and categories of their existence."[3]...

Clearly, the word "reform" is disingenuous when applied to the welfare changes of 1996; instead of improving the situation of the poor, reform "is punishment of individuals or restriction of their rights in order to improve their characters or behaviors, as in 'reform school.' This type of welfare reform has a long tradition" in both the United States and the United Kingdom.[4] As many authors have demonstrated, the notion that poverty or joblessness is a result of personal failings is particularly American, even as some European countries have shared the values of the Protestant work ethic to a lesser extent. This explains why our policies are far more punitive and individually oriented than in other liberal capitalist countries (although England comes close).[5]

As Sheila D. Collins and Gertrude Schaffner Goldberg discuss, the history of welfare or poor relief in the United States has had the following undemocratic characteristics:[6] outdoor relief is limited or denied (this is still true—many cities ban individual food donations and regulate outdoor bread lines);[7] work is provided under coercive conditions (workfare today is not voluntary, wages are below minimum wage, benefits are not provided, and workfare wages can be garnished to pay back welfare); there is an assumption that paupers are irresponsible and individually flawed (this assumption is still evident in the ascetic prescriptions of TANF[8] and nearly all other welfare programs); the notion that the provision of aid is a causal factor in the demand for it (this is evident today in talks about welfare dependency and cheating); authorities have required relatives who are often also poor to aid their poor relations (this is still true, particularly with entrance to a homeless shelter—the individual must prove that he or she has exhausted the list of relatives with whom to stay before entering the shelter);[9] aid is not viewed as an entitlement in the United States (and never has been, and furthermore, this is truer today than it was in the early part of the twentieth century); welfare relief varies from state to state (and always has); despite Supreme Court rulings that strike down residency requirements

---

[2]On "penal welfarism," or the connection between the welfare state and criminal justice, see Garland, *Culture of Control*. [Notes are Arnold's unless otherwise indicated.]

[3]Wolin, "Democracy and the Welfare State," 159.

[4]Sheila D. Collins and Gertrude Schaffner Goldberg, *Washington's New Poor Law* (New York: Apex Press, Council on International and Public Affairs, 2001), 6.

[5]See Wilson, *When Work Disappears*.

[6]Collins and Goldberg, *Washington's New Poor Law*, 9. The characteristics listed in this paragraph are Collins and Goldberg's; the parenthetical comments are mine.

[7]For example, San Francisco has arrested individuals for feeding the homeless. In many other cities, outdoor bread lines have been hotly contested.

[8]*TANF*: Temporary Assistance for Needy Families, the formal name for the U.S. welfare program. [Eds.]

[9]As a housing advocate in Boston's shelter system, I was required to go through a list of relatives and friends with whom shelter residents could stay. Among other problems this causes, staying with a relative or friend can endanger the terms of that person's lease.

as limiting freedom of travel, local authorities deny or limit assistance to newcomers (and always have), be they citizens or immigrants;[10] and, finally, welfare has "denied recipients political and civil rights in return for a meager dole"[11] (this is still true de facto if not de jure). These broad characteristics of welfare throughout U.S. history highlight not only the punitive character of the welfare system[12] but also the coercive nature of workfare. The crucial assumptions behind workfare programs are two: participants must be forced to work; and they have no motivation to do so and thus must be guided, shaped, and disciplined. This is why they are denied choices that ordinary workers would ideally have, such as what hours to work, what they will be paid, and where their wages will go.

It needs to be emphasized that workfare is dependent *not* on job creation but rather on a flexible labor market:

> Contemporary workfare policies rarely involve job creation on any signif-
> icant scale, along the lines of the old-fashioned public-works programs;
> they are more concerned with deterring welfare claims and necessitat-
> ing the acceptance of low-paid, unstable jobs in the context of increas-
> ingly "flexible" labor markets. Stripped down to its labor-regulatory
> essence, workfare is not about creating jobs for people that don't have
> them; it is about creating workers for jobs that nobody wants. In a
> Foucauldian[13] sense, it is seeking to make "docile bodies" for the new
> economy: flexible, self-reliant, and self-disciplining.[14]

Welfare and workfare indicate bare survival—recipients are not meant to rise even to lower-middle-class status. As Piven and Cloward note:

> In New York City, some 45,000 people, mainly women, sweep the streets
> and clean the subways and the parks. They do the work once done by
> unionized municipal employees. But instead of a paycheck and a living
> wage, they get a welfare check that leaves them far below the poverty
> level, and they have none of the benefits and protections of unionized
> workers. Perhaps just as bad, they have become public spectacles of ab-
> ject and degraded labor—of slave labor, many of them say.[15]

The word slavery is an exaggeration but it is not incidental: workers in Marx's analysis were also "free" to sell their labor and participate in a "free" market; but their limited choices, de facto political disenfran-chisement, lack of collective bargaining or representation (i.e., unions), and inhuman work conditions indicated a profound asymmetry of politi-cal power. These dynamics, which are present today just as in Marx's

---

[10]See Sanford F. Schram, "Introduction," in *Welfare Reform: A Race to the Bottom?* ed. Schram and Samuel H. Beer (Washington, D.C.: Woodrow Wilson Center Press, n.d.). Recent changes in TANF requirements (2006) may allow American-born recipients to move from state to state without cessation of welfare; however, it is unclear whether this will be imple-mented efficiently.

[11]Collins and Goldberg, *Washington's New Poor Law*, 9.

[12]See, for example, Garland, *Culture of Control*.

[13]*Foucauldian:* Resembling the ideas of French philosopher Michel Foucault (1926–1984); Foucault's *Discipline and Punish: The Birth of the Prison* (1975) theorized about Western sys-tems of punishment and control. [Eds.]

[14]Jamie Peck, *Workfare States* (New York: Guilford Press, 2001), 6.

[15]Richard Cloward and Frances Fox Piven in Peck, *Workfare States*, ix.

time, challenge any claims about "freedom." Today, workfare and welfare programs have taken away many of the rights (not necessarily in the legal sense but broadly conceived) that ordinary citizens enjoy, including the rights to privacy and individual moral choice as well as the right to determine work conditions.

Furthermore, if the new working class (low-tier workers) is viewed as part of the inner city, as composed of both formal citizens and migrants, it must be recognized that this same group is not only subject to welfare and workfare surveillance and control, but also to the War on Drugs, racial profiling, the War on Terror, immigration controls, and the resurgence of racial prejudice and sexism.... This set of power dynamics indicates a far more complex and intricate system of controls—one that in effect suspends the law through bureaucratic mechanisms in a systematic fashion (systematic meaning that the impact is long-lasting and that this population is treated consistently as a biological threat to national security).[16] Unlike the conditions at Guantánamo Bay (not to idealize conditions there), the ideational system that creates ethnic, racial, and gender antagonisms obscures these power dynamics and often inverts them, positing these groups as the true usurpers or exploiters (of "us": the welfare system, taxpayers' dollars, our moral sensibility, and so on).

All of these policies disproportionately affect low-tier workers and the very poor.[17] ... Similar to workfare policies and low-wage strategies, the U.S. guest-worker program combines these two elements: "flexible" work conditions; and heavy surveillance and political control, accompanied by the political powerlessness of workers. One of the more prominent sectors of the guest-worker program is agriculture; the United States has the most physically intensive agricultural system in the West, while at the same time, agricultural jobs have been rated by various authorities as the most and second most dangerous jobs in America.[18] Because many of these workers are on agricultural visas, they are monitored by the BCIS[19] as well as by local police forces, employers, and citizens' watch groups. Guest workers are tied to one employer, must be on site twenty-four hours a day, seven days a week, are provided housing that lacks both refrigeration and sewage, often live in tents or other makeshift housing, and have no access to doctors, electricity, or outside help. As of this writing, guest workers cannot strike, change employers, or bargain for wages.[20] If they are fired from their positions, they have less than a week to leave the country and no legal recourse. Meanwhile,

[16]See Arnold, *Homelessness, Citizenship, and Identity*, Chapter 4.
[17]See, for example, David L. Marcus, "Three Times and Out," *Boston Globe*, October 14, 1998, A1; Nancy Gertner and Daniel Kanstroom, "The Recent Spotlight on the INS Failed to Reveal Its Dark Side," *Boston Globe*, May 21, 2000, E1, E3.
[18]Other jobs rated among the most dangerous are mining and meatpacking work.
[19]*BCIS:* Bureau of Citizenship and Immigration Services, a component of the Homeland Security Agency. [Eds.]
[20]Legislation has been proposed to modify guest workers' conditions, but this is at the very beginning stages; moreover, the proposed legislation still does not go far enough to protect these workers from abuse, starvation, poor medical care, and exposure to the elements.

illegal immigrants in the meatpacking industry often work in factories that are freezing, isolated, and subject to deregulated (read "unsafe") working conditions. Often they are tracked by BCIS and citizens' watch groups and are deported or allowed to stay according to arbitrary criteria. Additionally, conditions in the Border Industrial Program, a transnational factory area established through a partnership between the United States and Mexico, are both "free"—that is, deregulated—and dangerous and exploitative for workers. Just as international companies in this program (*maquilas*) have enjoyed relaxed environmental and labor standards, female *maquiladora* workers have been subject to brutal conditions. Hundreds of these women have been rape-murdered or kidnapped. The murder investigations of these "women of Juárez" have been sluggish, but their border crossing is certainly policed. The lack of heat in these factories, the speeding up of conveyor belts so that injuries are commonplace, and the vulnerability of these workers to both the market and the police form the parameters of these workers' daily existence.[21] In all of these cases, workers are exploited and seemingly abandoned by the state; yet at the same time they are subject to much greater surveillance and control.

ENGAGING THE TEXT

1. Arnold writes in a formal style well suited to an intellectually sophisticated audience. Try writing a 100- to 200-word summary of her argument that would be accessible to high school readers.

2. Does Arnold persuade you that welfare and workfare are unreasonably invasive, punitive programs? What specific details does she cite to support her point of view? What level of supervision, if any, do you think would be appropriate for recipients of federal aid?

3. Arnold and the writers she quotes point to ways in which welfare and workfare resemble parole, lynching, reform schools, and slave labor. Discuss the rhetorical effect of such references, considering both their emotional impact and their logical validity.

4. Arnold's point of view is obviously not conservative. How would you characterize it—liberal, progressive, reformist, radical, revolutionary, or something else? Explain.

EXPLORING CONNECTIONS

5. Review Diana Kendall's "Framing Class, Vicarious Living, and Conspicuous Consumption" (p. 314). How would you expect media to "frame" welfare

---

[21]See Human Rights Watch, "Human Rights Watch Welcomes U.S. Government Meat and Poultry Study," http://hrw.org/English/docs/2005/02/03/usdomio117_txt.htm; "Abusive Child Labor Found in U.S. Agriculture," http//hrw.org/English/docs/2000/06/20/usdom580_txt.htm; NCRLC, "U.S. Agricultural Workers," http://www.ncrlc.com/Agricultural Workers.html.

recipients? Can you think of any specific examples of media representations of welfare recipients, or are these people invisible in the media?

6. Read "The New Jim Crow" by Michelle Alexander (p. 738). Explain why you think Arnold would agree or disagree with Alexander's claim that America's mass incarceration of black and brown men constitutes a "new Jim Crow" — that is, a system of legalized racial discrimination. How well does Alexander's term "invisible punishment" (p. 742) apply to parole, welfare, and workfare as described by Arnold?

7. Read Katherine Mangu-Ward's "The War on Negative Liberty" (p. 659) and Chris Norwood's "The Rise of Mass Dependency" (at bedfordstmartins.com /rereading/epages) and compare their assessments of government intervention with that offered by Arnold. What do you think these authors would do to address issues involving poverty and public health?

EXTENDING THE CRITICAL CONTEXT

8. Research welfare/workfare in your city or county. Report to the class on the types and amount of aid, the number of recipients, and demographic data such as age, gender, and race/ethnicity of recipients.

THE NEW AMERICAN DIVIDE
CHARLES MURRAY

America is a divided nation. We tend to see the gaps between us as fundamentally political or economic — Republicans versus Democrats, or Wall Street versus Main Street. Charles Murray, in contrast, sees the most essential differences as cultural; the new American divide is, at heart, the dissolution of a "common civic culture." His essay calls on Americans to rebuild a shared set of values that include marriage, hard work, and religious faith. Charles Murray (b. 1943), currently the W. H. Brady Scholar at the American Enterprise Institute, a conservative think tank, has authored several books on American culture, politics, and social structures. He is best known for his controversial 1994 bestseller *The Bell Curve: Intelligence and Class Structure in American Life* (coauthored with Richard J. Herrnstein), which explored connections between social class and IQ. "The New American Divide" echoes themes of his latest book, *Coming Apart: The State of White America, 1960–2010*, published in 2012.

AMERICA IS COMING APART. For most of our nation's history, whatever the inequality in wealth between the richest and poorest citizens, we maintained a cultural equality known nowhere else in the world—for whites, anyway. "The more opulent citizens take great care not to stand aloof from the people," wrote Alexis de Tocqueville, the great chronicler of American democracy, in the 1830s. "On the contrary, they constantly keep on easy terms with the lower classes: They listen to them, they speak to them every day."

Americans love to see themselves this way. But there's a problem: It's not true anymore, and it has been progressively less true since the 1960s.

People are starting to notice the great divide. The tea party sees the aloofness in a political elite that thinks it knows best and orders the rest of America to fall in line. The Occupy movement sees it in an economic elite that lives in mansions and flies on private jets. Each is right about an aspect of the problem, but that problem is more pervasive than either political or economic inequality. What we now face is a problem of cultural inequality.

When Americans used to brag about "the American way of life"— a phrase still in common use in 1960— they were talking about a civic culture that swept an extremely large proportion of Americans of all classes into its embrace. It was a culture encompassing shared experiences of daily life and shared assumptions about central American values involving marriage, honesty, hard work and religiosity.

Over the past 50 years, that common civic culture has unraveled. 5 We have developed a new upper class with advanced educations, often obtained at elite schools, sharing tastes and preferences that set them apart from mainstream America. At the same time, we have developed a new lower class, characterized not by poverty but by withdrawal from America's core cultural institutions.

To illustrate just how wide the gap has grown between the new upper class and the new lower class, let me start with the broader upper-middle and working classes from which they are drawn, using two fictional neighborhoods that I hereby label Belmont (after an archetypal upper-middle-class suburb near Boston) and Fishtown (after a neighborhood in Philadelphia that has been home to the white working class since the Revolution).

To be assigned to Belmont, the people in the statistical nationwide databases on which I am drawing must have at least a bachelor's degree and work as a manager, physician, attorney, engineer, architect, scientist, college professor or content producer in the media. To be assigned to Fishtown, they must have no academic degree higher than a high-school diploma. If they work, it must be in a blue-collar job, a low-skill service job such as cashier, or a low-skill white-collar job such as mail clerk or receptionist.

People who qualify for my Belmont constitute about 20% of the white population of the U.S., ages 30 to 49. People who qualify for my Fishtown constitute about 30% of the white population of the U.S., ages 30 to 49.

I specify white, meaning non-Latino white, as a way of clarifying how broad and deep the cultural divisions in the U.S. have become. Cultural inequality is not grounded in race or ethnicity. I specify ages 30 to 49—what I call prime-age adults—to make it clear that these trends are not explained by changes in the ages of marriage or retirement.

In Belmont and Fishtown, here's what happened to America's com- 10 mon culture between 1960 and 2010.

Marriage: In 1960, extremely high proportions of whites in both Belmont and Fishtown were married—94% in Belmont and 84% in Fishtown. In the 1970s, those percentages declined about equally in both places. Then came the great divergence. In Belmont, marriage stabilized during the mid-1980s, standing at 83% in 2010. In Fishtown, however, marriage continued to slide; as of 2010, a minority (just 48%) were married. The gap in marriage between Belmont and Fishtown grew to 35 percentage points, from just 10.

Single parenthood: Another aspect of marriage—the percentage of children born to unmarried women—showed just as great a divergence. Though politicians and media eminences are too frightened to say so, nonmarital births are problematic. On just about any measure of development you can think of, children who are born to unmarried women fare worse than the children of divorce and far worse than children raised in intact families. This unwelcome reality persists even after controlling for the income and education of the parents.

In 1960, just 2% of all white births were nonmarital. When we first started recording the education level of mothers in 1970, 6% of births to white women with no more than a high-school education—women, that is, with a Fishtown education—were out of wedlock. By 2008, 44% were nonmarital. Among the college-educated women of Belmont, less than 6% of all births were out of wedlock as of 2008, up from 1% in 1970.

Industriousness: The norms for work and women were revolutionized after 1960, but the norm for men putatively has remained the same: Healthy men are supposed to work. In practice, though, that norm has eroded everywhere. In Fishtown, the change has been drastic. (To avoid conflating this phenomenon with the latest recession, I use data collected in March 2008 as the end point for the trends.)

The primary indicator of the erosion of industriousness in the work- 15 ing class is the increase of prime-age males with no more than a high school education who say they are not available for work—they are "out of the labor force." That percentage went from a low of 3% in 1968 to 12% in 2008. Twelve percent may not sound like much until you think about the men we're talking about: in the prime of their working lives, their 30s and 40s, when, according to hallowed American tradition, every American man is working or looking for work. Almost one out of eight now aren't. Meanwhile, not much has changed among males with college educations. Only 3% were out of the labor force in 2008.

There's also been a notable change in the rates of less-than-full-time work. Of the men in Fishtown who had jobs, 10% worked fewer than 40 hours a week in 1960, a figure that grew to 20% by 2008. In Belmont, the number rose from 9% in 1960 to 12% in 2008.

Crime: The surge in crime that began in the mid-1960s and continued through the 1980s left Belmont almost untouched and ravaged Fishtown. From 1960 to 1995, the violent crime rate in Fishtown more than sextupled while remaining nearly flat in Belmont. The reductions in crime since the mid-1990s that have benefited the nation as a whole have been smaller in Fishtown, leaving it today with a violent crime rate that is still 4.7 times the 1960 rate.

Religiosity: Whatever your personal religious views, you need to realize that about half of American philanthropy, volunteering and associational memberships is directly church-related, and that religious Americans also account for much more nonreligious social capital than their secular neighbors. In that context, it is worrisome for the culture that the U.S. as a whole has become markedly more secular since 1960, and especially worrisome that Fishtown has become much more secular than Belmont. It runs against the prevailing narrative of secular elites versus a working class still clinging to religion, but the evidence from the General Social Survey, the most widely used database on American attitudes and values, does not leave much room for argument.

For example, suppose we define "de facto secular" as someone who either professes no religion at all or who attends a worship service no more than once a year. For the early GSS surveys conducted from 1972 to 1976, 29% of Belmont and 38% of Fishtown fell into that category. Over the next three decades, secularization did indeed grow in Belmont, from 29% in the 1970s to 40% in the GSS surveys taken from 2006 to 2010. But it grew even more in Fishtown, from 38% to 59%.

It can be said without hyperbole that these divergences put Belmont [20] and Fishtown into different cultures. But it's not just the working class that's moved; the upper middle class has pulled away in its own fashion, too.

If you were an executive living in Belmont in 1960, income inequality would have separated you from the construction worker in Fishtown, but remarkably little cultural inequality. You lived a more expensive life, but not a much different life. Your kitchen was bigger, but you didn't use it to prepare yogurt and muesli for breakfast. Your television screen was bigger, but you and the construction worker watched a lot of the same shows (you didn't have much choice). Your house might have had a den that the construction worker's lacked, but it had no StairMaster or lap pool, nor any gadget to monitor your percentage of body fat. You both drank Bud, Miller, Schlitz or Pabst, and the phrase "boutique beer" never crossed your lips. You probably both smoked. If you didn't, you did not glare contemptuously at people who did.

When you went on vacation, you both probably took the family to the seashore or on a fishing trip, and neither involved hotels with five stars. If you had ever vacationed outside the U.S. (and you probably hadn't), it was a one-time trip to Europe, where you saw eight cities in 14 days—not one of the two or three trips abroad you now take every year for business, conferences or eco-vacations in the cloud forests of Costa Rica.

You both lived in neighborhoods where the majority of people had only high-school diplomas—and that might well have included you. The people around you who did have college degrees had almost invariably gotten them at state universities or small religious colleges mostly peopled by students who were the first generation of their families to attend college. Except in academia, investment banking, a few foundations, the CIA and the State Department, you were unlikely to run into a graduate of Harvard, Princeton or Yale.

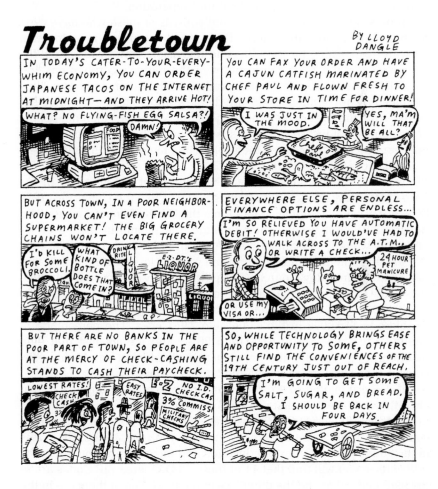

Even the income inequality that separated you from the construction worker was likely to be new to your adulthood. The odds are good that your parents had been in the working class or middle class, that their income had not been much different from the construction worker's, that they had lived in communities much like his, and that the texture of the construction worker's life was recognizable to you from your own childhood.

Taken separately, the differences in lifestyle that now separate 25
Belmont from Fishtown are not sinister, but those quirks of the upper-
middle class that I mentioned—the yogurt and muesli and the rest—are
part of a mosaic of distinctive practices that have developed in Belmont.
These have to do with the food Belmonters eat, their drinking habits,
the ages at which they marry and have children, the books they read
(and their number), the television shows and movies they watch (and
the hours spent on them), the humor they enjoy, the way they take
care of their bodies, the way they decorate their homes, their leisure
activities, their work environments and their child-raising practices.
Together, they have engendered cultural separation.

It gets worse. A subset of Belmont consists of those who have risen
to the top of American society. They run the country, meaning that
they are responsible for the films and television shows you watch, the
news you see and read, the fortunes of the nation's corporations and
financial institutions, and the jurisprudence, legislation and regulations
produced by government. They are the new upper class, even more detached from the lives of the great majority of Americans than the people
of Belmont—not just socially but spatially as well. The members of this
elite have increasingly sorted themselves into hyper-wealthy and hyper-
elite ZIP Codes that I call the SuperZIPs.

In 1960, America already had the equivalent of SuperZIPs in the
form of famously elite neighborhoods—places like the Upper East Side
of New York, Philadelphia's Main Line, the North Shore of Chicago and
Beverly Hills. But despite their prestige, the people in them weren't
uniformly wealthy or even affluent. Across 14 of the most elite places to
live in 1960, the median family income wasn't close to affluence. It was
just $84,000 (in today's purchasing power). Only one in four adults in
those elite communities had a college degree.

By 2000, that diversity had dwindled. Median family income had
doubled, to $163,000 in the same elite ZIP Codes. The percentage of
adults with B.A.s rose to 67% from 26%. And it's not just that elite
neighborhoods became more homogeneously affluent and highly educated—they also formed larger and larger clusters.

If you are invited to a dinner party by one of Washington's power
elite, the odds are high that you will be going to a home in Georgetown,
the rest of Northwest D.C., Chevy Chase, Bethesda, Potomac or McLean,
comprising 13 adjacent ZIP Codes in all. If you rank all the ZIP Codes
in the country on an index of education and income and group them by
percentiles, you will find that 11 of these 13 D.C.-area ZIP Codes are in
the 99th percentile and the other two in the 98th. Ten of them are in the
top half of the 99th percentile.

Similarly large clusters of SuperZIPs can be found around New 30
York City, Los Angeles, the San Francisco-San Jose corridor, Boston
and a few of the nation's other largest cities. Because running major
institutions in this country usually means living near one of these cities,
it works out that the nation's power elite does in fact live in a world that

is far more culturally rarefied and isolated than the world of the power elite in 1960.

And the isolation is only going to get worse. Increasingly, the people who run the country were born into that world. Unlike the typical member of the elite in 1960, they have never known anything but the new upper-class culture. We are now seeing more and more third-generation members of the elite. Not even their grandparents have been able to give them a window into life in the rest of America.

Why have these new lower and upper classes emerged? For explaining the formation of the new lower class, the easy explanations from the left don't withstand scrutiny. It's not that white working class males can no longer make a "family wage" that enables them to marry. The average male employed in a working-class occupation earned as much in 2010 as he did in 1960. It's not that a bad job market led discouraged men to drop out of the labor force. Labor-force dropout increased just as fast during the boom years of the 1980s, 1990s and 2000s as it did during bad years.

As I've argued in much of my previous work, I think that the reforms of the 1960s jump-started the deterioration. Changes in social policy during the 1960s made it economically more feasible to have a child without having a husband if you were a woman or to get along without a job if you were a man; safer to commit crimes without suffering consequences; and easier to let the government deal with problems in your community that you and your neighbors formerly had to take care of.

But, for practical purposes, understanding why the new lower class got started isn't especially important. Once the deterioration was under way, a self-reinforcing loop took hold as traditionally powerful social norms broke down. Because the process has become self-reinforcing, repealing the reforms

---

Top 10 SuperZIPs

In 'Coming Apart,' Charles Murray identifies 882 'SuperZIPs,' ZIP Codes where residents score in the 95th through the 99th percentile on a combined measure of income and education, based on the 2000 census. Here are the top-ranked areas:

1. **60043:** Kenilworth, Ill. (Chicago's North Shore)
2. **60022:** Glencoe, Ill. (Chicago's North Shore)
3. **07078:** Short Hills, N.J. (New York metro area)
4. **94027:** Atherton, Calif. (San Francisco-San Jose corridor)
5. **10514:** Chappaqua, N.Y. (New York metro area)
6. **19035:** Gladwyne, Pa. (Philadelphia's Main Line)
7. **94028:** Portola Valley, Calif. (S.F.-San Jose corridor)
8. **92067:** Rancho Sante Fe, Calif. (San Diego suburbs)
9. **02493:** Weston, Mass. (Boston suburbs)
10. **10577:** Purchase, N.Y. (New York metro area)

of the 1960s (something that's not going to happen) would change the trends slowly at best.

Meanwhile, the formation of the new upper class has been driven 35 by forces that are nobody's fault and resist manipulation. The economic value of brains in the marketplace will continue to increase no matter what, and the most successful of each generation will tend to marry each other no matter what. As a result, the most successful Americans will continue to trend toward consolidation and isolation as a class. Changes in marginal tax rates on the wealthy won't make a difference. Increasing scholarships for working-class children won't make a difference.

The only thing that can make a difference is the recognition among Americans of all classes that a problem of cultural inequality exists and that something has to be done about it. That "something" has nothing to do with new government programs or regulations. Public policy has certainly affected the culture, unfortunately, but unintended consequences have been as grimly inevitable for conservative social engineering as for liberal social engineering.

The "something" that I have in mind has to be defined in terms of individual American families acting in their own interests and the interests of their children. Doing that in Fishtown requires support from outside. There remains a core of civic virtue and involvement in working-class America that could make headway against its problems if the people who are trying to do the right things get the reinforcement they need—not in the form of government assistance, but in validation of the values and standards they continue to uphold. The best thing that the new upper class can do to provide that reinforcement is to drop its condescending "nonjudgmentalism." Married, educated people who work hard and conscientiously raise their kids shouldn't hesitate to voice their disapproval of those who defy these norms. When it comes to marriage and the work ethic, the new upper class must start preaching what it practices.

Changing life in the SuperZIPs requires that members of the new upper class rethink their priorities. Here are some propositions that might guide them: Life sequestered from anybody not like yourself tends to be self-limiting. Places to live in which the people around you have no problems that need cooperative solutions tend to be sterile. America outside the enclaves of the new upper class is still a wonderful place, filled with smart, interesting, entertaining people. If you're not part of that America, you've stripped yourself of much of what makes being American special.

Such priorities can be expressed in any number of familiar decisions: the neighborhood where you buy your next home, the next school that you choose for your children, what you tell them about the value and virtues of physical labor and military service, whether you become an active member of a religious congregation (and what kind you choose) and whether you become involved in the life of your community at a more meaningful level than charity events.

Everyone in the new upper class has the monetary resources to 40
make a wide variety of decisions that determine whether they engage
themselves and their children in the rest of America or whether they
isolate themselves from it. The only question is which they prefer to do.

That's it? But where's my five-point plan? We're supposed to trust
that large numbers of parents will spontaneously, voluntarily make the
right choice for the country by making the right choice for themselves
and their children?

Yes, we are, but I don't think that's naive. I see too many signs that
the trends I've described are already worrying a lot of people. If enough
Americans look unblinkingly at the nature of the problem, they'll fix it.
One family at a time. For their own sakes. That's the American way.

ENGAGING THE TEXT

1. As Murray notes, there is a real Fishtown neighborhood in Philadelphia and
a real Belmont near Boston (para. 6). Explain why Murray constructs fictional versions of these places and why he limits his data set to non–Latino
whites ages thirty to forty-nine (para. 9). Discuss the logic and the rhetorical
effectiveness of these strategies.

2. Explain why you agree or disagree with Murray's assessment that our "common civic culture has unraveled" (para. 5). What do you think your parents
or grandparents would say about this claim?

3. Debate the relative importance of cultural versus economic separation in
American society. Which gap is of greater concern to you, and why?

4. Analyze "The New American Divide" as an example of a "problem-solution"
essay, a genre frequently assigned in college classes. List the specific problems Murray cites, his explanations of their causes, and the solutions he
offers.

5. The range in affluence from Fishtown to "SuperZIPS" like Beverly Hills or
Georgetown is immense. How big a range can be found in the student body
at your college or university? Have you seen any evidence that the most affluent and least affluent students essentially belong to different cultures?

EXPLORING CONNECTIONS

6. Review "Class in America — 2009" by Gregory Mantsios (p. 281) and read
Patrick J. Buchanan's "Deconstructing America" (p. 593). Discuss how
Mantsios and Buchanan might respond to Murray's claim that "cultural inequality is not grounded in race or ethnicity" (para. 9). Whose interpretation
of U.S. culture do you find most persuasive, and why?

7. Write a letter to Murray from Maddie Parlier ("Making It in America," p. 333)
reflecting how you think she might respond to Murray's ideas on single parenthood, hard work, and religion.

8. The year 1960 marks the starting date of Murray's research and the ending date for Stephanie Coontz's "What We Really Miss About the 1950s" (p. 27). What picture does Murray paint of America in 1960, and how does Coontz's essay complicate or challenge Murray's perspective?

EXTENDING THE CRITICAL CONTEXT

9. Using Google Maps, pick a random street address in Belmont, Massachusetts, and look at the images you can find with the "street view" feature. Take notes on what you see, including the condition and style of the buildings, the types of homes or businesses, the private or public landscaping, and any vehicles or people that may show up in the image. Then do the same for Fishtown in Philadelphia. Compare notes with classmates and write a journal entry or short essay describing the physical environments of these two places.

10. In Chapter Four of his book *Coming Apart*—entitled "How Thick Is Your Bubble?"—Murray presents twenty-five questions designed to measure how well or how poorly upper-middle-class Americans understand the lives of ordinary Americans. Find the survey in the book or online, give it to several people in your community or at your school, and score/interpret the results according to Murray's guidelines. Assess whether the people you surveyed are living in a thick bubble, a thin bubble, or no bubble at all.

FROM THE GREAT DIVERGENCE: AMERICA'S GROWING INEQUALITY CRISIS AND WHAT WE CAN DO ABOUT IT

TIMOTHY NOAH

The "Great Divergence" describes thirty-three years of growing inequality in America between the very wealthy and everybody else. This trend toward widening gaps in wealth and income has been around so long that we may mistakenly assume it is natural or inevitable, but Noah insists it is neither. Noah also sounds an alarm about what he calls "The Great Divergence, Part 2"—a recent and dramatic widening of the inequality between ordinary Americans and the "undeniably rich," the "really rich," and the "stinking rich," who together are consuming ever-bigger slices of the American pie. Timothy Noah is a columnist and blogger for the *New Republic* and has worked at the *Wall*

Street Journal, the *Washington Monthly*, and *Slate*, where his series on the great divergence won the 2011 Hillman Prize for public service magazine journalism. The excerpt below is from his 2012 book based on the *Slate* series.

Introduction

> *The fact is that income inequality is real; it's been rising for more than twenty-five years.*
>
> —PRESIDENT GEORGE W. BUSH, JANUARY 2007

DURING THE PAST THIRTY-THREE YEARS the difference in America between being rich and being middle class became much more pronounced. People with high incomes consumed an ever-larger share of the nation's total income, while people in the middle saw their share shrink. For most of this time the phenomenon attracted little attention from the general public and the press because it occurred in increments over one third of a century. During the previous five decades—from the early 1930s through most of the 1970s—the precise opposite had occurred. The share of the nation's income that went to the wealthy had either shrunk or remained stable. At the first signs, during the early 1980s, that this was no longer happening, economists figured they were witnessing a fluke, an inexplicable but temporary phenomenon, or perhaps an artifact of faulty statistics. But they weren't. A democratization of incomes that Americans had long taken for granted as a happy fact of modern life was reversing itself. Eventually it was the steady growth in income inequality that Americans took for granted. The divergent fortunes of the rich and the middle class became such a fact of everyday life that people seldom noticed it, except perhaps to observe now and then with a shrug that life was unfair.

There were signs that this indifference was beginning to evaporate in the fall of 2011, when protestors turned up on Wall Street waving signs that said WE ARE THE BOTTOM 99 PERCENT. As I write, it's too early to say whether the Occupy Wall Street movement will have any lasting positive effect, but certainly the topic is becoming more difficult to ignore.

"I am 21 and scared of what the future will bring," read one testimonial posted online by a protester. "I work full time with no benefits and I am actively looking for a second job, because I am barely making it. I worry every month that I will not be able to afford rent. I am afraid of what will happen if I get sick. I am afraid I will never be able to go back to school." Another read: "My parents have worked hard their entire lives as small business owners. In hard times they ALWAYS paid their employees before themselves. They would like to retire soon, but can't afford to stay in the modest ranch house they have lived in for 35 years. We are currently making renovations to our house so they can move in and avoid Section 8 [low-income] housing." The day before these statements appeared on the Web, the *New York Times* evaluated for its more affluent readers the pluses and minuses of Kohler's new $6,400 luxury Numi toilet, which featured two flushing modes, an automatically rising toilet lid, and stereophonic sound.

We tend to think of the United States as a place that has grown more equal over time, not less, and in the most obvious ways that's true. When the republic was founded, African Americans were still held in bondage and were defined in the Constitution as representing three fifths of a human being. Only adult white male property owners could vote. Over the next two centuries full citizenship rights were extended gradually to people who didn't own property, to blacks, to women, and to Native Americans. In recent years, gay activists have fought at the state level for the right to same-sex marriage, and they've prevailed, at this writing, in six states and the District of Columbia. It seems just a matter of time before this right is extended in the rest of the country. Difficult to enforce, the principle that all men and women are equal before the law is even more difficult to refute. All the groups mentioned here experienced setbacks in their pursuit of legal equality, some lasting as long as a century. Few people belonging to any of these groups would argue that this pursuit ends with the removal of explicit legal barriers. Still, most would likely agree that over the long haul legal obstacles to full and equal participation in American life tend to diminish.

It was once possible to make a similar argument with respect to [5] economic obstacles. As late as 1979, the prevailing view among economists was that incomes in any advanced industrial democracy would inevitably become more equal or remain stable in their distribution. They certainly wouldn't become more *un*equal. That sorry fate was reserved for societies at an earlier stage of development or where the dictatorial powers of the state preserved privilege for the few at the expense of the many. In civilized, mature, and free nations, the gaps between rich, middle class, and poor did not increase.

That seemed the logical lesson to draw from U.S. history. The country's transformation from an agrarian society to an industrial one during the late nineteenth and early twentieth centuries had created a period of extreme economic inequality—one whose ramifications can still be glimpsed by, say, pairing a visit to George Vanderbilt's 125,000-acre Biltmore Estate in Ashville, North Carolina, with a trip to the Tenement Museum on Manhattan's Lower East Side. But from the early 1930s through the early 1970s, incomes became more equal, and remained so, while the industrial economy lost none of its rude vitality. As the 1970s progressed, that vitality diminished, but income distribution remained unchanged. "As measured in the official data," the Princeton economist Alan Blinder wrote in 1980, "income inequality was just about the same in 1977...as it was in 1947."[1] What Blinder couldn't know (because he didn't have more recent data) was that this was already beginning to change. Starting in 1979, incomes once again began to grow unequal. When the economy recovered in 1983, incomes grew even more unequal. They have continued growing more unequal to this day.

The United States is not the only advanced industrialized democracy where incomes have become more unequal in recent decades. The trend is global. A 2008 report by the Organisation for Economic Co-operation and Development, which represents thirty-four market-oriented democracies, concluded that since the mid-1980s, income inequality had increased in two thirds of the twenty-four OECD countries for which data were available, which included most of the world's leading industrial democracies.[2] But the level and growth rate of income inequality in the United States has been particularly extreme.

There are various ways to measure income distribution, and by all of them the United States ranks at or near the bottom in terms of equality. The most common measure, the Gini coefficient, is named for an Italian statistician named Corrado Gini (1884–1965). It measures distribution—of income or anything else—on a scale that goes from 0 to 1. Let's imagine, for instance, that we had fifty marbles to distribute among fifty children. Perfect equality of distribution would be if each child got one marble. The Gini coefficient would then be 0. Perfect inequality of distribution would be if one especially pushy child ended up with all fifty marbles. The Gini coefficient would then be 1. As of 2005, the United States' Gini coefficient was 0.38, which on the income-equality scale ranked this country twenty-seventh of the thirty OECD nations for which data were available. The only countries with more unequal income distribution were Portugal (0.42), Turkey (0.43), and Mexico (0.47). The same relative rankings were achieved when you calculated the ratio of the highest income below the threshold for the top 10 percent to the highest income below the threshold for the bottom 10 percent. The United States dropped to twenty-ninth place (just above Mexico) when you calculated the ratio of median income to the highest income below the threshold for the bottom 10 percent. When you calculated the percentage of national income that went to the top 1 percent, the United States was the undisputed champion. Its measured income distribution was more unequal than that of any other OECD nation.[3] As of 2007 (i.e., right before the 2008 financial crisis), America's richest 1 percent possessed nearly 24 percent of the nation's pretax income, a statistic that gave new meaning to the expression "Can you

[1]Alan Blinder, "The Level and Distribution of Economic Well-Being," Working Paper 488 (Cambridge, MA: National Bureau of Economic Research, 1980), 2. [All notes are Noah's except 4, 8, 14, 15, 19, 23, 25, 26.]
[2]*Growing Unequal? Income Distribution and Poverty in OECD Countries* (Paris: Organisation for Economic Co-operation and Development, 2008), 27.
[3]*Growing Unequal?*, 25, 32, 51–52.

spare a quarter?" (I include capital gains[4] as part of income, and will do so whenever possible throughout this book.) In 2008, the last year for which data are available, the recession drove the richest 1 percent's income share down to 21 percent.[5] To judge from Wall Street's record bonuses and corporate America's surging profitability in the years following the 2008 financial crisis, income share for the top 1 percent will resume its upward climb momentarily, if it hasn't already. We already know from census data that in 2010 income share for the bottom 40 percent fell and that the poverty rate climbed to its highest point in nearly two decades?[6]

In addition to having an unusually high *level* of income inequality, the United States has seen income inequality increase at a much faster *rate* than most other countries. Among the twenty-four OECD countries for which Gini-coefficient change can be measured from the mid-1980s to the mid-aughts, only Finland, Portugal, and New Zealand experienced a faster growth rate in income inequality. Of these, only Portugal ended up with a Gini rating worse than the United States'. Another important point of comparison is that some OECD countries saw income inequality *decline* during this period. France, Greece, Ireland, Spain, and Turkey all saw their Gini ratings go *down* (though the OECD report's data for Ireland and Spain didn't extend beyond 2000). That proves it is not woven into the laws of economics that an advanced industrial democracy must, during the present epoch, see its income-inequality level fall, or even stay the same. Some of these countries are becoming more economically egalitarian, not less, just as the United States did for much of the twentieth century.[7]

Many changes in the global economy are making incomes less   10
equal in many countries outside the United States, but the income-inequality trend of the past three decades has been unusually fierce here in the world's richest nation. Americans usually invoke the term "American exceptionalism" to describe what it is that makes our country so much more blessed than all others. But American exceptionalism can also describe ingrained aspects of our country's economy, or gov-

---

[4]*capital gain*: an increase from the purchase price to the sale price of an asset such as an investment or piece of property.

[5]Facundo Alvaredo, Tony Atkinson, Thomas Piketty, and Emmanuel Saez, "The World Top Incomes Database," http://g-mond.parisschoolofeconomics.eu/topincomes/. Hereafter referred to as WTID.

[6]*Income, Poverty, and Health Insurance Coverage in the United States: 2010* (Washington: U.S. Census Bureau, 2011), 10, 14.

[7]*Growing Unequal?*, 27, 51. Finland's very low Gini rating (0.27) ranks it the seventh most income-equal nation in the OECD, while New Zealand's very high Gini coefficient (0.34) ranks it a mere four places above the United States' dismal twenty-seventh out of thirty. Portugal's disturbingly high level of income inequality and high rate of increase in income inequality, which exceed those in the United States, appear to result largely from the fact that nearly 78 percent of its households are headed by people who lack a high school degree. By European standards, that's an extraordinarily low high school graduation rate. But even in poorly educated Portugal, the top 1 percent's income share is just a little more than half what it is in the United States. To achieve American-style income inequality, you need lots of poor people, which Portugal has, and lots of rich people, which it lacks.

ernment, or character, that put us at a disadvantage on the world stage. Income inequality is one of the more notable ways that the United States differs, in ways we can only regret, even from nations that resemble us more than they do not.

The Nobel Prize–winning economist Paul Krugman of Princeton (and the *New York Times* op-ed page) termed the age of inequality "the Great Divergence" in his 2007 book *The Conscience of a Liberal.* It has existed for my entire adult life. I graduated from college and moved to Washington, D.C., in 1980, one year after the Great Divergence began. Today I'm a middle-aged man with two nearly grown children. For thirty-two years I've covered politics and policy in the nation's capital for a variety of newspapers and magazines, and quite a lot has changed. When I started out, I typed my stories on an IBM Selectric. My editor scribbled changes in pencil and handed the story to a composer (sometimes me), who tapped the keys of a typesetting machine that groaned and shuddered as it turned the story into a long column of type on a glue-backed white sheet. The white sheet was then pasted onto large posterboards called "mechanicals" and shipped off to a printing press. The Soviet Union was an indestructible adversary, China was a poverty-ridden curiosity making its first baby steps toward joining the community of nations, and everybody thought sending Stinger missile launchers to Afghan rebels was a swell idea. Foreign policy intellectuals furrowed their brows over Eurocommunism, and feminists still believed they had a decent shot at adding an Equal Rights Amendment[8] to the Constitution. It was a different reality. But incomes were growing more unequal in America then, and they continue to grow more unequal in America today. That story hasn't changed at all.

What did change over the years were the speculative explanations as to *why* incomes were becoming more unequal. It was Ronald Reagan's fault. No, it was the inevitable result of a maturing global economy. No, it was caused by computers. No, it was caused by the twin epidemics of teenage pregnancy and divorce. Some people denied the Great Divergence was happening at all. Others said it was a fleeting phenomenon. Still others said all would be well once the economy became more productive (i.e., once there was a significant increase in output per hour worked). As time went on, the favored hypotheses kept changing. It was maddening. How can we address the problem if we don't even know what the problem *is*?

Gradually, however, a body of academic work, mainly by economists but also by political scientists and sociologists, has begun to accumulate. This book is an attempt to synthesize the best of that work for nonexperts who would like to know, at long last, what's been

[8]*Equal Rights Amendment:* a proposed amendment to the U.S. Constitution stipulating that "equality of rights under the law shall not be denied or abridged by the United States or by any State on account of sex." First introduced to Congress in 1923, the amendment passed both houses in 1972 but was never ratified by enough states to become law.

happening to the economy, especially in the United States. Economists are often treated skeptically by the public at large, mainly because it usually sees them when they're on TV attempting to predict the future. But while the economics profession isn't much better at soothsaying than any other, it performs an enormously valuable, greatly underappreciated service in documenting and interpreting the past. Economic trends are hard to interpret in real time because doing so requires data, and the best and most complete data sets often aren't available for five or ten years. By the time they are available, the world has moved on to fretting about newer trends. As a result, when the day arrives for us to understand better, say, the oil shocks of 1973, or the recession of 1982–83, we are preoccupied with trying to figure out the tech boom of the late 1990s or the housing bubble of the aughts. By "we," I mean all of American society but especially my own fraternity of political and policy-wonk journalists. History isn't news. But the Great Divergence has been going on for so long that it manages to be both. It's history because it began when Jimmy Carter was in the White House. It's also news because it's continuing while Barack Obama is president.

* * * * * * * *

IN 2003 THOMAS PIKETTY AND EMMANUEL Saez noticed a dimension to the Great Divergence that had nothing to do with the gap between college graduates and high school graduates, or the decline of labor unions, or the differing political philosophies of Democrats and Republicans. The causes of this newly discovered trend were so fundamentally different...that it's best to think of it as a separate and distinct phenomenon: the Great Divergence, Part 2.

What Piketty and Saez saw was that the very richest Americans 15 had, during the preceding two decades, swallowed up a lot more of the nation's collective income than had been previously understood. Prior to the publication of their groundbreaking paper "Income Inequality in the United States, 1913–1998," the data typically used to analyze U.S. income distribution came from monthly household income surveys conducted by the U.S. census. This data set, known to experts as the Current Population Survey, was very useful if you wanted to track income trends for households as divided into quintiles (five groups, richest to poorest). But it wasn't particularly useful if you wanted to break down the population into much smaller groups, especially at the top end of the income scale. There were two reasons for this. First, the Current Population Survey didn't distinguish among incomes of $1 million per year or more. Households that made that much money were "top-coded" as belonging to a single category. The second problem with the Current Population Survey was that it was based on sampling data. Sampling is very useful when you're measuring extremely large populations; that's why demographers are forever recommending that the Census Bureau's much better-known project, the decennial census, quit trying to count every last American—a method that's bound to miss some hard-to-find people—and instead conduct a scientifically rigorous sampling, which would be more accurate. But sampling becomes a lot less accurate when you're measuring trends within a very small subgroup of the larger population. And the proportion of households with annual incomes above $1 million is well under 1 percent.[9]

Rather than rely on the Current Population Survey for broad-brush data about the rich, Piketty and Saez did what Simon Kuznets had done prior to his groundbreaking 1954 analysis of U.S. income distribution. They looked at data from the Internal Revenue Service. Except perhaps for a very few criminals who possess a superhuman ability to hide enormous quantities of cash, *everyone* in the United States who makes $1 million or more files a yearly tax return, and the IRS keeps track of *precisely* how much each of these people rakes in. That solved the top-coding and sampling problems. The IRS data posed a different problem: Some people don't have to file income tax returns because they don't make enough money. Today that's a pretty small group of people at very low incomes, but prior to 1944 it was true of most people. Even so, Piketty and Saez found that anyone whose income put them in the top decile (the top 10 percent, which today would mean a combined family income of $109,000 or more) *always* had to file, going all the way back to 1916.[10] That enabled Piketty and Saez to create a field of study—you might call it "decile-ology"—examining America's top income decile over a longer period and slicing it into smaller and smaller subgroups ("fractiles")—the top 1 percent, the top 0.1 percent, the top 0.01 percent—than anyone had ever done before. Like Antonie van Leeuwenhoek peering into a droplet of lake water teeming with spirogyra and vorticella, Piketty and Saez put the top decile under their microscope and scrutinized various fractiles of rich Americans.

"If a $100,000-a-year household thinks itself to be middle class," the neoconservative writer Irving Kristol once wrote, "then it *is* middle class." This sentiment is widely held, but it makes no mathematical sense. Any family whose income exceeds that of 90 percent of all other families cannot sensibly be called anything but rich. To believe otherwise would oblige you to judge your child mediocre when his teacher

[9]Thomas Piketty and Emmanuel Saez, "Income Inequality in the United States, 1913–1998," *Quarterly Journal of Economics* 118, no. 1 (Feb. 2003), 1–39; Saez, "Striking It Richer: The Evolution of Top Incomes in the United States," *Pathways* (Palo Alto, CA: Stanford Center for the Study of Poverty and Inequality, 2008), 6–7, updated at http://elsa.berkeley.edu/~saez /saez-UStopincomes-2008.pdf; Paul Krugman, "On Tracking Inequality," *The Conscience of a Liberal* (blog), Sept. 19, 2006, at http://krugman.blogs.nytimes.com/2006/09/19/on -tracking-inequality/.

[10]Between 1913, when the income tax was introduced, and 1916 even many in the top decile were excused from having to file. Piketty and Saez therefore confined their analysis for this brief period to filers within the top 1 percent.

gives him an A.[11] But within the top decile distinctions are nonetheless worth making.

- *Sort of Rich.* Let's call these everyone making between $109,000 and $153,000. That situates them today in the bottom half of the top 10 percent.

- *Basically Rich.* That's everyone making between $153,000 and $368,000 (the bottom threshold for the top 1 percent).

- *Undeniably Rich.* That's everyone making between $368,000 and $1.7 million (the bottom threshold for the top 0.1 percent).

- *Really Rich.* That's everyone making between $1.7 million and $9.1 million (the bottom threshold for the top 0.01 percent).

- *Stinking Rich.* That's everybody in the top 0.01 percent, making $9.1 million or more.[12]

You can be Stinking Rich and still get snubbed by a hedge-fund manager who pulls down $10 million or more, but now we're down to about 8,400 households in America and narrower distinctions start to seem fetishistic.[13]

Piketty and Saez didn't employ the blunt terminology used here, but they sliced their top-decile sampling along these lines, and in so doing made the following discoveries (all numbers that follow are up-dated through 2008, the last year for which data are available):

- The American aristocracy is in one respect more like the rest of us than it used to be. "Before World War II," Piketty and Saez wrote, "the richest Americans were overwhelmingly rentiers deriving most of their income from wealth holdings (mainly in the form of divi-dends)." (A rentier is someone who lives off income from fixed as-sets like stocks, bonds, or real estate.) But today, Piketty and Saez found, at least as many are job holders deriving most of their in-come from their wages (a category of compensation in which they included stock options offered to employees in lieu of wages). Does

[11]Irving Kristol, "Some Personal Reflections on Economic Well-Being and Income Distribution," in *The American Economy in Transition,* ed. Martin Feldstein (Chicago: University of Chicago Press, 1980), 484. Note the publication date. Kristol's claim was even less persuasive in 1980, when $100,000 was the equivalent of $274,000 in current dollars. Were he still alive, Kristol might answer that my A-student analogy overlooks the contem-porary epidemic of grade inflation. Point taken.

[12]All calculations of fractile thresholds are from WTID (World Top Incomes Database), which when this book went to press was current through 2008, and include capital gains. The 2007–09 recession drove the thresholds down between 2007 and 2008, and almost certainly they came down a bit further in 2009, but those numbers are not yet available. Probably they rebounded with the economic recovery (such as it was) in 2010 and 2011. It should by now be clear, from the many citations here, that much of this book couldn't have been written without this fantastically useful Web tool.

[13]SOI Tax Stats, Historical Table 3, IRS Web page at http://www.irs.gov/taxstats/article /o„id=175800,00.html. The figure is for 2009.

that mean it became posh to have a job? A better way to put it is that having a job—the right job, anyway—became the way to get posh. That's encouraging in one sense: To roll in the dough you don't have to inherit it. But it's discouraging in another sense: You can't blame enormous income disparities on coupon-clipping Bertie Wooster[14] who exist outside the wage structure (and reality as most of us understand it). The wage structure *itself* is grossly misshapen.

- The rich, defined as the top 10 percent (which today means everyone making $109,000 or more), increased their share of national income during the Great Divergence from about one third (34 percent) to nearly one half (48 percent).

- The top 5 percent (Basically, Undeniably, Really, and Stinking Rich; today, everybody making at least $153,000) increased their share of national income during the Great Divergence from 23 to 37 percent.

- The top 1 percent (Undeniably, Really, and Stinking; today, everybody making at least $368,000) more than *doubled* their share of the national income during the Great Divergence, from 10 to 21 percent. A chart showing this found its way into President Obama's first budget, prompting the *Wall Street Journal* columnist Daniel Henninger to call it "the most politically potent squiggle along an axis since Arthur Laffer[15] drew his famous curve on a napkin in the mid-1970s." But where Laffer's squiggle was an argument to *lower* taxes, Piketty and Saez's (the conservative Henninger noted with some dismay) was an argument to *raise* them on the rich.[16] It was also what later inspired 2011's Occupy Wall Street protest slogan, "We are the 99 percent."

- The top 0.1 percent (Really and Stinking; today, everybody making at least $1.7 million) *tripled* their share of the national income during the Great Divergence, from 3 to 10 percent.

[14]*Bertie Wooster*: Bertram Wilberforce Wooster, a fictional character in a series of stories and novels by British author P. G. Wodehouse (1881–1975).

[15]*Arthur Laffer*: Arthur B. Laffer (b. 1940), American economist and a member of President Ronald Reagan's Economic Policy Advisory Board from 1981 to 1989. The Laffer Curve demonstrates that in a given economy there is a tax rate that will maximize revenue; because excessive taxes might discourage productivity, the "ideal" tax rate is not obvious.

[16]Another difference—there's no polite way to say this—is that the economics profession takes Piketty and Saez much more seriously than it ever took Laffer. As the journalist Jonathan Chait put it, "Laffer believed it was possible to simultaneously expand the economy and tamp down inflation by cutting taxes, especially the high tax rates faced by upper-income earners. Respectable economists—not least among them conservative ones—considered this laughable." See Jonathan Chait, *The Big Con: The True Story of How Washington Got Hoodwinked and Hijacked by Crackpot Economics* (Boston: Houghton Mifflin, 2007), 14.

- The top 0.01 percent (Stinking; today, everybody making at least $9.1 million) nearly *quadrupled* their share of the national income during the Great Divergence, from 1.4 to 5 percent.[17]

Notice a pattern? The richer you are, the faster you expand your slice of your country's income. Or as Saez put it to me, "The [inequality] phenomenon is more extreme the further you go up in the distribution," and it's "very strong once you pass that threshold of the top 1 percent."[18]

Perhaps you view "the rich get richer" as an inexorable fact of economic life, like compounding interest. But...the top-incomes-based divergence is not typical of past American history. And while it's true that an upward pattern in top-income shares has since 1979 been fairly common in other developed countries, it isn't universal. Top-income shares in these other countries are lower and, where they are increasing, do so less rapidly. An inequality trend driven by large and quickly growing income shares at the summit is not capitalism's norm....

[It is] not a fact of economic life that the income share of the very richest Americans must be as high as it is today; it is also not a fact of economic life that the very richest Americans must increase their income share over time or even maintain it at the same level. Their income share can dwindle over a long period, as it did in the decades after World War II, without hurting the economy. Dwindling income share for the very rich may even *help* the economy. "None of the bad consequences one might have expected from a drastic equalization of incomes actually materialized after World War II," Paul Krugman writes in *The Conscience of a Liberal*. "On the contrary, the Great Compression succeeded in equalizing incomes for a long period—more than thirty years. And the era of equality was also a time of unprecedented prosperity, which we have never been able to recapture. Trickle-up[19] economics has a better track record over America's last century than trickle-down....

The Great Divergence (Part 2) is a dramatic departure from the status quo that prevailed in the United States from the end of World War II through the early 1980s. Although top income shares are rising in many developed countries, nowhere are they rising as fast as in the United States. Also, nowhere (except Argentina) have top income shares reached the same high level as in the United States. Indeed, if you update income share for America's one-percenters to 2008, the United States pulls slightly ahead of Argentina—not that this is a competition any sensible country would want to win.

Who is it exactly who got rich?

---

[17]All these calculations, and the ones that follow, are from the WTID, include capital gains, and are current through 2008.
[18]Emmanuel Saez, interview with author, Aug. 18, 2010.
[19]*trickle-down economics*: the hypothesis that tax breaks and other benefits for corporations and the wealthy produce the best overall economy and thus indirectly help the middle and working classes.

A 2010 study by Jon Bakija, Adam Cole, and Bradley Heim, economists at Williams College, the U.S. Treasury, and Indiana University, respectively, looked at that question by examining income tax records for 2005. They found that among the Really and Stinking Rich—the top 0.1 percent, who currently make at least $1.7 million—43 percent were executives, managers, and supervisors at nonfinancial firms, and 18 percent were financiers. Together they accounted for the majority. The professions next in line were law (7 percent), medicine (6 percent), and real estate (4 percent).[20]

The skyrocketing increase in nonfinancial executive pay has been well documented. A *New York Times* survey of two hundred corporations with revenues of $10.78 billion or more found that in 2010 median compensation for chief executives was just under $11 million, a 23 percent increase over 2009. (The comparable median for all workers fell slightly during the same period.) The largest payout went to Philippe Dauman, president and chief executive of Viacom, the entertainment conglomerate that owns Paramount Pictures and Comedy Central. Dauman got $84.5 million, an amount that exceeds the entire 2011–12 town budget for North Haven, Connecticut. It takes a village to pay a corporate titan.[21] ...

The 43 percent of the Really and Stinking Rich who run America's nonfinancial corporations were very significant players in the Great Divergence (Part 2). No other occupational group had a larger membership among the top 0.1 percent. But, incredibly, the quadrupling of chief executives' pay during the 1990s wasn't enough to *increase* this group's presence among the Really and Stinking Rich once the run-up in top income shares began. Proportionally, its membership actually diminished slightly, from 48 percent in 1979 to 43 percent in 2005. The group to watch—the group that *expanded* its share of the top earners' pie—was the nation's financiers. Back in 1979, the financial sector represented only 11 percent of the Really and Stinking Rich. By 2005, financiers represented 18 percent.[22] That's because changes during this period in how

[20]These figures don't include capital gains....The study, alas, did not provide multiyear data that included capital gains. If you include capital gains for 2004—the paper doesn't show these figures for 2005—the percentages are only slightly different: 41 percent for nonfinancial executives, 18 percent for financiers, 6 percent for lawyers, and 4 percent for doctors. Jon Bakija, Adam Cole, and Bradley T. Heim, "Jobs and Income Growth of Top Earners and the Causes of Changing Income Inequality: Evidence from U.S. Tax Return Data," Williams College Economics Department Working Paper No. 2010–24 (Nov. 2010), 49–51, Tables 1–3. Membership in the somewhat less-exclusive top 1 percent had fewer nonfinancial executives (31 percent), more doctors (16 percent), fewer financiers (14 percent), and slightly more lawyers (8 percent).

[21]Pradnya Joshi, "We Knew They Got Raises. But This?," *New York Times*, July 2, 2011, at http://www.nytimes.com/2011/07/03/business/03pay.html?_r=2; "Usual Weekly Earnings of Wage and Salary Workers Fourth Quarter 2010," U.S. Bureau of Labor Statistics press release, Jan. 20, 2011, at http://www.bls.gov/news.release/archives/wkyeng_01202011.pdf; "North Haven Voters Have Until 8 P.M. to Cast Ballot on Budget," *New Haven Register*, May 17, 2011, at http://www.newhavenregister.com/articles/2011/05/17/news/metro/doc4dd2e6e1349b6751514042.txt.

[22]Bakija, Cole, and Heim, "Jobs and Income Growth of Top Earners," 51, Table 3.

nonfinancial corporations did business paled in comparison to changes in how Wall Street did business.

In their 2010 book *13 Bankers*, Simon Johnson, an economist at MIT's Sloan School of Management, and James Kwak, a former consultant at McKinsey and Company, describe the financial sector's astonishing growth over three decades through mergers and expansions into new businesses.

> Between 1980 and 2000, the assets held by commercial banks, securities firms, and the securitizations they created grew from [the equivalent of] 55 percent of GDP[23] to [the equivalent of] 95 percent. Financial sector profits grew even faster, from an average of 13 percent of all domestic corporate profits from 1978 to 1987 to an average of 30 percent from 1998 to 2007. The growth was faster still for the largest banks. Between 1990 and 1999, the ten largest bank holding companies' share of all bank assets grew from 26 percent to 45 percent, and their share of all deposits doubled from 17 percent to 34 percent. And they continued to grow. In 1998, the merged Travelers and Citibank had $700 billion in assets; at the end of 2007, Citigroup had $2.2 trillion in assets, not counting $1.1 trillion in off-balance-sheet assets, even after the spinoff of the Travelers insurance businesses. Bank of America was not far behind, growing from $570 billion after the NationsBank–Bank of America merger to $1.7 trillion at the end of 2007.[24]

In effect, Wall Street ate the economy. *Take General Electric:* You probably think of it as a maker of lightbulbs and appliances, right? And in 1980, manufacturing did indeed account for 92 percent of its profits. But by early 2008, GE's financial business accounted for 56 percent of its profits. (Its GE Capital subsidiary happens to be the largest nonbank lender in the United States.) Now consider General Motors: It makes cars, doesn't it? But before its financial arm, GMAC, got caught up in the subprime mortgage crisis of the late aughts, GMAC routinely accounted for 60 to 90 percent of the parent company's profits. (GM sold off GMAC but has since replaced it with a new financial division, GM Financial.) When the wildly leveraged[25] U.S. economy crashed and burned at the end of 2008, many predicted that Wall Street's era of economic dominance had ended. But by March 2011, the *Wall Street Journal* could report that the financial sector once again was creating about 30 percent of corporate profits in the United States. While still

---

[23]*GDP:* Gross Domestic Product, a measure of the value of all goods and services produced within a country.

[24]Simon Johnson and James Kwak, *13 Bankers: The Wall Street Takeover and the Next Financial Meltdown* (New York: Vintage, 2011; originally published by Pantheon in 2010), 85–86.

[25]*leveraged:* leveraging describes a variety of strategies for attempting to multiply financial gains; a simple example would be investing $10,000 and borrowing $90,000 to speculate on a $100,000 piece of real estate.

"If we don't decide what we're worth, who will?"

short of the 2002 peak, when finance generated fully 44 percent of corporate profits, 30 percent was the financial sector's average during the
subprime bubble.[26, 27] ...

Today it can feel as though we live in a society [in which] the first 30
principle isn't economic equality; it's economic inequality. Any effort to
minimize income differences is held politically suspect, an intrusion on
individual liberty. Whenever the government proposes any action that
might redistribute income downward, it must demonstrate that the most
economically favored will somehow benefit. If the favored few don't believe they'll benefit, they can usually persuade their allies in Congress

[26]*subprime bubble*: the recent period—roughly 2003–2006—during which both individual homebuyers and large institutions financed mortgages at low but adjustable rates;
the bubble burst as rising rates, declining real estate values, rising unemployment, and
tight credit markets led to mortgage defaults, foreclosures, and billions of dollars of losses
in real estate and mortgage-backed investments.

[27]Justin Lahart, "Has the Financial Industry's Heyday Come and Gone?," *Wall Street
Journal*, Apr. 28, 2008, at http://online.wsj.com/article/SB120933096635747945.html;
Christine Hauser, "G.E. Posts Earnings That Exceed Forecasts and Raises Dividend," *New York
Times*, Apr. 21, 2011, at http://www.nytimes.com/2011/04/22/business/22electric.html?_
r=2; David Welch, "G.M.'s Dwindling Options," *Businessweek*, Mar. 16, 2006, at http://www
.businessweek.com/autos/content/mar2006/bw2G060316_306932.htm; Kathleen Madigan,
"Like the Phoenix, U.S. Finance Profits Soar," *Real Time Economics* (blog), *Wall Street
Journal*, Mar. 25, 2011, at http://blogs.wsj.com/economics/2011/03/25/like-the-phoenix-u
-s-fmance-profits-soar/; Sameer Khatiwada, "Did the Financial Sector Profit at the Expense
of the Rest of the Economy? Evidence from the United States," Discussion Paper no. 206,
International Institute for Labor Studies, Jan. 1, 2010, 2, at http://digitalcommons.ilr.conhell
.edu/cgi/viewcontentcgi?article=1101&context=intl.

to block it. Under Senate filibuster rules, all it takes is forty-one nays. To repeat the admirably candid words of the Procter & Gamble lobbyist (and sometime presidential aide) Bryce Harlow, "When business really tries...it never loses a big battle in Washington."

But there's another strain in American politics, one that impressed the British essayist Henry Fairlie when he first arrived in the United States. It's the America in which a small child is as likely as a powerful president to address a complete stranger with an informal "Hi." Americans believe fervently in the value of social equality, and social equality is at risk when incomes become too dramatically unequal. It's the America that believes hard work should be rewarded, because if it isn't workers will have no reason to give their best. And it's an America that believes in equal opportunity for all to an extent that America has lately been unable to fulfill. There is even an America that recoils, on principle, from vast disparities in income. In years past, it was common to hear Americans describe with sharp disapproval societies starkly divided into the privileged and the destitute. They were oligarchies, or banana republics. Even if their leaders were democratically elected, these countries didn't seem very democratic. Is it my imagination, or do we hear less criticism of such societies today in the United States? Might it be harder for Americans, as gated communities spread across the land while middle-class enclaves disappear, to sustain in such discussions the necessary sense of moral superiority?...

Asking what the ideal distribution in America would be is a distraction from the real question, which is how we can align it a bit more successfully with our democratic ideals. You'd have to be blind not to see that we are headed in the wrong direction, and we've been heading that way for too long.

We can do better. We have done better before, and other leading industrialized democracies are doing better now. Let's get started while the vast disparities in how people live and what they have still have the power to offend our sense of fair play. The worst thing we could do to the Great Divergence is get used to it.

ENGAGING THE TEXT

1. What is the difference between the "Great Divergence" and what Noah terms the "Great Divergence, Part 2"? Explain why Noah is particularly concerned about Part 2.

2. Why is it so important, according to Noah, for economists to look back in time? Explain why you agree or disagree that data from the 1930s to the 1970s remains relevant today.

3. Noah compares the United States to many other countries, including Portugal, Turkey, Mexico, Finland, New Zealand, and Ireland. How does he use economic data from around the world to inform his argument? To what extent do you agree that the results of these comparisons are troubling?

4. In paragraph 2, Noah writes that "it's too early to say whether the Occupy Wall Street movement will have any lasting positive effect, but certainly the topic [of diverging incomes] is becoming more difficult to ignore." What positive effects might Noah have in mind here? From your perspective today, what lasting positive or negative effects has the Occupy movement produced?

5. Working in small groups, critique the definitions of wealth Noah borrows from Piketty and Saez and discuss how you would define and label the upper and middle classes in the United States. For example, do you agree that an annual income of $109,000 makes you "sort of rich"? If you revised the slogan "We are the 99 Percent" to be less snappy but more accurate, where would you draw the line between the rich and everyone else — at 90 percent, for example, or perhaps 99.5 percent?

6. Do you agree with Noah that something is clearly wrong when the gap between the rich and the rest of us grows wider? Why should average Americans care if the top 1 percent owns a quarter, a third, or even a half of the nation's total wealth?

EXPLORING CONNECTIONS

7. Compare Noah's analysis of the Great Divergence to Charles Murray's description of "The New American Divide" in the preceding essay (p. 347). How do they frame the issues? How similar is the data they use to support their arguments? Describe the tone each author uses in writing about the wealthiest Americans — for example, in Murray's description of the "SuperZIPS" and Noah's description of the Stinking Rich?

8. Drawing on this excerpt from *The Great Divergence* and on "The New American Divide" by Charles Murray (p. 347), debate the relative importance of the cultural gap and the economic gap between rich and ordinary Americans.

9. Read Eric Liu and Nick Hannauer's "Great Citizenship" (p. 750), and discuss how the wealth gap that Noah documents might affect the growth of democratic social networks in America. Can online social media make the United States a more democratic nation while the country becomes increasingly divided economically? Explain why you think the growth of social media is more likely to widen or narrow America's wealth gap.

EXTENDING THE CRITICAL CONTEXT

10. In Chapter 11 of *The Great Divergence*, entitled "What to Do," Noah describes several steps America might take to reduce income inequality. Discuss the four proposals listed below, assessing which you consider most sensible and politically viable:

    - "Soak the Rich" (For example, raise the marginal tax rate to 50 percent on annual incomes over $1 million, and up to a maximum of 70 percent on incomes over $20 million.)

- "Fatten Government Payrolls" (For example, repair aging infrastructure such as bridges and highways and establish an ambitious federal jobs program.)
- "Universalize Preschool" (Give all kids the benefits of early education, thus reducing educational inequality and perhaps boosting future economic productivity.)
- "Reregulate Wall Street" (For example, break up banks that are "too big to fail" so that taxpayers won't have to bail them out.)

How do Noah's solutions differ from those proposed by Charles Murray in "The New American Divide" (p. 347)?

11. In paragraph 6 Noah uses the Vanderbilt Estate in North Carolina and the Tenement Museum in Manhattan as examples of extreme wealth and poverty in the United States, but you may not have to travel very far to see a wide spectrum of wealth and poverty. Collaborate with classmates to draw a map of the geography of wealth in your town, city, or region. What does your map suggest about money, success, education, immigration status, or ethnicity?

FURTHER CONNECTIONS

1. How would you expect your county to compare with other counties in your state in terms of wealth? How would you expect your state to compare with other states? Research state and county data from the U.S. Census Bureau Web site (www.census.gov) and present or write up your findings. To what extent do you think you have had advantages or disadvantages because of where you were born or grew up?

2. The Merriam Webster Online Dictionary defines "wage slave" as "a person dependent on wages or a salary for a livelihood." Are you a wage slave now, and do you expect to be one in the future? Discuss the connotations of this term, and explain why you think the term is or is not a useful one in contemporary America. What are the alternatives to wage slavery?

3. This chapter of *Rereading America* has been criticized by conservatives for undermining the work ethic of American college students. Rush Limbaugh, for example, claimed that the chapter "presents America as a stacked deck," thus "robbing people of the ability to see the enormous opportunities directly in front of them." Do you agree? Write a journal entry or essay in which you explain how these readings have influenced your attitudes toward work and success.

4. **Connecting to the e-Pages.**   Write a short essay or make a video reflecting your personal vision of the American Dream. You will find inspiration and helpful models in the e-Pages: "Stephen Cruz," by Pulitzer Prize winner Studs Terkel, describes how one man redefines his understanding of success, and the video *The High Price of Materialism* explores the psychological price we pay for some of the goods we so eagerly consume. See bedfordstmartins.com/rereading /epages for these selections.

TRUE WOMEN
AND REAL MEN
Myths of Gender

Bree Scott-Hartland as Delphinia Blue, photo by Carolyn Jones
(From *Living Proof,* Abbeville Press, 1994)

FAST FACTS

1. Among men aged 15–44, 76.3% agree or strongly agree with the statement, "It is more important for a man to spend a lot of time with his family than to be successful at his career."

2. In a recent survey more young women than young men rated career high on their list of life priorities (66% to 59%).

3. The Centers for Disease Control reports that one in four women have experienced severe physical violence at the hands of an intimate partner at some point in their lives.

4. In 2009, according to the National School Climate Survey, 86% of lesbian, gay, bisexual, and transgender students experienced harassment at school; one in three skipped a day of school in the past month because they felt unsafe there.

5. 77% of teens 12–17 use social media; among young teenage girls (12–13 years old), 33% say that people their age are mostly unkind to each other on social networking sites, in contrast to 9% of boys the same age.

6. In 29 states, you can be fired based on your sexual orientation; in 35 states, you can be fired based on your gender identity and expression.

Sources: (1) Centers for Disease Control; (2) The Pew Research Center; (3) National Intimate Partner and Sexual Violence Survey: 2010 Summary Report; (4) Gay, Lesbian and Straight Education Network; (5) Pew Research Center; (6) Human Rights Campaign: *2011 Annual Report.*

COMMON SENSE TELLS US that there are obvious differences between females and males: after all, biology, not culture, determines whether you're able to bear children. But culture and cultural myths do shape the roles men and women play in our public and private relationships: we may be born female and male, but we are made women and men. Sociologists distinguish between sex and gender — between one's biological identity and the conventional patterns of behavior we learn to associate with each sex. While biological sex remains relatively stable, the definition of "appropriate" gender behavior varies dramatically from one cultural group or historical period to the next. The variations show up markedly in the way we dress. For example, in Thailand, men who act and dress like women are not only socially accepted but encouraged to participate in popular, male-only beauty pageants; in contemporary Anglo-American culture, on the other hand, cross-dressers are usually seen as deviant or ridiculous. Male clothing in late-seventeenth- and early-eighteenth-century England would also have failed our current "masculinity" tests: in that period, elaborate laces, brocades, wigs, and even makeup signaled wealth, status, and sexual attractiveness for men and women alike.

History shows us how completely our gender derives from cultural myths about what is proper for men and women to think, enjoy, and do. And history is replete with examples of how the apparent "naturalness" of gender has been used to regulate political, economic, and personal relations between the sexes.

Many nineteenth-century scientists argued that it was "unnatural" for women to attend college; rigorous intellectual activity, they asserted, would draw vital energy away from a woman's reproductive organs and make her sterile. According to this line of reasoning, women who sought higher education threatened the natural order by jeopardizing their ability to bear children and perpetuate the species. Arguments based on nature were likewise used to justify women's exclusion from political life. In his classic 1832 treatise on American democracy, James Fenimore Cooper remarked that women's domestic role and "necessary" subordination to men made them unsuitable for participation in public affairs. Thus denying women the right to vote was perfectly consistent with the principles of American democracy:

> In those countries where the suffrage is said to be universal, exceptions exist, that arise from the necessity of things. . . . The interests of women being thought to be so identified with those of their male relatives as to become, in a great degree, inseparable, females are, almost generally, excluded from the possession of political rights. There can be no doubt that society is greatly the gainer, by thus excluding one half its members, and the half that is best adapted to give a tone to its domestic happiness, from the strife of parties, and the fierce struggles of political controversies. . . . These exceptions, however, do not very materially affect the principle of political equality. (*The American Democrat*)

Resistance to gender equality has been remarkably persistent in the United States. It took over seventy years of hard political work by both black and white women's organizations to win the right to vote. But while feminists gained the vote for women in 1920 and the legal right to equal educational and employment opportunities in the 1970s, attitudes change even more slowly than laws. Contemporary antifeminist campaigns voice some of the same anxieties as their nineteenth-century counterparts over the "loss" of femininity and domesticity.

Women continue to suffer economic inequities based on cultural assumptions about gender. What's defined as "women's work" — nurturing, feeding, caring for family and home — is devalued and pays low wages or none at all. When women enter jobs traditionally held by men, they often encounter discrimination, harassment, or "glass ceilings" that limit their advancement. But men, too, pay a high price for their culturally imposed roles. Psychological research shows higher rates of depression among people of both sexes who adhere closely to traditional roles than among those who do not. Moreover, studies of men's mental and physical health suggest that social pressure to "be a man" (that is, to be emotionally controlled, powerful, and successful) can contribute to isolation, anxiety, stress, and illness, and may be partially responsible for men's shorter life spans. As sociologist Margaret Andersen observes, "traditional gender roles limit the psychological and social possibilities for human beings."

Even our assumption that there are "naturally" only two genders is a cultural invention that fails to accommodate the diversity of human experience. Some cultures have three or more gender categories. One of the best-known third genders is the American Indian *berdache*, a role that is found in as many as seventy North and South American tribes. The berdache is a biological male who takes the social role of a woman, does women's work (or in some cases both women's and men's work), and often enjoys high status in the society; the berdache has sex with men who are not themselves berdaches and in some cultures may also marry a man. Euro-American culture, by contrast, offers no socially acceptable alternative gender roles. As a result, gay men, lesbians, bisexuals, transsexuals, cross-dressers, and other gender rebels confront pervasive and often legally sanctioned discrimination similar to that once experienced by women. Just as many Americans in the past considered it "unnatural" and socially destructive for women to vote or go to college, many now consider it "unnatural" and socially destructive for gays and lesbians to marry, or for individuals to express a gender identity that violates conventional notions of masculinity or femininity.

This chapter focuses on cultural myths of gender and the influence they wield over human development and personal identity. The first three selections examine how dominant American culture defines female and male gender roles — and how those roles may define us. In "How the Americans Understand the Equality of the Sexes," Alexis de Tocqueville describes the status of American women in the early years of the Republic. Jamaica Kincaid's "Girl," a story framed as a mother's advice to her daughter, presents a more contemporary take on what it means to be raised a woman. Aaron H. Devor's "Becoming Members of Society" examines gender as a socially constructed category and discusses the psychological processes that underlie gender role acquisition.

The next selection, "Weeping for the Lost Matriarchy" by Kay Givens McGowan, asks us to re-evaluate our current understandings of both history and women's roles. It contends that Southeastern Native women had "economic and political power; spiritual equality; the right to proper health care, up to and including abortion on demand; the right to divorce on demand; and the right to call — and call off — war." This matriarchy was forcibly uprooted by colonists who often failed to comprehend what they were destroying.

The second half of the chapter opens with a series of conventional and unconventional images of women and men; this provides an opportunity to think about the ways that we "read" gender visually. Then three essays examine the power of the media to reflect our attitudes and shape our behavior. Jean Kilbourne's "'Two Ways a Woman Can Get Hurt': Advertising and Violence" argues that the objectification of women in ads constitutes a form of cultural abuse. Peggy Orenstein, in "Just Between You, Me, and My 622 BFFs," suggests that social networking can hurt young girls by promoting narcissism and discouraging empathy. She also worries that Facebook "friends" are taking the place of real friends in the real world. In "From Fly-Girls to Bitches and Hos," self-described "hip-hop feminist" Joan Morgan maintains that it's necessary to look behind the violent misogyny of many rap lyrics in order to understand and heal the pain of the African American men who compose and perform the songs. The chapter concludes with two essays about men. Michael Kimmel's "'Bros Before Hos': The Guy Code" lays out the "rules" of masculinity that govern and at times distort the behavior and emotions of young men. Hanna Rosin, in "The End of Men," offers a very different view: she profiles strong women who are thriving in the new economy, in contrast to their counterparts — underachieving, slacker men.

In the e-Pages, Jesse Green's "S/He" addresses transgenderism, the mismatch between "brain gender" and biological gender. Transgender kids raise difficult questions for parents: Should they allow their son or daughter to dress as the opposite sex after school and on weekends or at all times? Should they agree to puberty blockers (hormones that prevent the development of sexual maturity) for their child? How about sex-reassignment surgery? For the kids themselves, the answers seem more obvious. As one father says, "People would say, 'I can't believe you'd let your kid do that. That's abuse.' I'll tell you what's abuse: suicide." The e-Pages also include a video of a gay college student who talks about coming out, being harassed, and "experiencing opposition." See bedfordstmartins.com/rereading/epages for these two selections.

Sources

Andersen, Margaret L. *Thinking About Women: Sociological Perspectives on Gender.* 3rd ed. New York: Macmillan, 1993. Print.

Cooper, James Fenimore. *The American Democrat.* N.p.: Minerva Press, 1969. Print.

French, Marilyn. *Beyond Power: On Women, Men, and Morals.* New York: Ballantine Books, 1985. Print.

Giddings, Paula. *When and Where I Enter: The Impact of Black Women on Race and Sex in America.* New York: Bantam Books, 1984. Print.

Hubbard, Ruth. *The Politics of Women's Biology.* New Brunswick, NJ: Rutgers University Press, 1990. Print.

Lorber, Judith. *Paradoxes of Gender.* New Haven and London: Yale University Press, 1994. Print.

Weinrich, James D. and Walter L. Williams, "Strange Customs, Familiar Lives: Homosexualities in Other Cultures." *Homosexuality: Research Implications for Public Policy.* Ed. John C. Gonsiorek and James D. Weinrich. Newbury Park, CA: Sage, 1991. Print.

BEFORE READING

- Imagine for a moment that you were born female (if you're a man) or male (if you're a woman). How would your life be different? Would any of your interests and activities change? How about your relationships with other people? Write a journal entry describing your past, present, and possible future in this alternate gender identity.

- Collect and bring to class images of girls and boys, women and men taken from popular magazines and newspapers. Working in groups, make a collage of either male or female gender images; then compare and discuss your results. What do these media images tell you about what it means to be a woman or a man in this culture?

- Do a brief freewrite focusing on the performer in the frontispiece to this chapter. How would you describe this person's gender? In what ways does this image challenge traditional ideas about maleness and femaleness?

HOW THE AMERICANS UNDERSTAND THE EQUALITY OF THE SEXES

ALEXIS DE TOCQUEVILLE

In 1831, Alexis de Tocqueville (1805–1859), a French aristocrat, left Europe to study the American penal system. The young democracy that he observed in the United States left a deep impression on Tocqueville, and in 1835 he published his reflections on this new way of life in *Democracy in America* — a work that has since become the point of departure for many studies of American culture. In the following passage from *Democracy in America*, Tocqueville compares the social condition of American women to that of their European counterparts. Tocqueville's concept of equality and assumptions about women can seem foreign to modern readers, so it would be a good idea to take your time as you read this short passage.

I HAVE SHOWN HOW DEMOCRACY destroys or modifies the different inequalities which originate in society; but is that all? or does it not ultimately affect that great inequality of man and woman which has seemed, up to the present day, to be eternally based in human nature? I believe that the social changes which bring nearer to the same level the father and son, the master and servant, and, in general, superiors and inferiors, will raise woman, and make her more and more the equal of man. But here, more than ever, I feel the necessity of making myself clearly understood; for there is no subject on which the coarse and lawless fancies of our age have taken a freer range.

There are people in Europe who, confounding together the different characteristics of the sexes, would make man and woman into beings not only equal, but alike. They would give to both the same functions, impose on both the same duties, and grant to both the same rights; they would mix them in all things, —their occupations, their pleasures, their business. It may readily be conceived, that, by thus attempting to make one sex equal to the other, both are degraded; and from so preposterous a medley of the works of nature, nothing could ever result but weak men and disorderly women.

It is not thus that the Americans understand that species of democratic equality which may be established between the sexes. They admit that, as nature has appointed such wide differences between the physical and moral constitution of man and woman, her manifest design was to give a distinct employment to their various faculties; and they hold that improvement does not consist in making beings so dissimilar do pretty nearly the same things, but in causing each of them to fulfil their respective tasks in the best possible manner. The Americans have applied to the sexes the great principle of political economy which governs the manufactures of our age, by carefully dividing the duties of man from those of woman, in order that the great work of society may be the better carried on.

In no country has such constant care been taken as in America to trace two clearly distinct lines of action for the two sexes, and to make them keep pace one with the other, but in two pathways which are always different. American women never manage the outward concerns of the family, or conduct a business, or take a part in political life; nor are they, on the other hand, ever compelled to perform the rough labor of the fields, or to make any of those laborious exertions which demand the exertion of physical strength. No families are so poor as to form an exception to this rule. If, on the one hand, an American woman cannot escape from the quiet circle of domestic employments, she is never forced, on the other, to go beyond it. Hence it is, that the women of America, who often exhibit a masculine strength of understanding and a manly energy, generally preserve great delicacy of personal appearance, and always retain the manners of women, although they sometimes show that they have the hearts and minds of men.

Nor have the Americans ever supposed that one consequence of democratic principles is the subversion of marital power, or the confusion of the natural authorities in families. They hold that every association must have a head in order to accomplish its object, and that the natural head of the conjugal association is man. They do not therefore deny him the right of directing his partner; and they maintain that, in the smaller association of husband and wife, as well as in the great social community, the object of democracy is to regulate and legalize the powers which are necessary, and not to subvert all power.

This opinion is not peculiar to one sex, and contested by the other: I never observed that the women of America consider conjugal authority as a fortunate usurpation of their rights, nor that they thought themselves degraded by submitting to it. It appeared to me, on the contrary, that they attach a sort of pride to the voluntary surrender of their own will, and make it their boast to bend themselves to the yoke,—not to shake it off. Such, at least, is the feeling expressed by the most virtuous of their sex; the others are silent; and, in the United States, it is not the practice for a guilty wife to clamor for the rights of women, whilst she is trampling on her own holiest duties.[1]

It has often been remarked, that in Europe a certain degree of contempt lurks even in the flattery which men lavish upon women: although a European frequently affects to be the slave of woman, it may be seen that he never sincerely thinks her his equal. In the United States, men seldom compliment women, but they daily show how much they esteem them. They constantly display an entire confidence in the understanding of a wife, and a profound respect for her freedom; they have decided that her mind is just as fitted as that of a man to discover the plain truth, and her heart as firm to embrace it; and they have never sought to place her virtue, any more than his, under the shelter of prejudice, ignorance, and fear.

It would seem that, in Europe, where man so easily submits to the despotic sway of women, they are nevertheless deprived of some of the greatest attributes of the human species, and considered as seductive but imperfect beings; and (what may well provoke astonishment) women ultimately look upon themselves in the same light, and almost consider it as a privilege that they are entitled to show themselves futile, feeble, and timid. The women of America claim no such privileges.

Again, it may be said that in our morals we have reserved strange immunities to man; so that there is, as it were, one virtue for his use, and another for the guidance of his partner; and that, according to the opinion of the public, the very same act may be punished alternately as a crime, or only as a fault. The Americans know not this iniquitous division of duties and rights; amongst them, the seducer is as much dishonored as his victim.

It is true that the Americans rarely lavish upon women those eager attentions which are commonly paid them in Europe; but their conduct to women always implies that they suppose them to be virtuous and refined; and such is the respect entertained for the moral freedom of the sex, that in the presence of a woman the most guarded language is used, lest her ear should be offended by an expression. In America, a young unmarried woman may, alone and without fear, undertake a long journey. 10

The legislators of the United States, who have mitigated almost all the penalties of criminal law, still make rape a capital offence, and no crime is visited with more inexorable severity by public opinion. This may be accounted for; as the Americans can conceive nothing more precious than a woman's honor, and nothing which ought so much to

[1]Allusion to Mary Wollstonecraft (1759–1797), English radical, political theorist, and author of *Vindication of the Rights of Woman*, who argued that women should enjoy complete political, economic, and sexual freedom; Wollstonecraft scandalized the "polite" society of her day by living according to her feminist principles. [Eds.]

be respected as her independence, they hold that no punishment is too severe for the man who deprives her of them against her will. In France, where the same offence is visited with far milder penalties, it is frequently difficult to get a verdict from a jury against the prisoner. Is this a consequence of contempt of decency, or contempt of women? I cannot but believe that it is a contempt of both.

Thus, the Americans do not think that man and woman have either the duty or the right to perform the same offices, but they show an equal regard for both their respective parts; and though their lot is different, they consider both of them as beings of equal value. They do not give to the courage of woman the same form or the same direction as to that of man; but they never doubt her courage: and if they hold that man and his partner ought not always to exercise their intellect and understanding in the same manner, they at least believe the understanding of the one to be as sound as that of the other, and her intellect to be as clear. Thus, then, whilst they have allowed the social inferiority of woman to subsist, they have done all they could to raise her morally and intellectually to the level of man; and in this respect they appear to me to have excellently understood the true principle of democratic improvement.

As for myself, I do not hesitate to avow, that, although the women of the United States are confined within the narrow circle of domestic life, and their situation is, in some respects, one of extreme dependence, I have nowhere seen woman occupying a loftier position; and if I were asked, now that I am drawing to the close of this work, in which I have spoken of so many important things done by the Americans, to what the singular prosperity and growing strength of that people ought mainly to be attributed, I should reply, To the superiority of their women.

ENGAGING THE TEXT

1. What roles does Tocqueville assume are natural and appropriate for women? For men? Which of his assumptions, if any, seem contemporary? Which ones seem antiquated, and why?

2. How do American and European attitudes toward women differ, according to Tocqueville? In what ways does he suggest that American democracy is enabling women to become "more and more the equal of man" (para. 1)?

3. By the time Tocqueville wrote this selection, the first feminist manifesto, Mary Wollstonecraft's *Vindication of the Rights of Woman* (1792), had been read and discussed in Europe for over forty years. Which parts of Tocqueville's essay seem to be intended as a response to feminist arguments for women's equality?

4. Tocqueville finds some forms of equality between women and men more desirable than others. Which forms does he approve of, which does he disapprove of, and why?

EXPLORING CONNECTIONS

5. Read the selection by Aaron H. Devor (p. 387); how and why does Devor's understanding of gender roles differ from Tocqueville's assumption that the "great inequality of man and woman" appears to be "eternally based in human nature" (para. 1)?

6. Both Tocqueville and Thomas Jefferson (p. 497) attempt to justify or rationalize a particular form of inequality. What strategies does each writer use to build his case for the subjection of women or for the enslavement of blacks? Which of their arguments appear least effective to you as a modern reader, and why?

EXTENDING THE CRITICAL CONTEXT

7. Work in groups to list the specific tasks involved in maintaining a household in the 1830s (keep in mind that electricity, indoor plumbing, ready-made clothing, and prepared foods were not available). How credible is Tocqueville's claim that no American woman is "ever compelled...to make any of those laborious exertions which demand the exertion of physical strength" (para. 4)? How do you explain his failure to acknowledge the hard physical labor routinely performed by many women during this time?

GIRL

JAMAICA KINCAID

Although she now lives in New England, Jamaica Kincaid (b. 1949) retains strong ties, including citizenship, to her birthplace—the island of Antigua in the West Indies. After immigrating to the United States to attend college, she ended up educating herself instead, eventually becoming a staff writer for *The New Yorker*, the author of several critically acclaimed books, and an instructor at Harvard University. About the influence of parents on children she says, "The magic is they carry so much you don't know about. They know you in a way you don't know yourself." Some of that magic is exercised in the story "Girl," which was first published in *The New Yorker* and later appeared in Kincaid's award-winning collection *At the Bottom of the River* (1983). She has written and edited many volumes of nonfiction on subjects ranging from colonialism to gardening and travel. She has published four novels: *Annie John* (1985), *Lucy* (1990), *The Autobiography of My Mother* (1996), and *Mr. Potter* (2002).

WASH THE WHITE CLOTHES ON MONDAY and put them on the stone heap; wash the color clothes on Tuesday and put them on the clothesline to dry; don't walk barehead in the hot sun; cook pumpkin fritters[1] in very hot sweet oil; soak your little clothes right after you take them off; when buying cotton to make yourself a nice blouse, be sure that it doesn't have gum[2] on it, because that way it won't hold up well after a wash; soak salt fish overnight before you cook it; is it true that you sing benna in Sunday school?; always eat your food in such a way that it won't turn someone else's stomach; on Sundays try to walk like a lady and not like the slut you are so bent on becoming; don't sing benna[3] in Sunday school; you mustn't speak to wharf-rat boys, not even to give directions; don't eat fruits on the street—flies will follow you; *but I don't sing benna on Sundays at all and never in Sunday school*; this is how to sew on a button; this is how to make a buttonhole for the button you have just sewed on; this is how to hem a dress when you see the hem coming down and so to prevent yourself from looking like the slut I know you are so bent on becoming; this is how you iron your father's khaki shirt so that it doesn't have a crease; this is how you iron your father's khaki pants so that they don't have a crease; this is how you grow okra[4]—far from the house, because okra tree harbors red ants; when you are growing dasheen,[5] make sure it gets plenty of water or else it makes your throat itch when you are eating it; this is how you sweep a corner; this is how you sweep a whole house; this is how you sweep a yard; this is how you smile to someone you don't like too much; this is how you smile to someone you don't like at all; this is how you smile to someone you like completely; this is how you set a table for tea; this is how you set a table for dinner; this is how you set a table for dinner with an important guest; this is how you set a table for lunch; this is how you set a table for breakfast; this is how to behave in the presence of men who don't know you very well, and this way they won't recognize immediately the slut I have warned you against becoming; be sure to wash every day, even if it is with your own spit; don't squat down to play marbles—you are not a boy, you know; don't pick people's flowers—you might catch something; don't throw stones at blackbirds, because it might not be a blackbird at all; this is how to make a bread pudding; this is how to make doukona;[6] this is how to make pepper pot;[7] this is how to make a good medicine for a cold; this is how to make a good medicine to throw away a child before it even becomes a child; this is how to catch a fish; this is how to throw back a fish you don't like, and that way something bad won't fall on you; this is how to bully a man; this is how a man bullies you; this is how to love a man, and if this doesn't work there are other ways, and if they don't work don't feel too bad about giving up; this is how to spit up in the air if you feel like it, and this is how to move quick so that it doesn't fall on

[1]*fritters:* Small fried cakes of batter, often containing vegetables, fruit, or other fillings. [All notes are the editors'.]
[2]*gum:* Plant residue on cotton.
[3]*sing benna:* Sing popular music (not appropriate for Sunday school).
[4]*okra:* A shrub whose pods are used in soups, stews, and gumbo.
[5]*dasheen:* The taro plant, cultivated, like the potato, for its edible tuber.
[6]*doukona:* Plantain pudding; the plantain fruit is similar to the banana.
[7]*pepper pot:* A spicy West Indian stew.

you; this is how to make ends meet; always squeeze bread to make sure it's fresh; *but what if the baker won't let me feel the bread?*; you mean to say that after all you are really going to be the kind of woman who the baker won't let near the bread?

ENGAGING THE TEXT

1. What are your best guesses as to the time and place of the story? Who is telling the story? What does this dialogue tell you about the relationship between the characters, their values and attitudes? What else can you surmise about these people (for instance, ages, occupation, social status)? On what evidence in the story do you base these conclusions?

2. Why does the story juxtapose advice on cooking and sewing, for example, with the repeated warning not to act like a slut?

3. Explain the meaning of the last line of the story: "you mean to say that after all you are really going to be the kind of woman who the baker won't let near the bread?"

4. What does the story tell us about male-female relationships? According to the speaker, what roles are women and men expected to play? What kinds of power, if any, does the speaker suggest that women may have?

EXPLORING CONNECTIONS

5. To what extent would Tocqueville approve of the behaviors and attitudes that the mother is trying to teach her daughter in this selection?

6. What does it mean to be a successful mother in "Girl"? How does this compare to being a good mother or parent in "Looking for Work" (p. 22) or "An Indian Story" (see bedfordstmartins.com/rereading/epages)? Of all the parents in these narratives, which do you consider most successful, which least, and why?

EXTENDING THE CRITICAL CONTEXT

7. Write an imitation of the story. If you are a woman, record some of the advice or lessons your mother or another woman gave you; if you are a man, put down advice received from your father or from another male. Read what you have written aloud in class, alternating between male and female speakers, and discuss the results: How does parental guidance vary according to gender?

8. Write a page or two recording what the daughter might be thinking as she listens to her mother's advice; then compare notes with classmates.

BECOMING MEMBERS OF SOCIETY: LEARNING THE SOCIAL MEANINGS OF GENDER

AARON H. DEVOR

Gender is the most transparent of all social categories: we acquire gender roles so early in life and so thoroughly that it's hard to see them as the result of lessons taught and learned. Maleness and femaleness seem "natural," not the product of socialization. In this wide-ranging scholarly essay, Aaron H. Devor suggests that many of our notions of what it means to be female or male are socially constructed. He also touches on the various ways that different cultures define gender. A professor of sociology and Dean of Graduate Studies at the University of Victoria in British Columbia, Devor is a member of the International Academy of Sex Research and author of *FTM: Female-to-Male Transsexuals in Society* (1997). Born Holly Devor in 1951, Devor announced in 2002 his decision to live as a man and to adopt the name Aaron H. Devor. This selection is taken from his groundbreaking book, *Gender Blending: Confronting the Limits of Duality* (1989).

The Gendered Self

The task of learning to be properly gendered members of society only begins with the establishment of gender identity. Gender identities act as cognitive filtering devices guiding people to attend to and learn gender role behaviors appropriate to their statuses. Learning to behave in accordance with one's gender identity is a lifelong process. As we move through our lives, society demands different gender performances from us and rewards, tolerates, or punishes us differently for conformity to, or digression from, social norms. As children, and later adults, learn the rules of membership in society, they come to see themselves in terms they have learned from the people around them.

Children begin to settle into a gender identity between the age of eighteen months and two years.[1] By the age of two, children usually understand that they are members of a gender grouping and can correctly

---

[1]Much research has been devoted to determining when gender identity becomes solidified in the sense that a child knows itself to be unequivocally either male or female. John Money and his colleagues have proposed eighteen months of age because it is difficult or impossible to change a child's gender identity once it has been established around the age of eighteen months. Money and Ehrhardt, p. 243. [All notes are Devor's unless otherwise indicated.]

identify other members of their gender.[2] By age three they have a fairly firm and consistent concept of gender. Generally, it is not until children are five to seven years old that they become convinced that they are permanent members of their gender grouping.[3]

Researchers test the establishment, depth, and tenacity of gender identity through the use of language and the concepts mediated by language. The language systems used in populations studied by most researchers in this field conceptualize gender as binary and permanent. All persons are either male or female. All males are first boys and then men; all females are first girls and then women. People are believed to be unable to change genders without sex change surgery, and those who do change sex are considered to be both disturbed and exceedingly rare.

This is by no means the only way that gender is conceived in all cultures. Many aboriginal cultures have more than two gender categories and accept the idea that, under certain circumstances, gender may be changed without changes being made to biological sex characteristics. Many North and South American native peoples had a legitimate social category for persons who wished to live according to the gender role of another sex. Such people were sometimes revered, sometimes ignored, and occasionally scorned. Each culture had its own word to describe such persons, most commonly translated into English as "berdache." Similar institutions and linguistic concepts have also been recorded in early Siberian, Madagascan, and Polynesian societies, as well as in medieval Europe.[4]

Very young children learn their culture's social definitions of gender and gender identity at the same time that they learn what gender behaviors are appropriate for them. But they only gradually come to understand the meaning of gender in the same way as the adults of their society do. Very young children may learn the words which describe their gender and be able to apply them to themselves appropriately, but their comprehension of their meaning is often different from that used by adults. Five-year-olds, for example, may be able to accurately recognize their own gender and the genders of the people around them, but they will often make such ascriptions on the basis of role information, such as hair style, rather than physical attributes, such as genitals,

[2]Mary Driver Leinbach and Beverly I. Fagot, "Acquisition of Gender Labels: A Test for Toddlers," *Sex Roles* 15 (1986), pp. 655–66.

[3]Maccoby, pp. 225–29; Kohlberg and Ullian, p. 211.

[4]See Susan Baker, "Biological Influences on Human Sex and Gender," in *Women: Sex and Sexuality*, ed. Catherine R. Stimpson and Ethel S. Person (Chicago: University of Chicago Press, 1980), p. 186; Evelyn Blackwood, "Sexuality and Gender in Certain Native American Tribes: The Case of Cross-Gender Females," *Signs* 10 (1984), pp. 27–42; Vern L. Bullough, "Transvestites in the Middle Ages," *American Journal of Sociology* 79 (1974), 1381–89; J. Cl. DuBois, "Transsexualisme et Anthropologie Culturelle," *Gynecologie Pratique* 6 (1969), pp. 431–40; Donald C. Forgey, "The Institution of Berdache among the North American Plains Indians," *Journal of Sex Research* 11 (Feb. 1975), pp. 1–15; Walter L. Williams, *The Spirit and the Flesh: Sexual Diversity in American Indian Culture* (Boston: Beacon, 1986).

even when physical cues are clearly known to them. One result of this level of understanding of gender is that children in this age group often believe that people may change their gender with a change in clothing, hair style, or activity.[5]

The characteristics most salient to young minds are the more culturally specific qualities which grow out of gender role prescriptions. In one study, young school age children, who were given dolls and asked to identify their gender, overwhelmingly identified the gender of the dolls on the basis of attributes such as hair length or clothing style, in spite of the fact that the dolls were anatomically correct. Only 17 percent of the children identified the dolls on the basis of their primary or secondary sex characteristics.[6] Children five to seven years old understand gender as a function of role rather than as a function of anatomy. Their understanding is that gender (role) is supposed to be stable but that it is possible to alter it at will. This demonstrates that although the standard social definition of gender is based on genitalia, this is not the way that young children first learn to distinguish gender. The process of learning to think about gender in an adult fashion is one prerequisite to becoming a full member of society. Thus, as children grow older, they learn to think of themselves and others in terms more like those used by adults.

Children's developing concepts of themselves as individuals are necessarily bound up in their need to understand the expectations of the society of which they are a part. As they develop concepts of themselves as individuals, they do so while observing themselves as reflected in the eyes of others. Children start to understand themselves as individuals separate from others during the years that they first acquire gender identities and gender roles. As they do so, they begin to understand that others see them and respond to them as particular people. In this way they develop concepts of themselves as individuals, as an "I" (a proactive subject) simultaneously with self-images of themselves as individuals, as a "me" (a member of society, a subjective object). Children learn that they are both as they see themselves and as others see them.[7]

To some extent, children initially acquire the values of the society around them almost indiscriminately. To the degree that children absorb the generalized standards of society into their personal concept of what is correct behavior, they can be said to hold within themselves the attitude of the "generalized other."[8] This "generalized other" functions as a sort of monitoring or measuring device with which individuals may judge their own actions against those of their generalized conceptions of how members of society are expected to act. In this way members of society have available to them a guide, or an internalized observer, to turn the more private "I" into the object of public scrutiny, the "me." In

[5]Maccoby, p. 255.
[6]Ibid., p. 227.
[7]George Herbert Mead, "Self," in *The Social Psychology of George Herbert Mead,* ed. Anselm Strauss (Chicago: Phoenix Books, 1962, 1934), pp. 212–60.
[8]G. H. Mead.

this way, people can monitor their own behavioral impulses and censor actions which might earn them social disapproval or scorn. The tension created by the constant interplay of the personal "I" and the social "me" is the creature known as the "self."

But not all others are of equal significance in our lives, and therefore not all others are of equal impact on the development of the self. Any person is available to become part of one's "generalized other," but certain individuals, by virtue of the sheer volume of time spent in interaction with someone, or by virtue of the nature of particular interactions, become more significant in the shaping of people's values. These "significant others" become prominent in the formation of one's self-image and one's ideals and goals. As such they carry disproportionate weight in one's personal "generalized other."[9] Thus, children's individualistic impulses are shaped into a socially acceptable form both by particular individuals and by a more generalized pressure to conformity exerted by innumerable faceless members of society. Gender identity is one of the most central portions of that developing sense of self....

Gender Role Behaviors and Attitudes

The clusters of social definitions used to identify persons by gender are   10
collectively known as femininity and masculinity. Masculine characteristics are used to identify persons as males, while feminine ones are used as signifiers for femaleness. People use femininity or masculinity to claim and communicate their membership in their assigned, or chosen, sex or gender. Others recognize our sex or gender more on the basis of these characteristics than on the basis of sex characteristics, which are usually largely covered by clothing in daily life.

These two clusters of attributes are most commonly seen as mirror images of one another with masculinity usually characterized by dominance and aggression, and femininity by passivity and submission. A more even-handed description of the social qualities subsumed by femininity and masculinity might be to label masculinity as generally concerned with egoistic dominance and femininity as striving for cooperation or communion.[10] Characterizing femininity and masculinity in such a way does not portray the two clusters of characteristics as being in a hierarchical relationship to one another but rather as being two different approaches to the same question, that question being centrally concerned with the goals, means, and use of power. Such an alternative conception of gender roles captures the hierarchical and competitive

---

[9]Hans Gerth and C. Wright Mills, *Character and Social Structure: The Psychology of Social Institutions* (New York: Harcourt, Brace and World, 1953), p. 96.

[10]Egoistic dominance is a striving for superior rewards for oneself or a competitive striving to reduce the rewards for one's competitors even if such action will not increase one's own rewards. Persons who are motivated by desires for egoistic dominance not only wish the best for themselves but also wish to diminish the advantages of others whom they may perceive as competing with them. See Maccoby, p. 217.

masculine thirst for power, which can, but need not, lead to aggression, and the feminine quest for harmony and communal well-being, which can, but need not, result in passivity and dependence.

Many activities and modes of expression are recognized by most members of society as feminine. Any of these can be, and often are, displayed by persons of either gender. In some cases, cross gender behaviors are ignored by observers, and therefore do not compromise the integrity of a person's gender display. In other cases, they are labeled as inappropriate gender role behaviors. Although these behaviors are closely linked to sexual status in the minds and experiences of most people, research shows that dominant persons of either gender tend to use influence tactics and verbal styles usually associated with men and masculinity, while subordinate persons, of either gender, tend to use those considered to be the province of women.[11] Thus it seems likely that many aspects of masculinity and femininity are the result, rather than the cause, of status inequalities.

Popular conceptions of femininity and masculinity instead revolve around hierarchical appraisals of the "natural" roles of males and females. Members of both genders are believed to share many of the same human characteristics, although in different relative proportions; both males and females are popularly thought to be able to do many of the same things, but most activities are divided into suitable and unsuitable categories for each gender class. Persons who perform the activities considered appropriate for another gender will be expected to perform them poorly; if they succeed adequately, or even well, at their endeavors, they may be rewarded with ridicule or scorn for blurring the gender dividing line.

The patriarchal gender schema[12] currently in use in mainstream North American society reserves highly valued attributes for males and actively supports the high evaluation of any characteristics which might inadvertently become associated with maleness. The ideology which the schema grows out of postulates that the cultural superiority of males is a natural outgrowth of the innate predisposition of males toward aggression and dominance, which is assumed to flow inevitably from evolutionary and biological sources. Female attributes are likewise postulated to find their source in innate predispositions acquired in the evolution of the species. Feminine characteristics are thought to be intrinsic to the female facility for childbirth and breastfeeding. Hence, it is popularly believed that the social position of females is biologically mandated to be intertwined with the care of children and a "natural"

---

[11]Judith Howard, Philip Blumstein, and Pepper Schwartz, "Sex, Power, and Influence Tactics in Intimate Relationships," *Journal of Personality and Social Psychology* 51 (1986), pp. 102–09; Peter Kollock, Philip Blumstein, and Pepper Schwartz, "Sex and Power in Interaction: Conversational Privileges and Duties," *American Sociological Review* 50 (1985), pp. 34–46.

[12]*schema:* A mental framework, scheme, or pattern that helps us make sense of experience. [Eds.]

dependency on men for the maintenance of mother-child units. Thus the goals of femininity and, by implication, of all biological females are presumed to revolve around heterosexuality and maternity.[13]

Femininity, according to this traditional formulation, "would result in warm and continued relationships with men, a sense of maternity, interest in caring for children, and the capacity to work productively and continuously in female occupations."[14] This recipe translates into a vast number of proscriptions and prescriptions. Warm and continued relations with men and an interest in maternity require that females be heterosexually oriented. A heterosexual orientation requires women to dress, move, speak, and act in ways that men will find attractive. As patriarchy has reserved active expressions of power as a masculine attribute, femininity must be expressed through modes of dress, movement, speech, and action which communicate weakness, dependency, ineffectualness, availability for sexual or emotional service, and sensitivity to the needs of others.

Some, but not all, of these modes of interrelation also serve the demands of maternity and many female job ghettos. In many cases, though, femininity is not particularly useful in maternity or employment. Both mothers and workers often need to be strong, independent, and effectual in order to do their jobs well. Thus femininity, as a role, is best suited to satisfying a masculine vision of heterosexual attractiveness.

Body postures and demeanors which communicate subordinate status and vulnerability to trespass through a message of "no threat" make people appear to be feminine. They demonstrate subordination through a minimizing of spatial use: people appear feminine when they keep their arms closer to their bodies, their legs closer together, and their torsos and heads less vertical then do masculine-looking individuals. People also look feminine when they point their toes inward and use their hands in small or childlike gestures. Other people also tend to stand closer to people they see as feminine, often invading their personal space, while people who make frequent appeasement gestures, such as smiling, also give the appearance of femininity. Perhaps as an outgrowth of a subordinate status and the need to avoid conflict with more socially powerful people, women tend to excel over men at the ability to correctly interpret, and effectively display, nonverbal communication cues.[15]

[13]Chodorow, p. 134.

[14]Jon K. Meyer and John E. Hoopes, "The Gender Dysphoria Syndromes: A Position Statement on So-Called 'Transsexualism'," *Plastic and Reconstructive Surgery* 54 (Oct. 1974), pp. 444–51.

[15]Erving Goffman, *Gender Advertisements* (New York: Harper Colophon Books, 1976); Judith A. Hall, *Non-Verbal Sex Differences: Communication Accuracy and Expressive Style* (Baltimore: Johns Hopkins University Press, 1984); Nancy M. Henley, *Body Politics: Power, Sex and Non-Verbal Communication* (Englewood Cliffs, New Jersey: Prentice Hall, 1979); Marianne Wex, *"Let's Take Back Our Space": "Female" and "Male" Body Language as a Result of Patriarchal Structures* (Berlin: Frauenliteraturverlag Hermine Fees, 1979).

Speech characterized by inflections, intonations, and phrases that convey nonaggression and subordinate status also make a speaker appear more feminine. Subordinate speakers who use more polite expressions and ask more questions in conversation seem more feminine. Speech characterized by sounds of higher frequencies are often interpreted by listeners as feminine, childlike, and ineffectual.[16] Feminine styles of dress likewise display subordinate status through greater restriction of the free movement of the body, greater exposure of the bare skin, and an emphasis on sexual characteristics. The more gender distinct the dress, the more this is the case.

Masculinity, like femininity, can be demonstrated through a wide variety of cues. Pleck has argued that it is commonly expressed in North American society through the attainment of some level of proficiency at some, or all, of the following four main attitudes of masculinity. Persons who display success and high status in their social group, who exhibit "a manly air of toughness, confidence, and self-reliance" and "the aura of aggression, violence, and daring," and who conscientiously avoid anything associated with femininity are seen as exuding masculinity.[17] These requirements reflect the patriarchal ideology that masculinity results from an excess of testosterone, the assumption being that androgens supply a natural impetus toward aggression, which in turn impels males toward achievement and success. This vision of masculinity also reflects the ideological stance that ideal maleness (masculinity) must remain untainted by female (feminine) pollutants.

Masculinity, then, requires of its actors that they organize them- 20 selves and their society in a hierarchical manner so as to be able to explicitly quantify the achievement of success. The achievement of high status in one's social group requires competitive and aggressive behavior from those who wish to obtain it. Competition which is motivated by a goal of individual achievement, or egoistic dominance, also requires of its participants a degree of emotional insensitivity to feelings of hurt and loss in defeated others, and a measure of emotional insularity to protect oneself from becoming vulnerable to manipulation by others. Such values lead those who subscribe to them to view feminine persons as "born losers" and to strive to eliminate any similarities to feminine people from their own personalities. In patriarchally organized societies, masculine values become the ideological structure of the society as a whole. Masculinity thus becomes "innately" valuable and femininity serves a contrapuntal function to delineate and magnify the hierarchical dominance of masculinity.

[16]Karen L. Adams, "Sexism and the English Language: The Linguistic Implications of Being a Woman," in Women: A Feminist Perspective, 3rd edition, ed. Jo Freeman (Palo Alto, Calif.: Mayfield, 1984), pp. 478–91; Hall, pp. 37, 130–37.

[17]Elizabeth Hafkin Pleck, Domestic Tyranny: The Making of Social Policy Against Family Violence from Colonial Times to the Present (Cambridge: Oxford University Press, 1989), p. 139.

Body postures, speech patterns, and styles of dress which demonstrate and support the assumption of dominance and authority convey an impression of masculinity. Typical masculine body postures tend to be expansive and aggressive. People who hold their arms and hands in positions away from their bodies, and who stand, sit, or lie with their legs apart—thus maximizing the amount of space that they physically occupy—appear most physically masculine. Persons who communicate an air of authority or a readiness for aggression by standing erect and moving forcefully also tend to appear more masculine. Movements that are abrupt and stiff, communicating force and threat rather than flexibility and cooperation, make an actor look masculine. Masculinity can also be conveyed by stern or serious facial expressions that suggest minimal receptivity to the influence of others, a characteristic which is an important element in the attainment and maintenance of egoistic dominance.[18]

Speech and dress which likewise demonstrate or claim superior status are also seen as characteristically masculine behavior patterns. Masculine speech patterns display a tendency toward expansiveness similar to that found in masculine body postures. People who attempt to control the direction of conversations seem more masculine.[19] Those who tend to speak more loudly, use less polite and more assertive forms, and tend to interrupt the conversations of others more often also communicate masculinity to others. Styles of dress which emphasize the size of upper body musculature, allow freedom of movement, and encourage an illusion of physical power and a look of easy physicality all suggest masculinity. Such appearances of strength and readiness to action serve to create or enhance an aura of aggressiveness and intimidation central to an appearance of masculinity. Expansive postures and gestures combine with these qualities to insinuate that a position of secure dominance is a masculine one.

Gender role characteristics reflect the ideological contentions underlying the dominant gender schema in North American society. That schema leads us to believe that female and male behaviors are the result of socially directed hormonal instructions which specify that females will want to have children and will therefore find themselves relatively helpless and dependent on males for support and protection. The schema claims that males are innately aggressive and competitive and therefore will dominate over females. The social hegemony[20] of this ideology ensures that we are all raised to practice gender roles which will confirm this vision of the nature of the sexes. Fortunately, our training to gender roles is neither complete nor uniform. As a result, it is possible to point to multitudinous exceptions to, and variations on, these themes. Biological evidence is equivocal about the source of gender

[18]Goffman, *Gender Advertisements*; Hall; Henley; Wex.
[19]Adams; Hall, pp. 37, 130–37.
[20]*hegemony:* System of preponderant influence, authority, or dominance. [Eds.]

"We don't believe in pressuring the children. When the time is right, they'll choose the appropriate gender."

roles; psychological androgyny[21] is a widely accepted concept. It seems most likely that gender roles are the result of systematic power imbalances based on gender discrimination.[22]

ENGAGING THE TEXT

1. Devor charges that most languages present gender as "binary and permanent" (para. 3). Has this been your own view? How does Devor challenge this idea — that is, what's the alternative to gender being binary and permanent — and how persuasive do you find his evidence?

2. How, according to Devor, do children "acquire" gender roles? What are the functions of the "generalized other" and the "significant other" in this process?

3. Explain the distinction Devor makes between the "I" and the "me" (paras. 7 and 8). Write a journal entry describing some of the differences between your own "I" and "me."

---

[21]*androgyny:* The state of having both male and female characteristics. [Eds.]
[22]Howard, Blumstein, and Schwartz; Kollock, Blumstein, and Schwartz.

4. Using examples from Devor and from other reading or observation, list some "activities and modes of expression" (para. 12) that society considers characteristically female and characteristically male. Which are acceptable cross-gender behaviors, and which are not? Search for a "rule" that defines what types of cross-gender behaviors are tolerated.

5. Do some aspects of the traditional gender roles described by Devor seem to be changing? If so, which ones, and how?

EXPLORING CONNECTIONS

6. To what extent do Alexis de Tocqueville's views of women and men (p. 380) reflect the "patriarchal gender schema" as Devor defines it?

7. Drawing on Devor's discussion of gender role formation, analyze the difference between the "I" and the "me" of the girl in Jamaica Kincaid's story (p. 384).

8. How would Devor explain the humor of the cartoon on page 395? How do the details of the cartoon — the setting, the women's appearance, the three pictures on the coffee table — contribute to its effect?

9. Read Jesse Green's "S/He" in the e-Pages: How do transgender kids like Molly, Frieda, Isaac, and Nick challenge the view that gender is "binary and permanent" (Devor, para. 3)?

EXTENDING THE CRITICAL CONTEXT

10. As a class, identify at least half a dozen men living today who are widely admired in American culture. To what extent do they embody the "four main attitudes of masculinity" outlined by Devor (para. 19)?

11. Write an essay or journal entry analyzing your own gender role socialization. To what extent have you been pressured to conform to conventional roles? To what extent have you resisted them? What roles have "generalized others" and "sigificant others" played in shaping your identity?

WEEPING FOR THE LOST MATRIARCHY
KAY GIVENS McGOWAN

In this essay, Kay Givens McGowan asks us to reimagine colonial history from a Native American perspective. She argues that the tribes of the Southeastern United States represented true matriarchies that were destroyed by contact with patriarchal European culture. She provides a succinct overview of native history, from the Trail of Tears and Indian boarding schools to the current status of tribal people, with a particular emphasis on women. A lifelong activist of Mississippi Choctaw/Cherokee heritage, McGowan has worked at the local, national, and international levels on behalf of Native Americans. She helped found First Step, a domestic violence shelter in southeast Michigan, and DARE, the Downriver Anti-Rape Effort. For over thirty years, she has served on the national board of the Indian Youth Council, and with her twin sister, Faye Givens, founded the National Urban Indian Coalition. In 1995, she served as a delegate to the United Nations' Fourth World Conference on Women in Beijing, China; in 2005, she helped to draft the *United Nations Declaration on the Rights of Indigenous Peoples*. In collaboration with her sister, she has interviewed residents of the Indian boarding schools for a documentary, *The Indian Schools: The Survivors' Story*, which premiered in 2011. McGowan has a doctorate in cultural anthropology and is a lecturer in sociology and anthropology at Eastern Michigan University; this essay appeared in *Daughters of Mother Earth: The Wisdom of Native American Women* (2006), edited by Barbara Alice Mann and Winona LaDuke.

BEFORE THE EUROPEANS, Southeastern Natives lived in matriarchal cultures, but today, it is painful for us to examine our old societies. Too often, modern Native women are "strong" only in comparison to their disempowered brothers. What has been lost is everything. If, however, there is any hope of restoring Native society, of saving our children, our brothers—ourselves—knowing how we once lived may give us some guidance.

The great Native American civilizations of the Southeast of the present-day United States—importantly including the Cherokee, Choctaw, Chickasaw, Muscogee, and Seminole—were matriarchal societies. In them, women, as equals of the men, had power and influence. All of this changed with the coming of the Europeans, who assumed that Native people lived as Europeans did, in patriarchal systems, in which elite men defined the "appropriate way" for women to behave. They failed to understand the equality of the sexes in Native American societies, where women enjoyed high economic, social, and political status.

Economically, the Southeastern nations were agricultural people. Women farmed and controlled the crops that their work produced, so they were often the traders. This set of responsibilities was confusing to and frequently misunderstood by the early Europeans with whom they traded. In their imposed patriarchy, European men just assumed Native societies were like the male-dominated societies of Europe, in which the economy rested entirely in male hands.

Because they were farmers, however, Native women performed the work that low-status men did in Europe, where the farm work was done by serfs who never controlled the land and who were not entitled to its bounty. Each year, the crops belonged to their landlords. By contrast, Native women viewed the Earth as their Mother, who gave life to the plants, just as they, the women, gave life to their children. Instead of being drudges in a hierarchical and exploitative situation, as serfs were in Europe, Southeastern women considered the planting and harvesting of food rewarding, for the bounty realized was theirs to dispose of as they saw fit. In the matriarchal societies of the Southeast, women worked cooperatively for the good of everyone.

Rights to farmlands and their produce did not end the economic powers of Southeastern women. Women had ownership rights. For instance, they owned the houses, the crops, and the lineages. As eighteenth-century naturalist William Bartram observed in 1791 after visiting the Muskogees ("Creeks") and the Cherokees, "Marriage gives no right to the husband over the property of his wife."[1] That Native women could own property was a shock to the Europeans, who believed that men had the sole right to own and control all property. Even their women and children were considered their property.

When English and French traders sought skins, furs, corn, and other products, they had to trade with women, engendering apprehension and uncertainty in the Europeans. As a result, they often refused to trade with the women, but it was not until the mid-1700s that the heel of British oppression came to rest firmly on the backs of Native women. Being the greatest power in the "colonies" by 1763, the British dominated and controlled the territories, laying down the law not just on economic issues but also on social and political issues.

Socially, contrary to European patrilineal expectations, Southeastern societies traced their ancestry through the women. Children were born into the clan of their mother, where they remained their entire lives. This descent pattern is called matrilineal and was common in many more Native American societies than just the Southeastern. Across Turtle Island (North America), generations of mothers, daughters, and granddaughters formed large social units that made up the clans, as well as individual lineages.

The power of matrilineage was reinforced by our matrilocal residence patterns. When a couple married, they lived with, or very near, the woman's family. Often, a young bride, her mother, her sisters, and their families all lived with the bride's maternal grandmother. Matrilineage combined with a matrilocal residence pattern formed the basic family structure of Southeastern societies.

The descent pattern, along with the residence patterns, gave power to the women of the nation. When a woman married, she worked and bore children for her own lineage, not her husband's. Her role as mother was more important than her role as wife. Men might come and go, but children remained a woman's children for life.

If a woman tired of her man, she could take her children and leave—or rather, *he* could leave. In the case of a divorce, the husband returned to the clan house of his mother. The life of his children remained unchanged in the home of their mother, except that their father no longer lived there. Consequently, in divorce, the matrilocal residence pattern was nondisruptive to children, who were the most important consideration in Indian societies.

The women of the Southeastern nations had much more freedom than European women living in their nuclear families because all of the women of the Native family shared in the tasks of child care and child-rearing. From the perspective of the children, they had unconditional love from aunts and grandmothers, as well as from their biological mothers. They felt the security of a large extended family, which meant that there were a significant number of people they could count on the rest of their lives for help, love, acceptance, and security.

Southeastern women also had sexual freedom, unlike women in Europe. The Europeans had two notions about women. Either they were "decent," meaning chaste until marriage, or they were "indecent," that is, prostitutes who sold sex for money. The idea of sexually self-directed women was unheard-of in Europe. In stark contrast, Southeastern Native women had many options, including the right to have sex with anyone they chose.

In the late seventeenth and early eighteenth centuries, Native women often traveled with the *coureurs-de-bois* (French trappers), sometimes marrying them. In particular, Indian "hunting women" would accompany the French fur trappers, acting as interpreters, cooking, making clothing, cutting wood, and hauling water. In return, the men provided food, skins, and physical protection. More often than not, if they so desired, these hunting "wives" had sexual relations with the *coureurs-de-bois*, as well. In fact, it was the French traders who often needed the protection of the women's clan and nation, so there was reciprocity in these relationships based on mutual needs.

In other words, choice and direction in sexual relationships resided in the women. Southeastern women chose the men they wanted to have sexual relations with; the men did not choose them, for the freedom to choose was a woman's absolute right. Whereas the hunting wife was an institution throughout the Eastern woodlands, it had absolutely no counterpart in European culture.

Unmarried Native women also had the right to control their own fertility. They did not have to marry any man, nor was unmarried pregnancy considered immoral. The focus was on the child, not how it came to be, and every child was a sacred gift, not only to the mother but also to her clan. There was no stigma in having an "illegitimate" child, for in the non-Christian matriarchies of the Southeast, there was no such notion as bastardy. In fact, the free mating of the hunting wife was how the *Métis* Nation of Canada came to be. After the Treaty of Paris of 1763, which ended French colonialism in North America (not to be confused with the 1783 Treaty of Paris, which ended the American Revolution),

15

many of the French returned to France, leaving their *Métis*, or mixed-blood, children with their Native mothers, creating the modern *Métis* nation. (*Métis* is French for "half.")

Once the British gained more control over "the colonies," Christian missionaries immediately began imposing their values regarding chastity, marriage, and morality on Southeastern women, in particular. The patriarchal society of the British dictated that men would be economically and socially dominant in this new land. Men, of course, were allowed to enjoy the double standard that was, well, *standard* in Europe. In addition to English moral standards, especially in the area of sexuality, the English language was imposed, as well. Subordinate and less powerful nations met with extinction under British rule, but fighting for their continued existence, broken clans began regrouping and consolidating with one another under the ancient Native adoption laws.

Once their self-determination had been compromised, Southeastern peoples were denied political and economic power. Their land was taken, and their population decreased dramatically as a result of warfare, genocide, and disease, three components so mixed together that, sometimes, it is hard to sort them out from one another. Indian losses only intensified after the American Revolution, when the "Treaty Period" of Native history began under the new U.S. government. Imposed political, religious, economic, and marriage systems greatly changed the social order and the status of Southeastern women.

It is axiomatic that women hold the greatest power in societies where they are the economic producers exercising some control over the distribution of economic resources. Once English-style capitalism replaced Native communalism, however, the trade-and-barter society (or, more accurately, the gifting economies) of Southeastern peoples shifted to the cash economy of the United States. Native women could no longer trade but instead had to buy. Worst of all, as the Euro-Americans imposed their notion of "private property" and began buying instead of using land, British-style common law kicked in with its notion of land ownership, a punitive legal system, a penal code, and male-dominated courts of law.

The resultant economic shift inflicted serious damage on the Southeastern matriarchies, especially as the women lost their ancient right to the land. Both the economic trauma and the sociopolitical disruption being visited on the Southeast worked against matriarchy. By forcing an entirely new system on Southeastern Natives, the British system managed to replace the more progressive Southeastern lifeways with its own, regressive ways.

As Native women saw their social and economic control slipping 20 away, some noticed their political power was also at risk. By 1700, Native women who had enjoyed positions of leadership and equality were now experiencing the double jeopardy of being both discriminated against as women and treated unjustly as Natives by the newly arrived Euro-Americans. The harmony, cooperation, sharing, and generosity that characterized the Southeastern matriarchies gave way to internal colonialism.

Under Robert Blauner's theory, there are four basic characteristics of internal colonialism:

1. The colonized have a new social system imposed on them.

2. The Native culture is modified or destroyed.

3. The internal colony is controlled from the outside.

4. Racism prevails.[2]

All of these characteristics were present in the colonies by 1750.

After the American Revolution began in 1775, the political system of the United States changed from British colonial rule to the new, state-run "democracy" of America. For all the high-flown talk, however, the systems put in place by the Euro-Americans did not really change from those in place under the British. What did change was the political egalitarianism of the Southeast. Southeastern values were replaced with the invaders' values, Blauner's first and second stages of colonialism.

To understand how much was lost politically, it is first necessary to understand what once existed. In most cases, women in Southeastern cultures were noncombatants, but female fighters did exist, like Muscogee Coosaponakeesa ("Creek Mary"), who led her people in a successful campaign against the British in Savannah during the 1750s. Similarly, Cherokee Clan Mothers had the right to call and wage war. The office of *Da'nawagasta,* or "Sharp War," was held by a woman warrior who headed a women's military society. Women of influence, such as Coosaponakeesa, were harder to find in the late eighteenth century, after colonialism took firm hold.

Cherokee women also had the right to decide the fate of war captives, life-or-death decisions that were made by vote of the Women's Council and relayed to the district at large by the "War Woman," also known as the "Pretty Woman." Any decision over adoption had to be made by female clan heads, because a captive chosen to live was then adopted into one of the families, whose affairs were directed by the Clan Mothers.

The War Woman carried the title of Beloved Woman, and her power was great. The Women's Council, as distinguished from the district, village, or confederacy councils, was powerful in a number of political and sociospiritual ways. It may have had the deciding voice regarding which males served on the councils. Certainly the Women's Council was influential in national decisions, and its spokeswomen served as War Woman and Peace Woman, presumably holding offices in the towns designated as red towns (War) and white towns (Peace), respectively. Their other powers included the right to speak in the men's council, the right to choose whom and whether to marry, the right to bear arms, and the right to choose their extramarital occupations.[3] Under colonialism, the highly respected, political role of the Cherokees' Beloved Women sadly eroded.

Southeasterners recognized that the dramatic shifts in culture post-contact were related to the lack of power held by English women in their own society. Southeastern Natives even commented on it. In fact, Atagulkalu (Attakullaculla, "Leaning Wood"), a Cherokee diplomat who had spent time in England negotiating an agreement with King George II, called the British on their failure to include women in their councils in 1757.[4] The British turned away from his plea to include women, puzzled rather than enlightened. Due to this oblivion, the British were unable to grasp that Southeastern women held key roles as decision makers and consequently denied them any power to make decisions under colonial rule.

Native self-determination had been slipping away throughout the eighteenth century due to European imperialism. For instance, when the French left the county after the Treaty of Paris was signed in 1763, they ceded southern Alabama to England and Louisiana to Spain. Natives were never mentioned in or consulted for that first Treaty of Paris. Southeastern Natives believed that the Europeans were, thereby, dividing and ceding land that had never been European in the first place. All of the land involved was Native American land, yet they were powerless to stop the paper transfers of land.

The erosion of the power of Native women continued as the American Revolution toppled the major Southeastern nations. In 1775, after the Revolution had begun, European settlers believed that *all* the land, North and South, belonged rightfully to them. Native people did not see it that way. In most cases, Native Americans had not relinquished rights to their land, nor had they been defeated by the British or the Americans, both of whom claimed it. Certainly, nations like the Seminoles were not ready to concede anything to any European seizure.

Immediately after the Revolution, with its British concession of "the Northwest Territories" (Ohio, Michigan, Indiana, Illinois, and Wisconsin) at the 1783 Treaty of Paris, the new American government began the process of "removing" Indians to Ohio, the first dumping ground of the first removals, so that white settlers could move in. The settlers resorted to: 30

1. Warfare,

2. Organized raids on Indian settlements,

3. Blatant massacres, and

4. The destruction of the ecological base of Native survival.[5]

The Revolution brought chaos to Native Americans, both North and South. The new United States tried to rationalize its conquest and subjugation of Native people by posing as the benefactor and guardian of Indian people. The new Americans put forth the notion that uncivilized, non-christian Natives were incapable of caring for themselves but needed guidance to create "civilized" societies. The marginalization of the matriarchy was now complete. Outside of their national community, no one in power was even aware of the lost cultural tradition of matriarchy.

While claiming to be the guardian of Native Americans and their interests, the U.S. government crafted policies, laws, and cultural frameworks that were to demolish what was left of the matriarchies of the so-called Five Civilized Tribes of the Southeast: the Muscogee, the Choctaw, the Chickasaw, the Cherokee, and the newly formed Seminole Nation, which consisted of Muscogees allied with escaped African slaves. These actions by the United States also led to the largest land grab in American history.

The Red Stick Creeks, who were followers of Tecumseh, fought U.S. troops at Horseshoe Bend in 1813. After Tecumseh was killed, the survivors, known as Refugee Creeks, retreated to Spanish Florida. The Seminoles fought the longest war with the United States, from 1817 intermittently through 1842. They were never defeated. Andrew Jackson, so instrumental in the early wars against Southeastern nations, then pressed his genocidal policies by enforcing the Indian Removal Act (1830), authorizing the Bureau of Indian Affairs (BIA) to relocate all Eastern Natives west of the Mississippi River. Any nation that attempted to resist was to be relocated by military force.

All five of the large nations of the Southeast were removed at tremendous costs in lives and real dollars. The U.S. Army protected the rights of white settlers to take Native land, whereas the rights of Natives did not exist. In despair, the great nations of the American Southeast faced Removal, one after another, to "Indian Territory," a place the Choctaws called "home of the red man," or Oklahoma. By the lowest estimates, 25 percent of the population of each nation forced onto its particular "Trail of Tears" died of disease, exposure, and malnutrition en route. Approximately 50 percent of the entire Cherokee population—8,000 people—died during the forced march, most of the dead being women and children. The Choctaws' forced removal from Mississippi in 1836 was equally devastating, involving the loss of 15 percent of their population, or 6,000 out of 40,000 people. The Chickasaw suffered severe losses, as well. By contrast, the Muscogees and Seminoles are said to have suffered about a 50 percent mortality. For the Muscogees, this came primarily in the period immediately after Removal. For example, of the 10,000 or more of those who were resettled from 1836 to 1837, an incredible 3,500 died of bilious fevers.[6]

The Removal controversy dominated Native-settler relations from the 1820s until the Civil War began in 1861. Native men stood as the treaty signers, so that Southeastern women's former role as political equals and wartime decision makers, not to mention proprietors of the land, was denied to them. Importantly, traditionalists who did not sign remained at home, cherishing older ways that recognized women. Thus, for all of the federal muscle used in trying to force Southeastern peoples off their land, remnant bands of every nation escaped Removal, remaining in their traditional homelands, living in traditional ways. In the twenty-first century, the Cherokees, Choctaws, Muscogees, and Seminoles still have communities and a few reservations in their home-lands. To this day, remnant groups of Yuchi, Chickasaws, and others remain hidden in Mississippi, Tennessee, and elsewhere.

Wherever the survivors were, the psychological and spiritual scars of the Trail of Tears passed from one generation to the next. Now, such suffering is called intergenerational trauma, but although the suffer-ing has been named, no restitution has been made for it. The U.S. gov-ernment has never taken responsibility for the atrocities it committed against America's indigenous people. Instead, all that was ever received by way of an apology for Removal was lamely offered in September of 2000 by the then-head of the BIA, Kevin Gover, himself a Pawnee—an irony not lost on Indians.

Removal hardly ended the assault on Native self-determination. The lands in Indian Territory designated for the Five Civilized Tribes were manipulated into ever-smaller parcels by the government. This was because the government was taking away land promised the Southeastern Natives to give to other Natives being removed from other places in the East. When the Chickasaws arrived in Indian Territory, for instance, they bought land from their closest relatives, the Choctaws. Similarly, when the Seminoles arrived, they were given land bought from the Creeks. The land base of Indian Territory continued to shrink, as the Cherokees took in the Lenapes ("Delawares") in 1867 and the Shawnees in 1870. Some of the Catawbas, or eastern Lakotas, came to live with the Choctaws in 1871. The Caddos from Texas fled brutal treatment by coming on their own to Indian Territory. Each new arrival crowded the landscape. Importantly, Indian Territory was under the complete control of the federal government. Women were hardly even a blip on its radar.

In 1866, new treaties were imposed on the nations that fought on the side of the Confederacy during the Civil War, punishing them for fighting on the "wrong side." The western half of Indian Territory was thus taken away from the Confederate Choctaws, Chickasaws, and Cherokees, who had followed General Stan Watie of the Cherokees, the only Native General in the Confederacy, who led his all-Native division. Even as land was stripped from Confederate Natives, other Native land was being taken for the transcontinental railroads. Finally, because the U.S. government really had no plan for what to do with the Freedmen, or freed slaves, many were to be made citizens of the "Indian" nations and consequently allowed to claim land in "Indian Territory."[7] Every successive adjustment to laws or treaties led to smaller land hold-ings by the five large nations of the Southeast.

Having acquired nearly all of the Indian land holdings and confined Natives to reservations by 1871, Congress tired of making treaties with them. There really being no Natives left to contend the point effectively, Congress unilaterally ended the practice of treating with them. For their part, Southeastern Natives felt that the end was long overdue. Aside from the fact that nearly all extant treaties were fraudulent, none of the provisions of the 364 treaties with the Natives was ever honored by the U.S. government, anyway.

The next hundred years of Indian and U.S. government relations involved one failed program after another. The Dawes Act of 1887 intended to destroy the Native communities by dividing up and allotting 40 to 160 acres of land to individual Indian head of households. The "excess" land could then be sold to the settlers, and Indians would then become the holders of "private property," like their Euro-American neighbors. This was an assimilation tactic that was not only unsuccessful but also resulted in many Natives losing their allotted land. Because the concept of taxing land was foreign, Natives did not pay their property taxes and wound up forfeiting their land for back taxes.

More importantly, as an addendum to Dawes, the U.S. government passed a law in 1888 that declared that all Native women marrying Euro-American men had de facto agreed to abandon their Native identity.[8] Not only they but all their children lost their right to be Natives and live as Natives. This law hit Southeastern Native women very hard. A primary tactic for separating Natives from their land was for a settler man to marry a woman from one of the Five Civilized Tribes. He thereby gained her land because, under Euro-American law, the wife's property passed to her husband.

From 1871 until the present, then, nothing in the U.S. treatment of Indians has improved the status of Indian women. Consider the following "failed experiments":

- Federal suppression of Native American religion until the passage of the Indian Freedom of Religion Act of 1978 finally gave Indians the same rights to their beliefs that all other Americans have. Under this policy, Southeastern women were not only denied their spiritual traditions, but also their strong place as leaders in and practitioners of their traditional belief systems. Euro-American religion had no leadership roles for women.

- Indian children being taken from their families and placed in boarding schools to "save the child, but kill the Indian." This policy resulted in untold physical, psychological, and sexual abuse of female and male Native children.[9] The boarding schools contributed to the destruction of Native parents, families, and nations. The problems around parenting issues in Indian country today are a direct result of the Indian Boarding School era, which began in 1879 with the Carlisle Indian School and continues in a limited way up to the present. The trauma induced by this system contributed to the rise in alcoholism, suicide, and mental illness still prevalent in Indian country today.[10] Women bear the social brunt of these ills.

- Injustices such as the nonconsensual sterilization by the Indian Health Service of 40 percent of Native women of childbearing age without their knowledge, a practice that continued through the 1970s. The U.S. population control policy amounted to genocide by any standards.[11]

- Removal of Indian children from their families and placement in foster care. Estimates suggest that as many as 30 percent of all Indian children have been removed from their homes.[12]

- Shocking disparities in the area of health care. Compared to the mainstream population of the United States, Native Americans are more than four times as likely to die from diabetes; six times as likely to die from tuberculosis; and more than seven times as likely to die from alcoholism. Natives have a suicide rate four times the national average.[13]

Native women have been those most affected by all these impositions of colonialism. First and foremost, Southeastern women have seen their matriarchy destroyed. As women, they once had all the rights and powers that American women today are struggling to obtain, including economic and political power; spiritual equality; the right to proper health care, up to and including abortion on demand; the right to divorce on demand; and the right to call—and call off—war.

In 1986, Margaret Schuler summarized some of the major categories of human rights violations that frequently affect women:[14]

1. Economic exploitation (no minimum wage laws and no day care rights),

2. Lack of equal treatment of women by family law systems,

3. Denial of reproductive rights (including the right to contraceptive information, medically safe abortions, and the right to bear or not bear children), and

4. Violence and exploitation (including domestic violence, rape, sexual harassment, sex trafficking, and coerced prostitution).

Consistent with Schuler's findings, Indian women lack any sort of economic clout. According to the U.S. Department of Labor, unemployment for Native women in 1995 stood at 14.4 percent.[15] Because unemployment and poverty accompany each other, the national poverty rate for Native Americans was 24.5 percent in 2001.[16] Poverty and unemployment tend to entrap Native women when they find themselves in violent and abusive situations, as they very often do.

Among a population that is already reeling from unequal and inadequate health care, Native women find themselves at high risk for health-related problems from diabetes, heart disease, and diabetic eye disease to HIV/AIDS and cancer. Thus, not only have 40 percent of living

Native women been sterilized without their consent, but even those still fertile are so wracked by disease and poor health care that their chances of producing healthy offspring are minimized. Furthermore, they have much less time to give to a family. Whereas the average life expectancy for Euro-American women is eighty-one years, Native American women can expect to live little more than half that, or fifty-two years.

Native women are also victimized at alarming rates. According to statistics from the U.S. Department of Justice in 2004, Native American females are two and a half times more likely to be victims of a violent crime than any other group of females in the United States.[17] In 70 percent of these attacks, Native American female victims reported the attacker was either white or black. In cases of rape or sexual assault, Native victims reported that the offender was Euro-American in four out of five attacks. Unlike other groups of victims, they were more likely to be attacked by a stranger than an intimate partner, family member, or acquaintance, a circumstance that is virtually unheard of in crime statistics elsewhere. Finally, even though Native women make up 0.6 percent of the U.S. population, 1.5 percent of victims of violence are Indian women.[18]

These statistics can only mean that Native American women are the culturally designated victims, par excellence, of internal colonialism. Instead of the power brokers they were even two hundred years ago, Native women today are economically, socially, spiritually, and politically broken. They form a silent, marginalized, and oppressed minority, dependent upon equally dispossessed male partners for survival. The European model for this marginalization is so antiquated that not even Euro-American conservatives follow it. Although the regression is rarely discussed or noted in mainstream society, the position of Indian women in American society has regressed to the point that they suffer the lowest economic, educational, and social status of *any* group in American society.

Clearly, the matriarchy has fallen, and the losers are all of us—Euro-American, African American, Asian American, and Latino/a, as well as Native American. The vibrant model of matriarchy posed by Native women of the Southeast was rooted out precisely because of the threat that it offered the Euro-Christian model of hierarchical patriarchy. Now that the rest of the world has finally caught up with what Southeastern Indians knew all along, is it not time that the women of the Southeast regained their status as full members of the human community?

Notes

1. Mark Van Doren (ed.), *Travels of William Bartram* (1791; New York: Dover, 1955), p. 252. [All notes are McGowan's.]
2. Robert Blauner, *Racial and Ethnic Groups in America,* 3rd ed. (Dubuque, IA: Kendall Hunt, 1969), p. 15.
3. S. C. Williams (ed.), *Lieutenant Henry Timberlake's Memoirs, 1756–1765* (1927, reprint; Marietta, GA: Continental Book, 1948), p. 94.
4. Alice Beck Kehoe, *North American Indians: A Comprehensive Account,* 2nd ed. (Englewood Cliffs, NJ: Prentice Hall, 1992), p. 203.

5. Vine Deloria Jr., *Custer Died for Your Sins: An Indian Manifesto* (New York: Avon, 1969), pp. 61–63; Barbara Alice Mann, "The Greenville Treaty of 1795: Pen-and-Ink Witchcraft in the Struggle for the Old Northwest," in Bruce E. Johansen (ed.), *Enduring Legacies: Native American Treaties and Contemporary Controversies* (Westport, CT: Praeger, 2004), pp. 136–201.

6. Russell Thornton, "Cherokee Population Losses during the Trail of Tears: A New Perspective and a New Estimate," *Ethnohistory* 31 (1984): p. 291.

7. Kehoe, *North American Indians,* p. 199; Barbara Alice Mann, "'A Man of Misery': Chitto Harjo and the Senate Select Committee on Oklahoma Statehood," in Barbara Alice Mann (ed.), *Native American Speakers of the Eastern Woodlands: Selected Speeches and Critical Analyses* (Westport, CT: Greenwood, 2001), pp. 197–228. The classic source on this issue is Angie Debo, *And Still the Waters Run: The Betrayal of the Five Civilized Tribes,* 4th ed. (Princeton, NJ: Princeton University Press, 1991).

8. An Act in Relation to Marriage between White Men and Indian Women, 25 Stat. L., 392, 9 August 1888.

9. For an intensive look at boarding school problems, see *Native Americas* (Winter 2000). Most of the issue is dedicated to the boarding school experience. See Darren Bonaparte, "Running for Safety," *Native Americas* (Winter 2000): 15 for sexual abuse.

10. Ron Lewis and M. K. Ho, "Social Work with Native Americans," *Social Work* (September 1975): pp. 379–382.

11. Jim Vander Wall, "American Indian Women at the Center of the Indigenous Resistance in Contemporary North America," in M. Annette Jaimes (ed.), *The State of Native America: Genocide, Colonization and Resistance* (Boston: South End Press, 1992), p. 326; Sally S. Torphy, "Native American Women and Coerced Sterilization: On the Trail of Tears in the 1970's," *American Indian Cultures and Research Journal* 24, no. 2 (2000): pp. 1–22.

12. Terry Cross, *Indian Child Welfare Report* (Portland, OR: Indian Child Welfare Association, 2002), p. 6.

13. Rachel Joseph, "Indian Health Care Improvement Act Reauthorization Amendments of 2004," Hearing on SB 212/HR 2440 before the House Resources Committee, 107th Congress, Testimony of Rachel Joseph, Cochair, National Steering Committee, 2004, p. 127.

14. Margaret Schuler, "Women and the Law," in R. S. Gallin, M. Aronoff, and A. Ferguson (eds.), *Women and International Development,* Annual vol. 1 (Boulder, CO: Westview Press: 1986): pp. 155–187.

15. U.S. Department of Labor, Bureau of Indian Affairs, *1995 Annual Report, Quiet Crisis: Federal Funding and Un-met Needs in Indian Country* (Washington, DC: Government Printing Office, 2003), p. 32.

16. U.S. Census Bureau, *Poverty in the United States: 2001: Current Population Reports* (Washington, DC: Government Printing Office, 2002), p. 7.

17. U.S. Department of Justice, Bureau of Statistics, *American Indians and Crime* (Washington, DC: Bureau of Justices Statistics Clearinghouse, 2004), p. 1.

18. Ibid., p. 7.

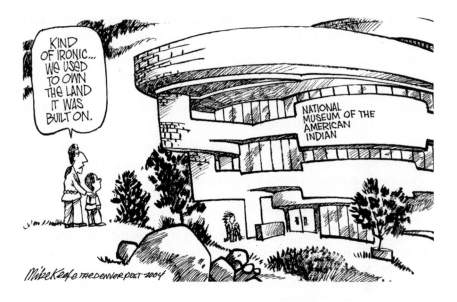

ENGAGING THE TEXT

1. Contrast the matriarchal pattern of Southeastern tribal life to British and American patriarchy. How did tribal customs like matrilineage, matrilocal residence patterns, women's sexual freedom, and communalism threaten "Euro-Christian hierarchical patriarchy"?

2. What is internal colonialism? How did the British, and later the American, government make use of internal colonialism to subdue the Southeastern tribes? How did European imperialism and the imposition of private property undermine female authority?

3. McGowan refers to "intergenerational trauma," the idea that "psychological and spiritual scars...[pass] from one generation to the next" (para. 36). How might the Trail of Tears, the Dawes Act, the Indian boarding schools, or the nonconsensual sterilization of Indian women affect multiple generations of a family? Write a journal entry in which you imagine the impact and trace the effects of one of these events.

4. What does McGowan mean when she says, "the matriarchy has fallen and the losers are all of us" (para. 49)? How did Southeastern tribal women enjoy "all the rights and powers that American women today are struggling to obtain"? (para. 43).

EXPLORING CONNECTIONS

5. The cartoon above points out the irony that the Museum of the American Indian was built on land that once belonged to Native Americans. Explore the Museum's Web site (http://nmai.si.edu/home/), and then write an

essay or journal entry explaining why you think McGowan would or would not approve of the exchange of Native American lands for the museum.

6. Hanna Rosin, in "The End of Men" (p. 471), observes that "The working class, which has long defined our notions of masculinity, is slowly turning into a matriarchy, with men increasingly absent from the home and women making all the decisions" (para. 13). Compare this view of matriarchy to the matriarchy McGowan describes.

7. Read Vincent Parrillo's analysis of prejudice (p. 504) and discuss which of the theories he presents might explain the racism directed at Native Americans at different points in their history.

EXTENDING THE CRITICAL CONTEXT

8. What would our society look like if the values of the Southeastern tribes had prevailed? Write a story or journal entry that envisions a contemporary culture based on matrilineal power. Compare your view to others produced by your classmates and discuss: Is this society a utopia, a dystopia, or something in between? What role do men play in these alternative societies?

9. The *Declaration on the Rights of Indigenous Peoples* was passed overwhelmingly by the United Nations in 2007. In December of 2010, the United States became the last country to endorse the *Declaration*. Do some quick Internet research on the *Declaration*: Why do you think official approval took so long?

VISUAL PORTFOLIO
READING IMAGES OF GENDER

4

VISUAL PORTFOLIO

READING IMAGES OF GENDER

1. What do you imagine is happening in the photo on page 411? Where are these boys, and who or what are they aiming at with their water guns? First, write a short narrative from the point of view of one of the boys explaining what led up to this moment and describing your thoughts and feelings. Then write an alternate account from a different point of view — perhaps that of someone who's a target of the water barrage or that of a social scientist (like Aaron H. Devor or Michael Kimmel) analyzing the significance of the scene. Share your stories and discuss the differences of interpretation they reveal.

2. Analyze the photo of the three young women holding up articles of clothing (p. 412). What do you think they are doing? How would you interpret their expressions and body language? Compare this image to the images of women in the two photos that follow: To what extent does each image reflect Devor's description of femininity?

3. Working in pairs or groups, develop an interpretation of the photo of the young woman looking in the mirror (p. 413). Take into account the framing of the photo, the setting, the young woman's outfit, her posture and expression, the direction of her gaze, and the fragmented reflection. Present these interpretations in class and evaluate the persuasiveness of each.

4. Imagine that you are one of the people in the picture of the four teens (p. 414) and freewrite about what is happening (or what has just happened). What are you thinking and feeling at this moment, and why? Compare your responses to those of classmates: Does the gender of the "character" you adopt affect your interpretation of the image? If so, how and why?

5. How old is the child with the computer (p. 415)? Does she seem to know what she's doing, or is this random play? How can you tell? In 2011, the Campaign for a Commercial-Free Childhood chose a tablet computer designed for babies as its worst toy of the year. Do you agree that computer use for babies and toddlers should be discouraged? Why? What benefits might there be to introducing small children to computers?

6. How would you describe the mood or feeling the photographer has captured in the picture of the father and child (p. 416)? How do the light, the setting, the stance, and the expression of each figure contribute to this impression?

7. Do you think that "Masculinity" would be an appropriate title for the picture of the man and child (p. 416)? Why or why not? Eli Reed, the photographer, titles

the photo simply, "Mississippi, 1991"; why do you think he chose to identify it by place and time rather than by theme?

8. The picture of the two soldiers kissing (p. 417) was taken shortly after the repeal of the "Don't Ask, Don't Tell" policy in the military. Note the details of the photo: the dropped backpack, the flowers around the neck of the Marine, the large flag in the background. What is the mood of the image? Why do you think the photographer chose to shoot the picture from this angle? The photo was posted on Facebook, and immediately went viral: Why do you think this image resonated so strongly with Americans?

"TWO WAYS A WOMAN CAN GET HURT": ADVERTISING AND VIOLENCE

JEAN KILBOURNE

> Most of us like to think of ourselves as immune to the power of ads — we know that advertisers use sex to get our attention and that they make exaggerated claims about a product's ability to make us attractive, popular, and success-ful. Because we can see through these subtle or not-so-subtle messages, we assume that we're too smart to be swayed by them. But Jean Kilbourne argues that ads affect us in far more profound and potentially damaging ways. The way that ads portray bodies — especially women's bodies — as objects condi-tions us to see each other in dehumanizing ways, thus "normalizing" attitudes that can lead to sexual aggression. Kilbourne (b. 1946) has spent most of her professional life teaching and lecturing about the world of advertising. She has produced award-winning documentaries on images of women in ads (*Killing Us Softly, Slim Hopes*) and tobacco advertising (*Pack of Lies*). She has also been a member of the National Advisory Council on Alcohol Abuse and Alcoholism and has twice served as an adviser to the surgeon general of the United States. Currently she serves on the Massachusetts Governor's Commission on Sexual and Domestic Abuse and is a senior scholar at the Wellesley Centers for Women (WCW) at Wellesley College. Her most recent book, coauthored by Diane E. Levin, is *So Sexy So Soon: The New Sexualized Childhood and What Parents Can Do to Protect Their Kids* (2008). The following selection is taken from her 1999 book *Can't Buy My Love: How Advertising Changes the Way We Think and Feel* (formerly titled *Deadly Persuasion*).

SEX IN ADVERTISING IS MORE ABOUT DISCONNECTION and dis-tance than connection and closeness. It is also more often about power than passion, about violence than violins. The main goal, as in pornog-raphy, is usually power over another, either by the physical dominance or preferred status of men or what is seen as the exploitative power of female beauty and female sexuality. Men conquer and women ensnare, always with the essential aid of a product. The woman is rewarded for her sexuality by the man's wealth, as in an ad for Cigarette boats in which the woman says, while lying in a man's embrace clearly after sex, "Does this mean I get a ride in your Cigarette?"

Sex in advertising is pornographic because it dehumanizes and objectifies people, especially women, and because it fetishizes prod-ucts, imbues them with an erotic charge—which dooms us to disap-pointment since products never can fulfill our sexual desires or meet our emotional needs. The poses and postures of advertising are often

Two Ways A Woman Can Get Hurt.

(Heartbreaker)

(Soap and water shave)

Skintimate® Shave Gel Ultra Protection formula contains 75% moisturizers, including vitamin E, to protect your legs from nicks, cuts and razor burn. So while guys may continue to be a pain, shaving most definitely won't.

SKINTIMATE® SHAVE GEL.
LOVE YOUR LEGS

borrowed from pornography, as are many of the themes, such as bondage, sadomasochism, and the sexual exploitation of children. When a beer ad uses the image of a man licking the high-heeled boot of a woman clad in leather, when bondage is used to sell neckties in the *New York Times*, perfume in *The New Yorker*, and watches on city

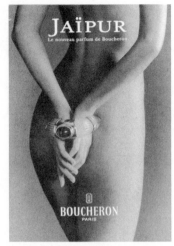

buses, and when a college magazine promotes an S&M Ball, pornography can be considered mainstream.

Most of us know all this by now and I suppose some consider it
kinky good fun. Pornography is more dangerously mainstream when its
glorification of rape and violence shows up in mass media, in films and
television shows, in comedy and music videos, and in advertising. Male
violence is subtly encouraged by ads that encourage men to be force-
ful and dominant, and to value sexual intimacy more than emotional
intimacy. "Do you want to be the one she tells her deep, dark secrets
to?" asks a three-page ad for men's cologne. "Or do you want to be her
deep, dark secret?" The last page advises men, "Don't be such a good
boy." There are two identical women looking adoringly at the man in
the ad, but he isn't looking at either one of them. Just what is the deep,
dark secret? That he's sleeping with both of them? Clearly the way to
get beautiful women is to ignore them, perhaps mistreat them.

"Two ways a woman can get hurt," says an ad for shaving gel,
featuring a razor and a photo of a handsome man. My first thought

is that the man is a batterer or date rapist, but the ad informs us that he is merely a "heartbreaker." The gel will protect the woman so that "while guys may continue to be a pain, shaving most definitely won't." Desirable men are painful—heartbreakers at best.

Wouldn't it be wonderful if, realizing the importance of relationships in all of our lives, we could seek to learn relational skills from women and to help men develop these strengths in themselves? In fact, we so often do the opposite. The popular culture usually trivializes these

sweat. Go all out. We'll keep up. New Old Spice Anti-Perspirant helps stop the sweat that causes odor. The proof? You're looking at her. For great odor protection, now you've got **proof** of its promises.

abilities in women, mocks men who have real intimacy with women (it is almost always married men in ads and cartoons who are jerks), and idealizes a template for relationships between men and women that is a recipe for disaster: a template that views sex as more important than anything else, that ridicules men who are not in control of their women (who are "pussy-whipped"), and that disparages fidelity and commitment (except, of course, to brand names).

Indeed the very worst kind of man for a woman to be in an intimate relationship with, often a truly dangerous man, is the one considered most sexy and desirable in the popular culture. And the men capable of real intimacy (the ones we tell our deep, dark secrets to) constantly have their very masculinity impugned. Advertising often encourages women to be attracted to hostile and indifferent men while encouraging boys to become these men. This is especially dangerous for those of us who have suffered from "condemned isolation" in childhood: like heat-seeking missiles, we rush inevitably to mutual destruction.

Men are also encouraged to never take no for an answer. Ad after ad implies that girls and women don't really mean "no" when they say it, that women are only teasing when they resist men's advances. "NO" says an ad showing a man leaning over a woman against a wall. Is she screaming or laughing? Oh, it's an ad for deodorant and the second word, in very small print, is "sweat." Sometimes it's "all in good fun," as in the ad for Possession shirts and shorts featuring a man ripping the clothes off a woman who seems to be having a good time.

And sometimes it is more sinister. A perfume ad running in several teen magazines features a very young woman, with eyes blackened by makeup or perhaps something else, and the copy, "Apply generously to your neck so he can smell the scent as you shake your head 'no.'" In

P♡SSESSION
SHIRTS AND SHORTS
1-800-229-GRVPO

other words, he'll understand that you don't really mean it and he can respond to the scent like any other animal.

Sometimes there seems to be no question but that a man should force a woman to have sex. A chilling newspaper ad for a bar in George-town features a closeup of a cocktail and the headline, "If your date won't listen to reason, try a Velvet Hammer." A vodka ad pictures a wolf hiding in a flock of sheep, a hideous grin on its face. We all know what wolves do to sheep. A campaign for Bacardi Black rum features

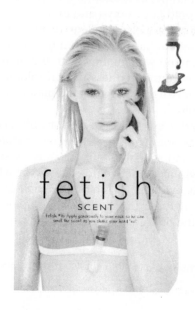

fetish
SCENT

shadowy figures almost obliterated by darkness and captions such as
"Some people embrace the night because the rules of the day do not
apply." What it doesn't say is that people who are above the rules do
enormous harm to other people, as well as to themselves.

These ads are particularly troublesome, given that between one- 10
third and three-quarters of all cases of sexual assault involve alcohol
consumption by the perpetrator, the victim, or both.[1] "Make strangers
your friends, and your friends a lot stranger," says one of the ads in
a Cuervo campaign that uses colorful cartoon beasts and emphasizes
heavy drinking. This ad is especially disturbing when we consider the
role of alcohol in date rape, as is another ad in the series that says, "The
night began with a bottle of Cuervo and ended with a vow of silence."
Over half of all reported rapes on college campuses occur when either
the victim or the assailant has been drinking.[2] Alcohol's role has different meaning for men and women, however. If a man is drunk when he
commits a rape, he is considered less responsible. If a woman is drunk
(or has had a drink or two or simply met the man in a bar), she is considered more responsible.

In general, females are still held responsible and hold each other
responsible when sex goes wrong—when they become pregnant or are
the victims of rape and sexual assault or cause a scandal. Constantly
exhorted to be sexy and attractive, they discover when assaulted that
that very sexiness is evidence of their guilt, their lack of "innocence."
Sometimes the ads play on this by "warning" women of what might
happen if they use the product. "Wear it but beware it," says a perfume

[1] Wilsnack, Plaud, Wilsnack, and Klassen, 1997, 262. [All notes are Kilbourne's unless
otherwise indicated.]
[2] Abbey, Ross, and McDuffie, 1991. Also Martin, 1992, 230–37.

ad. Beware what exactly? Victoria's Secret tempts young women with blatantly sexual ads promising that their lingerie will make them irresistible. Yet when a young woman accused William Kennedy Smith of raping her, the fact that she wore Victoria's Secret panties was used against her as an indication of her immorality. A jury acquitted Smith, whose alleged history of violence against women was not permitted to be introduced at trial.

It is sadly not surprising that the jury was composed mostly of women. Women are especially cruel judges of other women's sexual behavior, mostly because we are so desperate to believe we are in control of what happens to us. It is too frightening to face the fact that male violence against women is irrational and commonplace. It is reassuring to believe that we can avoid it by being good girls, avoiding dark places, staying out of bars, dressing "innocently." An ad featuring two young women talking intimately at a coffee shop says, "Carla and Rachel considered themselves open-minded and non-judgmental people. Although they did agree Brenda was a tramp." These terrible judgments from other women are an important part of what keeps all women in line.

If indifference in a man is sexy, then violence is sometimes downright erotic. Not surprisingly, this attitude too shows up in advertising. "Push my buttons," says a young woman, "I'm looking for a man who can totally floor me." Her vulnerability is underscored by the fact that she is in an elevator, often a dangerous place for women. She is young, she is submissive (her eyes are downcast), she is in a dangerous place, and she is dressed provocatively. And she is literally asking for it.

"Wear it out and make it scream," says a jeans ad portraying a man sliding his hands under a woman's transparent blouse. This could be a seduction, but it could as easily be an attack. Although the ad that ran in the Czech version of *Elle* portraying three men attacking a woman seems unambiguous, the terrifying image is being used to sell jeans *to women*. So someone must think that women would find this image

compelling or attractive. Why would we? Perhaps it is simply designed to get our attention, by shocking us and by arousing unconscious anxiety. Or perhaps the intent is more subtle and it is designed to play into the fantasies of domination and even rape that some women use in order to maintain an illusion of being in control (we are the ones having the fantasies, after all, we are the directors).

A camera ad features a woman's torso wrapped in plastic, her hands tied behind her back. A smiling woman in a lipstick ad has a padlocked chain around her neck. An ad for MTV shows a vulnerable young 15

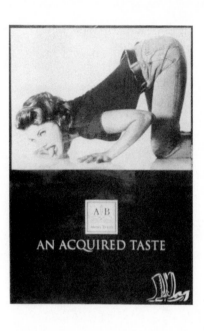

AN ACQUIRED TASTE

woman, her breasts exposed, and the simple copy "Bitch." A perfume ad features a man shadowboxing with what seems to be a woman.

Sometimes women are shown dead or in the process of being killed. "Great hair never dies," says an ad featuring a female corpse lying on a bed, her breasts exposed. An ad in the Italian version of *Vogue* shows a man aiming a gun at a nude woman wrapped in plastic, a leather briefcase covering her face. And an ad for Bitch skateboards, for God's sake, shows a cartoon version of a similar scene, this time clearly targeting young people. We believe we are not affected by these images, but most of us experience visceral shock when we pay conscious attention to them. Could they be any less shocking to us on an unconscious level?

Most of us become numb to these images, just as we become numb to the daily litany in the news of women being raped, battered, and killed. According to former surgeon general Antonia Novello, battery is the single greatest cause of injury to women in America, more common than automobile accidents, muggings, and stranger rapes combined, and more than one-third of women slain in this country die at the hands

La Borsa è la Vita

of husbands or boyfriends.[3] Throughout the world, the biggest problem for most women is simply surviving at home. The Global Report on Women's Human Rights concluded that "Domestic violence is a leading cause of female injury in almost every country in the world and is typically ignored by the state or only erratically punished."[4] Although usually numb to these facts on a conscious level, most women live in a state of subliminal terror, a state that, according to Mary Daly,[5] keeps us divided both from each other and from our most passionate, powerful, and creative selves.[6]

Ads don't directly cause violence, of course. But the violent images contribute to the state of terror. And objectification and disconnection create a climate in which there is widespread and increasing violence. Turning a human being into a thing, an object, is almost always the first step toward justifying violence against that person. It is very difficult, perhaps impossible, to be violent to someone we think of as an equal, someone we have empathy with, but it is very easy to abuse a thing. We see this with racism, with homophobia. The person becomes an object and violence is inevitable. This step is already taken with women. The violence, the abuse, is partly the chilling but logical result of the objectification.

An editorial in *Advertising Age* suggests that even some advertisers are concerned about this: "Clearly it's time to wipe out sexism in beer ads; for the brewers and their agencies to wake up and join the rest of America in realizing that sexism, sexual harassment, and the cultural portrayal of women in advertising are inextricably linked."[7] Alas, this editorial was written in 1991 and nothing has changed.

It is this link with violence that makes the objectification of women 20 a more serious issue than the objectification of men. Our economic system constantly requires the development of new markets. Not surprisingly, men's bodies are the latest territory to be exploited. Although we are growing more used to it, in the beginning the male sex object came as a surprise. In 1994 a "gender bender" television commercial in which a bevy of women office workers gather to watch a construction worker doff his shirt to quaff a Diet Coke led to so much hoopla that you'd have thought women were mugging men on Madison Avenue.[8]

There is no question that men are used as sex objects in ads now as never before. We often see nude women with fully clothed men in ads (as in art), but the reverse was unheard of, until recently. These days some ads do feature clothed and often aggressive women with nude men. And women sometimes blatantly objectify men, as in the Metroliner ad that says, "'She's reading Nietzsche,' Harris noted to

---

[3]Novello, 1991. Also Blumenthal, 1995.
[4]Wright, 1995, A2.
[5]*Mary Daly:* Radical feminist scholar and author (1928–2010). [Eds.]
[6]Weil, 1999, 21.
[7]Brewers can help fight sexism, 1991, 28.
[8]Kilbourne, 1994, F13.

bitch skateboards

himself as he walked towards the café car for a glass of cabernet. And as he passed her seat, Maureen looked up from her book and thought, 'Nice buns.'"

Although these ads are often funny, it is never a good thing for human beings to be objectified. However, there is a world of difference between the objectification of men and that of women. The most important difference is that there is no danger for most men, whereas objectified women are always at risk. In the Diet Coke ad, for instance, the women are physically separated from the shirtless man. He is the one in control. His body is powerful, not passive. Imagine a true role reversal of this ad: a group of businessmen gather to leer at a beautiful woman worker on her break, who removes her shirt before drinking her Diet Coke. This scene would be frightening, not funny, as the Diet Coke ad is. And why is the Diet Coke ad funny? Because we know it doesn't describe any truth. However, the ads featuring images of male violence against women do describe a truth, a truth we are all aware of, on one level or another.

When power is unequal, when one group is oppressed and discriminated against *as a group*, when there is a context of systemic and historical oppression, stereotypes and prejudice have different weight and meaning. As Anna Quindlen[9] said, writing about "reverse racism": "Hatred by the powerful, the majority, has a different weight—and often very different effects—than hatred by the powerless, the minority."[10] When men objectify women, they do so in a cultural context in which women are constantly objectified and in which there are consequences—from economic discrimination to violence—to that objectification.

For men, though, there are no such consequences. Men's bodies are not routinely judged and invaded. Men are not likely to be raped, harassed, or beaten (that is to say, men presumed to be heterosexual are not, and very few men are abused in these ways by women). How many men are frightened to be alone with a woman in an elevator? How many men cross the street when a group of women approaches? Jackson Katz, who writes and lectures on male violence, often begins his workshops by asking men to describe the things they do every day to protect themselves from sexual assault. The men are surprised, puzzled, sometimes amused by the question. The women understand the question easily and have no trouble at all coming up with a list of responses. We don't list our full names in the phone directory or on our mailboxes, we try not to be alone after dark, we carry our keys in our hands when we approach our cars, we always look in the back seat before we get in, we are wary of elevators and doorways and bushes, we carry pepper sprays, whistles, Mace.

Nonetheless, the rate of sexual assault in the United States is the highest of any industrialized nation in the world.[11] According to a 1998 study by the federal government, one in five of us has been the victim of rape or attempted rape, most often before our seventeenth birthday. And more than half of us have been physically assaulted, most often by the men we live with. In fact, three of four women in the study who responded that they had been raped or assaulted as adults said the perpetrator was a current or former husband, a cohabiting partner or a date.[12] The article reporting the results of this study was buried on page twenty-three of my local newspaper, while the front page dealt with a long story about the New England Patriots football team.

A few summers ago, a Diet Pepsi commercial featured Cindy Crawford being ogled by two boys (they seemed to be about twelve years old) as she got out of her car and bought a Pepsi from a machine. The boys made very suggestive comments, which in the end turned out to be about the Pepsi's can rather than Ms. Crawford's. There was no

[9]*Anna Quindlen:* Novelist and Pulitzer Prize–winning journalist who often writes about women's issues (b. 1953). [Eds.]
[10]Quindlen, 1992, E17.
[11]Blumenthal, 1995, 2.
[12]Tjaden and Thoennes, 1998.

where women are women
and men are
roadkill.

harley-davidson motorclothes

outcry: the boys' behavior was acceptable and ordinary enough for a soft-drink commercial.

Again, let us imagine the reverse: a sexy man gets out of a car in the countryside and two preteen girls make suggestive comments, seemingly about his body, especially his buns. We would fear for them and rightly so. But the boys already have the right to ogle, to view women's bodies as property to be looked at, commented on, touched, perhaps eventually hit and raped. The boys have also learned that men ogle primarily to impress other men (and to affirm their heterosexuality). If anyone is in potential danger in this ad, it is the woman (regardless of the age of the boys). Men are not seen as *property* in this way by women.

Nannette's
because they'll never be this age again

Indeed if a woman does whistle at a man or touches his body or even makes direct eye contact, it is still *she* who is at risk and the man who has the power.

"I always lower my eyes to see if a man is worth following," says the woman in an ad for men's pants. Although the ad is offensive to everyone, the woman is endangering only herself.

"Where women are women and men are roadkill," says an ad for motorcycle clothing featuring an angry-looking African American woman. Women are sometimes hostile and angry in ads these days, especially women of color who are often seen as angrier and more threatening than white women. But, regardless of color, we all know that women are far more likely than men to end up as roadkill—and, when it happens, they are blamed for being on the road in the first place.

Even little girls are sometimes held responsible for the violence against them. In 1990 a male Canadian judge accused a three-year-old girl of being "sexually aggressive" and suspended the sentence of her molester, who was then free to return to his job of baby-sitter.[13] The deeply held belief that all women, regardless of age, are really temptresses in disguise, nymphets, sexually insatiable and seductive, conveniently transfers all blame and responsibility onto women.

All women are vulnerable in a culture in which there is such widespread objectification of women's bodies, such glorification of disconnection, so much violence against women, and such blaming of the victim. When everything and everyone is sexualized, it is the powerless

[13]Two men and a baby, 1990, 10.

You already know the feeling.

BALI

who are most at risk. Young girls, of course, are especially vulnerable. In the past twenty years or so, there have been several trends in fashion and advertising that could be seen as cultural reactions to the women's movement, as perhaps unconscious fear of female power. One has been the obsession with thinness. Another has been an increase in images of violence against women. Most disturbing has been the increasing sexualization of children, especially girls. Sometimes the little girl is made up and seductively posed. Sometimes the language is suggestive. "Very cherry," says the ad featuring a sexy little African American girl who is wearing a dress with cherries all over it. A shocking ad in a gun magazine features a smiling little girl, a toddler, in a bathing suit that is tugged up suggestively in the rear. The copy beneath the photo says, "short BUTTS from FLEMING FIREARMS."[14] Other times girls are juxtaposed with grown women, as in the ad for underpants that says "You already know the feeling."

This is not only an American phenomenon. A growing national obsession in Japan with schoolgirls dressed in uniforms is called "Lolicon," after Lolita.[15] In Tokyo hundreds of "image clubs" allow Japanese men to act out their fantasies with make-believe schoolgirls. A magazine called *V-Club* featuring pictures of naked elementary-school girls competes with another called *Anatomical Illustrations of Junior High*

[14]Herbert, 1999, WK 17.
[15]*Lolita:* The title character of Vladimir Nabokov's 1955 novel, Lolita is a young girl who is sexually pursued by her stepfather. [Eds.]

School Girls.[16] Masao Miyamoto, a male psychiatrist, suggests that Japanese men are turning to girls because they feel threatened by the growing sophistication of older women.[17]

In recent years, this sexualization of little girls has become even more disturbing as hints of violence enter the picture. A three-page ad for Prada clothing features a girl or very young woman with a barely pubescent body, clothed in what seem to be cotton panties and perhaps a training bra, viewed through a partially opened door. She seems surprised, startled, worried, as if she's heard a strange sound or glimpsed someone watching her. I suppose this could be a woman awaiting her lover, but it could as easily be a girl being preyed upon.

The 1996 murder of six-year-old JonBenet Ramsey[18] was a gold mine for the media, combining as it did child pornography and violence. In November of 1997 *Advertising Age* reported in an article entitled "JonBenet keeps hold on magazines" that the child had been on five magazine covers in October, "Enough to capture the Cover Story lead for the month. The pre-adolescent beauty queen, found slain in her home last Christmas, garnered 6.5 points. The case earned a *triple play* [italics mine] in the *National Enquirer*, and one-time appearances on *People* and *Star*."[19] Imagine describing a six-year-old child as "pre-adolescent."

Sometimes the models in ads are children, other times they just 35 look like children. Kate Moss was twenty when she said of herself, "I look twelve."[20] She epitomized the vacant, hollow-cheeked look known

[16]Schoolgirls as sex toys, 1997, 2E.
[17]Ibid.
[18]*JonBenet Ramsey:* Six-year-old beauty-pageant winner who was sexually molested and murdered in her Boulder, Colorado, home in 1996. [Eds.]
[19]Johnson, 1997, 42.
[20]Leo, 1994, 27.

as "heroin chic" that was popular in the mid-nineties. She also often looked vulnerable, abused, and exploited. In one ad she is nude in the corner of a huge sofa, cringing as if braced for an impending sexual assault. In another she is lying nude on her stomach, pliant, available, androgynous enough to appeal to all kinds of pedophiles. In a music video she is dead and bound to a chair while Johnny Cash sings "Delia's Gone."

It is not surprising that Kate Moss models for Calvin Klein, the fashion designer who specializes in breaking taboos and thereby getting himself public outrage, media coverage, and more bang for his buck. In 1995 he brought the federal government down on himself by running a campaign that may have crossed the line into child pornography.[21] Very young models (and others who just seemed young) were featured in lascivious print ads and in television commercials designed to mimic child porn. The models were awkward, self-conscious. In one commercial, a boy stands in what seems to be a finished basement. A male voiceover tells him he has a great body and asks him to take off his shirt. The boy seems embarrassed but he complies. There was a great deal of protest, which brought the issue into national consciousness but which also gave Klein the publicity and free media coverage he was looking for. He pulled the ads but, at the same time, projected that his jeans sales would almost double from $115 million to $220 million that year, partly because of the free publicity but also because the controversy made his critics seem like prudes and thus positioned Klein as the daring rebel, a very appealing image to the majority of his customers.

Having learned from this, in 1999 Klein launched a very brief advertising campaign featuring very little children frolicking in their underpants, which included a controversial billboard in Times Square.[22]

[21]Sloan, 1996, 27.
[22]Associated Press, 1999, February 18, A7.

Although in some ways this campaign was less offensive than the earlier one and might have gone unnoticed had the ads come from a department store catalog rather than from Calvin Klein, there was the expected protest and Klein quickly withdrew the ads, again getting a windfall of media coverage. In my opinion, the real obscenity of this campaign is the whole idea of people buying designer underwear for their little ones, especially in a country in which at least one in five children doesn't have enough to eat.

Although boys are sometimes sexualized in an overt way, they are more often portrayed as sexually precocious, as in the Pepsi commercial featuring the young boys ogling Cindy Crawford or the jeans ad portraying a very little boy looking up a woman's skirt. It may seem that I am reading too much into this ad, but imagine if the genders were reversed. We would fear for a little girl who was unzipping a man's fly in an ad (and we would be shocked, I would hope). Boys are vulnerable to sexual abuse too, but cultural attitudes make it difficult to take this seriously. As a result, boys are less likely to report abuse and to get treatment.

Many boys grow up feeling that they are unmanly if they are not always "ready for action," capable of and interested in sex with any woman who is available. Advertising doesn't cause this attitude, of course, but it contributes to it. A Levi Strauss commercial that ran in Asia features the shock of a schoolboy who discovers that the seductive young woman who has slipped a note into the jeans of an older student is his teacher. And an ad for BIC pens pictures a young boy wearing X-ray glasses while ogling the derriere of an older woman. Again, these ads would be unthinkable if the genders were reversed. It is increasingly difficult in such a toxic environment to see children, boys or girls, as *children*.

In the past few years there has been a proliferation of sexually gro- 40
tesque toys for boys, such as a Spider Man female action figure whose
exaggerated breasts have antennae coming out of them and a female
Spawn figure with carved skulls for breasts. Meantime even children
have easy access to pornography in video games and on the World
Wide Web, which includes explicit photographs of women having intercourse with groups of men, with dogs, donkeys, horses, and snakes;
photographs of women being raped and tortured; some of these women
made up to look like little girls.

It is hard for girls not to learn self-hatred in an environment in which
there is such widespread and open contempt for women and girls. In
1997 a company called Senate distributed clothing with inside labels
that included, in addition to the usual cleaning instructions, the line
"Destroy all girls." A Senate staffer explained that he thought it was

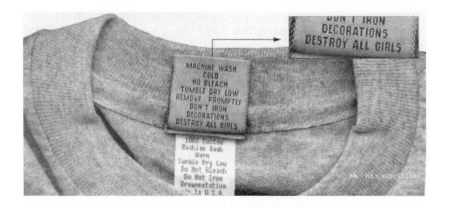

"kind of cool."[23] Given all this, it's not surprising that when boys and girls were asked in a recent study to write an essay on what it would be like to be the other gender, many boys wrote they would rather be dead. Girls had no trouble writing essays about activities, power, freedom, but boys were often stuck, could think of nothing.

It is also not surprising that, in such an environment, sexual harassment is considered normal and ordinary. According to an article in the journal *Eating Disorders*:

> In our work with young women, we have heard countless accounts of this contempt being expressed by their male peers: the girls who do not want to walk down a certain hallway in their high school because they are afraid of being publicly rated on a scale of one to ten; the girls who are subjected to barking, grunting and mooing calls and labels of "dogs, cows, or pigs" when they pass by groups of male students; those who are teased about not measuring up to buxom, bikini-clad [models]; and the girls who are grabbed, pinched, groped, and fondled as they try to make their way through the school corridors.
>
> Harassing words do not slide harmlessly away as the taunting sounds dissipate....They are slowly absorbed into the child's identity and developing sense of self, becoming an essential part of who she sees herself to be. Harassment involves the use of words as weapons to inflict pain and assert power. Harassing words are meant to instill fear, heighten bodily discomfort, and diminish the sense of self.[24]

It is probably difficult for those of us who are older to understand how devastating and cruel and pervasive this harassment is, how different from the "teasing" some of us might remember from our own childhoods (not that that didn't hurt and do damage as well). A 1993 report by the American Association of University Women found that 76 percent of female students in grades eight to eleven and 56 percent of male students said they had been sexually harassed in school.[25] One

[23]Wire and *Times* staff reports, 1997, D1.
[24]Larkin, Rice, and Russell, 1996, 5–26.
[25]Daley and Vigue, 1999, A12.

high-school junior described a year of torment at her vocational school: "The boys call me slut, bitch. They call me a ten-timer, because they say I go with ten guys at the same time. I put up with it because I have no choice. The teachers say it's because the boys think I'm pretty."[26]

High school and junior high school have always been hell for those who were different in any way (gay teens have no doubt suffered the most, although "overweight" girls are a close second), but the harassment is more extreme and more physical these days. Many young men feel they have the right to judge and touch young women and the women often feel they have no choice but to submit. One young woman recalled that "the guys at school routinely swiped their hands across girls' legs to patrol their shaving prowess and then taunt them if they were slacking off. If I were running late, I'd protect myself by faux shaving—just doing the strip between the bottom of my jeans and the top of my cotton socks."[27]

Sexual battery, as well as inappropriate sexual gesturing, touching, and fondling, is increasing not only in high schools but in elementary and middle schools as well.[28] There are reports of sexual assaults by students on other students as young as eight. A fifth-grade boy in Georgia repeatedly touched the breasts and genitals of one of his fellow students while saying, "I want to get in bed with you" and "I want to feel your boobs." Authorities did nothing, although the girl complained and her grades fell. When her parents found a suicide note she had written, they took the board of education to court.[29]

A high-school senior in an affluent suburban school in the Boston area said she has been dragged by her arms so boys could look up her skirt and that boys have rested their heads on her chest while making lewd comments. Another student in the same school was pinned down on a lunch table while a boy simulated sex on top of her. Neither student reported any of the incidents, for fear of being ostracized by their peers.[30] In another school in the Boston area, a sixteen-year-old girl, who had been digitally raped by a classmate, committed suicide.[31]

According to Nan Stein, a researcher at Wellesley College:

> Schools may in fact be training grounds for the insidious cycle of domestic violence.... The school's hidden curriculum teaches young women to suffer abuse privately, that resistance is futile. When they witness harassment of others and fail to respond, they absorb a different kind of powerlessness—that they are incapable of standing up to injustice or acting in solidarity with their peers. Similarly, in schools boys receive permission, even training, to become batterers through the practice of sexual harassment.[32]

[26]Hart, 1998, A12.
[27]Mackler, 1998, 56.
[28]Daley and Vigue, 1999, A1, A12.
[29]Shin, 1999, 32.
[30]Daley and Vigue, 1999, A12.
[31]Daley and Abraham, 1999, B6.
[32]Stein, 1993, 316–17.

This pervasive harassment of and contempt for girls and women constitute a kind of abuse. We know that addictions for women are rooted in trauma, that girls who are sexually abused are far more likely to become addicted to one substance or another. I contend that all girls growing up in this culture are sexually abused—abused by the pornographic images of female sexuality that surround them from birth, abused by all the violence against women and girls, and abused by the constant harassment and threat of violence. Abuse is a continuum, of course, and I am by no means implying that cultural abuse is as terrible as literally being raped and assaulted. However, it hurts, it does damage, and it sets girls up for addictions and self-destructive behavior. Many girls turn to food, alcohol, cigarettes, and other drugs in a misguided attempt to cope.

As Marian Sandmaier said in *The Invisible Alcoholics: Women and Alcohol Abuse in America*, "In a culture that cuts off women from many of their own possibilities before they barely have had a chance to sense them, that pain belongs to all women. Outlets for coping may vary widely, and may be more or less addictive, more or less self-destructive. But at some level, all women know what it is to lack access to their own power, to live with a piece of themselves unclaimed."[33]

Today, every girl is endangered, not just those who have been phys- [50] ically and sexually abused. If girls from supportive homes with positive role models are at risk, imagine then how vulnerable are the girls who have been violated. No wonder they so often go under for good—ending up in abusive marriages, in prison, on the streets. And those who do are almost always in the grip of one addiction or another. More than half of women in prison are addicts and most are there for crimes directly related to their addiction. Many who are there for murder killed men who had been battering them for years. Almost all of the women who are homeless or in prisons and mental institutions are the victims of male violence.[34]

Male violence exists within the same cultural and sociopolitical context that contributes to addiction. Both can be fully understood only within this context, way beyond individual psychology and family dynamics. It is a context of systemic violence and oppression, including racism, classism, heterosexism, weightism, and ageism, as well as sexism, all of which are traumatizing in and of themselves. Advertising is only one part of this cultural context, but it is an important part and thus is a part of what traumatizes.

Sources

Abbey, A., Ross, L., and McDuffie, D. (1991). Alcohol's role in sexual assault. In Watson, R., ed. *Addictive behaviors in women.* Totowa, NJ: Humana Press.
Associated Press (1999, February 18). Calvin Klein retreats on ad. *Boston Globe*, A7.

[33]Sandmaier, 1980, xviii.
[34]Snell, 1991.

Blumenthal, S. J. (1995, July). *Violence against women*. Washington, DC: Department of Health and Human Services.

Brewers can help fight sexism (1991, October 28). *Advertising Age*, 28.

Daley, B., and Vigue, D. I. (1999, February 4). Sex harassment increasing amid students, officials say. *Boston Globe*, A1, A12.

Hart, J. (1998, June 8). Northampton confronts a crime, cruelty. *Boston Globe*, A1, A12.

Herbert, B. (1999, May 2). America's littlest shooters. *New York Times*, WK 17.

Johnson, J. A. (1997, November 10). JonBenet keeps hold on magazines. *Advertising Age*, 42.

Kilbourne, J. (1994, May 15). "Gender bender" ads: Same old sexism. *New York Times*, F13.

Larkin, J., Rice, C., and Russell, V. (1996, Spring). Slipping through the cracks: Sexual harassment. *Eating Disorders: The Journal of Treatment and Prevention*, vol. 4, no. 1, 5–26.

Leo, J. (1994, June 13). Selling the woman-child. *U.S. News and World Report*, 27.

Mackler, C. (1998). Memoirs of a (sorta) ex-shaver. In Edut, O., ed. (1998). *Adios, Barbie*. Seattle, WA: Seal Press, 55–61.

Novello, A. (1991, October 18). Quoted by Associated Press, AMA to fight wife-beating. *St. Louis Post Dispatch*, 1, 15.

Quindlen, A. (1992, June 28). All of these you are. *New York Times*, E17.

Sandmaier, M. (1980). *The invisible alcoholics: Women and alcohol abuse in America*. New York: McGraw-Hill.

Schoolgirls as sex toys. *New York Times* (1997, April 16), 2E.

Shin, A. (1999, April/May). Testing Title IX. *Ms.*, 32.

Sloan, P. (1996, July 8). Underwear ads caught in bind over sex appeal. *Advertising Age*, 27.

Snell, T. L. (1991). *Women in prison*. Washington, DC: U.S. Department of Justice.

Stein, N. (1993). No laughing matter: Sexual harassment in K-12 schools. In Buchwald, E., Fletcher, P. R., and Roth, M. (1993). *Transforming a rape culture*. Minneapolis, MN: Milkweed Editions, 311–31.

Tjaden, R., and Thoennes, N. (1998, November). *Prevalence, incidence, and consequences of violence against women: Findings from the National Violence Against Women Survey*. Washington, DC: U.S. Department of Justice.

Two men and a baby (1990, July/August). *Ms.*, 10.

Vigue, D. J., and Abraham, Y. (1999, February 7). Harassment a daily course for students. *Boston Globe*, B1, B6.

Weil, L. (1999, March). Leaps of faith. *Women's Review of Books*, 21.

Wilsnack, S. C., Plaud, J. J., Wilsnack, R. W., and Klassen, A. D. (1997). Sexuality, gender, and alcohol use. In Wilsnack, R. W., and Wilsnack, S. C., eds. *Gender and alcohol: Individual and social perspectives*. New Brunswick, N.J.: Rutgers Center of Alcohol Studies, 262.

Wire and Times Staff Reports (1997, May 20). Orange County skate firm's "destroy all girls" tags won't wash. *Los Angeles Times*, D1.

Wright, R. (1995, September 10). Brutality defines the lives of women around the world. *Boston Globe*, A2.

ENGAGING THE TEXT

1. What parallels does Kilbourne see between advertising and pornography? How persuasive do you find the evidence she offers? Do the photos of the ads she describes strengthen her argument? Why or why not?

2. Why is it dangerous to depict women and men as sex objects, according to Kilbourne? Why is the objectification of women *more* troubling, in her view? Do you agree?

3. How does Kilbourne explain the appeal of ads that allude to bondage, sexual aggression, and rape — particularly for female consumers? How do you respond to the ads reproduced in her essay?

4. What does Kilbourne mean when she claims that the depiction of women in advertising constitutes "cultural abuse"? How does she go about drawing connections between advertising images and social problems like sexual violence, harassment, and addiction? Which portions of her analysis do you find most and least persuasive, and why?

EXPLORING CONNECTIONS

5. Media images constitute part of the "generalized other" — the internalized sense of what is socially acceptable and unacceptable — described by Aaron H. Devor (p. 387). In addition to the violent and sexualized images Kilbourne examines, what other images or messages about gender do you encounter regularly in the media? Which ones have been most influential in the development of your "generalized other"?

6. Drawing on the essays by Kilbourne and Joan Morgan (p. 455), write an essay exploring the power of media to promote or curb violence.

EXTENDING THE CRITICAL CONTEXT

7. Kilbourne claims that popular culture idealizes dangerous, exploitative, or dysfunctional relationships between women and men. Working in small groups, discuss the romantic relationships depicted in movies you've seen recently. Does her critique seem applicable to those films? List the evidence you find for and against her argument and compare your results with those of other groups.

8. In her analysis of two ads (the Diet Pepsi commercial featuring Cindy Crawford and the Diet Coke ad with the shirtless construction worker), Kilbourne applies a gender reversal test in order to demonstrate the existence of a double standard. Try this test yourself on a commercial or ad that relies on sexual innuendo. Write a journal entry describing the ad and explaining the results of your test.

9. Working in pairs or small groups, survey the ads in two magazines — one designed to appeal to a predominantly female audience and one aimed at a largely male audience. What differences, if any, do you see in the kinds of images and appeals advertisers use in the two magazines? How often do you see the kinds of "pornographic" ads Kilbourne discusses? Do you find any ads depicting the "relational skills" that she suggests are rarely emphasized in popular culture?

④

JUST BETWEEN YOU, ME, AND MY 622 BFFS
PEGGY ORENSTEIN

> In this passage from *Cinderella Ate My Daughter: Dispatches from the Front Lines of the New Girly-Girl Culture* (2011), Peggy Orenstein looks at girls in the age of Facebook and is disturbed by what she sees. Orenstein contends that social media can distort personality development, encouraging self-absorption, lack of empathy, and the "performance" of sexuality. The inevitable mistakes teenagers make can live on indefinitely in cyberspace, and the anonymity of online comments can foster cyberbullying. Orenstein (b. 1961), is a contributing writer for the *New York Times*. She has written extensively about gender issues in *School Girls: Young Women, Self-Esteem and the Confidence Gap* (1994), and *Flux: Women on Sex, Work, Kids, Love and Life in a Half-Changed World* (2000). Her memoir, *Waiting for Daisy* (2007), was a *New York Times* best-seller.

...ERIN, WHO IS FOURTEEN, has been online since she was in third grade. "I used to love doing the painting pages on the Dragon Tales site," she said, laughing. "I did them until I was much too old."

Erin and three of her friends were sitting in her family's Albany, California, living room. Her mother had set out an array of healthy snacks for us—hummus with carrots, fresh strawberries—but the girls shunned those for a bucket of shamrock-shaped, green frosted sugar cookies bought at the grocery store in celebration of Saint Patrick's Day. Each one here today had been online since she was seven or eight. Each carried her cell phone as if it were a fifth limb. Each owned an iPod touch. Each used computers daily, often in the privacy of her bedroom. Naturally, they all had Facebook accounts, which, judging from my communication with them, they checked numerous times during the school day. They'd had some amazing experiences online: one of the girls, Katie, fourteen, who had been adopted as an infant, told me she had found her birth mother on Facebook. So she'd friended her. "It was an open adoption, so I always knew her name," Katie explained, "but she'd never visited or anything. She was only seventeen when I was born." The two ended up meeting in person some months later, when the woman passed through San Francisco. "It was cool," Katie said, though she had no plans to see the woman again. The casual way she related the story confused me. Finding your birth mother with a few clicks—on Facebook, of all things—would seem momentous, yet Katie was treating it like it was no big deal. Maybe she was just playing it cool, but I wondered whether the unlimited possibility for connection had somehow devalued its worth.

Each of these girls had more than 400 friends on the networking site—one, Felicia, had 622—which was so unremarkable that I almost didn't note it. But really? Six hundred twenty-two friends? There were only about 250 students in her entire grade at school. One of my favorite books as a child was Joan Walsh Anglund's[1] *A Friend Is Someone Who Likes You.* These days, a better title might be *A Friend Is Someone You Have Actually Met in Person.* There is no way Felicia could know all those people offline, though she claimed to have at least *met* each of them. Even so, 622 people can witness everything she writes, every picture she posts. Six hundred twenty-two people can pass that information on to *their* 622 friends. Six hundred twenty-two people are watching her, judging her, at least in theory, every hour of every day. How does that influence a child's development?

Apparently, quite a bit. In short order—a matter of a few years—social networking and virtual worlds have transformed how young people, male as well as female, conceptualize both their selves and their relationships. According to Adriana Manago, a researcher at the Children's Digital Media Center in Los Angeles who studies college students' behavior on MySpace and Facebook, young people's real-life identities[2] are becoming ever more externally driven, sculpted in response to feedback from network "friends." Obviously, teens have always tested out new selves among their peers, but back in the dark ages (say, in the year 2000), any negative response was fleeting and limited to a small group of people they actually knew. Now their thoughts, photos, tastes, and activities are laid out for immediate approval or rejection by hundreds of people, many of whom are relative strangers. The self, Manago said, becomes a brand, something to be marketed to others rather than developed from within. Instead of intimates with whom you interact for the sake of the exchange, friends become your consumers, an audience for whom you perform.

The impact, back in the offline world, appears to be an uptick in narcissistic tendencies among young adults. In the largest study[3] of its kind, a group of psychologists found that the scores of the 16,475 college students who took the Narcissistic Personality Inventory[4] between 1982 and 2006 have risen by 30 percent. A full two-thirds of today's young adults rank above average; excessive self-involvement is associated with difficulty in maintaining romantic relationships, dishonesty,

5

---

[1]*Joan Walsh Anglund:* Children's book author and illustrator (b. 1926). [All notes are Orenstein's except 1, 4, 5, 6, 13, 15–17, and 20.]

[2]Author's interview with Adriana Manago, Department of Psychology and Children's Digital Media Center, UCLA, May 7, 2010; Adriana Manago, Michael B. Graham, Patricia M. Greenfield, and Goldie Salimkhan, "Self-Presentation and Gender on MySpace."

[3]"Study Sees Rise in Narcissism Among Students," *Day to Day*, February 27, 2007, www .npr.org/templates/story/story.php?storyId=7618722&ps=rs; Associated Press, "College Students Think They're *So* Special," February 27, 2007, www.msnbc.msn.com/id/17349066/.

[4]*Narcissistic Personality Inventory:* The most widely used psychological test for narcissism, a disorder that involves an inflated sense of self-importance and extreme preoccupation with the self.

and lack of empathy. And, it turns out, empathy, too, seems[5] in measurably shorter supply: an analysis of seventy-two studies performed on almost 14,000 college students between 1979 and 2009 showed a drop in that trait, with the sharpest decline occurring since 2000. Social media may not have instigated that trend, but by encouraging self-promotion over self-awareness, they could easily accelerate it.

I don't mean to demonize new technology. I enjoy Facebook myself. Because of it, I am in touch with old friends and relatives who are scattered around the globe. It has also served as a handy vehicle to promote my work, to alert the readers among my "friends" that I have published something new. Yet I am also aware of the ways Facebook and the microblogging site Twitter subtly shifted my self-perception. Online, I carefully consider how any comments or photos I post will shape the persona I have cultivated; offline, I have caught myself processing my experience as it occurs, packaging life as I live it. As I loll in the front yard with Daisy[6] or stand in line at the supermarket or read in bed, part of my consciousness splits off, viewing the scene from the outside and imagining how to distill it into a status update or a Tweet. Apparently, teenagers are not the only ones at risk of turning the self into a performance, though since their identities are less formed, one assumes the potential impact will be more profound.

Girls, especially, are already so accustomed to disconnecting from their inner experience, observing themselves as others might. Unlike earlier generations, though, their imagined audience is all too real: online, every girl becomes a mini-Miley[7] complete with her own adoring fan base that she is bound to maintain. In fact, if you try to choose the screen name "Miley" in a virtual world, you will be told no dice, though you can be Miley1819 or higher, if you would like. According to Manago, girls attract the most positive feedback when they post provocative photos[8] or create hot avatars—as long as they don't go too far. Just as with real celebs, then, girls online engage in perpetual, public negotiation between appearing "beautiful, sexy, yet innocent" (which they reportedly want) and coming off as "a slut" in front of hundreds of people (which they do not). Perhaps that high-wire act, as much as anything, reveals the lie of girls' popular culture: if the sexualization and attention to appearance truly "empowered" girls, they would emerge from childhood with more freedom and control over their sexuality. Instead, they seem to have less: they have learned that sexiness confers power—unless you use it (or are perceived as using it). The fastest way to take a girl down remains, as ever, to attack her looks or sexual

[5]"Empathy: College Students Don't Have as Much as They Used to, Study Finds," *Science Daily*, May 29, 2010, www.sciencedaily.com/releases/2010/05/100528081434.htm.
[6]*Daisy*: Orenstein's daughter.
[7]*Mini-Miley*: Miley Cyrus, actress and singer-songwriter.
[8]Author's interview with Adriana Manago; Manago et al., "Self-Presentation and Gender on MySpace."

behavior: Ugly. Fat. Slut. Whore. Those are the teen girl equivalent of kryptonite.

Erin and her friends have their own ideas about how to strike the right balance. Jessica, fourteen, explained, "I never put up a picture *just* of me. That's slutty."

I asked how merely posting a solo shot of herself could qualify as "slutty." "Well," she responded, "it's self-centered, though, which is kind of the same thing."

She pulled up the profile of one of her classmates to show me what she meant. The other girls crowded around the screen. How strange, I thought; I don't know this girl and never will, but here I was rifling through her photos, reading what other people thought of them. One snapshot showed her leaning forward in a bikini top; in another, she posed with one shoulder thrust coyly toward the viewer. "Look at her," said Felicia, disgusted. "She's dyed her hair *blond*. Badly. And look at that." She pointed to a close-up shot of the girl mugging for the camera with a boy. "He is in her bed! Her *bed*!"

Felicia did not stint on comments about other girls, even though she herself had been branded a slut in eighth grade by classmates who were jealous of the boy she was dating. Also, she has large breasts, which had developed early, and, really, isn't that enough? Her tormentors targeted her both in person and electronically, even creating a Facebook page called "Felicia's a Whore." "I tried to act like it didn't bother me," she said, tersely. "But it was not a lovely situation." Nor an uncommon one. The girls showed me another friend's Formspring page: a free application that allows your Facebook "friends" to ask questions or post comments about you—anonymously. That means that while the person who says "Can I see ur tits live?" or "U r a bitch!" is someone you know (or at least someone you have friended), you can never know exactly *who*. Think of it as the online equivalent of a bathroom stall with all the raunchiness and lord-of-the-flies viciousness that implies. The mind reels at the idea of such technology in the hands of teenage girls, who are already masters of—and suckers for—stealth aggression.

In the early days of the Web, people feared their daughters would be stalked by strangers online, but the far bigger threat has turned out to come from neighbors, friends, peers. In the first high-profile case[9] of cyberbullying, a Missouri girl, Megan Meier, hung herself in her bedroom after a romance with a boy she had met on MySpace—but had never spoken to or seen in person—went sour. "You're the kind of boy a girl would kill herself over," Meier wrote in her final post, twenty minutes before her suicide. She was just three weeks shy of her fourteenth birthday. The boy, it was later discovered, did not exist: he had been fabricated by Meier's neighbor, forty-seven-year-old Lori Drew, to punish the girl for spreading rumors about Drew's own daughter. Four years

[9]Jennifer Steinhauer, "Verdict in MySpace Suicide Case," *The New York Times*, November 27, 2008, p. A25.

later, in 2010, fifteen-year-old Phoebe Prince[10] put cyberbullying back in the headlines: she hung herself after enduring months of sexual slurs in her South Hadley, Massachusetts, high school hallways, as well as via text message and on Facebook. A few months later, Alexis Pilkington,[11] a popular seventeen-year-old soccer player from Long Island, also took her life after a series of cybertaunts, which persisted on a memorial page created after her death.

Most cases of online harassment do not go that far, but the upsurge of abuse is disturbing. A 2009 poll conducted by the Associated Press and MTV found that half of young people[12] aged fourteen to twenty-four reported experiencing digital abuse, with girls significantly more likely to be victimized than boys. Two-thirds of those who were the target of rumors and hearsay were "very upset" or "extremely upset" by the experience, and they were more than twice as likely as their peers to have considered suicide.

Gossip and nasty notes may be painful staples of middle school and high school girls' lives, but YouTube, Facebook, instant messaging, texting, and voice mail can raise cruelty to exponential heights. Rumors can spread faster and further and, as the case of Phoebe Prince illustrates, there is nowhere to escape their reach—not your bedroom, not the dinner table, not while going out with your friends. The anonymity of the screen may also embolden bullies: the natural inhibitions one might feel face-to-face, along with any sense of accountability, fall away. It is easy, especially among young people, for behavior to spin out of control. Further, this risks exposing them to consequences they did not—or could not—anticipate.

Portraying girls as victims, particularly of other girls, is distressing, 15 but it is also comfortable, familiar territory. What happens when girls, under the pretext of sexual self-determination, seem to victimize themselves? A 2008 survey by the National Campaign to Prevent Teen and Unplanned Pregnancy found that 39 percent[13] of teens had sent or posted sexually suggestive messages (or "sexts"), and 22 percent of teenage girls had electronically sent or posted nude or seminude photos of themselves. At first I was skeptical of those figures: the teen sext-

[10]Brian Ballou and John Ellement, "9 Charged in Death of South Hadley Teen, Who Took Life After Bullying," *The Boston Globe*, March 29, 2010, www.boston.com/news/local /breaking_news/2010/03/holding_for_pho.html.

[11]Oren Yaniv, "Long Island Teen's Suicide Linked to Cruel Cyberbullies, Formspring .me Site: Police," *Daily News*, March 25, 2010, www.nydailynews.com/news/ny_crime /2010/03/25/2010-03-25_li_teens_suicide_linked_to_cruel_cyberbullies_police.html; "Cyber Bullies Harass Teen Even After Suicide," *The Huffington Post*, March 24, 2010, www .huffingtonpost.com/2010/03/24/alexis-pilkington-faceboo_n_512482.html.

[12]Associated Press and MTV, "A Thin Line: Executive Summary," MTV, December 2009, www.athinline.org/MTV-AP_Digital_Abuse_Study_Executive_Summary.pdf. A report by the Pew Internet and American Life Project put the rates of cyberbullying at one-third of teens; 38 percent of girls in that survey experienced harassment versus 26 percent of boys. Amanda Lenhart, *Cyberbullying*, www.pewinternet.org/reports/2007/cyberbullying.aspx.

[13]The National Campaign to Prevent Teen and Unplanned Pregnancy, *Sex and Tech: Executive Summary*.

ing "epidemic" had the earmarks of media-generated hype, the kind of moral panic that breaks out whenever girls have the audacity to act sexually. Young ladies flashing skin and propositioning boys? Heavens to Betsy, hie them to a nunnery![14]

Then, mere days after that report was released, a friend of mine found a photo on her fourteen-year-old son's computer of one of his female classmates—a ninth-grader—naked from the waist up. She was not even a girl he knew well. "We're trying to teach our son that women are not playthings," my friend said. "How are we supposed to do that if a girl sends him something like this?"

Good question. How is one to explain such behavior? Part of me, I had to admit, was taken by the girl's bravado: that at age fourteen, she felt confident enough in her body to send a nudie shot to a boy she barely knew. Was it possible that this was a form of progress, a sign that at least some of today's girls were taking charge of their sexuality, transcending the double standard? I wanted to believe it, but the conclusion didn't sit right.

I checked in with Deborah Tolman, a professor of human sexuality studies at Hunter College who for years has been my go-to gal on all matters of girls and desire. As it happened, she had been wrestling with these very questions and had come up with a theory: girls like the one I have described are not connecting more deeply to their own feelings, needs, or desires. Instead, sexual entitlement itself has become objectified; like identity, like femininity, it, too, has become a performance, something to "do" rather than to "experience." Teasing and turning boys on might give girls a certain thrill, even a fleeting sense of power, but it will not help them understand their own pleasure, recognize their own arousal, allow them to assert themselves in intimate (let alone casual) relationships.

Previously, I mentioned that early sexualization can derail girls' healthy development, estrange them from their own erotic feelings. Ninth-graders texting naked photos may be one result. Another might be the annual "slut list"[15] the senior girls at an affluent high school in Millburn, New Jersey, compile of incoming freshmen (which made national news after they posted it on Facebook in 2009); being chosen is at once an honor and a humiliation, marking a girl as "popular" even as it accuses her of lusting after her brother or wanting someone to "bend me over and knock me up." That detached sexuality may also contribute to an emerging phenomenon that Tolman is studying, which she called, bluntly, Anal Is the New Oral. "All girls are now expected to have oral sex in their repertoire," she explained. "Anal sex is becoming the new 'Will she do it or not?' behavior, the new 'Prove you love me.' And still,

[14]*Hie them to a nunnery*: Variation on Hamlet's words to Ophelia in *Hamlet* Act III, scene 1; a "nunnery" was actually a whorehouse.

[15]Tina Kelley, "A Rite of Hazing Now Out in the Open," *The New York Times*, September 18, 2009, p. A13; Tina Kelley, "When the Cool Get Hazed," *The New Tork Times*, September 27, 2009, p. WK5.

girls' sexual pleasure is not part of the equation." That is such a fundamental misunderstanding of romantic relationships and sexuality—as
a mother, it plunges me into despair. I find myself improbably nostalgic for the late 1970s, when I came of age. Fewer of us competed on
the sports field, raised our hands during math class, or graduated from
college. No one spoke the word "vagina," whether in a monologue or
not.[16] And there was that Farrah flip[17] to contend with. Yet in that oh-so-
brief window between the advent of the pill and the fear of AIDS, when
abortion was both legal and accessible to teenagers, there was—at
least for some of us—a kind of *Our Bodies, Ourselves*[18] optimism about
sex. Young women felt an almost solemn, political duty to understand
their desire and responses, to explore their own pleasure, to recognize
sexuality as something rising from within. And young men—at least
some of them—seemed eager to take the journey with us, to rewrite
the rules of masculinity so they would prize mutuality over conquest.
That notion now seems as quaint as a one-piece swimsuit on a five-
year-old. "By the time they are teenagers," Tolman said, "the girls I talk
to respond to questions about how their bodies feel—questions about
sexuality or desire—by talking about how their bodies look. They will
say something like 'I felt like I looked good.'" My fear for my daughter,
then, is not that she will someday act in a sexual way; it is that she will
learn to act sexually against her own self-interest.

Most young women, thankfully, are not out there making person-   20
alized *Playboy* centerfolds. The ones who are may well be the ones
engaging in other risky behaviors offline; the statistics on sexting, for
instance, are similar, demographically, to those on binge drinking.
Megan Meier, the girl[19] who committed suicide in 2006, had a history
of depression, as did Alexis Pilkington. Phoebe Prince seems to have[20]
been a self-cutter. Does that make them anomalies, or canaries in a coal
mine[21]? What about the thirteen-year-old girl "in love" who sends a hot
shot to her boyfriend without considering what he will do with it after
she dumps him? Or the girl who one time—just one time—does a stupid, thoughtless thing. Which of us hasn't been that girl? In the old days
that One Stupid Thing might have sparked ugly rumors, but it could
also fade away. The bad judgment you showed when you got drunk at
a party and danced topless on a table was ephemeral. But my friend's

---

[16]*No one spoke the word "vagina" whether in a monologue or not:* Refers to *The
Vagina Monologues* (1996), a feminist play by Eve Ensler.

[17]*Farrah flip:* Hairstyle popularized by actress Farrah Fawcett, known for her long,
feathered hair.

[18]*Our Bodies, Ourselves:* Feminist classic published in 1971, dealing with many aspects of women's health and sexuality.

[19]Steinhauer, "Verdict in MySpace Suicide Case"; "Cyber Bullies Harass Teen Even
After Suicide."

[20]Emily Bazelon, "What Really Happened to Phoebe Prince?" *Slate*, July 20, 2010,
www.slate.com/id/2260952.

[21]*Canaries in a coal mine:* Miners used to take a caged canary with them into the
coal mine; if toxic gasses were present, the canary would sicken or die. Hence, an early
warning.

son, were he so inclined, could forward his classmate's photo to one of his friends, who could forward it to two of his friends and, as in that 1970s shampoo commercial, so on and so on, until all three thousand-plus kids at their high school had a copy—and maybe all the kids in the next town as well. And that, as much as the act itself, is the problem: the indelibility of it, the never-ending potential for replication, the loss of control over your image and identity right when, as a teenager, you need it most.

Electronic media have created a series of funhouse mirrors. They both forge greater intimacy and undermine it—sometimes simultaneously. Determining what, exactly, is going on at any given time is confusing enough for an adult, let alone a child. The ten-year-old daughter of another friend of mine recently invited a pal for a sleepover. Rather than playing in person, the girls wanted to spend the evening using the family's computers—a desktop downstairs, a laptop upstairs—to send each other messages on the virtual world Webkinz.com. Was that just a latter-day version of one of my favorite childhood activities—putting a message in a basket and lowering it down the laundry chute on a string from the second story of my house to the basement, where my best friend awaited? Or was it something else, the beginnings of alienation from living, breathing friends, from the messiness and reciprocity of authentic relationships? Watching the unparalleled social experiment being conducted on our children, it's worth considering—for boys as well as girls—how Internet use enhances their *real* lives, their *real* friendships, their contributions to the *real* world. And if we can't answer all of that in a satisfying way, maybe it is time to give their second lives some second thought.

ENGAGING THE TEXT

1. How does a person "become a brand" in the online world? What other changes in personality and values can be linked to social media, according to Orenstein?

2. Megan Meier, Phoebe Prince, and Alexis Pilkington committed suicide following episodes of cyberbullying. Why are teenage girls particularly vulnerable to digital abuse, in Orenstein's view?

3. Is "sexting" a matter of freedom of expression and sexual power? Why or why not?

4. One of the things that worries Orenstein most is the "indelibility" of online images—the fact that a potentially embarrassing picture you post to one friend can be forwarded to two of his friends, who then forward it to their friends, and so forth. How legitimate is her concern about "loss of control over your image"? (para. 20). Is there anything you can do to prevent this happening, other than forswearing social media entirely? Brainstorm strategies for maintaining privacy online.

5. How do electronic media "both forge greater intimacy and undermine it"? (para. 21). What seems to be Orenstein's overall view of social media, particularly for teenagers? Do you agree with her assessment? List the pros and cons of e-media, and share with your classmates.

EXPLORING CONNECTIONS

6. What is Lalo Alcaraz suggesting in "Life begins at fetusbook," the cartoon on page 453? What are the implications of the umbilical cord attached to the corporate logo? Do you think children should have unrestricted access to Facebook, MySpace, and Twitter? Why or why not?

7. Review Aaron H. Devor's "Becoming Members of Society" (p. 387). How does Orenstein's view of online "performance" reflect or complicate Devor's view of the personal "I" and the social "me"? Of the generalized and significant other?

8. To what extent does Alex Williams (p. 93) share Orenstein's concerns about narcissism and self-absorption as a result of engagement in social media? How do their concerns differ? What benefits, if any, do they see in teenagers' use of electronic media?

EXTENDING THE CRITICAL CONTEXT

9. What has been your experience of social media? Have you ever been involved in a case of cyberbullying or known someone who was? Write a journal entry in which you describe the circumstances and reflect on the experience.

10. Research what can be done to prevent cyberbullying and teen suicide: What role can parents, schools, and other teens play in identifying teenagers at risk? What laws might be applicable to cyberbullies? What school policies have been effective in addressing cyberbullying? What can victims themselves do? Some places to start:

   • National Suicide Prevention Hotline (www.suicidepreventionlifeline.org)

   • The Jed Foundation (www.jedfoundation.org)

   • National Organization for People of Color Against Suicide (www.nopcas .com)

   • The Trevor Project (www.thetrevorproject.org)

FROM FLY-GIRLS TO BITCHES AND HOS

JOAN MORGAN

As a music writer and fan of hip-hop, Joan Morgan loves the power of rap. As a feminist, she is troubled by the pervasive sexism of its lyrics. The misogyny of rap, she argues, is a symptom of crisis in the black community; it must be confronted and understood, not simply condemned, as a step toward healing the pain that it both expresses and inflicts. This passage comes from her collection of essays, *When Chickenheads Come Home to Roost: A Hip-Hop Feminist Breaks It Down* (1999). Formerly the executive editor of *Essence*, she has also written for the *Village Voice, Vibe, Ms.,* and *Spin*.

> *Feminist criticism, like many other forms of social analysis, is widely considered part of a hostile white culture. For a black feminist to chastise misogyny in rap publicly would be viewed as divisive and counterproductive. There is a widespread perception in the black community that public criticism of black men constitutes collaborating with a racist society....*
>
> —MICHELE WALLACE, "When Black Feminism
> Faces the Music, and the Music Is Rap,"
> The *New York Times*[1]

LORD KNOWS OUR LOVE JONES for hip-hop is understandable. Props given to rap music's artistic merits, its irrefutable impact on pop culture, its ability to be alternately beautiful, poignant, powerful, strong, irreverent, visceral, and mesmerizing—homeboy's clearly got it like that. But in between the beats, booty shaking, and hedonistic abandon, I have to wonder if there isn't something inherently unfeminist in supporting a music that repeatedly reduces me to tits and ass and encourages pimping on the regular. While it's human to occasionally fall deep into the love thang with people or situations that simply aren't good for you, feminism alerted me long ago to the dangers of romancing a misogynist (and ridiculously fine, brilliant ones with gangsta leans are no exception). Perhaps the nonbelievers were right, maybe what I'd been mistaking for love and commitment for the last twenty years was really nothing but a self-destructive obsession that made a mockery of my feminism....

I guess it all depends on how you define the f-word. My feminism places the welfare of black women and the black community on its list

---

[1]Michele Wallace, "When Black Feminism Faces the Music, and the Music Is Rap," the *New York Times*, July 29, 1990. [All notes are Morgan's.]

of priorities. It also maintains that black-on-black love is essential to the survival of both.

We have come to a point in our history, however, when black-on-black love—a love that's survived slavery, lynching, segregation, poverty, and racism—is in serious danger. The stats usher in this reality like taps before the death march: According to the U.S. Census Bureau, the number of black two-parent households has decreased from 74 percent to 48 percent since 1960. The leading cause of death among black men ages fifteen to twenty-four is homicide. The majority of them will die at the hands of other black men.[2]

Women are the unsung victims of black-on-black crime. A while back, a friend of mine, a single mother of a newborn (her "babyfather"—a brother—abdicated responsibility before their child was born) was attacked by a pit bull while walking her dog in the park. The owner (a brother) trained the animal to prey on other dogs and the flesh of his fellow community members.

A few weeks later my mom called, upset, to tell me about the murder of a family friend. She was a troubled young woman with a history of substance abuse, aggravated by her son's murder two years ago. She was found beaten and burned beyond recognition. Her murderers were not "skinheads," "The Man," or "the racist white power structure." More likely than not, they were brown men whose faces resembled her own.

Clearly, we are having a very difficult time loving one another.

Any feminism that fails to acknowledge that black folks in nineties America are living and trying to love in a war zone is useless to our struggle against sexism. Though it's often portrayed as part of the problem, rap music is essential to that struggle because it takes us straight to the battlefield.

My decision to expose myself to the sexism of Dr. Dre, Ice Cube, Snoop Dogg, or the Notorious B.I.G. is really my plea to my brothers to tell me who they are. I need to know why they are so angry at me. Why is disrespecting me one of the few things that make them feel like men? What's the haps, what are you going through on the daily that's got you acting so foul?

As a black woman and a feminist I listen to the music with a willingness to see past the machismo in order to be clear about what I'm *really* dealing with. What I hear frightens me. On booming track after booming track, I hear brothers talking about spending each day high as hell on malt liquor and Chronic. Don't sleep. What passes for "40 and a blunt" good times in most of hip-hop is really alcoholism, substance abuse, and chemical dependency. When brothers can talk so cavalierly about killing each other and then reveal that they have no expectation to see their twenty-first birthday, that is straight-up depression *masquerading* as machismo.

Anyone curious about the processes and pathologies that form the psyche of the young, black, and criminal-minded needs to revisit our

5

10

[2]Joan Morgan, "Real Love," *Vibe*, April 1996, p. 38.

dearly departed Notorious B.I.G.'s first album, *Ready to Die*. Chronicling the life and times of the urban "soldier," the album is a blues-laden soul train that took us on a hustler's life journey. We boarded with the story of his birth, strategically stopped to view his dysfunctional, warring family, his first robbery, his first stint in jail, murder, drug-dealing, getting paid, partying, sexin', rap-pin', mayhem, and death. Biggie's player persona might have momentarily convinced the listener that he was livin' phat without a care in the world but other moments divulged his inner hell. The chorus of "Everyday Struggle": *I don't wanna live no more / Sometimes I see death knockin' at my front door* revealed that "Big Poppa" was also plagued with guilt, regret, and depression. The album ultimately ended with his suicide.

The seemingly impenetrable wall of sexism in rap music is really the complex mask African Americans often wear both to hide and express the pain. At the close of this millennium, hip-hop is still one of the few forums in which young black men, even surreptitiously, are allowed to express their pain.

When it comes to the struggle against sexism and our intimate relationships with black men, some of the most on-point feminist advice I've received comes from sistas like my mother, who wouldn't dream of using the term. During our battle to resolve our complicated relationships with my equally wonderful and errant father, my mother presented me with the following gem of wisdom, "One of the most important lessons you will ever learn in life and love, is that you've got to love people for what they are—not for who you would like them to be."

This is crystal clear to me when I'm listening to hip-hop. Yeah, sistas are hurt when we hear brothers calling us bitches and hos. But the real crime isn't the name-calling, it's their failure to love us—to be our brothers in the way that we commit ourselves to being their sistas. But recognize: Any man who doesn't truly love himself is incapable of loving us in the healthy way we need to be loved. It's extremely telling that men who can only see us as "bitches" and "hos" refer to themselves only as "niggas."

In the interest of our emotional health and overall sanity, black women have got to learn to love brothers realistically, and that means differentiating between who they are and who we'd like them to be. Black men are engaged in a war where the real enemies—racism and the white power structure—are masters of camouflage. They've conditioned our men to believe the enemy is brown. The effects of this have been as wicked as they've been debilitating. Being in battle with an enemy that looks just like you makes it hard to believe in the basics every human being needs. For too many black men there is no trust, no community, no family. Just self.

Since hip-hop is the mirror in which so many brothers see themselves, it's significant that one of the music's most prevalent mythologies is that black boys rarely grow into men. Instead, they remain perpetually postadolescent or die. For all the machismo and testosterone in the music, it's frighteningly clear that many brothers see themselves as 15 powerless when it comes to facing the evils of the larger society, accepting responsibility for their lives, or the lives of their children.

So, sista friends, we gotta do what any rational, survivalist-minded person would do after finding herself in a relationship with someone whose pain makes him abusive. We've gotta continue to give up the love but *from a distance that's safe.* Emotional distance is a great enabler of unconditional love and support because it allows us to recognize that the attack, the "bitch, ho" bullshit—isn't personal but part of the illness.

And the focus of black feminists has got to change. We can't afford to keep expending energy on banal discussions of sexism in rap when sexism is only part of a huge set of problems. Continuing on our previous path is akin to demanding that a fiending, broke crackhead not rob you blind because it's *wrong* to do so.

If feminism intends to have any relevance in the lives of the majority of black women, if it intends to move past theory and become functional it has to rescue itself from the ivory towers of academia. Like it or not, hip-hop is not only the dominion of the young, black, and male, it is also the world in which young black women live and survive. A functional game plan for us, one that is going to be as helpful to Shequanna on 142nd as it is to Samantha at Sarah Lawrence, has to recognize hip-hop's ability to articulate the pain our *community* is in and use that knowledge to create a redemptive, healing space.

Notice the emphasis on "community." Hip-hop isn't only instrumental in exposing black men's pain, it brings the healing sistas need right to the surface. Sad as it may be, it's time to stop ignoring the fact that rappers meet "bitches" and "hos" daily—women who reaffirm their depiction of us on vinyl. Backstage, the road, and the 'hood are populated with women who would do anything to be with a rapper sexually for an hour if not a night. It's time to stop fronting like we don't know who rapper Jeru the Damaja was talking about when he said:

> Now a queen's a queen but a stunt's a stunt
> You can tell who's who by the things they want

Sex has long been the bartering chip that women use to gain protec- 20
tion, material wealth, and the vicarious benefits of power. In the black community, where women are given less access to all of the above, "trickin'" becomes a means of leveling the playing field. Denying the justifiable anger of rappers—men who couldn't get the time of day from these women before a few dollars and a record deal—isn't empowering and strategic. Turning a blind eye and scampering for moral high ground diverts our attention away from the young women who are being denied access to power and are suffering for it.

It might've been more convenient to direct our sistafied rage attention to "the sexist representation of women" in those now infamous Sir Mix-A-Lot videos, to fuss over *one* sexist rapper, but wouldn't it have been more productive to address the failing self-esteem of the 150 or so half-naked young women who were willing, unpaid participants? And what about how flip we are when it comes to using the b-word to describe each other? At some point we've all been the recipients of competitive, unsisterly, "bitchiness," particularly when vying for male attention.

Since being black and a woman makes me fluent in both isms, I sometimes use racism as an illuminating analogy. Black folks have finally gotten to the point where we recognize that we sometimes engage in oppressive behaviors that white folks have little to do with. Complexion prejudices and classism are illnesses which have their *roots* in white racism but the perpetrators are certainly black.

Similarly, sistas have to confront the ways we're complicit in our own oppression. Sad to say it, but many of the ways in which men exploit our images and sexuality in hip-hop is done with our permission and cooperation. We need to be as accountable to each other as we believe "race traitors" (i.e., one hundred or so brothers in blackface cooning in a skinhead's music video) should be to our community. To acknowledge this doesn't deny our victimization but it does raise the critical issue of whose responsibility it is to end our oppression. As a feminist, I believe it is too great a responsibility to leave to men.

A few years ago, on an airplane making its way to Montego Bay, I received another gem of girlfriend wisdom from a sixty-year-old self-declared nonfeminist. She was meeting her husband to celebrate her thirty-fifth wedding anniversary. After telling her I was twenty-seven and very much single, she looked at me and shook her head sadly. "I feel sorry for your generation. You don't know how to have relationships, especially the women." Curious, I asked her why she thought this was. "The women of your generation, you want to be right. The women of my generation, we didn't care about being right. We just wanted to win."

Too much of the discussion regarding sexism and the music focuses on being right. We feel we're *right* and the rappers are wrong. The rappers feel it's their *right* to describe their "reality" in any way they see fit. The store owners feel it's their *right* to sell whatever the consumer wants to buy. The consumer feels it's his *right* to be able to decide what he wants to listen to. We may be the "rightest" of the bunch but we sure as hell ain't doing the winning.

I believe hip-hop can help us win. Let's start by recognizing that its illuminating, informative narration and its incredible ability to articulate our collective pain is an invaluable tool when examining gender relations. The information we amass can help create a redemptive, healing space for brothers and sistas.

We're all winners when a space exists for brothers to honestly state and explore the roots of their pain and subsequently their misogyny, sans judgment. It is criminal that the only space our society provided for the late Tupac Shakur to examine the pain, confusion, drug addiction, and fear that led to his arrest and his eventual assassination was in a prison cell. How can we win if a prison cell is the only space an immensely talented but troubled young black man could dare utter these words: "Even though I'm not guilty of the charges they gave me, I'm not innocent in terms of the way I was acting. I'm just as guilty for not doing things. Not with this case but with my life. I had a job to do and I never showed up. I was so scared of this responsibility that I was running away from it."[3] We have to do better than this for our men.

And we have to do better for ourselves. We desperately need a space to lovingly address the uncomfortable issues of our failing self-esteem, the ways we sexualize and objectify ourselves, our confusion about sex and love and the unhealthy, unloving, unsisterly ways we treat each other. Commitment to developing these spaces gives our community the potential for remedies based on honest, clear diagnoses.

As I'm a black woman, I am aware that this doubles my workload—that I am definitely going to have to listen to a lot of shit I won't like—but without these candid discussions, there is little to no hope of exorcising the illness that hurts and sometimes kills us.

ENGAGING THE TEXT

1. What qualities of hip-hop music and rap artists does Morgan admire or appreciate? What fears does she have for rap's female fans and for the artists themselves? To what extent do you agree with Morgan's assessment of the misogyny, anger, and despair expressed by hip-hop?

2. What evidence does Morgan offer that "black folks in nineties America are living and trying to love in a war zone"? How does she explain the causes of the violence she describes? How persuasive do you find her analysis, and why?

3. How do you interpret Morgan's call for establishing "a redemptive, healing space" for confronting the pain expressed by hip-hop? What kind of "space" is she talking about, and how would you go about establishing it?

4. What audience is Morgan addressing and what persuasive strategies—of both argument and style—does she use to appeal to that audience? What do you find effective or ineffective about her approach?

5. While Morgan asserts that we need to examine the lives of rappers like Notorious B.I.G. to understand the roots of their misogyny, critics might counter that she is simply making excuses for intolerable attitudes. Write an essay explaining why you agree or disagree with Morgan's argument.

EXPLORING CONNECTIONS

6. Compare Jean Kilbourne's analysis of sexism and violence in advertising (p. 420) to Morgan's discussion of the same themes in rap. What are the

[3]Kevin Powell, "The Vibe Q: Tupac Shakur, Ready to Live," *Vibe*, April 11, 1995, p. 52.

causes and consequences of "pornographic" depictions of women in popular culture according to each writer? Do you think Kilbourne would concur with Morgan about how we should respond to these images? Why or why not?

7. See "'Bros Before Hos': The Guy Code" (below) and compare the features of Michael Kimmel's "Guy Code" to the images of masculinity portrayed by hip-hop artists.

EXTENDING THE CRITICAL CONTEXT

8. Survey the current issues of several magazines aimed at fans of rap music. What images do they present of women, men, and human relationships? How often do they reflect the themes that Morgan discusses? What other themes and patterns do you find? To what extent, if any, have the subjects and attitudes of hip-hop artists changed since the 1990s?

9. Examine the lyrics of several female rappers and compare them to those of the male rappers Morgan mentions. What similarities and differences do you find in the subjects they address and the feelings they express? If you're not a fan of rap, you may want to consult an online hip-hop dictionary for help in decoding some of the language (www.rapdict.org).

"BROS BEFORE HOS": THE GUY CODE
MICHAEL KIMMEL

According to sociologist Michael Kimmel, "guys" —young men, ages sixteen to twenty-six— represent a distinct social group. In *Guyland: The Perilous World Where Boys Become Men* (2008), he investigates the values, rites, and preoccupations of these young men. This selection from the book details the code of masculinity that guys are expected to follow. Kimmel (b. 1951) has written or edited more than a dozen books on men and masculinity as well as editing the journal *Men and Masculinities*; he teaches at the State University of New York at Stony Brook. He is also a spokesperson for the National Organization for Men Against Sexism (NOMAS) and has served as an expert witness for the U.S. Department of Justice in two key sex discrimination cases against military academies which had excluded women. His most recent work, coauthored by Michael Kaufman, is *The Guy's Guide to Feminism* (2011).

WHENEVER I ASK YOUNG WOMEN what they think it means to be a woman, they look at me puzzled, and say, basically, "Whatever I want." "It doesn't mean anything at all to me," says Nicole, a junior at Colby College in Maine. "I can be Mia Hamm, I can be Britney Spears, I can be Madame Curie or Madonna. Nobody can tell me what it means to be a woman anymore."

For men, the question is still meaningful—and powerful. In countless workshops on college campuses and in high-school assemblies, I've asked young men what it means to be a man. I've asked guys from every state in the nation, as well as about fifteen other countries, what sorts of phrases and words come to mind when they hear someone say, "Be a man!"[1]

The responses are rather predictable. The first thing someone usually says is "Don't cry," then other similar phrases and ideas—never show your feelings, never ask for directions, never give up, never give in, be strong, be aggressive, show no fear, show no mercy, get rich, get even, get laid, win—follow easily after that.

Here's what guys say, summarized into a set of current epigrams. Think of it as a "Real Guy's Top Ten List."

1. "Boys Don't Cry"

2. "It's Better to be Mad than Sad"

3. "Don't Get Mad—Get Even"

4. "Take It Like a Man"

5. "He Who has the Most Toys When he Dies, Wins"

6. "Just Do It," or "Ride or Die"

7. "Size Matters"

8. "I Don't Stop to Ask for Directions"

9. "Nice Guys Finish Last"

10. "It's All Good"

The unifying emotional subtext of all these aphorisms involves 5 never showing emotions or admitting to weakness. The face you must show to the world insists that everything is going just fine, that everything is under control, that there's nothing to be concerned about (a contemporary version of Alfred E. Neuman of *MAD* magazine's "What, me worry?"). Winning is crucial, especially when the victory is over other men who have less amazing or smaller toys. Kindness is not an option, nor is compassion. Those sentiments are taboo.

This is "The Guy Code," the collection of attitudes, values, and traits that together composes what it means to be a man. These are the rules that govern behavior in Guyland, the criteria that will be used to evaluate whether any particular guy measures up. The Guy Code revisits what psychologist William Pollack called "the boy code" in his

---

[1]*hear someone say, "Be a man!":* This workshop idea was developed by Paul Kivel of the Oakland Men's Project. I am grateful to Paul for demonstrating it to my classes. [All notes are Kimmel's.]

bestselling book *Real Boys*[2]—just a couple of years older and with a lot more at stake. And just as Pollack and others have explored the dynamics of boyhood so well, we now need to extend the reach of that analysis to include late adolescence and young adulthood.

[2]*Real Boys:* See William Pollack, *Real Boys: Rescuing Our Sons from the Myths of Boyhood* (New York: Henry Holt, 1998).

In 1976, social psychologist Robert Brannon summarized the four basic rules of masculinity:[3]

1. "No Sissy Stuff!" Being a man means not being a sissy, not being perceived as weak, effeminate, or gay. Masculinity is the relentless repudiation of the feminine.

2. "Be a Big Wheel." This rule refers to the centrality of success and power in the definition of masculinity. Masculinity is measured more by wealth, power, and status than by any particular body part.

3. "Be a Sturdy Oak." What makes a man is that he is reliable in a crisis. And what makes him so reliable in a crisis is not that he is able to respond fully and appropriately to the situation at hand, but rather that he resembles an inanimate object. A rock, a pillar, a species of tree.

4. "Give 'em Hell." Exude an aura of daring and aggression. Live life out on the edge. Take risks. Go for it. Pay no attention to what others think.

Amazingly, these four rules have changed very little among successive generations of high-school and college-age men. James O'Neil, a developmental psychologist at the University of Connecticut, and Joseph Pleck, a social psychologist at the University of Illinois, have each been conducting studies of this normative definition of masculinity for decades. "One of the most surprising findings," O'Neil told me, "is how little these rules have changed."

Being a Man Among Men

Where do young men get these ideas? "Oh, definitely, my dad," says Mike, a twenty-year-old sophomore at Wake Forest. "He was always riding my ass, telling me I had to be tough and strong to make it in this world."

"My older brothers were always on my case," says Drew, a twenty-four-year-old University of Massachusetts grad. "They were like, always ragging on me, calling me a pussy, if I didn't want to play football or wrestle. If I just wanted to hang out and like play my Xbox, they were constantly in my face." 10

"It was subtle, sometimes," says Warren, a twenty-one-year-old at Towson, "and other times really out front. In school, it was the male teachers, saying stuff about how explorers or scientists were so courageous and braving the elements and all that. Then, other times, it was phys-ed class, and everyone was all over everyone else talking about 'He's so gay' and 'He's a wuss.'"

[3]*four basic rules of masculinity:* See Robert Brannon and Deborah David, "Introduction" to *The Forty-Nine Per Cent Majority* (Reading, MA: Addison-Wesley, 1976).

"The first thing I think of is my coach," says Don, a twenty-six-year-old former football player at Lehigh. "Any fatigue, any weakness, any sign that being hit actually hurt and he was like 'Waah! [fake crying] Widdle Donny got a boo boo. Should we kiss it guys?' He'd completely humiliate us for showing anything but complete toughness. I'm sure he thought he was building up our strength and ability to play, but it wore me out trying to pretend all the time, to suck it up and just take it."

The response was consistent: Guys hear the voices of the men in their lives—fathers, coaches, brothers, grandfathers, uncles, priests—to inform their ideas of masculinity.

This is no longer surprising to me. One of the more startling things I found when I researched the history of the idea of masculinity in America for a previous book was that men subscribe to these ideals not because they want to impress women, let alone any inner drive or desire to test themselves against some abstract standards. They do it because they want to be positively evaluated by other men. American men want to be a "man among men," an Arnold Schwarzenegger-like "man's man," not a Fabio-like "ladies' man." Masculinity is largely a "homosocial" experience: performed for, and judged by, other men.

Noted playwright David Mamet explains why women don't even enter the mix. "Women have, in men's minds, such a low place on the social ladder of this country that it's useless to define yourself in terms of a woman. What men need is men's approval." While women often become a kind of currency by which men negotiate their status with other men, women are for possessing, not for emulating.

The Gender Police

Other guys constantly watch how well we perform. Our peers are a kind of "gender police," always waiting for us to screw up so they can give us a ticket for crossing the well-drawn boundaries of manhood. As young men, we become relentless cowboys, riding the fences, checking the boundary line between masculinity and femininity, making sure that nothing slips over. The possibilities of being unmasked are everywhere. Even the most seemingly insignificant misstep can pose a threat or activate that haunting terror that we will be found out.

On the day the students in my class "Sociology of Masculinity" were scheduled to discuss homophobia, one student provided an honest and revealing anecdote. Noting that it was a beautiful day, the first day of spring after a particularly brutal Northeast winter, he decided to wear shorts to class. "I had this really nice pair of new Madras shorts," he recounted. "But then I thought to myself, these shorts have lavender and pink in them. Today's class topic is homophobia. Maybe today is not the best day to wear these shorts." Nods all around.

Our efforts to maintain a manly front cover everything we do. What we wear. How we talk. How we walk. What we eat (like the recent

flap over "manwiches"—those artery-clogging massive burgers, dripping with extras). Every mannerism, every movement contains a coded
gender language. What happens if you refuse or resist? What happens
if you step outside the definition of masculinity? Consider the words
that would be used to describe you. In workshops it generally takes less
than a minute to get a list of about twenty terms that are at the tip of
everyone's tongues: wimp, faggot, dork, pussy, loser, wuss, nerd, queer,
homo, girl, gay, skirt, Mama's boy, pussy-whipped. This list is so effort-
lessly generated, so consistent, that it composes a national well from
which to draw epithets and put-downs.

Ask any teenager in America what is the most common put-down
in middle school or high school? The answer: "That's so gay." It's said
about anything and everything—their clothes, their books, the music or
TV shows they like, the sports figures they admire. "That's so gay" has
become a free-floating put-down, meaning bad, dumb, stupid, wrong.
It's the generic bad thing.

Listen to one of America's most observant analysts of masculinity, 20
Eminem. Asked in an MTV interview in 2001 why he constantly used
"faggot" in every one of his raps to put down other guys, Eminem told
the interviewer, Kurt Loder,

> The lowest degrading thing you can say to a man when you're battling
> him is to call him a faggot and try to take away his manhood. Call him
> a sissy, call him a punk. "Faggot" to me doesn't necessarily mean gay
> people. "Faggot" to me just means taking away your manhood.[4]

But does it mean homosexuality? Does it really suggest that you
suspect the object of the epithet might actually be attracted to another
guy? Think, for example, of how you would answer this question: If you
see a man walking down the street, or meet him at a party, how do you
"know" if he is homosexual? (Assume that he is not wearing a T-shirt
with a big pink triangle on it, and that he's not already holding hands
with another man.)

When I ask this question in classes or workshops, respondents invariably provide a standard list of stereotypically effeminate behaviors.
He walks a certain way, talks a certain way, acts a certain way. He's well
dressed, sensitive, and emotionally expressive. He has certain tastes in
art and music—indeed, he has *any* taste in art and music! Men tend
to focus on the physical attributes, women on the emotional. Women
say they "suspect" a man might be gay if he's interested in what she's
talking about, knows something about what she's talking about, or is
sensitive and a good listener. One recently said, "I suspect he might be
gay if he's looking at my eyes, and not down my blouse." Another said
she suspects he might be gay if he shows no sexual interest in her, if he
doesn't immediately come on to her.

---

[4]*The lowest...your manhood:* Richard Kim, "A Bad Rap?" in *The Nation*, March 5,
2001, p. 5.

Once I've established what makes a guy "suspect," I ask the men in the room if any of them would want to be thought of as gay. Rarely does a hand go up—despite the fact that this list of attributes is actually far preferable to the restrictive one that stands in the "Be a Man" box. So, what do straight men do to make sure that no one gets the wrong idea about them?

Everything that is perceived as gay goes into what we might call the Negative Playbook of Guyland. Avoid everything in it and you'll be all right. Just make sure that you walk, talk, and act in a different way from the gay stereotype; dress terribly; show no taste in art or music; show no emotions at all. Never listen to a thing a woman is saying, but express immediate and unquenchable sexual interest. Presto, you're a real man, back in the "Be a Man" box. Homophobia—the fear that people might *misperceive* you as gay—is the animating fear of American guys' masculinity. It's what lies underneath the crazy risk-taking behaviors practiced by boys of all ages, what drives the fear that other guys will see you as weak, unmanly, frightened. The single cardinal rule of manhood, the one from which all the other characteristics—wealth, power, status, strength, physicality—are derived is to offer constant proof that you are not gay.

Homophobia is even deeper than this. It's the fear *of* other men— that other men will perceive you as a failure, as a fraud. It's a fear that others will see you as weak, unmanly, frightened. This is how John Steinbeck put it in his novel *Of Mice and Men*: 25

> "Funny thing," [Curley's wife] said. "If I catch any one man, and he's alone, I get along fine with him. But just let two of the guys get together an' you won't talk. Jus' nothin' but mad." She dropped her fingers and put her hands on her hips. "You're all scared of each other, that's what. Ever'one of you's scared the rest is goin' to get something on you."[5]

In that sense, homosexuality becomes a kind of shorthand for "unmanliness"—and the homophobia that defines and animates the daily conversations of Guyland is at least as much about masculinity as it is about sexuality.

But what would happen to a young man if he were to refuse such limiting parameters on who he is and how he's permitted to act? "It's not like I want to stay in that box," says Jeff, a first-year Cornell student at my workshop. "But as soon as you step outside it, even for a second, all the other guys are like, 'What are you, dude, a fag?' It's not very safe out there on your own. I suppose as I get older, I'll get more secure, and feel like I couldn't care less what other guys say. But now, in my fraternity, on this campus, man, I'd lose everything."

The consistency of responses is as arresting as the list is disturbing: "I would lose my friends." "Get beat up." "I'd be ostracized." "Lose my self-esteem." Some say they'd take drugs or drink. Become withdrawn,

---

[5]John Steinbeck, *Of Mice and Men* (New York: Scribner's, 1937), p. 57.

sullen, a loner, depressed. "Kill myself," says one guy. "Kill them," responds another. Everyone laughs, nervously. Some say they'd get mad. And some say they'd get even. "I dunno," replied Mike, a sophomore at Portland State University. "I'd probably pull a Columbine. I'd show them that they couldn't get away with calling me that shit."

Guys know that they risk everything—their friendships, their sense of self, maybe even their lives—if they fail to conform. Since the stakes are so enormous, young men take huge chances to prove their manhood, exposing themselves to health risks, workplace hazards, and stress-related illnesses. Here's a revealing factoid. Men ages nineteen to twenty-nine are three times less likely to wear seat belts than women the same age. Before they turn nineteen though, young men are actually *more* likely to wear seat belts. It's as if they suddenly get the idea that as long as they're driving the car, they're completely in control, and therefore safe.[6] Ninety percent of all driving offenses, excluding parking violations, are committed by men, and 93 percent of road ragers are male.[7] Safety is emasculating! So they drink too much, drive too fast, and play chicken in a multitude of dangerous venues.

The comments above provide a telling riposte to all those theories 30 of biology that claim that this definition of masculinity is "hard-wired," the result of millennia of evolutionary adaptation or the behavioral response to waves of aggression-producing testosterone, and therefore inevitable. What these theories fail to account for is the way that masculinity is coerced and policed relentlessly by other guys. If it were biological, it would be as natural as breathing or blinking. In truth, the Guy Code fits as comfortably as a straightjacket.

Boys' Psychological Development: Where the Guy Code Begins

Masculinity is a constant test—always up for grabs, always needing to be proved. And the testing starts early. Recently, I was speaking with a young black mother, a social worker, who was concerned about a conversation she had had with her husband a few nights earlier. It seems that her husband had taken their son to the barber, which, she explained to me, is a central social institution in the African American community. As the barber prepared the boy's hair for treatment, using, apparently some heat and some painful burning chemicals, the boy began to cry. The barber turned to the boy's father and pronounced, "This boy is a wimp!" He went on, "This boy has been spending too much time with his mama! Man, you need to put your foot down. You have got to get this boy away from his mother!"

[6]*completely in control, and therefore safe:* Eric Nagourney, "Young Men with No Attachments" in *New York Times*, January 4, 2005.
[7]*and 93 percent of road ragers are male:* Mary Blume, "The Feminist Future of the Automobile" in *International Herald Tribune*, October 8, 2004, p. 11.

That evening the father came home, visibly shaken by the episode, and announced to his wife that from that moment on the boy would not be spending as much time with her, but instead would do more sports and other activities with him, "to make sure he doesn't become a sissy."

After telling me this story, the mother asked what I thought she should do. "Gee," I said, "I understand the pressures that dads feel to 'toughen up' their sons. But how old is your boy, anyway?"

"Three and a half," she said.

I tried to remind her, of course, that crying is the natural human response to pain, and that her son was behaving appropriately. But her story reminded me of how early this pressure starts to affect an emotionally impervious manly stoicism.

Ever since Freud, we've believed that the key to boys' development is separation, that the boy must switch his identification from mother to father in order to "become" a man. He achieves his masculinity by repudiation, dissociation, and then identification. It is a perilous path, but a necessary one, even though there is nothing inevitable about it—and nothing biological either. Throw in an overdominant mother, or an absent father, and we start worrying that the boy will not succeed in his masculine quest.

Boys learn that their connection to mother will emasculate them, turn them into Mama's Boys. And so they learn to act *as if* they have made that leap by pushing away from their mothers. Along the way they suppress all the feelings they associate with the maternal—compassion, nurturance, vulnerability, dependency. This suppression and repudiation is the origin of the Boy Code. It's what turns those happy, energetic, playful, and emotionally expressive five-year-olds into sullen, withdrawn, and despondent nine-year-olds. In the recent spate of bestselling books about boys' development, psychologists like William Pollack, James Garbarino, Michael Thompson, Dan Kindlon, and others, argue that from an early age boys are taught to refrain from crying, to suppress their emotions, never to display vulnerability. As a result, boys feel effeminate not only if they *express* their emotions, but even if they *feel* them. In their bestseller, *Raising Cain*, Kindlon and Thompson describe a "culture of cruelty" in which peers force other boys to deny their emotional needs and disguise their feelings. It's no wonder that so many boys end up feeling emotionally isolated.

These books about boys map the inner despair that comes from such emotional numbness and fear of vulnerability. Pollack calls it the "mask of masculinity," the fake front of impervious, unemotional independence, a swaggering posture that boys believe will help them to present a stoic front. "Ruffled in a manly pose," the great Irish poet William Butler Yeats put it in his poem "Coole Park" (1929), "For all his timid heart."

The ruffling starts often by age four or five, when he enters kindergarten, and it gets a second jolt when he hits adolescence. Think of the messages boys get: Stand on your own two feet! Don't cry! Don't be a sissy! As one boy in Pollack's book summarizes it: "Shut up and take it, or you'll be sorry." When I asked my nine-year-old son, Zachary, what he thought of when I said "be a man" he said that one of his friends said something about "taking it like a man. So," he explained, "I think it means acting tougher than you actually are."

Recently a colleague told me about a problem he was having. It [40] seems his seven-year-old son, James, was being bullied by another boy on his way home from school. His wife, the boy's mother, strategized with her son about how to handle such situations in the future. She suggested he find an alternate route home, tell a teacher, or perhaps even tell the boy's parents. And she offered the standard "use your words, not your fists" conflict-reducer. "How can I get my wife to stop treating James like a baby?" my colleague asked. "How will he ever learn to stand up for himself if she turns him into a wimp?"

The Boy Code leaves boys disconnected from a wide range of emotions and prohibited from sharing those feelings with others. As they grow older, they feel disconnected from adults, as well, unable to experience the guidance towards maturity that adults can bring. When they turn to anger and violence it is because these, they believe, perhaps rightly, are the only acceptable forms of emotional expression allowed them. Just as the Boy Code shuts boys down, the Guy Code reinforces those messages, suppressing what was left of boyhood exuberance and turning it into sullen indifference.

No wonder boys are more prone to depression, suicidal behavior, and various other forms of out-of-control or out-of-touch behaviors than girls are. No wonder boys drop out of school and are diagnosed as emotionally disturbed four times more often as girls, get into fights twice as often, and are six times more likely than girls to be diagnosed with Attention Deficit and Hyperactivity Disorder (ADHD).[8]

ENGAGING THE TEXT

1. What are the "rules" associated with the Guy Code, according to Kimmel? To what extent do these rules reflect your own understanding of what it means to be a man? Discuss Kimmel's assertion that "the Guy Code fits as comfortably as a straightjacket" (para. 30).

2. Outline the psychology of the Guy Code: How do boys become men, according to Kimmel, and how does their development affect their emotional lives and relationships with others?

3. Kimmel writes that "masculinity is coerced and policed relentlessly by other guys" (para. 30). Write a journal entry detailing any encounters you've observed or experienced that involve such "gender police." What happened,

[8]*No wonder...Hyperactivity Disorder:* See, for example, Brad Knickerbocker, "Young and Male in America: It's Hard Being a Boy" in *Christian Science Monitor*, April 29, 1999.

and how did you react at the time? Did the incident(s) have any lasting effect on your thinking or behavior? If so, how and why?

4. Kimmel argues that homophobia plays a central role in defining and reinforcing the Guy Code. What evidence do you see that young men are or are not pressured "to offer constant proof that [they] are not gay" (para. 24)?

EXPLORING CONNECTIONS

5. In what ways does Kimmel's analysis of American masculinity help to explain the violence and misogyny described by Jean Kilbourne (p. 420) and Joan Morgan (p. 455)? What other factors contribute to these problems?

6. How does the image on page 463 reflect both the rewards and the costs of the Guy Code? How do you interpret the meaning and placement of the "Think again" message?

EXTENDING THE CRITICAL CONTEXT

7. Working in small groups, try to come up with a list of "rules" you associate with being a woman. As a class, debate whether or not a Girl Code exists, and if so, what it consists of and how it's taught and reinforced.

8. For one full day, keep track of every time you hear the word "gay" used as a pejorative term in conversation or in the media. In each case, is the speaker male or female? Who or what is he or she referring to? Is he joking or serious? Bring your notes to class to compare with others' observations. Do your findings bear out Kimmel's assertion that "Homophobia ... is the animating fear of American guys' masculinity" (para. 24)?

THE END OF MEN

HANNA ROSIN

Hanna Rosin's "The End of Men" created a firestorm when it first appeared as the cover story of the *Atlantic Monthly* (July/August 2010). Feminist critics said that her emphasis on women's success distracted from the real problems facing them, and many men found the idea that men were "toast" insulting. In her wide-ranging essay, Rosin asserts that the postindustrial economy favors women over men. Relying on interviews and statistics, she touches on the decline of the Marlboro Man, the rise of female professionals, the decreasing influence of manufacturing, and the failure of men to adapt to the changing needs of the new economy. Rosin is a senior editor at the *Atlantic*, which has featured other controversial articles by her, including "The Case Against

Breastfeeding." She is currently working on a book-length version of "The End of Men"; her first book, *God's Harvard: A Christian College on a Mission to Save America,* was published in 2007. Her work has also appeared in the *New Republic,* the *New Yorker, GQ,* and the *Washington Post.*

IN THE 1970s the biologist Ronald Ericsson came up with a way to separate sperm carrying the male-producing Y chromosome from those carrying the X. He sent the two kinds of sperm swimming down a glass tube through ever-thicker albumin barriers. The sperm with the X chromosome had a larger head and a longer tail, and so, he figured, they would get bogged down in the viscous liquid. The sperm with the Y chromosome were leaner and faster and could swim down to the bottom of the tube more efficiently. Ericsson had grown up on a ranch in South Dakota, where he'd developed an Old West, cowboy swagger. The process, he said, was like "cutting out cattle at the gate." The cattle left flailing behind the gate were of course the X's, which seemed to please him. He would sometimes demonstrate the process using cartilage from a bull's penis as a pointer.

In the late 1970s, Ericsson leased the method to clinics around the U.S., calling it the first scientifically proven method for choosing the sex of a child. Instead of a lab coat, he wore cowboy boots and a cowboy hat, and doled out his version of cowboy poetry. (*People* magazine once suggested a TV miniseries based on his life called *Cowboy in the Lab.*) The right prescription for life, he would say, was "breakfast at five-thirty, on the saddle by six, no room for Mr. Limp Wrist." In 1979, he loaned out his ranch as the backdrop for the iconic "Marlboro Country" ads because he believed in the campaign's central image — "a guy riding on his horse along the river, no bureaucrats, no lawyers," he recalled when I spoke to him this spring. "He's the boss." (The photographers took some 6,500 pictures, a pictorial record of the frontier that Ericsson still takes great pride in.)

Feminists of the era did not take kindly to Ericsson and his Marlboro Man veneer. To them, the lab cowboy and his sperminator portended a dystopia of mass-produced boys. "You have to be concerned about the future of all women," Roberta Steinbacher, a nun-turned-social-psychologist, said in a 1984 *People* profile of Ericsson. "There's no question that there exists a universal preference for sons." Steinbacher went on to complain about women becoming locked in as "second-class citizens" while men continued to dominate positions of control and influence. "I think women have to ask themselves, 'Where does this stop?'" she said. "A lot of us wouldn't be here right now if these practices had been in effect years ago."

Ericsson, now 74, laughed when I read him these quotes from his old antagonist. Seldom has it been so easy to prove a dire prediction wrong. In the '90s, when Ericsson looked into the numbers for the two dozen or so clinics that use his process, he discovered, to his surprise, that couples were requesting more girls than boys, a gap that has persisted, even though Ericsson advertises the method as more effective for producing boys. In some clinics, Ericsson has said, the ratio is now as high as 2 to 1. Polling data on American sex preference is sparse, and does not show a clear preference for girls. But the picture from the doctor's office unambiguously does. A newer method for sperm selection, called MicroSort, is currently completing Food and Drug Administration clinical trials. The girl requests for that method run at about 75 percent.

Even more unsettling for Ericsson, it has become clear that in choosing the sex of the next generation, *he* is no longer the boss. "It's the women who are driving all the decisions," he says—a change the MicroSort spokespeople I met with also mentioned. At first, Ericsson says, women who called his clinics would apologize and shyly explain that they already had two boys. "Now they just call and [say] outright, 'I want a girl.' These mothers look at their lives and think their daughters will have a bright future their mother and grandmother didn't have, brighter than their sons, even, so why wouldn't you choose a girl?"

Why wouldn't you choose a girl? That such a statement should be so casually uttered by an old cowboy like Ericsson—or by anyone, for that matter—is monumental. For nearly as long as civilization has existed, patriarchy—enforced through the rights of the firstborn son—has been the organizing principle, with few exceptions. Men in ancient Greece tied off their left testicle in an effort to produce male heirs; women have killed themselves (or been killed) for failing to bear sons. In her iconic 1949 book, *The Second Sex*, the French feminist Simone de Beauvoir suggested that women so detested their own "feminine condition" that they regarded their newborn daughters with irritation and disgust. Now the centuries-old preference for sons is eroding—or even reversing. "Women of our generation want daughters precisely because we like who we are," breezes one woman in *Cookie* magazine. Even Ericsson, the stubborn old goat, can sigh and mark the passing of an era. "Did male dominance exist? Of course it existed. But it seems to be gone now. And the era of the firstborn son is totally gone."

Ericsson's extended family is as good an illustration of the rapidly shifting landscape as any other. His 26-year-old granddaughter—"tall, slender, brighter than hell, with a take-no-prisoners personality"—is a biochemist and works on genetic sequencing. His niece studied civil engineering at the University of Southern California. His grandsons, he says, are bright and handsome, but in school "their eyes glaze over. I have to tell 'em: 'Just don't screw up and crash your pickup truck and get some girl pregnant and ruin your life.'" Recently Ericsson joked with the old boys at his elementary-school reunion that he was going to have a sex-change operation. "Women live longer than men. They do better in this economy. More of 'em graduate from college. They go into space and do everything men do, and sometimes they do it a whole lot better. I mean, hell, get out of the way—these females are going to leave us males in the dust."

Man has been the dominant sex since, well, the dawn of mankind. But for the first time in human history, that is changing—and with shocking speed. Cultural and economic changes always reinforce each other. And the global economy is evolving in a way that is eroding the historical preference for male children, worldwide. Over several centuries, South Korea, for instance, constructed one of the most rigid patriarchal societies in the world. Many wives who failed to produce male heirs were abused and treated as domestic servants; some families prayed to spirits to kill off girl children. Then, in the 1970s and '80s, the government embraced an industrial revolution and encouraged women to enter the labor force. Women moved to the city and went to college. They advanced rapidly, from industrial jobs to clerical jobs to professional work. The traditional order began to crumble soon after. In 1990, the country's laws were revised so that women could keep custody of their children after a divorce and inherit property. In 2005, the court ruled that women could register children under their own names. As recently as 1985, about half of all women in a national survey said they "must have a son." That percentage fell slowly until 1991 and then plummeted to just over 15 percent by 2003. Male preference in South Korea "is over," says Monica Das Gupta, a demographer and Asia expert at the World Bank. "It happened so fast. It's hard to believe it, but it is." The same shift is now beginning in other rapidly industrializing countries such as India and China.

Up to a point, the reasons behind this shift are obvious. As thinking and communicating have come to eclipse physical strength and stamina as the keys to economic success, those societies that take advantage of the talents of all their adults, not just half of them, have pulled away from the rest. And because geopolitics and global culture are, ultimately, Darwinian,[1] other societies either follow suit or end up marginalized. In 2006, the Organization for Economic Cooperation and Development devised the Gender, Institutions and Development Database, which measures the economic and political power of women in 162 countries. With few exceptions, the greater the power of women, the greater the country's economic success. Aid agencies have started to recognize this relationship and have pushed to institute political quotas in about 100 countries, essentially forcing women into power in an effort to improve those countries' fortunes. In some war-torn states, women are stepping in as a sort of maternal rescue team. Liberia's president, Ellen Johnson Sirleaf, portrayed her country as a sick child in need of her care during her campaign five years ago. Postgenocide Rwanda elected to heal itself by becoming the first country with a majority of women in parliament.

---

[1]*Darwinian:* Refers to Charles Darwin (1809–1882), whose theory of competition and natural selection is often (mis)used to apply to society.

In feminist circles, these social, political, and economic changes are [10] always cast as a slow, arduous form of catch-up in a continuing struggle for female equality. But in the U.S., the world's most advanced economy, something much more remarkable seems to be happening. American parents are beginning to choose to have girls over boys. As they imagine the pride of watching a child grow and develop and succeed as an adult, it is more often a girl that they see in their mind's eye.

What if the modern, postindustrial economy is simply more congenial to women than to men? For a long time, evolutionary psychologists have claimed that we are all imprinted with adaptive imperatives from a distant past: men are faster and stronger and hardwired to fight for scarce resources, and that shows up now as a drive to win on Wall Street; women are programmed to find good providers and to care for their offspring, and that is manifested in more-nurturing and more-flexible behavior, ordaining them to domesticity. This kind of thinking frames our sense of the natural order. But what if men and women were fulfilling not biological imperatives but social roles, based on what was more efficient throughout a long era of human history? What if that era has now come to an end? More to the point, what if the economics of the new era are better suited to women?

Once you open your eyes to this possibility, the evidence is all around you. It can be found, most immediately, in the wreckage of the Great Recession,[2] in which three-quarters of the 8 million jobs lost were lost by men. The worst-hit industries were overwhelmingly male and deeply identified with macho: construction, manufacturing, high finance. Some of these jobs will come back, but the overall pattern of dislocation is neither temporary nor random. The recession merely revealed—and accelerated—a profound economic shift that has been going on for at least 30 years, and in some respects even longer.

Earlier this year, for the first time in American history, the balance of the workforce tipped toward women, who now hold a majority of the nation's jobs. The working class, which has long defined our notions of masculinity, is slowly turning into a matriarchy, with men increasingly absent from the home and women making all the decisions. Women dominate today's colleges and professional schools—for every two men who will receive a B.A. this year, three women will do the same. Of the 15 job categories projected to grow the most in the next decade in the U.S., all but two are occupied primarily by women. Indeed, the U.S. economy is in some ways becoming a kind of traveling sisterhood: upper-class women leave home and enter the workforce, creating domestic jobs for other women to fill.

The postindustrial economy is indifferent to men's size and strength. The attributes that are most valuable today—social intelligence, open

---

[2]*The Great Recession:* The financial collapse of 2008 is considered to be the most serious economic crisis since the Great Depression.

communication, the ability to sit still and focus—are, at a minimum, not predominantly male. In fact, the opposite may be true. Women in poor parts of India are learning English faster than men to meet the demands of new global call centers. Women own more than 40 percent of private businesses in China, where a red Ferrari is the new status symbol for female entrepreneurs. Last year, Iceland elected Prime Minister Johanna Sigurdardottir, the world's first openly lesbian head of state, who campaigned explicitly against the male elite she claimed had destroyed the nation's banking system, and who vowed to end the "age of testosterone."

Yes, the U.S. still has a wage gap, one that can be convincingly 15 explained—at least in part—by discrimination. Yes, women still do most of the child care. And yes, the upper reaches of society are still dominated by men. But given the power of the forces pushing at the economy, this setup feels like the last gasp of a dying age rather than the permanent establishment. Dozens of college women I interviewed for this story assumed that they very well might be the ones working while their husbands stayed at home, either looking for work or minding the children. Guys, one senior remarked to me, "are the new ball and chain." It may be happening slowly and unevenly, but it's unmistakably happening: in the long view, the modern economy is becoming a place where women hold the cards.

In his final book, *The Bachelors' Ball*, published in 2007, the sociologist Pierre Bourdieu describes the changing gender dynamics of Béarn, the region in southwestern France where he grew up. The eldest sons once held the privileges of patrimonial loyalty and filial inheritance in Béarn. But over the decades, changing economic forces turned those privileges into curses. Although the land no longer produced the impressive income it once had, the men felt obligated to tend it. Meanwhile, modern women shunned farm life, lured away by jobs and adventure in the city. They occasionally returned for the traditional balls, but the men who awaited them had lost their prestige and become unmarriageable. This is the image that keeps recurring to me, one that Bourdieu describes in his book: at the bachelors' ball, the men, self-conscious about their diminished status, stand stiffly, their hands by their sides, as the women twirl away.

The role reversal that's under way between American men and women shows up most obviously and painfully in the working class. In recent years, male support groups have sprung up throughout the Rust Belt and in other places where the postindustrial economy has turned traditional family roles upside down. Some groups help men cope with unemployment, and others help them reconnect with their alienated families. Mustafaa El-Scari, a teacher and social worker, leads some of these groups in Kansas City. El-Scari has studied the sociology of men and boys set adrift, and he considers it his special gift to get them to open up and reflect on their new condition. The day I visited one of his classes, earlier this year, he was facing a particularly resistant crowd.

None of the 30 or so men sitting in a classroom at a downtown Kansas City school have come for voluntary adult enrichment. Having failed to pay their child support, they were given the choice by a judge to go to jail or attend a weekly class on fathering, which to them seemed the better deal. This week's lesson, from a workbook called *Quenching the Father Thirst*, was supposed to involve writing a letter to a hypothetical estranged 14-year-old daughter named Crystal, whose father left her when she was a baby. But El-Scari has his own idea about how to get through to this barely awake, skeptical crew, and letters to Crystal have nothing to do with it.

Like them, he explains, he grew up watching Bill Cosby[3] living behind his metaphorical "white picket fence" — one man, one woman, and a bunch of happy kids. "Well, that check bounced a long time ago," he says. "Let's see," he continues, reading from a worksheet. What are the four kinds of paternal authority? Moral, emotional, social, and physical. "But you ain't none of those in that house. All you are is a paycheck, and now you ain't even that. And if you try to exercise your authority, she'll call 911. How does that make you feel? You're supposed to be the authority, and she says, 'Get out of the house, bitch.' She's calling you 'bitch'!"

The men are black and white, their ages ranging from about 20 to 40. A couple look like they might have spent a night or two on the streets, but the rest look like they work, or used to. Now they have put down their sodas, and El-Scari has their attention, so he gets a little more philosophical. "Who's doing what?" he asks them. "What is our role? Everyone's telling us we're supposed to be the head of a nuclear family, so you feel like you got robbed. It's toxic, and poisonous, and it's setting us up for failure." He writes on the board: $85,000. "This is her salary." Then: $12,000. "This is your salary. Who's the damn man? Who's the man now?" A murmur rises. "That's right. She's the man."

Judging by the men I spoke with afterward, El-Scari seemed to have pegged his audience perfectly. Darren Henderson was making $33 an hour laying sheet metal, until the real-estate crisis hit and he lost his job. Then he lost his duplex — "there's my little piece of the American dream" — then his car. And then he fell behind on his child-support payments. "They make it like I'm just sitting around," he said, "but I'm not." As proof of his efforts, he took out a new commercial driver's permit and a bartending license, and then threw them down on the ground like jokers, for all the use they'd been. His daughter's mother had a $50,000-a-year job and was getting her master's degree in social work. He'd just signed up for food stamps, which is just about the only social-welfare program a man can easily access. Recently she'd seen him waiting at the bus stop. "Looked me in the eye," he recalled, "and just drove on by."

---

[3] *Bill Cosby:* William Henry Cosby, comedian well known for his family sitcom, *The Cosby Show.*

The men in that room, almost without exception, were casualties of the end of the manufacturing era. Most of them had continued to work with their hands even as demand for manual labor was declining. Since 2000, manufacturing has lost almost 6 million jobs, more than a third of its total workforce, and has taken in few young workers. The housing bubble masked this new reality for a while, creating work in construction and related industries. Many of the men I spoke with had worked as electricians or builders; one had been a successful real-estate agent. Now those jobs are gone too. Henderson spent his days shuttling between unemployment offices and job interviews, wondering what his daughter might be doing at any given moment. In 1950, roughly one in 20 men of prime working age, like Henderson, was not working; today that ratio is about one in five, the highest ever recorded.

Men dominate just two of the 15 job categories projected to grow the most over the next decade: janitor and computer engineer. Women have everything else—nursing, home health assistance, child care, food preparation. Many of the new jobs, says Heather Boushey of the Center for American Progress, "replace the things that women used to do in the home for free." None is especially high-paying. But the steady accumulation of these jobs adds up to an economy that, for the working class, has become more amenable to women than to men.

The list of growing jobs is heavy on nurturing professions, in which women, ironically, seem to benefit from old stereotypes and habits. Theoretically, there is no reason men should not be qualified. But they have proved remarkably unable to adapt. Over the course of the past century, feminism has pushed women to do things once considered against their nature—first enter the workforce as singles, then continue to work while married, then work even with small children at home. Many professions that started out as the province of men are now filled mostly with women—secretary and teacher come to mind. Yet I'm not aware of any that have gone the opposite way. Nursing schools have tried hard to recruit men in the past few years, with minimal success. Teaching schools, eager to recruit male role models, are having a similarly hard time. The range of acceptable masculine roles has changed comparatively little, and has perhaps even narrowed as men have shied away from some careers women have entered. As Jessica Grose wrote in *Slate*,[4] men seem "fixed in cultural aspic."[5] And with each passing day, they lag further behind.

As we recover from the Great Recession, some traditionally male 25 jobs will return—men are almost always harder-hit than women in economic downturns because construction and manufacturing are more cyclical than service industries—but that won't change the long-term

[4] *Slate:* Online magazine that deals with politics and culture, often with a humorous bent.
[5] *aspic:* Gelatin mold.

trend. When we look back on this period, argues Jamie Ladge, a business professor at Northeastern University, we will see it as a "turning point for women in the workforce."

The economic and cultural power shift from men to women would be hugely significant even if it never extended beyond working-class America. But women are also starting to dominate middle management, and a surprising number of professional careers as well. According to the Bureau of Labor Statistics, women now hold 51.4 percent of managerial and professional jobs—up from 26.1 percent in 1980. They make up 54 percent of all accountants and hold about half of all banking and insurance jobs. About a third of America's physicians are now women, as are 45 percent of associates in law firms—and both those percentages are rising fast. A white-collar economy values raw intellectual horsepower, which men and women have in equal amounts. It also requires communication skills and social intelligence, areas in which women, according to many studies, have a slight edge. Perhaps most important—for better or worse—it increasingly requires formal education credentials, which women are more prone to acquire, particularly early in adulthood. Just about the only professions in which women still make up a relatively small minority of newly minted workers are engineering and those calling on a hard-science background, and even in those areas, women have made strong gains since the 1970s.

Office work has been steadily adapting to women—and in turn being reshaped by them—for 30 years or more. Joel Garreau picks up on this phenomenon in his 1991 book, *Edge City*, which explores the rise of suburbs that are home to giant swaths of office space along with the usual houses and malls. Companies began moving out of the city in search not only of lower rent but also of the "best educated, most conscientious, most stable workers." They found their brightest prospects among "underemployed females living in middle-class communities on the fringe of the old urban areas." As Garreau chronicles the rise of suburban office parks, he places special emphasis on 1978, the peak year for women entering the workforce. When brawn was off the list of job requirements, women often measured up better than men. They were smart, dutiful, and, as long as employers could make the jobs more convenient for them, more reliable. The 1999 movie *Office Space* was maybe the first to capture how alien and dispiriting the office park can be for men. Disgusted by their jobs and their boss, Peter and his two friends embezzle money and start sleeping through their alarm clocks. At the movie's end, a male co-worker burns down the office park, and Peter abandons desk work for a job in construction.

Near the top of the jobs pyramid, of course, the upward march of women stalls. Prominent female CEOs, past and present, are so rare that they count as minor celebrities, and most of us can tick off their names just from occasionally reading the business pages: Meg Whitman at eBay, Carly Fiorina at Hewlett-Packard, Anne Mulcahy and

Ursula Burns at Xerox, Indra Nooyi[6] at PepsiCo; the accomplishment is considered so extraordinary that Whitman and Fiorina are using it as the basis for political campaigns. Only 3 percent of *Fortune* 500 CEOs are women, and the number has never risen much above that.

But even the way this issue is now framed reveals that men's hold on power in elite circles may be loosening. In business circles, the lack of women at the top is described as a "brain drain" and a crisis of "talent retention." And while female CEOs may be rare in America's largest companies, they are highly prized: last year, they outearned their male counterparts by 43 percent, on average, and received bigger raises.

Even around the delicate question of working mothers, the terms of the conversation are shifting. Last year, in a story about breast-feeding, I complained about how the early years of child rearing keep women out of power positions. But the term *mommy track*[7] is slowly morphing into the gender-neutral *flex time*, reflecting changes in the workforce. For recent college graduates of both sexes, flexible arrangements are at the top of the list of workplace demands, according to a study published last year in the *Harvard Business Review*. And companies eager to attract and retain talented workers and managers are responding. The consulting firm Deloitte, for instance, started what's now considered the model program, called Mass Career Customization, which allows employees to adjust their hours depending on their life stage. The program, Deloitte's Web site explains, solves "a complex issue—one that can no longer be classified as a woman's issue."

"Women are knocking on the door of leadership at the very moment when their talents are especially well matched with the requirements of the day," writes David Gergen in the introduction to *Enlightened Power: How Women Are Transforming the Practice of Leadership.* What are these talents? Once it was thought that leaders should be aggressive and competitive, and that men are naturally more of both. But psychological research has complicated this picture. In lab studies that simulate negotiations, men and women are just about equally assertive and competitive, with slight variations. Men tend to assert themselves in a controlling manner, while women tend to take into account the rights of others, but both styles are equally effective, write the psychologists Alice Eagly and Linda Carli, in their 2007 book, *Through the Labyrinth.*

Over the years, researchers have sometimes exaggerated these differences and described the particular talents of women in crude gender stereotypes: women as more empathetic, as better consensus-seekers and better lateral thinkers; women as bringing a superior moral

30

---

[6]*Meg Whitman...Carly Fiorina...Anne Mulcahy...Ursula Burns...Indra Nooyi:* Of these powerful women executives, only Ursula Burns and Indra Nooyi still hold the positions Rosin mentions; Meg Whitman is now CEO of Hewlett-Packard, Carly Fiorina is engaged in political and philanthropic work, and Anne Mulcahy now chairs the board of trustees at Save the Children.

[7]*mommy track:* Refers to flexible scheduling that allows women to work and raise children.

sensibility to bear on a cutthroat business world. In the '90s, this field of feminist business theory seemed to be forcing the point. But after the latest financial crisis, these ideas have more resonance. Researchers have started looking into the relationship between testosterone and excessive risk, and wondering if groups of men, in some basic hormonal way, spur each other to make reckless decisions. The picture emerging is a mirror image of the traditional gender map: men and markets on the side of the irrational and overemotional, and women on the side of the cool and levelheaded.

We don't yet know with certainty whether testosterone strongly influences business decision-making. But the perception of the ideal business leader is starting to shift. The old model of command and control, with one leader holding all the decision-making power, is considered hidebound. The new model is sometimes called "post-heroic," or "transformational" in the words of the historian and leadership expert James MacGregor Burns. The aim is to behave like a good coach, and channel your charisma to motivate others to be hardworking and creative. The model is not explicitly defined as feminist, but it echoes literature about male-female differences. A program at Columbia Business School, for example, teaches sensitive leadership and social intelligence, including better reading of facial expressions and body language. "We never explicitly say, 'Develop your feminine side,' but it's clear that's what we're advocating," says Jamie Ladge.

A 2008 study attempted to quantify the effect of this more-feminine management style. Researchers at Columbia Business School and the University of Maryland analyzed data on the top 1,500 U.S. companies from 1992 to 2006 to determine the relationship between firm performance and female participation in senior management. Firms that had women in top positions performed better, and this was especially true if the firm pursued what the researchers called an "innovation intensive strategy," in which, they argued, "creativity and collaboration may be especially important"—an apt description of the future economy.

It could be that women boost corporate performance, or it could be that better-performing firms have the luxury of recruiting and keeping high-potential women. But the association is clear: innovative, successful firms are the ones that promote women. The same Columbia-Maryland study ranked America's industries by the proportion of firms that employed female executives, and the bottom of the list reads like the ghosts of the economy past: shipbuilding, real estate, coal, steelworks, machinery.

If you really want to see where the world is headed, of course, looking at the current workforce can get you only so far. To see the future—of the workforce, the economy, and the culture—you need to spend some time at America's colleges and professional schools, where a quiet revolution is under way. More than ever, college is the gateway to economic success, a necessary precondition for moving into the upper-middle class—and increasingly even the middle class. It's this broad, striving middle class that defines our society. And demographically, we can see with absolute clarity that in the coming decades the middle class will be dominated by women.

We've all heard about the collegiate gender gap. But the implications of that gap have not yet been fully digested. Women now earn 60 percent of master's degrees, about half of all law and medical degrees, and 42 percent of all M.B.A.s. Most important, women earn almost 60 percent of all bachelor's degrees—the minimum requirement, in most cases, for an affluent life. In a stark reversal since the 1970s, men are now more likely than women to hold only a high-school diploma. "One would think that if men were acting in a rational way, they would be getting the education they need to get along out there," says Tom Mortenson, a senior scholar at the Pell Institute for the Study of Opportunity in Higher Education. "But they are just failing to adapt."

This spring, I visited a few schools around Kansas City to get a feel for the gender dynamics of higher education. I started at the downtown campus of Metropolitan Community College. Metropolitan is the kind of place where people go to learn practical job skills and keep current with the changing economy, and as in most community colleges these days, men were conspicuously absent. One afternoon, in the basement cafeteria of a nearly windowless brick building, several women were trying to keep their eyes on their biology textbook and ignore the text messages from their babysitters. Another crew was outside the ladies' room, braiding each other's hair. One woman, still in her medical-assistant scrubs, looked like she was about to fall asleep in the elevator between the first and fourth floors.

When Bernard Franklin took over as campus president in 2005, he looked around and told his staff early on that their new priority was to "recruit more boys." He set up mentoring programs and men-only study groups and student associations. He made a special effort to bond with male students, who liked to call him "Suit." "It upset some of my feminists," he recalls. Yet, a few years later, the tidal wave of women continues to wash through the school—they now make up about 70 percent of its students. They come to train to be nurses and teachers—African American women, usually a few years older than traditional college students, and lately, working-class white women from the suburbs seeking a cheap way to earn a credential. As for the men? Well, little has changed. "I recall one guy who was really smart," one of the school's counselors told me. "But he was reading at a sixth-grade level and felt embarrassed in front of the women. He had to hide his books from his friends, who would tease him when he studied. Then came the excuses. 'It's spring, gotta play ball.' 'It's winter, too cold.' He didn't make it."

It makes some economic sense that women attend community colleges—and in fact, all colleges—in greater numbers than men. Women ages 25 to 34 with only a high-school diploma currently have a median income of $25,474, while men in the same position earn $32,469. But it makes sense only up to a point. The well-paid lifetime union job has 40 been disappearing for at least 30 years. Kansas City, for example, has shifted from steel manufacturing to pharmaceuticals and information technologies. "The economy isn't as friendly to men as it once was," says Jacqueline King, of the American Council on Education. "You would think men and women would go to these colleges at the same rate." But they don't.

In 2005, King's group conducted a survey of lower-income adults in college. Men, it turned out, had a harder time committing to school, even when they desperately needed to retool. They tended to start out behind academically, and many felt intimidated by the schoolwork. They reported feeling isolated and were much worse at seeking out fellow students, study groups, or counselors to help them adjust. Mothers going back to school described themselves as good role models for their children. Fathers worried that they were abrogating their responsibilities as breadwinner.

The student gender gap started to feel like a crisis to some people in higher-education circles in the mid-2000s, when it began showing up not just in community and liberal-arts colleges but in the flagship public universities—the UCs and the SUNYs and the UNCs. Like many of those schools, the University of Missouri at Kansas City, a full research university with more than 13,000 students, is now tipping toward 60 percent women, a level many admissions officers worry could permanently shift the atmosphere and reputation of a school. In February, I visited with Ashley Burress, UMKC's student-body president. (The other three student-government officers this school year were also women.) Burress, a cute, short, African American 24-year-old grad student who is getting a doctor-of-pharmacy degree, had many of the same complaints I heard from other young women. Guys high-five each other when they get a C, while girls beat themselves up over a B-minus. Guys play video games in each other's rooms, while girls crowd the study hall. Girls get their degrees with no drama, while guys seem always in danger of drifting away. "In 2012, I will be Dr. Burress," she said. "Will I have to deal with guys who don't even have a bachelor's degree? I would like to date, but I'm putting myself in a really small pool."

UMKC is a working- and middle-class school—the kind of place where traditional sex roles might not be anathema. Yet as I talked to students this spring, I realized how much the basic expectations for men and women had shifted. Many of the women's mothers had established their careers later in life, sometimes after a divorce, and they had urged their daughters to get to their own careers more quickly. They would be a campus of Tracy Flick,[8] except that they seemed neither especially brittle nor secretly falling apart.

Victoria, Michelle, and Erin are sorority sisters. Victoria's mom is a part-time bartender at a hotel. Victoria is a biology major and wants to be a surgeon; soon she'll apply to a bunch of medical schools. She

[8]*Tracy Flick:* Fictional character from the film *Election* (1999).

doesn't want kids for a while, because she knows she'll "be at the hospital, like, 100 hours a week," and when she does have kids, well, she'll "be the hotshot surgeon, and he"—a nameless he—"will be at home playing with the kiddies."

Michelle, a self-described "perfectionist," also has her life mapped 45 out. She's a psychology major and wants to be a family therapist. After college, she will apply to grad school and look for internships. She is well aware of the career-counseling resources on campus. And her fiancé?

> MICHELLE: He's changed majors, like, 16 times. Last week he wanted to be a dentist. This week it's environmental science.
>
> ERIN: Did he switch again this week? When you guys have kids, he'll definitely stay home. Seriously, what does he want to do?
>
> MICHELLE: It depends on the day of the week. Remember last year? It was bio. It really is a joke. But it's not. It's funny, but it's not.

Among traditional college students from the highest-income families, the gender gap pretty much disappears. But the story is not so simple. Wealthier students tend to go to elite private schools, and elite private schools live by their own rules. Quietly, they've been opening up a new frontier in affirmative action, with boys playing the role of the underprivileged applicants needing an extra boost. In 2003, a study by the economists Sandy Baum and Eban Goodstein found that among selective liberal-arts schools, being male raises the chance of college acceptance by 6.5 to 9 percentage points. Now the U.S. Commission on Civil Rights has voted to investigate what some academics have described as the "open secret" that private schools "are discriminating in admissions in order to maintain what they regard as an appropriate gender balance."

Jennifer Delahunty, the dean of admissions and financial aid at Kenyon College, in Ohio, let this secret out in a 2006 *New York Times* op-ed. Gender balance, she wrote back then, is the elephant in the room. And today, she told me, the problem hasn't gone away. A typical female applicant, she said, manages the process herself—lines up the interviews, sets up a campus visit, requests a visit with faculty members. But the college has seen more than one male applicant "sit back on the couch, sometimes with their eyes closed, while their mom tells them where to go and what to do. Sometimes we say, 'What a nice essay his mom wrote,'" she said, in that funny-but-not vein.

To avoid crossing the dreaded 60 percent threshold, admissions officers have created a language to explain away the boys' deficits: "Brain hasn't kicked in yet." "Slow to cook." "Hasn't quite peaked." "Holistic picture." At times Delahunty has become so worried about "overeducated females" and "undereducated males" that she jokes she is getting conspiratorial. She once called her sister, a pediatrician, to vet her latest theory: "Maybe these boys are genetically like canaries in a coal mine,[9] absorbing so many toxins and bad things in the environment that their DNA is shifting. Maybe they're like those frogs—they're more vulnerable or something, so they've gotten deformed."

Clearly, some percentage of boys are just temperamentally unsuited to college, at least at age 18 or 20, but without it, they have a harder time finding their place these days. "Forty years ago, 30 years ago, if you were one of the fairly constant fraction of boys who wasn't ready to learn in high school, there were ways for you to enter the mainstream economy," says Henry Farber, an economist at Princeton. "When you woke up, there were jobs. There were good industrial jobs, so you could have a good industrial, blue-collar career. Now those jobs are gone."

Since the 1980s, as women have flooded colleges, male enroll- 50 ment has grown far more slowly. And the disparities start before college. Throughout the '90s, various authors and researchers agonized over why boys seemed to be failing at every level of education, from elementary school on up, and identified various culprits: a misguided feminism that treated normal boys as incipient harassers (Christina Hoff Sommers); different brain chemistry (Michael Gurian); a demanding, verbally focused curriculum that ignored boys' interests (Richard Whitmire). But again, it's not all that clear that boys have become more dysfunctional—or have changed in any way. What's clear is that schools, like the economy, now value the self-control, focus, and verbal aptitude that seem to come more easily to young girls.

Researchers have suggested any number of solutions. A movement is growing for more all-boys schools and classes, and for respecting the individual learning styles of boys. Some people think that boys should be able to walk around in class, or take more time on tests, or have tests and books that cater to their interests. In their desperation to reach out to boys, some colleges have formed football teams and started engineering programs. Most of these special accommodations sound very much like the kind of affirmative action proposed for women over the years—which in itself is an alarming flip.

Whether boys have changed or not, we are well past the time to start trying some experiments. It is fabulous to see girls and young women poised for success in the coming years. But allowing generations of boys to grow up feeling rootless and obsolete is not a recipe for a peaceful future. Men have few natural support groups and little access to social welfare; the men's-rights groups that do exist in the U.S. are taking on an angry, antiwoman edge. Marriages fall apart or never happen at all, and children are raised with no fathers. Far from being celebrated, women's rising power is perceived as a threat.

What would a society in which women are on top look like? We already have an inkling. This is the first time that the cohort of Americans

[9]*canaries in a coal mine:* Miners used to take a caged canary with them into the coal mine; if toxic gasses were present, the canary would sicken or die; hence an early warning.

ages 30 to 44 has more college-educated women than college-educated men, and the effects are upsetting the traditional Cleaver-family dynamics.[10] In 1970, women contributed 2 to 6 percent of the family income. Now the typical working wife brings home 42.2 percent, and four in 10 mothers—many of them single mothers—are the primary breadwinners in their families. The whole question of whether mothers should work is moot, argues Heather Boushey of the Center for American Progress, "because they just do. This idealized family—he works, she stays home—hardly exists anymore."

The terms of marriage have changed radically since 1970. Typically, women's income has been the main factor in determining whether a family moves up the class ladder or stays stagnant. And increasing numbers of women—unable to find men with a similar income and education—are forgoing marriage altogether. In 1970, 84 percent of women ages 30 to 44 were married; now 60 percent are. In 2007, among American women without a high-school diploma, 43 percent were married. And yet, for all the hand-wringing over the lonely spinster, the real loser in society—the only one to have made just slight financial gains since the 1970s—is the single man, whether poor or rich, college-educated or not. Hens rejoice; it's the bachelor party that's over.

The sociologist Kathryn Edin spent five years talking with low- 55 income mothers in the inner suburbs of Philadelphia. Many of these neighborhoods, she found, had turned into matriarchies, with women making all the decisions and dictating what the men should and should not do. "I think something feminists have missed," Edin told me, "is how much power women have" when they're not bound by marriage. The women, she explained, "make every important decision"—whether to have a baby, how to raise it, where to live. "It's definitely 'my way or the highway,'" she said. "Thirty years ago, cultural norms were such that the fathers might have said, 'Great, catch me if you can.' Now they are desperate to father, but they are pessimistic about whether they can meet her expectations." The women don't want them as husbands, and they have no steady income to provide. So what do they have?

"Nothing," Edin says. "They have nothing. The men were just annihilated in the recession of the '90s, and things never got better. Now it's just awful."

The situation today is not, as Edin likes to say, a "feminist nirvana." The phenomenon of children being born to unmarried parents "has spread to barrios and trailer parks and rural areas and small towns," Edin says, and it is creeping up the class ladder. After staying steady for a while, the portion of American children born to unmarried parents jumped to 40 percent in the past few years. Many of their mothers are struggling financially; the most successful are working and going to

---

[10]*Cleaver-family dynamics:* Refers to the family in *Leave It to Beaver;* mom stayed at home and vacuumed in pearls and high heels.

school and hustling to feed the children, and then falling asleep in the elevator of the community college.

Still, they are in charge. "The family changes over the past four decades have been bad for men and bad for kids, but it's not clear they are bad for women," says W. Bradford Wilcox, the head of the University of Virginia's National Marriage Project.

Over the years, researchers have proposed different theories to explain the erosion of marriage in the lower classes: the rise of welfare, or the disappearance of work and thus of marriageable men. But Edin thinks the most compelling theory is that marriage has disappeared because women are setting the terms—and setting them too high for the men around them to reach. "I want that white-picket-fence dream," one woman told Edin, and the men she knew just didn't measure up, so she had become her own one-woman mother/father/nurturer/provider. The whole country's future could look much as the present does for many lower-class African Americans: the mothers pull themselves up, but the men don't follow. First-generation college-educated white women may join their black counterparts in a new kind of middle class, where marriage is increasingly rare.

As the traditional order has been upended, signs of the profound 60 disruption have popped up in odd places. Japan is in a national panic over the rise of the "herbivores," the cohort of young men who are rejecting the hard-drinking salaryman life of their fathers and are instead gardening, organizing dessert parties, acting cartoonishly feminine, and declining to have sex. The generational young-women counterparts are known in Japan as the "carnivores," or sometimes the "hunters."

American pop culture keeps producing endless variations on the omega male, who ranks even below the beta in the wolf pack. This often-unemployed, romantically challenged loser can show up as a perpetual adolescent (in Judd Apatow's *Knocked Up* or *The 40-Year-Old Virgin*), or a charmless misanthrope (in Noah Baumbach's *Greenberg*), or a happy couch potato (in a Bud Light commercial). He can be sweet, bitter, nostalgic, or cynical, but he cannot figure out how to be a man. "We call each other 'man,'" says Ben Stiller's character in *Greenberg*, "but it's a joke. It's like imitating other people." The American male novelist, meanwhile, has lost his mojo and entirely given up on sex as a way for his characters to assert macho dominance, Katie Roiphe explains in her essay "The Naked and the Conflicted." Instead, she writes, "the current sexual style is more childlike; innocence is more fashionable than virility, the cuddle preferable to sex."

At the same time, a new kind of alpha female has appeared, stirring up anxiety and, occasionally, fear. The cougar trope started out as a joke about desperate older women. Now it's gone mainstream, even in Hollywood, home to the 50-something producer with a starlet on his arm. Susan Sarandon and Demi Moore have boy toys, and Aaron Johnson, the 19-year-old star of *Kick-Ass*, is a proud boy toy for a woman 24 years his senior. The *New York Times* columnist Gail Collins recently wrote that the cougar phenomenon is beginning to look like it's not about desperate women at all but about "desperate young American men who are latching on to an older woman who's a good earner." *Up in the Air*, a movie set against the backdrop of recession-era layoffs, hammers home its point about the shattered ego of the American man. A character played by George Clooney is called too old to be attractive by his younger female colleague and is later rejected by an older woman whom he falls in love with after she sleeps with him—and who turns out to be married. George Clooney! If the sexiest man alive can get twice rejected (and sexually played) in a movie, what hope is there for anyone else? The message to American men is summarized by the title of a recent offering from the romantic-comedy mill: *She's Out of My League.*

In fact, the more women dominate, the more they behave, fittingly, like the dominant sex. Rates of violence committed by middle-aged women have skyrocketed since the 1980s, and no one knows why. High-profile female killers have been showing up regularly in the news: Amy Bishop,[11] the homicidal Alabama professor; Jihad Jane and her sidekick, Jihad Jamie;[12] the latest generation of Black Widows,[13] responsible for suicide bombings in Russia. In Roman Polanski's *The Ghost Writer*, the traditional political wife is rewritten as a cold-blooded killer at the heart of an evil conspiracy. In her recent video *Telephone*, Lady Gaga, with her infallible radar for the cultural edge, rewrites *Thelma and Louise* as a story not about elusive female empowerment but about sheer, ruthless power. Instead of killing themselves, she and her girlfriend (played by Beyoncé) kill a bad boyfriend and random others in a homicidal spree and then escape in their yellow pickup truck, Gaga bragging, "We did it, Honey B."

The Marlboro Man, meanwhile, master of wild beast and wild country, seems too far-fetched and preposterous even for advertising. His modern equivalents are the stunted men in the Dodge Charger ad that ran during this year's Super Bowl in February. Of all the days in the year, one might think, Super Bowl Sunday should be the one most dedicated to the cinematic celebration of macho. The men in Super Bowl ads should be throwing balls and racing motorcycles and doing whatever it is men imagine they could do all day if only women were not around to restrain them.

Instead, four men stare into the camera, unsmiling, not moving except for tiny blinks and sways. They look like they've been tranquilized, like they can barely hold themselves up against the breeze. Their lips do not move, but a voice-over explains their predicament—how   65

---

[11] *Amy Bishop:* Denied tenure, Amy Bishop took out a gun and opened fire at a faculty meeting, killing three colleagues and injuring three others.

[12] *Jihad Jane...Jihad Jamie:* Colleen Renee LaRose (a.k.a Jihad Jane) and 18-year-old Mohammed Hassan Khalid conspired to kill a Swedish cartoonist who had drawn a cartoon that offended some Muslims.

[13] *Black Widows:* Name popularly given to female Chechen extremists.

they've been beaten silent by the demands of tedious employers and enviro-fascists and women. Especially women. "I will put the seat down, I will separate the recycling, I will carry your lip balm." This last one—lip balm—is expressed with the mildest spit of emotion, the only hint of the suppressed rage against the dominatrix. Then the commercial abruptly cuts to the fantasy, a Dodge Charger vrooming toward the camera punctuated by bold all caps: MAN'S LAST STAND. But the motto is unconvincing. After that display of muteness and passivity, you can only imagine a woman—one with shiny lips—steering the beast.

Candorville

ENGAGING THE TEXT

1. Why does Rosin begin her essay by profiling the "cowboy" biologist, Ronald Ericsson?

2. What evidence does Rosin offer that the era of male dominance is over? What evidence does she present that it is still in place? To what extent does female economic dominance extend to the middle class? To the upper class?

3. What role has the Great Recession played in the economic shift Rosin describes—away from valuing "strength and stamina" and toward valuing "thinking and communicating" (para. 9)? How have changes in the types of job skills demanded by the postindustrial economy affected men? How have they affected women?

4. Rosin cites a number of international examples to support her point about changes in the global economy. How do the decline of male birth preference in South Korea, the rate of women learning English in

India, and the elections of Ellen Johnson Sirleaf in Rwanda and of Johanna Sigurdardottir in Iceland bolster her argument? Can you think of different examples that suggest continued male dominance?

5. Some private colleges are now offering a kind of affirmative action for men in order to maintain an "appropriate" gender balance; in addition, people are calling for "more all-boys schools and classes," and for "special accommodations" of specifically male learning styles (para. 51). Do you think that such measures are warranted? Debate in class.

6. What image of men does this essay present? Examine each reference Rosin makes to males: Do you find her depiction fair or unfair? Why?

7. Rosin offers examples of the new "alpha female" and "omega male" that she says are becoming more common. Do you agree with her analysis? What alternative examples could you offer of "alpha males" and "omega females"? Which do you see more often in current media?

EXPLORING CONNECTIONS

8. In his "Candorville" cartoon (p. 489) Darrin Bell lists a number of measures — against Planned Parenthood, equal pay, and contraceptive coverage — that many states are considering or have already passed. To what extent do you think these measures reflect a backlash against women's increasing power and independence?

9. Role play or write an imaginary conversation among Rosin, Aaron H. Devor (p. 387), Jean Kilbourne (p. 420), and Michael Kimmel (p. 461) concerning contemporary women's and men's roles.

10. Review Adam Davidson's "Making It in America" (p. 333): Does Maddie's experience reflect the rise of women that Rosin describes? How easy or difficult would it be for her to gain the experience she needs to move from "unskilled" to "skilled" worker status?

EXTENDING THE CRITICAL CONTEXT

11. Do some informal research in response to the question, "What if the modern, postindustrial economy is simply more congenial to women than to men?" (para. 11). For example, scan the Bureau of Labor Statistics' "Table 14: Employed persons by detailed industry and sex, 2010 annual averages" (www.bls.gov/cps/wlf-table14-2011.pdf). What patterns, if any, do you see in these figures? What other sources of data can you find about women, men, and work? Based on your findings, how immediate or distant does the "end of men" appear to you?

FURTHER CONNECTIONS

1. Compare the rhetorical strategies and effectiveness of any two of the selections in this chapter. What is each writer's purpose and what audience is he or she addressing? To what extent and how does each author appeal to readers' reason and emotions? What kind of persona does each writer project? What kinds of evidence does each author rely on? How persuasive or compelling do you find each selection, and why?

2. Research the issue of domestic violence. How is it defined? How prevalent is domestic violence nationwide, in your state, and in your community? What are the risk factors for abusers and their victims? Investigate the resources in your community that offer assistance to victims of domestic abuse: hotlines, shelters, organizations, and government agencies that provide counseling or legal aid. Do these services focus on punishing abusers or "curing" them? Write a paper evaluating the effectiveness of different approaches to protecting victims from abusive partners.

3. Research the status of women in the field or profession you plan to pursue. Are women's salaries and compensation comparable to those of men with similar credentials and experience? What is the ratio of women to men in the field as a whole, in entry-level positions, and in executive or high-status positions? Interview at least one woman in this line of work: In what ways, if any, does she feel that her work experience has differed from a man's? Report your findings to the class.

4. Title IX, the law mandating equal funding for women's sports at publicly funded schools, has been praised for opening new opportunities for women athletes and criticized for siphoning money away from some popular men's sports. Research the impact of Title IX on athletics programs at your college or university: How has the picture of women's and men's sports changed since 1972, the year Title IX was enacted? Have women's and men's athletics attained equality at your school?

5. Some religious groups argue that laws and policies that prohibit harassment of or discrimination against homosexuals infringe on their religious freedom. Investigate a specific case in which a religious organization has made this claim. What arguments have been advanced on both sides of the case? What values and assumptions underlie these arguments? What rights and freedoms are at stake for each party in the dispute?

6. **Connecting to the e-Pages.** "S/He" portrays some of the difficulties that transgender people encounter, from unsympathetic schools to parents who want to help their kids but don't quite know how. What resources in your area or at your school are designed to support trans people? Are support groups available? Does your school have policies concerning harassment? What Internet resources can you find? See bedfordstmartins.com/rereading/epages.

5

CREATED EQUAL
The Myth of the Melting Pot

FAST FACTS

1. In 2010, 15% of all new marriages were interracial or interethnic.

2. 24% of Blacks and 21% of Latinos, in contrast to 8% of whites, live in poverty; 18% of people of color, compared to 43% of whites, have retirement accounts.

3. From 2007 to 2010, the Native American unemployment rate rose nearly eight percentage points, to 15%, over one and a half times the increase for white workers.

4. In 2011, there were 1,018 hate groups active in the United States, up from 926 in 2008.

5. As of 2010, 13% of Americans were foreign-born; over a quarter lived in California.

6. Over the last ten years, Asian immigration has risen from 19% to 36%. In 2010, more Asians than Latinos immigrated to the United States.

Sources: (1) and (6): Pew Research Center; (2) United for a Fair Economy: "The State of the Dream," 2009; (3) Economic Policy Institute: "Different Race, Different Recession: American Indian Unemployment in 2010"; (4) Southern Poverty Law Center; (5) American Community Survey Reports: "Foreign-Born Population in the United States: 2010."

THE MYTH OF THE MELTING POT predates the drafting of the U.S. Constitution. In 1782, a year before the Peace of Paris formally ended the Revolutionary War, J. Hector St. John de Crèvecoeur envisioned the young American republic as a crucible that would forge its disparate immigrant population into a vigorous new society with a grand future:

> What, then, is the American, this new man? He is neither an European, or the descendant of an European....He is an American, who leaving behind him all his ancient prejudices and manners, receives new ones from the new mode of life he has embraced, the new government he obeys, and the new rank he holds....Here individuals of all nations are melted into a new race of men, whose labours and posterity will one day cause great changes in the world.

Crèvecoeur's metaphor has remained a powerful ideal for many generations of American scholars, politicians, artists, and ordinary citizens. Ralph Waldo Emerson, writing in his journal in 1845, celebrated the national vitality produced by the mingling of immigrant cultures: "In this continent — asylum of all nations, — the energy of...all the European tribes, — of the Africans, and of the Polynesians — will construct a new race, a new religion, a new state, a new literature." An English Jewish writer named Israel Zangwill, himself an immigrant, popularized the myth in his 1908 drama, *The Melting Pot.* In the play, the hero rhapsodizes, "Yes East and West, and North and South, the palm and the pine, the pole and the equator, the crescent and the cross — how the great Alchemist melts and fuses them with his purging flame! Here shall they all unite to build the Republic of Man and the Kingdom of God." The myth was perhaps most vividly dramatized, though, in a pageant staged by Henry Ford in the early 1920s. Decked out in the costumes of their native lands, Ford's immigrant workers sang traditional songs from their homelands as they danced their way into an enormous replica of a cast-iron pot. They then emerged from the other side wearing identical "American" business suits, waving miniature American flags, and singing "The Star-Spangled Banner."

The drama of becoming an American has deep roots: immigrants take on a new identity — and a new set of cultural myths — because they want to become members of the community, equal members with all the rights, responsibilities, and opportunities of their fellow citizens. The force of the melting pot myth lies in this implied promise that all Americans are indeed "created equal." However, the myth's promises of openness, harmony, unity, and equality were deceptive from the beginning. Crèvecoeur's exclusive concern with the mingling of *European* peoples (he lists the "English, Scotch, Irish, French, Dutch, Germans, and Swedes") utterly ignored the presence of some three-quarters of a million Africans and African Americans who then lived in this country, as well as the tribal peoples who had lived on the land for thousands of years before European contact. Crèvecoeur's vision of a country embracing "all nations" clearly applied only to northern European nations. Benjamin Franklin, in a 1751 essay, was more blunt: since Africa, Asia, and most of America were inhabited by dark-skinned people, he argued, the American colonies should consciously try to increase the white population and keep out the rest: "Why increase the Sons of Africa, by Planting them in America, where we have so fair an opportunity, by excluding Blacks and Tawneys, of increasing the lovely White...?" If later writers like Emerson and Zangwill saw a more inclusive cultural mix as a source of hope and renewal for the United States, others throughout this country's history have, even more than Franklin, feared that mix as a threat.

The fear of difference underlies another, equally powerful American myth — the myth of racial supremacy. This is the negative counterpart of the melting pot ideal: instead of the equal and harmonious blending of cultures, it proposes a racial and ethnic hierarchy based on the "natural superiority" of Anglo-Americans. Under the sway of this myth, differences become signs of inferiority, and "inferiors" are treated as childlike or even subhuman. This myth has given rise to some of the most shameful passages in our national life: slavery, segregation, and lynching; the near extermination of tribal peoples and cultures; the denial of citizenship and constitutional rights to African Americans, American Indians, Chinese and Japanese immigrants; the brutal exploitation of Mexican and Asian laborers. The catalog of injustices is long and painful. The melting pot ideal itself has often masked the myth of racial and ethnic superiority. "Inferiors" are expected to "melt" into conformity with Anglo-American behavior and values. Henry Ford's pageant conveys the message that ethnic identity is best left behind — exchanged for something "better," more uniform, less threatening.

This chapter explores the interaction between these two related cultural myths: the myth of unity and the myth of difference and hierarchy. It examines how the categories of race and ethnicity are defined and how they operate to divide us. These issues become crucial as the population of the United States grows increasingly diverse. The selections here challenge you to reconsider the fate of the melting pot myth as we enter the era of multi-ethnic, multicultural America. Can we learn to accept and honor our differences?

The first half of the chapter focuses on the origins and lingering consequences of racism. It opens with a selection by Thomas Jefferson that unambiguously expresses the myth of racial superiority. Pondering the future of freed slaves, Jefferson concludes that because blacks "are inferior to whites in the endowments both of body and mind," they should be prevented from intermarrying and "staining the blood" of the superior race. Surveying the most common psychological and sociological theories of prejudice, Vincent N. Parrillo, in "Causes of Prejudice," provides a series of frameworks for understanding the roots of racial conflict. JoYin Shih's "Chyna and Me" offers a personal narrative about growing up Chinese and conflicted about her identity; she feels more akin to African American students than she does to other Asians. An essay by Cheryl I. Harris and Devon Carbado, "Loot or Find: Fact or Frame?" examines how assumptions about race ultimately distorted media coverage of Hurricane Katrina. In "Barack Obama: Miles Traveled, Miles to Go," Erin Aubry Kaplan recounts both the initial excitement and the ultimate frustration that accompanied the election of our first black president.

The second half of the chapter offers a Visual Portfolio that gives individual faces to abstractions like race and discrimination. The images challenge us to ponder the centrality of race in American culture and to rethink the ways we "read" identity. The readings in this section address the emerging myth of the "new melting pot." First, George M. Fredrickson presents an overview of race relations in American history; "Models of Ethnic Relations: A Historical Perspective" shows how concepts of ethnic hierarchy, assimilation, pluralism, and separatism have shaped group identities and interactions over time. David Treuer, in a selection from *Rez Life*, "An Indian's Journey Through Reservation Life," talks about the negative consequences of forced assimilation and presents a new kind of Indian activism — the effort to restore Native languages and cultures. In "Deconstructing America" Patrick Buchanan sounds the alarm about the hazards of immigration and diversity, arguing that the United States is becoming dangerously divided by race, ethnicity, and culture. Rubén Martínez probes the personal, cultural, and political significance of the U.S.–Mexican border in "The Crossing," which focuses on his encounter with a seriously ill, undocumented immigrant in the Sonoran desert of New Mexico.

The e-Pages present two selections that vigorously contest stereotypes. Maysan Haydar, in "Veiled Intentions: Don't Judge a Muslim Girl By Her Covering," discusses her reasons for wearing the hijab, or traditional headscarf, of Muslim women. Hint: It has nothing to do with fundamentalism. In the YouTube video *More Than That*, a group of students from the Pine Ridge Reservation counters media depictions of reservation poverty and crime with messages of hope, resilience, and self-reliance. See bedfordstmartins.com /rereading/epages for these two selections.

Sources

Franklin, John Hope. *Race and History: Selected Essays, 1938–1988*. Baton Rouge: Louisiana State University Press, 1989. 321–31. Print.

Gordon, Milton M. *Assimilation in American Life: The Role of Race, Religion, and National Origins*. New York: Oxford University Press, 1964. Print.

Njeri, Itabari. "Beyond the Melting Pot." *Los Angeles Times* 13 Jan. 1991: E1+. Print.

Pitt, Leonard. *We Americans*. 3rd ed. Vol. 2. Dubuque: Kendall/Hunt, 1987. Print.

Takaki, Ronald. "Reflections on Racial Patterns in America." In *From Different Shores: Perspectives on Race and Ethnicity in America*. Ed. Ronald Takaki. New York: Oxford University Press, 1987. 26–37. Print.

BEFORE READING

- Survey images in the popular media (newspapers, magazines, TV shows, movies, and pop music) for evidence of the myth of the melting pot. Do you find any figures in popular culture who seem to endorse the idea of a "new melting pot" in the United States? How closely do these images reflect your understanding of your own and other ethnic and racial groups? Explore these questions in a journal entry, then discuss in class.

- Alternatively, you might investigate the metaphors that are being used to describe racial and ethnic group relations or interactions between members of different groups on your campus and in your community. Consult local news sources and campus publications, and keep your ears open for conversations that touch on these issues. Do some freewriting about what you discover and compare notes with classmates.

- What is your emotional response to the frontispiece photo? How do you interpret the photograph's meaning? What do the woman's body language and expression suggest about her situation? What is the significance of the flag blanket? Jot down your impressions and note the visual details that support your "reading" of the picture. Then compare your responses in small groups: How much consistency or variation do you find in your interpretations?

FROM NOTES ON THE STATE OF VIRGINIA
THOMAS JEFFERSON

Thomas Jefferson is probably best known as the author of the Declaration of Independence. As third president of the United States (1801–1809), Thomas Jefferson (1743–1826) promoted westward expansion in the form of the Louisiana Purchase and the Lewis and Clark Expedition. In addition to his political career he was a scientist, architect, city planner (Washington, D.C.), and founder of the University of Virginia. This passage from his *Notes on the State of Virginia* (1785) reveals a very different and, for many readers, shocking side of Jefferson's character — that of a slave owner and defender of white supremacy. Here he proposes that the new state of Virginia gradually phase out slavery rather than abolish it outright. He also recommends that all newly emancipated slaves be sent out of the state to form separate colonies, in part to prevent racial conflict and in part to prevent intermarriage with whites. Jefferson was not the first and was far from the last politician to advocate solving the nation's racial problems by removing African Americans from its boundaries. In 1862, the Great Emancipator himself, Abraham Lincoln, called a delegation of black leaders to the White House to enlist their support in establishing a colony for African Americans in Central America. Congress had appropriated money for this project, but it was abandoned after the governments of Honduras, Nicaragua, and Costa Rica protested the plan.

MANY OF THE LAWS which were in force during the monarchy being relative merely to that form of government, or inculcating principles inconsistent with republicanism, the first assembly which met after the establishment of the commonwealth appointed a committee to revise the whole code, to reduce it into proper form and volume, and report it to the assembly. This work has been executed by three gentlemen,[1] and reported.... The following are the most remarkable alterations proposed:

To change the rules of descent, so as that the lands of any person dying intestate shall be divisible equally among all his children, or other representatives, in equal degree.

To make slaves distributable among the next of kin, as other movables....

To emancipate all slaves born after the passing [of] the act. The bill reported by the revisers does not itself contain this proposition; but an amendment containing it was prepared, to be offered to the legislature whenever the bill should be taken up, and farther directing, that they should continue with their parents to a certain age, then to be brought up, at the public expense, to tillage, arts, or sciences, according to their geniuses, till the females should be eighteen, and the males twenty-one years of age, when they should be colonized to such place as the circumstances of the time should render most proper, sending them out with arms, implements of household and of the handicraft arts, seeds, pairs of the useful domestic animals, &c., to declare them a free and independent people, and extend to them our alliance and protection, till they have acquired strength; and to send vessels at the same time to other parts of the world for an equal number of white inhabitants; to induce them to migrate hither, proper encouragements were to be proposed. It will probably be asked, Why not retain and incorporate the

---

[1]*executed by three gentlemen:* Jefferson was one of the three men who wrote this set of proposed revisions to the legal code of Virginia. [All notes are the editors'.]

blacks into the State, and thus save the expense of supplying by importation of white settlers, the vacancies they will leave? Deep-rooted prejudices entertained by the whites; ten thousand recollections, by the blacks, of the injuries they have sustained; new provocations; the real distinctions which nature has made; and many other circumstances, will divide us into parties, and produce convulsions, which will probably never end but in the extermination of the one or the other race. To these objections, which are political, may be added others, which are physical and moral. The first difference which strikes us is that of color. Whether the black of the negro resides in the reticular membrane between the skin and scarf-skin, or in the scarf-skin itself; whether it proceeds from the color of the blood, the color of the bile, or from that of some other secretion, the difference is fixed in nature, and is as real as if its seat and cause were better known to us. And is this difference of no importance? Is it not the foundation of a greater or less share of beauty in the two races? Are not the fine mixtures of red and white, the expressions of every passion by greater or less suffusions of color in the one, preferable to that eternal monotony, which reigns in the countenances, that immovable veil of black which covers the emotions of the other race? Add to these, flowing hair, a more elegant symmetry of form, their own judgment in favor of the whites, declared by their preference of them, as uniformly as is the preference of the Oranootan[2] for the black woman over those of his own species. The circumstance of superior beauty, is thought worthy of attention in the propagation of our horses, dogs, and other domestic animals; why not in that of man? Besides those of color, figure, and hair, there are other physical distinctions proving a difference of race. They have less hair on the face and body. They secrete less by the kidneys, and more by the glands of the skin, which gives them a very strong and disagreeable odor. This greater degree of transpiration, renders them more tolerant of heat, and less so of cold than the whites. Perhaps, too, a difference of structure in the pulmonary apparatus, which a late ingenious experimentalist has discovered to be the principal regulator of animal heat, may have disabled them from extricating, in the act of inspiration, so much of that fluid from the outer air, or obliged them in expiration, to part with more of it. They seem to require less sleep. A black after hard labor through the day, will be induced by the slightest amusements to sit up till midnight, or later, though knowing he must be out with the first dawn of the morning. They are at least as brave, and more adventuresome. But this may perhaps proceed from a want of forethought, which prevents their seeing a danger till it be present. When present, they do not go through it with more coolness or steadiness than the whites. They are more ardent after their female; but love seems with them to be more an eager desire, than a tender delicate mixture of sentiment and sensation. Their griefs are transient. Those numberless afflictions, which render it doubtful whether heaven has

[2]*Oranootan:* Orangutan.

given life to us in mercy or in wrath, are less felt, and sooner forgotten with them. In general, their existence appears to participate more of sensation than reflection. To this must be ascribed their disposition to sleep when abstracted from their diversions, and unemployed in labor. An animal whose body is at rest, and who does not reflect, must be disposed to sleep of course. Comparing them by their faculties of memory, reason, and imagination, it appears to me that in memory they are equal to the whites; in reason much inferior, as I think one could scarcely be found capable of tracing and comprehending the investigations of Euclid; and that in imagination they are dull, tasteless, and anomalous. It would be unfair to follow them to Africa for this investigation. We will consider them here, on the same stage with the whites, and where the facts are not apochryphal on which a judgment is to be formed. It will be right to make great allowances for the difference of condition, of education, of conversation, of the sphere in which they move. Many millions of them have been brought to, and born in America. Most of them, indeed, have been confined to tillage, to their own homes, and their own society; yet many have been so situated, that they might have availed themselves of the conversation of their masters; many have been brought up to the handicraft arts, and from that circumstance have always been associated with the whites. Some have been liberally educated, and all have lived in countries where the arts and sciences are cultivated to a considerable degree, and all have had before their eyes samples of the best works from abroad. The Indians, with no advantages of this kind, will often carve figures on their pipes not destitute of design and merit. They will crayon out an animal, a plant, or a country, so as to prove the existence of a germ in their minds which only wants cultivation. They astonish you with strokes of the most sublime oratory; such as prove their reason and sentiment strong, their imagination glowing and elevated. But never yet could I find that a black had uttered a thought above the level of plain narration; never saw even an elementary trait of painting or sculpture. In music they are more generally gifted than the whites with accurate ears for tune and time, and they have been found capable of imagining a small catch.[3] Whether they will be equal to the composition of a more extensive run of melody, or of complicated harmony, is yet to be proved. Misery is often the parent of the most affecting touches in poetry. Among the blacks is misery enough, God knows, but no poetry. Love is the peculiar œstrum of the poet. Their love is ardent, but it kindles the senses only, not the imagination. Religion, indeed, has produced a Phyllis Whately [sic];[4] but it

---

[3]The instrument proper to them is the Banjar, which they brought hither from Africa, and which is the original of the guitar, its chords being precisely the four lower chords of the guitar. [Jefferson's note]

[4]*Phyllis Whately:* Phillis Wheatley (175?–1784) was born in Africa but transported to the United States and sold as a slave when she was a young child. Her *Poems on Various Subjects, Religious and Moral* (1773) was the first book of poetry to be published by an African American.

could not produce a poet. The compositions published under her name are below the dignity of criticism. The heroes of the Dunciad[5] are to her, as Hercules to the author of that poem. Ignatius Sancho[6] has approached nearer to merit in composition; yet his letters do more honor to the heart than the head. They breathe the purest effusions of friendship and general philanthropy, and show how great a degree of the latter may be compounded with strong religious zeal. He is often happy in the turn of his compliments, and his style is easy and familiar, except when he affects a Shandean[7] fabrication of words. But his imagination is wild and extravagant, escapes incessantly from every restraint of reason and taste, and, in the course of its vagaries, leaves a tract of thought as incoherent and eccentric, as is the course of a meteor through the sky. His subjects should often have led him to a process of sober reasoning; yet we find him always substituting sentiment for demonstration. Upon the whole, though we admit him to the first place among those of his own color who have presented themselves to the public judgment, yet when we compare him with the writers of the race among whom he lived and particularly with the epistolary class in which he has taken his own stand, we are compelled to enroll him at the bottom of the column. This criticism supposes the letters published under his name to be genuine, and to have received amendment from no other hand; points which would not be of easy investigation. The improvement of the blacks in body and mind, in the first instance of their mixture with the whites, has been observed by every one, and proves that their inferiority is not the effect merely of their condition of life....

The opinion that they are inferior in the faculties of reason and imagination, must be hazarded with great diffidence. To justify a general conclusion, requires many observations, even where the subject may be submitted to the anatomical knife, to optical glasses, to analysis by fire or by solvents. How much more then where it is a faculty, not a substance, we are examining; where it eludes the research of all the senses; where the conditions of its existence are various and variously combined; where the effects of those which are present or absent bid defiance to calculation; let me add too, as a circumstance of great tenderness, where our conclusion would degrade a whole race of men from the rank in the scale of beings which their Creator may perhaps have given them. To our reproach it must be said, that though for a century and a half we have had under our eyes the races of black and

---

[5]*the heroes of the Dunciad:* In the mock epic poem *The Dunciad* (1728), English satirist Alexander Pope (1688–1744) lampoons his literary rivals as fools and dunces.

[6]*Ignatius Sancho:* Born on a slave ship, Ignatius Sancho (1729–1780) became a servant in the homes of several English aristocrats, where he educated himself and became acquainted with some of the leading writers and artists of the period. He later became a grocer in London and devoted himself to writing. His letters were collected and published in 1782.

[7]*Shandean:* In the style of Laurence Sterne's comic novel, *The Life and Opinions of Tristram Shandy* (1758–1766). Sancho admired Sterne's writing and corresponded regularly with him.

of red men, they have never yet been viewed by us as subjects of natural history. I advance it, therefore, as a suspicion only, that the blacks, whether originally a distinct race, or made distinct by time and circumstances, are inferior to the whites in the endowments both of body and mind. It is not against experience to suppose that different species of the same genus, or varieties of the same species, may possess different qualifications. Will not a lover of natural history then, one who views the gradations in all the races of animals with the eye of philosophy, excuse an effort to keep those in the department of man as distinct as nature has formed them? This unfortunate difference of color, and perhaps of faculty, is a powerful obstacle to the emancipation of these people. Many of their advocates, while they wish to vindicate the liberty of human nature, are anxious also to preserve its dignity and beauty. Some of these, embarrassed by the question, "What further is to be done with them?" join themselves in opposition with those who are actuated by sordid avarice only. Among the Romans emancipation required but one effort. The slave, when made free, might mix with, without staining the blood of his master. But with us a second is necessary, unknown to history. When freed, he is to be removed beyond the reach of mixture.

ENGAGING THE TEXT

1. Jefferson proposes colonizing—that is, sending away—all newly emancipated slaves and declaring them "a free and independent people" (para. 4).

In what ways would their freedom and independence continue to be limited, according to this proposal?

2. Jefferson predicts that racial conflict in the United States "will probably never end but in the extermination of the one or the other race" (para. 4). Which of the divisive issues he mentions, if any, are still sources of conflict today? Given the history of race relations from Jefferson's time to our own, do you think his pessimism was justified? Why or why not?

3. Jefferson presents what seems on the surface to be a systematic and logical catalog of the differences he sees between blacks and whites; he then attempts to demonstrate the "natural" superiority of whites based on these differences. Working in pairs or small groups, look carefully at his observations and the conclusions he draws from them. What flaws do you find in his analysis?

EXPLORING CONNECTIONS

4. Examine the Joel Pett cartoon on page 502. How have race relations changed since Jefferson's time? To what extent do racist attitudes persist? Explain your answer.

5. Consider the picture of Jefferson's descendants on page 57. Write a journal entry or essay comparing the image of Jefferson you received in American history classes to the impression you get from the photo and from the passage above. How do you account for the differences?

6. Working in groups, write scripts for an imaginary meeting between Jefferson and Malcolm X (p. 189) and present them to the class. After each group has acted out its scenario, compare the different versions of the meeting. What does each script assume about the motives and character of the two men?

EXTENDING THE CRITICAL CONTEXT

7. Read the Declaration of Independence (p. 624) in Chapter Six and compare Jefferson's most famous document to the lesser-known passage reprinted here. How do the purposes of the two texts differ? What ideas and principles, if any, do they have in common, and where do they conflict?

8. Write a letter to Jefferson responding to this selection and explaining your point of view. What would you tell him about how and why attitudes have changed between his time and ours?

9. Influenced by the heroic image of Jefferson as a champion of freedom and democracy, civic leaders have named libraries, schools, and other public institutions after him for the last two hundred years. Debate whether or not it is appropriate to honor Jefferson in this way given the opinions expressed in this passage.

CAUSES OF PREJUDICE

VINCENT N. PARRILLO

What motivates the creation of racial categories? In the following selection, Vincent Parrillo reviews several theories that seek to explain the motives for prejudiced behavior—from socialization theory to economic competition. As Parrillo indicates, prejudice cannot be linked to any single cause: a whole network of forces and frustrations underlies this complex set of feelings and behaviors. Parrillo (b. 1938) is a professor of sociology at William Paterson University in New Jersey. His books include *Rethinking Today's Minorities* (1991), *Diversity in America* (2008, 3rd ed.), and *Understanding Race and Ethnic Relations* (2010, 4th ed.). He has also written and produced two award-winning documentaries for PBS television. This excerpt originally appeared in *Strangers to These Shores* (2010, 10th ed.).

PREJUDICIAL ATTITUDES may be either positive or negative. Sociologists primarily study the latter, however, because only negative attitudes can lead to turbulent social relations between dominant and minority groups. Numerous writers, therefore, have defined *prejudice* as an attitudinal "system of negative beliefs, feelings, and action-orientations regarding a certain group or groups of people."[1] The status of the strangers is an important factor in the development of a negative attitude. Prejudicial attitudes exist among members of both dominant and minority groups. Thus, in the relations between dominant and minority groups, the antipathy felt by one group for another is quite often reciprocated.

Psychological perspectives on prejudice—whether behaviorist, cognitive, or psychoanalytic—focus on the subjective states of mind of individuals. In these perspectives, a person's prejudicial attitudes may result from imitation or conditioning (behaviorist), perceived similarity–dissimilarity of beliefs (cognitive), or specific personality characteristics (psychoanalytic). In contrast, sociological perspectives focus on the objective conditions of society as the social forces behind prejudicial attitudes and behind racial and ethnic relations. Individuals do not live in a vacuum; social reality affects their states of mind.

Both perspectives are necessary to understand prejudice. As psychologist Gordon Allport argued,[2] besides needing a close study of

---

[1] Reported by Daniel Wilner, Rosabelle Price Walkley, and Stuart W. Cook, "Residential Proximity and Intergroup Relations in Public Housing Projects," *Journal of Social Issues* 8(1) (1952): 45. See also James W. Vander Zanden, *American Minority Relations*, 3rd ed. (New York: Ronald Press, 1972), p. 21. [All notes are Parrillo's.]

[2] Gordon W. Allport, *The Nature of Prejudice* (Reading, MA: Addison-Wesley, 1954), pp. 13–14.

habits, perceptions, motivation, and personality, we need an analysis of social settings, situational forces, demographic and ecological variables, and legal and economic trends.[3] Psychological and sociological perspectives complement each other in providing a fuller explanation of intergroup relations.

The Psychology of Prejudice

The psychological approach to prejudice is to examine individual behavior. We can understand more about prejudice among individuals by focusing on four areas of study: levels of prejudice, self-justification, personality, and frustration.

Levels of Prejudice. Bernard Kramer suggested that prejudice exists on three levels: cognitive, emotional, and action orientation.[4] The **cognitive level of prejudice** encompasses a person's beliefs and perceptions of a group as threatening or nonthreatening, inferior or equal (e.g., in terms of intellect, status, or biological composition), seclusive or intrusive, impulse gratifying, acquisitive, or possessing other positive or negative characteristics. Mr. X's cognitive beliefs are that Jews are intrusive and acquisitive. Other illustrations of cognitive beliefs are that the Irish are heavy drinkers and fighters, African Americans are rhythmic and lazy, and the Poles are thick-headed and unintelligent.

Generalizations shape both ethnocentric and prejudicial attitudes, but there is a difference. *Ethnocentrism* is a generalized rejection of all outgroups on the basis of an ingroup focus, whereas *prejudice* is a rejection of certain people solely on the basis of their membership in a particular outgroup.

In many societies, members of the majority group may believe that a particular low-status minority group is dirty, immoral, violent, or law breaking. In the United States, the Irish, Italians, African Americans, Mexicans, Chinese, Puerto Ricans, and others have at one time or another been labeled with most, if not all, of these adjectives. In most European countries and in the United States, the group lowest on the socioeconomic ladder has often been depicted in caricature as also lowest on the evolutionary ladder. The Irish and African Americans in the United States and the peasants and various ethnic groups in Europe have all been depicted in the past as apelike:

> The Victorian images of the Irish as "white Negro" and simian Celt, or a combination of the two, derived much of its force and inspiration from physiognomical beliefs ... [but] every country in Europe had its equivalent of "white Negroes" and simianized men, whether or not they happened

[3]Gordon W. Allport, "Prejudice: Is It Societal or Personal?" *Journal of Social Issues* 18 (1962): 129–30.

[4]Bernard M. Kramer, "Dimensions of Prejudice," *Journal of Psychology* 27 (April 1949): 389–451.

to be stereotypes of criminals, assassins, political radicals, revolutionaries, Slavs, gypsies, Jews or peasants.[5]

The **emotional level of prejudice** encompasses the feelings that a minority group arouses in an individual. Although these feelings may be based on stereotypes from the cognitive level, they represent a more intense stage of personal involvement. The emotional attitudes may be negative or positive, such as fear/envy, distrust/trust, disgust/admiration, or contempt/empathy. These feelings, based on beliefs about the group, may be triggered by social interaction or by the possibility of interaction. For example, whites might react with fear or anger to the integration of their schools or neighborhoods, or Protestants might be jealous of the lifestyle of a highly successful Catholic business executive.

An **action-orientation level of prejudice** is the positive or negative predisposition to engage in discriminatory behavior. A person who harbors strong feelings about members of a certain racial or ethnic group may have a tendency to act for or against them—being aggressive or nonaggressive, offering assistance or withholding it. Such an individual would also be likely to want to exclude or include members of that group both in close, personal social relations and in peripheral social relations. For example, some people would want to exclude members of the disliked group from doing business with them or living in their neighborhood. Another manifestation of the action-orientation level of prejudice is the desire to change or maintain the status differential or inequality between the two groups, whether the area is economic, political, educational, social, or a combination. Note that an action orientation is a predisposition to act, not the action itself.

Self-Justification. **Self-justification** involves denigrating a person 10 or group to justify maltreatment of them. In this situation, self-justification leads to prejudice and discrimination against members of another group.

Some philosophers argue that we are not so much rational creatures as we are rationalizing creatures. We require reassurance that the things we do and the lives we live are proper, that good reasons for our actions exist. If we can convince ourselves that another group is inferior, immoral, or dangerous, we may feel justified in discriminating against its members, enslaving them, or even killing them.

History is filled with examples of people who thought their maltreatment of others was just and necessary: As defenders of the "true faith," the Crusaders killed "Christ-killers" (Jews) and "infidels" (Muslims). Participants in the Spanish Inquisition imprisoned, tortured, and executed "heretics," "the disciples of the Devil." Similarly, the Puritans burned witches, whose refusal to confess "proved they were evil"; pioneers

---

[5]L. Perry Curtis Jr., *Apes and Angels: The Irishman in Victorian Caricature* (Washington, DC: Smithsonian Press, 1971).

exploited or killed Native Americans who were "heathen savages"; and whites mistreated, enslaved, or killed African Americans, who were "an inferior species." According to U.S. Army officers, the civilians in the Vietnamese village of My Lai were "probably" aiding the Viet Cong; so in 1968, U.S. soldiers fighting in the Vietnam War felt justified in slaughtering over 300 unarmed people there, including women, children, and the elderly. In recent years suicide bombers and terrorists have killed innocent civilians, also justifying their actions through their religious fanaticism.

Some sociologists believe that self-justification works the other way around. That is, instead of self-justification serving as a basis for subjugating others, the subjugation occurs first and the self-justification follows, resulting in prejudice and continued discrimination.[6] The evolution of racism as a concept after the establishment of the African slave trade would seem to support this idea. Philip Mason offers an insight into this view:

> A specialized society is likely to defeat a simpler society and provide a lower tier still of enslaved and conquered peoples. The rulers and organizers sought security for themselves and their children; to perpetuate the power, the esteem, and the comfort they had achieved, it was

Candorville © Darrin Bell. © 2006 The Washington Post. All rights reserved. Reprinted with permission.

[6]See Marvin B. Scott and Stanford M. Lyman, "Accounts," *American Sociological Review* 33 (February 1968): 40–62.

necessary not only that the artisans and labourers should work contentedly but that the rulers should sleep without bad dreams. No one can say with certainty how the myths originated, but it is surely relevant that when one of the founders of Western thought set himself to frame an ideal state that would embody social justice, he—like the earliest city dwellers—not only devised a society stratified in tiers but believed it would be necessary to persuade the traders and work-people that, by divine decree, they were made from brass and iron, while the warriors were made of silver and the rulers of gold.[7]

Another example of self-justification serving as a source of prejudice is the dominant group's assumption of an attitude of superiority over other groups. In this respect, establishing a prestige hierarchy—ranking the status of various ethnic groups—results in differential association. To enhance or maintain self-esteem, a person may avoid social contact with groups deemed inferior and associate only with those identified as being of high status. Through such behavior, self-justification may come to intensify the social distance between groups.... *Social distance* refers to the degree to which ingroup members do not engage in social or primary relationships with members of various outgroups.

Personality.   In 1950, in *The Authoritarian Personality*, T. W. Adorno   15 and his colleagues reported a correlation between individuals' early childhood experiences of harsh parental discipline and their development of an **authoritarian personality** as adults.[8] If parents assume an excessively domineering posture in their relations with a child, exercising stern measures and threatening to withdraw love if the child does not respond with weakness and submission, the child tends to be insecure and to nurture much latent hostility against the parents. When such children become adults, they may demonstrate **displaced aggression,** directing their hostility against a powerless group to compensate for their feelings of insecurity and fear. Highly prejudiced individuals tend to come from families that emphasize obedience.

The authors identified authoritarianism by the use of a measuring instrument called an F scale (the *F* stands for potential fascism). Other tests included the A-S (anti-Semitism) and E (ethnocentrism) scales, the latter measuring attitudes toward various minorities. One of their major findings was that people who scored high on authoritarianism also consistently showed a high degree of prejudice against all minority groups. These highly prejudiced people were characterized by rigidity of viewpoint, dislike for ambiguity, strict obedience to leaders, and intolerance of weakness in themselves and others.

No sooner did *The Authoritarian Personality* appear than controversy began. H. H. Hyman and P. B. Sheatsley challenged the meth-

[7]Philip Mason, *Patterns of Dominance* (New York: Oxford University Press, 1970), p. 7. See also Philip Mason, *Race Relations* (New York: Oxford University Press, 1970), pp. 17–29.
[8]T. W. Adorno, Else Frankel-Brunswik, Daniel J. Levinson, and R. Nevitt Sanford, *The Authoritarian Personality* (New York: Harper & Row, 1950).

odology and analysis.[9] Solomon Asch questioned the assumptions that the F scale responses represented a belief system and that structural variables (e.g., ideologies, stratification, and mobility) do not play a role in shaping personality.[10] E. A. Shils argued that the authors were interested only in measuring authoritarianism of the political right while ignoring such tendencies in those at the other end of the political spectrum.[11] Other investigators sought alternative explanations for the authoritarian personality. D. Stewart and T. Hoult extended the framework beyond family childhood experiences to include other social factors.[12] H. C. Kelman and Janet Barclay pointed out that substantial evidence exists showing that lower intelligence and less education also correlate with high authoritarianism scores on the F scale.[13]

Despite the critical attacks, the underlying conceptions of *The Authoritarian Personality* were important, and research into personality as a factor in prejudice has continued. Subsequent investigators refined and modified the original study. Correcting scores for response bias, they conducted cross-cultural studies. Respondents in Germany and Near Eastern countries, where more authoritarian social structures exist, scored higher on authoritarianism and social distance between groups. In Japan, Germany, and the United States, authoritarianism and social distance were moderately related. Other studies suggested that an inverse relationship exists between social class and F scale scores: the higher the social class, the lower the authoritarianism.[14]

Although studies of authoritarian personality have helped us understand some aspects of prejudice, they have not provided a causal explanation. Most of the findings in this area show a correlation, but the findings do not prove, for example, that harsh discipline of children causes them to become prejudiced adults. Perhaps the strict parents were themselves prejudiced, and the child learned those attitudes from them—or, as George Simpson and J. Milton Yinger say,

> One must be careful not to assume too quickly that a certain tendency—rigidity of mind, for example—that is correlated with prejudice necessarily causes that prejudice....The sequence may be the other way around....It is more likely that both are related to more basic factors.[15]

[9]H. H. Hyman and P. B. Sheatsley, "The Authoritarian Personality: A Methodological Critique," in R. Christie and M. Jahoda (eds.), *Studies in the Scope and Method of "The Authoritarian Personality"* (Glencoe, IL: Free Press, 1954).

[10]Solomon E. Asch, *Social Psychology* (Englewood Cliffs, NJ: Prentice Hall, 1952), p. 545.

[11]E. A. Shils, "Authoritarianism: Right and Left," in *Studies in the Scope and Method of "The Authoritarian Personality."*

[12]D. Stewart and T. Hoult, "A Social-Psychological Theory of 'The Authoritarian Personality,'" *American Journal of Sociology* 65 (1959): 274.

[13]H. C. Kelman and Janet Barclay, "The F Scale as a Measure of Breadth of Perspective," *Journal of Abnormal and Social Psychology* 67 (1963): 608–15.

[14]For an excellent summary of authoritarian studies and literature, see John P. Kirscht and Ronald C. Dillehay, *Dimensions of Authoritarianism: A Review of Research and Theory* (Lexington, KY: University of Kentucky Press, 1967).

[15]George E. Simpson and J. Milton Yinger, *Racial and Cultural Minorities: An Analysis of Prejudice and Discrimination* (New York: Harper & Row, 1953), p. 91.

For some people, prejudice may indeed be rooted in subconscious [20] childhood tensions, but we simply do not know whether these tensions directly cause a high degree of prejudice in the adult or whether other powerful social forces are the determinants. Whatever the explanation, authoritarianism is a significant phenomenon worthy of continued investigation. Recent research, however, has stressed social and situational factors, rather than personality, as primary causes of prejudice and discrimination.[16]

Yet another dimension of the personality component is the role of self-esteem. Galinsky and Ku found that those with high self-esteem evaluated an outgroup more positively than those with low self-esteem.[17] Major, Kaiser, and McCoy reported that individuals' awareness of potential discrimination against themselves provided self-esteem protection, in contrast to the lower self-esteem experienced by those less aware of such external factors affecting themselves.[18] It would thus appear that the level of one's self-esteem affects attitudes both about oneself and others.

Frustration. Frustration is the result of relative deprivation in which expectations remain unsatisfied. **Relative deprivation** is a lack of resources, or rewards, in one's standard of living in comparison with those of others in the society. A number of investigators have suggested that frustrations tend to increase aggression toward others.[19] Frustrated people may easily strike out against the perceived cause of their frustration. However, this reaction may not be possible because the true source of the frustration is often too nebulous to be identified or too powerful to act against. In such instances, the result may be displaced aggression; in this situation, the frustrated individual or group usually redirects anger against a more visible, vulnerable, and socially sanctioned target that is unable to strike back. Minorities meet these criteria and are thus frequently the recipients of displaced aggression by the dominant group.

Blaming others for something that is not their fault is known as **scapegoating.** The term comes from the ancient Hebrew custom of using a goat during the Day of Atonement as a symbol of the sins of the people. In an annual ceremony, a priest placed his hands on the head of a goat and listed the people's sins in a symbolic transference of guilt; he then chased the goat out of the community, thereby freeing the people

---

[16]See, for example, Thomas F. Pettigrew, "Intergroup Contact Theory," *Annual Review of Psychology* 49 (1998): 65–85.

[17]See Adam D. Galinsky and Gillian Ku, "The Effects of Perspective-Taking on Prejudice: The Moderating Role of Self-Evaluation," *Personality and Social Psychology Bulletin* 30 (May 2004): 594–604.

[18]Brenda Major, Cheryl R. Kaiser, and Shannon K. McCoy, "It's Not My Fault: When and Why Attributions to Prejudice Protect Self-Esteem," *Personality and Social Psychology Bulletin* 29 (June 2003): 772–81.

[19]See Russell G. Geen, *Human Aggression*, 2nd ed. (Berkshire, England: Open University Press, 2001).

of sin.[20] Since those times, the powerful group has usually punished the scapegoat group rather than allowing it to escape.

There have been many instances throughout world history of minority groups serving as scapegoats, including the Christians in ancient Rome, the Huguenots in France, the Jews in Europe and Russia, and the Puritans and Quakers in England. Gordon Allport suggests that certain characteristics are necessary for a group to become a suitable scapegoat. The group must be (1) highly visible in physical appearance or observable customs and actions; (2) not strong enough to strike back; (3) situated within easy access of the dominant group and, ideally, concentrated in one area; (4) a past target of hostility for whom latent hostility still exists; and (5) the symbol of an unpopular concept.[21]

Some groups fit this typology better than others, but minority racial and ethnic groups have been a perennial choice. Irish, Italians, Catholics, Jews, Quakers, Mormons, Chinese, Japanese, blacks, Puerto Ricans, Mexicans, and Koreans have all been treated, at one time or another, as the scapegoat in the United States. Especially in times of economic hardship, societies tend to blame some group for the general conditions, which often leads to aggressive action against the group as an expression of frustration. For example, a study by Carl Hovland and Robert Sears found that, between 1882 and 1930, a definite correlation existed in the South between a decline in the price of cotton and an increase in the number of lynchings of blacks.[22]

For over twenty years, Leonard Berkowitz and his associates studied and experimented with aggressive behavior. They concluded that, confronted with equally frustrating situations, highly prejudiced individuals are more likely to seek scapegoats than are nonprejudiced individuals. Another intervening variable is that personal frustrations (marital failure, injury, or mental illness) make people more likely to seek scapegoats than do shared frustrations (dangers of flood or hurricane).[23]

Some experiments have shown that aggression does not increase if the frustration is understandable.[24] Other experiments have found that people become aggressive only if the aggression directly relieves their frustration.[25] Still other studies have shown that anger is a more likely

[20]Leviticus 16:5–22.

[21]Gordon W. Allport, *The Nature of Prejudice* (Cambridge, MA: Addison-Wesley, 1954), pp. 13–14.

[22]Carl I. Hovland and Robert R. Sears, "Minor Studies of Aggression: Correlation of Lynchings with Economic Indices," *Journal of Psychology* 9 (Winter 1940): 301–10.

[23]See Leonard Berkowitz, "Whatever Happened to the Frustration-Aggression Hypothesis?" *American Behavioral Scientist* 21 (1978): 691–708; L. Berkowitz, *Aggression: A Social Psychological Analysis* (New York: McGraw-Hill, 1962).

[24]D. Zillman, *Hostility and Aggression* (Hillsdale, NJ: Erlbaum, 1979); R. A. Baron, *Human Aggression* (New York: Plenum Press, 1977); N. Pastore, "The Role of Arbitrariness in the Frustration-Aggression Hypothesis," *Journal of Abnormal and Social Psychology* 47 (1952): 728–31.

[25]A. H. Buss, "Instrumentality of Aggression, Feedback, and Frustration as Determinants of Physical Aggression," *Journal of Personality and Social Psychology* 3 (1966): 153–62.

result if the person responsible for the frustrating situation could have acted otherwise.[26] Clearly the results are mixed, depending on the variables within a given social situation.

Frustration–aggression theory, although helpful, is not completely satisfactory. It ignores the role of culture and the reality of actual social conflict and fails to show any causal relationship. Most of the responses measured in these studies were of people already biased. Why did one group rather than another become the object of the aggression? Moreover, frustration does not necessarily precede aggression, and aggression does not necessarily flow from frustration.

The Sociology of Prejudice

The sociological approach to prejudice is not to examine individual behavior, as psychologists do, but rather to examine behavior within a group setting. Sociologist Talcott Parsons provided one bridge between psychology and sociology by introducing social forces as a variable in frustration–aggression theory. He suggested that both the family and the occupational structure may produce anxieties and insecurities that create frustration.[27] According to this view, the growing-up process (gaining parental affection and approval, identifying with and imitating sexual role models, and competing with others in adulthood) sometimes involves severe emotional strain. The result is an adult personality with a large reservoir of repressed aggression that becomes *free-floating*—susceptible to redirection against convenient scapegoats. Similarly, the occupational system is a source of frustration: Its emphasis on competitiveness and individual achievement, its function of conferring status, its requirement that people inhibit their natural impulses at work, and its ties to the state of the economy are among the factors that generate emotional anxieties. Parsons pessimistically concluded that minorities fulfill a functional "need" as targets for displaced aggression and therefore will remain targets.[28]

Perhaps most influential in staking out the sociological position on prejudice was Herbert Blumer, who suggested that prejudice always involves the "sense of group position" in society. Agreeing with Kramer's delineation of three levels of prejudice, Blumer argued that prejudice can include beliefs, feelings, and a predisposition to action, thus motivating behavior that derives from the social hierarchy.[29] By emphasizing his-

[26]J. R. Averill, "Studies on Anger and Aggression: Implications for Theories of Emotion," *American Psychologist* 38 (1983): 1145–60.

[27]Talcott Parsons, "Certain Primary Sources and Patterns of Aggression in the Social Structure of the Western World," in *Essays in Sociological Theory* (New York: Free Press, 1964), pp. 298–322.

[28]For an excellent review of Parsonian theory in this area, see Stanford M. Lyman, *The Black American in Sociological Thought: A Failure of Perspective* (New York: Putnam, 1972), pp. 145–69.

[29]Herbert Blumer, "Race Prejudice as a Sense of Group Position," *Pacific Sociological Review* 1 (1958): 3–7.

torically established group positions and relationships, Blumer shifted the focus away from attitudes and personality compositions of individuals. As a social phenomenon, prejudice rises or falls according to issues that alter one group's position vis-à-vis that of another group.

Socialization. In the **socialization process,** individuals acquire the values, attitudes, beliefs, and perceptions of their culture or subculture, including religion, nationality, and social class. Generally, the child conforms to the parents' expectations in acquiring an understanding of the world and its people. Being impressionable and knowing of no alternative conceptions of the world, the child usually accepts these concepts without questioning. We thus learn the prejudices of our parents and others, which then become part of our values and beliefs. Even when based on false stereotypes, prejudices shape our perceptions of various peoples and influence our attitudes and actions toward particular groups. For example, if we develop negative attitudes about Jews because we are taught that they are shrewd, acquisitive, and clannish—all-too-familiar stereotypes—as adults we may refrain from business or social relationships with them. We may not even realize the reason for such avoidance, so subtle has been the prejudice instilled within us.

People may learn certain prejudices because of their pervasiveness. The cultural screen that we develop and through which we view the surrounding world is not always accurate, but it does permit transmission of shared values and attitudes, which are reinforced by others. Prejudice, like cultural values, is taught and learned through the socialization process. The prevailing prejudicial attitudes and actions may be deeply embedded in custom or law (e.g., the **Jim Crow laws** of the 1890s and early twentieth century establishing segregated public facilities throughout the South, which subsequent generations accepted as proper and maintained in their own adult lives).

Although socialization explains how prejudicial attitudes may be transmitted from one generation to the next, it does not explain their origin or why they intensify or diminish over the years. These aspects of prejudice must be explained in another way.

Economic Competition. People tend to be more hostile toward others when they feel that their security is threatened; thus, many social scientists conclude that economic competition and conflict breed prejudice. Certainly, considerable evidence shows that negative stereotyping, prejudice, and discrimination increase markedly whenever competition for available jobs increases.

An excellent illustration relates to the Chinese sojourners in the nineteenth-century United States. Prior to the 1870s, the transcontinental railroad was being built, and the Chinese filled many of the jobs made available by this project in the sparsely populated West. Although they were expelled from the region's gold mines and schools and could obtain no redress of grievances in the courts, they managed to convey to some whites the image of being clean, hard-working, law-abiding people. The completion of the railroad, the flood of former Civil War soldiers into the job market, and the economic depression of 1873 worsened their situation. The Chinese became more frequent victims of open discrimination and hostility. Their positive stereotype among some whites was widely displaced by a negative one: They were now "conniving," "crafty," "criminal," "the yellow menace." Only after they retreated into Chinatowns and entered specialty occupations that minimized their competition with whites did the intense hostility abate.

One pioneer in the scientific study of prejudice, John Dollard, demonstrated how prejudice against the Germans, which had been virtually nonexistent in a small U.S. industrial town, arose when times got bad:

> Local Whites largely drawn from the surrounding farms manifested considerable direct aggression toward the newcomers. Scornful and derogatory opinions were expressed about the Germans, and the native Whites had a satisfying sense of superiority toward them....The chief element in the permission to be aggressive against the Germans was rivalry for jobs and status in the local woodenware plants. The native Whites felt definitely crowded for their jobs by the entering German groups and in case of bad times had a chance to blame the Germans who by their presence provided more competitors for the scarcer jobs. There seemed to be no traditional pattern of prejudice against Germans unless the skeletal suspicion of all out-groupers (always present) be invoked in this place.[30]

Both experimental studies and historical analyses have added credence to the economic-competition theory. Muzafer Sherif directed several experiments showing how intergroup competition at a boys' camp led to conflict and escalating hostility.[31] Donald Young pointed out that, throughout U.S. history, in times of high unemployment and thus intense job competition, nativist movements against minorities have flourished.[32] This pattern has held true regionally—against Asians on the West Coast, Italians in Louisiana, and French Canadians in New England—and nationally, with the antiforeign movements always peaking during periods of depression. So it was with the Native American Party in the 1830s, the Know-Nothing Party in the 1850s, the American Protective Association in the 1890s, and the Ku Klux Klan after World War I. Since the passage of civil rights laws on employment in the twentieth century, researchers have consistently detected the strongest antiblack prejudice among working-class and middle-class whites who feel threatened by blacks entering their socioeconomic group in

[30]John Dollard, "Hostility and Fear in Social Life," *Social Forces* 17 (1938): 15–26.

[31]Muzafer Sherif, O. J. Harvey, B. Jack White, William Hood, and Carolyn Sherif, *Intergroup Conflict and Cooperation: The Robbers Cave Experiment* (Norman: University of Oklahoma Institute of Intergroup Relations, 1961). See also M. Sherif, "Experiments in Group Conflict," *Scientific American* 195 (1956): 54–58.

[32]Donald Young, *Research Memorandum on Minority Peoples in the Depression* (New York: Social Science Research Council, 1937), pp. 133–41.

noticeable numbers.[33] It seems that any group applying the pressure of job competition most directly on another group becomes a target of its prejudice.

Once again, a theory that offers some excellent insights into prejudice—in particular, that adverse economic conditions correlate with increased hostility toward minorities—also has some serious shortcomings. Not all groups that have been objects of hostility (e.g., Quakers and Mormons) have been economic competitors. Moreover, why is hostility against some groups greater than against others? Why do the negative feelings in some communities run against groups whose numbers are so small that they cannot possibly pose an economic threat? Evidently, values besides economic ones cause people to be antagonistic to a group perceived as an actual or potential threat.

Social Norms. Some sociologists have suggested that a relationship exists between prejudice and a person's tendency to conform to societal expectations.[34] **Social norms**—the norms of one's culture—form the generally shared rules defining what is and is not proper behavior in one's culture. By learning and automatically accepting the prevailing prejudices, an individual is simply conforming to those norms.

This theory holds that a direct relationship exists between degree   40 of conformity and degree of prejudice. If so, people's prejudices should decrease or increase significantly when they move into areas where the prejudicial norm is different. Evidence supports this view. Thomas Pettigrew found that southerners in the 1950s became less prejudiced against blacks when they interacted with them in the army, where the social norms were less prejudicial.[35] In another study, Jeanne Watson found that people moving into an anti-Semitic neighborhood in New York City became more anti-Semitic.[36]

John Dollard's study, *Caste and Class in a Southern Town* (1937/ 1957), provides an in-depth look at the emotional adjustment of whites and blacks to rigid social norms.[37] In his study of the processes, functions, and maintenance of accommodation, Dollard detailed the "carrot-and-stick" method social groups employed. Intimidation—sometimes even severe reprisals for going against social norms—ensured compliance. However, reprisals usually were unnecessary. The advantages whites

---

[33] Andrew Greeley and Paul Sheatsley, "The Acceptance of Desegregation Continues to Advance," *Scientific American* 210 (1971): 13–19; T. F. Pettigrew, "Three Issues in Ethnicity: Boundaries, Deprivations, and Perceptions," in M. Yinger and S. J. Cutler (eds.), *Major Social Issues: A Multidisciplinary View* (New York: Free Press, 1978); R. D. Vanneman and T. F. Pettigrew, "Race and Relative Deprivation in the United States," *Race* 13 (1972): 461–86.

[34] See Harry H. L. Kitano, "Passive Discrimination in the Normal Person," *Journal of Social Psychology* 70 (1966): 23–31.

[35] Thomas Pettigrew, "Regional Differences in Anti-Negro Prejudice," *Journal of Abnormal and Social Psychology* 59 (1959): 28–36.

[36] Jeanne Watson, "Some Social and Psychological Situations Related to Change in Attitude," *Human Relations* 3 (1950): 15–56.

[37] John Dollard, *Caste and Class in a Southern Town*, 3rd ed. (Garden City, NY: Doubleday Anchor Books, 1957).

and blacks gained in psychological, economic, or behavioral terms served to perpetuate the caste order. These gains in personal security and stability set in motion a vicious circle. They encouraged a way of life that reinforced the rationale of the social system in this community.

Two 1994 studies provided further evidence of the powerful influence of social norms. Joachim Krueger and Russell W. Clement found that consensus bias persisted despite the availability of statistical data and knowledge about such bias.[38] Michael R. Leippe and Donna Eisenstadt showed that induced compliance can change socially significant attitudes and that the change generalizes to broader beliefs.[39]

Although the social-norms theory explains prevailing attitudes, it does not explain either their origins or the reasons new prejudices develop when other groups move into an area. In addition, the theory does not explain why prejudicial attitudes against a particular group rise and fall cyclically over the years.

Although many social scientists have attempted to identify the causes of prejudice, no single factor provides an adequate explanation. Prejudice is a complex phenomenon, and it is most likely the product of more than one causal agent. Sociologists today tend either to emphasize multiple-cause explanations or to stress social forces encountered in specific and similar situations—forces such as economic conditions, stratification, and hostility toward an outgroup.

ENGAGING THE TEXT

1. Review Parrillo's discussion of the cognitive, emotional, and action-oriented levels of prejudice. Do you think it's possible for an individual to hold prejudiced beliefs that do *not* affect her feelings and actions? Why or why not?

2. How can prejudice arise from self-justification? Offer some examples of how a group can assume an attitude of superiority in order to justify ill-treatment of others.

3. How, according to Parrillo, might personal factors like authoritarian attitudes, low self-esteem, or frustration promote the growth of prejudice?

4. What is the "socialization process," according to Parrillo? In what different ways can socialization instill prejudice?

5. What is the relationship between economic competition and prejudice? Do you think prejudice would continue to exist if everyone had a good job with a comfortable income?

---

[38]Joachim Krueger and Russell W. Clement, "The Truly False Consensus Effect: An Ineradicable and Egocentric Bias in Social Perception," *Journal of Personality and Social Psychology* 67 (1994): 596–610.

[39]Michael R. Leippe and Donna Eisenstadt, "Generalization of Dissonance Reduction: Decreasing Prejudice through Induced Compliance," *Journal of Personality and Social Psychology* 67 (1994): 395–414.

EXPLORING CONNECTIONS

6. Which of the causes of prejudice that Parrillo describes are reflected in the comments about immigrants in Darrin Bell's cartoon (p. 507)? What is Bell saying about the nature of anti-immigrant attitudes in U.S. history? What does he suggest about immigrants themselves?

EXTENDING THE CRITICAL CONTEXT

7. List the various groups that you belong to (racial, economic, cultural, social, familial, and so forth) and arrange them in a status hierarchy. Which groups were you born into? Which groups did you join voluntarily? Which have had the greatest impact on your socialization? Which groups isolate you the most from contact with outsiders?

8. Working in small groups, research recent news stories for examples of incidents involving racism or prejudice. Which of the theories described by Parrillo seem most useful for analyzing the motives underlying these events?

9. Visit the Southern Poverty Law Center Web site to learn which hate groups are active in your state. As an individual or class project, do further research on these groups. How do they operate and whom do they target? What efforts by law enforcement, government, civil rights organizations, or community groups are being made to combat their influence? Which of these seem most likely to be effective, and why? What further steps, if any, do you think should be taken?

CHYNA AND ME

JOYIN C SHIH

> JoYin Shih writes about the difficulties of growing up Chinese in America. She resists identifying with the stereotype of the good student—the polite, passive nerd. She resents her mother's reaction when a teacher insists that she speak Chinese so the class can experience her culture; instead of condemning the teacher's insensitivity, her mother argues that JoYin should be ashamed that she doesn't speak better Chinese. Feeling boxed in by her identity, JoYin envies African Americans for their outspoken anger at social injustice. This story was originally published in *Afro Asia: Revolutionary Political and Cultural Connections between African Americans and Asian Americans* (2008), edited by Fred Ho and Bill V. Mullen.

MR. ZEIGLER, MY THIRD GRADE TEACHER, had just ordered me to stand in front of the class along with Lillian. I stumbled up the aisle toward the front of the room, exposed and framed by the green chalk-board. Turning on my heel, I faced the rest of the class, all thirty-eight kids sitting in their rows, shades of skin varied like a box of mixed white to dark chocolates.

"Go on," Mr. Z. encouraged, "Talk in your language so that the rest of the class can hear a bit of culture." I stared at his sincere request, trying to pick out meanness akin to the all-too-familiar peer taunting "Chinese, Japanese, Dirty knees..." but there was none. The Ziggy[1] doll that Mr. Z. kept on his desk smiled its dumb "I'm a nice guy, you gotta love me...or at least feel sorry for me" smile, as I bit my lip, want-ing to be a good student, and Lillian, who was a good student, hung her head. Our similar long, black hair hung at our faces like limp cur-tains pulled back for a sorry show. I heard Lillian's breath heave in and stutter up into a high-pitched sob. *Oh no you don't*, I remember think-ing, *don't you dare cry, you little ninny*. But, of course, the breathing quickened into juts of snot and tears and I fixed my gaze on our elder accusingly. "Mr. Ziegler," I was ashamed at the waver in my own voice, "Lillian is Korean and I'm Chinese...and besides, she's adopted."

The teacher cleared his throat and quickly ushered us back to our seats with a herding gesture of his arms. "Mmm, well, why don't you write a report about what it's like to be Chinese."

Over recess time, I produced two sentences:

Chinese is hard work. I eat rice and play the piano everyday and 5 *kids think I am weird.*

On the bus ride home from school, Griff, my spelling bee rival, ad-vised me, "You oughtta tell your parents on Z. If he ever asked anyone in class to stand up and tell 'im what it's like to be black, my Daddy'd raise hell."

"It'd be the talk of the PTA, for sure," his little sister agreed.

That evening, though, my mother shrugged her shoulders, "He didn't mean any harm. He isn't *racist*," she emphasized the word as if it were too terrible to assign anyone, let alone my teacher. "They just don't understand. Besides, you should be ashamed that you can't speak more Chinese." I tucked away the blame into my own pocket, the rights and reasons of anger jostled and messed. It began a collection of frus-tration and misled feelings of discrimination.

Four or five times a year, my father would drive my mother, older brother, and me to visit his sister, *Goo-goo,* in New York City. On the playgrounds of West 125th St., I befriended a black girl with shiny cheeks and hair twisted into fun sculptures tipped on the ends with plastic, candy-colored barrettes. Her mother called her Chyna, like fine China, her precious baby girl. Ironically, Chyna had a toughness she had donned from having three older brothers and two pit bulls at home. When a kid on the playground teased that her mother had shaped her

---

[1]*Ziggy:* Bland cartoon character who cheerfully endures minor misfortunes. [All notes are the editors'.]

hair like alien antennae, she spat back. "At least my momma does more'n' wails on me, you silly nigger," and a deft, Afro-aimed wad of gum hurtled from her mouth with more precision than any ten-year-old I knew had, including my much-idolized older brother. The antagonist, pissed and a bit shamed for the jab, started cussing up a slew of insults, but I was still struck by Chyna's casual, "you silly nigger." The latter word being what plowed me down: Nigger. It was a no-no word from where I was living in Maryland, among the mixed black and white who consciously and carefully dwelt on the fine line of the Progressive North and the Ignorant South. It was worse than saying any of the four-letter curse words that I only dared to spell out when I was really mad. The early lyrics of rap hadn't reached my ears yet and "reclamation"[2] was only a word in the spelling bee. This girl has balls, I thought, or the equivalent of what a nine-year-old me would think.

I tried to punch the same line a few days later on my brother during a squabble, "You silly Chink," to which my father bawled and slapped out of me any rebellious inclination to try that line again. I got a lengthy lecture about how unfair he was treated in the workplace; that his hard work and high education would still be passed over when promotions came around. Even now, I can't say the word "Chink" without wincing. It just doesn't sound empowering or provoke the same admiration that I felt for Chyna's words.

My teenage years were spent in a mall-centered town of northern New Jersey, where the high school was attended by only a handful of minorities. I permed my jet-black hair and then sprayed gallons of "Sun In" bleach onto it, while flipping through a *Vogue* in which Iman and Naomi Campbell[3] were the only tokens. I didn't yet know there was such a thing as Asian fever (an exclusive desire for Asian women), and, to be quite honest, when the idea was first introduced to me I welcomed it as pretty fine praise and affirmation until my later college years taught me to examine the twisted undercurrents. I didn't have a single Asian friend during high school, and when my public speaking/debate team visited with schools that were populated with East and South Asian students, I eyed the cliques with uncertainty and unease. I had bought into believing the stereotypes of my background. Academic success meant nerd. Playing the piano was discipline and "good" in a bad, uncool way. Quiet and polite was socially inept and passive. The unease also came from the development that much of my identity was dependent on being different. I had internalized the defenses so much that it worried me to be racially similar. I looked at the photos of streets in Beijing, crammed with bicycle traffic, black eyes, and black hair, and I was secretly scared that I would get lost in the multitudes if I were to be transported there, to "people of my own kind."

[2]*reclamation:* Rap artists have reclaimed the word, "nigger," just as an earlier generation of activists reclaimed the word, "black."
[3]*Iman and Naomi Campbell:* Among the first black supermodels.

Even when I had attended Saturday Chinese school in Maryland, I felt like an imposter. "Grace is already on the fifth level in her piano studies and Jenny is at the top of her math class and won the science award." Mothers would compare us like prize pigs at a farm auction. I clung to my mother and hung my head at her approving nods toward the other specimens of blue-ribbon children. With my piano skills *Für Elise*[4] stuttered out like a mangled musicbox, and my school grades were high, but unremarkably so. It made me angry that such competitiveness was laced in the Chinese community, but that heads turned with tight lips from social injustice. I remember hearing the women speak of the Ivy League colleges that their children applied to. Some universities were limiting the number of Asian students that could be accepted, almost a reverse affirmative action. It was strange to me that the issue was spoken of as though this were a great compliment to how many good students there were with yellow skin. I didn't want to be part of a community that could wag its head with a modest smile at such discrimination.

It was the "outsider" complex that drove my adolescent experience toward the punk rock and goth scenes, arenas that were not only Eurocentric but to the degree that plaster-white complexions and British accents were the desired ideal. It must have been at a hardcore club when I encountered my first Nazi skinhead. He was a big, rangy fellow, whose pants still hung to his ass despite the stringy suspenders. The skinhead, whom I'll call Nick, toted a thick and slightly crooked swastika on his forearm. Throughout the first two sets of identically angry bands I noticed that Nick kept jutting his chin my way, and whenever he leapt into the mosh pit, he always jostled his way out a bit closer to the corner I was standing in. Wary of his lumbering advancement, I checked around to be sure of my own troop of vampyric comrades backing me. I cupped my hand to Moshe, my mohawked friend who insisted on the nickname "Mosh." "There might be trouble," I remarked, being seriously sixteen and thinking of the pepper spray that I had in my purse, which was left on the bar across the crowd of ruckus. Mosh chuckled, "Nah, that's Big Nick, I went to grade school with him. He's not really into it." "It" being Nazi; being for this New Jersey kid like any other club that you might join and outgrow—the Mouseketeers,[5] for example. (I don't mean to imply with this one example that all Nazi skinheads are so flimsy in their beliefs, but the ones I have met in the Northeast have more often than not turned out to be middle-class kids who haven't had the same beaten-in, outright racism that is passed on like a bad gene from generation to generation as it is in more rural parts of the country, where white sheets are not a Jerry Springer[6] joke.)

---

[4] *Für Elise:* Piano solo by Ludwig von Beethoven (1770–1827).
[5] *Mouseketeers:* Teenage cast members of Disney's *Mickey Mouse Club.*
[6] *Jerry Springer:* Host of a tabloid-style talk show.

After one bellowed-out lyric, Nick gives a hardy kick in the center of the pit and jumps out next to me. He grunts, wipes his red forehead (razor burn?), and grins down at me with a set of steel-aligned teeth. "What's your name?" he hollers down through the guitar solo blare.

"JOYIN!"

"What?!" It's not just the noise level, I'm used to spelling out my name and saying it at least three times slow, as if leading my listener through a first reader's book.

"JOO-YINN."

Big Nick shakes his head, "I'll just call you JOY, okay? Can I get you a drink, Joy?"

For once, the name isn't the issue that annoys me. It's that this jackass with the most offensive hate message scrawled into his flesh is hitting on me. I'm fuming and I know that in this club, with the amps spewing out repetitive lyrics about a blind society, there was no way that I could administer my finely tuned, debate club tactics and try to make sense of what was going on in Big Nick's cerebellum. So I just yelled and pointed at the swastika, "NAZI!"

"Yeah!" Big Nick smiled back and saluted as if I were praising his Popeye muscles.

I pointed to myself, "CHINESE!" (Me, Jane. You, Fuckhead.)

"I LIKE CHINESE." I think he meant food, because I doubt that he mingled in the Chinese Cultural Center much.

I pointed to myself again, almost out of sheer mockery, "MINORITY."

He got the point and quickly blinked his eyes at me and shook his head, "BUT YOU'RE A MODEL MINORITY!"

Those two words stunned me more than the time Chyna ranted out the word "nigger," but it was an altogether different shock. It took something that sounded like praise and invoked a shame in me, while Chyna had taken a word that had a history of shame and invoked a connection, a proud one, albeit teasing. I felt like a scandal, like someone "passing" into a social privilege that I did not want yet could not deny.

It was just a couple of years later when I packed my bags, found an apartment in Harlem, and grabbed out desperately at the words to fit my anger in college. The first movements of identification were not clearly pursued. At a quick and skeptical glance, the Asian clubs at the university still seemed academic, social, or Christian. They seemed to lack the intensity and anger that the African American groups had. Again, I bought the stereotype. Everywhere I turned I felt boxed in, even by the boys and men who pursued me because of my Asianness. I felt that they were looking at my black hair and almond-shaped eyes for something exotic, something far beyond the New Jersey home that I really came from. I remember that a Caucasian hallmate once explained to me the subsets of Asian Women: "You've got your dowdy girls who shrink away from you in the elevator, and will blush all the while they help you with the lab report. There are the Gucci girls, usually Korean or Japanese, who are a real expensive date. They have twenty pairs of black shoes and usually stick with their own, anyhow. Then there's the Joy Luck Club,[7] who are the best bets for dates because they're sick of their domineering Chinese fathers." (I've recently heard that this person moved to Korea and is a rather popular television celebrity there.)

I don't mean to say that I assimilated into the black Harlem community; I couldn't and wasn't quite pretentious enough to believe that I could. I was attending Columbia University, one of the best and most-privileged colleges in the nation, but out of some illusion of self-preservation I had decided to live off campus, a few blocks higher into Harlem yet still at the safe edge of its perimeters.

Black culture meant strength to me. I made my way down the street from the bodegas and African cafés to the literature classes of Baldwin and Achebe.[8] At the university I envied the hip, independent black women whom I befriended on campus. Through my eyes they were soulful, strong, and spoke their minds, like my childhood friend Chyna. I saw African American students wearing colorful garb, growing their dreds, beating their drums, and saying "This is who I am." My feet itched to the sounds of hip hop and the lyrics seemed to match my own heated sentiments. But when I looked around for my Asian brothers and sisters, I saw them donning khakis and polos, assimilating for good jobs.

"Asian Americans are known for their success in business, education, and emphasis on family values. What is there to be angry about? It's a compliment." My mother still tries to convince me. I resented it, though, as many kids, not just minorities, with privileges resent their handed-down sweaters of ease that blanket personal struggles and hardships. I yearned for the ferocity of black anger, the right to that obvious and unifying spirit. The ability to protest was far more appealing and righteous to me than the polite assimilation of the Asian American community.

Coming to terms with my ethnicity relied heavily on breaching the gap that I had set up between myself and other Asians. On campus, I finally became close friends with other Asian women. The first comforts were simple. "Isn't it nice to eat together?" we grinned at each other, gnawing on our cold soy-chicken feet. "No one to make faces at us." At our dinner table, though, our familiar issues came forth with the platters of familiar food. We compared notes on childhoods (we all wince at the echoes of the teasing "dirty knees" song), adolescence (how many of us permed and bleached our hair?), and the present. I found myself with symptoms of my own sort of yellow fever, seeking out black-haired, sleek-eyed comrades to claim as my "sistas."

30

---

[7]*Joy Luck Club: The Joy Luck Club* (1989), a novel by Amy Tan, depicted four Chinese immigrant mothers and their American-born daughters.

[8]*Baldwin and Achebe:* James Arthur Baldwin (1924–1987) American novelist, essayist, and social critic, whose works include *Go Tell It on the Mountain* (1953), *Notes of a Native Son* (1955), and *The Fire Next Time* (1963); Chinua Achebe (b. 1930) Nigerian novelist, poet, professor and critic, best known for *Things Fall Apart* (1958).

After years of shifting layers of identity I embrace my Chinese heritage. Yet I still question the issues of discomfort and discrimination and acknowledge the ever-changing relations in the cultures around me. From the African American community I gained a sense of right to empower and to protest. From the Asian American community I gained a sense of affirmation and sharing of experiences. Living among and as part of the urban collage, I enjoy the motley group of cultures and recognize the struggles of each group and individual, but, most importantly, I am able to look in the mirror and recognize my own.

ENGAGING THE TEXT

1. What is wrong with the third grade teacher's request to "Talk your language" (para. 2)? What motivates his request? Is he, in fact, racist? Why or why not?

2. What is the difference between Chyna's use of the word "nigger" and JoYin's use of the word "Chink"? Why is JoYin's father upset by her use of the word?

3. Why does the skinhead's remark that JoYin is a model minority "invoke a shame" in her (para. 25)? Why does her mother embrace the term? To what extent do you think the differences between JoYin and her mother are generational?

4. Why does JoYin envy the African American students at Columbia? How does she finally come to terms with her own culture?

EXPLORING CONNECTIONS

5. Visit Bedford's e-Pages (bedfordstmartins.com/rereading/epages) for Chapter Five of *Rereading America* and discuss the role of stereotyping in "Chyna and Me" and in Maysan Haydar's "Veiled Intentions." What stereotypes does each woman encounter, and how does she deal with them?

6. Would Joan Morgan (p. 455) agree with Shih that Chyna's use of the word "nigger" is empowering? What does this term signify for Morgan? Is it ever all right to use this word? If so, when and why? If not, why not?

7. Compare JoYin's attitude toward her parents and toward school to the narrator's and to Teresa's in "Para Teresa" (p. 198). What does it mean to each of these women to be "minorities" in a white dominated world? What do they struggle with or against?

EXTENDING THE CRITICAL CONTEXT

8. Do some research on the model minority myth. Why is it misleading? What differences among individuals and immigrant groups does it mask? How is it used against Asian Americans? Against other minority groups? Write an essay or give a report about what you discover.

9. Interview friends, family members, or fellow students to create your own oral history on the subject of racial identity. What terms are applied to them (e.g., white, Caucasian, cracker, European American, Polack, honky, Anglo, kraut,

white trash, Mick, redneck, frog)? Do they prefer a particular term? Do any offend them? Why? Ask your subjects to describe a time when they had to re-evaluate their thoughts or feelings about their own racial group. What experiences made them conscious of their race? Share and edit these oral histories in small groups, and then assemble them into a class anthology.

LOOT OR FIND: FACT OR FRAME?
CHERYL I. HARRIS AND DEVON W. CARBADO

In 2005, Hurricane Katrina slammed into the Gulf Coast, killing more than 1,800 people and destroying thousands of homes and businesses. Hardest hit was New Orleans, where the hurricane damage was compounded by massive flooding caused by the failure of the city's levee system. Although residents were ordered to evacuate before the storm hit, many—overwhelmingly black and poor—lacked the resources to escape, and were trapped for days in attics, on roofs, on freeway overpasses, and in overcrowded emergency shelters. In this article, Cheryl I. Harris and Devon W. Carbado (b. 1965) analyze the media coverage of this disaster and the public response to the stories that emerged from the crisis in New Orleans. Both Harris and Carbado teach at UCLA's School of Law; they have written widely on constitutional issues, civil rights, gender, and critical race theory. Harris, who has also worked in the area of international human rights, served for several years as cochair for the National Conference of Black Lawyers. In 2005 she received the Distinguished Professor Award for Civil Rights Education from the ACLU Foundation of Southern California. Carbado has edited or coedited several books, including *Time on Two Crosses: The Collected Writings of Bayard Rustin* (2003), *Race Law Stories* (2008), *The Long Walk to Freedom: Runaway Slave Narratives* (2012), and *Acting White? Rethinking Race in Post-Racial America* (2013). He has won multiple awards for distinguished teaching.

Evidence of Things Seen

What do [the images on p. 525] represent? What facts do they convey? We could say that image A depicts a man who, in the aftermath of Katrina, is wading through high waters with food supplies and a big black plastic bag. We might say that image B depicts a man and woman,

This chapter draws from and builds upon Cheryl I. Harris, "White Washing Race; Scapegoating Culture," *California Law Review* (2006) (forthcoming) (book review). [All notes are Harris and Carbado's unless otherwise indicated.]

A

B

both wearing backpacks. They, too, are wading through high waters in the aftermath of Katrina, and the woman appears to be carrying food supplies.

This is not how these images were presented in the press. The captions that appeared with the two photos, both of which ran on Yahoo! news, were quite different. The caption for image A read: "A young man walks through chest-deep flood water after looting a grocery store in New Orleans." The caption for image B read: "Two residents wade through chest-deep waters after finding bread and soda from a local grocery store after Hurricane Katrina came through the area." The caption for image A, then, tells us that a crime has been committed; the caption for image B tells that a fierce, poignant struggle for survival is under way—the subjects have just found food. Image A depicts a young black man; image B shows a white man and woman.

The images and their respective captions almost immediately stirred up significant controversy. People complained that the captions accompanying the images were racially suggestive: black people "loot" and white people "find." *Boston Globe* correspondent Christina Pazzanese wondered, "I am curious how one photographer knew the food was looted by one but not the other. Were interviews conducted as they swam by?"[1]

[1]Cited in Aaron Kinney, " 'Looting' or 'finding'?" *Salon*, September 1, 2005.

Not everyone agreed, however, that the images and captions reflected a racial problem. As one commentator put it:

> It's difficult to draw any substantiated conclusions from these photos' captions. Although they were both carried by many news outlets, they were taken by two different photographers and came from two different services, the Associated Press (AP) and the Getty Images via Agence France-Presse (AFP). Services make different stylistic standards for how they caption photographs, or the dissimilar wordings may have been due to nothing more than the preferences of different photographers and editors, or the difference might be the coincidental result of a desire to avoid repetitive wording (similar photographs from the same news services variously describe the depicted actions as "looting," "raiding," "taking," "finding" and "making off"). The viewer also isn't privy to the contexts in which the photographs were taken—it's possible that in one case the photographer actually saw his subject exiting an unattended grocery store with an armful of goods, while in the other case the photographer came upon his subjects with supplies in hand and could only make assumptions about how they obtained them.[2]

For the most part, this controversy focused on a question of fact. Did 5 the black person really loot the goods he was carrying? Did the white man and white woman really find the food they were carrying? Indeed, the director of media relations at the Associated Press suggested that, as to image A, "he [the photographer] saw the person go into the shop and take the goods....that's why he wrote 'looting' in the article."[3] In other words, the fact of the matter was that the black man in image A was a looter.

The photographer of image B, Chris Graythen, maintained,

> I wrote the caption about the two people who "found" the items. I believed in my opinion, that they did simply find them, and not "looted" them in the definition of the word. The people were swimming in chest deep water, and there were other people in the water, both white and black. I looked for the best picture. There were a million items floating in the water—we were right near a grocery store that had 5+ feet of water in it. It had no doors. The water was moving, and the stuff was floating away. These people were not ducking into a store and busting down windows to get electronics. They picked up bread and Cokes that were floating in the water. They would have floated away anyhow.[4]

To some extent, the credibility of Graythen's explanation is beside the point here. That is, the loot-or-find problem of image A and image B cannot fully be addressed with reference to the individual intent of those who either took the picture or produced the accompanying interpretive text. Indeed, it is entirely plausible that had the photos appeared without

[2]www.snopes.com/Katrina/photos/looters.asp.
[3]Cited in Kinney, " 'Looting' or 'finding'?"
[4]Ibid.

any captions, they would have been read the same way.[5] This is because while neither "loot" nor "find" is written on either image, in the context of public disorder, the race of the subjects inscribes those meanings.

The "Color-Blind" Frame

Drawing on facts about both Hurricane Katrina and the public's response to it, this [essay] queries whether efforts to change the racial status quo and eliminate inequality should or can rely solely on facts or empiricism. There is a growing sense within the civil rights community that more empirical research is needed to persuade mainstream Americans that racism remains a problem in American society and that the elimination of racial disadvantage is not a do-it-yourself project. The idea seems to be that if only more Americans knew certain "facts" (for example, about the existence of implicit bias) they would be more inclined to support civil rights initiatives (for example, affirmative action). We agree that more empirical research is needed. Facts are important—indeed crucial—since so much of public opinion is grounded in misinformation. We simply do not think that there is a linear progression between raw empiricism and more enlightened public opinion about race and racism. Put another way, we do not believe that facts speak for themselves.

It is precisely the recognition that facts don't speak for themselves that helps to explain why scholars across academic fields and politicians across the political spectrum continue to pay significant attention to the social and cognitive processes that shape how we interpret facts. Of the variety of theories—in sociology, political science, law, anthropology, psychology, and economics—that attempt to explain these processes, most share the idea that we interpret events through frames—interpretational structures that, consciously and unconsciously, shape what we see and how we see it. In the words of one scholar, framing refers to "understanding a story you already know and saying, 'Oh yeah, that one.'"[6] As we process and make sense of an event, we take account of and simultaneously ignore facts that do not fit the frame, and sometimes we supply ones that are missing. Thus, it is sometimes said that "frames trump facts."[7]

---

[5]One study of local television news stories on crime and public opinion illustrates the strong association between criminal behavior and racial identity. Participants were shown an identical news story under three different conditions: one group witnessed a version in which the perpetrator was white; another group saw a version in which the perpetrator was black; and a third group viewed a version in which there was no picture of the perpetrator. Following the screening, the participants in the first, white-perpetrator group were less likely to recall having seen a suspect than subjects in the second, black-perpetrator group. Among those in the third group, who saw no image of the perpetrator, over 60 percent erroneously recalled seeing a perpetrator, and in 70 percent of those cases viewers identified that nonexistent image as black. See Franklin Gilliam Jr. and Shanto Iyengar, "Prime Suspects: The Influence of Local Television News on the Viewing Public," *American Journal of Political Science* 44 (2000):560.

[6]Roger Schank, "Tell Me a Story," *Narrative and Intelligence* 71 (1995).

[7]A more nuanced formulation suggests, "Like well-accepted theories that guide our interpretation of data, schemas incline us to interpret data consistent with our biases." See Jerry Kang, "Trojan Horses of Races," *Harvard Law Review* 118 (2005):1489,1515.

The most relevant and dominant frame is color blindness, or the belief 10
that race is *not* a factor in how we make sense of the world. Color blindness is a kind of metaframe that comprises three interwoven racial scripts:
(1) because of *Brown v. Board of Education*[8] and the civil rights reforms it
inaugurated, racism is by and large a thing of the past; (2) when racism
does rear its ugly head, it is the product of misguided and irrational behavior on the part of self-declared racial bigots, who are few and far between; and (3) racial consciousness—whether in the form of affirmative
action or Jim Crow[9]–like racism—should be treated with suspicion, if
not rejected outright. The gradual ascendancy and eventual racial dominance of color blindness frames the facts of racial inequality (manifested,
for example, in disparities in wealth and educational outcomes between
blacks and whites) as a function of something other than racism. Because
scientists have largely repudiated the notion of biological inferiority, color
blindness frames the problem of racial disadvantage in terms of conduct.
The problem is not genes but culture, not blood but behavior: were black
people to engage in normatively appropriate cultural practices—work
hard, attend school, avoid drugs, resist crime—they would transcend
their current social status and become part of the truly advantaged. On
this view, black disadvantage is both expected and deserved—a kind of
natural disaster not produced by racism.

At least initially, Katrina challenged the supremacy of color blindness. The tidal wave of suffering that washed over New Orleans
seemed incontrovertible evidence of the salience of race in contemporary U.S. society.[10] The simple fact that the faces of those left to fend for
themselves or die were overwhelmingly black raised questions about
the explanatory power of color blindness under which race is deemed
irrelevant.[11] Racial suffering was everywhere. And black people were

[8]*Brown v. Board of Education:* The 1954 landmark Supreme Court case that outlawed
segregated schools. [Eds.]

[9]*Jim Crow:* System of legalized segregation that dominated the South from 1866 to the
mid 1960s. Black Americans were denied access to schools, voting, and public restrooms
and transportation as well as subjected to systemic racism and violence. [Eds.]

[10]We do not intend to ignore the tremendous loss suffered in the Gulf region more
broadly: we focus on New Orleans because of its unique position in the national imagination, as well as its pre-Katrina racial demographics. Indeed, New Orleans was not just a
city that had come to be predominantly black; it was a city that was culturally marked
as black. As one noted historian has stated, "The unique culture of south Louisiana derives from black Creole culture." Quoted in "Buffetted by Katrina, City's Complex Black
Community Struggles to Regroup," Associated Press, October 4, 2005, www.msnbc.com.

[11]Or fend for themselves and be punished for it. A particularly harrowing account of
official indifference and hostility comes from the ordeal of two emergency room workers
who had the misfortune of being in New Orleans for a conference when Hurricane Katrina
struck. After their hotel in the French Quarter closed, they, along with several hundred others, collected money to hire buses for their evacuation, but the buses were prevented from
entering the city. When the workers attempted to flee on foot, they were directed to wait on
the interstate for rescue that never came. Neither the police nor the National Guard provided
them with food or water. When the group managed to find food for themselves and set up a
makeshift camp, they were repeatedly dispersed at gunpoint by the police. When they attempted to walk across the bridge into the neighboring city of Gretna, they were again turned
back at gunpoint by Gretna police. See Larry Bradshaw and Lorrie Beth Slonsky, "Trapped
in New Orleans," September 6, 2005, www.counterpunch.org/bradshaw09062005.html.

dying—prime time live. One had to close one's eyes, or willfully blind oneself, not to see this racial disaster. Everyone, it seemed, except government officials, was riveted. And there was little disagreement that Katrina exposed shameful fissures in America's social fabric; that the precipitating event was an act of God, not the cultural pathology of the victims; and that the government's response, at least in the initial phases, was woefully inadequate. Seasoned mainstream journalists wept and railed, while ordinary Americans flooded relief organizations with money.

The tragedy of Katrina created a rupture in the racial-progress narrative that had all but erased the suffering of poor black people from the political landscape. In contrast to the pre-Katrina picture, black people were perceived to be innocent victims. Black people were perceived to have a legitimate claim on the nation-state. Black people were perceived to be deserving of government help. Katrina—or the *facts* the public observed about its effects—disrupted our tendency to *frame* black disadvantage in terms of cultural deficiency. But how did that happen? And doesn't this disruption undermine our central point about facts and frames?

Not at all. Frames are not static. Epic events like Katrina push up against and can temporarily displace them. All those people. All that suffering. This can't be America. How could we let this happen? That question—how could we let this happen?—reflected a genuine humanitarian concern for fellow human beings. Moreover, the compelling facts about Katrina raised a number of questions about racial inequality previously suppressed under color blindness. Indeed, as the humanitarian crisis peaked with the retreating floodwaters, a debate over the role of race in the disaster quickly emerged. The unrelenting spectacle of black suffering bodies demanded an explanation. Why were those New Orleans residents who remained trapped during Katrina largely black and poor? Was it, as hip-hop artist Kanye West argued, a case of presidential indifference to, or dislike of, poor black people?[12] Or was it, as Ward Connerly[13] asserted, the predictable consequence of a

---

[12]On a nationally broadcast telethon to raise money for the victims of Katrina, Kanye West departed from the scripted remarks to say, "I hate the way they portray us in the media. You see a black family: it says they are looting. You see a white family; it says they have been looking for food. And you know, it has been five days, because most of the people are black, and even for me to complain about it, I would be a hypocrite, because I have tried to turn away from the TV because it is too hard to watch. So now I am calling my business manager right now to see what is the biggest amount I can give. And just imagine if I was down there and those are my people down there." Commenting on the slow pace of the government's response, he said, "George Bush doesn't care about black people." NBC immediately cut to another star on the program and censored West's remarks from the West Coast feed of the program. It also issued the following disclaimer: "Kanye West departed from the scripted comments that were prepared for him, and his opinions in no way represent the views of the networks. It would be most unfortunate if the efforts of the artists who participated tonight and the generosity of millions of Americans who are helping those in need are overshadowed by one person's opinion." "Rapper Kanye West Accuses Bush of Racism; NBC Apologizes," *CBC Arts*, September 3, 2005, www.cbc.ca/story/arts /national/2005/09/03/Arts/kanye_west_katrina20050903.html.

[13]*Ward Connerly:* Conservative African American political activist (b. 1939). [Eds.]

natural disaster that befell a city that just happened to be predominantly black? Was it, as Linda Chavez[14] claimed, the result of a culture of dependency combined with local bureaucratic incompetence? Was race a factor in determining who survived and who did not?[15] Or did class provide a better explanation?[16] Finally, could we ever fully understand Katrina without meaningfully engaging the legacy of slavery?[17] These and other, similar questions were pushed into the foreground by the force of Katrina's devastation.

But the frame of color blindness did not disappear. It manifested itself in the racial divide that emerged with respect to how people answered the foregoing questions. While there is some intraracial diversity of opinion among public figures about the role of race and racism in explaining what happened, there remains a striking racial difference in how the disaster is viewed. According to public opinion polls, whites largely reject the notion that race explains the governmental disregard, while blacks assert that the fact that the victims were black and poor was a significant part of the story.[18] This difference over the difference that race makes reflects competing racial frames. Thus, while the facts of what happened in Katrina's aftermath unsettled the familiar color-blind racial script that poor black people were the authors of their own plight, those facts did not ultimately dis-

[14]*Linda Chavez:* The first Latina (b. 1947) nominated to the U.S. Cabinet, now an author and conservative political commentator. [Eds.]

[15]This was Howard Dean's view. In an address to the National Baptist Convention he stated, "As survivors are evacuated, order is restored, the water slowly begins to recede, and we sort through the rubble, we must also begin to come to terms with the ugly truth that skin color, age and economics played a deadly role in who survived and who did not." "Excerpts of DNC Chairman Howard Dean's Remarks to the National Baptist Convention of America, Inc.," U.S. Newswire, September 8, 2005, www.usnewswire.com.

[16]While some have argued that class was a more salient factor than race in explaining who was affected, we do not think that given the country's history of de jure and de facto racial subordination, race can be so neatly disaggregated from class. Particularly in the context of New Orleans—a city that was predominantly black and predominantly poor—the fact that those left on the overpasses and in the Superdome were black had everything to do with why they were poor. The point is not to reproduce another unhelpful version of the race-versus-class debate but to avoid sublimating the racial dimension of the issues raised by Katrina. Recent survey analysis suggests that race was in fact a crucial factor in explaining who was in harm's way. See "Katrina Hurts Blacks and Poor Victims Most," CNN/*USA Today*/Gallup Poll, October 25, 2005.

[17]Both the Reverend Jesse Jackson and Representative Cynthia McKinney drew a link between the events in the Gulf and slavery. In response to a question by Anderson Cooper on CNN about whether race was a determinative factor in the federal government's response to Katrina, Jackson replied, "It is at least a factor. Today I saw 5,000 African Americans on the I-10 causeway desperate, perishing, dehydrated, babies dying. It looked like Africans in the hull of a slave ship. It was so ugly and so obvious. Have we missed this catastrophe because of indifference and ineptitude or is it a combination of both? And certainly I think the issue of race as a factor will not go away from this equation." Jesse Jackson, Remarks on *360 Degrees*, CNN, September 2, 2005. In an address on the floor of the House of Representatives on September 8, 2005, Representative McKinney said, "As I saw the African Americans, mostly African-American families ripped apart, I could only think about slavery, families ripped apart, herded into what looked like concentration camps." Cynthia McKinney, "Text of Remarks Delivered on the Floor of the House on Sept. 8, 2005," reprinted in "A Few Thoughts on the State of Our Nation," September 12, 2005, www.counterpunch.org/mckinney09122005.html.

[18]"Huge Racial Divide over Katrina and Its Consequences," Report of the Pew Research Center for People and the Press, September 8, 2005, 2; available at http://people-press.org/reports/display.php3?Report ID=255.

place core ideas embedded in the color-blind frame: race is irrelevant and racism largely does not exist. Most whites were able to see black people as victims, but they were unwilling to link their victim status to race or racism. A more acceptable story was that black people in New Orleans suffered only because of bureaucratic inefficiencies in the wake of a natural disaster. Race simply could not be a factor. Katrina then only partially destabilized the frame of color blindness. To the extent that our starting point for thinking about race is that it does not matter, other racial frames or scripts more easily fit within the overarching frame. These frames can both explicitly invoke race and, even more powerfully, implicitly play the race card. After the initial uncertainty, what emerged in the wake of Katrina was the frame of "law and order" —a racial script that permeated the debate over the iconic photographs with which we began our essay, and over the post-Katrina relief efforts. The media were both author and reader of events in ways that both challenged and underwrote this racial frame.

A Picture Is Worth a Thousand Words

Recall Chris Graythen's response to the racial controversy concerning   15
the images with which we began this chapter. With regard to image B, Graythen asserted that he "looked for the best picture." More specifically, Graythen searched for an image that would best narrate a particular factual story: that people were wading through water to find food. According to Graythen, both whites and blacks were finding food in the chest-high water. Unlike pre-Katrina New Orleans, this space was racially integrated. Graythen searched this racially integrated body of water for a picture that would most successfully convey the idea of people finding food (as distinct from people "ducking into a store and busting down windows to get electronics"). Graythen's "best picture" —his "Oh yeah, that one" —emerged when he saw the two white people photographed in image B. Their images best fit the caption that Graythen already had in mind, people wading through water to find food. Because people are more likely to associate blacks with looting ("ducking into a store and busting down windows to get electronics") than with finding food, Graythen's selection makes sense. Indeed, one can infer from Graythen's decision to photograph white people that it was easier to frame white people as despondent people finding food than it was to frame black people in that way. To put the point slightly differently, there would be some dissonance between the image of black people in those high waters and a caption describing people finding food. This dissonance is not about facts—whether in fact the black people were finding food; the dissonance is about frames—the racial association between black people and looting, particularly on the heels of a natural disaster or social upheaval.

Two caveats before moving on. First, nothing above is intended to suggest that Graythen's decision to photograph the two white people was racially conscious—that is, intentionally motivated by race. Frames operate both consciously and unconsciously; his selection of whites to photograph (and his "natural selection" against blacks) converged with existing racial frames about criminality and perpetrators, on the one hand, and law-abidingness and victims, on the other. The two photos were perfect mirror images of each other. But only image B could convey a story of survival against adversity; image A was inconsistent with that script. The presence of a black man with a big plastic bag in the context of a natural disaster is already inscribed with meaning. In that sense, the black man in image A did not require a caption to be framed; nor did the white man and woman in image B. The stereotype of black criminality was activated by image A and the many images like it, which showed the central problem in New Orleans not to be the lack of humanitarian aid, but the lack of law and order.

The second caveat: our analysis should not be read as an argument against empiricism or a claim that facts are irrelevant. We simply mean to say that racial frames shape our perceptions of the facts. This does not mean that we are overdetermined by frames or that we are unable to escape their interpretative strictures. Rather, the point is that dependence on "just the facts" will seldom be enough to dislodge racial frames.[19] Partly this is because racial frames are installed not as the result of empiricism, but in spite of it. Consider color blindness. It is the dominant racial frame for understanding race not because of facts but because of a well-financed political project to entrench and naturalize a color-blind understanding of American race relations.[20] Accordingly, something more than facts is required to undo the racial work color blindness continues to perform; and something more than facts is required to dislodge the normativity of color blindness itself.

From Rescue to Occupation: Seeing the Invisible

> *I'd rather have them here dead than alive. And at least they're not robbing you and you [don't] have to worry about feeding them.*[21]
> —A RESIDENT OF ST. GABRIEL WHEN ASKED FOR HER REACTIONS TO THE DECISION TO DESIGNATE THE TOWN AS A COLLECTIVE MORGUE

[19]As Gary Blasi contends, "If we store social categories in our heads by means of prototypes or exemplars rather than statistics, then our basic cognitive mechanisms not only predispose us toward stereotypes…, but also limit the potentially curative effect of information that contradicts the statistical assumptions about base rates that are embedded in our stereotypes." Gary Blasi, "Advocacy Against the Stereotype," *UCLA Law Review* 49 (2002):1241, 1256–57.

[20]See Lee Cokorinos, *The Assault on Diversity* (Institute for Democracy Studies, 2002), tracing the network of conservative activists and organizations that have waged a well-funded campaign over two decades to change the corpus of civil rights laws, end affirmative action, and reframe the political discourse on race and racism.

[21]This should not suggest that she was without any compassion. She went on to say, "[The bodies] have to go somewhere. These are people's families. They have to—they still have to have dignity." It's precisely our point that one can have compassion and still see black people through racial frames. *Paula Zahn Now*, CNN, September 8, 2005.

To the extent that our discussion of the problem of racial frames has largely examined representational issues, one mighty reasonably ask: What are the material consequences of this problem? And how, if at all, did it injure black New Orleanians in the wake of Hurricane Katrina? The answer relates to two interconnected frames: the frame of law and order and the frame of black criminality. Working together, these frames rendered black New Orleanians dangerous, unprotectable, and unrescuable.

In the immediate aftermath of Katrina, the media pointedly criticized the slow pace at which the federal government was responding to the disaster. But the critical stance was short-lived and quickly gave way to a focus on the breakdown of law and order, a frame that activated a familiar stereotype about black criminality. While initially blacks were seen as victims of Hurricane Katrina and a failed governmental response, this victim status proved to be highly unstable. Implicit in the frame that "this can't be America" is the notion that the neglect in the wake of Katrina was a violation of the duty of care owed to all citizens of the nation. This social contract includes blacks as citizens; and indeed the claim by blacks, "We are American" — a statement vigorously asserted by those contained in the convention center[22] — responded to and relied upon that frame.[23]

As time progressed, the social currency of the image of blacks as citizens of the state to whom a duty of care is owed diminished. It rubbed uneasily against the more familiar racial framing of poor black people as lazy, undeserving, and inherently criminal. Concern over the looting of property gradually took precedence over the humanitarian question of when people might be rescued and taken off of the highways and rooftops. Thus, while armed white men were presumed to be defending their property, black men with guns constituted gangs of violent looters who had to be contained. Under this frame, the surrounding towns and parishes that constituted potential refuge for black New Orleans residents who had no means to evacuate before the storm became no-go areas because of concerns about black criminality.

A particularly stark example of this came during the CNN interview on September 8 between Christiane Amanpour[24] and the resident of St. Gabriel quoted above. The sentiment that dead blacks were better than live ones was enforced not only by local authorities who, like the Gretna police, turned people away at gunpoint, but by the National Guard and other local authorities who purportedly denied the Red Cross

[22]See Michael Ignatieff, "The Broken Contract," *New York Times*, September 25, 2005 (reporting that a woman held at the convention center asserted, "We are American" during a TV interview, demonstrating both anger and astonishment that she would have to remind Americans of that fact and that the social contract had failed).

[23]Note that this frame is simultaneously inclusionary and exclusionary. To the extent that it asserts black citizenship, it seeks to include black people within the nation-state. However, it excludes noncitizens, black as well as others, from the circle of care based on lack of formal American belonging. This is deeply problematic but it reveals the limited space within which blacks could assert legitimate claims on national empathy.

[24]*Christiane Amanpour:* Chief International Correspondent for CNN News. [Eds.]

permission to enter the city shortly after the storm because of concerns about the safety of the rescuers.[25]

These fears were grounded in what ultimately proved to be grossly exaggerated or completely unsubstantiated media accounts of violence and attacks particularly in the Superdome and the convention center.[26] The tone of these reports were hyperbolic, evoking all of the familiar racial subtexts: FOX News, for example, issued a news report the day before the Superdome was evacuated that "there were many reports of robberies, rapes, car-jackings, rioters and murder and that violent gangs are roaming the streets at night, hidden by the cover of darkness." The *Los Angeles Times* was no less sensational, reporting that National Guard troops had to take rooftop positions to scan for snipers and armed mobs as gunfire rang out.[27] These reports were taken as authoritative by police and other law enforcement officials. Indeed, even the mayor of the city, Ray Nagin, who is black, spoke of "hundreds of armed gang members" killing and raping people inside the Superdome, such that the crowd had descended to an "almost animalistic state.[28]

We are not arguing that there was no violence. There was. But the frames of black criminality and law and order overdetermined how we interpreted both the extent and nature of that violence. For example, consider how the "facts" about rape were interpreted and discussed. Recently, advocacy groups for victims of sexual assault have begun to challenge the official count of reported rapes—four—as unrealistically low. A national database newly created by the National Sexual Violence Resource Center reports more than forty sexual assaults, while another victim's rights organization has reported more than 150 post-Katrina violent crimes, of which about one-third were sexual assaults, including those committed in the homes of host families.[29] This suggests that reports of sexual assaults were underreported. Paradoxically, at the same time that reports of rape were cited to confirm stereotypes of black criminality, the black women victims of *actual* rapes suffered an unconscionable degree of official disregard. While accounts of rape were

[25]See Anna Johnson, "Jackson Lashes Out at Bush over Hurricane Response, Criticizes Media for Katrina Coverage," AP Alert, September 3, 2005 (reporting that the Red Cross asserted that it could not enter New Orleans on orders from the National Guard and local authorities). A principal reason for the delay was that government officials believed that they had to prepare a complicated military operation rather than a relief effort. See "Misinformation Seen Key in Katrina Delays," UPI Top Stories, September 30, 2005.

[26]See Brian Thevenot and Gordon Russell, "Reports of Anarchy at the Superdome Overstated," *Seattle Times*, September 26, 2005 (reporting that "the vast majority of reported atrocities committed by evacuees have turned out to be false, or at least unsupported by any evidence, according to key military, law enforcement, medical and civilian officers in a position to know." See also Andrew Gumbel, "After the Storm, US Media Held to Account for Exaggerated Tales of Katrina Chaos," *Los Angeles Times*, September 28, 2005.

[27]Susannah Rosenblatt and James Rainey, "Reports of Post-Katrina Mayhem May Have Been Overblown," *Los Angeles Times*, September 27, 2005.

[28]Thevenot and Russell, "Reports of Anarchy."

[29]See "40 Rapes Reported in Hurricane Katrina, Rita Aftermath," NewOrleans Channel.com, wsdu, http://msnbc.msn.com/id/10590305; Nancy Cook Lauer, "Rape-Reporting Procedure Missing After Hurricane" Women's eNews, www.womensenews.org/article.cfm /dyn/aid/2448.

invoked as signs of the disintegration of social order in New Orleans, some of the black women who experienced sexual violence were unable to file reports with law enforcement officials despite their efforts to do so, notwithstanding the city's ostensible mission to maintain law and order to protect victims from crime.

One of the more prominent examples of this official disregard was Charmaine Neville, a member of the family of renowned New Orleans musicians, who was raped by a roving group of men who invaded her community in the Lower Ninth Ward while she and her neighbors struggled unsuccessfully over a series of days to be evacuated and to obtain medical care.[30] Neville's searing account of what happened to her is a clear indictment of the government for its neglect: "What I want people to understand is that if we hadn't been left down there like animals that they were treating us like, all of those things would not have happened." Neville reported that her efforts to tell law enforcement officers and the National Guard of her assault were ignored. Neville's prominence and her fortuitous encounter with a member of the Catholic archdiocese in New Orleans during an interview at a local news station meant that her assault received media attention. Others did not.

Obviously, we are not excusing the conduct of the rapists or blaming that conduct on the government. Our point is simply that the overall governmental response in the aftermath of Katrina, shaped as it was by the racial frame of law and order, created conditions of possibility for rape and increased the likelihood that those rapes would be unaddressed. The sexual assaults against women—the vast majority of them black—became markers of black disorder, chaos, and the "animalistic" nature of New Orleans residents; but black women themselves could not occupy the position of victims worthy of rescue. Their injuries were only abstractions that were marshaled to make the larger point about the descent of New Orleans into a literal and figurative black hole. Black women's rape was invoked but not addressed. To borrow from Kimberle Crenshaw, their stories of rape were "voyeuristically included" in a law-and-order campaign.[31] Their specific injury—the fact that they were actually victims—was largely ignored.

The government focused its attention on violence directed against property and violence directed against the rescuers—reports of which have proven to be false or grossly embellished. While these acts of violence could fit comfortably within the frame of law and order, violence against black women's bodies could not. Images of black criminality could work concomitantly with and help to instantiate the law-and-order frame that relies on black disorder; images of black women as innocent victims could do neither. The frames of law and order and black

[30]See Charmaine Neville, "How We Survived the Flood," transcript of interview given to New Orleans media outlets, September 5, 2005, www.counterpunch.org/neville09072005.html.

[31]Kimberle Crenshaw, "Mapping the Margins: Intersectionality, Identity Politics, and Violence Against Women of Color," *Stanford Law Review* 43 (1991): 1241, 1261.

criminality influenced both the exaggeration (overreporting) and the marginalization (underreporting) of violent crimes in ways that make clear that facts don't speak for themselves.

In another example of the law-and-order and black-criminality frames at work in New Orleans, the characterization of the Superdome and the convention center as unsafe facilitated the shift from humanitarian rescue mission to military occupation and security. In part because of the perception of the severe security threat to rescuers, no food, water, or medical care was provided to the convention center until a force of a thousand soldiers and police in full battle gear was sent in to secure the center on September 2 at noon. They were able to do so in twenty minutes and encountered absolutely no resistance, though thousands of people were in the building.

Only one shooting was confirmed in the Superdome, when a soldier shot himself during a scuffle with an attacker. Though New Orleans police chief Eddie Compass reported that he and his officers had retrieved more than thirty weapons from criminals who had been shooting at the rescuers, he later modified his statement to say that this had happened to another unit, a SWAT team at the convention center. The director of the SWAT team, however, reported that his unit had heard gunshots only one time and that his team had recovered no weapons despite aggressive searches.

In retrospect, it is clear that the media both mischaracterized and exaggerated the security threat to the rescue mission. Certainly the chaos in the wake of Katrina and the breakdown of the communications network helped develop a climate in which rumors could and did flourish. Yet under similarly difficult conditions during other natural disasters and even war, reporters have adhered to basic journalistic standards. That they did not under these conditions could be explained as an isolated case of failure under extremely trying circumstances. That might very well be so. Yet, the important part of this story is not that the media failed to observe the basic rules of journalism; it is that the story they told was one people were all too ready to accept. It was a narrative that made sense within the commonly accepted racial frames of law and order and black criminality.

These frames made it difficult for us to make sense of reported 30 instances of "guys who looked like thugs, with pants hanging down around their asses," engaged in frantic efforts to get people collapsing from heat and exhaustion out of the Superdome and into a nearby makeshift medical facility. These images did not make racial sense. There was no ready-made social frame within which the image of black male rescuers could be placed. Existing outside of standard racial frames, black male rescuers present a socially unintelligible image. That we have trouble *seeing* "guys who look like thugs" as rescuers is not a problem of facts. It is a problem of frames. Indeed, the very use of the term "thug" already frames the fact of what they might be doing in a particular way.

Conclusion

Lessons from Hurricane Katrina include those about preparedness for natural disasters; coordination among local, state, and federal rescue efforts; and a nation's capacity for empathy and compassion. While it is less than clear that all of these lessons are being learned, we are at least discussing these lessons. Not so with respect to race. As a nation, we rarely talk about race and Katrina anymore. It is almost unspeakable to do so.

Yet, Katrina offers profound insights into how race operates in American society, insights into how various facts about our social life are racially interpreted through frames. As a result of racial frames, black people are both visible (as criminals) and invisible (as victims). Racial frames both capture and displace us—discursively and materially. More than shaping whether we see black people as criminal or innocent, perpetrator or victim, these frames shape whether we see black people at all. Indeed, one might reasonably ask: Where have all the black people gone, long time passing? It is not hyperbolic to say that post-Katrina black New Orleanians have become a part of an emerging social category: the disappeared. A critical lesson of Katrina is that civil rights advocacy groups need to think harder about frames, particularly when making interventions into natural disasters involving African Americans.

As Michele Landis Dauber reminds us, the template for the American social welfare system has been disaster relief, and the extent to which people are entitled to any form of government resources has always depended upon the claimants' ability to "narrat[e] their deprivation as a disaster—a sudden loss for which the claimant is not responsible."[32] In the case of Katrina, this disaster-relief conception of welfare would seem to promote an immediate national response to aid the hurricane victims. The problem for black people and for other nonwhites, however, as Dauber herself notes, is that racial minorities' claims to victim status have always been fraught "because they are highly likely to be cast as a 'disaster' for the dominant racial group.[33] Implicit in Dauber's analysis is the idea that the move to realign America's racial discourse and policy away from its current distortions must confront the complex problem of racial frames. The existence of racial frames makes it enormously difficult to incorporate "just the facts" into an argument about racism. Those facts will rarely, if ever, be able to escape completely the interpretational reach and normative appeal of racial frames about color blindness and black cultural dysfunctionality.

What is required is likely to be more in the nature of a social movement than a social survey. Facts will always play a crucial role, but just as the successes of the civil rights movement were born of organized

---

[32]Michele Landis Dauber, "Fate, Responsibility, and 'Natural' Disaster Relief: Narrating the American Welfare State," *Law and Society* 33 (1999):257, 264.

[33]Ibid., 307.

struggle, so too must our efforts to shift racial frames ground themselves in a broader and more organic orientation than raw empiricism. People came to see the facts of de jure segregation differently not because new facts emerged about its harms but because new interpretations of those facts were made possible by social organization on the ground that pushed the courts toward a new consensus. We believe the same is true today.

"You look like this sketch of someone who's thinking about committing a crime."

The New Yorker Collection 2000 David Sipress from cartoonbank.com. All Rights Reserved.

ENGAGING THE TEXT

1. What is an interpretive frame? According to Harris and Carbado, what role did framing play in the controversy over the two photos of Hurricane Katrina victims wading through the water? What alternative explanations of the photos and their captions are mentioned in the article? Which explanation seems most plausible to you, and why?

2. Harris and Carbado identify several unspoken assumptions underlying the "metaframe" of color blindness. What are they, and how do they affect the way "color blind" people explain racial inequality? Do you agree that color blindness is a problem? Why or why not?

3. In what ways did Hurricane Katrina challenge existing racial frameworks? How did the public understanding of the disaster change over time, and what role did framing play in those evolving interpretations?

4. How were the interpretive frames of the government and media at odds with facts in the aftermath of Hurricane Katrina? How persuasive do you find Harris and Carbado's argument that "frames trump facts" (para. 9)?

5. Harris and Carbado contend that that it's essential to "shift racial frames" (para. 34) in order to combat racial injustice. How would you go about trying to change the frame of color blindness? Brainstorm strategies and discuss their feasibility and likelihood of success.

EXPLORING CONNECTIONS

6. In the cartoon on page 538, what frame is suggested by the policeman's comment to the black "suspect"? What frame does the cartoonist rely on as the source of humor here?

7. Read the essay by Michelle Alexander and analyze the role of "framing" in the criminal justice system. How might the perception of blacks as criminals stack the deck against black defendants?

EXTENDING THE CRITICAL CONTEXT

8. Write a journal entry describing an experience that made you question a preconception you had about another race, ethnicity, or nationality. What did you believe about the group before this experience, and what happened to make you question your view? Did you change as a result? If so, how and why?

9. Read news reports, editorials, blogs, or letters to the editor that address a current incident or issue that creates controversy over race (for example, charges of racial profiling, police brutality, insensitive remarks by a public figure, or "reverse discrimination"). How are the facts of the situation framed by participants, politicians, and pundits? What evidence, if any, do you see of the color-blindness frame? What other frames do you detect? Compare notes in class and discuss your observations.

10. As a class project, develop and conduct a mini-survey on color blindness on your campus. For example, you might ask participants to agree or disagree with a series of short statements like these: "Racism is a serious problem today" or "It's better not to talk about race." Compile your results and write a paper discussing what you found and what further questions your survey raises.

11. Watch the award-winning documentary *Trouble the Water*. How does the film's depiction of Hurricane Katrina and its aftermath differ from the mainstream media accounts discussed by Harris and Carbado?

BARACK OBAMA: MILES TRAVELED, MILES TO GO

ERIN AUBRY KAPLAN

In 2008 America did something exceptional — electing Barack Obama as president of the United States. His first inaugural, attended by well over a million people, broke all records for events in Washington, DC. But even before he took office, he faced unprecedented challenges: The collapse of the housing and financial markets, a gridlocked Congress, and two wars — in Afghanistan and Iraq. Republicans swore to make him a one-term president, while "birthers" claimed that he was born in Kenya, not the United States, and hence was ineligible to hold office. Erin Aubry Kaplan details these and other conflicts in her essay, which considers Obama's first term as president from a personal point of view. She recounts her wonder at hearing the words "President Obama," but at the same time acknowledges that his election has done nothing to address the poverty and crime afflicting large portions of the black community. She understands the forces limiting Obama's ability to act, but still rages against his failure of nerve. A journalist and essayist, Kaplan was the first weekly African American op-ed columnist for the *Los Angeles Times* from 2005 to 2007. She was previously a staff writer for the *L.A. Weekly*, and has been a regular contributor to *Salon.com*, *Essence*, and *Ms*. This piece is taken from her recent essay collection, *Black Talk, Blue Thoughts, and Walking the Color Line: Dispatches from a Black Journalista* (2011).

I. 2009

It hits me most when I'm in the car. At the top of the hour, any hour, on any day of the week in the wake of January twentieth, the newscast leads with a report of President Obama. What he said or did, what he's thinking, or what issues he's grappling with in the near future. I stare at the dashboard: President Obama! *Who?* I almost laugh in astonishment. I thrill with a feeling, too rich and heady to contain in the small space of my Chrysler, at having gotten away with something I had no right to get away with; it feels like getting a shot of pure oxygen when you've been breathing bad air so long, the good stuff almost kills you. I would die happy breathing this, so happy it wouldn't feel like death but a kind of effortless transcendence that religion always promises but that reality has slyly delivered ahead of it. I'd be damned happy to be dead. Maybe I am.

Who in the hell would have thought? Who would have thought at all that they'd be here for *this?* President Obama. I sigh big, adjust my grip on the wheel, shake my head to clear it. But I'm eager for it to fill up again. Eager to contemplate, again, how Barack was close to me forty years ago in ways that I couldn't have imagined until today. Yes, he was there all along. But for a quirk of geography (I was in L.A.; he was five hours across the water in Hawaii), he could have been in third grade with me, one smart, unbottled black boy among many in the very early '70s, one of relatively few boys who succeeded, one of even fewer who made it big. But never mind—in the beginning, Barack Obama was Gerald, was Gabriel, was Dwayne, was Stephen, Joe, David, Kevin, Patrick, and Derrick. They were all there, and all equally possible. Wherever they are now, I hope they burn with the old sense of open road as much as I do when the realization of *President Obama* lands on me in the middle of traffic, as it does routinely. I almost have to brake from the impact. It makes me remember. It is glorious.

And then it passes. The newscast segues into a talk show or a song, and then I'm simply in the car, driving. I'm going along a boulevard toward home, a largely black neighborhood on the outskirts of South Central.[1] Almost against my will, I look at what I'm returning to. I reluctantly take stock of the red graffiti that cuts across pale brick walls like flesh wounds, idle storefronts, young black men congregated around the open door of a tattoo shop like it's a church hall. The distance between all of this and Barack and the new way he's supposed to be showing us is frustrating, crazy-making. Does no one see? In all the praise, and even in the doubt of Barack, there has been almost no acknowledgement of this whole black netherworld of grinding sameness, non-movement, hope gone slack. It's a world that belongs to all black people, wherever they end up, and to the rest of America, this world of weak schooling and even weaker job prospects and prison stints that have threatened black people always; this generation is no different. The burden and blame for this state of affairs is all of ours. This is what we are loath to admit, to see, that Barack is extraordinary, but he is not our difference. Not yet. For black people so hungry for victory, the most I can say is that Barack is certainly *of* us, a shining example of us, but he is not all of us. The strange truth is that we secured a black president before we secured justice for the vast majority of black people; of course, nobody thought things would happen in this order, but they have, and now we are groping for the way forward. Some say that there is no more need for a way forward, that a particularly murky chapter of black struggle has finally come to an end. What struggle is that? The struggle to become president? There was never any such thing. In the scheme of things that had to be done, it wasn't important.

There are reasons for that. I count those reasons in my last mile home: grown men half-heartedly selling chocolate bars out of boxes on street medians, tough boys mincing along like geishas in pants with

---

[1] *South Central:* South Central Los Angeles, an inner-city neighborhood. [All notes are editors'.]

waists pulled low, girls indifferent to each. None of them have what Barack and I had—an absolute belief in possibility and, consequently, in ourselves. We never divested ourselves of that belief, it never left us, whether we left the communities we grew up in or whether we stayed. I'm still here. I am not the difference, either. I would like to be. I would like President Barack Obama to make my difference possible. In those moments in the car when the radio seizes me and I'm wonder-struck for thirty seconds out of the day, it doesn't seem like much to ask for at all.

II. 2010

Obama is shrinking. It started happening the moment he took office, when he officially crossed over from the airy magic of the possible to the dirty, deoxygenated, thoroughly racialized workaday grind of American politics; all those new white converts started falling away from him like party confetti falling to earth. In the harsh light of the morning after, Obama looked suddenly out of place. It was obvious. The natty suits and close-cropped hair, the practiced thoughtfulness, the measured rise and fall of his voice meant to give shape to the vague chaos of two wars in the Middle East and the much clearer chaos of a failing economy, the way he lifted his chin during public addresses and press conferences as if trying to literally put himself above it all—all the things that had stirred people's imagination became, on the other side of the inaugural, targets for doubt and derision. It's all been exhausting to watch. Of course, there was no way for a black man to look in place as a president, because there had never been one before. I expected that. But I also expected the novelty to wear off fairly quickly and for "Obama" to become synonymous with "president." It had happened for everyone else who'd held the office in my lifetime, even for the short-lived and unremarkable presidents like Ford and Bush II; like them or despair about them, Americans accepted them as their leaders. The acceptance starts with the title "President," but it goes much deeper than that. An agreed-upon sense of collective investment in the person in charge is what makes a nation—to say nothing of a democracy—possible.

But what's happened, and not happened, in the very brief era of Obama is unprecedented and unsettling. In some ways he is still not really president. Rather than fusing, the words "president" and "Obama" have only become more estranged over the last year and a half as it's become increasingly clear that the *idea* of President Obama is more powerful and persuasive than Obama the man could ever be. There's no comparison between the two, and likely never was. It's true that a campaigning politician is a much more romantic figure than that same politician after he's elected; it's also true that almost nobody expects that politician, especially one gaining an office for the first time, to fully measure up to the pre-election magic. But Obama is a marked exception to this. Eighteen months on, it turns out that people not only wanted him to measure up to the magic, they wanted him to improve on it—in retrospect, the much-analyzed "hope and change" campaign was taken by the public as a reasonable starting point, not as the usual overreaching that new presidents are allowed to adjust downward, to a certain degree. Obama's goldenness wasn't supposed to tarnish even a little; it was supposed to spin itself into platinum. In a country that's been worshipping at the altar of individualism for the last forty years, Obama's political fortune was widely viewed more as a privilege given to him by a generous (and anxious) public than a right made possible by his innate qualities. Even among his supporters, the attitude was therefore: he owes us. Starting *now*.

High expectations are fine, necessary, especially in bad times. But they often mask resentment or a fatal skepticism, and this is the wall—the barely concealed flip side of hope and change—that the post-candidate Obama ran into. The wall is that much more formidable for anyone or anything that challenges the racial status quo, and Obama does that simply by being black. He was always a paradox: the man whose ascension to the presidency was either going to resolve or resurrect for a new century the whole matter of racial justice. As a country, we much prefer resolution. We like events that dramatize racial resolution in memorable ways—for example, the 1954 *Brown v. Board of Education* U.S. Supreme Court decision.[2] We think of this as one of the finest hours in our judicial history, a sweeping application of hope and change that finally retired the era of Jim Crow. But that decision was a comma, not a period. What we never talk about is the fact that after 1954 public schools across the country desegregated very slowly, and integration in many ways never happened at all. Brown precipitated a big shift, all right, but it was a shift away from the spirit of the ruling, not toward it. Whites fled public schools before desegregation had time to take root as a new reality; conditioned by years of black fear and loathing, they refused to submit to what they saw as a radical experiment, and so deserted their own places and even their own self-interest rather than allow the experiment any real margin of error. The same thing has happened with the first black president. From the beginning of his time in office, Obama's declining poll numbers have shown that non-black voters are simply not willing to grant him any margin of error. Of course, that stinginess is partly due to circumstances: Obama arrived with more major national and international crises to fix or deflect than any other president in history. He was expected to quell rising anxiety from all quarters—Democrat, Republican, liberal, progressive, conservative, pacifist, hawkish—about the ultimate fate of a country that everybody wants to believe has unlimited capacity to heal, recover, and progress. The expectation that Obama, or anyone, could right this long-foundering ship in a year's time, or four or even eight years' time, is absurd.

[2] *Brown v. Board of Education:* U.S. Supreme Court decision outlawing segregation.

But the other part of the public's unforgiving attitude is tied to ancient reservations about color. In the real world, blacks in charge are given little room to fail, even less room to be mediocre; the sanctioned margin of error for leaders is tiny, and for black men it's nonexistent. People of color are not really people in these situations, but symbols—question marks representing whether the race has the right stuff or not. President Obama in the White House, the seat of American power, is that symbol writ about as large as possible: he is a president operating constantly under the hot lights of both celebrity and racial scrutiny. It's a burden he was bound to carry. But being a symbol has also dehumanized and diminished him, even among his admirers. This is not a new dynamic, or a new effect. We're all guilty of dehumanizing black people, even in good times; we distance ourselves from their complex reality by seeing them first as constructs and symbols described by the hopes, fears, and fetishes we project onto them. Dictating who blacks are and what they should be allows whites to retain their cultural supremacy and to contain their eternal fear of blacks as the ultimate other, likeable, maybe, but unknown and unknowable. Those blacks who don't fit the preferred construct—welfare queen, hip-hop thug, college grad, post-racial redeemer—are marginalized or ignored. It's all part of a psychological and spiritual inequality that has always defined race relations and that black people continually struggle against, whether they're a prisoner on death row or president in the White House. And the higher they rise in modern times, the closer they come to white folks and the greater their struggle—and the less they seem able to fight.

I watch Obama battle his own symbolism on a daily basis, watch him trying as artfully as possible to counter the notion that he's either a hero or hedonist (post-election, it's mostly hedonist) that people infinitely prefer to flesh and blood. It's interesting to compare this treatment to that of Obama's predecessor, George W. Bush. For eight years Bush, despite being widely despised, was granted plenty of latitude, shades of gray, and even forgiveness by media and by the voters, including those he made steadily worse off with his policies. Why? Bush was familiar. Maybe he was an idiot, but to many voters he was *their* idiot, the underachieving fuck-up that everybody knew in school and could relate to as such, even if they didn't invite him to parties. The bottom line is Bush was a recognizable entity to a majority of Americans; Obama is not. People don't talk about Obama's personal quirks or life philosophy or vulnerabilities, nor do they seem interested. A deep identification between voters and the person in charge is the real power in politics, and Obama doesn't have it by virtue of his color. This doesn't mean he doesn't have admirers. Lots of Americans were suitably impressed and even moved by his bootstraps success story and how he came to terms with his own racial history, but few people have lived that story. Others were moved by his charisma and exotica (a black American man without the freighted black American name of Johnson or Jackson), and on that basis alone gave him a chance. But—would they have had a beer with him? Could he have lived in their neighborhood with ten other families that looked like his? Those whites who hated Bush as president likely wouldn't have objected to him living in their midst.

Obama is not Bush, and that was, and in some way remains, as much of an obstacle as it was a political advantage in 2008. Yes, against immeasurable odds and against the lessons of our own history, he did become president, and I suppose we can be proud of that. But we have misread the depth and nature of our act. America hired Obama; it didn't take him to its heart or invite him into where it lives. We feel about him pretty much what we feel about other black people in workplaces where they are scarce or, as in Obama's case, where they are the pioneering First One — we give them a chance, applaud ourselves for our vision and generosity, and then settle quickly into watching them for missteps. It's a schizophrenic attitude: we are encouraged by the black person's potential enough to give him a job, but are ever wary of giving him power. This is why as soon as Obama stepped into the White House, he had to be punished. Whites are used to controlling black opportunity, to giving and taking it as they see fit. President Obama in that way was never president-in-waiting, he was an opportunity — the bright and capable intern who deserved a shot. But being in charge was not part of the deal.

It seems ridiculous to have to keep asserting this, but Obama's election did not put the finishing touches on racial justice. America hasn't achieved nearly enough racial justice to even think in such terms. What Obama and the new century have really given us is a third run at Reconstruction (the second being the civil rights era of the 1950s and 1960s). But this one is going sour much more quickly, in part because news cycles and event cycles move much more quickly. But it's going sour also because a black man assuming national and international power at a moment of such great national fear and uncertainty is proving to be a noxious mix. Fear and uncertainty have moved steadily from the margins to become full-time occupations, and discrediting President Barack Hussein Obama has become so common a practice, it's a whole new discipline unto itself, complete with on-the-job training and benefits. Critics are quick to say they're not just unhappy with Obama, they're unhappy with the whole federal government he represents. But in the minds of too many, Obama and the sins and excesses of government are inseparable; in fact, they're the same thing. We've all been trained to see the fed as the main helpmeet of undeserving blacks, so a black man actually heading the whole government is, for conservatives and lots of others who lean that way, a nightmarish conflation of race and politics (for those somewhat less conservative, including Democrats, it may not be a nightmare; but it is at the very least unappetizing food for thought). Obama's smallest move to help or empathize with the needy is openly challenged as a liberal impulse, but subliminally, and more importantly, it's challenged as a *black* liberal impulse, which we all understand is the most unrestrained kind.

In this new era of Reconstruction, the reinvigoration of a states'-rights, anti-central-government movement has found expression in the so-called Tea Party,[3] which is not the Klan of old but has quite comfortably harbored elements of it. This being the twenty-first century, everybody denies being racist—the label is hopelessly old-fashioned in the high-tech age of Twitter and Facebook. But how else to explain the pettiness and distortions that have characterized so much anti-Obama-ism? Hysteria about Big Government is one thing; that goes back centuries and rises and falls on a historical continuum. But there has been equal hysteria about manufactured, race-driven controversies about Obama's American citizenship, his shadowy Muslim-ism and sufficient lack of Christian faith,[4] his emotional opaqueness (betraying the preferred stereotype that blacks should be cool on the surface, but volcanic underneath), his mother-in-law moving into the White House, his daughters' hairstyles, his wife's gall in taking a European vacation. The political opposition that I knew would be fierce has been beyond reason. Calling the modest steps Obama has taken toward health-care reform socialism, fascism, and the end of America as we know it was so absurd I have to assume that what really offended people was not the reform at all, which we didn't actually get, but the fact Obama carried it out against the wishes of those who didn't approve of his hiring. This is why the fight against "Obamacare,"[5] etc. dug in deeper by the week and was animated by such fury: he had broken the rules of black opportunity. He is that worst of all things, an arrogant black man. Protesters didn't quite feel free to say that, but they did the next best thing by waving signs that depicted Obama as dastardly figures such as Hitler, Osama bin Laden, the bloody-mouthed Joker from the "Batman" movie. One irony among many is how the epic fight against health-care reform played out so personally against Obama, when it was really all about what he symbolizes. Media painted the fight as a segment of the American people against one man, but it wasn't. It was the opposite, or something more complicated than that—the American people against their better angels.

This is painful to say, but none of the racial oppressiveness excuses what Obama is doing wrong as president, or not doing enough of. Call me naive, but I expected more of him (did I have a choice?). Yes, he came to office a career centrist Democrat, but it's disappointing to see that his presidency has not yet unleashed or substantially encouraged a progressive side many of us thought we had glimpsed beneath the mask of racial accommodation. (Certainly I thought the progressivism

---

[3] *Tea Party:* Conservative political party emphasizing small government and an "originalist" interpretation of the Constitution.

[4] *Controversies about Obama's American citizenship, his shadowy Muslim-ism, and sufficient lack of Christian faith:* The false beliefs that Obama was born in Kenya, is a secret Muslim, and isn't a Christian are surprisingly widespread.

[5] *Obamacare:* The Affordable Care Act (2010), which mandates that everyone have health care insurance.

was there, was sure I had seen it when Obama visited Los Angeles way back in 2006. He came to a park in the core black neighborhood of Crenshaw; I drove down there to pick up some bath towels at a store near the park and to see what all the fuss was about. By the end of the rally, listening to Obama rail easily against the injustice of too many people of color being in prison, I nearly swooned. He made his points with his suit jacket off, chin up, white business shirt rolled up at the cuffs and gleaming in the sun. As far as I know, he never made them again.) He has shown himself to be more manager than leader, more married to the status quo than his rhetoric had us believe. He even expanded on the status quo in unnerving, Bush-like ways: bailing out giant corporate miscreants with taxpayer money, casting the disastrous war in Afghanistan as a moral undertaking the same way Bush cast the invasion of Iraq. And there is Obama's failure of nerve in taking and holding a position on smaller but still significant issues—racial profiling, equal treatment of Muslims. Too often he's taken the right stance and then, after some hasty temperature-taking of public opinion, backslid into a compromised space that ultimately gets him nothing. He is not able to trust [his] own assessment of things, and that undermines him most of all. Obama doesn't seem to know how far he can or should go, what he can get away with; it's as if he is testing various facets of himself to see which will work best in the uncharted territory of being a black president. But this kind of tinkering is disastrous. It doesn't achieve change. It was obvious from the beginning that certain folks would hate him for whatever he did—so why does he not lead and make a difference? I don't think Obama would mind making a difference. But I'm not at all sure that he wants to make a difference more than he wants to secure a legacy at the table of American power. The best scenario I can concoct at this point is that he wants to do both, fulfilling an old black-empowerment adage that you can do well for yourself and do good at the same time. But Obama doesn't seem to understand, or he refuses to accept, that doing well for himself and doing good for the people isn't possible in the divisive, disillusioned, almost radioactive climate in which he became president. It may never be possible.

One more thing: What about black people? What about us? Obama may turn out to be the strangest bit of black history we've ever had. He is without a doubt the most spectacular example of black achievement to date, but his impact on the distressed state of black people in the twenty-first century will be almost nil. That's disorienting, a giant vacuum of a fact that no black person dares to go near lest he or she get sucked into a void of disappointment we have not known before—and we have known disappointment. Since the ecstasy of the inauguration has faded, black people seem to have no idea how to feel about Obama. Our votes helped carry him to the promised land, but now he is gone from us, or we have let him go. We are listless and depressed, left to wonder: Is Obama proof that the system works, or evidence that it has outfoxed black people yet again? Is the joke on us? I realize that, since the inauguration, I have not talked very extensively about Obama with other black people. There seems to be not much to say. He is not in our running conversations in the way that Martin Luther King or Jackie Robinson or even Malcolm X was; we recognized those lives and those fates as our own. Obama's life in many ways is *his* own. His presidential run was a singular vision, a challenge he set for himself, not an outgrowth of black discontent or an affirmation of black resolve. Such is the individualism we are privy to now—selfhood that Martin and Malcolm could have hardly imagined.

Obama may not be a reflection of us. But he *is* us. He knows we're here, just beyond his presidential reach. He signifies it constantly with that stern, preacherly stance, with rhetoric that lingers in sing-song when he wants to make a point, with eyes that habitually rove over an audience while he talks—seeking out a witness—with the way he consciously clasps hands together or folds arms across himself when he's exasperated with white folks but can't show it. That is surely us. We have all stood where he stands now. But as president, Obama stands in another country. At this point, black folk can only observe him from miles away and wish him the best and hope that whatever good he does, we will benefit too: we pray that where he goes, we will be able to follow. This laissez-faire wishfulness is so far the extent of our hope, and it isn't much. It ought to be more, much more. We thought our store of hope would get a fresh infusion from Obama's triumph, but instead it has rendered us oddly helpless, more at a loss than before because deliverance looks tantalizingly near. Obama has come at a cost. He has achieved a great height that required that he officially separate himself (if he hadn't done it already) from the daily cares and concerns of other black people, as though shrugging off unnecessary weight as he moved further up a mountain. Willingly or not, he's done that. What do the rest of us black folk do now with our strangely resilient faith in the American system and its promises of equal consideration? Even the most cynical among us have never known how *not* to believe.

The anemic state of black hope, briefly resuscitated by the events of 2008, has been years in the making. Hope has decreased in direct proportion to the growth of our middle and educated classes and the occasionally spectacular success of one of our members. Between the '60s and now we convinced ourselves that we don't need it anymore, that collective black energy and self-interest eventually had to go the way of hippie communes. We've grown to accept as a price for being comfortable the stigma of empathizing with other, less fortunate black people who are not. Obama understands that stigma, and though he may not agree with it, he abides by it. He is not a black politician because he cannot be. Though even if he were, black people would still expect him to do little for us, so accustomed have we grown to black elected leadership giving us platitudes and performance, but not leadership. Like tolerance built up in the blood over many years to certain viruses, we have developed a great tolerance and even affection for all the brave talk about the primacy of community; we are used to our politicians sounding radical on our block and then blunting the message in another part of town because, we're told, that's how the game is played, that's how we can get over. Except that compromise and selective brave talk have never gotten us over. Our needs are not only not taken seriously by our own, they're not *taken.* We have seen this so regularly in the last fifty years, in the long, sustained golden age of black representation, it's hard to feel any outrage now about what Obama is not doing for us. We have long understood, even if we don't officially accept it, that self-suppression and abandonment are key and unquestioned ingredients of modern black success, like literacy in the home and algebra before eighth grade. So of course blacks don't really talk about Obama or keep close tabs. But even at a distance, it's hard to watch a black man in charge handling his own people and his own history with rubber gloves like it's all one big infection, some kind of hazardous waste that has to be detoxified with words and declarations before it can be buried underground in concrete. Obama is not the first to do it, but he's become the most skilled at appealing to blacks at certain moments while simultaneously keeping them at arm's length, reaching out but not daring to risk an embrace of any kind. For Obama to be "outed" as a black sympathizer would be in a way worse than being outed as a gay man or as a Muslim. Being perceived as truly black would mean defeat, pure and simple. So, once again, we have lost.

In the summer of 2010, the *Los Angeles Times* described Obama as a kind of Velcro president when it came to race—despite his attempts to treat it like any other issue on the table, racial questions (starting with his own genetic makeup) and controversies were sticking to him like flies to flypaper. When he did say something, it was invariably characterized as radical or inappropriate, and he and his administration overcorrected to an almost embarrassing degree—hastily modifying a remark Obama made about a cop who arrested a well-known black scholar in his own home,[6] preemptively firing a black government bureaucrat who had allegedly said bigoted things about white folks[7] (she hadn't). What's really been happening is that Obama is still trying to climb out from under the shadow of Jeremiah Wright, his former pastor and black activist who stirred the wrath of the anti-Obama critics early on. Obama quelled racial fears enough to be elected, but he is still tarred with the sin of Wright,[8] who he can't shake as a doppelganger even though whites applauded candidate Obama's eloquent 2008 disquisition that was meant to pit racial reason and circumspection against

---

[6]*A cop who arrested a well-known black scholar in his own home:* Obama criticized the police for racial profiling after Harvard Professor Henry Louis Gates Jr. was handcuffed and arrested for "breaking in" to his own home.

[7]*A black government bureaucrat who had allegedly said bigoted things about white folks (she hadn't):* Shirley Sherrod was forced to resign due to a misleading video edited by a right-wing blogger; once the full video was reviewed, Obama apologized and offered her a new position, which she declined.

[8]*Jeremiah Wright:* Wright became a source of controversy when videos of his fiery sermons condemning American racism came to light.

Wright's narrow-minded racial madness. That speech was almost for naught. As president, the new neo-cons, led by sportscaster-turned-anti-Reconstructionist Glenn Beck, lost no time in calling Obama a racist who hates white people and possibly white "culture"; Tea Partyers felt free to call him every bad name—fascist, socialist, Hitler, Joker, Muslim/non-American terrorist—except nigger. But that is often what they meant. They meant a misbehaving, thieving, silver-tongued trickster nigger, a modern-day Br'er Rabbit trying to best the farmer while appearing to be his friend. So obsessed are the neo-cons with the idea of this deception, racial fury is building in the country as swiftly as funnel clouds, though the media tends not to remark on it. At a rally held in New York City to protest Attorney General Eric Holder's proposal to try terrorist detainees in criminal court, rather than detain them indefinitely in Guantanamo Bay, one of the more agitated protesters at the rally suggested that Holder, a black man, be lynched. I read about this terrorist threat in the leftish but evenhanded *New Yorker* magazine. Though it shocked me, the story didn't remark on it; it was simply presented as one detail among many in the fight to try, or not to try, Muslims detained for terrorism. I didn't read about the lynching remark anywhere else.

But my apprehension isn't just about would-be lynchers or Tea Partyers or devotees of Glenn Beck. It's also about plain Americans, even liberals—especially liberals—who help to corrupt the legitimacy of a President Obama with their silence and indifference. I'm sure they don't see themselves as racist and probably consider the very word distasteful. But they feel no compulsion to speak out against the racial hostility and resistance that Obama attracts. That lack of compulsion is most glaring in the president's fellow Democrats, who talk plenty about unity and respect, but who are leery of even raising the vote-losing idea that some of their constituents might be racially unenlightened. And while Obama has lots of hard-working hires in his administration, none effectively represent him; no one feels like his proxy. George Bush had Cheney, Rumsfeld, and Karl Rove,[9] but Obama has no one. Every bad moment sticks to him because there's really nothing and no one between him and all the inclement political weather out there, no barrier islands to break the hurricanes. Obama has been to the mountaintop, and it is raining. It's been raining there a long time. James Baldwin[10] said as much forty years ago when he responded to Robert Kennedy's suggestion that someone like Baldwin might be elected president one day: "What really exercises my mind is not this hypothetical day on which some other Negro 'first' will become the first Negro president,"

---

[9]*Cheney, Rumsfeld, and Karl Rove:* Former Vice President Dick Cheney; former Secretary of Defense Donald Rumsfeld; and former Senior Advisor and Deputy Chief of Staff Karl Rove, also known as "Bush's brain."

[10]*James Baldwin:* James Arthur Baldwin (1924–1987), American novelist, essayist, and social critic, whose works include *Go Tell It on the Mountain* (1953), *Notes of a Native Son* (1955), and *The Fire Next Time* (1963).

said Baldwin. "What I am really curious about is just what kind of country will he be president of?"

Still: I'm furious Obama can't represent me in the way I wanted him to, expected him to. Who else *but* him? He is me, as well as David and Joe and the rest of us who were solemnly handed off the dream in the '60s and '70s; we took it without much idea of what to do with it, but now—well, now we have the most high-profile black American leader in history, more watched and studied than Martin Luther King, and I am not a priority? It's an abomination. And yet I understand, we understand. Black people understand without wanting to or agreeing to. We close one eye, shift Obama away from the raging center of things, and we instantly see what kind of cul-de-sac he's stuck in. Anybody black with any kind of ambition has been stuck like that, boxed in, arm twisted up behind the back. For all my reservations about Obama the president, my heart can't help but go out to Obama the man on this one; he tries so hard to duck under the razor wire of prejudice and difference, but he keeps getting cut. None of his maneuvers matter. He stands up straight and holds his head high, does all those things we were told to do when we were kids, back when the 1960s lit the torch and we were its flames finally being blown upward by a new breath of freedom and self-determination; all that unequivocal *Hell yes, we can!* was our new half-patriotic, half-defiant pledge of allegiance. But we look back and see that a lot of that was just brave talk; *Yes, we can* was fine for us, but it didn't have a lot of takers in the real world. Many of us in Obama's generation and generations after remain in the stuffy ether of potential, convinced that we might still set the world ablaze with a new consciousness and finally purify it of its sins, set it in a new direction. We are still waiting.

But of course it will take time. Black folks will give Obama time; we 20 are used to things taking indefinable amounts of time, to seeing time as almost biblical when it comes to improvement for us. Meanwhile, we content ourselves with the fact that Obama is our brother—not in the details of his personal narrative or even his philosophy, maybe, but in the historical, quasi-biblical black struggle for acceptance and true equality that other Americans expected Obama to put to rest. He has not, and we're glad of that. Of course we don't want him to fail—or, God forbid, to be mediocre. But I am nonetheless relieved that his incomplete story, and ours, are joined together.

One of the more memorable discussions about the logistics of black American success happens in a scene that comes late in the Michael Mann movie *Ali*. As the Champ, played by Will Smith, prepares for the famous Rumble in the Jungle in Zaire, he argues with his wife about his friendship with boxing promoter and hustler extraordinaire Don King. His wife snaps that King doesn't give a shit about Africa and black empowerment, that he's a capitalist who "talks black, lives white, and cares about green." Ali doesn't deny this, but he defends King by saying that in order to accomplish what he, Ali, wants to accomplish, he's got to use everybody who's willing to go along with some piece of his vision, "honkies and bad-ass niggers, too." That reminded me of Obama's multicultural approach to his campaign; he learned early that the South Side of Chicago, or the east side of Oakland or the central part of L.A., could never get it done alone. He had to enlist anybody who would go along with some piece of his vision. This is what initially filled me, the idea that Obama could point all these anybodies in a single direction, get them to actually follow him and people like him—David and Joe and Derrick—instead of fearing their intentions or freezing them in a construct that forever puts them at the margin of things. The rub was Obama's goal in bringing us all together. Ali's larger goal in Zaire was clear: to bring some uniquely American uplift to a country and a continent that was struggling to stand on new legs of post-colonial freedom. I'm not sure what Obama's goal was. I'm still not. What I do know is that the time in which he came to power does not belong to black folks; the moment is not ours. Nor can President Obama, a presence that is flawed but still intoxicating, make it ours. We have to do that. He is not the best we have, though he is the highest, but even from that lofty height he has made it clear that we have much more climbing to do before we finally get over.

ENGAGING THE TEXT

1. Why does Kaplan divide her essay into two sections, "2009" and "2010"? What different perceptions of President Obama are suggested by these

dates? In the first section, what does she feel is at once "glorious" and "crazy-making" (para. 3) about his success? How does the second section offer a more complex view of his presidency?

2. According to Kaplan, the Supreme Court decision *Brown v. Board of Education* represented "a comma, not a period" in the history of desegregation. What does she mean by this? In what ways does she believe "the same thing has happened with the first black president" (para. 7)?

3. Kaplan contrasts Americans' attitudes toward President Obama and his immediate predecessor. What does she see as George W. Bush's advantage in public opinion? What are Obama's disadvantages? Do you agree with her assessment? Why or why not?

4. Kaplan explains the extreme opposition to President Obama's policies as a form of racism. How does she distinguish between ordinary political extremism and racially-tinged extremism? Explain why you agree or disagree with her analysis.

5. In what ways has President Obama distanced himself from the concerns of black Americans? In what ways has he embraced his blackness? How does Kaplan explain his ambivalence?

EXPLORING CONNECTIONS

6. What does the Pett cartoon on page 552 say about the status of race in America? What does it suggest about the legacy of Martin Luther King, Jr.? What does it imply about the relative importance of Black History Month?

7. To what extent do the causes of prejudice identified by Vincent N. Parrillo (p. 504) seem to be at work in the violent reactions of the Tea Party to President Obama that Kaplan describes? How useful are these theories at explaining the responses of Obama supporters?

8. Analyze the role played by Harris and Carbado's racial "frames" (p. 524) in Kaplan's discussion of President Obama. How did Obama's election reinforce the "racial-progress narrative" (para. 12)? How do the conspiracy theories about Obama's citizenship reflect Harris and Carbado's observation that facts are "seldom enough to dislodge racial frames" (para. 17)? What frames are at work here?

EXTENDING THE CRITICAL CONTEXT

9. Compare one of Obama's speeches to a predominantly white audience (like the House Republicans) to one of his speeches to a largely black audience (like the NAACP). Does he present himself differently? Does his language or accent vary? Does he appear more at ease with one audience or the other? These speeches, and many others, are available on YouTube.

VISUAL PORTFOLIO

READING IMAGES OF THE MELTING POT

VISUAL PORTFOLIO

READING IMAGES OF THE MELTING POT

1. The photo "Please don't kill my sons" was taken at one of the many protest demonstrations following the shooting of Trayvon Martin, the African American teenager who was killed in February 2012 by a Sanford, Florida, neighborhood-watch coordinator. What does the sign suggest about the vulnerability of black men? Do some quick Internet research about African Americans killed by police in the current year. How do you explain the results?

2. Write a narrative that explains the situation pictured in the second image of the portfolio (p. 555). What is happening and what led up to this scene? Who are these people and what are their relationships? Identify specific details of setting, dress, body language, and facial expression that support your interpretation. Compare narratives and discuss the assumptions that inform the stories as well as the persuasiveness of the evidence they are based on.

3. How many different ways could you describe the ethnic or cultural identity of each of the four friends on page 556 based on the visual cues provided by the photo? What knowledge or assumptions about race, ethnicity, and culture underlie your interpretations?

4. Do you find the T-shirt, "Go Fightin' Whites," funny or offensive? An intramural basketball team in Colorado adopted the team name as a protest against Indian mascots like the Fightin' Redskins. Then in 2012, the Oregon State Board of Education threatened to withhold state funding from any high school that had a Native-themed mascot. Did the Oregon policy go too far, or is retiring Indian mascots long overdue?

5. How might Cheryl I. Harris and Devon W. Carbado read the significance of the images on pages 493 and 558, which were taken in New Orleans following Hurricane Katrina?

6. What messages do you think the photo on page 558 conveys about power, survival, and American values? Why do you think the photographer chose to focus on the figures in the foreground? How would the effect of the image change if the entire scene were clearly in focus? If the shot had been taken from a different angle — from above, for example, or from the side of the street?

7. The image on page 559 depicts a section of the fence that divides the United States from Mexico. What sense does the picture give you of the photographer's views of immigration, the fence, the border, and the relationship between the two countries? What details of the picture itself — angle, lighting, proportion, position of the figures — suggest these views?

8. How do you think the people in the "Close the Border" photo (p. 560) would explain the motives for their protest? What motives might Vincent N. Parrillo (p. 504) or George M. Fredrickson (p. 565) attribute to them? Write an imaginary conversation among the protesters and the two writers.

9. Analyze the imagery of the sign "The Doctor Will See You Now" from a Tea Party Patriots demonstration against healthcare reform. What is implied by casting President Obama as the Joker in *Batman*? Is there any significance to his being depicted in a form of whiteface? Does this image support or call into question Erin Aubry Kaplan's notion that these protests cast "the American people against their better angels" (para. 13)?

10. The Obamas' visit to the Lincoln Memorial took place the night before inauguration day, 2009. What is the intended symbolism of this photo (p. 562)? How do you respond to it? What political and civic purposes were served by the visit, and by photographs like this one?

MODELS OF AMERICAN ETHNIC RELATIONS: A HISTORICAL PERSPECTIVE

GEORGE M. FREDRICKSON

Are Irish Americans white? The answer is so self-evident that the question seems absurd, but as historian George Fredrickson notes, the idea of "whiteness" has in the past excluded many Europeans, including the Irish. A survey of ethnic and racial categories in American history shows how much they change with the politics and prejudices of the time. Yet citizenship, civil rights, even human status have been granted or withheld on the basis of these shifting definitions. Fredrickson examines four models of ethnic relations — hierarchy, assimilation, pluralism, and separatism — that have defined how groups perceived as different from each other should interact. Fredrickson (1934–2009) wrote extensively about race in the history of the United States and South Africa, served as president of the Organization for American Historians, and taught for many years at Stanford University. His books include *The Inner Civil War* (1965), *The Black Image in the White Mind* (1972), *White Supremacy* (1981), *Black Liberation* (1995), and *Racism: A Short History* (2002).

THROUGHOUT ITS HISTORY, the United States has been inhabited by a variety of interacting racial or ethnic groups. In addition to the obvious "color line" structuring relationships between dominant whites and lower-status blacks, Indians, and Asians, there have at times been important social distinctions among those of white or European ancestry. Today we think of the differences between white Anglo-Saxon Protestants and Irish, Italian, Polish, and Jewish Americans as purely cultural or religious, but in earlier times these groups were sometimes thought of as "races" or "subraces" — people possessing innate or inborn characteristics and capabilities that affected their fitness for American citizenship. Moreover, differences apparently defined as cultural have sometimes been so reified[1] as to serve as the functional equivalent of physical distinctions. Indians, for example, were viewed by most nineteenth-century missionaries and humanitarians as potentially equal and similar to whites. Their status as noncitizens was not attributed to skin color or physical appearance; it was only their obdurate adherence to "savage ways" that allegedly stood in the way of their possessing equal rights and being fully assimilated. Analogously, conservative opponents of affirmative action and other antiracist policies in the 1990s may provide a "rational" basis for prejudice and discrimination by attributing the disadvantages and alleged shortcomings

---

[1] *reified:* Treated as if real, concrete, but actually abstract. [All notes are editors'.]

of African Americans to persistent cultural "pathology" rather than to genetic deficiencies (D'Souza 1995).

It can therefore be misleading to make a sharp distinction between race and ethnicity when considering intergroup relations in American history. As I have argued extensively elsewhere, ethnicity is "racialized" whenever distinctive group characteristics, however defined or explained, are used as the basis for a status hierarchy of groups who are thought to differ in ancestry or descent (Fredrickson 1997, ch. 5).

Four basic conceptions of how ethnic or racial groups should relate to each other have been predominant in the history of American thought about group relations—ethnic hierarchy, one-way assimilation, cultural pluralism, and group separatism. This [essay] provides a broad outline of the historical career of each of these models of intergroup relations, noting some of the changes in how various groups have defined themselves or been defined by others.

Ethnic Hierarchy

Looking at the entire span of American history, we find that the most influential and durable conception of the relations among those American racial or ethnic groups viewed as significantly dissimilar has been hierarchical. A dominant group—conceiving of itself as society's charter membership—has claimed rights and privileges not to be fully shared with outsiders or "others," who have been characterized as unfit or unready for equal rights and full citizenship. The hierarchical model has its deepest roots and most enduring consequences in the conquest of Indians and the enslavement of blacks during the colonial period (Axtell 1981; Jordan 1968). But it was also applied in the nineteenth century to Asian immigrants and in a less severe and more open-ended way to European immigrants who differed in culture and religion from old-stock Americans of British origin (Higham 1968; Miller 1969). The sharpest and most consequential distinction was always between "white" and "nonwhite." The first immigration law passed by Congress in 1790 specified that only white immigrants were eligible for naturalization. This provision would create a crucial difference in the mid-nineteenth century between Chinese "sojourners," who could not become citizens and voters, and Irish immigrants, who could.

Nevertheless, the Irish who fled the potato famine of the 1840s by emigrating to the United States also encountered discrimination. Besides being Catholic and poor, the refugees from the Emerald Isle were Celts rather than Anglo-Saxons, and a racialized discourse,[2] drawing on British precedents, developed as an explanation for Irish inferiority to Americans of English ancestry (Knobel 1986). The dominant group during the nineteenth and early twentieth centuries was not simply white

5

---

[2]*racialized discourse:* Language that defines a group of people as a race and attributes distinctive "racial" characteristics to them.

but also Protestant and Anglo-Saxon. Nevertheless, the Irish were able to use their right to vote and the patronage they received from the Democratic Party to improve their status, an option not open to the Chinese. Hence, they gradually gained the leverage and respectability necessary to win admission to the dominant caste, a process that culminated in Al Smith's nomination for the presidency in 1928 and John F. Kennedy's election in 1960.

The mass immigration of Europeans from eastern and southern Europe in the late nineteenth and early twentieth centuries inspired new concerns about the quality of the American stock. In an age of eugenics,[3] scientific racism,[4] and social Darwinism,[5] the notion that northwestern Europeans were innately superior to those from the southern and eastern parts of the continent—to say nothing of those light-skinned people of actual or presumed west Asian origin (such as Jews, Syrians, and Armenians)—gained wide currency. A determined group of nativists, encouraged by the latest racial "science," fought for restrictive immigration policies that discriminated against those who were not of "Nordic" or "Aryan" descent (Higham 1968). In the 1920s the immigration laws were changed to reflect these prejudices. Low quotas were established for white people from nations or areas outside of those that had supplied the bulk of the American population before 1890. In the minds of many, true Americans were not merely white but also northern European. In fact, some harbored doubts about the full claim to "whiteness" of swarthy immigrants from southern Italy.

After immigration restriction had relieved ethnic and racial anxieties, the status of the new immigrants gradually improved as a result of their political involvement, their economic and professional achievement, and a decline in the respectability of the kind of scientific racism that had ranked some European groups below others. World War II brought revulsion against the genocidal anti-Semitism and eugenic experiments of the Nazis, dealing a coup de grâce to the de facto hierarchy that had placed Anglo-Saxons, Nordics, or Aryans at the apex of American society. All Americans of European origin were now unambiguously white and, for most purposes, ethnically equal to old-stock Americans of Anglo-Saxon, Celtic, and Germanic ancestry. Hierarchy was now based exclusively on color. Paradoxically, it might be argued, the removal of the burden of "otherness" from virtually all whites made more striking and salient than ever the otherness of people of color, especially African Americans.

---

[3]*eugenics:* Movement that advocated improving the human race by encouraging genetically "superior" people to reproduce and promoting the sterilization of "undesirables," including minorities, poor people, and those with mental and physical disorders.
[4]*scientific racism:* Refers to various efforts to find some scientific basis for white superiority, the results of which were inevitably bad science.
[5]*social Darwinism:* The belief that Darwin's theory of evolution and natural selection applies to society; thus the existence of extreme wealth and poverty (whether of individuals or nations) is rationalized as a "natural" result of competition and the survival of the fittest.

The civil rights movement of the 1960s was directed primarily at the legalized racial hierarchy of the southern states. The Civil Rights Acts of 1964 and 1965 brought an end to government-enforced racial segregation and the denial of voting rights to blacks in that region. But the legacy of four centuries of white supremacy survives in the disadvantaged social and economic position of blacks and other people of color in the United States. The impoverished, socially deprived, and physically unsafe ghettos, barrios, and Indian reservations of this nation are evidence that ethnic hierarchy in a clearly racialized form persists in practice if not in law.

One-Way Assimilation

Policies aimed at the assimilation of ethnic groups have usually assumed that there is a single and stable American culture of European, and especially English, origin to which minorities are expected to conform as the price of admission to full and equal participation in the society and polity of the United States (Gordon 1964, ch. 4). Assimilationist thinking is not racist in the classic sense: it does not deem the outgroups in question to be innately or biologically inferior to the ingroup. The professed goal is equality—but on terms that presume the superiority, purity, and unchanging character of the dominant culture. Little or nothing in the cultures of the groups being invited to join the American mainstream is presumed worthy of preserving. When carried to its logical conclusion, the assimilationist project demands what its critics have described—especially in reference to the coercive efforts to "civilize" Native Americans—as "cultural genocide."

Estimates of group potential and the resulting decisions as to which 10 groups are eligible for assimilation have varied in response to changing definitions of race. If an ethnic group is definitely racialized, the door is closed because its members are thought to possess ineradicable traits (biologically or culturally determined) that make them unfit for inclusion. At times there have been serious disagreements within the dominant group about the eligibility of particular minorities for initiation into the American club.

Although one-way assimilationism was mainly a twentieth-century ideology, it was anticipated in strains of nineteenth-century thinking about Irish immigrants, Native Americans, and even blacks. Radical white abolitionists and even some black antislavery activists argued that prejudice against African Americans was purely and simply a result of their peculiarly degraded and disadvantaged circumstances and that emancipation from slavery would make skin color irrelevant and open the way to their full equality and social acceptability (Fredrickson 1987, ch. 1). These abolitionists had little or no conception that there was a rich and distinctive black culture that could become the source of a positive group identity, and that African modes of thought and behavior had been adapted to the challenge of surviving under slavery.

LA CUCARACHA   by LALO ALCARAZ

If the hope of fully assimilating blacks into a color-blind society was held by only a small minority of whites, a majority probably supposed that the Irish immigrants of the 1840s and 1850s could become full-fledged Americans, if they chose to do so, simply by changing their behavior and beliefs. The doctrine of the innate inferiority of Celts to Anglo-Saxons was not even shared by all of the nativists who sought to slow down the process of Irish naturalization (Knobel 1986). A more serious problem for many of them was the fervent Catholicism of the Irish; Anglo-Protestant missionaries hoped to convert them en masse. The defenders of unrestricted Irish immigration came mostly from the ranks of the Democratic Party, which relied heavily on Irish votes. Among them were strong believers in religious toleration and a high wall of separation between church and state. They saw religious diversity as no obstacle to the full and rapid Americanization of all white-skinned immigrants.

The most sustained and serious nineteenth-century effort to assimilate people who differed both culturally and phenotypically[6] from the majority was aimed at American Indians. Frontier settlers, military men who fought Indians, and many other whites had no doubts that Indians were members of an inherently inferior race that was probably doomed to total extinction as a result of the conquest of the West. Their views were graphically expressed by General Philip Sheridan when he opined that "the only good Indian is a dead Indian." But an influential group of eastern philanthropists, humanitarian reformers, and government officials thought of the Indians as having been "noble savages" whose innate capacities were not inferior to those of whites. Thomas Jefferson, who had a much dimmer view of black potentialities, was one of the first to voice this opinion (Koch and Peden 1944, 210–11). For these ethnocentric humanitarians, the "Indian problem" was primarily cultural rather than racial, and its solution lay in civilizing the "savages" rather than exterminating them. Late in the century, the assimilationists adopted policies designed to force Indians to conform to Euro-American cultural norms; these included breaking up communally held reservations into privately owned family farms and sending Indian children to boarding schools where they were forbidden to speak their

[6]*phenotypically:* Physically.

own languages and made to dress, cut their hair, and in every possible way act and look like white people. The policy was a colossal failure; most Native Americans refused to abandon key aspects of their traditional cultures, and venal whites took advantage of the land reforms to strip Indians of much of their remaining patrimony[7] (Berkhofer 1978; Hoxie 1984; Mardock 1971).

In the early twentieth century, the one-way assimilation model was applied to the southern and eastern European immigrants who had arrived in massive numbers before the discriminatory quota system of the 1920s was implemented. While some nativists called for their exclusion on the grounds of their innate deficiencies, other champions of Anglo-American cultural homogeneity hoped to assimilate those who had already arrived through education and indoctrination. The massive "Americanization" campaigns of the period just prior to World War I produced the concept of America as a "melting pot" in which cultural differences would be obliterated. The metaphor might have suggested that a new mixture would result—and occasionally it did have this meaning—but a more prevalent interpretation was that non-Anglo-American cultural traits and inclinations would simply disappear, making the final brew identical to the original one (Gordon 1964, ch. 5).

Before the 1940s, people of color, and especially African Americans, were generally deemed ineligible for assimilation because of their innate inferiority to white ethnics, who were now thought capable of being culturally reborn as Anglo-Americans. Such factors as the war-inspired reaction against scientific racism and the gain in black political power resulting from mass migration from the South (where blacks could not vote) to the urban North (where the franchise was again open to them) led to a significant reconsideration of the social position of African Americans and threw a spotlight on the flagrant denial in the southern states of the basic constitutional rights of African Americans. The struggle for black civil rights that emerged in the 1950s and came to fruition in the early 1960s was premised on a conviction that white supremacist laws and policies violated an egalitarian "American Creed"—as Gunnar Myrdal had argued in his influential wartime study *An American Dilemma* (1944). The war against Jim Crow[8] was fought under the banner of "integration," which, in the minds of white liberals at least, generally meant one-way assimilation. Blacks, deemed by Myrdal and others as having no culture worth saving, would achieve equal status by becoming just like white Americans in every respect except pigmentation.

When it became clear that the civil rights legislation of the 1960s had failed to improve significantly the social and economic position of blacks in the urban ghettos of the North, large numbers of African Americans rejected the integrationist ideal on the grounds that it had

[7] *patrimony:* Inheritance.
[8] *Jim Crow:* Collective term for southern segregation laws.

been not only a false promise but an insult to the culture of African Americans for ignoring or devaluing their distinctive experience as a people. The new emphasis on "black power" and "black conscious- ness" conveyed to those whites who were listening that integration had to mean something other than one-way assimilation to white middle- class norms if it was to be a solution to the problem of racial inequality in America (Marable 1991; Van Deburg 1992).

It should be obvious by now that the one-way assimilation model has not proved to be a viable or generally acceptable way of adjusting group differences in American society. It is based on an ethnocentric ideal of cultural homogeneity that has been rejected by Indians, blacks, Asians, Mexican Americans, and even many white ethnics. It reifies and privi- leges one cultural strain in what is in fact a multicultural society. It should be possible to advocate the incorporation of all ethnic or racial groups into a common civic society without requiring the sacrifice of cultural dis- tinctiveness and diversity.

Cultural Pluralism

Unlike assimilationists, cultural pluralists celebrate differences among groups rather than seek to obliterate them. They argue that cultural diversity is a healthy and normal condition that does not preclude equal rights and the mutual understandings about civic responsibilities needed to sustain a democratic nation-state. This model for American ethnic relations is a twentieth-century invention that would have been virtually inconceivable at an earlier time. The eighteenth and nine- teenth centuries lacked the essential concept of the relativity of cultures. The model of cultural development during this period was evolution- ary, progressive, and universalistic. People were either civilized or they were not. Mankind was seen as evolving from a state of "savagery" or "barbarism" to "civilization," and all cultures at a particular level were similar in every way that mattered. What differentiated nations and eth- nic groups was their ranking on the scale of social evolution. Modern Western civilization stood at the apex of this universal historical pro- cess. Even nineteenth-century black nationalists accepted the notion that there were universal standards of civilization to which people of African descent should aspire. They differed from white supremacists in believing that blacks had the natural capability to reach the same heights as Caucasians if they were given a chance (Moses 1978).

The concept of cultural pluralism drew on the new cultural anthro- pology of the early twentieth century, as pioneered by Franz Boas. Boas and his disciples attempted to look at each culture they studied on its own terms and as an integrated whole. They rejected theories of social evolution that ranked cultures in relation to a universalist conception of "civilization." But relativistic cultural anthropologists were not neces- sarily cultural pluralists in their attitude toward group relations within

American society. Since they generally believed that a given society or community functioned best with a single, integrated culture, they could favor greater autonomy for Indians on reservations but also call for the full assimilation of new immigrants or even African Americans. Boas himself was an early supporter of the National Association for the Advancement of Colored People (NAACP) and a pioneering advocate of what would later be called racial integration.

An effort to use the new concept of culture to validate ethnic diver- [20] sity within the United States arose from the negative reaction of some intellectuals to the campaign to "Americanize" the new immigrants from eastern and southern Europe in the period just before and after World War I. The inventors of cultural pluralism were cosmopolitan critics of American provincialism or representatives of immigrant communities, especially Jews, who valued their cultural distinctiveness and did not want to be melted down in an Americanizing crucible. The Greenwich Village intellectual Randolph Bourne described his ideal as a "transnational America" in which various ethnic cultures would interact in a tolerant atmosphere to create an enriching variety of ideas, values, and lifestyles (Bourne 1964, ch. 8). The Jewish philosopher Horace Kallen, who coined the phrase "cultural pluralism," compared the result to a symphony, with each immigrant group represented as a section of the orchestra (Higham 1984, ch. 9; Kallen 1924). From a different perspective, W. E. B. DuBois celebrated a distinctive black culture rooted in the African and slave experiences and heralded its unacknowledged contributions to American culture in general (Lewis 1993). But the dominant version advocated by Kallen and Bourne stopped, for all practical purposes, at the color line. Its focus was on making America safe for a variety of European cultures. As a Zionist, Kallen was especially concerned with the preservation of Jewish distinctiveness and identity.

Since it was mainly the viewpoint of ethnic intellectuals who resisted the assimilationism of the melting pot, cultural pluralism was a minority persuasion in the twenties, thirties, and forties. A modified version reemerged in the 1950s in Will Herberg's (1960) conception of a "triple melting pot" of Protestants, Catholics, and Jews. The revulsion against Nazi anti-Semitism and the upward mobility of American Jews and Catholics inspired a synthesis of cultural pluralism and assimilationism that made religious persuasion the only significant source of diversity among white Americans. Herberg conceded, however, that black Protestants constituted a separate group that was not likely to be included in the Protestant melting pot. He therefore sharpened the distinction between race or color and ethnicity that was central to postwar thinking about group differences. Nevertheless, Herberg's view that significant differences between, say, Irish and Italian Catholics were disappearing was challenged in the 1960s and later, especially in the "ethnic revival" of the 1970s, which proclaimed that differing national origins among Euro-Americans remained significant and a valuable source of cultural variations.

The "multiculturalism" of the 1980s operated on assumptions that were similar to those of the cultural pluralist tradition, except that the color line was breached and the focus was shifted from the cultures and contributions of diverse European ethnic groups to those of African Americans, Mexican Americans, Asian Americans, and Native Americans. Abandonment of the earlier term "multiracialism" signified a desire to escape from the legacy of biological or genetic determinism and to affirm that the differences among people who happened to differ in skin color or phenotype were the result of their varying cultural and historical experiences. Under attack was the doctrine, shared by assimilationists and most earlier proponents of cultural pluralism, that the cultural norm in the United States was inevitably European in origin and character. Parity was now sought for groups of Asian, African, and American Indian ancestry. This ideal of cultural diversity and democracy was viewed by some of its critics as an invitation to national disunity and ethnic conflict (Schlesinger 1992). But its most thoughtful proponents argued that it was simply a consistent application of American democratic values and did not preclude the interaction and cooperation of groups within a common civic society (Hollinger 1995). Nevertheless, the mutual understandings upon which national unity and cohesion could be based needed to be negotiated rather than simply imposed by a Euro-American majority.

Group Separatism

Sometimes confused with the broadened cultural pluralism described here is the advocacy of group separatism. It originates in the desire of a culturally distinctive or racialized group to withdraw as much as possible from American society and interaction with other groups. Its logical outcome, autonomy in a separate, self-governing community, might conceivably be achieved either in an ethnic confederation like Switzerland or in the dissolution of the United States into several ethnic nations. But such a general theory is a logical construction rather than a program that has been explicitly advocated. Group separatism emanates from ethnocentric concerns about the status and destiny of particular groups, and its advocates rarely if ever theorize about what is going to happen to other groups. Precedents for group separatism based on cultural differences can be found in American history in the toleration of virtually autonomous religious communities like the Amish and the Hutterites[9] and in the modicum of self-government and immunity from general laws accorded to Indian tribes and reservations since the 1930s.

The most significant and persistent assertion of group separatism in American history has come from African Americans disillusioned

[9] *the Amish and the Hutterites:* Religious groups that reject the values and technology of contemporary society, living in relatively isolated, self-sufficient farming communities.

with the prospects for equality within American society. In the nineteenth century, several black leaders and intellectuals called on African Americans to emigrate from the United States in order to establish an independent black republic elsewhere; Africa was the most favored destination. In the 1920s, Marcus Garvey created a mass movement based on the presumption that blacks had no future in the United States and should identify with the independence and future greatness of Africa, ultimately by emigrating there. More recently, the Nation of Islam has proposed that several American states be set aside for an autonomous black nation (Fredrickson 1995, chs. 2, 4, 7). At the height of the black power movement of the 1960s and early 1970s, a few black nationalists even called for the establishment of a noncontiguous federation of black urban ghettos—a nation of islands like Indonesia or the Philippines, but surrounded by white populations rather than the Pacific Ocean.

The current version of black separatism—"Afrocentrism"[10]—has not as yet produced a plan for political separation. Its aim is a cultural and spiritual secession from American society rather than the literal establishment of a black nation. Advocates of total separation could be found among other disadvantaged groups. In the late 1960s and 1970s Mexican American militants called for the establishment of the independent Chicano nation of Aztlán[11] in the American Southwest (Gutierrez 1995, 184–85) and some Native American radicals sought the reestablishment of truly independent tribal nations.

Group separatism might be viewed as a utopian vision or rhetorical device expressing the depths of alienation felt by the most disadvantaged racial or ethnic groups in American society. The extreme unlikelihood of realizing such visions has made their promulgation more cathartic than politically efficacious. Most members of groups exposed to such separatist appeals have recognized their impracticality, and the clash between the fixed and essentialist[12] view of identity that such projects entail and the fluid and hybrid quality of group cultures in the United States has become increasingly evident to many people of color, as shown most dramatically by the recent movement among those of mixed parentage to affirm a biracial identity. Few African Americans want to celebrate the greater or lesser degree of white ancestry most of them possess, but many have acknowledged not only their ancestral ties to Africa but their debt to Euro-American culture (and its debt to them). Most Mexican Americans value their cultural heritage but do not have the expectation or even the desire to establish an independent Chicano nation in the Southwest. Native Americans have authentic historical and legal claims to a high degree of autonomy but

[10]*Afrocentrism:* An academic movement intended to counter the dominant European bias of Western scholarship; Afrocentric scholars seek to show the influence of African cultures, languages, and history on human civilization.

[11]*Aztlán:* Includes those parts of the United States once governed by Mexico.

[12]*essentialist:* Refers to the idea that group characteristics are innate, or "essential," rather than cultural.

generally recognize that total independence on their current land base is impossible and would worsen rather than improve their circumstances. Asian Americans are proud of their various cultures and seek to preserve some of their traditions but have shown little or no inclination to separate themselves from other Americans in the civic, professional, and economic life of the nation. Afrocentrism raises troubling issues for American educational and cultural life but hardly represents a serious threat to national unity.

Ethnic separatism, in conclusion, is a symptom of racial injustice and a call to action against it, but there is little reason to believe that it portends "the disuniting of America." It is currently a source of great anxiety to many Euro-Americans primarily because covert defenders of ethnic hierarchy or one-way assimilation have tried to confuse the broad-based ideal of democratic multiculturalism with the demands of a relatively few militant ethnocentrists for thoroughgoing self-segregation and isolation from the rest of American society.

Of the four models of American ethnic relations, the one that I believe offers the best hope for a just and cohesive society is a cultural pluralism that is fully inclusive and based on the free choices of individuals to construct or reconstruct their own ethnic identities. We are still far from achieving the degree of racial and ethnic tolerance that realization of such an ideal requires. But with the demographic shift that is transforming the overwhelmingly Euro-American population of thirty or forty years ago into one that is much more culturally and phenotypically heterogeneous, a more democratic form of intergroup relations is a likely prospect, unless there is a desperate reversion to overt ethnic hierarchicalism by the shrinking Euro-American majority. If that were to happen, national unity and cohesion would indeed be hard to maintain. If current trends continue, minorities of non-European ancestry will constitute a new majority sometime in the next century. Well before that point is reached, they will have the numbers and the provocation to make the country virtually ungovernable if a resurgent racism brings serious efforts to revive the blatantly hierarchical policies that have prevailed in the past.

References

Axtell, James. (1981). *The European and the Indian: Essays in the Ethnohistory of Colonial North America.* New York: Oxford University Press.

Berkhofer, Robert F., Jr. (1978). *The White Man's Indian: Image of the American Indian from Columbus to the Present.* New York: Alfred A. Knopf.

Bourne, Randolph S. (1964). *War and the Intellectuals: Collected Essays, 1915–1919.* New York: Harper Torch.

D'Souza, Dinesh. (1995). *The End of Racism: Principles for a Multiracial Society.* New York: Free Press.

Fredrickson, George M. (1987). *The Black Image in the White Mind: The Debate on Afro-American Character and Destiny, 1817–1914.* Middletown, Conn.: Wesleyan University Press.

———. (1995). *Black Liberation: A Comparative History of Black Ideologies in the United States and South Africa.* New York: Oxford University Press.

————. (1997). *The Comparative Imagination: On the History of Racism, Nationalism, and Social Movements.* Berkeley: University of California Press.

Gordon, Milton M. (1964). *Assimilation in American Life: The Role of Race, Religion, and National Origins.* New York: Oxford University Press.

Gutierrez, David. (1995). *Walls and Mirrors: Mexican Americans, Mexican Immigrants, and the Politics of Ethnicity.* Berkeley: University of California Press.

Herberg, Will. (1960). *Protestant-Catholic-Jew: An Essay in American Religious Sociology.* Garden City, N.Y.: Anchor Books.

Higham, John. (1968). *Strangers in the Land: Patterns of American Nativism, 1860–1925.* New York: Atheneum.

————. (1984). *Send These to Me: Jews and Other Immigrants in Urban America.* Baltimore: Johns Hopkins University Press.

Hollinger, David. (1995). *Postethnic America: Beyond Multiculturalism.* New York: Basic Books.

Hoxie, Frederick E. (1984). *A Final Promise: The Campaign to Assimilate the Indians, 1880–1920.* Lincoln: University of Nebraska Press.

Jordan, Winthrop D. (1968). *White Over Black: American Attitudes Toward the Negro, 1550–1812.* New York: University of North Carolina Press.

Kallen, Horace. (1924). *Culture and Democracy in the United States: Studies in the Group Psychology of American Peoples.* New York: Boni & Liveright.

Koch, Adrienne, and Peden, William (eds.). (1944). *The Life and Selected Writings of Thomas Jefferson.* New York: Modern Library.

Knobel, Dale T. (1986). *Paddy and the Republic: Ethnicity and Nationality in Antebellum America.* Middletown, Conn.: Wesleyan University Press.

Lewis, David Levering. (1993). *W. E. B. DuBois: Biography of a Race, 1868–1919.* New York: Henry Holt.

Marable, Manning. (1991). *Race, Reform, and Rebellion: The Second Reconstruction in Black America.* Jackson, Miss.: University of Mississippi Press.

Mardock, Robert W. (1971). *The Reformers and the American Indian.* Columbia: University of Missouri Press.

Miller, Stuart Creighton. (1969). *The Unwelcome Immigrant: The American Image of the Chinese, 1785–1882.* Berkeley: University of California Press.

Moses, Wilson Jeremiah. (1978). *The Golden Age of Black Nationalism, 1850–1925.* Hamden, Conn.: Archon Books.

Myrdal, Gunnar. (1944). *An American Dilemma.* New York: Harper and Row.

Schlesinger, Arthur M., Jr. (1992). *The Disuniting of America.* New York: Norton.

Van Deburg, William L. (1992). *New Day in Babylon: The Black Power Movement and American Culture, 1965–1975.* Chicago: University of Chicago Press.

ENGAGING THE TEXT

1. How does Fredrickson distinguish between race and ethnicity? How and under what circumstances can ethnicity become "racialized" (para. 2)?

2. What does Fredrickson mean by "the burden of 'otherness'"? Summarize the ways in which racial categories and definitions of "whiteness" have changed during the course of American history.

3. What are some of the ways that ethnic hierarchy has been eliminated? In what ways does it persist, according to Fredrickson? What evidence can you think of that would support or challenge this contention?

4. Fredrickson writes that "assimilationist thinking is not racist in the classic sense" (para. 9) — thereby implying that such thinking may be racist in some other sense. What does he mean by this? Do you agree?

5. How does Fredrickson distinguish cultural pluralism from assimilation? How did earlier forms of pluralism differ from the current concept of multiculturalism?

6. Why does Fredrickson reject the claim that an emphasis on ethnic identity threatens the unity and stability of American society? Why does a Euro-American backlash against ethnic diversity pose a greater risk in his view? Have you observed any recent examples of either divisiveness or backlash? Compare your observations with those of classmates.

EXPLORING CONNECTIONS

7. Write an essay examining the ways in which various models of ethnic relations can be seen operating in one or more of the following selections:

   Richard Rodriguez, "The Achievement of Desire" (see bedfordstmartins .com/rereading/epages)

   Malcolm X, "Learning to Read" (p. 189)

   Studs Terkel, "Stephen Cruz" (see bedfordstmartins.com/rereading/epages)

   Kay Givens McGowan, "Weeping for the Lost Matriarchy" (p. 396)

   JoYin C Shih, "Chyna and Me" (p. 517)

   Erin Aubry Kaplan, "Barack Obama: Miles Traveled, Miles to Go" (p. 540)

   Michelle Alexander, "The New Jim Crow" (p. 738)

8. What model or models of ethnic relations do you see represented in the cartoon by Lalo Alcaraz on page 569?

9. Examine the Visual Portfolio on pages 554–62. Identify the model of ethnic relations you see embodied in each image and explain your reasoning.

EXTENDING THE CRITICAL CONTEXT

10. If your campus or community is involved in a debate concerning affirmative action, immigration, bilingual education, multiculturalism, or ethnic studies, analyze several opinion pieces or position papers on the issue. What models of ethnic relations are expressed or assumed by each side of the debate?

FROM REZ LIFE: AN INDIAN'S JOURNEY THROUGH RESERVATION LIFE

DAVID TREUER

Out of the 300-plus native languages originally spoken in the United States, only about half remain, and many of them are dying. David Treuer is acutely aware of this loss. In the following passage, he focuses on the efforts of Ojibwe language activists to revive their native language and preserve their culture. But Treuer is at heart a storyteller. In addition to profiling Keller Paap, the "recovering rock star" who leads the Ojibwe language immersion program, he weaves in stories about "blood quantum" the American Indian Movement of the 1960s and 1970s. (the way tribal membership is determined), the Carlisle school, and the Cherokee Freedmen. Treuer has won fellowships from the National Endowment for the Humanities, the Bush Foundation and the Guggenheim Foundation. A professor of literature and creative writing at the University of Southern California, he has produced several well-received novels; a book of essays, *Native American Fiction: A User's Manual* (2006); and *Rez Life: An Indian's Journey Through Reservation Life* (2012), from which this selection is taken.

I AM NOT SUPPOSED TO BE ALIVE. Native Americans were supposed to die off, as endangered species do, a century ago. Our reservations aren't supposed to exist either; they were supposed to be temporary in many ways, and, under assault by the Dawes Act[1] in the nineteenth century and by termination policy during the Eisenhower era[2] in the twentieth century, they were supposed to disappear, too.

But I am not dead after all, and neither is rez life despite the coldest wishes of a republic since two centuries before I was born. We stubbornly continue to exist. There were just over 200,000 Native Americans alive at the dawn of the twentieth century; as of the 2000 census, we number more than 2 million. If you discount population growth by immigration, we are the fastest-growing segment of the U.S. population. But even as our populations are growing, something else, I fear, is dying: our cultures.

Among my fellow Indians, this is not a popular thing to say. Most of us immediately sneer at warnings of cultural death, calling the very idea

---

[1]*Dawes Act:* The General Allotment Act of 1887, sponsored by Senator Henry L. Dawes of Massachusetts, divided Indian land into individual allotments; "excess" land was purchased by the government and sold to non–Indians. Individual land ownership effectively diluted tribal power.

[2]*termination policy during the Eisenhower era:* From 1953 to 1966, over 100 tribes lost their tribal status, over a million acres of land were removed from trust, and over 33,000 native people were relocated from reservations to large cities.

further proof that "the man" is still trying to kill us, but now with attitudes and arguments rather than discrimination and guns. Any Indian caught worrying that we might indeed vanish can expect to be grouped with the self-haters. While many things go into making a culture — kinship, history, religion, place — the disappearance of our languages suggests that our cultures, in total, may not be here for much longer.

For now, many Native American languages still exist, but most of them just barely, with only a very few living speakers, all of them old. On January 21, 2008, Marie Smith Jones, the last living fluent speaker of Eyak, one of about twenty remaining Native Alaskan languages, died at the age of eighty-nine. Linguists estimate that when Europeans first came to North America, more than 300 Native American languages were spoken here. Today, there are only about 150. Of those languages, only twenty are spoken by children. Only three languages — Dakota, Dene, and Ojibwe — have a vibrant community of speakers. Within a century, if nothing is done, hardly any Native languages will remain, though the surviving ones will include my language, Ojibwe.

Cultures change, of course. Sometimes they change slowly, in response to such factors as warming temperatures, differences in food sources, or new migration patterns. At other times, cultural changes are swift — the result of colonialism, famine, migration, or war. But at some point (which no one is anxious to identify exactly), a culture ceases to be a culture and becomes an ethnicity — that is, it changes from a life system that develops its own terms into one that borrows, almost completely, someone else's.

To claim that Indian cultures can continue without Indian languages only hastens our end, even if it makes us feel better about ourselves. Our cultures and our languages — as unique, identifiable, and particular entities — are linked to our sovereignty. If we allow our own wishful thinking and complacency to finish what George Armstrong Custer began, we will lose what we've managed to retain: our languages, land, laws, institutions, ceremonies, and, finally, ourselves. Cultural death matters because if the culture dies, we will have lost the chance not only to live on our own terms (something for which our ancestors fought long and hard) but also to live in our own terms.

If my language dies, our word for bear, "makwa," will disappear, and with it the understanding that "makwa" is derived from the word for box, "makak" (because black bears box themselves up, sleeping, for the winter). So too will the word for namesake, "niiyawen'enh." Every child who gets an Ojibwe name has namesakes, sometimes as many as six or eight of them. Throughout a child's life, his or her namesakes function somewhat like godparents, giving advice and help, good for a dollar to buy an Indian taco at a powwow. But they offer something more too. The term for "my body," "niiyaw" (a possessive noun: ni- = "I/mine"; -iiyaw = "body/soul"), is incorporated into the word for a namesake because the idea (contained by the word and vice versa) is that when you take part in a naming, you are giving a part of your soul, your body, to the person being named. So, to say "my namesake," niiyawen'enh, is to say "my fellow body, myself." If these words are lost, much will happen, but also very little will happen. We will be able to go to Starbucks, GameStop, Walmart, and Home Depot. We will still use Crest Whitestrips. Some of us will still do our taxes. Some of us still won't. The mechanics of life as it is lived by modern Ojibwes will remain, for the most part, unchanged. The languages we lose, when we lose them, are always replaced by other languages. And all languages can get the job of life done. But something else might be lost and there might be more to the job of life than simply living it.

At Waadookodaading Ojibwe Language Immersion School at Lac Courte Oreilles (LCO) Reservation in Wisconsin, people are doing something about this. You drive past a lot of natural beauty between Hayward and the school—a lot of maple and pine; deep, clear lakes—most of it owned by whites. At the school, in two yellow modular buildings built with tribal funds in what used to be the corner of the school parking lot, a cultural revival is occurring. On the hot day in May when I visited the school I saw silhouettes of students drawn in chalk on the wooden decking that connects the buildings. The third and fourth grades were studying solar movement as part of their science curriculum, all done in Ojibwe, and done only here. Inside, the classroom walls are covered with signs in the Ojibwe language. A smartboard, linked to the teacher's laptop, provides state-of-the-art learning opportunities.

One of the teachers who helped start the immersion program is a lanky, tall, excitable man named Keller Paap. When these teachers started the school in 2000 they had only a few students in kindergarten. Now, there are about twenty students in the program between kindergarten and fourth grade. After greeting the fourth-grade students in the classroom, Keller brings them to the music room in the main school building, where they all sing along with Keller's guitar playing to welcome the new day. They speak, sing, argue, and flirt with each other in Ojibwe at a level that eludes most adults at LCO and every other Ojibwe reservation across the United States. After the morning singing they head back to the classroom and begin working on their science unit. "Ahaw," asks Keller. "Awegonesh ge-ayaayambam da-agawaateyaag?" [So. What do all you need to make a shadow?]

One girl says, shyly, "Andaatewin."   10

"Mii gwayak," says Keller. "Awegonesh gaye? Giizis ina?"

"Ahaw," says a playful boy, without a hint of shame or bashfulness.

"Mii go gaye apiichaawin," says another kid, in a spurt of intuition.

This classroom is light-years ahead of most tribal language programs, which are still stuck on "bezhig, niizh, niswi," and "makwa, waabooz, waagosh" ("one, two, three" and "bear, rabbit, fox"). They aren't listing things in Ojibwe at Waadookodaading; they are thinking in Ojibwe.

Keller; his wife, Lisa LaRonge; Alex Decoteau; and the other teachers at Waadookodaading are, together, saving Ojibwe culture. Keller Paap is one of a few activists who have devoted their lives to saving the Ojibwe language. He is an unlikely hero. Raised in a suburb of Minneapolis, college-educated, a recovering rock star (he is an accomplished guitarist), he has given up all financial security, all his other possible prospects, everything, in order to move to LCO to open an Ojibwe-language immersion school. He is a new kind of activist for a new kind of reservation community.

Indian activism used to be a tough guy's game. In the late 1960s and early 1970s the American Indian Movement (AIM) rose from urban Indian populations across the country. Cleveland, Minneapolis, Chicago, Oakland, and Los Angeles had been destinations for Indians relocated during the 1950s, and they became the seed plots for a surge of Indian activism. Relocation, a government-sponsored program, yet another switchback in the U.S. government's long road toward freeing itself of Indians and of all responsibility toward us, was a policy that sought to integrate Indians into the mainstream workforce by severing their relationship to their reservation communities. The relocation program promised jobs, education, and housing in up-and-coming American cities. Very little of this was forthcoming. Instead, Indians were crowded into ghettos, fought for work, fought for education, and suffered. It should be said that many Indians flourished in cities in the 1950s and many still flourish there today; more than half of all Indians live in urban areas. Still, the common notion that reservations are prisons should be revised; it was the city that became a prison for many Indians. They were stuck in a city and could not get out. They hadn't the money to move back to the reservation and yet they had little reason to stay. Franklin Avenue, Gowanus Canal, Chicago's South Side—these became signifiers of rough life as important as the reservations the Indians had come from. Out of this situation, which was supposed to gradually make Indians as Indians "disappear," came AIM.

Clyde Bellecourt, Dennis Banks, George Mitchell, and Herb Powless, among others, founded AIM in 1968. Its rationale and goals were: the U.S. government has never had the interests of American Indians in mind or at heart, and any attempt to work within the system or with the system is bound to fail. Unlike the black civil rights movement, AIM had no great strength of numbers, economic capital, or visibility to use in getting its point across. The answer: bold, graphic takeovers and marches. Within seven years AIM had marched on and taken over Alcatraz Island (more accurately, a group of Bay Area Indians took over Alcatraz and some of the high-profile AIM leadership came toward the end of the takeover); the Bureau of Indian Affairs (BIA) headquarters in Washington, D.C.; Mount Rushmore; and a replica of the *Mayflower*. At each event the AIMsters dressed in cowboy boots, tight jeans, buckskin jackets, and headbands and issued passionate, even poetic, statements about the continued mistreatment of American Indians. Often, light-skinned Indians were told they couldn't belong to AIM or had to march in the back. AIM was always concerned with its image. Its activism was a kind of art—street theater that was visual and often violent and that conveyed clear messages about the mistreatment of Indians.

The most shocking and visible moment for AIM, and the moment that marked its decline, was its standoff with the federal government at the Jumping Bull Compound on the Pine Ridge Reservation in South Dakota, which left two federal agents dead. Leonard Peltier was charged with and convicted of murder and is still serving a sentence at Leavenworth. Afterward, marked by vicious infighting and infiltrated by the FBI, AIM became, in the opinion of many, aimless. And not everyone had approved of AIM in the first place. During the 1970s anger at the Red Lake Reservation chairman, Roger Jourdain, at his policies, and at embezzlement by other employees fueled riots at Red Lake. Jourdain's house was burned down and cars were shot through with bullets. AIM tried to muscle in on the unrest and was rebuffed. The traditional community of Ponemah took a stand against AIM. As Eugene Stillday recounts, a number of veterans (of World War II, Korea, and Vietnam) from Ponemah gathered at The Cut—a narrow place in the road, bordered by the lake on one side and a large swamp on the other. They barricaded the road, built sandbag bunkers, and kept constant guard, armed with deer rifles and shotguns. Carloads of AIMsters drove up the road, were stopped, and after looking at the faces of the Ponemah veterans chose to turn around and go elsewhere.

This was what passed for activism in the late 1960s and 1970s. Keller Paap, on the other hand, is an unlikely activist. He was raised in a comfortable suburb: White Bear Lake, on the north side of St. Paul. His mother is from Red Cliff Reservation in Wisconsin; his father is of German ancestry. After graduating from high school in White Bear Lake he started college, stopped, and devoted himself to becoming a rock and roller. Keller *looks* like a rock star. He's tallish (six feet and change), thin, and bony, with long black hair, wide cheekbones and lips, and long tapered fingers that were made to hold a guitar and to play it well. When someone is talking to him about the Ojibwe language, the glazed look that comes over his eyes must be the same look he had during a guitar solo. It is not difficult to imagine him wearing a bandanna, like Steven Van Zandt,[3] or the same purse-lipped expression when he is focused on his guitar. During the day the kids sometimes start spacing out during their lessons and Keller jumps up, thumbs his iPod while gushing at the kids in Ojibwe, finds Herbie Hancock's "Rockit," and gets his kids to kick off their shoes and try to do the "robot," the "scarecrow," and "the moon walk." During the early 1980s Keller spent a lot of time

---

[3]*Steven Van Zandt:* Rock musician and actor, best known as a member of Bruce Springsteen's E Street Band.

practicing his break-dancing moves. Later, he and his friends followed the Grateful Dead.[4]

I first met Paap in 1994 at the University of Minnesota, where he was finishing his undergraduate degree. He was a student in the Ojibwe-language class offered through the department of American Indian Studies. At the time he didn't seem all that interested in the language.

"Back then I thought it was sort of cool," he says. "I was Ojibwe, my people were from Red Cliff, and this was our language, and it felt good to study it."

That good feeling quickly became a passion.

"It all started with hanging out with Dennis Jones, the Ojibwe-language instructor at the U. I traveled around with him and recorded his mom and worked on translating her stories. And, man! The intricacy! The crazy complexity of the language totally got me. I mean, hanging out with Nancy, and Rose Tainter, and Delores Wakefield—all those elders, sitting around the kitchen table drinking Red Rose tea and talking—it felt comfortable, like it was with my uncles and cousins and relatives up at Red Cliff when I was a kid. Even more than music, even more than the guitar, the complexity and music of the language and the feeling of belonging to something totally caught me."[5]

Catch him it did. Soon after graduating he worked as a teaching assistant for the language program. He met his wife there. Lisa LaRonge is from LCO Reservation, due south of Red Cliff. Like Keller she is tall, with long brown hair. Like Keller, she has gone through many incarnations before devoting herself to the language. They moved to Lisa's reservation in 1998 and, with a few others, opened an Ojibwe-language immersion school—Waadookodaading ("we help each other"). Waadookodaading has been in operation for ten years now, as one of only a few schools generating fluent speakers of the Ojibwe language. Strangely, many other Ojibwe-language activists have some kind of artistic pedigree. Leslie Harper—who along with her sister Laurie, Adrian Liberty, and elders like Johnny Mitchell founded the Niigaane Immersion program at Leech Lake—is a writer and a former Miss Indian Minneapolis. Liberty is a drummer—his band Powermad was featured in David Lynch's *Wild at Heart*.

The goal of these activists seems odd to many: in communities rife with drugs, violence, gangs, domestic abuse, suicide, and high dropout rates, Ojibwe-language immersion seems like a perverse luxury.

Odd or not, what these fighters are after is something very different from what AIM was after in the 1960s and 1970s. AIM wanted the world to stand up and take notice of the injustices we suffered and continue to suffer. By taking notice public opinion might actually sway policy. Language activists look in the other direction—instead of looking out

---

[4]*The Grateful Dead:* Founded in 1965 in the San Francisco Bay area; one of the longest lasting rock bands with some of the most dedicated followers (Deadheads).
[5]Interview with Keller Paap, August 2009, Scattergood Lake.

at the government and the mainstream and trying to convince them of something, they are looking in and are trying to convince their fellow Indians of something else. As my brother has put it on a number of occasions, "The U.S. government has spent millions of dollars trying to take our language away from us. Why would we expect the government to give it back? It's up to us to give it back to ourselves."

The U.S. government did indeed spend millions of dollars and many years trying to stamp out indigenous languages, mostly through subtle discriminatory practices (such as hiring and education) but the government also used unsubtle means, the most destructive of which was the institution of Indian boarding schools. As Native American languages endured a sustained assault, Indian identity—those elusive bonds that wed self and society and that make a people—took the greatest number of hits. Many Indians see this as proof of the spiteful, harmful attitude the feds have always had toward Indians. But governments really aren't spiteful just to be spiteful. They are like animals—they do what they do out of self-interest. And for many years, Indians were a threat—a constant, powerful, very real, very physical threat—to American imperial expansion. We were, quite simply, either in the way or powerful enough to pose a threat if provoked. The process by which Indians were dealt with only sometimes took the form of war. In many other instances Indians were subjected to a process of "Americanization." In place from colonial days, Americanization was aimed at creating a uniform public body, one that shared the same values and lifestyles and put the same premium on work, saving, expansion, and accumulation of capital. However, for Indians, the late nineteenth century and the early twentieth century was a dark time, in many ways because of the boarding schools.

In 1878–1879, the U.S. government built and funded the first of twenty-six federally controlled Indian boarding schools. Carlisle Indian Industrial School, in Carlisle, Pennsylvania, came to epitomize the boarding school era, which for many Indians was one of the darkest times in our history. The idea of the boarding schools was to forcibly break the family bonds that, in the opinion of many, kept Indians from becoming civilized and part of the American public. Carlisle drew students from more than 140 different tribes. The students had their hair cut short. Their names were changed. They were forbidden to speak their Native languages. No Indian religions were allowed at the school—attendance at Christian services was compulsory. Students were beaten for speaking their languages. Many were abused. By 1902, with twenty-six schools in operation, more than 6,000 Indian children had been removed from their homes and sent hundreds of miles away from their communities. When boarding schools and the policies that supported them were finally abolished in the 1970s, hundreds of thousands of Indians had been sent there. Carlisle alone admitted more than 12,000 students by the time of its closing in 1918.

Attendance at boarding schools was not compulsory. Parents had to agree to let their children go. But their permission was often effected through coercion. Indian agents, who got bonuses for collecting children for school, threatened to withhold annuities or supplies. They blacklisted Indian families who refused to send their children along. Some parents, like my great-grandmother, could not afford to feed their children, and while their Indianness was under assault at these boarding schools at least their children would have something to eat. After the schools had been in existence for a few decades the pressure to send children away became a norm. If you wanted your children to have a chance at a job or an education you sent them away. It simply was what was done. Agents from the BIA were extremely effective at coercing families into letting their children go.…

Forced assimilation in the form of allotment[6] and boarding schools   30
had terrible effects on reservation life and Indian lives. But as bad as the U.S. government has been in its treatment of Indians, sometimes Indians are as bad or even worse to one another. One really fucked-up aspect of Indian life is that, unlike any other minority, Indians have rules, based on genetics and "blood quantum," that determine whether or not someone is *officially* an Indian.…

"Blood quantum" is a strange way to determine who is and who is not officially Indian. And whatever impact this might have on how one feels about one's identity, such exclusions have direct and sometimes dire consequences.…There have been blood quantum laws on the books since the eighteenth century, most notably in Virginia, where it was illegal to mix with Indians and blacks. Ironically, "one drop" laws (one drop of black blood made you black) were reversed for Indians: they had to prove they had a certain fraction of Indian blood in order to qualify for enrollment and membership and to receive their treaty rights. But it wasn't until the 1930s that blood quantum became a widespread marker for racial descent, on which hung the issue of an Indian's nationality. Until then, for hundreds of years, Indian tribes had various means of including or excluding someone. Many tribes, mine among them, practiced widespread "adoptions." Indian children (and often white children) were captured or kidnapped and formally adopted into Ojibwe families to replace children and men lost in war or lost to disease. That's what happened to John Tanner in the mid-eighteenth century. He was abducted by Shawnee in the Ohio River valley when he was about ten years old, was marched into northern Ohio and Michigan, and later was sold to an Ojibwe family. He grew up among the Ojibwe, spoke our language, married an Ojibwe woman, and made his life with

---

[6]*Allotment:* Refers to the effect of the Dawes Act; individual land ownership was designed to encourage Native Americans to assimilate into American society.

us. Not that it was always a happy life for him—his Shawnee captors beat him, left him for dead, smeared feces on his face, and piled other humiliations on him during his captivity. His Ojibwe family was only marginally more loving, until he proved he could hunt and provide for them. Indians from other tribes were adopted or married in and they enjoyed not only an Indian identity but the rights secured by the tribes and bands they joined.

Such fluid cultural boundaries became more rigid in the twentieth century. As part of the IRA,[7] which brought constitutional government to many tribes, the tribes could set their own blood quantum requirements for enrollment (half, one-fourth, one-sixteenth, or whatever), but only in consultation with, and with the approval of, the BIA. Since its inception, even though Indians are the fastest-growing segment of the U.S. population, official Indians in some tribes are declining. That is, many tribes are getting smaller.

Now many tribes are shrinking by their own efforts. The Mdewakanton Sioux Community has roughly 250 enrolled members. This number has remained quite static for the last twenty years—interestingly, the period when the tribe has run multibillion-dollar Mystic Lake Casino. The Mdewakanton is supposed to be a community reserved for the descendants of Dakota Indians who sided with the U.S. government during the Dakota Conflict of 1862. In payment for their support and their reluctance to join their tribesmen they were given land near present-day Shakopee, Minnesota. However, a lawsuit working its way through the courts alleges that there are more than 20,000 eligible enrollees (according to blood quantum rules on the books) living in the United States and Canada who meet the tribal enrollment criteria and can prove membership to the band at Shakopee. These descendants have appealed to the tribe and been rejected. The tribe doesn't want them and doesn't want to enroll them. In their case this is not a matter of "identity" but a matter of resources. If enrolled they would be entitled, along with the 250 officially enrolled members, to per capita payments, which would drop from $80,000 a month down to $1,000 a month. It is easy to see why the Indians in power and enrolled at Shakopee don't want to open their arms to their tribal brothers. They are as greedy as any other Americans; I can't think of many people who after a lifetime of struggle would gladly give up $1.2 million a year in exchange for the moral high ground.[8]

Who gets to be an official Indian and who is an unofficial Indian is sometimes a matter of identity and insecurity about that identity. Sometimes it is a matter of economics and greed. In both instances tribal enrollment confuses race (descent) and culture (environment).

---

[7]*IRA:* The Indian Reorganization Act (1934) terminated the allotment system, limited the sale of American Indian lands, and granted limited tribal sovereignty.

[8]Kevin Diaz, *Minneapolis Star Tribune*, November 10, 2009, http://www.startribune .com/politics/state/69722942.html.

Being enrolled won't necessarily make you more culturally Indian. And not being enrolled won't make you less so. But enrollment and nonenrollment can make you more or less poor and can determine where and how you live.

One of the strangest and most fascinating instances of the question "Who is and who isn't Indian?" is the case of the Cherokee Freedmen.

The forced removal of Cherokee and the other four members of the Five Civilized Tribes from their lands in Georgia, Florida, Tennessee, Kentucky, and South Carolina in the 1820s and 1830s to the Indian Territories on what was known as the Trail of Tears has become a symbolic moment in American history. The Trail of Tears has come to signify American injustice, Indian-hating presidents, paternalistic Supreme Court justices, and the Indians' plight in general. It has been written about, sung about, painted, reenacted. The Trail of Tears was brutal. Of the 15,000 Indians who were forced to march to Indian Territory in the dead of winter, 4,000 died along the way—from starvation, hypothermia, typhus, or pneumonia. One can envision the long line of the downtrodden and disposed staggering through blizzards and fording icy rivers. The Cherokee and allied tribes were forced to march because they had been dispossessed. Their 5,000 black slaves were forced to march because they were the personal property of the Indians. Once they reached Oklahoma, the black slaves continued to be slaves until emancipation. During the Civil War the Cherokee Nation was divided. Some Cherokee sided with the Union, others with the Confederacy. After the Union victory the Cherokee Nation was forced to the negotiating table, largely as punishment for supporting the Confederacy, and forced to sign a treaty. One stipulation of the treaty of 1866 was that former Cherokee slaves, known as Freedmen, were to be given full citizenship in the Cherokee Nation. As members of the Cherokee Nation, the Freedmen would be entitled to all the rights and benefits of Cherokee citizens, such as allotments, the right to vote in tribal elections, the right to stand for office, and receipt of annuities.

A little over 100 years later the Cherokee Nation wanted to remove the descendants of the Freedmen from the rolls and deprive them of tribal membership. This meant that these descendants—who considered themselves culturally (if not completely racially) Cherokee, who had lived and worked on Cherokee lands, who had the same values and language as the Cherokee—would no longer be eligible to vote, hold office, receive federal housing assistance, or receive whatever casino profits might come their way. One can smell divisive greed in the air again, though one senses something else, too: the Cherokee in Oklahoma have long had one of the most welcoming, inclusive, and progressive enrollment policies. Unlike the St. Croix Band of Ojibwe in Wisconsin, the Cherokee Nation requires only proof of descent from the "Dawes rolls," a list of Cherokee and other Civilized Tribe members compiled in 1893 and closed in 1907 for the purpose of allotment.

The Dawes rolls had included a few categories of tribal membership: by blood; by marriage; and, specifically, Freedmen or descendants of Freedmen, and Delaware Indians adopted into the Cherokee Nation. There is no minimum blood quantum requirement. Such a policy has been a blessing and a curse to the Cherokee. With more than 250,000 enrolled members living in almost every state in the Union, they have remarkable power of presence and numbers and a much more flexible understanding than any other tribe of what it might mean to be Indian. They also suffer from encroachment and the constant threat of cultural dissolution through acculturation—many who want to be Indian claim to be Cherokee, not because they are but because it's easy. Hence the popular refrain we all hear at parties: my grandmother was a Cherokee princess. (No one seriously claims to be descended from a Hopi princess, a Dakota princess, or an Inuit princess.)

In the late 1980s the Cherokee Nation tried to disenroll the descendants of the Freedmen. The case went to federal court, which ruled in *Nero v. Cherokee Nation* that tribes had the right to determine the criteria of their own tribal membership. This ran counter to a century of policy that said tribes could determine the criteria for membership but only in "consultation" with the BIA. Many members of the Cherokee Nation were (and are) divided over the issue, and in 2006 the Cherokee Nation Judicial Appeals Tribunal maintained that the Freedmen were potentially eligible for enrollment. The Cherokee Nation put the issue to a referendum, and as a result a constitutional amendment was passed in 2007 that limited membership in the Cherokee Nation to those who were Cherokee, Shawnee, or Delaware by blood, listed on the Dawes rolls.

The wheels on the bus go round and round. The Black Congressional Caucus got involved. It saw the exclusion of the Cherokee Freedmen as an instance of exclusion based on race. As the case worked its way through the courts, Representative Diane Watson of California introduced legislation that would block $300 million in federal funding and annul all gaming compacts between the Cherokee and the state of Oklahoma until the Cherokee Nation reinstated the Freedmen. The basis for the legislation is about as potent an irony as exists in the history of Indian-white relations: the Cherokee were being punished for breaking a treaty they made in "good faith" with the United States![9]

The U.S. government and the state government of Oklahoma don't 40 want to be too hasty or too autocratic in dealing with the Cherokee Nation—if only because the Cherokee suffered so much, before, during, and after the Trail of Tears. But haven't the Cherokee Freedmen—not just disposed, but the dehumanized *property* of the dispossessed—suffered more? In 1828, leading up to the Trail of Tears, the Cherokee had standing in U.S. courts. Their slaves did not. Tribal enrollment has been,

[9]See http://www.time.com/time/nation/article/0,8599,1635873,00.html.

from the beginning, a way of determining who can claim economic benefits that devolve from treaties. From the start, enrollment and Indian citizenship have been institutions created by the U.S. government as a way of limiting its responsibility toward Indians and eventually getting out of the "Indian business." But it couldn't always control the ways in which tribes sought to define themselves. Blood quantum was supposed to be a way out for the government. But this has been tricky. The Dawes rolls (and this fact seems to have been lost) were created as a means of fractionalizing collective Cherokee landholdings and opening up the Indian Territories for white settlement. When the white bureaucrats made the rolls, they listed people who looked Cherokee as Cherokee, and those who looked black (even if these were mixed black and Cherokee) as black. The Dawes rolls were based on blood, but only on how blood "looked" (and here we remember the anthropologists scratching the chests of White Earth Indians and measuring their skulls). From the beginning, the rolls were flawed and were designed to cheat Indians. One wonders: why rely on them now for any purpose? Enrollment has become a kind of signifier for Indians that says (or is believed to say) what someone's degree of Indianness is. But this is a relatively recent development. One wonders: by fighting about enrollment at all, aren't we just adopting a system of exclusion that helps the U.S. government but doesn't help us? And couldn't the Cherokee have won a little something from everyone had they thought of the problems of race, identity, and enrollment differently? After all, very few nations in the world base citizenship on race. It can be based on many things—such as language, a naturalization process, an oath, residency, or all of the above. Couldn't the Cherokee Nation say: since we were slaveholders, we have a moral debt to the descendants of the people we wrongly enslaved? Couldn't the Cherokee say: in order to pay that debt we will allow the Freedmen to remain on the rolls as citizens of the Cherokee Nation (or even limited citizens, nonvoting citizens, or whatever), though they are not racially Cherokee? This way the Cherokee would have sacrificed some autonomy and spread some resources a little thinner but would have made right a historical wrong and emerged as the moral victors in the enrollment issue.

Many Indian tribes, many reservations, are stronger than they have ever been before. Gaming has something to do with that. So do numbers. But we are not so strong that we can afford to waste our people. We are not so strong that we can keep excluding one another. But that's exactly what tribes often do....

In part, impatience with the sometimes self-serving identity politics is what motivates language-immersion activists such as Keller Paap. They feel that if they are able to bring language back to the center of our sense of ourselves, all the other complicated politics of self, all the other markers of authenticity, will fall away. They feel that the government's attempt at assimilation created the destructive, diseased social fabric in which we are wrapped today. And so the work that Keller Paap, Lisa LaRonge,...Adrian Liberty, Leslie Harper, and others are doing to bring the Ojibwe language back is, essentially, an antiassimilationist movement. In many ways it turns around what AIM started. (One of AIM's cries was "Indian pride"—and AIMsters didn't style themselves as BIA bureaucrats with short hair and bolo ties.) The renewed interest in tribal cultures and tribal language runs against hundreds of years of government policy....

For language activists, the language is the key to everything else—identity, life and lifestyle, home and homeland. Most language activists are also traditional Indians, but very modern traditional Indians, as likely to attend a ceremony as they are to have smartphones on which they record language material and Indian ceremonial music they are trying to learn. This new traditionalism is not a turning back of the clock, but a response to it; modernism (and modern, global capitalism) is a great obliterator of cultural difference and a great infuser of a new kind of class difference, and language activism is one way Indians are not only protecting themselves and their rights but also creating meaning in their lives. For Keller Paap and his family, this means tapping maple trees, ricing, hunting, collecting wild leeks, blasting Hendrix and Chris Whitley from the tinny speakers of their VW Westy van, and competing every year in the Birkebeiner cross-country ski race held in Hayward, Wisconsin. It means choosing to live their modern lives, with all those modern contradictions, in the Ojibwe language—to choose Ojibwe over English, whether for ceremony or for karaoke....

If we lose our language and the culture that goes with it, I think, something more will be lost than simply a bouquet of discrete understandings about bears or namesakes, more than an opportunity to speak to my children and friends in public without anyone eavesdropping. If the language dies, we will lose something personal, a degree of understanding that resides, for most fluent speakers, on an unconscious level. We will lose our sense of ourselves and our culture. There are many aspects of culture that are extralinguistic—that is, they exist outside or in spite of language: kinship, legal systems, governance, history, personal identity. But there is very little that is extralinguistic about a story, about language itself. I think what I am trying to say is that we will lose beauty—the beauty of the particular, the beauty of the past and the intricacies of a language tailored for our space in the world. That Native American cultures are imperiled is important and not just to Indians. It is important to everyone, or should be. When we lose cultures, we lose American plurality—the productive and lovely discomfort that true difference brings.

ENGAGING THE TEXT

1. What is lost, according to Treuer, when a language dies? Why does he focus on the Ojibwe word for "namesake" (para. 7)? What connection does he see between language and culture?

2. What differences does Treuer note between the goals of the AIM activists and the language activists? Does Ojibwe-language immersion seem to you to be "a perverse luxury" (para. 25), given the serious problems of reservation life that Treuer cites? Debate in class.

3. Since attendance at Indian boarding schools wasn't compulsory, how and why did Indian agents coerce parents into sending their children to the schools?

4. What is "blood quantum," and why is it so vital to determining who is and is not Indian? How does it differ from the "one drop rule"?

5. Who were the Cherokee Freedmen? What history complicates their designation as Cherokee? Should they remain as citizens of the Cherokee Nation? Why or why not?

6. In what sense is the "new traditionalism" a response to modernism? To what extent do you agree with Treuer's claim that the preservation of Native American cultures is "important to everyone" (para. 43)?

EXPLORING CONNECTIONS

7. What does Matt Bors, the cartoonist on page 591, suggest about the historical forgetfulness of American culture? Compare the image of Indians here and in the cartoon by Mike Keefe on page 409: Which depiction, if either, gives a more realistic portrait of Native Americans? Is it possible for cartoonists to avoid stereotypes and still be funny?

8. Treuer asserts that "the government's forced assimilation created the destructive, diseased social fabric in which we are wrapped today" (para. 42). How do the selections by Kay Givens McGowan (p. 396 in Chapter Four) and George M. Fredrickson (p. 565) support this observation? Are the efforts of language activists enough to begin restoring the social fabric of tribal peoples? Why or why not?

9. How does Gatto's concept of "schooling" — as opposed to education (p. 141) — apply to the Indian boarding schools? How would Treuer define real education?

EXTENDING THE CRITICAL CONTEXT

10. Visit Bedford's e-Pages for this chapter of *Rereading America* (bedfordst martins.com/rereading/epages) and watch the video, *More Than That*, created by two classes on the Pine Ridge Reservation in South Dakota. The video, originally designed as a response to a *20/20* news special depicting impoverished reservation life, presents a very different view. What message do the students in the video convey about their values? What perception of Native Americans do they appear to be reacting to?

11. To see some of the language activists Treuer mentions and to hear more about their efforts to preserve the Ojibwe language, watch any or all segments of *First Speakers: Restoring the Ojibway Language*, a special from Twin Cities Public Television: www.tpt.org/?a=productions&id=3. How does actually hearing the Ojibway language compare to reading about it? What other differences do you detect between the video and the essay?

12. Research the language that was originally spoken by the native inhabitants of your area. Is it a living language? What efforts, if any, are being made to preserve or restore it?

13. Watch an episode or read the transcript of an episode of *We Shall Remain*, the five-part PBS series on Native American history. How does the series represent American Indians? How does this treatment compare to the treatment of Native Americans in popular films like *Windtalkers*, *Pocahontas*, or *Dances with Wolves* that are based on historical events?

DECONSTRUCTING AMERICA

PATRICK J. BUCHANAN

One of the most influential and outspoken conservative voices in the United States, Patrick J. Buchanan (b. 1938) lives and breathes politics. He served as a senior advisor to Presidents Nixon, Ford, and Reagan, and has campaigned for the presidency himself three times — as a candidate in the Republican primaries of 1992 and 1996 and as the nominee of the Reform Party in 2000. Six of his ten books have been best-sellers. The titles speak for themselves: they include *The Great Betrayal: How American Sovereignty and Social Justice Are Being Sacrificed to the Gods of the Global Economy* (1998); *The Death of the West: How Dying Populations and Immigrant Invasions Imperil Our Country and Civilization* (2002); *Where the Right Went Wrong: How Neoconservatives Subverted the Reagan Revolution and Hijacked the Bush Presidency* (2004); *State of Emergency: The Third World Invasion and Conquest of America* (2006); and *Suicide of a Superpower: Will America Survive to 2025?* (2011). Buchanan founded the *American Conservative* magazine, writes a syndicated column on politics, and appears daily on cable TV news shows as a political analyst. The following selection is taken from his 2007 book, *Day of Reckoning: How Hubris, Ideology, and Greed Are Tearing America Apart.*

> *Yet at present, the United States is unwinding strand by strand, rather like the Soviet Union.*
>
> — WILLIAM REES-MOGG, 1992[1]

> *The histories of bilingual and bicultural societies that do not assimilate are histories of turmoil, tension and tragedy.*
>
> — SEYMOUR MARTIN LIPSET[2]

IN 2007, ON THE 400TH ANNIVERSARY of the Jamestown[3] settlement, Queen Elizabeth II arrived to commemorate the occasion. But it took some fancy footwork by Her Majesty to run the Powhatan gauntlet.[4]

---

[1]Daniel Patrick Moynihan, *Pandaemonium: Ethnicity in International Politics* (New York: Oxford University Press, 1994), p. 24. [All notes are Buchanan's unless otherwise indicated.]

[2]Stanley Monteith, "The Diabolic Plan," Reprise of Richard Lamm's Address, "A Plan to Destroy America," May 2006. RaidersNewsNetwork.com

[3]*Jamestown:* Founded in 1607, Jamestown, Virginia, was the first permanent English settlement in North America. [Eds.]

[4]*Powhatan gauntlet:* The Powhatan tribe led a confederacy of more than thirty other tribes during the period of the Jamestown settlement; the gauntlet refers to a tribal initiation ritual in which young men submitted to an extended period of severe physical and mental discipline before emerging as mature men and recognized leaders. [Eds.]

CREATED EQUAL

CANDORVILLE By Darrin Bell

For the queen had been there before, fifty years ago, for the 350th anniversary, in a less progressive era. As the Associated Press reported, "the last time the queen helped Virginia mark the anniversary of its colonial founding, it was an all-white affair in a state whose government was in open defiance of a 1954 Supreme Court order to desegregate public schools."[5]

That was the time of massive resistance to integration in Virginia. And the queen was quick to recognize and embrace the change: "Since I visited Jamestown in 1957, my country has become a much more diverse society just as the Commonwealth of Virginia and the whole United States of America have also undergone a major social change."[6]

Both nations are indeed more diverse. But the most recent reminder of diversity in Virginia, to which the queen alluded, was the massacre of thirty-two students and teachers at Virginia Tech by an immigrant madman.

And now that London is Londonistan,[7] Muslim imams preach hatred of the West in mosques, and Pakistani subway bombers find support in their madrassas.[8] Race riots are common in the northern industrial cities. Crime rates have soared. In parts of London, people fear to walk. Yes, the Britain of Tony Blair and Gordon Brown[9] is more diverse than the Britain of Victoria and Lord Salisbury,[10] Lloyd George and Churchill.[11] Is it also a better, lovelier, stronger, more respected nation than the Britannia that ruled the waves and a fourth of the world? 5

[5] "Queen Elizabeth Sees Virginia Anew," May 3, 2007, Associated Press, MSNBC .com.

[6] Ibid.

[7] *Londonistan:* Ironic reference to the large immigrant Pakistani population of London. [Eds.]

[8] *madrassas:* Islamic religious schools. [Eds.]

[9] *Tony Blair and Gordon Brown:* Blair (b. 1953) served as the British prime minister, 1997–2007; he was succeeded by Brown (b. 1951). [Eds.]

[10] *Victoria and Lord Salisbury:* Queen Victoria (1819–1901) was Britain's longest-reigning monarch; Robert Cecil, Third Marquess of Salisbury (1830–1903) served as her prime minister three times. [Eds.]

[11] *Lloyd George and Churchill:* David Lloyd George (1863–1945) was Britain's prime minister during much of World War I, 1916–1922; Sir Winston Churchill served as prime minister throughout World War II, 1940–1945, and again in the early 1950s, 1951–1955. [Eds.]

The prevailing orthodoxy demands that we parrot such platitudes. And Her Majesty was careful to conform. "Fifty years on, we are now in a position to reflect more candidly on the Jamestown legacy," said the queen, as she began to reflect less candidly on that legacy.[12]

Here, at Jamestown, "Three great civilizations came together for the first time—western European, native American and African."[13]

Well, that is certainly one way of putting it.

Even Her Majesty must have smiled inwardly as she delivered this comic rendition of history. For the Jamestown settlers were not Western Europeans but English Christians. They despised French Catholics and the great event in their lives had been the sinking of the Spanish Armada. And the first decision taken at Jamestown was to build a fort to protect them from Chief Powhatan's tribe, whom they thought might massacre them, as they suspected Indians had massacred the Roanoke[14] colony. Their leader, Capt. John Smith, would escape being clubbed to death by Powhatan, thanks only to the princess Pocahontas. Or so Smith liked to tell the tale. In 1622, the Indians succeeded in massacring a third of all the inhabitants of Jamestown.[15]

As for the Africans, they arrived in 1619 in slave ships, and were not freed for 246 years. Then they were segregated for a century.

Jamestown was no coming together of "three great civilizations." It was the beginning of centuries of imperial conquest by British Christians who drove the pagan Indians westward, repopulated their lands, and imposed their own faith, customs, laws, language, and institutions upon their New World. Jamestown was the beginning of America—and of the British Empire.

"With the benefit of hindsight, we can see in that event [Jamestown] the origins of a singular endeavor—the building of a great nation, founded on the eternal values of democracy and equality," said the queen.[16]

A great nation did indeed arise from Jamestown, but, intending no disrespect to Her Majesty, democracy and equality had nothing to do with it. The House of Burgesses, formed in 1619, was restricted to white males, men of property. The American Revolution was not fought for equality, but to be rid of British rule. Four of the first five presidents— Washington, Jefferson, Madison, and Monroe—were Virginia slaveholders. Exactly two and a half centuries after Jamestown, in 1857, came Chief Justice Roger B. Taney's *Dred Scott* decision declaring that slaves were not Americans and that none of them had any of the rights

[12]Patrick J. Buchanan, "Queen's Fancy PC Footwork in Jamestown," May 7, 2007. VDARE.com

[13]Ibid.

[14]*Roanoke:* Located in what is now North Carolina, Roanoke Island was the site of the first attempts by the English to settle in North America. The first group of settlers, in 1585, encountered such hardship that they returned to England the following year; a small group of men who remained were killed by Indians. The second group of colonists, in 1587, mysteriously vanished. [Eds.]

[15]"From Jamestown's Swamp: Pocahontas Was the Least of It," editorial, *Washington Post*, May 12, 2007, p. A14.

[16]Ibid.

of American citizens. Few Americans then, certainly not Abe Lincoln, believed in social or political equality.

Now, if, in 1957 — 350 years after Jamestown, 100 years after *Dred Scott*—the state of Virginia had a declared policy of massive resistance to racial integration, how can the queen claim that Jamestown or Virginia or America were always about "the eternal values of democracy and equality"?

History contradicts the politically correct version the queen had to 15 recite about the Jamestown settlement—and raises another question.

If Jamestown and Virginia were not about democracy, equality, and diversity for the 350 years between 1607 and 1957, who invented this myth that America was always about democracy, equality, and diversity? And what was their motive?

At Jamestown the queen performed a service to America of which she was surely unaware. By radically revising her views of fifty years ago, about what Jamestown was, the queen revealed the real revolution that occurred between the era of Eisenhower and that of George W. Bush.

It is a revolution in thought and belief about who we are as a nation. In the half century since massive resistance, Virginia has indeed become a radically changed society. No longer does Richmond proudly call herself the Capital of the Confederacy. Lee-Jackson Day is out. Martin Luther King Day is in. The Confederate flag flies nowhere. On Monument Avenue, which features the statues of Robert E. Lee, "Stonewall" Jackson, J. E. B. Stuart, and Jefferson Davis,[17] a statue of Arthur Ashe, an African American tennis player, has been added.[18] "Carry Me Back to Old Virginny" was retired by the legislature as the state song ten years before the queen's return. Within days of her arrival in 2007, the Virginia legislature apologized for slavery.

Virginia 2007 is ashamed of who she was in 1957. But how then can Virginia be proud of what Jamestown was in 1607? For the first Jamestown was not some multicultural village but the first outpost of an imperial nation determined to settle and conquer North America for English Christians, to wipe out or drive out Indians who got in its way, and to bring in Africans as slaves to do the labor English settlers would not do.

An Inconvenient Truth

The point here is unpleasant to modernity but critical to recognize: The 20 United States, the greatest republic since Rome, and the British Empire, the greatest empire since Rome, may be said to have arisen from that

---

[17] *Robert E. Lee...and Jefferson Davis:* Lee (1807–1870), Jackson (1824–1863), and Stuart (1833–1864) were Confederate generals; Davis (1808–1889) served as president of the Confederate States. [Eds.]
[18] "Multimedia Tour: Monument Ave," *Discover Richmond.* discoverrichmond.com

three-cornered fort the Jamestown settlers began to build the day they arrived. But that republic and that empire did not rise because the settlers and those who followed believed in diversity, equality, and democracy, but because they rejected diversity, equality, and democracy. The English, the Virginians, the Americans were all "us-or-them" people.

They believed in the superiority of their Christian faith and English culture and civilization. And they transplanted that unique faith, culture, and civilization to America's fertile soil. Other faiths, cultures, and civilizations—like the ones the Indians had here, or the Africans brought, or the French had planted in Quebec, or the Spanish in Mexico—they rejected and resisted with cannon, musket, and sword. This was *our* land, not anybody else's.

But today America and Britain have embraced ideas about the innate equality of all cultures, civilizations, languages, and faiths, and about the mixing of all tribes, races, and peoples, that are not only ahistorical, they are suicidal for America and the West. For all over the world, rising faiths like Islam, rising movements like the indigenous peoples' movement rolling out of Latin America to Los Angeles, rising powers like China reaching for Asian and world hegemony—ignore the kumbaya we preach, and look to what our fathers practiced when *they* conquered the world.

What the queen said at Jamestown 2007 was that we are not the same people we were in 1957. She is right. For we now reject as repellent and ethnocentric the idea that the British who founded our republic and created the British Empire were not only unique but superior to other peoples and civilizations. And to show the world how resolutely we reject those old ideas, we threw open our borders in the last forty years to peoples of all creeds, cultures, countries, and civilizations, inviting them to come and convert the old America into the most multicultural, multilingual, multiethnic, multiracial nation in history—"The First Universal Nation"[19] of Ben Wattenberg's[20] warblings. But if the Jamestown settlers had believed in equality and diversity, and had shared their fort with the Indians, the settlers would never have been heard from again.

No matter the lies we tell ourselves and teach our children, no great republic or empire—not Persia, Rome, Islam, Spain, France, Britain, Russia, China, the United States—ever arose because it embraced democracy, diversity, and equality. None. The real question is not whether the values the queen celebrated at Jamestown created America—they had nothing to do with it—but whether America can survive having embraced them....

[19] *The First Universal Nation:* Title of a 1990 book by Ben Wattenberg which argued that the United States, due to its increasing ethnic diversity, is becoming a "universal" country. [Eds.]
[20] *Ben Wattenberg:* Conservative author (b. 1933) and host of a number of PBS television shows dealing with current events. [Eds.]

The Disuniting of America

America is today less a nation than an encampment of suspicious and 25
hostile tribes quarreling viciously over the spoils of politics and power.
We live on the same land, under the same set of laws, but we are no
longer the one people of whom John Jay[21] wrote in *Federalist* No. 2.

> Providence has been pleased to give this one connected country to one
> united people—a people descended from the same ancestors, speaking
> the same language, professing the same religion, attached to the same
> principles of government, very similar in their manners and customs,
> and who, by their joint counsels, arms, and efforts, fighting side by side
> throughout a long and bloody war, have nobly established their general
> liberty and independence.[22]

"This country and this people seem to have been made for each
other," Jay wrote, calling his countrymen "a band of brethren." Even before the Constitution had been ratified, Jay regarded Americans as "one
united people," "one connected country," "brethren," of common blood.[23]

But what held this "one united people" together—a common heritage, history, faith, language, manners, customs, and culture—today pulls
us apart.

Are we united by language? Children in Chicago are taught in two
hundred languages. Our fastest growing media are Spanish speaking.
Half the 9 million in Los Angeles County speak a language other than
English in their homes. Today's vile talk on radio and television, in the
movies, magazines, and books, would have been an embarrassment in
a marine barracks fifty years ago.

Are we united by faith? While 99 percent Protestant in 1789, we are
now Protestant, Catholic, Jewish, Mormon, Muslim, Hindu, Buddhist,
Taoist, Shintoist, Santería, Sikh, New Age, voodoo, agnostic, atheist,
Rastafarian. The mention of the name of Jesus by the preachers President Bush chose to give invocations at his inauguration evoked cries
of "insensitive," "divisive," "exclusionary." A *New Republic* editorial
lashed out at these "crushing Christological thuds" from the inaugural
stand.[24]

Many of the Christian churches have split asunder over abortion, 30
female bishops, homosexual clergy, and gay marriage.

In 2007, after a court battle by the American Civil Liberties Union,
the U.S. Department of Veterans Affairs agreed to add the five-point star
of the Wiccan neo-pagan religion to the list of thirty-eight "emblems

---

[21]*John Jay:* Founding father (1745–1829) and first chief justice of the United States.
[Eds.]
[22]James Madison, Alexander Hamilton, John Jay, *The Federalist Papers*, with an
introduction by Willmore Kendall and George W. Carey (New Rochelle, N.Y.: Arlington
House), p. 38.
[23]Ibid.
[24]Jeff Jacoby, "The Role of Religion in Government: Invoking Jesus at the Inauguration," *Boston Globe*, Feb. 2, 2001, p. A15; Patrick J. Buchanan, *The Death of the West*
(New York: St. Martin's Press, 2002), p. 144.

of belief" allowed on VA grave markers. The thirty-eight include "symbols for Christianity, Buddhism, Islam and Judaism, as well as... for...Sufism Reoriented, Eckiankar and the Japanese faith Seicho-No-Ie."[25]

Are we united by a common culture? To the contrary. We are in a raging culture war in which peaceful coexistence is a myth.

In the nineteenth century, America was torn apart by slavery and the tariff. Those issues were settled in a civil war that resulted in 600,000 dead. Today, America is divided over issues of race, ethnicity, religion, language, culture, history, morality, the very things that once defined us and united us as a people and a nation.

Protestants and Catholics, a hundred years ago, disagreed passionately over whether beer, wine, and spirits were wicked. Today, we Americans disagree over whether annihilating 45 million unborn babies in the womb since *Roe v. Wade*[26] is a mark of progress or a monstrous national evil causing us to echo Jefferson, "I tremble for my country when I reflect that God is just."

In the 1960s, to do penance for all her sins, from Jamestown on, the 35 United States threw open its doors to peoples of all colors, continents, and creeds. And today, the America of John F. Kennedy, 89 percent white and 10 percent of African descent, an essentially biracial country united by a common culture, creed, history, and tradition, is gone. We threw it away.

Today, America is twice as populous as in 1950—with 300 million people. Instead of 1 to 2 million Hispanics, there are 45 million, with 102 million expected by 2050, concentrated in a Southwest that 58 percent of Mexicans say belongs to them. Our population is down to 67 percent European, and falling; 14.5 percent Hispanic and rising rapidly, 13 percent black and holding, and 4.5 percent Asian and rising. By 2040, Americans of European descent will be less than half the population, when, as President Bill Clinton told an audience of cheering California students, we will all belong to minorities. White Americans are already a minority in California, New Mexico, Texas, Hawaii. Twelve to 20 million illegal aliens are in the country. We may not have believed in diversity in the old America, but we are practicing it now. But has all this diversity made us a stronger nation than we were in the time of Eisenhower and Kennedy?

In October 2006, the *Financial Times* reported the findings of Robert Putnam, author of *Bowling Alone*, on diversity in America.

A bleak picture of the corrosive effects of ethnic diversity has been revealed in research by Harvard University's Robert Putnam, one of the world's most influential political scientists.

[25]Scott Bauer, "VA Allows Wiccan Symbols on Headstones," April 23, 2007, Associated Press. Yahoo.News.
[26]*Roe v. Wade:* The 1973 Supreme Court case that legalized abortion. [Eds.]

His research shows that the more diverse a community is, the less likely its inhabitants are to trust anyone—from their next-door neighbour to the mayor.

The core message...was that, "in the presence of diversity, we hunker down," he said. "We act like turtles. The effect of diversity is worse than had been imagined. And it's not just that we don't trust people who are not like us. In diverse communities, we don't trust people who do look like us."

Prof. Putnam found trust was lowest in Los Angeles, "the most diverse human habitation in human history...."[27]

The city Professor Putnam references, Los Angeles, was the scene of the Academy Award–winning film *Crash*, which portrayed a feral zone in which whites, blacks, Asians, and Hispanics clashed violently again and again, as they could not understand one another or communicate with one another.

Wrote columnist John Leo, after perusing the report, "Putnam adds a crushing footnote: his findings 'may underestimate the real effect of diversity on social withdrawal.'"[28]

With another 100 million people anticipated in the United States 40 by 2050, most of them immigrants and their children, legal and illegal, Putnam's findings are ominous. If the greater the diversity the greater the mistrust, Balkanization beckons—for all of us.

Is diversity a strength? In the ideology of modernity, yes. But history teaches otherwise. For how can racial diversity be a strength when racial diversity was behind the bloodiest war in U.S. history and has been the most polarizing issue among us ever since?

Our most divisive Supreme Court decision, *Dred Scott*, was about race. The War Between the States was about race. Reconstruction was about race. Segregation was about race. The riots in Harlem, Watts, Newark, Detroit, then Washington, DC, and a hundred other cities after the assassination of Dr. King were about race. The riot in Los Angeles following the Simi Valley jury's acquittal of the cops who beat Rodney King was about race. Forced busing, affirmative action, quotas, profiling are about race. The O. J. trial, the Tawana Brawley and Duke rape-case hoaxes, and the Don Imus affair[29] were about race. When Gunnar Myrdal wrote his classic *American Dilemma*, about the crisis of our democracy, the subject was—race.

All Americans believe slavery was evil and the denial of equal justice under law was wrong. But because they were wrong, does that make

---

[27]John Lloyd, "Study Paints Bleak Picture of Ethnic Diversity," Oct. 8, 2006. FT.com
[28]John Leo, "Bowling with Our Own," *City Journal*, Summer 2007, vol. 17, no. 3.
[29]*"The O. J. trial...the Don Imus affair:"* In 1995, O. J. Simpson was found not guilty of murder after a long and highly publicized criminal trial; in 1986, a New York grand jury found that Tawana Brawley's claim that she was raped and brutalized by white men was fabricated; in 2006, another African American woman charged that she had been raped by a group of white Duke University lacrosse players, but the charges were dropped the following year; talk-radio host Don Imus was fired in 2007 after making racist comments about female African American basketball players. In each case, opinions tended to divide along racial lines. [Eds.]

what we are doing—inviting the whole world to come to America—right or wise?

Today, tens of thousands of corporate and government bureaucrats monitor laws against discrimination and laws mandating integration in housing and employment. To achieve equality, Americans are sacrificing freedom. Police are ever on the lookout for hate crimes. Hardly a month passes without some controversy or crime rooted in race being forced through cable TV and talk radio onto the national agenda. How does all this make us a more united, stronger people?

Among the educated and affluent young, resegregation is in vogue. 45 Columnist Leo writes that at UCLA, racially separate graduations have become the norm. "The core reason," he writes, "is the obvious one."

> On campus, assimilation is a hostile force, the domestic version of American imperialism. On many campuses, identity-group training begins with separate freshman orientation programs for nonwhites, who arrive earlier and are encouraged to bond before the first Caucasian freshmen arrive. Some schools have separate orientations for gays as well. Administrations tend to foster separatism by arguing that bias is everywhere, justifying double standards that favor identity groups.[30]

Leo concludes on a note of despair, "As in so many areas of national life, the preposterous is now normal."[31]

Quo Vadis,[32] America?

Again, history teaches that multiethnic states are held together either by an authoritarian regime or a dominant ethnocultural core, or they are ever at risk of disintegration in ethnic conflict.

The Soviet Union, Czechoslovakia, and Yugoslavia, artificial nations all, disintegrated when the dictatorships collapsed.

In democracies it is an ethnocultural core that holds the country together. England created a United Kingdom of English, Scots, Welsh, and Irish, with England predominant. Now that Britain is no longer great, the core nations have begun to pull apart, to seek their old independence, as the English have begun to abandon the land they grew up in.

In "Vanishing England," in August 2007, columnist Cal Thomas 50 reported a startling fact: Between June 2005 and June 2006, 200,000 British citizens (the equivalent of a million Americans) left their country for good, as more than a half million legal immigrants and unknown thousands of illegals entered. "Britons give many reasons for leaving, but their stories share one commonality," Thomas wrote; "life in Britain has become unbearable for them."[33] There is the lawlessness and the constant threat of Muslim terror, but also

---

[30]John Leo, "Let the Segregation Commence...Separatist Graduations Proliferate at UCLA," June 13, 2007, *City Journal*, Spring 2007, vol. 17, no. 2.

[31]Ibid.

[32]*Quo Vadis:* Latin phrase meaning "Where are you going?" [Eds.]

[33]Cal Thomas, "Vanishing England," *Washington Times*, Aug. 29, 2007, p. A17.

the loss of a sense of Britishness, exacerbated by the growing refusal of public schools to teach the history and culture of the nation to the next generation. What it means to be British has been watered down in a plague of political correctness that has swept the country faster than hoof-and-mouth disease. Officials says they do not wish to "offend" others.[34]

Intellectuals deceive themselves if they believe the new trinity of their faith—democracy, equality, and diversity—can replace the old idea of what it meant to be a Briton, what it meant to be an Englishman.

In the thirteen North American colonies, the ethnocultural core was British-Protestant, with a smattering of Germans whose growing numbers alarmed Ben Franklin. After the wave of Irish from 1845 to 1849, and the steady German influx, and then the great wave from Southern and Eastern Europe between 1890 and 1920, America was no longer British-Protestant, but a European-Christian nation whose institutions, language, and culture remained British. Bismarck said the most important fact of the twentieth century would be that the North Americans spoke English. Indeed, that is why we fought on Britain's side in two world wars. Despite our eighteenth- and nineteenth-century quarrels and wars, the Brits were still "the cousins."

By 1960, 88.6 percent of our nation was of European stock and 95 percent Christian. America had never been a more united nation. African Americans had been assimilated into the Christian faith and national culture if not fully into society. While Jews, perhaps 4 percent of the population, were non-Christians, their parents or grandparents had come from European Christian nations.

Since the cultural revolution of the 1960s and the Immigration Act of 1965, however, the ethnocultural core has begun to dissolve. Secularism has displaced Christianity as the faith of the elites. The nation has entered a post-Christian era. There is no longer a unifying culture. Rather, we are fighting a culture war. And the European ethnic core is shrinking. From near 90 percent in 1960, it is down to 67 percent today, and will be less than 50 percent by 2040.

Here we come to the heart of the matter.   55

Quo Vadis, America? Where are you going?

If we have no common faith and are divided by morality and culture, and are separated by ethnicity and race, what holds us together? Especially in light of Putnam's report that "diversity" dilutes "social capital," erodes community, and engenders mutual mistrust.

Realizing we are divided on the things that constitute a true nation—blood and soil, tradition and faith, history and heroes—intellectuals have sought to construct, in lieu of the real nation, the nation of the heart that is passing away, an artificial nation, a nation of the mind, an ideological nation, a creedal nation, united by a belief in the new trinity: diversity, democracy, and equality. As Christianity is purged

[34]Ibid.

from the public schools, this civil religion is taught in its stead. The dilemma of those who conjured up this civil religion and creedal nation, liberals and neoconservatives, is that it has no roots and does not touch the heart. Americans will not send their sons to fight and die for such watery abstractions.

ENGAGING THE TEXT

1. What kind of "revolution" (para. 17) does Buchanan believe has occurred in the United States and Britain in the fifty years between Queen Elizabeth's two visits to Jamestown? What illustrations of social change does he offer? How would you characterize his attitude toward these changes?

2. Why does Buchanan object to Queen Elizabeth's reference to the Jamestown colony as a meeting of "three great civilizations" (para. 7)? In his view, what is the real significance of Jamestown?

3. How does Buchanan differentiate between earlier groups of immigrants to the United States and those who have come since the 1965 Immigration Act? What effects does he believe immigrants are having on this country? Do you agree with his assessment? Why or why not?

4. Buchanan suggests that a nation based on "democracy, diversity, and equality" (para. 24) is unlikely to thrive or even to survive. Debate the merits of the logic and evidence he presents in support of his claim.

5. According to Buchanan, laws prohibiting discrimination, hate crimes, and segregated housing and employment require "sacrificing freedom" (para. 44) in order to attain greater equality. How and for whom is freedom restricted by such laws? Explain why you think the tradeoff is or is not worthwhile.

EXPLORING CONNECTIONS

6. Which of the models of ethnic relations described by George M. Fredrickson (p. 565) does Buchanan appear to endorse, which does he reject, and why? How would you describe his ideal vision of America?

7. To what extent would David Treuer (p. 578) agree with Buchanan about the history of the United States and our treatment of Native Americans? To what extent would he agree or disagree about the significance of diversity in modern America?

EXTENDING THE CRITICAL CONTEXT

8. Buchanan mentions the practice, on some campuses, of holding separate orientations or graduation ceremonies for different "identity groups" (para. 45). If your school offers such functions, organize a group or whole class project and interview students, family members, and faculty who have attended one of these events. Pool your interview notes: do you find any consistency or patterns of response in your interviewees' comments about

the event? Write a paper based on your research assessing the purpose and value of separate functions.

9. Buchanan quotes a newspaper article reporting on research done by political scientist Robert Putnam. Look up Putnam's original article, "*E Pluribus Unum*: Diversity and Community in the Twenty-first Century" (available online). Discuss the extent to which Putnam's research supports or challenges Buchanan's contention that diversity undermines social cohesion.

THE CROSSING
RUBÉN MARTÍNEZ

Although the United States prides itself on being a nation of immigrants, Americans' attitudes toward immigrants can be complex and contradictory. One recent poll showed opinion evenly divided over whether immigration helps or hurts the country, and while Americans overwhelmingly oppose illegal immigration, a consistent majority believes that undocumented workers fill jobs that citizens don't want. In this essay, adapted from his book *Burning Sand* (2006), Rubén Martínez explores the cultural contradictions that arise in our representations of the border and of those who cross it searching for a better life. Martínez is an award-winning journalist and associate professor of creative writing at the University of Houston. His earlier books include *The Other Side: Notes from the New L.A., Mexico City and Beyond* (1993), *Crossing Over: A Mexican Family on the Migrant Trail* (2002), and *The New Americans* (2004).

I AM, AGAIN, on the line.

I've been drawn to it my entire life, beginning with frequent childhood jaunts across it to Tijuana and back—that leap from the monochrome suburban grids of Southern California to the Technicolor swirl of urban Baja California and back. I am an American today because of that line—and my parents' will to erase it with their desire.

I return to it again and again because I am from both sides. So for me, son of a mother who emigrated from E1 Salvador and a Mexican American father who spent his own childhood leaping back and forth, the line is a sieve. And it is a brick wall.

It defines me even as I defy it. It is a book without a clear beginning or end, and despite the fact that we refer to it as a "line," it is not even linear; to compare it to an actual book I'd have to invoke Cortázar's[1] *Hopscotch*. This line does and does not exist. It is a historical, political,

---

[1]*Cortázar:* Julio Florencio Cortázar (1914–1986), Argentine writer known for his short stories.

economic, and cultural fact. It is a laughable, puny, meaningless thing. It is a matter of life and death. And it is a matter of representation. It is a very productive trope[2] in both American and Mexican pop.

The cowboy crosses the line to evade the law, because he imagines 5 there is no law in the South. The immigrant crosses the line to embrace the future because he imagines there is no past in the North. Usually rendered by the River (the Rio Grande/Río Bravo—its name changes from one shore to the other), the line appears again and again in film and literature and music from both sides.

Just a few: Cormac McCarthy and Carlos Fuentes, Marty Robbins and Los Tigres del Norte, Sam Peckinpah and Emilio "El Indio" Fernández, Charles Bowden and Gloria Anzaldúa.[3]

In the Western, the moment of the crossing (the lawless gang fleeing the lawmen, their horses' hooves muddying the muddy waters all the more) is heralded by a stirring musical figure, brassy and percussive, leaping several tonal steps with each note. Once we're safely on the other side, the melodic strings of Mexico take over. The swaggering American will have his way with a Mexican señorita. The post-colonial[4] representations of borderlands literature—produced by Mexicans and Americans alike—have yet to soften the edges of this Spring Break syndrome. The whorehouse-across-the-river is there for a spurned Jake Gyllenhaal to get off with smooth-skinned brown boys in an otherwise liberatory *Brokeback Mountain*. Americans fictional and real always fantasize remaining in that racy, lazy South, but business or vengeance or a respectable marriage (the señorita is a puta, and you can't marry a puto[5] on either side of the border) usually call the cowboy back home.

The Mexican or Chicano production is an inverted mirror of the same. The climax of Cheech Marin's *Born in East L.A.* (and dozens of Mexican B-movies) fulfills every migrant's fantasy of a joyous rush of brown humanity breaching a hapless Border Patrol, the victory of simple desire over military technology that occurs thousands of times a day on the border and feeds the paranoid vision of a reconquista[6] (which, a handful of crackpot Chicano nationalists notwithstanding, has been largely invented by the likes of the Minutemen,[7] white dudes with real

---

[2]*trope:* Figure of speech, such as metaphor.

[3]*Cormac McCarthy...Gloria Anzaldúa:* Cormac McCarthy (b. 1933), American novelist known for writing about the Southwest; Carlos Fuentes (b. 1928), Mexican essayist and fiction writer; Marty Robbins (1925–1982), American country-western singer; Los Tigres del Norte, Grammy-winning musical group formed in the late 1960s; Sam Peckinpah (1925–1984), American writer, director, and producer of western films and television series; Emilio Fernández (1903–1968), Mexican actor, writer, and director; Charles Bowden (b. 1945), American nonfiction writer and editor; Gloria Anzaldúa (1942–2004), Chicana writer and editor, best known for *Borderlands/La Frontera: The New Mestiza* (1987).

[4]*post-colonial:* Refers to the time following the independence of a colony; postcolonial literature often deals with the impact and legacy of colonial rule.

[5]*puta/puto:* Whore.

[6]*reconquista:* Reconquest; much of the American southwest once belonged to Mexico.

[7]*Minutemen:* Self-appointed anti-immigrant guardians of the U.S. borders, particularly in the southwest. This contemporary group has adopted the name of the well-known American military unit that fought in the Revolutionary War.

economic insecurities unfortunately marinated in traditional border-lands racism).

Every step across the line is a breach of one code or another. Some of these laws are on the books; some have never been written down; some are matters more private than public.

I've been drawn to that line my whole life. Sometimes it's a meta- 10 phor. Sometimes it's not.

This time, I am close to the line on the Buenos Aires National Wildlife Refuge in southern Arizona. It is a late August afternoon, a day that will not make headlines because there are no Minuteman patrols out hunting migrants, no Samaritans out seeking to save them. Nor is there, for the moment, any Border Patrol in the immediate vicinity. The land is as its public designation intended: a unique Sonoran desert hab-itat bizarrely and beautifully traversed by grasslands that are home to hundreds of unique species, including the endangered pronghorn an-telope; it is also an outstanding birding location. But there are no bird-ers in the dead of summer. The birders and the Minutemen have no wish to be out in temperatures that often rise to more than 110 degrees. (Some Samaritans who belong to a group called No More Deaths are indeed in the area, but the day's final patrol is probably heading back to the church-based group's campground near the town of Arivaca, which borders the refuge.)

I park at the Arivaca Creek trailhead. The interpretive sign tells of the possibility of hearing the "snap of vermilion flycatchers snatching insects on the wing." It also tells of another species, a relative new-comer to this "riparian ribbon":

"Visitors to BANWR are advised to remain alert for illegal activ-ity associated with the presence of undocumented aliens (UDAs). There is also increased law enforcement activity by several agencies & organizations."

The bulleted visitor guidelines advise not to let the "UDAs ap-proach you or your vehicle," a Homeland Security variation of "do not feed the wildlife."

The humidity from recent monsoonal deluges is stifling, making 15 100 degrees feel much hotter—and wetter. The reed-like branches of ocotillos have sprouted their tiny lime-green leaves, hiding their terrifi-cally sharp thorns. Moss flourishes on arroyo stones. Mosquitoes zip and whine through the thick air. The desert jungle.

I tell myself that I'll take a short stroll; it's getting late. I climb the trail from the creek bed, which is dominated by mammoth cotton-wood trees, south toward the red dirt hills—a trail used by birders and "UDAs" alike. I can imagine an Audubon guide leading a gaggle of khaki-clad tourists peering through binoculars, first at a vermilion flycatcher and then at a Mexican rushing through a mesquite thicket, *Profugus mexicanus*. On the line everything seems to attract its opposite or, more accurately, everything seems to attract a thing that seems to have no relation to it, not parallel universes but saw-toothed eruptions, the crumpled metal of a collision. These pairings occur not just near the political border—I am about 11 miles from the boundary between the United States of America and the United States of Mexico—but throughout the West. The border is no longer a line. Its ink has diffused, an ambiguous veil across the entire territory.

Take the microcosm of the BANWR and its immediate vicinity. The birders and the migrants, the Samaritans and the Minutemen. Hunters and stoners. A "dude ranch" that charges city slickers up to $2,500 a week. Retirees of modest means. Hellfire Protestants and Catholic penitents and New Age vortex-seekers. Living here or passing through are Americans and Native Americans and Mexicans and Mexican Americans and Mexican Indians, all of varying shades and accents, and there are Iranians and Guatemalans and Chinese. This kind of situation was once affectionately referred to as the Melting Pot. But no, it is more like speaking in tongues, speaking in Babel.[8] The tower is crumbling. Melting pot meltdown.

I climb into the red hills as the sun nears the horizon. The sky at the zenith is a stunning true blue. Reaching a saddle, I stumble on to a huge migrant encampment—water jugs and backpacks and soiled underwear and tubes of toothpaste and a brand-new denim jacket finely embroidered with the name of a car club, opened cans of refried beans, bottles of men's cologne, Tampax, tortillas curled hard in the heat. The things they carried and left behind because 11 miles into the 50-mile hike they'd begun to realize the weight of those things, and they'd resolved to travel lighter. If something was to go wrong and they got lost and hyperthermic, they might even begin stripping the clothes off their backs.

It is possible, too, that they've just broken camp; it is possible that they saw me coming and are hiding behind one of the saddle's humps. I call out: ¡No soy migra![9] This is a line from the script of the Samaritan Patrol, who, like the activists of No More Deaths, scour the desert searching for migrants in distress. They call out so that the fearful migrants might reveal themselves to receive food and water. It is a good line in the borderlands; I can't think of a better one. The real problem is, what am I going to say if someone actually responds? Buenas tardes señoras y señores, soy periodista y quería entervistarles, si es que no les es mucha molestia[10]...the journalist's lame introduction. Of course, they would have no reason to stop and speak to me—just the opposite. Indeed, why would they believe that I am not migra? And what if the smugglers are hauling a load of narcotics instead of humans? What

---

[8]*Babel:* Refers to an ancient city whose inhabitants tried to build a tower to heaven, which God destroyed. He then made the people speak different languages so that they could no longer work together.

[9]*¡No soy migra!:* I'm not immigration ("la migra" refers generically to any branch or agent of the U.S. immigration authority, such as the Border Patrol).

[10]*Buenas tardes...mucha molestia:* Good afternoon, ladies and gentlemen, I'm a journalist and would like to interview you, if it's not too much trouble.

if they are carrying weapons? This is not idle paranoia—this desert is armed with Mexican and American government-issue sidearms and the assault rifles of the paramilitary brigades on both sides. It is no surprise that there is bloodshed. Assault, rape, torture, and murder are common.

In any event, I have nothing to offer the trekkers; they have not run out of water yet (though by tomorrow, after 15 or 20 miles, they well might). I am suddenly ashamed, as if I've intruded on a tremendously private moment, as if I've stumbled upon a couple in erotic embrace, bodies vulnerable to the harshness of the landscape and my gaze.

The sun sets, a funnel of gold joining cerulean canopy to blood-red earth. The land is completely still. I hold my breath. I realize that I want them to appear. I want to join them on the journey. The Audubon birder needs the vermilion flycatcher; right now, the writer needs a mojado.[11]

The migrant stumbles through the desert and I after him—he's on a pilgrimage and I'm in pursuit of him. Thus I am the literary migra: I will trap the mojado within the distorting borders of representation—a problem no writer has ever resolved. But aren't I also representing the origins of my own family's journey? Don't I also return to the line because it was upon my parents and grandparents' crossing it that I became possible?

¡No soy migra! I call out again.

There is no response. I sweat profusely, soaking through my UNM[12] Lobos T-shirt. Even my jeans hang heavy with moisture. Swatting mosquitoes, I retrace my footsteps back to the car.

I drive west in the dimming light. There is no one on this road but me.

Suddenly, a flutter in my peripheral vision. And now a figure stumbles out of the desert green to remind me that the border is, above all else, a moral line. He crawls from the brush and waves to me from the south side of the road. I stop the truck and roll down my window. He is a plaintive-looking fellow in his thirties, with thick black curls, a sweaty and smudged moon of a face. He has large brown eyes ringed by reddened whites. He is wearing a black T-shirt, blue jeans, and white tennis shoes. He carries a small blue vinyl bag.

¿Qué pasó? I ask. What happened?

With the first syllables of his response I can tell that he is from El Salvador. It is an accent that splits the difference between the typically muted tones of the Latin American provinces and the urgent desire of urban speech. It is the accent of my mother and her family; it is the Spanish accent I associate most with my childhood.

He says his name is Victor and that he had hiked about 12 miles into U.S. territory and could not make it any farther. His migrant crew had traveled all night and started up again late in the afternoon—just a

---

[11]*mojado:* Wetback.
[12]*UNM:* University of New Mexico.

U.S. Immigration Policy

couple of hours ago—but he'd become extremely fatigued and his vision began to blur.

Soy diabético,[13] says Victor.   30

Immediately I grab my phone to dial 911. It chirps a complaint: there is no signal. I think: Hypoglycemia, he needs something sweet. I think this because of the hundreds of plot lines in television dramas I've watched since I was a kid. In the backseat I have enough supplies to keep a dozen hikers going for at least a day in the desert—power bars, fruit cups, tins of Vienna sausages, peanut butter crackers, bags of trail mix, several bottles of Gatorade and gallon-jugs of drinking water. I expect him to tear ravenously into the strawberry-flavored bar I give him, but he eats it very slowly, taking modest sips of water between bites.

I flip open the cellphone again. Still no signal.

The particulars of a problem begin to form in my mind. Although I am not a medical expert, it is apparent that Victor needs urgent attention. But there is no way to contact medical personnel. The only option is to drive Victor to the nearest town, which is Arivaca, about 10 miles away. I become aware that by doing so, both Victor and I will be risking apprehension by the Border Patrol. More than one border denizen has told me that merely giving a migrant a ride can place one in a tenuous legal situation.

---

[13] *Soy diabético:* I'm diabetic.

U.S. Code (Title 8, Chapter 12, Subchapter II, Part VIII, Section 1324) stipulates that an American citizen breaks the law when "knowing or in reckless disregard of the fact that an alien has come to, entered, or remains in the United States in violation of law, transports, or moves or attempts to transport or move such alien within the United States by means of transportation or otherwise, in furtherance of such violation of law."

The ethical calculation is simple enough. The law might contradict 35 my moral impulse, but the right thing to do is obvious. I also tell myself that in the event of apprehension by the Border Patrol, the truth of the situation will suffice. I am a Samaritan, after all, not a coyote. The truth will suffice at least for me, that is: I will go free, and Victor will be deported.

I tell Victor to get in the car.

The night falls fast. Soon the only things we can see through the bug-splattered windshield are the grainy blacktop ahead and the tangle of mesquites lining the road. I keep expecting more migrants to appear in the headlights and wave us down. At any given moment on this stretch of borderland there may be hundreds of migrants attempting passage.

It is a winding road and I'm a conservative driver, so there's time for small talk. Victor is much more animated now. He says he is feeling better.

He is from Soyapango, a working-class suburb of San Salvador that I remember well from my time in the country during the civil war, when it had the reputation of being a rebel stronghold. Right now, Victor is 1,800 miles from Soyapango.

¿Y a qué se dedica usted? He asks what I do for a living. 40

I reply that I am a writer, and then there is silence for about a quarter of a mile.

The Border Patrol will appear any minute now, I think to myself.

His large round eyes glisten, reflecting the light from my dashboard. More questions. ¿Cómo se llama el pueblo al que vamos? ¿Qué lejos queda Phoenix? ¿Qué lejos queda Los Angeles? What's the name of the town we're heading to? How far is Phoenix? How far is Los Angeles? Phoenix: where the coyote told him he'd be dropped off at a safe house. Los Angeles: where his sister lives. He has memorized a phone number. It begins with the area code 818. Yes, he is feeling quite fine now, Victor says, and he realizes that I can't drive him all the way to L.A. But Phoenix is only 100 miles away. That's like from San Salvador to Guatemala City.

There is still no Border Patrol in sight. This does not make any sense. There are hundreds of agents on duty in what is called the Tucson Sector, the busiest and deadliest crossing along the U.S.–Mexico line. Is it the changing of the guard? Are the agents on dinner break? Are they tracking down Osama bin Laden, disguised as a Mexican day laborer?

Now, I realize, the problem is a bit different. Victor is apparently no longer experiencing a medical emergency, although I cannot be absolutely certain of this. The law is ambiguous on the matter of Samaritan aid. I am aware of a pending federal court case against two young No More Deaths activists, Shanti Sellz and Daniel Strauss, who recently attempted to conduct a "medical evacuation" by taking two apparently ailing migrants directly to a hospital rather than handing them over to the BP. Federal prosecutors decided that the activists were transporting the migrants "in furtherance" of their illegal presence in the U.S. and indicted the pair on several felony charges. The activists and their supporters say that the ethical imperative of offering aid in the context of a medical emergency supersedes the letter of immigration law—a moral argument without juridical precedent on the border. The activists are clearly hoping to set one.

But the law is decidedly less ambiguous about what Victor is now asking me to do. If I drive him to Phoenix and put him in touch with his sister, I will clearly have provided transportation "in furtherance of" his illegal presence. He is no longer asking for medical aid.

The air-conditioning chills the sweat on the wet rag that my Lobos T-shirt has become. It seems that there are now several possibilities, several problems. It seems that there are many right and wrong things to do. The scenarios tumble through my mind.

Risk the trip to Phoenix. (Where is that BP checkpoint on I-19? Is it north or south of Arivaca Junction? I look into the sky—are there thunderheads? Checkpoints often close when it rains.) What if Victor is actually still sick and on the verge of a seizure—shouldn't I turn him over to the BP? But will the BP give him the medical care he needs? And, not least of all, what of Victor's human right to escape the living hell that is Soyapango (poverty and crime there today are taking nearly as much a toll as the civil war did)? If Victor has that essential human right to seek a better life for himself and his family, what is my moral duty when he literally stumbles into my life on the border? Am I willing to risk federal charges to fulfill an ethical responsibility that I decide trumps the laws of my country?

I slow down to a crawl as we near the outskirts of Arivaca, a town famed for a 60s-era commune and the weed-growing hippies that hung on long past the Summer of Love. It will all end here in Arivaca, I tell myself. The BP trucks will be lined up outside the one small grocery store in town, or maybe up at the Grubsteak, which is presided over by a gregarious Mexican who waits on the graying hippies and handful of outsider artists who arrived years ago thinking they'd found the grail of Western living, long before chaos came to the border.

But when I pull up to the store, there is only the heat of the night and a flickering street lamp gathering a swarm of moths. I notice a few local kids—white, shaved heads—standing by a pay phone. Now it occurs to me that there is a possible solution to this mess. In the rush of events, I'd forgotten that No More Deaths had a camp about four miles east of town. Because it is a faith-based organization, the camp was baptized "Ark of the Covenant." Since 2004, No More Deaths had re- cruited student activists—like Sellz and Strauss, the pair under federal indictment—from around the country to come to southern Arizona and walk the lethal desert trails. There would be activists there with more experience than I in these matters. They could easily consult the doc- tors and lawyers supporting their cause to determine the right thing to do—or at least their version of the right thing.

I walk into the store. I tell Victor to stay inside the car. The clerk be- hind the counter is reading the newspaper, head cupped in her hands and elbows leaning on the food scale next to the cash register.

I briefly blurt out my story.

She asks me where Victor is. In the car, I say. Immediately she tells me that the BP can impound my vehicle, they can file charges. She tells me that she can call the Border Patrol for me. She seems to know ex- actly what the right thing to do is. The only thing to do. She places her hand on the phone.

A few seconds later I'm back in the heat of the night and I ask the first passerby, a young blond woman named Charity, for directions to the Ark of the Covenant. Do you have a map? She asks. She means a local map. No. Now she is drawing one on a page of my reporter's notebook. She draws many lines. Here there is a hill, she says; here, a llama ranch. She says a quarter of a mile, then a couple of miles, then three-quarters of a mile and left and right and across. It is a moonless night. Good luck, she says.

I climb back in the truck, I turn the ignition. I give Victor the note- book with the map. In a minute we're out of town and on to the first dirt road of the route. Still no BP in sight. The map is accurate. I pass by the llama ranch, barely catching the sign in the dimness. 55

For several minutes I ride on impulse—no thoughts at all. But as I turn left just where Charity told me to, a thought powerful enough to take my foot off the gas seizes me.

I can't ride into the Ark of the Covenant with Victor in the truck. What I'd forgotten in my haste was the political reality of the moment: the feds had called No More Deaths' bluff and were going after them in court. I remembered hearing from a couple of activists that before and since the arrests of Sellz and Strauss, there had been constant BP surveillance on the encampment.

If the BP were to see me dropping off Victor at the camp now, would they, could they use this as more evidence of running a de facto smuggling operation? Perhaps this could strengthen the federal case against Sellz and Strauss. And what if there was a conviction? And what if a judge ordered the camp closed?

Now I was weighing Victor's singular rights and desire and the goals and strategy of an activist movement that had helped dozens of migrants in distress over the past two summers and that could continue to help many more. The problem was, my cellphone was dead. The problem was my desire to capture a mojado. The problem was, I didn't have enough information to know what the "right" decision was. I had placed myself on the line, and I wasn't ready for what it would ask of me.

I slow down, and the dust kicked up by the tires envelops the truck. 60 Victor and I turn to each other.

Fifteen minutes later, I pull up, for the second time, to the convenience store in Arivaca. The clerk is still reading the paper. I tell her to call the Border Patrol. I tell her that Victor has diabetes and symptoms of hypoglycemia.

She picks up the phone: "We've got a diabetic UDA."

I walk out to Victor, who is standing next to my truck, staring into the black desert night. He asks me again how far it is to Tucson. I tell him that he'll die if he tries to hike.

I tell myself that Victor is probably living and working somewhere in America now. It is quite possible that he attempted to cross over again after his apprehension by the Border Patrol, and that he succeeded. This thought does and does not comfort me.

I tell myself I did the right thing. I tell myself I did the wrong thing. 65 I tell myself that every decision on the line is like that, somewhere in between.

ENGAGING THE TEXT

1. What different meanings — personal, geographic, cultural, metaphoric — does Martínez associate with the border? Why does he emphasize this complexity? In what ways is he "on the line" (para. 1)?

2. How does Martínez's role as a journalist influence his decisions and actions? To what extent does his family history affect his thinking and behavior?

3. Martínez refers to trapping his subject "within the distorting borders of representation" (para. 22). How does he represent or misrepresent Victor? How might Victor represent himself differently?

4. What is the effect of Martínez's use of the derogatory word "mojado" in the passage describing his search for an undocumented immigrant to interview? Why do you think he chooses to use the term here and in paragraph 59 and not elsewhere in the essay?

5. Debate the ethical dilemma Martínez faces: Does the moral imperative to obtain medical assistance for Victor outweigh Martínez's legal obligation to turn him over to the Border Patrol? Write a journal entry explaining what you would have done in Martínez's place, and why. Share your responses in class.

EXPLORING CONNECTIONS

6. Which of George M. Fredrickson's models of ethnic relations (p. 565) appear to be operating along the U.S.–Mexican border as Martínez describes it? Do you see evidence of more than one model coexisting?

7. How might Martínez respond to the depiction of immigrants in the preceding essay by Patrick J. Buchanan? Write an imaginary letter from Martínez to Buchanan expressing these views.

8. In "U.S. Immigration Policy" (p. 609) what is the cartoonist suggesting about American attitudes and laws regarding immigration? To what extent does Martínez share the cartoonist's view? How does his perspective differ?

EXTENDING THE CRITICAL CONTEXT

9. Write an essay comparing Martínez's representation of the U.S.–Mexican border to another depiction that you are familiar with in music, film, or literature.

10. Work in groups to research the Minutemen and No More Deaths. What is the history and purpose of each organization? What appear to be their primary values?

11. Examine the language used by news reporters, politicians, and pro- and anti-immigrant groups in discussing immigration issues: How are documented and undocumented immigrants portrayed? What metaphors are used to describe the number of immigrants entering the United States (e.g., flood) and what are their implications?

FURTHER CONNECTIONS

1. Research the history of the native peoples of your state. Learn as much as you can about a specific aspect or period of that history. What tribal groups inhabited the area before Europeans arrived? What is known about the cultures and languages of these tribes? How much and why did the native population decrease following European contact? What alliances and treaties were made between the tribes and the newcomers as non-natives began to occupy native lands? To what extent were treaties upheld or abandoned, and why? How were local native populations affected by relocation, the establishment of reservations, the creation of Indian boarding schools, the Dawes Act, or other legislation? What role has the Bureau of Indian Affairs played in protecting or failing to protect tribal interests? What issues are of greatest concern to the tribes in your area today? Write up the results of your research and present them to the class.

2. Some states and communities have responded to the rise in illegal immigration by enacting laws or ordinances that ban any language other than English, deny government services to undocumented immigrants, and penalize citizens (such as employers, landlords, and merchants) who "assist" them. Has your state or community adopted any such regulations? Research the arguments for and against such legislation and discuss your findings in class. Which arguments are the most compelling, and why?

3. Investigate a recent conflict between ethnic, racial, or cultural groups on your campus or in your community. Research the issue, and interview people on each side. What event triggered the conflict? How do the groups involved perceive the issue differently? What tension, prior conflict, or injustice has contributed to the conflict and to the perceptions of those affected by it? Has the conflict been resolved? If so, write a paper discussing why you feel that the resolution was appropriate or not. If the conflict is continuing, write a paper proposing how a fair resolution might be reached.

4. Contentious debates over issues like affirmative action often hinge on whether or not the debaters accept the idea of structural racism (also called systemic racism). Proponents argue that structural racism is largely responsible for persistent racial disparities in wealth, income, home ownership, education, health care, and life expectancy. Investigate the concept of structural racism: What is it? How does it differ from individual racism or intentional discrimination? What evidence and examples of systemic racism do proponents cite? How do opponents of the concept explain racial inequalities, and what

supporting evidence do they offer? Argue a position: Is it necessary to address structural discrimination in order to achieve racial equality in the United States?

5. **Connecting to the e-Pages.**   Working in groups, create a short video in which you challenge a stereotype of your own group. Use your imagination: What misperceptions of athletes, Latinos, sorority girls, African Americans, or math majors have been bothering you? How does the reality of the group differ from the stereotype? For example, how might you translate Maysan Haydar's "Veiled Intentions" into images? Or how could you recast *More Than That* to address anti-Asian stereotypes? See bedfordstmartins.com/rereading/epages for these selections.

LAND OF LIBERTY
American Myths of Freedom

Freedom of Speech, from Norman Rockwell's *Four Freedoms*, 1943

FAST FACTS

1. The 2011 State of the First Amendment poll by the McCormick Tribune Foundation showed that while 62% of Americans can identify freedom of speech as part of the Bill of Rights, only 19 % recall that the Bill of Rights also includes freedom of religion, and 17%, freedom of the press. Thirty percent of those surveyed couldn't identify any First Amendment rights.

2. According to a 2010 McClatchy poll, 51% of Americans would be willing to give up some of their First Amendment rights to make the country safe from terrorism.

3. In 2006, Transportation Security Administration (TSA) airport screeners in New Jersey succeeded in detecting only 2 of 22 suspicious devices during government security tests. According to a 2010 ABC News report about a man who boarded a Texas flight with a loaded gun, TSA test failure rates approach 70% at some U.S. airports.

4. A 2012 *New York Times* report on dependency in America noted that nearly half of all U.S. households received government benefits in 2010. Citizens in so-called "red states," which generally support fiscally conservative economic and political policies, typically receive more in government support than they pay in federal taxes, while those in "blue states" pay more federal taxes than they receive in government benefits.

5. With 730 prison inmates for every 100,000 citizens, the United States has the highest incarceration rate in the world, as compared to Russia with 522 inmates per 100,000, Iran with 333, China with 122, and Japan with 55.

6. In 2010, white males were incarcerated at a rate of 678 inmates per 100,000 general population, Hispanic males at a rate of 1,755 per 100,000, and black males at a rate of 4,347 per 100,000. In 2009, blacks accounted for 39.4% of all U.S. prison inmates.

7. It's estimated that 15,000 to 17,000 slaves are trafficked into the United States each year, making the United States one of the top three destinations for the modern slave trade. California, Florida, New York, Nevada, and Ohio are considered "particularly vulnerable" to human trafficking.

Sources: (1) First Amendment Center, "State of the First Amendment 2011" (www .firstamendmentcenter.org/sofa); (2) McClatchy-Ipsos Poll (www.mcclatchydc .com/2010/01/12/82156/poll-most-americans-would-trim.html); (3) "Airport screeners fail to see most test bombs," *Seattle Times*, October 28, 2006; Kevin Quinn (December 17, 2010), ABC News KTRK-TV/DT Houston.; (4) Binyamin

Applebaum and Robert Gebeloff, "Even Critics of Safety Net Increasingly Depend on It," *New York Times* (February 11, 2012, p. A–1); (5) International Centre for Prison Studies (March 18, 2010), "Prison Brief—Highest to Lowest Rates," *World Prison Brief* (London: King's College London School of Law); (6) U.S. Bureau of Justice Statistics; (7) Coalition to Abolish Slavery and Trafficking Web site, "About the Problem." (www.castla.org/key-stats)

This will be the day when all of God's children will be able to sing with a new meaning, "My country, 'tis of thee, sweet land of liberty, of thee I sing. Land where my fathers died, land of the pilgrim's pride, from every mountainside, let freedom ring."

— MARTIN LUTHER KING, JR.

At the conclusion of his famous "I Have a Dream" speech, delivered in the summer of 1963 on the steps of the Lincoln Memorial, Martin Luther King Jr., sought to rally the crowd by evoking the most powerful theme in America's cultural mythology—the idea of personal liberty. King knew that any child would recognize the lines he quoted from Samuel Francis Smith's "America." From our earliest days in elementary school, we learn about the Pilgrims who fled Europe seeking freedom in the New World and about the colonists who fought the Revolutionary War to free themselves from British rule. We read how the Civil War brought about the end of slavery and how King's own words inspired a generation of African Americans to stand up for their rights. We're taught that America was founded on freedom. But the relationship between the ideal of freedom and the reality of life in America has never been simple or straightforward.

It's hard to appreciate what America must have meant to religious dissenters like the Puritans in sixteenth-century Europe. Persecuted by what they saw as a corrupt and authoritarian church, the Pilgrims viewed America through the biblical stories of exile, enslavement, and liberation they had read in the Old Testament: they came to see themselves as the new "children of Israel," "the chosen people" destined to venture into the wilderness of a "New Eden." Just as Christ had come to redeem creation from sin, they saw themselves as his agents, freeing humanity from the sordidness and decadence of the "Old World." But the Pilgrims sought a very narrow kind of emancipation: they came to America in pursuit of religious—not personal—liberty; they sought freedom of worship, not the kind of individual liberty that has become the hallmark of American independence. Indeed, in the rigidity of their religious doctrines, the authoritarianism of their social structure, their distrust of difference, and their contempt for worldly pleasures, they seem an unlikely source of inspiration for the American creed of "Life, Liberty, and the pursuit of Happiness."

Some historians trace the American concept of freedom not to the Puritan settlements of New England but to the American Indian cultures the Puritans and other European settlers displaced. Beginning with Christopher Columbus,

European explorers were amazed by the personal freedom enjoyed by the Native Americans they encountered: they could scarcely comprehend a life apparently unrestrained by rigid social distinctions, gender roles, financial obligations, religious doctrines, or state regulations. In a 1503 letter to Lorenzo de Medici, Amerigo Vespucci described these remarkable people who seemed to live in harmony with nature:

> The inhabitants of the New World do not have goods of their own, but all things are held in common. They live together without king, without government, and each is his own master.... There is a great abundance of gold, and by them it is in no respect esteemed or valued.... Surely if the terrestrial paradise be in any part of the earth, I esteem that it is not far distant from these parts.

Europeans raised in cultures dominated by the authority of monarchy, aristocracy, and the church were particularly impressed by the relative freedom of native children. American Indian families often encouraged their sons and daughters to develop a strong sense of independence and personal liberty. Iroquois children, for example, were taught to resist overbearing authority and were rarely punished severely; they were also taught that all tribal members — male, female, adult, and child — were equal and that possessions were to be shared by the entire community. Such attitudes contrasted sharply with those imported to the New World by the Pilgrims, who believed that a child's natural stubbornness and pride had to be broken down through education, discipline, and corporal punishment.

The examples of freedom and equality provided by societies like the Iroquois and the Huron sparked the European imagination and, as some scholars suggest, placed liberty at the top of the Western world's political agenda for the next four hundred years. To political philosophers like Jean-Jacques Rousseau, the "noble savage" was living proof that human beings were born free "in a state of nature" and that tyranny and slavery were the result of social corruption: if tyranny and injustice were not natural or god-given features of human life, then it would be possible — even necessary — for subjects to rebel against royal domination and reclaim their natural "inalienable" human rights. To political activists like Thomas Paine, the freedom and equality enjoyed within many American Indian cultures demonstrated that society could be organized without aristocracy, monarchy, and ecclesiastical authority. The first great advocate of both American independence and the abolition of slavery, Paine based many of his revolutionary ideas on his intimate knowledge of Iroquois customs and values.

The example of America's original inhabitants may have inspired the settlers to take up arms and fight for their own "natural" rights, but, as historian Howard Zinn has pointed out, the Revolutionary War had devastating consequences for Native Americans:

> What did the Revolution mean to the Native Americans, the Indians? They had been ignored by the fine words of the Declaration, had not been considered equal, certainly not in choosing those who would govern the American territories in which they lived, nor in being able to pursue happiness as they had pursued it for centuries before the white Europeans arrived. Now, with the British out of the way, the Americans could

begin the inexorable process of pushing the Indians off their lands, killing them if they resisted. In short...the white Americans were against British imperial control in the East, and for their own imperialism in the West.

It is one of history's most profound ironies that America's war for independence, the first war ever fought in the name of individual liberty, hastened the destruction of the very societies that had inspired the modern myth of freedom.

America's ambivalence toward the principle of freedom also found expression in the nation's newly drafted Constitution. The American Revolution's idealization of freedom had made slavery appear hypocritical to some patriots; as Abigail Adams wrote during the war, "I wish most sincerely there was not a slave in the province; it always appeared a most iniquitous scheme to me to fight ourselves for what we are daily robbing and plundering from those who have as good a right to freedom as we have." Such feelings prevailed in Vermont, where slavery was outlawed a year after the colonies declared their independence. However, economic and political considerations took precedence over human rights as the Constitutional Convention debated the slavery issue in 1787.

Outright abolition was never discussed at the convention — it would have been politically unacceptable to the many delegates who owned slaves. The question that did arise was whether the United States should continue to allow the importation of Africans for slave labor. Several representatives argued that it was "inconsistent with the principles of the revolution and dishonorable to the American character to have such a feature in the Constitution." But delegates from the South contended that more slaves not only were essential for developing southern agriculture but also would provide economic benefits for the northern states. Thus, a document that sought to "secure the blessings of liberty to ourselves and our posterity" also legitimized the sale and ownership of one human being by another.

The ideal of freedom was compromised again when liberties explicitly protected by the Constitution were denied in practice. The First Amendment guarantee of free speech, for example, was not actively enforced until well into the twentieth century. Dissenters — abolitionists, political activists, labor organizers, feminists, and birth control advocates, among others — were frequently arrested, harassed, fined, denied permits, or otherwise prevented from speaking publicly. The problem was so widespread that, in 1915, a government-sponsored investigative committee reported that

> on numerous occasions in every part of the country, the police of cities and towns have either arbitrarily or under the cloak of a traffic ordinance, interfered with, or prohibited public speaking, both in the open and in halls, by persons connected with organizations of which the police or those from whom they receive their orders, did not approve. In many instances such interference has been carried out with a degree of brutality which would be incredible if it were not vouched for by reliable witnesses.

But while the United States has often failed to uphold the rights of all citizens, the ideals of liberty and self-determination set out in the Declaration and Constitution have inspired many to fight for — and sometimes win — their ["unalienable"] rights. Popular movements throughout the nation's history have organized, marched, struck, sued, and practiced civil disobedience when established political channels failed them. A determined, seventy-five-year campaign by American feminists won women the vote in 1920, and systematic protests and court challenges by the labor movement in the 1930s gave us many of our current protections of free speech. Denied equal protection under the law, equal access to economic opportunity, equal education, and even an equal chance to vote, African Americans sought redress in the courts and on the streets of America for decades, eventually winning substantive legal reforms during the civil rights movement of the 1960s.

Today, battles over individual rights and the meaning of freedom continue to rage across the nation's cultural landscape. On the political right, the Tea Party and Libertarian movements claim that big government is robbing us of the pure, unbridled liberty the framers promised in the Constitution and the Bill of Rights. As they see it, freedom in America is being whittled away by excessive taxation and government spending on social "safety-net" programs, which ultimately breed weakness and dependency in the American character. They complain that overly protective "nanny state" bureaucrats limit our choices by regulating everything from the kinds of light bulbs we can buy to the level of sugar in our kids' morning cereal. They even wonder if the current climate of political correctness doesn't stifle free speech and thought. Of course critics on the left are no less passionate about the threats they see to freedom in contemporary America. Since the 9/11 attacks, civil libertarians have grown increasingly uneasy about the expansion of government police and surveillance powers in the name of homeland security. When federal agents can "data mine" our bank records, monitor the books we borrow at local libraries, and detain suspects indefinitely without charge, many Americans wonder exactly how free we still are. The rise of the Internet and social networking has compounded these fears. Net users generally agree that access to online information should be as free as possible, but does that include even the most personal information we confide online — including every purchase we make, every Web site we browse, or every idea or person we "like" on social media sites?

"Land of Liberty" invites you to explore the meaning of freedom in contemporary American culture and to examine recent threats to our civil rights. The chapter begins with a quartet of readings that provide historical context for your exploration of freedom in America. Drafted by Thomas Jefferson more than two centuries ago, the Declaration of Independence expresses the revolutionary spirit of the new republic in its call to arms against British rule. The Preamble to the Constitution and the Bill of Rights expand on the vision of liberty that animates the Declaration of Independence by detailing the proper role and limits of government power and the essential rights of every American citizen. Our brief survey of the roots of American freedoms closes with an intensely personal interpretation of the Founders' revolutionary intentions. In "Freedom Is Intended as a Challenge," feminist and social critic Naomi Wolf reminds us that real freedom today demands constant vigilance and personal sacrifice, just as it did in 1776.

The next section of the chapter focuses on recent threats to the freedoms guaranteed in the First Amendment. In "The Decline of American Press Freedom," Anne Applebaum surveys several cases of corporate self-censorship in response to pressure from foreign powers, claiming along the way that

American executives have lost the courage to stand up for free speech. Juan Williams continues this theme in "Defying the PC Police," as he wonders if American culture in general has become too polarized and politically correct to support the honest and open exchange of ideas essential to democracy. Next, the chapter shifts its focus to issues involving freedom of choice. In "The War on Negative Liberty," Katherine Mangu-Ward charges that our own good intentions are leading us to restrict the essential rights of others — including the right to make bad choices. Philosopher Martha C. Nussbaum carries the argument further in "Whether from Reason or Prejudice: Taking Money for Bodily Services." She challenges us to put good intentions aside and to think rationally about why America continues to criminalize women who choose prostitution as a career. An excerpt from ACLU president Susan N. Herman's book *Taking Liberties* completes the first half of the chapter by examining the impact of the USA PATRIOT Act on First Amendment guarantees. Herman's account of Sami, an Arab engineering student falsely accused of terrorist activities, offers you the chance to consider how far you'd compromise the Bill of Rights in the name of national security.

The second half of *Land of Liberty: American Myths of Freedom* opens with the chapter's Visual Portfolio. Here you'll find images that evoke some of the tensions that arise in a nation dedicated to individual liberty and free expression. Next comes a series of selections questioning whether America today really is as free as we assume. In "George Orwell...Meet Mark Zuckerberg," Lori Andrews investigates the world of data-aggregators, companies that secretly track every move you make online and then sell your virtual profile to the highest bidder. Next, Kevin Bales and Ron Soodalter present an idea that's even more disturbing. In "Slavery in the Land of the Free," they claim that human trafficking is alive and well today in homes, farms, and factories across the country. Michelle Alexander rounds off the last section of the chapter with "The New Jim Crow," her account of how the mass incarceration of black and brown men has created a permanently disenfranchised "undercaste" in American society.

The chapter closes with "Great Citizenship," Eric Liu and John Hanauer's rallying call for all Americans to practice "civic ecology" by taking responsibility for the social impact of every individual choice. Addressing the power of social networking as a source of political and cultural change, "Great Citizenship" connects with ideas in almost every selection in the chapter.

To continue your exploration of freedom in contemporary American culture, visit the e-Pages for *Rereading America* at bedfordstmartins.com/rereading /epages. Here you'll find *The Declaration of Interdependence*, a crowdsourced video that offers a global revision of America's founding document. You'll also find "The Rise of Mass Dependency," Chris Norwood's exposé of how big government and the "medical industrial complex" conspire to transform the United States into a country of utterly dependent — but immensely profitable — invalids.

Sources

Bennett, Lerone Jr. *Before the Mayflower: A History of Black America*, rev. 5th ed. New York: Viking Penguin, 1984.

Kairys, David. "Freedom of Speech." In *The Politics of Law: A Progressive Critique*, David Kairys, ed. New York: Pantheon Books, 1982.

Ketchem, Ralph, ed. *The Anti-Federalist Papers and the Constitutional Convention Debates*. New York: Mentor Books, 1986.

Kumar, Krishan. *Utopia and Anti-Utopia in Modern Times*, Oxford: Basil Blackwell, 1987.

Weatherford, Jack. *Indian Givers: How the Indians of the Americas Transformed the World*. New York: Ballantine Books, 1988.

Zinn, Howard. *A People's History of the United States*. New York: Harper and Row, 1980.

BEFORE READING

- Working in groups, spend a few minutes brainstorming a list of all the words and ideas that come to mind when you think of the idea of liberty. Compare the results of your brainstorming session in class and discuss what they suggest about how Americans view freedom today.

- Return to the frontispiece of this chapter and discuss what you think Norman Rockwell was trying to convey in *Freedom of Speech*. Who is the man standing in the middle of the painting, and who are the people around him? What can you tell about them from their dress and expressions? What's the situation, and what do you think the speaker is saying? In general, how does Rockwell depict the exercise of our right to free speech? How realistic is this depiction?

- Review the "Fast Facts" located at the beginning of this chapter. Which strike you as the most surprising? Why? What do these isolated facts suggest about the condition of freedom in the United States today? Which would you like to learn more about or dispute?

THE DECLARATION OF INDEPENDENCE

THE PREAMBLE TO THE CONSTITUTION OF THE UNITED STATES

THE BILL OF RIGHTS

A decade after drafting the Declaration of Independence, Thomas Jefferson wrote a letter to John Adams's son-in-law, reminding him that "The tree of liberty must from time to time be refreshed with the blood of patriots and tyrants." In his lifetime, Jefferson (1743–1826) was many things: politician, diplomat, scientist, architect, city planner, founder of the University of Virginia, lifelong slave owner, and third president of the United States. But as the Declaration of Independence demonstrates, he was also a committed revolutionary. Drafted by Jefferson in 1776 to justify the colonies' revolt against British tyranny, the Declaration of Independence has become one of the nation's fundamental expressions of American freedom.

Ratified by Congress in 1788, the Constitution of the newly formed United States attempted to translate the Declaration's notion of liberty into practical terms. The Preamble to the Constitution offers an amazingly compact statement of the purposes and, by implication, the limits of democratic government. The Bill of Rights expands on that vision in a series of ten amendments appended to the Constitution in 1791. Proposed in 1789 by James Madison as a safeguard against government tyranny, the Bill of Rights enumerates the specific liberties guaranteed to every American. While it was originally meant to apply only to the rights of white land-owning men, its provisions were augmented by the Fourteenth Amendment in 1868, which extended constitutional guarantees to "all persons born or naturalized in the United States" — including Native Americans, former slaves, and women.

The Declaration of Independence
Thomas Jefferson

The Unanimous Declaration of the Thirteen United States of America.

When in the Course of human events, it becomes necessary for one people to dissolve the political bands which have connected them with another, and to assume among the powers of the earth, the separate and equal station to which the Laws of Nature and of Nature's God entitle them, a decent respect to the opinions of mankind requires that they should declare the causes which impel them to the separation.—We hold these truths to be self-evident, that all men are created equal, that they are endowed by their Creator with certain unalienable Rights, that among these are Life, Liberty and the pursuit of Happiness.—That to secure these rights, Governments are instituted among Men, deriving their just powers from the consent of the governed.—That whenever any Form of Government becomes destructive of these ends, it is the Right of the People to alter or to abolish it, and to institute new Government, laying its foundation on such principles and organizing its powers in such form, as to them shall seem most likely to effect their Safety and Happiness. Prudence, indeed, will dictate that Governments long established should not be changed for light and transient causes; and accordingly all experience hath shewn, that mankind are more disposed to suffer, while evils are sufferable, than to right themselves by abolishing the forms to which they are accustomed. But when a long train of abuses and usurpations, pursuing invariably the same Object[1] evinces a design to reduce them under absolute Despotism, it is their right, it is their duty, to throw off such Government, and to provide new Guards for their future security.—Such has been the patient sufferance of these Colonies; and such is now the necessity which constrains them to alter their former Systems of Government. The history of the present King of Great Britain is a history of repeated injuries and usurpations, all having in direct object the establishment of an absolute Tyranny over these States. To prove this, let Facts be submitted to a candid world.——He has refused his Assent to Laws, the most wholesome and necessary for the public good.——He has forbidden his Governors to pass Laws of immediate and pressing importance, unless suspended in their operation till his Assent should be obtained; and when so suspended, he has utterly neglected to attend to them.——He has refused to pass other Laws for the accommodation of large districts of people, unless those people would relinquish the right of Representation in the Legislature, a right inestimable to them and formidable to tyrants only.——He has called together legislative bodies at places unusual, uncomfortable, and distant from the depository of their public Records, for the sole purpose of fatiguing them into compliance with his measures.——He has dissolved Representative Houses repeatedly, for opposing with manly firmness his invasions on the rights of the people.——He has refused for a long time, after such dissolutions, to cause others to be elected; whereby the Legislative powers, incapable of Annihilation, have returned to the People at large for their exercise; the State remaining in the mean time exposed to all the dangers of invasion from without, and convulsions within.——He has endeavoured to prevent the population of these States; for that purpose obstructing the Laws for Naturalization of Foreigners; refusing to pass others to encourage their migrations hither, and raising the conditions of new Appropriations of Lands.——He has obstructed the Administration of Justice, by refusing his Assent to Laws for establishing Judiciary powers.——He has made Judges dependent on his Will alone, for the tenure of their offices, and the amount and payment of their salaries.——He has erected a multitude of New Offices, and sent hither swarms of Officers to harass our people, and eat out their substance.——He has kept among us, in times of peace, Standing Armies without the Consent of our legislatures.——He has affected to render the Military independent of and superior to the Civil power.——He has combined with others to subject us to a jurisdiction foreign to our constitution, and unacknowledged by our laws; giving his Assent to their Acts of pretended Legislation:—For Quartering large bodies of armed troops among us:—For protecting them, by a mock Trial, from punishment for any Murders which they should commit on the Inhabitants of these States:—For cutting off our Trade with all parts of the world:—For imposing Taxes on us

[1]*Object:* Goal, purpose. [Eds.]

without our Consent:—For depriving us in many cases, of the benefits of Trial by Jury:—For transporting us beyond Seas to be tried for pretended offences:—For abolishing the free System of English Laws in a neighbouring Province, establishing therein an Arbitrary government, and enlarging its Boundaries so as to render it at once an example and fit instrument for introducing the same absolute rule into these Colonies:—For taking away our Charters, abolishing our most valuable Laws, and altering fundamentally the Forms of our Governments:—For suspending our own Legislatures, and declaring themselves invested with power to legislate for us in all cases whatsoever.—He had abdicated Government here, by declaring us out of his Protection and waging War against us:—He has plundered our seas, ravaged our Coasts, burnt our towns, and destroyed the lives of our people.—He is at this time transporting large Armies of foreign Mercenaries to compleat the works of death, desolation and tyranny, already begun with circumstances of Cruelty & Perfidy scarcely paralleled in the most barbarous ages, and totally unworthy the Head of a civilized nation.—He has constrained our fellow Citizens taken Captive on the high Seas to bear Arms against their Country, to become the executioners of their friends and Brethren, or to fall themselves by their Hands.—He has excited domestic insurrections amongst us, and has endeavoured to bring on the inhabitants of our frontiers, the merciless Indian Savages, whose known rule of warfare, is an undistinguished destruction of all ages, sexes and conditions. In every stage of these Oppressions We have Petitioned for Redress in the most humble terms: Our repeated Petitions have been answered only by repeated injury. A Prince, whose character is thus marked by every act which may define a Tyrant, is unfit to be the ruler of a free people. Nor have We been wanting in attentions to our British brethren. We have warned them from time to time of attempts by their legislature to extend an unwarrantable jurisdiction over us. We have reminded them of the circumstances of our emigration and settlement here. We have appealed to their native justice and magnanimity, and we have conjured them by the ties of our common kindred to disavow these usurpations, which would inevitably interrupt our connections and correspondence. They too have been deaf to the voice of justice and of consanguinity. We must, therefore, acquiesce in the necessity, which denounces our Separation, and hold them, as we hold the rest of mankind, Enemies in War, in Peace Friends.

We, THEREFORE, the Representatives of the UNITED STATES OF AMERICA, in General Congress Assembled, appealing to the Supreme Judge of the world for the rectitude of our intentions, do, in the Name and by Authority of the good People of these Colonies, solemnly publish and declare, That these United Colonies are, and of Right ought to be FREE AND INDEPENDENT STATES; that they are Absolved from all Allegiance to the British Crown, and that all political connection between them and the State of Great Britain, is and ought to be totally dissolved; and that as Free and Independent States, they have full Power to levy

War, conclude Peace, contract Alliances, establish Commerce, and to do all other Acts and Things which Independent States may of right do.——And for the support of this Declaration, with a firm reliance on the protection of divine Providence, we mutually pledge to each other our Lives, our Fortunes and our sacred Honor.

Preamble to the Constitution

We the People of the United States, in Order to form a more perfect Union, establish Justice, insure domestic Tranquility, provide for the common defence, promote the general Welfare, and secure the Blessings of Liberty to ourselves and our Posterity, do ordain and establish this Constitution for the United States of America.

The Bill of Rights

Amendment I

Congress shall make no law respecting an establishment of religion, or prohibiting the free exercise thereof; or abridging the freedom of speech, or of the press; or the right of the people peaceably to assemble, and to petition the Government for a redress of grievances.

Amendment II

A well regulated Militia, being necessary to the security of a free State, the right of the people to keep and bear Arms, shall not be infringed.

Amendment III

No Soldier shall, in time of peace be quartered in any house, without the consent of the Owner, nor in time of war, but in a manner to be prescribed by law.

Amendment IV

The right of the people to be secure in their persons, houses, papers, and effects, against unreasonable searches and seizures, shall not be violated, and no Warrants shall issue, but upon probable cause, supported by Oath or affirmation, and particularly describing the place to be searched, and the persons or things to be seized.

Amendment V

No person shall be held to answer for a capital, or otherwise infamous crime, unless on a presentment or indictment of a Grand Jury, except in cases arising in the land or naval forces, or in the Militia, when in actual service in time of War or public danger; nor shall any person be subject for the same offence to be twice put in jeopardy of life or limb; nor shall be compelled in any criminal case to be a witness against himself, nor be deprived of life, liberty, or property, without due process of law; nor shall private property be taken for public use, without just compensation.

Amendment VI

In all criminal prosecutions, the accused shall enjoy the right to a speedy and public trial, by an impartial jury of the State and district wherein the crime shall have been committed, which district shall have been previously ascertained by law, and to be informed of the nature and cause of the accusation; to be confronted with the witnesses against him; to have compulsory process for obtaining witnesses in his favor, and to have the Assistance of Counsel for his defence.

Amendment VII

In Suits at common law, where the value in controversy shall exceed twenty dollars, the right of trial by jury shall be preserved, and no fact tried by a jury, shall be otherwise re-examined in any Court of the United States, than according to the rules of the common law.

Amendment VIII

Excessive bail shall not be required, nor excessive fines imposed, nor cruel and unusual punishments inflicted.

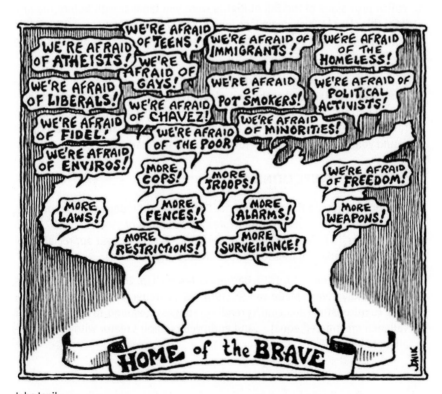

John Jonik

Amendment IX

The enumeration in the Constitution, of certain rights, shall not be construed to deny or disparage others retained by the people.

Amendment X

The powers not delegated to the United States by the Constitution, nor prohibited by it to the States, are reserved to the States respectively, or to the people.

ENGAGING THE TEXT

1. What do you think Jefferson meant when he wrote that "all men are created equal" in the Declaration of Independence? How might this claim be interpreted?

2. Try to summarize the entire Declaration in a paragraph. Compare your results in small groups and discuss the differences in your impressions of what the document says.

3. What do you think Jefferson meant when he said that we have the right to "Life, Liberty, and the pursuit of Happiness"? What might "Happiness" mean in this context? What aspects of the Preamble might help to clarify this?

4. Which provisions of the Bill of Rights were you familiar with before reading it for this class? Which seem less memorable and why? How might the Bill of Rights be seen as a logical response to the specific tyrannies outlined in the Declaration?

5. In an 1879 letter to James Madison, Jefferson observed that every constitution naturally "expired" at the end of nineteen years because a new generation of citizens needed a new set of laws. Working in groups, write your own revision of the Bill of Rights. What rights would you omit and what new rights would you include to update it for the current generation?

EXPLORING CONNECTIONS

6. How does Jefferson the drafter of the Declaration of Independence compare with Jefferson the author of the *Notes on the State of Virginia* (p. 497)? To what extent do Jefferson's personal views on race affect your appreciation of him as a champion of freedom and individual rights?

7. How might Malcolm X (p. 189), Barbara Ehrenreich (p. 267), Gregory Mantsios (p. 281), Kay Givens McGowan (p. 396), David Treuer (p. 578), and Stephen Cruz (bedfordstmartins.com/rereading/epages), respond to the claim that "all men are created equal...and endowed by their Creator with certain unalienable rights"?

EXTENDING THE CRITICAL CONTEXT

8. After doing some online research, compare the provisions of the U.S. Bill of Rights with other famous "bills," including, for example, the Canadian Charter of Rights and Freedoms, Chapter Two of the Constitution of South Africa, or the United Nations' Universal Declaration of Human Rights. What differences do you note between these statements of fundamental human liberties and the U.S. Bill of Rights? Which do you prefer and why?

FREEDOM IS INTENDED AS A CHALLENGE

NAOMI WOLF

Do you recall the first time you were asked to read the Declaration of Independence? For many Americans, meeting the Founding Fathers is a less-than-memorable experience. As Naomi Wolf suggests in this selection, the Declaration we study in school is often presented as a bloodless museum piece with no real connection to our daily lives. But Wolf clearly thinks otherwise. In her contemporary re-reading of the Declaration, she discovers a call to arms that challenges every American to make personal sacrifices for the cause of freedom. A feminist and social critic, Wolf (b. 1962) is the author of seven books, including *The Beauty Myth: How Images of Beauty Are Used Against Women* (1991), *The End of America: Letter of Warning to a Young Patriot* (2007), and *Give Me Liberty: A Handbook for American Revolutionaries* (2008), the source of this selection. She is also cofounder of the American Freedom Campaign, a grassroots democracy movement dedicated to defending freedom and the Constitution.

Oh, Freedom…Oh, Freedom over me.
— AFRICAN-AMERICAN SPIRITUAL

The Declaration of Independence: Your Contract as Liberty's Warrior

The American contract is codified in Thomas Jefferson's short but stunning Declaration of Independence. Jefferson wrote it as a distillation of sentiments that were common among his fellow colonists:

We hold these Truths to be self-evident, that all Men are created equal, that they are endowed by their Creator with certain unalienable Rights, that among these are Life, Liberty, and the Pursuit of Happiness.—That to secure these Rights, Governments are instituted among Men, deriving their just Powers from the Consent of the governed, that whenever any Form of Government becomes destructive of these Ends, it is the Right of the People to alter or to abolish it, and to institute new Government, laying its Foundation on such Principles, and organizing its Powers in such Form, as to them shall seem most likely to effect their Safety and Happiness. Prudence, indeed, will dictate that Governments long established should not be changed for light and transient Causes; and accordingly all Experience hath shewn, that Mankind are more disposed to suffer, while Evils are sufferable than to right themselves by abolishing the Forms to which they are accustomed. But when a long Train of Abuses and Usurpations, pursuing invariably the same Object, evinces a Design to reduce them under absolute Despotism, it is their Right, it is their Duty, to throw off such Government, and to provide new Guards for their future Security.

This language, while beautiful, is quite difficult; it is the formal language of a very formal century far removed from our own. Most of the "fake patriotism" bullet points we get from the Declaration focus on its first sentence and an early clause in it, the famous "Life, Liberty, and the Pursuit of Happiness." (Or as a Svedka vodka ad has it, "Life, Liberty, and the Pursuit of Happy Hour." Or as a Cadillac ad puts it, "Life, Liberty and the Pursuit.")

Since our attention is usually called to that opening shot, most of us think of the Declaration as being no more disturbing or personally demanding than a nicely lit HBO special about 1776. We tend to think that the Declaration intends something pleasant and benign: people like to pursue their individual pleasures, God wants it to work out this way, and everyone's interests are best served by our having the right to do so. Out of context, this phrase evokes a smiley-faced, noncombative, self-absorbed version of the American task.

But it turns out that the Declaration of Independence is about our continual duty as Americans to rebel—not so much about our continual enjoyment as Americans of the pleasures of shopping and team sports. Indeed, historian Pauline Maier points out in *American Scripture: Making the Declaration of Independence* that the Declaration of Independence's first long sentence asserts above all the "right of revolution."[1]

What Is "the Pursuit of Happiness"?

The founders saw two ideas, individuality and happiness—as in "the Pursuit of Happiness" above—as being closely related.

5

---

[1]Maier, op. cit., 134–35. On the Declaration's "duty to rebel," see p. 137. On its use of "happiness," see p. 167. [All notes are Wolf's, except 8–10.]

But again, our contemporary understanding of both these terms is far distorted from how the founders intended us to interpret them: we tend to think of both as lifestyle opportunities—scope for personal preferences to play out upon. A whole marketing wavelength around us is all about this predicate of "individuality" and "happiness": MySpace, MyTunes, MyFavorites, my personal checking, my monogram, my pet, my cubicle, my retirement goals. In contemporary America, "happiness" is what you get when you activate your "liberty" to express your "individuality." "Happiness" today is often defined as personal satisfaction that stops with the individual, and even personal pleasure and joy.

But to Jefferson and his Enlightenment contemporaries, the "individual" and "happiness" had different meanings than what we assume they do today. To Jefferson, "happiness" would not have been the opposite of the eighteenth-century term "melancholy," which today we would call sadness or depression. Rather, to many of the founders, "happiness" was a fortunate state of enfranchisement in the context of an open, just society. This sense of the word descended to the revolutionary generation from Greek literature: to the founders, "happiness" meant the development of one's full power as an individual, and one's respecting of the "sacred rights" and consciences of others in a condition of freedom.[2] (Robert Kennedy picked up this definition when he wrote, "Long ago the Greeks defined happiness as 'the exercise of vital powers along lines of excellence in a life affording them scope.'")[3]

For instance, Jefferson wrote in 1787: "Happy for us, that when we find our constitutions defective & insufficient to secure the *happiness* of our people, we can assemble with all the coolness of philosophers & set it to rights, while every other nation on earth must have recourse to arms to amend or restore their constitutions."[4] In 1803 he defined the nation's well-being in terms of people's "liberty" and "security," which in turn make them feel "*at...ease*" and lead them to act on behalf of a whole. In 1814, he wrote to a friend, Miles King, using "happiness" in the context of honesty, kindness, and respect for others' personal and religious freedoms: "He [God] formed us moral agents....he is far above our power; but that we may promote the *happiness* of those with whom he has placed us in society, by acting honestly toward all, benevolently to those who fall within our way, respecting sacredly their rights, bodily and mental, and cherishing especially their freedom of conscience, as we value our own."[5,6]

---

[2]Ibid., 214, on how "memories tend to fade after 'life, liberty and the pursuit of happiness.'"

[3]Maxwell Taylor Kennedy, *Make Gentle the Life of This World: The Vision of Robert F. Kennedy* (New York: Broadway Books, 1998), 14.

[4]Kaminski, op. cit., 50, 133, 138, 302.

[5]Ibid., 121.

[6]Ibid., 302.

So the right to "the Pursuit of Happiness" we inherit is not a plea-sure pursuit such as catalog shopping or an indulgence in a personal lifestyle choice, whether a doll collectors' convention or an S&M gala.

To most of us, nonetheless, the first clause alone *is* the Declaration 10 of Independence. We remember it because our civics textbooks and politicians stick to this section; but we also remember it because the modern ear can more easily understand the words of the opening clause than those of the second half.

But then—the rest of the text! If you read to the end and trans-late into contemporary English—which I bet your middle school civics textbooks never did for you—you will find that Jefferson put together a most radical document with most challenging implications for every one of us. And Pauline Maier points out that what Jefferson was doing by constructing his paragraph as he did—using an eighteenth-century way of building a set of ideas so the most important one comes last—makes it all the more indefensible to take the first famous clause out of context.

So the rest of Jefferson's passage is just as crucial for us to under-stand—Maier would say even more crucial. And it illuminates a com-pletely different role for us.

With translation for a modern reader, it means something like this:

> That to guarantee these rights for themselves, men create governments that derive their rightful [or "proper"] power from the consent of those who are governed; that whenever any form of government starts to be destructive to the goals of life, liberty, and the pursuit of happiness, the people have a *right* to change *or even destroy* that form of govern-ment; and the people have a right then to create a new form of govern-ment—one that is founded upon the kind of principles, and that takes the kind of shape, that seems to them to be most likely to guarantee their safety and good fortune.
>
> It is obviously not prudent to change or to destroy long-established governments for superficial reasons, or in response to [difficult] circum-stances that are transient; and experience shows that it is human nature for people to put up with suffering if the suffering is bearable. But when a long series of abuses and violations of their rights appears to be di-rected at one primary goal—that of reducing a given people to having to live under conditions of absolute despotism—*then it is the people's right—indeed, it is their duty*—to throw off this kind of government, so as to establish new forms of protection for their security in the future.

This part of the declaration is not saying: "Hurrah, you are born free, enjoy your bingo or your yoga as you see fit." Nor is it simply jus-tifying in ringing terms the domestic political decision to separate the fate of the young North American colonies from the oppressive "pro-tection" of mother England. Rather, it is saying something darker and more personally demanding: you have a sacred obligation to take the most serious possible steps and undergo the most serious kinds of per-sonal risks in defense of this freedom that is your natural right; and you *must* rise up against those who seek to subdue you—wherever and whenever they appear.

Did Mrs. Jones in eighth grade put that on your test? I didn't think so. My own civics class had no such focus on personal resistance. Was that mandate in the shaded box in your textbook? Or was there, much more likely, a photo of the actual unexplicated and illegible parchment document? Maier makes the point that the document itself, starting at the fifty-year anniversary after the Revolution, became and remains today a kind of sacred relic for a secular nation—but that the relic has itself been promoted and publicized often at the expense of anyone explaining the more rebellious message it intended to convey to us, the heirs of Jefferson's revolutionary manifesto.[7]

The pretty but illegible scroll that had become so iconic was in my textbook in middle school. That translated mandate to protest and confront abusive power? Didn't make it in. The Fourth of July gives us fireworks and speeches—not, usually, a reminder that we inherit a sworn duty to rebel at injustice.

If we actually learned this entire passage as the nation's and our own personal manifesto, would we tolerate today the state spying on us illegally? Would we tolerate the passage of laws today that allow the executive to bypass the people's representatives entirely—giving Americans effectively a condition of being subject to taxation and other commitments without representation? Would we be okay with our rights and liberties being chipped away? Would we change the channel?

The more I read the Declaration, the more unsettled I became. Did this mean that I was not free to sit by, check out, scan the catalogs, go on a long vacation, tend my own garden when I was sick of the mess on the homefront? Did this mean that I personally had to step up to confront abusive power?

How altogether different and more difficult an experience of oneself and one's country it would be if a "declaration of independence" for Americans means accepting a personal commitment to defend liberty. Jefferson left us not a guarantee of a life basking in a lawn chair, but rather a guarantee of a life of personal upheaval and sacrifice when necessary.

I kept going over and over Jefferson's language. I was looking, I realized, for a loophole. Did the philosopher of Monticello[8] make any allowance for my personal complacency? Didn't the language somewhere let me off the hook? Didn't he know I was *busy*?

No, I was forced to conclude, not anywhere. Thomas Jefferson implicated *me*.

And you too.

---

[7]Maier, op. cit., 215.
[8]*Monticello:* Jefferson's Virginia home.

"Liberation" is not only about a historical moment in the past. It is, as African-American slaves knew for centuries, a destination of the mind. Jews who were not alive during the historical liberation from Egypt understood this too, as have many others. So the Declaration's specific call to liberation from George III's tyranny[9] is also a timeless contract that implicates each one of us forever, bestowing upon us certain rights but charging us too with certain responsibilities, and not at one moment of time but continually. This meant I was going to have to feel more outrage and less detachment, do more fighting and less settling. And there wasn't a time when my commitment could expire; it wasn't "one revolution" or "in your college days" that we were asked to fight. It is whenever our country—meaning, liberty—needed us. Even when we are old. Even when we are sick of it. Even if we have done it before.

Jefferson and Adams[10] both lived long, productive lives. Both men fought for and won the first revolution and served their country as leaders; in old age, both longed to be left in peace, the former at his farm in Monticello and the latter at his estate in Massachusetts.[11]

But both stepped up again and again to aid the nation when called 25 to, very much against their personal inclinations, because they understood the status of "being an American" existentially, that it means that one has signed on to fight the permanent revolution.

So real patriotism means understanding that the Declaration of Independence charges us *categorically* and *always* as Americans to rise up in person against threats to liberty. A friend remarked that the words in the Declaration seemed to force one to ask of oneself, "Am I a revolutionary on behalf of freedom?"

I realized that he was right. That *is* the question that the Declaration demands that each of us ask ourself.

Well, am I willing to be?

Are you?

ENGAGING THE TEXT

1. What's wrong with the way most Americans interpret the Declaration of Independence today, in Wolf's opinion? How would you describe her view of the average American? To what extent would you agree with her?

2. How, according to Wolf, did the Founding Fathers understand the meaning of "Happiness"? How does this notion differ from our common understanding of the word today?

---

[9]*George III's tyranny:* George William Frederick (1738–1820), king of Great Britain during the American Revolution.

[10]*Adams:* John Adams (1735–1826), American Founding Father and second president of the United States (1797–1801).

[11]Joseph J. Ellis, *Founding Brothers: The Revolutionary Generation* (New York: Vintage Books, 2000), 206–48.

3. To what extent would you agree with Wolf that the government has "chipped away" at our civil liberties? How, exactly, do you think the government limits your own personal freedom?

4. What do you think Wolf means when she claims that liberation is "a destination of the mind" (para. 23)? What, overall, does Wolf seem to want? What do you think it would be like to live in a world where every American was a "revolutionary on behalf of freedom"?

EXPLORING CONNECTIONS

5. Revisit the one-paragraph summary of the Declaration that you wrote earlier. To what extent does your summary convey what Wolf terms the "darker and more personally demanding" vision of freedom as "permanent revolution" (para. 14) and the duty to rebel personally against tyranny?

6. Which of the selections you've read so far in this course best embody the spirit of personal resistance that Wolf identifies with real liberty? Why or in what sense do the authors of these selections strike you as particularly free?

EXTENDING THE CRITICAL CONTEXT

7. Working in groups, make online or print collages of images from popular magazines or Web sites that express the way that Americans today understand the idea of freedom. Compare your work in class and discuss whether it supports or challenges Wolf's view of current American attitudes.

8. In groups, discuss what you recall about your encounters with the Declaration and Constitution in school. Based on your experiences, do you think Wolf is right when she suggests that U.S. schools present the Declaration as a kind of "sacred relic"? How should these historical documents be taught?

THE DECLINE OF AMERICAN PRESS FREEDOM
ANNE APPLEBAUM

The revolutionaries who wrote the Declaration of Independence and the Bill of Rights saw free speech as the foundation of American democracy. If "We the people" were to make critical decisions about the nation's future, all citizens needed to express their ideas freely and to hear differing points of view. That's why the First Amendment stresses free speech, freedom of the press, and the right of peaceable assembly. Of course, the history of the First Amendment has been filled with conflict and litigation. But the framers of the Constitution couldn't possibly have foreseen that the Bill of Rights would be tested in an era of global mass communication and transnational capitalism. As Anne Applebaum suggests in this selection, American corporations today seem all too willing to compromise First Amendment freedoms in response to threats from abroad, whether it's the risk of violent retaliation for printing cartoons of Mohammed or the loss of profits in economically booming but politically repressive places like Moscow or Beijing. Applebaum (b. 1964) is a journalist who writes regularly for the *Washington Post* and *Slate* magazine. Her publications include *Between East and West: Across the Borderlands of Europe* (1994) and *Gulag: A History* (2003), winner of the Pulitzer Prize for nonfiction in 2004.

IN 1949, when George Orwell wrote his dystopian novel *1984*, he gave its hero, Winston Smith, a job at the Ministry of Truth. All day long, Winston clips politically unacceptable facts, stuffs them into little pneumatic tubes, and then pushes the tubes down a chute. Beside him sits a woman in charge of finding and erasing the names of people who have been "vaporized." And their office, Orwell wrote, "with its fifty workers or thereabouts, was only one sub-section, a single cell, as it were, in the huge complexity of the Records Department."

It's odd to read *1984* in 2010, because it makes one realize that the politics of Orwell's vision aren't at all outdated. There are still plenty of governments in the world that go to extraordinary lengths to shape what their citizens read, think, and say, just like Orwell's Big Brother. But the technology envisioned in *1984* is so—well—1980s. Paper? Pneumatic tubes? Nowadays, none of that is necessary: it can all be done electronically, or through telephone calls, or using commercial pressure. In the modern world, censorship can take many forms, even reaching across international boundaries. And it has already begun to affect the American press, and American publishing, far more than is commonly understood.

To see what I mean, look closely at a decision taken by Yale University Press in the summer of 2009. Deep in the month of August, its editors quietly issued a statement confirming that there would be a change to the content of one of their forthcoming books, *The Cartoons that Shook the World*. The book was a scholarly account of the international controversy that followed a Danish newspaper's 2005 publication of twelve cartoons depicting the Prophet Mohammed. The book contained a significant amount of new material. Among other things, the Danish author, Jytte Klausen, argued that the controversy had been manipulated by Danish imams[1] who showed their followers false, sexually offensive depictions of Mohammed alongside the real ones, which were not inherently offensive at all.

She also argued that others—including the Egyptian government—used the cartoons to create "outrage" in the form of riots, boycotts, and anti-Danish protests, which they deployed for their own political ends. She consulted with several Muslim scholars who agreed that the protests were not evidence of authentic Muslim religious anger, but were rather political games. Later, she would write that she had "good reason" to believe that the publication of the cartoons need not have been interpreted offensively, and that republication of them by a scholarly press was not threatening or dangerous.

Nevertheless, the Yale press, "after careful consideration," decided   5
not to publish the cartoons. In a statement, the normally independent press declared that it had consulted Yale University, and that the university had in turn consulted "counterterrorism officials in the United States and in the United Kingdom, U.S. diplomats who had served as ambassadors in the Middle East, foreign ambassadors from Muslim countries, the top Muslim official at the United Nations, and senior scholars in Islamic studies." To the intense disappointment of Klausen as well as of the book's original editor—who had himself consulted lawyers and who supported printing the book—the university decided that the risk of terrorism was too great to allow the publication of the twelve cartoons.

Predictably, a minor controversy ensued. Some Yale alumni, myself included, signed a letter of protest. The *New York Times* and others printed angry criticism. But the university stuck to its decision, citing fears of violence and possible terrorist attacks on the Yale campus. John Negroponte, former CIA director, former ambassador to Baghdad, and

---

[1]*imams:* Islamic religious leaders. [All notes are the editors', unless otherwise indicated.]

class of '60, even applauded the Yale press for its "brave" refusal to print the images.

Equally predictably, the story faded. But Yale's decision to bow to pressure from unnamed and unknowable terrorists has further consequences. Although there was no direct threat—just a fear that someone, someday, might present one—the university has now set a standard for others. Yale's press is one of the best in the country: if its editors won't publish the Danish cartoons, why should anyone else? Indeed, one of Yale's strongest and most frequently cited arguments for not publishing the cartoons was the fact that most major U.S. newspapers refused to publish them in 2005. Now the bar is higher: if not only the *New York Times*, not only the *Washington Post*, but even Yale University Press refuse to publish them, then that makes it much harder for anybody else to treat the cartoon controversy as a legitimate matter for scholarly and political debate.

But Yale's decision was not an unusual one either. On the contrary, it is only one of a number of recent incidents that illustrate the increasing power of illiberal groups and regimes—not only Islamic terrorists but authoritarian foreign governments and the companies aligned with them—to place de facto[2] controls on American publishers, newspapers, and media companies, constraining once-sacred American rights to free speech, and once-inviolable American traditions of press freedom.

Indeed, the vague threat of "terrorism" is only one tool that foreign entities use to control free speech, and it is not necessarily the most powerful. Yale's decision attracted a good deal of attention, but in fact the university was merely cowardly. It thought it was acting in the interests of its students' safety. By contrast, the motives of other Americans who have lately tried to suppress information on behalf of foreign entities are often murkier.

A case in point is another decision, also taken in the summer of 2009. At that time, *GQ* magazine was debating whether it should publish an article titled "Vladimir Putin's Dark Rise to Power," by Scott Anderson. The article, based on extensive reporting, argued that Russian security services had helped plan and execute a series of bomb explosions in Moscow in 2000. These explosions, which killed dozens of people, were blamed on Chechen[3] terrorists. Subsequently, then-Russian president Vladimir Putin also used the explosions as a justification for the launch of the second Chechen war.

So conveniently timed were these terrorist attacks, in fact, that even at the time many in Moscow suspected the secret services had a hand in them, and much circumstantial evidence is available to support this thesis. Nevertheless, in Russia, discussion of this evidence remains

[2]*de facto:* As opposed to *de jure*, an activity deemed legal because it is common practice and not a matter of written law.
[3]*Chechen:* Related to the Chechen Republic, a semi-autonomous area in southern Russia that has sought independence since the dissolution of the Soviet Union in 1991.

officially taboo. Obviously, if Russian special forces acting on the authority of the Russian president were involved in killing Russian citizens, this is a very controversial matter indeed.

Eventually, Anderson's article making this case did appear in the September 2009 American edition of the magazine, but not anywhere else. Condé Nast, the U.S. media company that owns *GQ*, banned the article from appearing in the magazine's Russian edition, banned it from appearing in other foreign editions, and banned it from appearing on any Condé Nast website. In addition, the company ordered all of its magazines and affiliates around the world—magazines such as the *New Yorker* and *Wired*, among others—to refrain from mentioning or promoting the article in any way. In an e-mail sent to senior editors and later quoted by National Public Radio, company lawyers even forbade company employees to physically carry the U.S. edition of the magazine into Russia or to show it to any Russian government officials, journalists, or advertisers.

Clearly, Condé Nast's motives had nothing to do with security, and everything to do with Russian advertisers, many of whom are one way or another linked to the Russian government. And of course the company was made to look foolish: within days, Anderson's article was scanned, translated, and published in English and Russian on multiple websites. But perhaps that didn't matter. What Condé Nast seems to have wanted was to appear to be groveling before their Russian subscribers and advertisers.

In this, they succeeded. And, as in the case of Yale's decision, Condé Nast's humiliating act of self-censorship sets a precedent. If one of the largest and richest media companies in the country is not willing to take the chance of offending Putin, why should anyone else? The same, of course, is true for Russians: if American journalists writing about Russia in American publications cannot feel confident that their work will be supported, why should Russians, who risk so much more, feel any braver? Ultimately, a tame, censored Russian press is a disaster for the American companies that work in Russia and Americans who live there, since such a press will not dare to expose the culture of corruption that makes doing business in Russia so difficult for foreigners. But clearly, Condé Nast wasn't thinking that far down the line.

None of these flirtations with censorship compares, however, with 15 the lengths to which American companies have been persuaded to go in aiding and abetting censorship in China. Once upon a time, visionaries predicted that, in the twenty-first century, authoritarian and totalitarian regimes would no longer be able to operate, so overwhelmed would they be by the flood of free information available on the Internet. China in particular was often cited as the perfect example, a place where free markets would bring free information that would ultimately destroy the communist regime.

If it hasn't worked out that way, the fault lies partly in the decisions of some of America's best-known media and software companies, many of which have collaborated with the Chinese government's increasingly sophisticated Internet censorship regime for much of the past decade. In fact, the "Great Firewall," the vast Chinese Internet filter, was originally created with the help of Cisco Systems, an American company. Among other things, Cisco provided the Chinese government with technology designed to block traffic to individual pages within a particular web-site, so that you can read about Tibet's architectural heritage[4] and never know you missed the description of the Dalai Lama[5] at all. Cisco[6] shows no remorse: in a 2005 interview, a company spokesman told me that this is the "same equipment technology that your local library uses to block pornography," and besides, "We're not doing anything illegal."

Others have also complied. Since 2002, Yahoo! has been volun-tarily controlling its own search engine in China. The company signed a "public pledge of self-discipline" when it entered the Chinese market, in exchange for being allowed to place its servers on the Chinese main-land. At around the same time, Microsoft agreed to alter the Chinese version of its blog tool, MSN Spaces, at the behest of the Chinese gov-ernment. In practice, this means that Chinese bloggers who try to post a forbidden word— "Tiananmen,"[7] say, or "democracy" —receive a warn-ing stating that "this message contains a banned expression, please delete."

After much agonizing, mighty Google also joined them. The com-pany had been operating a Chinese version of google.com, with U.S.-based servers, for many years. But the service was difficult for ordinary Chinese users to access, so in 2006, the company decided to launch Google.cn. In order to be allowed to do so, it too pledged to abide by Chinese rules on banned websites. Anywhere else in the world, type the name of "Falun Gong,"[8] the banned Chinese spiritual movement, into Google, and thousands of results, chat rooms, and blogs turn up. On Google.cn, "Falun Gong" produces nothing.

What has been the result of this American compliance with Chinese edicts? Far from appeasing the regime, it appears to have emboldened the Chinese government to expand its censorship program. Pressure has been put on individual companies: in 2005, the Chinese govern-ment demanded that Yahoo! hand over the e-mail account information of a Chinese journalist who had leaked documents to a U.S.-based web-site—documents describing Chinese restrictions on media coverage

---

[4]*Tibet's architectural heritage:* Tibet is a semi-autonomous region in Central Asia, north of the Himalayan mountains, which has resisted control by the People's Republic of China since it was incorporated into mainland China in 1950.

[5]*Dalai Lama:* Tenzin Gyatso (b. 1935), the 14th Dalai Lama, is a Buddhist spiritual leader who became the head of the Tibetan government in exile after fleeing Chinese-controlled Tibet in 1959.

[6]*Cisco:* Cisco Systems is an American multinational corporation that manufactures and sells computer networking equipment.

[7]*Tiananmen:* In 1989, a seven-week-long series of protests for political reform and free-dom of the press paralyzed Tiananmen Square in central Beijing, in the People's Republic of China.

[8]*Falun Gong:* A spiritual movement banned by the Chinese Communist Party in 1999.

of the fifteenth anniversary of the Tiananmen Square uprising. Yahoo! agreed to help; the journalist received a ten-year jail sentence for "leaking state secrets."

At about the same time, the Chinese government also demanded 20 that Microsoft delete the writings of a free-speech advocate from its blog software. Microsoft complied with this request also, even though the company's servers are based in the United States. In other words, a Chinese government demand had forced an American company to change information on American servers based on American soil, possibly setting a precedent.

Since then, pressure has expanded over the system as a whole. Throughout 2009, U.S. sites such as YouTube (owned by Google) or Flickr (owned by Yahoo!) suddenly and inexplicably disappeared from Chinese servers, usually at a time when some politically sensitive event was taking place in China. (YouTube could not be viewed in China for many months, for example, after videos of Chinese soldiers beating Uighur[9] demonstrators in the rebellious province of Xinjiang began to circulate on the service.)

More generalized harassment has also been directed at Google, which in the summer of 2009 was accused of "spreading pornography." As a result, both of its sites, google.cn and google.com in Chinese, were completely blocked. Off the record, the company suspects that the real source of these accusations is its main Chinese competitor, Baidu, which of course benefits directly whenever Google suffers from technical difficulties. But in the murky and corrupt world of Chinese business and politics — made murkier and more corrupt by the lack of a completely free press — this accusation was difficult to prove.

In June 2009, the Chinese made an attempt to go even further. The government issued orders requiring all personal computers sold in the country to include a special form of filtering software, Green Dam, designed to filter out "unhealthy information" from the Internet. Allegedly aimed, once again, at "pornography," the software would have allowed the government to access its citizens' individual computers, preventing them from reading a constantly updated list of banned websites. It would also have allowed the government to monitor the browsing habits of individuals. "It's like downloading spyware onto your computer," one Hong Kong Internet expert explained, "but the government is the spy."

Full of bugs, and liable to freeze screens, Green Dam would have made all personal computers more difficult to use in general. As if that were not enough, the time allotted to load the software onto new computers was very short—the original deadline gave manufacturers one month—which presented enormous technical problems to any hardware

---

[9]*Uighur:* A Suni Muslim ethnic minority group in Eastern and Central Asia that has in recent years staged violent protests against alleged abuses by authorities of the People's Republic of China.

company selling in China. Nevertheless, two companies—Lenovo, based in China, and Acer, based in Taiwan—complied.

In this case, however, the U.S. companies—computer hardware companies this time, and not merely makers of software and search engines—decided to fight back. Acting as a group, they went to the U.S. trade representative and the commerce secretary, who in turn protested to the Chinese government and threatened to take the issue to the World Trade Organization. After a few weeks, the Chinese government backed off. Although Green Dam remains mandatory in Chinese schools and in Internet cafes, personal computers are not forced to use it—at least not yet. But although that story ended more or less happily, it is worth pausing for a moment to imagine what would have happened had those U.S. companies not banded together, and had they not protested the Chinese government's demands. The software would have been loaded; everyone in China would eventually be forced to use a computer containing government spyware; and the Chinese government would have been strengthened, once again, in its resolve to force foreign companies to collaborate in the mass censorship and limitations on free speech that it places on its own people. U.S. companies would have maintained their ability to sell in China, but over time might well have lost out to the Chinese companies, which are more willing to work closely with the Chinese government to get the results it wants.

And, in the winter of 2010, another crisis showed exactly how this can and will happen: in January, Google announced its intention to pull out of China altogether. The company said that it had been subject to an extraordinary series of cyber-attacks, aimed at entering and spying on the company's servers—as well as gaining access to the email accounts of Chinese and Tibetan dissidents. The company decided to take a principled stand on the issue: its CEO, Eric Schmidt, told *Newsweek* that "this was not a business decision." But, in fact, it was not clear whether Google's announcement was made for moral reasons, or because Chinese cyberhacks threaten the company's critical intellectual property—software codes, documents—as well as its reputation for security.

As of this writing, Google's final decision had not been made, and the company said it was talking to the Chinese government. But the dramatic announcement, coupled with the "Green Dam" fiasco do make one thing clear: large American companies still have the power and strength to challenge the Chinese government, at least when they act together—or at least when they have the size and strength of Google. As the cases of Yale University Press and Condé Nast well illustrate, smaller American companies no longer necessarily have this power, or at least they do not have the courage to find out whether they do. For the record, I note that weakness in the face of rich authoritarians is not an exclusively American trait: the Finnish company Nokia and the German company Siemens have sold cell phone monitoring and silencing equipment to the Iranian government. But the American corporate involvement in China is broader and deeper than that of almost any other country.

I don't want to imply, by discussing all of these stories together, that they are exactly the same. Many nuances exist. Yale does seem to have agonized over its decision not to publish the cartoons; Google, too, has publicly agonized over how it should operate in China, and has argued in the past that at the very least the company can provide Chinese consumers with *more* information, if not *complete* information. Nevertheless, these stories do point, more generally, to something new: even a decade ago it would have been hard to imagine an American university press refusing to print something out of fear of foreign terrorism, or that a large and respectable American company would agree to participate in mass censorship at all.

Indeed, two decades ago, even three and four decades ago, the American press had a reputation for standing up to totalitarian regimes. Moscow correspondents for American newspapers regularly investigated, and then printed, stories that infuriated the governments of the Soviet Union and the Warsaw Pact; as a result, Eastern European dissidents sought out American correspondents. In 1972, *New York Times* correspondent Hedrick Smith and *Washington Post* correspondent Robert Kaiser conducted the historic first interview with Aleksandr Solzhenitsyn.[10] In 1984, another *New York Times* correspondent hosted a party in Warsaw for Adam Michnik,[11] one of the country's most notorious dissidents, on the occasion of his release from jail. Their bosses knew about these escapades, and approved: when Nick Daniloff, a correspondent for *U.S. News and World Report* was arrested and accused of spying in Moscow, the magazine retained former Secretary of State Cyrus Vance as defense attorney; Daniloff remembers getting "great support" from Mortimer Zuckerman, the owner of the magazine. There was no suggestion of conforming to the demands of these totalitarian regimes. Why should there be?

But the world has changed, the financial power of illiberal regimes 30 has grown, the reach of international terrorism stretches further than it once did, and globalization has some unexpected consequences. Among other things, globalization means that consumers of the luxury goods so expensively advertised in Condé Nast magazines increasingly do not live in the United States—hence, the company's need to tailor its content to the tastes of the rich in Russia, China, the Gulf States, and other parts of the world that do not respect the rights of the free press or admire American traditions of investigative journalism. The kinds of

---

[10]*Alexander Solzhenitsyn:* Russian author and dissident (1918–2008) whose writings exposed the brutality of the Soviet concentration camp system.

[11]*Adam Michnik:* Polish historian and essayist (b. 1946) and a leader in the Polish anticommunist movement prior to the fall of the Soviet Union in 1991.

pressures put on newspaper owners are much different from what they used to be.

This shift represents a major cultural change, and it is not one that a law or congressional resolution can correct. On the contrary, the only solution to the new threats to American press freedom lies in organized resistance, as in the case of the Chinese software edicts, and in the widening of debate on this growing threat. Talking and writing help, since many of these decisions are easy enough to justify on an individual basis. But companies confronted by the long-term consequences of their refusals to publish may eventually come to think differently. Sergey Brin, one of Google's founders, said even before the 2010 announcement that it was "a mistake" for Google to enter China, partly because of the continued pressure the company has experienced, but also partly because of the negative consequences on Google's image in its most important market, the United States. A company that once claimed its motto was "Don't Be Evil" proved itself willing at least to dabble in some very evil practices—and, as it turned out, subjected itself to serious security threats as well.

Fortunately, still enough Americans were committed to the principle of free speech to point this out. The more these issues are debated and discussed, in the U.S. media as well as in Congress, the more likely that companies will think twice before making the wrong choices. Attacks on press freedom have always been best countered with more press freedom. That, at least, hasn't yet changed.

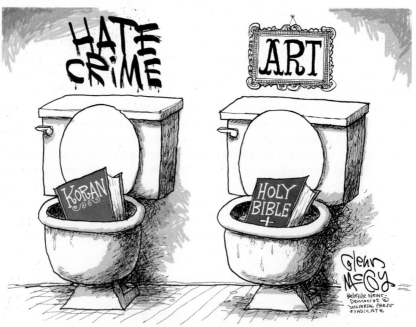

ENGAGING THE TEXT

1. What are the arguments for and against U.S.-based Internet firms like Google, Cisco, and Yahoo! continuing to do business in authoritarian nations like China? To what extent does globalization threaten our own Bill of Rights?

2. Applebaum criticizes corporations like Condé Nast, Cisco, Google, and Microsoft for caving in to pressure from foreign authoritarian regimes. Do you agree that U.S. corporations have a responsibility to support the principles of American democracy in other countries? Why or why not?

3. When the actions of U.S.-based corporations result in the imprisonment or death of dissidents in authoritarian nations like China, should these companies or their executives be held responsible? If so, by whom?

4. What solution does Applebaum offer to the problem of global censorship? How effective do you think her approach to the problem would be? What, if anything, do you think should be done to encourage U.S.-based corporations to resist censorship by foreign powers?

EXPLORING CONNECTIONS

5. Draft an additional amendment for inclusion in the Bill of Rights (p. 628) guaranteeing that U.S. individuals and corporations respect the human rights of foreign nationals. What freedoms would you include in your amendment? How could such an amendment be enforced?

6. How might Naomi Wolf (p. 631) interpret the cases of censorship that Applebaum presents? In what ways can individual Americans resist the kind of censorship Applebaum describes?

EXTENDING THE CRITICAL CONTEXT

7. Go online to view the cartoons that Yale University Press deleted from Jytte Klasen's book, *The Cartoons that Shook the World* (2009). Do you think Yale was right to ban these images in response to complaints from Muslim groups? Why or why not?

DEFYING THE PC POLICE

JUAN WILLIAMS

> *"Look, Bill, I'm not a bigot. You know the kind of books I've written about the civil rights movement in this country. But when I get on the plane, I got to tell you, if I see people who are in Muslim garb and I think, you know, they are identifying themselves first and foremost as Muslims, I get worried. I get nervous."*

On October 18, 2010, just two days after making this statement during an interview on FOX News's *The O'Reilly Factor*, Juan Williams lost his job. He was fired by National Public Radio because NPR management deemed his remarks "inconsistent with our editorial standards and practices" and because his words had "undermined his credibility as a news analyst with NPR." Within hours of his firing, Williams became the focus of a national debate about free speech and political correctness. For many, his termination by NPR symbolized all that's wrong in a nation where worry about offending others trumps First Amendment guarantees. Indeed many Americans today feel that political correctness in the media and in our schools and colleges threatens to undermine the free exchange of ideas that is the foundation of American democracy. An award-winning journalist and political analyst, Williams (b. 1954) now works on the FOX News Channel and writes regularly for the *Washington Post*, the *New York Times*, and the *Wall Street Journal*. His books include *Eyes on the Prize: America's Civil Rights Years, 1954–1965* (1987), *Thurgood Marshall: American Revolutionary* (1998), and *Muzzled: The Assault on Honest Debate* (2011), the source of this selection.

BARTENDERS ARE TOLD to avoid discussing two subjects with drinkers: religion and politics. The reason is pretty obvious. If the bartender offends a customer's religious or political beliefs, the bartender might lose a tip. Even worse, the customer might stop drinking and walk out. The very worst case is if the customer keeps drinking, stays, and begins an argument that drags everyone in the place into a fight and ruins the night for the bar. A bunch of drunks arguing and then punching one another is bad news. It's easy to see how the situation could get out of control. Given the potential for conflict and the incentive of getting money in the tip jar, it's in the interest of the bartender to limit talk to sports and celebrity gossip.

I, however, am not a bartender.

My job is to be better informed than the average citizen and tell you directly what a professional analyst and newsman thinks is really going on behind the headlines. That is what I try to do. The best news analysts describe for their audience the motivations, the desires, the inside baseball behind the basics of a daily news story—the who, what, where, when, and why. My views must be based on good reporting about current events, inside and sometimes off-the-record conversations with sources, and my past experiences. The goal is a strong presentation of all those elements in a logical manner that allows the viewer to understand how I am putting puzzling events together and why I'm thinking that way. To do my job at the highest level, I tell audiences what I know, what I think, and, yes, what I feel about people looking for advantage in power struggles, military engagements, and racial and cultural wars (the very thing NPR's Vivian Schiller and Ellen Weiss[1] criticized me for). The only reason to listen to a professional news analyst is to get into the edgy flow of the political debate about the story—a sense of where the story is going, the insights, the ideas, and the spin, as well as the charges of sham, deceit, and corruption. Audiences dialing up news programs in search of in-depth understanding of the news don't want bartenders.

When Schiller, Weiss, and like-minded news executives claim they are upholding high standards of journalism, they are actually forcing all reporters, commentators, and analysts to tell stories from one approved perspective. It is a perspective that amounts to liberal orthodoxy. They are being politically correct.

It begins with the journalists being forced to act like bartenders. They write and speak in such a way that they avoid having anyone complain—especially powerful people with a constituency. Journalists do this because of weak knees among their bosses, the news executives and managers, who live in fear that some power player will call or write to complain that they didn't like what they read, saw, or heard on the news. So the power players' hypocrisy and lies are allowed to go unchallenged.

The power player might be a big bank or a brokerage house on Wall Street claiming to look out for America while making money by closing down American industry and shipping jobs overseas. The powerful might also be an activist, say, Al Sharpton; a politician, such as Sarah Palin; or the White House press secretary. But there are other examples that can be more difficult to see. For example, what do you do with the story of a big-city summer jobs program for poor kids in which the young people sit around all day doing nothing and still collect a check at the end of the week? Do you report on the scam or keep a politically correct silence about how the city keeps young people from stirring up trouble during the hot summer months? Here is another example of stories that go untold while journalists pretend to be bartenders. People stand to applaud the tremendous sacrifice of American

[1]*Vivian Schiller and Ellen Weiss:* Former president and vice president of National Public Radio, both of whom resigned in the wake of the Williams incident. [All notes are the editors' unless otherwise indicated.]

soldiers even as polls show an overwhelming majority in opposition to any talk about renewing a universal draft or even a two-year national service commitment for young people. Few point out the inconsistency. No one wants to be the skunk at the garden party. No one wants to say the emperor has no clothes. No one wants to lose a tip. Similarly, our representatives in Congress refuse to deal with immigration reform. Yet it is commonplace for them to hire illegal immigrants as babysitters, contractors, and housecleaners (as well as to allow them to pick lettuce or work in factories in their districts or states). And politicians condemn drug dealers while the nation refuses to discuss why the United States is the top market in the world for consumption of illegal drugs.

The acceptance of hypocrisy and outright fabrication in journalism is a threat to the nation. It marks the end of free expression and the flow of information and ideas that are the basis for the informed debate that is essential to democracy. Much of the media plays along as baseball players, their heads as big as pumpkins, pretend not to use steroids, as bankers get rich even as they wreck the economy by giving mortgages to people who can't afford the monthly payments, as pornographic movies outsell Hollywood movies, without a word about the impact on culture, children, and families. Everyone becomes complicit in the silence.

"Politically correct" is a major theme of our times that extends far beyond journalism. Over the past few decades, the rules of bartender etiquette have been applied to the national conversation in bizarre and dangerous ways. The pernicious rule governing all conversation and debate is that even if the person you are talking to is not directly offended by your opinions, someone else within earshot might be. And if the two people are alone, their comments might be repeated or relayed at some later time in some other place and might offend someone somewhere else. In this PC environment, the preferred course of action is to not voice opinions on any controversial topic unless you know you are in the company of people with similar opinions. Always play the bartender. Americans are constantly walking on eggshells under these rules. Like the bartender, they reasonably conclude that it is better to go along to get along. Honest and constructive discussion is not worth the price they might pay if their opinions are deemed politically incorrect.

So how did we get to this point? What happened to the American ideal of being free to speak truth to the powerful? How did we become so damn politically correct that we stopped having honest conversations and debate?

"Political correctness" is one of the most controversial terms in the 10 lexicon of today's public discourse. As politics have become more bitterly polarized in recent years, even the meaning of the term "politically correct" seems to change depending on who is speaking and who is listening. In recent years, the Right and the Left seem to have their own stable of historians, sociologists, and even linguists that they trot out to deliver expertise that supports their views on who is guilty of being politically incorrect.

Both the left wing and the right wing are heavily invested in the fight over what it means to be "politically correct." That is because the winner of that fight earns the right to decide the vocabulary of acceptable terms and labels. It allows one side or the other to own the debate, control the airwaves, and stir a base of funders and grassroots fans. This fight is the backdrop to nearly every debate in America today. As for the middle ground, it is shunned as a kind of no-man's-land.

Every issue is loaded with a set of "with us or against us" terms. Even within groups of like-minded people, we are told what we can say and can't say. I sometimes feel out of place saying "happy holidays" to my colleagues at Fox because in conservative circles that term can be taken as evidence that you are part of the effort to undermine Christmas. NPR banned the use of the term "pro-life" because the liberal managers felt it put a happy face on the antiabortion message. They were willing to sacrifice the term "pro-choice," used by supporters of abortion rights, rather than accept "pro-life" (afterward, they would point out that people who support abortion rights aren't antilife). This same crazy dynamic applies to political fights. When I point out that Israel is an occupying force with settlements outside its borders, I am called an anti-Semite; and as you know, when I confess to a fear of Islamic extremism, I am called an anti-Muslim bigot.

By definition, political correctness means—and here I am quoting the *Oxford English Dictionary*—"the avoidance, often considered as taken to extremes, of forms of expression or action that are perceived to exclude, marginalize, or insult groups of people who are socially disadvantaged or discriminated against." Historians have found instances where the words "politically correct" appeared in print as early as the 1700s. The early meaning was much more literal and referred solely to the accuracy of a statement. Offense, real or perceived, did not figure into the definition. For example, "New York has more votes than Rhode Island in the Electoral College" was once known as a "politically correct" statement.

PC began to take on its new, more familiar meaning in the 1960s and 1970s. At first it was a term of self-criticism used by people on the Left, including civil rights activists and leaders of campus groups organizing against the Vietnam War, but especially in the cultural battles being fought over women's rights by leading feminists. The idea back then was that it was ironic for feminists committed to breaking down old social barriers to put up new walls by insisting that women all had to grow hair on their legs, burn their bras, and give up lipstick. That extreme attitude was condemned by women sympathetic to the movement with the dismissive use of the term "politically correct." And the idea was a winner because it brought more people to the movement by allowing women to set their own pace for their liberation from male domination.

What also became apparent during the sixties was the importance 15 of the emerging TV news coverage of left-wing social movements and the strategic importance of controlling the language used by reporters. The general idea, which has some basis in psychology and linguistic theory, is that there is a real connection among language, thought, and action. It was a first glimpse of future culture wars as leaders in liberal movements began insisting on new language in the name of fairness but with the real goal of changing politics and society by establishing a vocabulary of acceptable terms and language for people who cared about equality and justice. Soon it was not acceptable for the television network correspondents covering the civil rights movement to talk about "Negroes" or "Colored people." The proper reference was to "blacks" and later "African Americans." The movement for equal rights for Indians became a "Native Americans" movement. People began to refer to the chairman of a group as the "chairperson" or simply "the chair" in recognition that the chair could be a woman.

Comedians including Lenny Bruce, Richard Pryor, and George Carlin lampooned America's hypocrisy in banning from radio and TV the same vulgar epithets and profanity that were being used every day at home and on the street. Carlin became famous for his routine "The Seven Words You Can Never Say on Television." He skewered the American acceptance of euphemistic language that obscured reality, from sexual practices to racism, that Americans did not want to talk about.

The people jiggering with the engine of popular language used by news correspondents, politicians, and comedians in the sixties succeeded in making everyday people more aware of racism, sexism, and stereotypes of all sorts. This could be described as the post–World War II era of the opening of the American mind. The big idea was increased awareness leading to empathy, a new conception of how America could improve its practice of democratic ideals and finally effect real change in the form of civil rights laws and equal opportunities for women in the workplace. Discomfort in the nation with racial segregation and the government's questionable conduct of the Vietnam War provided a fertile environment for these ideas that challenged the established political order to take root. There was a superficial feel to some of these linguistic changes, but anyone who dismissed them as a passing fad had it wrong. The changes in popular language soon became changes in our textbook accounts of history; literature was scrutinized for its "Eurocentric canon" promoting the "white male power structure."

In a burst, universities agreed to create whole new academic departments, such as Black Studies, Latino Studies, and Women's Studies. "Critical theory" courses also became prominent during that time, essentially teaching that the transformation of Western society can be achieved through unremitting and deconstructive criticism of every institution in Western society. Critical theorists did not view institutions in the traditional sense as just business, government, education, and the like. They viewed these institutions as representations of social inequality when it came to race, class, gender, sexual orientation, and politics.

To left-wing intellectuals, this new "critical theory" approach revealed major American institutions as defenders of the status quo—protecting the wealthy, the powerful, and racial majorities. The animating idea behind "critical theory" is that these institutions should be deconstructed in the name of achieving genuine equality.

David Horowitz, a sixties campus leftist turned conservative writer, has written extensively about this period of history. He became a conservative because he was repulsed by the ever-widening constraints of politically correct behavior that made it impossible for him to express a different point of view to his fellow left-wingers without being dismissed as a sellout working for "the man" or an "Uncle Tom."

Horowitz was just one voice in a brewing backlash that extended 20 far beyond the American campus. Conservatives began to point out that the culture of political correctness was a hammer to bludgeon national politics and news reports into conformity with a liberal point of view. The right wing felt the left wing had co-opted the debate by finding a way to shut up people who defended American traditions and conservative principles. As a result, the political right wing began to fight politically correct campus "speech codes" and "hate codes," complaining that American colleges and universities basically indoctrinated top students in leftist thinking. Nobel Prize-winning writer Saul Bellow told *The New Yorker* that political correctness was "free speech without debate." Novelist Doris Lessing, another Nobel Prize winner, called political correctness "the offspring of Marxist dialectics."

After liberal Democratic president Jimmy Carter was rejected in favor of the Republican conservative Ronald Reagan, who had fought political correctness on California's college campuses as governor, the right wing became outspoken in rejecting liberals as an angry minority tearing down American institutions and traditions. With the help of Christian conservative groups like the Moral Majority, the Right convinced people that Christianity, by far the most popular religion in the United States, was under siege by a minority of liberal secularists in the name of political correctness. Even though it had its own rules setting limits on any criticism of Christianity, the right wing positioned itself as anti-political correctness. The conservatives became holy warriors with a mission to protect the faith from the secular PC attack machine. The strategy at work for conservatives was to give political correctness a bad name and, by extension, give liberalism a bad name. To conservatives, political correctness embodied everything that was wrong and evil about liberalism. They hung this idea around their opponents' necks like an albatross and watched with relish as it dragged liberalism into disrepute and damaged left-wing politics.

The intense racial tensions of the era became part of the jousting. The idea of forced racial equality—specifically quotas—became part of the conversation as evidence that political correctness included giving jobs to unqualified people in the name of equal rights. Playing to residual racism in the postintegration South, conservatives convinced a large segment of white voters, the majority in the region, that they were being threatened by liberal Democrats, who represented Northerners, Jews, immigrants, and racial minorities, especially black people. This was the premise of Jesse Helms's famous television advertisement in his North Carolina Senate campaign against Harvey Gantt. A pair of white hands crumples up a job rejection letter as a narrator says, "You needed that job. You were the best qualified, but they had to give it to a minority because of a racial quota." Even black radio talk show host Larry Elder picked up on the angst of whites when he questioned why the phrase "white trash" was acceptable when it was forbidden to talk that way about blacks, Hispanics, or Asians. The argument that whites have never been an enslaved and despised minority in the country failed to halt the slide in political correctness, because the counterargument undermined the heart of the argument for political correctness—equality for all. In addition, Jews, Irish, Italians, and other white ethnicities had their stories of discrimination and oppression. The serious message being loudly heard across American culture by the 1990s was that political correctness was not just an instance of fun and games among the intellectual class. To conservative white men and some white women, political correctness, affirmative action, and even talk of reparations for slavery were a very threatening reality that made it harder to get a job and get their children into college. It generally made them feel as if they had slipped under the thumb of an intellectual regime alien to their upbringing, their traditions, and their pride in America as the leading force for right in the world.

During Reagan's tenure in the White House, the Republican Party had found it could make huge political gains by playing to the so-called culture wars, in which conservatives became victims of liberal attacks on traditions and institutions central to American life. The most salient examples of the culture wars were incidents of excessive political correctness—such as calls not to have schools teach great books because they were written by "dead white men." But they extended into so-called political wedge issues, such as abortion, gun rights, and gay rights, which gave voters a stark choice of identifying with one side or the other. Conservative politicians found that a lot of white working-class Americans decided to side with them in the comfort of the voting booth because of discomfort with the fast pace of social change required by political correctness.

Members of the Right practiced ideological judo by using the ferocity of left-wing adherence to every politically correct position to mock the Left as self-righteous and given to censorship. They cast liberalism as the opposite of freedom, individual rights, and constitutional protections. University of Chicago professor Allan Bloom wrote a best-selling book, *The Closing of the American Mind,* which argued that political correctness in American schools was undermining academic freedom, intellectual debate, and overall scholarship. Bloom asked how anyone could speak or write in any course of study without fear of offending the high priests of political correctness. Democratic presidential candidate Michael Dukakis was asked by CNN's Bernie Shaw if he would want the death penalty for a man who raped and murdered his wife. Dukakis could not bring himself to say yes. It would have been a repudiation of liberal opposition to the death penalty. Conservatives pounced.

The backlash against politically correct thinking became pronounced in the early 1990s. The *New York Times* published articles about several incidents of PC run wild. "At San Francisco State University, a black professor was reviled by students for teaching in the political science department rather than in black studies," according to one story. The *Times* also found instances where a Harvard student was not only rebuked by other students but punished by the school's administration for hanging a Confederate flag out the window. At Stanford, students demanded an end to core curriculum in Western civilization and demanded a new approach called "Cultures, Ideas and Values" that the *Times* said focused on "non-European, non-white studies."

This coincided with long-standing efforts that had largely been initiated in the 1970s to eliminate American Indian names for sports teams. Major schools, including Marquette, Stanford, the University of Massachusetts, and the University of Wisconsin at La Crosse, all changed their nicknames over this time period. Marquette, for example, changed from "the Warriors" to "the Golden Eagles." All of this aggravated alumni and traditionalists. In this new world it was a crime to say that a person was blind. To be politically correct you had to say that person was "visually challenged." A handicapped person was "physically challenged," and a retarded person was only to be described as "mentally challenged." ...

Now it is largely the Left that decries limits on free speech such as those imposed by the Patriot Act after 9/11. And it was not just the law giving liberals rightful fits but also the conservative push to shut down debate about the terrorist attacks and halt criticism of the U.S. military response in Afghanistan and Iraq. The most famous instance occurred when Bill Maher on his late-night show, by then on ABC network television but appropriately still called *Politically Incorrect,* said with his usual fearlessness, "We [Americans] have been the cowards, lobbing cruise missiles from two thousand miles away. That's cowardly. Staying in the airplane when it hits the building, say what you want about it, it's not cowardly." Ironically, when he made these statements, Maher was *agreeing* with a conservative guest, Dinesh D'Souza, when he said that the 9/11 hijackers were not cowards because they stayed in the airplanes as they hit the buildings. If Maher had not affirmed D'Souza's comment about the perverse bravery of the terrorists, nothing might have ever come of it. D'Souza, with his conservative street cred, wasn't going to be lambasted as a traitor, was he? ABC was reportedly pressured to fire Maher after advertisers threatened to pull their sponsorship from his program, and Maher's show was canceled the following year, in large part due to ratings and advertising troubles presumed to have resulted from the backlash against his comments. Bush White House press secretary Ari Fleischer criticized Maher and, in a controversial statement of his own, warned people from the lectern in the White House briefing room to be careful about what they say.

That was seen by the Left and much of the rest of the country as a chilling threat to First Amendment rights. The Far Left began hauling out analogies between the Bush White House and Joe McCarthy, the Wisconsin senator who smeared liberals in the 1950s with largely baseless charges of being communist sympathizers. Instead of being called insensitive or offensive for violating a speech code under the rules of politically correct behavior, conservatives attacked antiwar protesters as people who hated America. Even the language being used in newspapers to describe the U.S. war effort became an issue when Vice President Cheney insisted that waterboarding terrorists—flooding a suspect's covered head with water to create the sensation of drowning—was not "torture." Scott Horton, writing in *Harper's* magazine, said the decision by the top editor of the *New York Times*, Bill Keller, not to label waterboarding as torture amounted to following "politically correct" dictates coming from conservatives. "This is not merely being politically correct; it is being politically subordinate. . . . Bill Keller's political correctness couldn't be more clear cut. . . . This is precisely the sort of political manipulation of language that George Orwell warned against in 'Politics and the English Language.' " . . .

At its core, political correctness relies on tribalism, an "us versus them" mentality. It is about cultivating identity groups and placing people into convenient boxes where they think and act and speak in predictable ways. In recent years, people and groups from all points on the political spectrum have used this fragmentation to their advantage. They use it to attain and expand their political power, whether it's by generating media attention or raising money. They use it to insulate and protect their constituents so that whenever a controversy comes along, they can go to the appropriate box and produce victims who will echo their sense of outrage.

The tremendous growth of media, with cable TV and the Internet offering niche outlets to fit any specific political taste—thereby atomizing the idea of a big-tent, mainstream media where everyone can tell their story and hear the other side—and decades of greater class divisions and political polarization have brought us to this point. There is no clear incentive for anyone involved to change the tone and the nature of the conversation. Politicians who utilize PC tactics regularly win at the ballot box. Lobbyists and special-interest advocacy groups are more influential and better funded than ever before. Their favorite weapon is to charge any opposing camp with being insensitive and even offensive—in other words, politically incorrect. Television ratings and Web traffic numbers are shattering records and soaring with any report about politically insensitive statements, such as the burst of online hits after Ann Coulter labeled the 9/11 widows "witches" and "harpies"

30

or Tucker Carlson pronounced himself a Christian who nonetheless thought football player Michael Vick should have been "executed" for staging dogfights. This problem did not happen overnight, and it will not be fixed overnight.

The goal of these political tactics is changing America to fit one's preferred vision—making sure one's ideas come out on top. The genius of America is that reactionary groups rarely achieve progress. But good arguments, persistence, and appeals to conscience that challenge the majority at critical junctures—see the civil rights movement and particularly Dr. Martin Luther King Jr.—actually *change* the majority and become "mainstream." This dynamic was first expressed by James Madison in Federalist No. 10. The idea is that only the best ideas and movements will survive and have the wide-scale appeal to rise and withstand exposure to vigorous national debate....

ENGAGING THE TEXT

1. How does Williams view the proper role of the journalist? What, in his opinion, prevents journalists from fulfilling this role? How do you think journalists should deal with their own values and biases?

2. What does Williams mean when he says that we now live in a "PC environment" ruled by "bartender etiquette." To what extent would you agree that "Americans are constantly walking on eggshells" today (para. 8)?

3. Williams notes that the language we use affects public policy and social attitudes. Do you think that the use of "politically correct" terms, like "African American," "Native American," and "physically challenged"—or the avoidance of demeaning racial- or gender-related language—reflects a genuine change in American attitudes and values? Or is all of this just another form of censorship?

4. Ultimately what does Williams think that PC culture is doing to us? Do you agree? Do you think society would benefit if all Americans felt empowered to say anything on their minds, regardless of the situation or the words they chose? Why or why not?

EXPLORING CONNECTIONS

5. How do you imagine the authors of the Declaration (p. 625) and the Bill of Rights (p. 628) would feel about political correctness? Is there a difference, in your view, between freedom of speech and the freedom to say anything you want to say?

6. What connection can you see between the kind of corporate self-censorship Anne Applebaum describes (p. 638) and the political correctness Williams detects in American culture? Is Yale's decision to censor the Mohammed cartoons or Google's decision to collaborate with Chinese authorities just another form of political correctness?

7. Would you consider curbing of the kind of antifemale violence in advertising that Jean Kilbourn describes in Chapter Four (p. 420) as a form of PC censorship? What can't advertisers do or say in ads today? Should they have complete freedom?

8. How might Michael Kimmel's analysis of male stereotypes in Chapter Four (p. 461) challenge the notion that people who express sexist ideas are demonstrating their "freedom"?

EXTENDING THE CRITICAL CONTEXT

9. Do some research to find out if your college has a formal speech code for professors and students. If you have a formal code, to what extent do you think it censors free speech? In general, how "PC" is the student and the classroom culture on your campus? Would you change it if you could, and why?

10. Research examples of censorship at American colleges over the past three or four years. What kinds of situations typically involve censorship? Who is typically censored? By whom and why? How often do these cases appear to involve what Williams would term "excessive political correctness"?

11. Which of the following would you ban at your college and why?

   • Burning the U.S. flag

   • The public use of offensive racial- or gender-related language or images

   • The controversial use of religious images in signs, publications, or works of art

   • Images of animals being killed or tortured

   • Images of fetuses being aborted

   • X-rated films in classes or the cinema club

   • The ability to access pornographic material on college computers

   • Display of the Confederate flag

   • Display of symbols associated with hate groups like the Ku Klux Klan

THIS MODERN WORLD
by TOM TOMORROW

THE WAR ON NEGATIVE LIBERTY
KATHERINE MANGU-WARD

You may not know it, but in the 1960s, college classrooms and libraries often came equipped with ashtrays. Today it's hard to imagine a world where students could light up just about anywhere on campus. Since the birth of modern environmentalism and growing awareness about the risks of tobacco and other consumer goods, Americans have gotten used to government regulators making decisions to protect public health—from the amount of ozone our cars can emit to the level of trans fats in our favorite snack food. But for many Americans, the so-called "nanny state" has gone too far in its desire to shield us from every conceivable harm. In fact, government regulation is now seen by some, including the author of this selection, as a profound threat to our fundamental freedoms. Kathrine Mangu-Ward is a Libertarian journalist who has written for the *Washington Post*, the *Wall Street Journal*, and the *Weekly Standard*. A graduate of Yale University, she is currently the managing editor of *Reason* magazine and Reason.com.

IN EARLY 2001, near Jalalabad, Afghanistan, a group of women gathered to eat ice cream in secret. Since agents of the Taliban's[1] Department for the Promotion of Virtue and Prevention of Vice often attacked Afghan women caught enjoying a scoop in public, the group took the precaution of ducking into a neglected restaurant in the back of a bazaar and settled within a protective wall of hanging sheets. Once inside, they carefully lifted their burqas[2] and spooned up forbidden bowls of vanilla ice cream. American playwright and activist Eve Ensler, who described this scene in her book, *The Good Body*, recounts the warning of her guide, Sunita: "If we get caught, it could mean a flogging or even an execution. It depends on what kind of mood the Taliban are in today." Rumors that Taliban men were circling the bazaar in pickup trucks soon set the women to flight, their ice cream barely finished.

Ice Cream in Brooklyn

Now imagine a place as far from Taliban-controlled Afghanistan as possible. It's August 2009, and the ice cream man is jingling through Brooklyn's Prospect Park. An idyllic American scene, yet parents are on edge. Vicki Sell, mother of three-year-old Katherine, told the *New York Times* she considers the behavior of the bell-ringing vendors "predatory." The jingle, say the Brooklyn parents, turns children into whining beggars. The sugar and additives in the ice cream make them hyperactive monsters. And the ice cream peddler lurks in the area long after his line of initial customers is gone, forcing parents to rebuff a new barrage of pleas every few minutes. Sell says she has repeatedly called the city's 311 complaint line in an effort to evict the unlicensed vendors, and would like to see them banned from the park.

At first glance, any comparison between the gentle beeping of a Brooklyn mom dialing 311 on her iPhone and the roar of the Taliban pickup truck seems absurd. But it remains true that both want the same thing—a targeted ban on ice cream.

The Taliban forbids ice cream to women for symbolic reasons. It is decadent, Western, and hard to eat gracefully in a burqa. In Afghanistan, the state seeks not just political control, not just personal obedience, but dominion over the souls of the men and women who live under the watchful eyes of the virtue police. To ban ice cream consumption in public is to proclaim that the sphere of individual liberty does not extend even to the inner folds of the women's voluminous burqas. For those women, any freedom that can be found must be minuscule, fleeting, and necessarily illusory, collapsed into a few furtive bites of ice cream.

---

[1] *Taliban:* A conservative, militant Islamist group opposing the United States in the war in Afghanistan. [All notes are the editors' unless otherwise indicated.]
[2] *burqas:* Head-to-foot outer garments worn by Muslim women.

By contrast, the Brooklyn moms support bans for purely practical reasons. Dealing with the ice cream truck is inconvenient, and they would rather not bother. Whether or not they succeed in banning the jingle of the ice cream man, as Americans they will continue to operate within a vast sphere of liberty. Their children scamper around in a world of free association, free speech, and free movement. They have robust expectations that they will enjoy a large degree of privacy in their own homes and move largely unmolested in public.

Yet there is a strange kinship between the Taliban and the Brooklyn parents. Both worry about what is lost in the pursuit of corporeal pleasures. They sense the oppressiveness of unhealthy desires. They are daunted by the prospect of taking responsibility for setting their own limits. The Taliban might brandish the language of virtue and vice in pursuit of total control, but their alarm at the prospect of helplessness in the face of temptation is just as real as that of the Brooklyn parents. And so the response is the same: A call for the state to set limits for them on their own seemingly inconsequential behaviors—and for everyone else around them.

The Brooklyn parents undoubtedly consider themselves to be freedom-loving Americans. But how could people who cherish freedom clamor for the state to take away their choices? Isaiah Berlin's now-familiar distinction[3] between the two types of liberty helps clear up the confusion. Negative liberty, or "freedom from," hinges on the idea of noninterference. True liberty, say John Stuart Mill,[4] Benjamin Constant,[5] Friedrich Hayek,[6] and others who champion this view, consists in carving out the largest possible area where individuals will be left alone to do as they please.

The Brooklyn moms have an entirely different concept of liberty, one that Berlin calls positive liberty: the freedom to fulfill your potential. The liberty of Jean-Jacques Rousseau,[7] Karl Marx,[8] and John Rawls[9] senses threats not only from an encroaching state or violent individuals, but from circumstances like poverty or ignorance as well. Under this conception of liberty—often used to support causes such as universal health insurance and unemployment benefits—freedom can be threatened by someone's own bad inclinations or unhealthy habits.

---

[3]*Isaiah Berlin's now-familiar distinction:* Sir Isaiah Berlin (1909–1997) was a British social critic, philosopher, and essayist who presented the ideas of positive and negative liberty in "Two Concepts of Liberty," a 1958 lecture at Oxford University.

[4]*John Stuart Mill:* British philosopher and political economist (1806–1873).

[5]*Benjamin Constant:* Henri-Benjamin Constant de Rebecque (1767–1830), Swiss-born French politician and early champion of political liberalism.

[6]*Friedrich Hayek:* Friedrich August Hayek (1899–1992) was an Austrian-born economist and political philosopher known for his support of liberalism and free market capitalism.

[7]*Jean-Jacques Rousseau:* Swiss-born philosopher, writer, and composer (1712–1778) whose ideas on democratic government influenced the French Revolution.

[8]*Karl Marx:* Karl Heinrich Marx (1818–1883), German philosopher, economist, and historian whose works inspired the development of modern socialism and communism.

[9]*John Rawls:* John Bordley Rawls (1921–2002), American philosopher known for his work on social justice.

"Once I take this view" that even one's own desires can threaten liberty, writes Berlin, "I am in a position to ignore the actual wishes of men or societies, to bully, oppress, torture in the name, and on behalf, of their 'real' selves, in the secure knowledge that whatever is the true goal of man (happiness, performance of duty, wisdom, a just society, self-fulfillment) must be identical with his freedom—the free choice of his 'true,' albeit often submerged and inarticulate, self."

This is why the Taliban and the Brooklyn moms can come to the same conclusion about ice cream bans. While they disagree on the parts of the self that need to be checked or limited—and the Brooklyn moms prefer democracy to determine those limits—they agree that state intervention to limit highly personal choices will make people better, and even freer. 10

Cigarettes in New York

Positive liberty has been ascendant in the United States since the early twentieth century. All around us, dings and dents appear in the surface of the sphere of negative liberty, disfiguring it, perhaps beyond recognition.

Consider the case of smoking bans. Setting aside health concerns about secondhand smoke, much of the discussion about restricting smokers rests on the desirability of discouraging them from harming themselves with their irresponsible behavior. When New York's ban on smoking in bars or restaurants sends smokers out into the cold and rainy streets, that's a feature, not a bug. As the list of places where smoking is not permitted grows longer, smoking becomes less appealing. Choice remains, but unhealthy impulses are circumscribed by increasingly restrictive rules. The same arguments are made for increasing taxes on cigarettes—to extract additional tax money from smokers is to do them a favor. After all, they shouldn't be spending that money on cigarettes in the first place. Supporters of smoking bans nearly always present their view, at least in part, as altruism. And the smokers themselves often buy into the argument. In his 1998 book on smoking regulation, *For Your Own Good,* Jacob Sullum quotes a Kentucky smoker on a cigarette tax increase in 1990: "I hope they price them out of my range, because I am really wanting to stop."

Those who lobby for and approve of smoking bans and ice cream-free zones don't see the ever-growing list of banned behaviors as an infringement of liberty. Instead, restrictions like these are a convenient and practical solution to the problem of what Berlin called "the divided self." All people have both good and bad impulses. The bad impulses can be powerful, stopping us from making good choices just as surely as a law might. This is why mothers want the ice cream truck's jingle taken away—to minimize the chance of bad choices not only in their children, but also in themselves. After all, holding firm against the onslaught of whining is a tough task. Those who propose nanny-state[10] bans and taxes often see themselves simply as removing temptations, reshaping desires, or otherwise limiting the availability of "bad options." They seek to realize a form of positive liberty.

Three years after the smoking ban, the New York City Board of Health voted to ban the use of trans fats in food served in restaurants. The logic behind the ban was identical to the justification of smoking bans. Although the science is clear on the harmfulness of these particular fats, people will not spontaneously give them up—trans fats are just too delicious in donuts, fried chicken, and pie crusts. Regulation requiring calorie counts on menus continues down this road, albeit more subtly. These mandates deprive people of the choice to remain ignorant. What was a punch line just a few years back ("What are they going to do next, ban donuts?") becomes a reality before the joke, or the donuts, have time to get stale. The trans fat ban was accomplished under the supervision of New York City Health Commissioner Thomas Frieden, now the head of the national Centers for Disease Control and Prevention. Fully assuming the role of parent, Frieden told the *Financial Times* that he felt "when anyone dies at an early age from a preventable cause in New York City, it's my fault."

A softer form of the same view has recently come on the scene 15 under the name "libertarian paternalism." As described by legal scholar Cass Sunstein, now the head of the U.S. Office of Information and Regulatory Affairs, and University of Chicago economist Richard Thaler in their 2008 book *Nudge,* the state should expand its practice of deciding which inclinations are good and which are bad, and then nudging citizens in the direction of the good (while not explicitly outlawing the bad). Call it positive liberty light.

Foie Gras[11] in Chicago

A new tax on Twinkies or hot dogs, both bêtes noires[12] of antiobesity crusaders, takes only a small chunk out of the sphere of negative liberty. The general population won't take much notice one way or the other, and those who do will be divided between the negative- and positive-liberty view. But any limit on Twinkie consumption is a hard blow to the competitive eater. There's always something else delicious on the menu if foie gras is banned, as it was briefly in Chicago from 2006 to 2008, but it's a sad loss for the chef who has been striving to perfect his searing technique for decades—and for his customers.

---

[10]*nanny-state:* British term for overprotective and intrusive government.

[11]*Foie Gras:* The sale of foie gras, a paste made from the livers of force-fed geese, has been banned by several city and state governments.

[12]*bêtes noire:* French for "black beast," a *bête noire* is a person or thing that is detested or avoided.

The Taliban doesn't care if it's a hot day, or if you have a sweet tooth, or if you've been looking forward to ice cream all week. In free societies where a philosophy of positive liberty is ascendant, the dynamic plays out differently, but the idea is the same. A handful of people may be disappointed when they don't find foie gras on the menu. But if their culinary whims interfere with the larger goals of maximizing the chances of self-actualization, the Chicago City Council couldn't care less.

"The smaller is the domain where choices among alternatives are made collectively," Anthony de Jasay wrote in 1997, "the smaller will be the probability that any individual's preference gets overruled." Yet people leap in eagerly to assist the state in overruling choices of which they disapprove. The Energy Policy Act of 1992 limited American showerheads to 2.5 gallons per minute. Recently, *Consumer Reports* went looking for the best showerhead. They found one from a British manufacturer that was stellar. Too good to be legal, in fact, since the fixture's multiple heads cause it to exceed water-use limits. The product reviewers at the magazine took it upon themselves to "contact" the Environmental Protection Agency. Rather than enjoying a bit of essentially harmless duck-and-weave around the law, citizens report on each other for violations—even while acknowledging that those violations have offered a far better product.

In a similar sad tale, European Parliament Directive 2005/32/EG banned the sale and importation of one-hundred-watt incandescent bulbs starting September 1, 2009, with lower wattages phasing out over time. Getting caught selling wasteful old-style bulbs brings a whopping seventy-thousand-dollar fine. A functionally identical ban goes into effect in the United States in 2012, justified by the need to reduce energy use in the face of global warming.

Compact fluorescents do use much less energy than their old-fashioned incandescent cousins. Never mind that the flickery blue of fluorescents in America's (cost-conscious) office buildings have become synecdoche[13] for the soul-crushing aspects of life as part of a large bureaucratic organization. They manage to illuminate things, anyway. Plus, they reduce electricity bills for most people. We should be happy! In the face of such scientific urgency and budgetary practicality, a 1783 reply from British Prime Minister William Pitt's pronouncement might sound old-fashioned and out of date: "Necessity is the plea for every infringement of human freedom. It is the argument of tyrants. It is the creed of slaves." After all, if there is only one kind of lightbulb in the stores, that is the kind of bulbs that people will buy. As the memory of the old choices fade, people often do not feel like slaves at all. Certainly, they do not experience freedom differently than they did before environmentally friendly compact fluorescent bulbs were invented, and

20

[13]*synecdoche:* A figure of speech in which a part of something is used to refer to the whole; for example, "farm hand" is a synecdoche for farm worker.

they could only choose incandescents for their table lamps. The average person who prefers the old bulbs can even stockpile enough bulbs to light their houses for a good while. Sales of incandescent bulbs were up 150 percent in the European Union in August 2009, but stashes of the bulbs won't last forever.

Once again, however, individuals with preferences slightly outside the ordinary lose out in the pursuit of positive liberty. The EU ban makes no exception for artists or museums. Yet to substitute long-lasting, environmentally friendly compact fluorescent bulbs into exhibits like Felix Gonzalez-Torres's 1993 installation *Untitled (Strange Music)*—a stark jumble of old-fashioned incandescent bulbs intended to burn out and be replaced—would change the piece beyond recognition.

By and large, citizens will remain unmoved by the plight of the work of Gonzalez-Torres, or the bulb-intensive creations of artists like Laszlo Moholy-Nagy, Olafur Eliasson, Carsten Höller, or Jorge Pardo.[14] Given the steady stream of bans "for your own good," and the still-absent squads of jackbooted thugs breaking into our homes, most of the time Americans (and this goes double for Europeans) acquiesce—after all, there's a kid in the background whining for ice cream, and it's distracting.

This is why advocates of negative liberty must add a caveat. Not only must I be free from interference with what I would like to do today, I must have a reasonable expectation I will be free to do what I like within my sphere of liberty tomorrow as well. Perhaps I, too, will want to become a modern lightbulb artist. Surely this should be one of the choices available to a free person. The incursions associated with positive liberty make no promises about where they draw the line on interference in the name of freeing the good self from the tyranny of the bad self. As Edmund Burke[15] put it, "The great inlet by which a colour for oppression has entered into the world is by one man's pretending to determine concerning the happiness of another."

A Cup of Tea in Boston

Positive liberty is ascendant in part because it is so easy to let the fights over daily inconveniences or restrictions slide. Larger infringements, when long-established, go uncontested as well. Extract thousands of dollars from their paychecks each month, and the American people will collectively shrug. But every now and then, the people will leap to the defense of liberty. Catch them at the right moment, and people can get exercised about the most unexpected things.

---

[14]*Laszlo Moholy-Nagy, Olafur Eliasson, Carsten Höller ... Jorge Pardo:* Famous twentieth-century artists.

[15]*Edmund Burke:* Irish statesman, author, and philosopher (1729–1797) who was the founder of modern British conservativism.

Sometimes the smallest, seemingly silliest infringements on per- 25 sonal liberty can be the most effective recruitment tools for the cause of liberty. The greatest example in history of a people fighting tooth-and-claw for negative liberties, of course, started with a tax on tea. A small tax on a luxury good should have been irrelevant to the American colonists in the face of larger concerns about the conduct of their distant government. Most of the colonists were drinking smuggled tea anyway. But the refusal of Boston's Royal Governor Thomas Hutchinson to give in to public pressure, as other officials had, and send the taxed tea back to Britain, was a small act weighted with symbolism. The British didn't want to lift the tax on Americans largely because it wanted to symbolically assert that it *could* tax Americans. The colonists responded to this symbolism with some of their own, and hoisted the tea into the harbor.

One might be forgiven for wondering if modern Americans would have the gumption to follow the steps of the Boston tea party patriots. But while it's not quite the same magnitude, Americans—New Yorkers, to be specific—did recently show a little of the old inclination to bang a few dents out of the sphere of negative liberty. This chapter may have started with ice cream. But in the end, all discussions about Americans and liberty must come back to caffeinated beverages.

Tone deaf and cash strapped, newly minted New York governor David Paterson looked around for things to tax at the end of 2008. Unlike the tax that inspired the Boston tea party, Paterson's proposal to tax full-sugar soda at an additional 15 percent wasn't a power grab. It was just more of the same. Paterson saw a great opportunity for a little more positive liberty—people want to be thin, yet they drink soda—plus a chance to make some money. The rebellion was nothing much: a few bloggers got angry, a couple of newspapers published editorials, a poll or two was taken, and that was enough to signal a little electoral discontent. So the already insecure new governor let the tax go. He took recourse instead in a public-service ad campaign showing goopy fat pouring out of a soda bottle, with a reminder to "cut back on soda and other sugary beverages" lest you "drink yourself fat." A great triumph for the negative conception of liberty? Hardly. But it's something, a reminder that as much as negative liberty may be out of fashion these days, for each American begging the government to take away their cigarettes and ice cream, there are still some folks who will occasionally throw an elbow when government tries to infringe on their personal decisions.

ENGAGING THE TEXT

1. Why does Mangu-Ward compare the Brooklyn moms who want to ban ice-cream vendors to the Taliban? Is this a fair comparison? What differences, if any, do you see between the motives and methods of these two groups?

2. What is the difference between positive and negative liberty, as presented by Mangu-Ward? How does positive liberty encroach upon or limit negative liberty in her view?

3. Mangu-Ward suggests that mandating warning labels on cigarettes and ingredient labels on snack foods amounts to "libertarian paternalism." Do you think that these labels limit our freedom and that we should have the "choice to remain ignorant"?

4. In general, would you agree that we have let the "nanny state" go too far in attempting to protect us from our "unhealthy impulses"? Which of the following should the government be allowed to control for the general welfare? Why?

   • The toxin levels in drinking water

   • The size of soda servings at fast-food restaurants

   • The availability of drugs

   • Automobile safety standards and equipment

   • Gasoline mileage standards

   • Cell phone use

   • Smoking in public

   • The flow rate of showerheads and toilets

   • Light bulb wattage and design

   • The minimum age of employment

   • The minimum age of marriage

   • The gender of marriage partners

EXPLORING CONNECTIONS

5. What kinds of liberties, positive or negative, did the Founding Fathers have in mind when they wrote the Declaration of Independence (p. 625) and the Constitution (p. 628)? Does the right to "Life, Liberty, and the pursuit of Happiness" include the right of individuals to make bad decisions regardless of their impact on "the general Welfare"?

6. Given her rereading of the Declaration and her interpretation of the "pursuit of Happiness" (p. 631), how might Naomi Wolf view Mangu-Ward's concerns about the loss of choice in contemporary American society? When Wolf complains about "our rights and liberties being chipped away," what kinds of rights does she have in mind?

7. Drawing on Juan Williams (p. 648) and Mangu-Ward, write a journal entry or a brief essay on whether you think our collective desire to impose positive values and behaviors on others threatens our essential freedoms.

EXTENDING THE CRITICAL CONTEXT

8. Look up the history of the Boston Tea Party online to learn more about the motives behind the incident. Was the Tea Party protesting excessive

taxation, as Mangu-Ward suggests, or a lack of legislative representation? What difference does this make in our view of the event — and what does it says about the role of government?

9. Visit the Bedford e-Pages for this chapter of *Rereading America* (bedford stmartins.com/rereading/epages) and read "The Rise of Mass Dependency," AIDS activist Chris Norwood's analysis of the tacit partnership between big government and the "medical industrial complex." Drawing on Norwood's exploration of the type 2 diabetes epidemic and Katherine Mangu-Ward's analysis of the growing American "nanny state" (p. 659), write an essay about the growth of dependency in contemporary American society. Are Americans losing their sense of independence and self-reliance? Are we becoming too dependent on big government and big business?

WHETHER FROM REASON OR PREJUDICE: TAKING MONEY FOR BODILY SERVICES

MARTHA C. NUSSBAUM

During the 2012 Nevada presidential primary, staffers at Reno, Nevada's famous Bunny Ranch turned out in force in support of their favorite candidate—Ron Paul. It makes sense for so-called "sex workers" to back a small-government Libertarian because prostitution remains one of the few relatively common occupations in the United States still forbidden by law. But why? As Martha Nussbaum argues in the following selection, banning prostitution might make about as much sense as criminalizing housecleaning or factory work. Nussbaum's rigorous analysis of prostitution as a matter of rational choice challenges us to rethink the boundary between morality and prejudice—and to reconsider the wisdom of state interference in all relations between consenting adults. Currently the Ernst Freund Distinguished Service Professor of Law and Ethics at the University of Chicago, Nussbaum (b. 1947) is one of the nation's preeminent philosophers. The winner of numerous academic awards and recipient of over forty honorary degrees, she specializes in ancient Greek and Roman philosophy and has published or edited more than thirty books on issues like women's rights, disability and the law, animal rights, religious violence, education, and human development. Her most recent publications include *Not for Profit: Why Democracy Needs the Humanities* (2010) and *Creating Capabilities: The Human Development Approach* (2011).

ALL OF US, with the exception of the independently wealthy and the unemployed, take money for the use of our bodies.[1] Professors, factory workers, lawyers, opera singers, prostitutes, doctors, legislators—we all do things with parts of our bodies, for which we receive a wage in return.[2] Some people get good wages and some do not; some have a relatively high degree of control over their working conditions and some

---

[1] I am grateful to the students in my seminar on sexual autonomy and law for all that their discussions contributed to the formulation of these ideas, to Sibyl Schwarzenbach and Laurie Shrage for discussions that helped me think about how to approach this topic, and to Elizabeth Anderson, Gertrud Fremling, Richard Posner, Mark Ramseyer, Eric Schliesser, Elizabeth Schreiber, Steven Schulhofer, Alan Soble, and Cass Sunstein for valuable comments on an earlier draft of this article. [All notes are Nussbaum's, except 3, 5, 7, 8, 12, 16, 17, 19, 27, 34, 35, 37, and 42.]

[2] Even if one is a Cartesian dualist, as I am not, one must grant that the human exercise of mental abilities standardly requires the deployment of bodily skills. Most traditional Christian positions on the soul go still further: Thomas Aquinas, for example, holds that souls separated from the body have only a confused cognition and cannot recognize particulars. So my statements about professors can be accepted even by believers in the separable soul.

have little control; some have many employment options and some have very few. And some are socially stigmatized and some are not.

The stigmatization of certain occupations may be well founded, based on convincing well-reasoned arguments. But it may also be based on class prejudice or stereotypes of race or gender. Stigma may also change rapidly, as these background beliefs and prejudices change. Adam Smith,[3] in *The Wealth of Nations*, writes that there are "some very agreeable and beautiful talents" that are admirable so long as no pay is taken for them, "but of which the exercise for the sake of gain is considered, whether from reason or prejudice, as a sort of publick prostitution." For this reason, he continues, opera singers, actors, and dancers must be paid an "exorbitant" wage to compensate them for the stigma involved in using their talents "as the means of subsistence." "Should the publick opinion or prejudice ever alter with regard to such occupations," he concludes, "their pecuniary[4] recompence would quickly diminish."[5] Smith was not altogether right about the opera market, but his discussion is revealing for what it shows us about stigma.[6] Today few professions are more honored than that of opera singer; yet only two hundred years ago that public use of one's body for pay was taken to be a kind of prostitution. Looking back at that time, we now think that the judgments and emotions underlying the stigmatization of singers were irrational and objectionable, like prejudices against members of different classes and races. Nor do we see the slightest reason to suppose that the unpaid artist is a purer and truer artist than the paid artist. We think it entirely right and reasonable that high art should receive a high salary. If a producer of opera should take the position that singers should not be paid—on the grounds that receiving money for the use of their talents involves an illegitimate form of commodification[7] and even market alienation[8] of those talents—we would think that this producer was a slick exploiter, out to make a profit from the ill treatment of vulnerable and impressionable artists.[9] On the whole we think

[3] *Adam Smith:* (1723–1790) Scottish social philosopher, whose *The Wealth of Nations* (1776) is considered the first work of free market economics.

[4] *pecuniary:* Relating to money.

[5] Adam Smith, in R. H. Campbell, and A. S. Skinner, eds. *An Inquiry into the Nature and Causes of the Wealth of Nations* (Indianapolis, 1981), I.x.b.25. In Adam Smith, in J. C. Bryce, ed., *Lectures on Rhetoric and Belles Lettres* (Oxford, England, 1983), ii.230, Smith points out that in ancient Greece acting was "as creditable...as it is discreditable now."

[6] He expresses the view that the relevant talents are not so rare and that when stigma is removed many more people will compete for the jobs, driving down wages; this is certainly true today of acting, but far less so of opera, where "the rarity and beauty of the talents" remains at least one dominant factor.

[7] *commodification:* The transformation of things that are typically not seen as "goods," such as human relationships, into products for sale.

[8] *alienation:* In the economic theory of Karl Marx (1818–1883), the separation of things that normally belong together, such as the alienation of workers from the power to control their own lives in a capitalist system.

[9] Such arguments have often been used in the theatre; they were used, for example, in one acting company of which I was a member in order to persuade actors to kick back their (union-mandatory) salaries to the owners. This is fairly common in theater, where the union is weak and actors are so eager for employment that they are vulnerable to such arguments.

that, far from cheapening or ruining talents, the presence of a contract guarantees conditions within which the artist can develop.[10]

It is widely believed, however, that taking money or entering into contracts in connection with the use of one's sexual and reproductive capacities is genuinely bad. Feminist arguments about prostitution, surrogate motherhood, and even marriage contracts standardly portray financial transactions in the area of female sexuality as demeaning to women and as involving a damaging commodification and market alienation of women's sexual and reproductive capacities.[11] The social meaning of these transactions is said to be both that these capacities are turned into objects for the use and control of men and also that the activities themselves are being turned into commodities, and thereby robbed of the type of value they have at their best.

One question we shall have to face is whether these descriptions of our current judgments and intuitions are correct. But even if they are, what does this tell us? Many things and people have been stigmatized in our nation's history, often for very bad reasons. An account of the actual social meaning of a practice is therefore just a door that opens onto the large arena of moral and legal evaluation. It invites us to raise Smith's question: are these current beliefs the result of reason or prejudice? Can they be defended by compelling moral arguments? And, even if they can, are these the type of moral argument that can form a basis for a legal restriction? Smith, like his Greek and Roman Stoic forebears,[12] understood that the evaluations that ground emotional responses and ascriptions of social meaning in a society are frequently corrupt—deformed by self-interest, resentment, and mere unthinking habit. The task he undertook, in *The Theory of Moral Sentiments,* was to devise procedures and strategies of argument through which one might separate the rationally defensible emotions from the irrational and prejudiced. In so proceeding, Smith and the Stoics were correct.

[10]The typical contract between major U.S. symphony orchestras and the musicians' union, for example, guarantees year-round employment to symphony musicians, even though they do not play all year; this enables them to use summer months to play in low-paying or experimental settings in which they can perform contemporary music, chamber music, do solo and concerto work, and so forth. It also restricts hours of both rehearsal and performance during the performing season, leaving musicians free to teach students, attend classes, work on chamber music with friends, and otherwise enrich their work. It also mandates blind auditions (that is, players play behind a curtain—with the result that the employment of female musicians has risen dramatically over the past twenty or so years since the practice was instituted).

[11]See Elizabeth Anderson, *Value in Ethics and Economics* (Cambridge, Mass., 1993); Elizabeth Anderson, "Is Women's Labor a Commodity?" *Philosophy and Public Affairs* 19 (1990), 71–92; Margaret Jane Radin, *Contested Commodities: The Trouble with the Trade in Sex, Children, Bodily Parts, and Other Things* (Cambridge, Mass., 1996); Margaret Jane Radin, "Market-Inalienability," *Harvard Law Review* 100 (1987), 1849–1937; Cass R. Sunstein, "Neutrality in Constitutional Law: With Special Reference to Pornography, Abortion, and Surrogacy," *Columbia Law Review* 92 (1992), 1–52; Cass R. Sunstein, *The Partial Constitution* (Cambridge, Mass., 1993), 257–290. For contrasting feminist perspectives on the general issue of contract, see Jean Hampton, "Feminist Contractarianism," in *A Mind of One's Own: Feminist Essays on Reason and Objectivity* (Boulder, Colo., 1993), 227–255; Susan Moller Okin, *Justice, Gender, and the Family* (New York, 1989).

[12]*"Stoic forebearers":* The Greco-Roman Stoic philosophers believed that destructive emotions could be overcome through the development of rational self-control.

Social meaning does no work on its own: it offers an invitation to normative moral and political philosophy.

Here we will investigate the question of sexual "commodification" by focusing on the example of prostitution.[13] I shall argue that a fruitful debate about the morality and legality of prostitution should begin from a broader analysis of our beliefs and practices with regard to taking pay for the use of the body and from a broader awareness of the options and choices available to poor working women. The former inquiry suggests that at least some of our beliefs about prostitution are as irrational as the beliefs Smith reports about singers; it will therefore help us to identify the elements in prostitution that are genuinely problematic. Most, though not all, of the genuinely problematic elements turn out to be common to a wide range of activities engaged in by poor working women. The second inquiry will suggest that many of women's employment choices are so heavily constrained by poor options that they are hardly choices at all. This should bother us. The fact that a woman with plenty of choices becomes a prostitute should not bother us, provided that there are sufficient safeguards against abuse and disease, safeguards of a type that legalization would make possible.

The most urgent issue raised by prostitution is that of employment opportunities for working women and their control over the conditions of their employment. The legalization of prostitution, far from promoting the demise of love, is likely to make things a little better for women who have too few options to begin with.[14] The really helpful thing for feminists to ponder, if they deplore the nature of these options, will be how to provide more options for these women, through education, skills training, and job creation. These unsexy topics are insufficiently addressed by feminist philosophers in the United States, but they are inevitable in any practical project dealing with real-life prostitutes and their female children.[15] This suggests that at least some of our feminist theory may be insufficiently grounded in the reality of working-class lives, and

---

[13]I shall use the terms "prostitution" and "prostitute" throughout because of their familiarity, although a number of international women's organizations now avoid it for reasons connected to those in this article, preferring the term "commercial sex worker" instead. For one recent example, see *Reproductive Health in Developing Countries: Expanding Dimensions, Building Solutions*, report of the Panel on Reproductive Health, National Research Council, Amy O. Tsui, Judith N. Wasserheit, and John G. Haaga, eds. (Washington, D.C., 1997), 30, stressing the wide variety of practices denoted by the term "commercial sex," and arguing that some studies show economic hardship as a major factor, but some do not.

[14]Among feminist discussions of prostitution, my approach is close to that of Sibyl Schwarzenbach, "Contractarians and Feminists Debate Prostitution," *New York University Review of Law and Social Change* 18 (1990–1991), 103–129, and to Laurie Shrage, "Prostitution and the Case for Decriminalization," *Dissent,* Spring 1996, 41–45, in which Shrage criticizes her earlier view expressed in "Should Feminists Oppose Prostitution?" *Ethics* 99 (1989), 347–361.

[15]To give just one example, the Annapurna Mahila Mandel project in Bombay offers job training and education in a residential school setting to the daughters of prostitutes; they report that in five years they have managed to arrange reputable marriages for one thousand such girls.

too focused on sexuality as an issue in its own right, as if it could be extricated from the fabric of poor people's attempts to survive....

Prostitution is not a single thing. It can only be well understood in its social and historical context. Ancient Greek *hetairai*[16] such as Pericles'[17] mistress Aspasia have very little in common with a modern call girl.[18] Even more important, within a given culture there are always many different types and levels of prostitution: in ancient Greece, the *hetaira*, the brothel prostitute, the streetwalker; in modern America, the self-employed call girl, the brothel prostitute, the streetwalker (and each of these at various levels of independence and economic success). It is also evident that most cultures contain a continuum of relations between women and men (or between same-sex pairs) that have a commercial aspect–ranging from the admitted case of prostitution to cases of marriage for money or expensive dates at the end of which sexual favors are expected. In most cultures, marriage itself has a prominent commercial aspect: the prominence of dowry murder[19] in contemporary Indian culture, for example, testifies to the degree to which a woman is valued, above all, for the financial benefits one can extract from her family.[20] Here we will focus on contemporary America, on female prostitution only, and on explicitly commercial relations of the sort that are illegal under current law.

We will consider the prostitute by situating her in relation to several other women who take money for bodily services:

1. A factory worker in the Perdue chicken factory who plucks feathers from nearly frozen chickens.

2. A domestic servant in a prosperous upper-middle-class house.

3. A nightclub singer in middle-range clubs who often sings songs requested by the patrons.

---

[16]*hetairai:* In ancient Greece, the *hetairai* were a class of well-educated, independent women skilled in art and music who made their livelihood by serving as professional companions to powerful men.

[17]*Pericles:* (495–429 BCE), the most famous Greek statesman during the Golden Age of Athens.

[18]Aspasia was a learned and accomplished woman who apparently had philosophical and political views; she is said to have taught rhetoric and to have conversed with Socrates. But she could not perform any of the functions of a citizen both because of her sex and because of her foreign birth. Her son Pericles was subsequently legitimated and became a general. More recently, some scholars have questioned whether Aspasia was in fact a *hetaira*, and some now think her a well-born foreign woman. But other *hetairai* in Greece were well educated and had substantial financial assets; the two women recorded as students in Plato's Academy were both *hetairai*, as were most of the women attested as students of Epicurus, including one who was apparently a wealthy donor.

[19]*dowry murder:* In India, the murder of young brides because their families do not provide sufficient "dowry"—the money or goods a woman brings to a marriage.

[20]See Martha Nussbaum, "Religion and Women's Human Rights," in Paul Weithmann, ed., *Religion and Contemporary Liberalism* (Notre Dame, Ind., 1997), 93–137.

4. A professor of philosophy who gets paid for lecturing and writing.

5. A skilled masseuse employed by a health club (with no sexual services on the side).

6. A "colonoscopy artist" who gets paid for having her colon examined with the latest instruments in order to test out their range and capability.

By considering similarities and differences between the prostitute and these other bodily actors, we can more easily identify the distinctive features of prostitution as a form of bodily service.

We will not address the issue of child prostitution or nonconsensual prostitution (e.g., young women sold into prostitution by their parents, forcible drugging and abduction, and so forth). We will look only at the type of choice to be a prostitute that is made by a woman over the age of consent, frequently in a situation of great economic duress.

1. *The prostitute and the factory worker.* Both prostitution and factory work are usually low-paid jobs; but in many instances a woman faced with the choice can (at least over the short haul) make more money in prostitution than in factory work. (This would probably be even more true if prostitution were legalized and the role of pimps thereby restricted, though the removal of risk and some stigma might at the same time depress wages, to some extent offsetting that advantage for the prostitute.) Both face health risks, but the health risk in prostitution can be very much reduced by legalization and regulation, whereas the particular type of work the factory worker is performing carries a high risk of damage to the nerves in the hands, a fact about it that appears unlikely to change. The prostitute may well have better working hours and conditions than the factory worker, especially if prostitution were legalized. She has a degree of choice about which clients she accepts and what activities she performs, whereas the factory worker has no choices—she must perform the same motions again and again for years. The prostitute also performs a service that requires skill and responsiveness to new situations, whereas the factory worker's repetitive motion exercises relatively little human skill and contains no variety.[21]

The factory worker, however, is unlikely to be the target of violence, whereas the prostitute needs—and does not always get—protection from violent customers. (Again, this situation can be improved by legalization: prostitutes in the Netherlands have a call button wired up to the police.) The factory worker's occupation, moreover, has no clear connection with stereotypes of gender—though this might not have been the case. In many parts of the world, manual labor is strictly segmented

---

[21]It is probably, however, a developed skill to come to work regularly and to work regular hours each day.

by sex, and more routinized, low-skill tasks are given to women.[22] The prostitute's activity does derive some of its attraction from stereotypes of women as sluttish and immoral, and it may in turn perpetuate such stereotypes. The factory worker suffers no invasion of her internal private space, whereas the prostitute's activity involves such (consensual) invasion. Finally the prostitute suffers from social stigma, whereas the factory worker does not—at least among people of her own social class. For all these reasons, many women, faced with the choice between factory work and prostitution, choose factory work, despite its other disadvantages.

2. *The prostitute and the domestic servant.* In domestic service as in prostitution, one is hired by a client and one must do what that client wants or fail at the job. In both, one has a limited degree of latitude to exercise skills as one sees fit, and both jobs require the exercise of some developed bodily skills. In both, one is at risk of enduring bad behavior from one's client, though the prostitute is more likely to encounter physical violence. Certainly both are traditionally professions that enjoy low respect, from society and from the client. Domestic service on the whole is likely to have worse hours and lower pay than (at least many types of) prostitution but it probably contains fewer health risks. It also involves no invasion of intimate bodily space, as prostitution (consensually) does.

Both prostitution and domestic service are associated with a type of social stigma. In the case of domestic service, the stigma is related to class: it is perceived as an occupation only for the lowest classes.[23] Domestic servants are in a vast majority of cases female, so the occupation is socially coded by sex. In the United States domestic service is very often racially coded as well. Not only in the South but also in many parts of the urban North African-American women often hold these low-paying occupations. In my home in suburban Philadelphia in the 1950s and 1960s, the only African Americans we saw were domestic servants, and the only domestic servants we saw were African American. The perception of the occupation as associated with racial stigma ran very deep, producing difficult tensions and resentments that made domestic service seem to be incompatible with dignity and self-respect. . . .

[22]Consider, for example, the case of Jayamma, a brick worker in Trivandrum, Kerala, India (discussed by Leela Gulati, *Profiles of Female Poverty* (Oxford, England, 1981), 35–62), whom I met on March 21, 1997, when she was approximately sixty-five years old. For approximately forty years, Jayamma worked as a brick carrier carrying heavy loads of bricks on her head all day from one place to another. Despite her strength, fitness, and reliability, she could never advance beyond that job because of her sex, whereas men were quickly promoted to the less physically demanding and higher-paying tasks of brick molding and truck loading.

[23]This appears to be a ubiquitous feature: in India, the mark of "untouchability" is the performance of certain types of cleaning, especially those dealing with bathroom areas. Mahatma Gandhi's defiance of caste manifested itself in the performance of these menial services.

3. *The prostitute and the nightclub singer.* Both of these people use [15] their bodies to provide pleasure, and the customer's pleasure is the primary goal of what they do.[24] This does not mean that a good deal of skill and art is not involved, and in both cases it usually is. Both have to respond to requests from the customer though (in varying degrees depending on the case) both may also be free to improvise or to make suggestions.

How do they differ? The prostitute faces health risks and risks of violence not faced by the singer. She also allows her bodily space to be invaded, as the singer does not. It may also be that prostitution is always a cheap form of an activity that has a higher better form, whereas this need not be the case in popular vocal performance (though of course it might be).[25] The nightclub singer, furthermore, does not appear to be participating in, or perpetuating, any type of gender hierarchy—though in former times this would not have been the case, singers being seen as "a type of publick prostitute" and their activity often associated with anxiety about the control of female sexuality. Finally, there is no (great) moral stigma attached to being a nightclub singer, though at one time there certainly was.

4. *The prostitute and the professor of philosophy.* These two figures have a very interesting similarity: both provide bodily services in areas that are generally thought to be especially intimate and definitive of selfhood. Just as the prostitute takes money for sex, which is commonly thought to be an area of intimate self-expression, so the professor takes money for thinking and writing about what she thinks—about morality, emotion, the nature of knowledge—all parts of a human being's intimate search for understanding the world and herself. It was precisely for this reason that some medieval thinkers saw philosophizing for money as a moral problem: it should be a pure spiritual gift and is degraded by the receipt of a wage. The fact that we do not think that the professor (even one who regularly holds out for the highest salary offered) thereby alienates her mind or turns her thoughts into commodities—even when she writes a paper for a specific conference or volume—should put us on our guard about making similar conclusions in the case of the prostitute.

In both cases the performance involves interaction with others, and the form of the interaction is not altogether controlled by the person. In both cases there is at least an element of producing pleasure

---

[24]This does not imply that there is one thing, pleasure, varying only by quantity, that they produce. With Mill (and Plato and Aristotle), I think that pleasures differ in quality, not only in quantity.

[25]This point was suggested to me by Elizabeth Schreiber. I am not sure whether I endorse it: it all depends on whether we really want to say that sex has one highest goal. Just as it would have been right, in an earlier era, to be skeptical about the suggestion that the sex involved in prostitution is "low" because nonreproductive, so too it might be good to be skeptical about the idea that prostitution sex is "low" because it is nonintimate. Certainly nonintimacy is present in many noncommercial sexual relationships and is sometimes desired as such.

or satisfaction (note the prominent role of teaching evaluations in the employment and promotion of professors), though in philosophy there is also a countervailing tradition of believing that the goal of the interaction is to produce dissatisfaction and unease. (Socrates would not have received tenure in a modern university.) It may appear at first that the intimate bodily space of the professor is not invaded—but we should further explore this idea. When someone's unanticipated argument goes into one's mind, is this not both intimate and bodily? (And far less consensual, often, than the penetration of prostitute by customer.) Both performances involve skill. It might plausibly be argued that the professor's involves a more developed skill, or at least a more expensive training—but we should be cautious here. Our culture is all too ready to think that sex involves no skill and is simply "natural," a view that is surely false and is not even seriously entertained by many cultures.[26]

The professor's salary and working conditions are usually a great deal better than those of all but the most elite prostitutes. The professor has a fair amount of control over the structure of her day and her working environment, but she also has fixed mandatory duties, as the prostitute, when self-employed, does not. If the professor is in a nation that protects academic freedom,[27] she has considerable control over what she thinks and writes, though fads, trends, and peer pressure surely constrain her to some extent. The prostitute's need to please her customer is usually more exigent and permits less choice. In this way, she is more like the professor of philosophy in Cuba than like her American counterpart—but the Cuban professor appears to be worse off, since she cannot say what she really thinks even when off the job.[28] Finally, the professor of philosophy, if female, both enjoys reasonably high respect in the community and also might be thought to bring credit to all women, in that she succeeds at an activity commonly thought to be the preserve only of males. She thus subverts traditional gender hierarchy, whereas the prostitute, while suffering stigma herself, may be thought to perpetuate gender hierarchy.

5. *The prostitute and the masseuse.* These two bodily actors seem very closely related. Both use a skill to produce bodily satisfaction in the client. Unlike the nightclub singer, both do this through a type of bodily contact with the client. Both need to be responsive to what the client wants, and to a large degree take direction from the client as to how to handle his or her body. The bodily contact involved is rather intimate, though the internal space of the masseuse is not invaded. The type of bodily pleasure produced by the masseuse may certainly have

[26]Thus the *Kama Sutra*, with its detailed instructions for elaborately skilled performances, strikes most Western readers as slightly comic since the prevailing romantic ideal of "natural" sex makes such contrivance seem quite unsexy.

[27]*academic freedom:* The principle that professors should have complete freedom of thought and expression in the classroom so that college classrooms will not be controlled by the state or special interests.

[28]We might also consider the example of a skilled writer who writes advertising copy.

an erotic element, though in the type of "respectable" masseuse considered here, it is not directly sexual.

The difference is primarily one of respectability. Practitioners of   20
massage have fought for, and have to a large extent won, the right to be
considered as dignified professionals who exercise a skill. Their trade
is legal, it is not stigmatized, and practitioners generally do not believe
that they degrade their bodies or turn their bodies into commodities by
using their bodies to give pleasure to customers. They have positioned
themselves alongside physical therapists and medical practitioners, dis-
sociating themselves from the erotic dimension of their activity. As a
consequence of this successful self-positioning, they enjoy better working hours, better pay, and more respect than most prostitutes. What,
then, is the difference? One is having sex, and the other is not. But what
sort of difference is this? Is it a difference we want to defend? Are our
reasons for thinking it so crucial really reasons, or are they simply ves-
tiges of moral prejudice? These questions call up a number of distinct
beliefs: the belief that women should not have sex with strangers; the
belief that commercial sex is inherently degrading and makes a woman
a degraded woman; the belief that women should not have to have
sex with strangers if they do not want to; and the general belief that
women should have the option to refuse sex with anyone they do not
really choose. Some of these beliefs are worth defending and some are
not. . . . We need to sort them out and to make sure that our policies are
not motivated by views we are not really willing to defend.

6. *The prostitute and the colonoscopy artist.* This hypothetical occupation is included for a reason that should now be evident: it involves
the consensual invasion of one's bodily space. (The example is not so
hypothetical: medical students need models when they are learning to
perform internal exams, and young actors do earn a living playing such
roles.[29]) The colonoscopy artist uses her skill at tolerating the fiber-optic
probe without anaesthesia to make a living. In the process, she permits an aperture of her body to be penetrated by another person's activity—far more deeply penetrated than is generally the case in sex. She
runs some bodily risk, since she is being used to test untested instruments, and she will probably have to fast and empty her colon regularly
enough to incur some malnutrition and some damage to her excretory
function. Her wages may not be very good—for this is probably not a
profession characterized by what Smith called "the beauty and rarity
of talents," and it may also involve some stigma, given that people are
inclined to be disgusted by the thought of intestines.

Yet, on the whole, we do not think that this is a base trade or one
that makes the woman who does it a fallen woman. We might want to

---

[29]See Terri Kapsalis, *Public Privates: Performing Gynecology from Both Ends of the
Speculum* (Durham, N.C., 1997); Terri Kapsalis, "In Print: Backstage at the Pelvic Theater,"
Chicago Reader, April 18, 1997, 46. While a graduate student in performance studies at
Northwestern, Kapsalis made a living as a "gynecology teaching associate," serving as the
model patient for medical students learning to perform pelvic and breast examinations.

ban or regulate it if we thought it was too dangerous, but we would not be moved to ban it for moral reasons. Why not? Some people would point to the fact that it neither reflects nor perpetuates gender hierarchy, and this is certainly true. (Even if being a woman is crucial to a person's selection for the job—they need to study, for example, both male and female colons—it will not be for reasons that seem connected with the subordination of women.) Surely a far greater part of the difference is that most people do not think anal penetration by a doctor in the context of a medical procedure is immoral, whereas lots of people do think that vaginal or anal penetration in the context of sexual relations is (except under special circumstances) immoral.[30] A woman who goes in for that is therefore an immoral and base woman.

Prostitution has many features that link it with other forms of bodily service. It differs from these other activities in many subtle ways but the biggest difference consists in the fact that it is more widely stigmatized. Professors no longer get told that selling their teaching is a *turpis quaestus*.[31] Opera singers no longer get told that they are unacceptable in polite society. Even the masseuse has won respect as a skilled professional. What is different about prostitution? Two factors stand out as sources of stigma. One is that prostitution is widely held to be immoral; the other is that prostitution is frequently bound up with gender hierarchy—with ideas that women and their sexuality are in need of male domination and control, and the related idea that women should be available to men to provide an outlet for their sexual desires. The immorality view would be hard to defend today as a justification for the legal regulation of prostitution, and perhaps even for its moral denunciation. People thought prostitution was immoral because they thought nonreproductive and especially extramarital sex was immoral. The prostitute was seen, typically, as a dangerous figure whose whole career was given over to lust. But female lust was and often still is commonly seen as bad and dangerous, so prostitution was seen as bad and dangerous. Some people would still defend these views today, but it seems inconsistent to do so if one is not prepared to repudiate other forms of nonmarital sexual activity on an equal basis. We have to grant that the most common reason for the stigma attached to prostitution is a weak reason, at least as a public reason: a moralistic view about female sexuality that is rarely consistently applied and that seems unable to justify restriction on the activities of citizens who have different views of what is good and proper. At any rate, it seems difficult to use the stigma so incurred to justify perpetuating the stigma through criminalization, unless one is prepared to accept a wide range of morals laws that interfere with

---

[30]The same goes for vaginal penetration, according to Kapsalis. She says that the clinical nature of the procedure more than compensates for "society's queasiness with female sexuality." (Kapsalis, "In Print," 46).

[31]"*a turpis quaestus*": Latin: "dishonorable profit or gain" or "base occupation."

chosen consensual activities—something that most feminist attackers of prostitution rarely wish to do.

More promising as a source of good moral arguments might be the stigma incurred by the connection of prostitution with gender hierarchy. Only a small minority of people view prostitution in a negative light because of its collaboration with male supremacy; for only a small minority of people at any time have been reflective feminists, concerned with the eradication of inequality. Such people will view the prostitute as they view veiled women, or women in *purdah*[32]: with sympathetic anger as victims of an unjust system. This reflective feminist critique does not explain why prostitutes are held in disdain—both because it is not pervasive enough and because it leads to sympathy rather than to disdain.

Gender hierarchy actually explains stigma in a very different way, a way that turns out in the end to be just another form of the immorality charge. People committed to gender hierarchy, and determined to ensure that the dangerous sexuality of women is controlled by men, frequently have viewed the prostitute—a sexually active woman—as a threat to male control of women. They therefore become determined either to criminalize the occupation or, if they also think that male sexuality needs such an outlet (and that this outlet ultimately defends marriage by giving male desire a safely debased outlet) to keep it within bounds by close regulation. Criminalization and regulation are not straightforwardly opposed; they can be closely related strategies. In a similar manner, prostitution is generally conceived as not the enemy but the ally of marriage: the two are complementary ways of controlling women's sexuality. The result is that social meaning is deployed in order that female sexuality be kept in bounds carefully set by men. The stigma attached to the prostitute is an integral part of such bounding.

A valuable illustration of this thesis is given by Alain Corbin's fascinating and careful study of prostitutes in France in the late nineteenth century.[33] Corbin shows that the interest in legal regulation of prostitution was justified by the alleged public interest in reining in and making submissive a female sexuality that was always potentially dangerous to marriage and social order. Kept in carefully supervised houses known as *maisons de tolérance*,[34] prostitutes were known by the revealing name of *filles soumises*,[35] a phrase that most obviously designated them as registered, "subjugated" to the law, but that also connoted their controlled and confined status. What this meant was that they were

---

[32]purdah: The practice in Islam of concealing women from men who are not related to them.

[33]Alain Corbin, *Women for Hire: Prostitution and Sexuality in France After 1850*, Alan Sheridan, trans. (Cambridge, Mass., 1990).

[34]*maisons de tolérance:* French: "houses of tolerance."

[35]*filles soumises: Fille soumise* is the French term for "prostitute," literally meaning "subjugated girl."

controlled and confined, so that they themselves could provide a safe outlet for desires that threatened to disrupt the social order. The underlying aim of the regulationist project, argues Corbin was "the total repression of sexuality."[36] Regulationists tirelessly cited St. Augustine's[37] dictum: "Abolish the prostitutes and the passions will overthrow the world; give them the rank of honest women and infamy and dishonor will blacken the universe."[38] In other words: stigma has to be attached to prostitutes because of the necessary hierarchy that requires morality to subjugate vice, and the male to subjugate the female. Separating the prostitute from the "good woman," the wife whose sexuality is monogamous and aimed at reproduction, creates a system that maintains male control over female desire.[39]

This attitude to prostitution has modern parallels. One instructive example is from Thailand in the 1950s, when Field Marshal Sarit Thanarat began a campaign of social purification, holding that "uncleanliness and social impropriety...led to the erosion of social orderliness."[40] In theory Thanarat's aim was to criminalize prostitution by the imposition of prison terms and stiff fines, in practice the result was a system of medical examination and "moral rehabilitation" that shifted the focus of public blame from the procurers and traffickers to prostitutes themselves. Unlike the French system, the Thai system did not encourage registered prostitution; but it was similar in its public message that the problem of prostitution is a problem of "bad" women, and in its reinforcement of the message that female sexuality is a cause of social disruption unless tightly controlled.

Sex hierarchy commonly causes stigma not through feminist critique but through a far more questionable set of social meanings, meanings that anyone concerned with justice for women should call into question. For it is these same meanings that are also used to justify the seclusion of women, the veiling of women, and the genital mutilation of women. Together, the social meanings uphold the view that women are essentially immoral and dangerous and can be controlled by men only if men carefully engineer things so that women do not get out of bounds. The prostitute, seen as the uncontrolled and sexually free woman, is perceived as particularly dangerous as she is both necessary to society

[36]See Corbin, *Women*, 29. Representative views of the authors of regulationism include the view that "debauchery is a fever of the senses carried to the point of delirium; it leads to prostitution (or to early death...)" and that "there are two natural sisters in the world: prostitution and riot" (373).

[37]*St. Augustine:* St. Augustine of Hippo (354–430), Algerian-born Roman theologian and philosopher whose works shaped the development of early Christianity.

[38]Augustine, *De ordine* 2.4.12.

[39]For a more general discussion of the relationship between prostitution and various forms of marriage, see Richard Posner, *Sex and Reason* (Cambridge, Mass., 1992), 130–133.

[40]Sukanya Hantrakul, "Thai Women: Male Chauvinism à la Thai," *Nation*, November 16, 1992, cited with further discussion in *A Modern Form of Slavery: Trafficking of Burmese Women and Girls into Brothels in Thailand*, Asia Watch Women's Rights Project (New York, 1993).

and in need of constant subjugation. If she is seen as an honest woman, a woman of dignity, she will destroy society. If she is marginalized, she may be tolerated for the service she provides (or, in the Thai case, she may provide an engrossing public spectacle of "moral rehabilitation").

All this diverts attention from some very serious crimes, such as the use of kidnapping, coercion, and fraud to entice women into prostitution. For these reasons international human rights organizations, such as Human Rights Watch and Amnesty International, have avoided taking a stand against prostitution as such, and have focused their energies on the issues of trafficking and financial coercion.[41]

It appears, then, that the stigma associated with prostitution has 30 an origin that feminists have good reason to connect with unjust background conditions and to decry as both unequal and irrational, based on a hysterical fear of women's unfettered sexuality. There may be other good arguments against the legality of prostitution, but the existence of widespread stigma all by itself does not appear to be among them. So long as prostitution is stigmatized, people are injured by that stigmatization, and it is a real injury to a person not to have dignity and self-respect in her own society. But that real injury, as with the comparable real injury to the dignity and self-respect of interracial couples, or of lesbians and gay men, is not best handled by continued legal strictures against the prostitute. It can be better dealt with by fighting discrimination against these people and taking measures to promote their dignity. As the Supreme Court determined in a mixed-race custody case, "Private biases may be outside the reach of the law, but the law cannot, directly or indirectly, give them effect."[42] . . .

The stigma traditionally attached to prostitution is based on a collage of beliefs most of which are not rationally defensible and which should be especially vehemently rejected by feminists: beliefs about the evil character of female sexuality, the rapacious character of male sexuality, the essentially marital and reproductive character of "good" women and "good" sex. Worries about subordination more recently raised by feminists are much more serious concerns but they apply to many types of work poor women do. Concerns about force and fraud should be extremely urgent concerns of the international women's movement. Where these conditions do not apply, feminists should view prostitutes as (usually) poor working women with few options, not as threats to the intimacy and commitment that many women and men seek. This does not mean that we should not be concerned about ways in which

---

[41]See *A Modern Form of Slavery: The Human Rights Watch Global Report on Women's Human Rights* (New York, 1995), 196–273, especially 270–273. The pertinent international human rights instruments take the same approach, including the International Covenant on Civil and Political Rights, the Convention on the Elimination of All Forms of Discrimination Against Women, and the Convention for the Suppression of Traffic in Persons and the Exploitation of the Prostitution of Others.

[42]*Palmore v. Sidoti*, 466 U.S. 429 (1984).

prostitution as currently practiced, even in the absence of force and fraud, undermines the dignity of women, just as domestic service in the past undermined the dignity of members of a given race or class. But the correct response to this problem seems to be to work to enhance the economic autonomy and the personal dignity of members of that class, not to rule off-limits an option that may be the only livelihood for many poor women and to further stigmatize women who already make their living this way.

In grappling further with these issues, we should begin from the realization there is nothing *per se* wrong with taking money for the use of one's body. That is the way most of us live and formal recognition of that fact through contract is usually a good thing for people, protecting their security and their employment conditions. What seems wrong is that relatively few people in the world have the option to use their body in their work in what Marx[43] would call a "truly human" manner of functioning, by which he meant having some choices about the work to be performed, some reasonable measure of control over its conditions and outcome, and also the chance to use thought and skill, rather than just to function as a cog in a machine. Women in many parts of the world are especially likely to be stuck at a low level of mechanical functioning, whether as agricultural laborers, as factory workers, or as prostitutes. The real question is how to expand the options and opportunities such workers face, how to increase the humanity inherent in their work, and how to guarantee that workers of all sorts are treated with dignity. In the further pursuit of these questions, we need, on balance, more studies of women's credit unions and fewer studies of prostitution.

ENGAGING THE TEXT

1. Why does Nussbaum introduce her analysis of the case for prostitution by discussing historical attitudes towards actors, dancers, and singers? What's her point, and why is it crucial to her argument?

2. How, according to Nussbaum, do the working conditions of voluntary (not coerced) prostitutes compare with those of factory workers and domestic servants? What are the limitations of these jobs in her view? To what extent would you agree?

3. In what ways is being a prostitute like being a college philosophy professor? What does Nussbaum mean when she says a professor's work is potentially more "invasive" than the work of a prostitute? Would you agree, and why or why not?

[43]*Marx:* Karl Heinrich Marx (1818–1883), German philosopher, economist, historian, journalist, and revolutionary socialist.

4. In what sense can prostitution be seen as an "ally" to marriage, according to Nussbaum? Why does she view both marriage and prostitution as ways of enforcing what she terms "gender hierarchy"? Why, in her opinion, can voluntary prostitution be seen as a threat to male-dominated society?

5. Aside from what Nussbaum calls issues of "prejudice," what are the genuinely problematic aspects of prostitution in your view? If prostitution were legalized, what specific safeguards could be provided to address these issues? Should the government also extend similar safeguards to women working in other potentially hazardous situations, like factories or domestic service?

6. Ultimately, do you think women should have the right to choose prostitution as a career? Do you agree with Nussbaum that legalization would make things "better for women who have too few options to begin with"?

EXPLORING CONNECTIONS

7. How might the distinction that Katherine Mangu-Ward draws between positive and negative liberty (p. 659) help clarify why we continue to criminalize prostitution? To what extent are laws against voluntary, consensual sexual activities similar to laws regulating smoking in public or the size of soft drinks?

8. How do the working conditions of waitresses, as described by Barbara Ehrenreich in Chapter Three (p. 267), and female factory workers like Maddie, as described by Adam Davidson (p. 333), compare with those of Nussbaum's voluntary prostitute? Which of these jobs do you think is the most physically, psychologically, or morally demeaning? What could be done to give women in these jobs more freedom and more control over their lives?

EXTENDING THE CRITICAL CONTEXT

9. Research the prostitution industry and the life conditions of prostitutes in one or more nations where the practice has been legalized, like Germany, Canada, France, Greece, Israel, Ireland, Mexico, Turkey, Peru, or Venezuela. To what extent do the results of your research suggest that the criminalization of prostitution is a matter of moral prejudice?

FROM TAKING LIBERTIES: THE WAR ON TERROR AND THE EROSION OF AMERICAN DEMOCRACY

SUSAN N. HERMAN

After the attacks of September 11, 2001, Americans experienced what can only be described as a collective state of shock. For the first time in half a century, the nation found itself under assault on its own soil, and the reaction was both swift and extreme. In less than a month, U.S. troops entered Afghanistan to root out al-Quaeda and oppose the Taliban, which had provided al-Quaeda terrorists with safe haven. Then, just a few weeks later, President George W. Bush signed the USA Patriot Act. Originally intended to strengthen the nation's ability to fight terrorism, the Patriot Act has been seen by many as an unprecedented threat to American liberty. This selection offers a dramatic example of how the Patriot Act can go wrong. The story of Sami, a Saudi Arabian student at the University of Idaho who is mistakenly labeled a terrorist by government agents, raises serious questions about the Patriot Act and the cost of freedom. Susan N. Herman, the author of this selection, became president of the American Civil Liberties Union in 2008 after serving for twenty years on the ACLU's Board of Directors. A specialist in issues of constitutional law and terrorism, she is also the Centennial Professor of Law at Brooklyn Law School. Her recent publications include *Taking Liberties: The War on Terror and the Erosion of American Democracy* (2011).

> *They were doing things I didn't ever think government agents would do.*
>
> —LIZ BRANDT, UNIVERSITY OF IDAHO LAW SCHOOL (2010)

> *What angers me most is that these are resources that could be spent pursuing real bad guys.*
>
> —DAVID MANNERS, *former CIA station chief for Jordan* (2004)

> *The part that surprised me was when I read the First Amendment instructions.*
>
> —JOHN STEGER, *Idaho juror* (2004)

JOHN STEGER, a retired Idaho forest worker, did not expect that he would be sitting in judgment on the Patriot Act or on the First Amendment when he was called for jury duty in April 2004. The case he was assigned to hear was a criminal prosecution against Sami Omar al-Hussayen, a thirty-four-year-old University of Idaho doctoral student whose Saudi name and origins must have seemed exotic in Idaho, a highly conservative state where Arabs make up less than two-tenths of 1 percent of the population.

Sami, who was in the country on a student visa, had been living in Moscow, Idaho (population about 20,000), for five years, along with his wife, Maha, and their three young boys while he worked toward his degree in computer studies. As a Muslim student leader, Sami had led a candlelight vigil on the Idaho campus shortly after 9/11, condemning the attacks as an affront to Islam. His neighbors knew him as a gentle man, the last person anyone would suspect of terrorist sympathies. But Sami was on trial for providing "material support" to terrorists because he volunteered as a webmaster for the Islamic Assembly of North America, a Michigan-based organization, among other groups. The Islamic Assembly described its websites as designed to "[s]pread the correct knowledge of Islam; [and] [w]iden the horizons and understanding...among Muslims concerning different Islamic contemporary issues."[1] To serve this educational mission, Sami had set up links so that people could look at a wide variety of sources firsthand, including some anti-American speeches, articles, and "fatwas" (interpretations of Islamic law by Muslim clerics) that advocated criminal activity and suicide operations. Sami said that he didn't himself know what all the sources said, as he did not read them all—he was just posting links, like a journalist reporting what others have said.

Why had the government focused on Sami? One of the Bush Administration's[2] immediate post-9/11 ideas about how to prevent terrorism was to disrupt terrorism-financing networks. Sections of the Patriot Act and a September 2001 Executive Order aimed to starve terrorists by going after the donors and networks that supported them. Suspecting that terrorism-financing networks existed within the United States—there was talk of a pipeline of money flowing from Brooklyn mosques to Al Qaeda[3]—government agents set out to discover who was running those networks. It was certainly no coincidence that Sami was a Muslim and worked with an Islamic charity. Islamic charities were a prime focus of the government's attention. But although many other Muslim charities were put on government watchlists or simply put out of business, the Islamic Assembly was not on any watchlist. Other Patriot Act provisions allowed the government to study Sami's banking records, and so the FBI also learned that he had made substantial con-

---

[1]Al-Kidd v. Ashcroft, 580 F.3d 949, 953 (9th Cir. 2009), aff'd en banc, 598 F.3d 1129 (9th Cir. 2010), cert. granted,__U.S. __, 131 S. Ct. 415 (2010). [All notes are Herman's, except 5, 8, 11, 12, 14, 16, 20, 23, 24, 27, and 28.]

[2]the Bush administration: George Walker Bush (b. 1946) served as forty-third president of the United States from 2001 until 2009.

[3]Al Qaeda: The global militant Islamist network that was responsible for the September 11, 2001 attacks on the United States, founded by Osama bin Laden in 1988.

tributions to Islamic charities.[4] Of course, giving generously to charity is a religious obligation for all faithful Muslims, just as it is for observant Catholics and Jews.

As it turned out, the agents were looking too hard. The FBI misinterpreted various facts as conforming to their theory that Sami was a terrorist mastermind. For example, investigators hypothesized that Sami's studies were really just a cover for his coming to the United States to raise money for terrorists. As support for this suspicion, they pointed to the fact that he had switched dissertation advisors in the middle of the school year—an unusual thing to do and a sign, they concluded, that he was stalling and that his dissertation was fictitious. But the actual reason Sami switched advisors was that his initial advisor was battling cancer. He found a new advisor so that he could finish his dissertation on schedule. Sami, a serious student who was maintaining a 3.8 average, was only a few months from completing his dissertation when the FBI entered his life.

Having focused on Sami, the government agents pulled out all the stops to come up with evidence to support their theory. Using yet another Patriot Act expansion of authority, they got the Foreign Intelligence Surveillance Court[5] to let them tap Sami's phone and to review his e-mails—even though they did not have probable cause to believe that he had committed any crime. Over the course of a year, they intercepted about 10,000 telephone calls and 20,000 e-mails involving Sami, his wife, and his family. In this context too, agents misinterpreted innocuous information, perhaps due to mistranslations. For instance, during one telephone conversation, Maha told a friend of her delight on discovering that a Kraft cheese product her children had enjoyed in Saudi Arabia was also available in Idaho. This comment was taken as evidencing an anti-American attitude—that the only thing she liked about America was Kraft cheese.

Despite the mountain of information the FBI gathered about Sami, they evidently did not come up with any concrete evidence to show that the organizations with which Sami was associated were financing

---

[4]My account of the circumstances surrounding Sami al-Hussayen's arrest relies on interviews with lawyer David Nevin and Idaho Law Professor Liz Brandt, on court records, and on the admirable reporting of Maureen O'Hagan in *A Terrorism Case That Went Awry*, SEATTLE TIMES, Nov. 22, 2004, http://seattletimes.nwsource.com/html/localnews /2002097570_sami22m.html, and by other reporters including Bob Fick, *Idaho Graduate Student Acquitted of Using Internet to Support Terrorism*, SEATTLE TIMES, June 11, 2004, http://seattletimes.nwsource.com/html/localnews/2001952936_webstudentacquitedl0.html; *Sami al-Hussayen Case*, IDAHO PUB. TELEVISION, May 27, 2004, http://idahoptv.org/dialogue /diaShowPage.cfm?versionID=118747 (discussion with four reporters covering the trial); Betsy Hiel, *Trial Ties Suspect to Calls for Jihad*, PITTSBURGH TRIBUNE-REV., May 16, 2004, http://www.pittsburghlive.eom/x/pittsburghtrib/news/middleeastreports/s_194369.html; and Betsy Z. Russell in the IDAHO SPOKESMAN-REVIEW, *e.g., Sami Al-Hussayen on His Way Home*, July 22, 2004, http://www.spokesman.com/stories/2004/jul/22/sami-al-hussayen -on-his-way-home/.

[5]*Foreign Intelligence Surveillance Court*: A U.S. federal court created by the 1978 Foreign Intelligence Surveillance Act (FISA) to oversee requests for warrants permitting physical and electronic surveillance of suspected foreign agents in the United States.

terrorism or that Sami approved of terrorism—no less supported it. Therefore, when Sami was arrested, he was not arrested on terrorism or even material support charges. He was arrested for immigration fraud, charged with lying on his student visa forms. According to the government, Sami lied in saying that he had come to the United States "for the sole purpose of" study and not to work—a promise they said was violated by his webmaster duties. Second, the government alleged that Sami had not complied with a post-9/11 requirement that men[6] entering the country provide the government with a list of organizations to which they belong or which they support[7] because he had not listed the Islamic Assembly. According to Sami's lawyers, this was the first time anyone had ever been charged with a crime for not telling the government about their volunteer charity work.

Sami's arrest in February 2003 sent shock waves through the university town. As many as a hundred federal, state, and local officials stormed the Idaho campus at 4:00 A.M., wearing flak jackets and brandishing large weapons. One frightened child in a family housing unit next to Sami's, on seeing the swarm of armed agents, screamed, "Mommy, the war is starting!" Idaho, founded as a land-grant[8] school, attracted students from the Middle East and developing nations who came to acquire skills in areas like agriculture and engineering, and so there were some 175 to 200 Arab students enrolled at that time. In addition to waking Sami and his family, agents rang the doorbells of all of the other Arab students at Idaho—referring to them as Sami's "associates"—to question them about whether they knew anything about terrorism or terrorism financing. This started at about 5:00 A.M. and continued until all had been questioned. These students reported being threatened with jail or deportation if they refused to answer questions; one reported being interrogated for seven hours. Dragnet interrogation of Arabs and Muslims was one technique the FBI adopted after 9/11, questioning thousands of people who were not actually suspected of anything—except of possibly knowing other Arabs and Muslims.[9] Immigration status—these students were dependent on their student visas—was a useful lever for getting people to submit to questioning they otherwise would have had a right to decline.

No one other than Sami was charged with anything. Liz Brandt, a member of the faculty at Idaho's law school who found herself enlisting

---

[6]Bureau of Consular Affairs, U.S. Dep't of State, A New Form DS 157, Supplemental Nonimmigrant Visa Application (2002), http://travel.state.gov/visa/laws/telegrams /telegrams_1432.html. The requirement applies to "all male nonimmigrant visa applicants between the ages of 16 and 45."

[7]See 18 U.S.C. §§ 1001(a)(2); 1546(a) & 3238 (2006).

[8]Land-grant school: Land-grant colleges and universities were created under the auspices of the Morrill Acts of 1862 and 1890, which provided federal land to the states for the creation of institutions dedicated primarily to the teaching of agriculture, science, and engineering.

[9]See Fox Butterfield, A Nation Challenged: The Interviews; A Police Force Rebuffs F.B.I. on Querying Mideast Men, N.Y. TIMES, Nov. 21, 2001, http://www.nytimes.com/2001/11 /21/us/nation-challenged-interviews-police-force-rebuffs-fbi-querying-mideast-men.html.

lawyers for the interrogated students to consult, recalls that the event was promoted to the media as the successful discovery of a sleeper cell in Idaho. Attorney General John Ashcroft fed that impression, describing Sami as part of a "terrorist threat to Americans that is fanatical, and it is fierce."[10] People who did not know Sami, Brandt says, tended to trust the government and to assume that Sami "must have done something really wrong." But, she adds, people who knew Sami never believed that he could be guilty of supporting terrorism. "When I heard the charges, I thought, this just can't be. It was like a War of the Worlds hoax."[11]

The prosecutors argued that Sami was so dangerous that he should be denied bail pending his trial. But the federal magistrate judge who reviewed their arguments was not persuaded. Sami, who had been living a peaceful life with his family, did not seem likely to flee. The entire family was completely integrated into the community. The boys, ages nine, six, and three at the time, attended local schools and played soccer and skateboarded with neighboring children. Sami worked with food banks and an organization supporting military families. Maha had developed close friends. (After Sami's arrest, the community formed a "protective shell" around the family, says Liz Brandt. Maha did not know how to drive, so neighbors regularly took her to the supermarket, for example, and everyone worked hard to soothe the children, who were traumatized by their experience and by seeing their father in jail.)

The magistrate judge ordered that Sami be allowed to await the trial at home. Instead of releasing him, however, the government tried another tack. The day after the federal magistrate judge ordered him freed, the government asked an immigration court judge to order that Sami be deported (on the theory that he was working in addition to studying) and to lock him up until his deportation. The immigration judge agreed, ordering that Sami be held pending his deportation and so Sami spent seventeen months incarcerated, in solitary confinement, locked in his cell for twenty-three hours a day while awaiting his trial. Immigration charges were also brought against Maha, whose immigration status was dependent on Sami's. As bewildered and shocked as Sami was by the charges against him, he told his lawyer, "They can do whatever they want with me. They can put me in prison for the rest of my life, but not my wife and children." Maha agreed to "voluntarily" return to Saudi Arabia in exchange for the government's agreement not to lock her up too. In November 2003, she was given three months to leave the country. This agreement was designed to allow her to remain in the country during Sami's trial. But when the trial was later postponed for several months, the government refused to allow Maha and

[10]O'Hagan, *supra* note 2.
[11]"*a War of the Worlds hoax*": Refers to the 1938 radio broadcast of an adaptation of H. G. Wells's famous science fiction novel *War of the Worlds*, which convinced many Americans that Martians had actually invaded the United States.

the children an extension. Sami therefore had to face the rest of his time in jail and the ordeal of a nine-week felony trial without his family. He occupied himself in jail by working on his dissertation, still hoping that he would be able to complete his degree.

Over a year after Sami's arrest, the government decided that it had enough evidence to add terrorism-related charges — based on the material support laws — to the immigration charges. The indictment now alleged that the website Sami worked on encouraged contributions to Hamas,[12] a Palestinian group blacklisted as a "foreign terrorist organization."[13] (The government's theory about which terrorists Sami was supporting shifted more than once, from Al Qaeda to Hamas to Chechnyan[14] rebels.) Using the broad net of the Patriot Act, the government charged Sami with the crime of providing "expert advice or assistance" to terrorists.[15] Sami did have expertise in computer studies. But had he actually provided material support to Hamas or any other terrorists? The government's view was that all the jury needed to believe to convict Sami was that he had used his expert skills as a webmaster in a manner that would enable people to encounter hateful ideas, perhaps be persuaded, and perhaps then offer their support. The potential sentence Sami faced was up to fifteen years on each of three terrorism-related charges, and up to twenty-five years on each immigration fraud charge.

In an opening statement at trial, prosecutor Kim Lindquist told the jury that Sami was supporting terrorists in Israel, Chechnya, and other locations through a network of websites used to recruit terrorists, to raise money, and to spread incendiary rhetoric. Juror John Steger's first reaction: "When he got done, I thought, this guy's going to be in jail for life."

As Sami's lawyer, David Nevin, pointed out, however, the government's theory was so broad that it ran up against the Constitution's guarantee of freedom of speech. The First Amendment had been interpreted to prohibit prosecuting people for advocating ideas unless their advocacy is intended to and is likely to incite imminent unlawful action — the so-called *Brandenburg* doctrine.[16] If Sami could be found guilty of a crime for posting fatwas on a website, Nevin argued, CNN

---

[12]*Hamas:* A Palestinian political party classified as a terrorist organization by the United States.

[13]United States v. al-Hussayen, Second Superseding Indictment, No. CR 03-048 at 8–9, (D. Idaho Mar. 4, 2004), http://news.findlaw.com/hdocs/docs/terrorism/usal-hussyn304sind2 .pdf.

[14]*Chechnyan rebels:* Since the dissolution of the Soviet Union in 1991, the Chechen Republic, a semi-autonomous area in southern Russia, has sought independence from the Russian Federation, often by resorting to terrorist activities.

[15]Providing Material Support to Terrorists, 18 U.S.C. § 2339A.

[16]*the Brandenburg Doctrine:* In its 1969 *Brandenburg v. Ohio* ruling (395 U.S. 444), the U.S. Supreme Court held that the government cannot punish inflammatory speech unless it is likely to incite "imminent lawless action," thus clarifying that speech that advocates but is unlikely to incite violence is still protected by the First Amendment.

could also be found guilty for airing speeches by Osama bin Laden.[17] Ironically, an Israeli terrorism expert who served as a prosecution witness testified at the trial that he himself had posted much of the very same material on his own website,[18] as had the BBC[19] on its website. A lot of people were interested in knowing how jihadists[20] explained themselves. Nevin asked the judge to dismiss the prosecution on the ground that it violated the First Amendment. The judge denied the motion, saying that an opinion explaining this decision would follow. No opinion ever followed.

Material Support of Terrorism

The law that was used against Sami had become progressively more hostile to First Amendment values. The first material support law, enacted in 1994,[21] made it a crime to give terrorists concrete assistance like weapons or cash. That statute contained several critical exceptions: (1) people could not be prosecuted for humanitarian assistance, like providing medical care, to someone "not directly involved in such violations"; and (2) investigations could not be initiated on the basis of "activities protected by the First Amendment, including expressions of support or the provision of financial support for the nonviolent political, religious, philosophical, or ideological goals or beliefs of any person or group."[22] If someone supported a group that engaged in both terrorist and nonterrorist activities—like running a nursery school—the prosecution could only get a conviction by showing that the accused intended to support terrorism and that there was an actual connection between the donation and terrorist activities. And people could not be targeted on the basis of their religion or their associations.

Looking back, that was the legislative equivalent of a baby step. The first major expansion of this material support statute was signed into law by President Bill Clinton in 1996 as part of the Antiterrorism and Effective Death Penalty Act of 1996—a response to the Oklahoma City bombing.[23] This revision spared prosecutors the burden of showing intent to promote terrorism and of showing how terrorist organizations

[17]Betsy Z. Russell, *Free Speech or Terrorism?* IDAHO SPOKESMAN-REV., May 4, 2004, http://www.spokesman.com/blogs/boise/2004/may/04/free-speech-or-terrorism/.
[18]Betsy Z. Russell, *Eye on Boise: Expert Cross-Examined,* IDAHO SPOKESMAN-REV., May 20, 2004, http://www.spokesman.com/blogs/boise/2004/may/20/expert-cross-examined/.
[19]*BBC:* the British Broadcasting Corporation.
[20]*jihadists:* A term commonly used to designate members of radical Islamist groups dedicated to violent action in opposition to the State of Israel and other Western powers.
[21]Violent Crime Control and Law Enforcement Act of 1994, Pub. L. No. 103–322, § 120005(a), 108 Stat. 1796, 2022 (1994).
[22]*Id.* at § 120005(c)(2).
[23]*the Oklahoma City bombing:* In the most violent case of domestic terrorism in U.S. history, Timothy McVee and Terry McNichols detonated a homemade bomb in a truck parked outside the Alfred P. Murrah Federal Building in Oklahoma City in 1995, killing 168.

actually used donations, on the theory that money was fungible.[24] If a terrorist did not have to pay for medical treatment, the theory went, the money saved could be used to buy bombs. The provision guaranteeing special protection for First Amendment activities was eliminated. These revisions made it considerably easier to get convictions but left less space for freedom of speech.

Five years later, the Patriot Act expanded the definition of material support to include any form of "expert advice or assistance" — spreading the dragnet wider and making the prosecutor's job that much easier.[25] "Expert advice or assistance" covers some acts that should certainly be criminal and in fact already were under other laws, like teaching terrorists to make bombs. But this term is so vague and open-ended that it has obvious potential for also capturing other kinds of conduct, including humanitarian aid. A doctor who provides medical treatment to a terrorist would seem to fit that description—or maybe a computer whiz. The statute contained no definition of "expert advice or assistance" at the time, so it was hard to tell what the limits of this concept might be, if there were any at all. Sami's prosecution was the first occasion on which the government relied on the Patriot Act's "expert advice or assistance" provision.

Throughout nine weeks of testimony and arguments, John Steger and his fellow jurors—three other men and eight women, including a banker, a PhD in education, and the owner of a lumberyard—didn't hear any evidence that seemed to them to substantiate the material support charges. "There was not a word spoken that indicated he supported terrorism," said John. The prosecution claimed that the charity's website featured links to other websites inviting donations to organizations like Hamas; the defense explained that those links had once existed but had been removed before Sami became webmaster. The prosecutor argued that it did not matter under the law whether or not Sami intended to aid terrorists as long as he knew that the website he worked on solicited donations, but there was no evidence to support that contention either. The prosecutor also argued, correctly, that the material support law did not require the government to show that anyone had clicked on a link leading to Hamas or had actually made a donation to a terrorist organization. This case could be brought only because the government did not have to prove very much at all under the post-Patriot Act material support laws.[26] But the jury found that the prosecution's proof did not even meet that low standard.

---

[24]*fungible:* In economic theory, a good or commodity is considered fungible if its individual parts or units can be easily substituted; thus paper money is fungible because any dollar bill can be replaced by any other dollar bill.

[25]Patriot Act § 805(2)(B).

[26]The only witness called by the defense was a former CIA official who testified that the website was analytical and did not bear the marks of terrorist-recruiting enterprises. *See* Betsy Z. Russell, *Terrorism Case Goes to Jury,* IDAHO SPOKESMAN-REV., June 2, 2004, http://spokesmanclassifieds.com/pf.asp?date=060204&ID=s1525547.

The jurors came to understand that this trial was not just about terrorism but also about the First Amendment. "We talked," John said, "about that we weren't going to step on anybody's rights to hold the opinion they had." As the jurors learned or rediscovered, First Amendment law protects the right to read or to voice hateful opinions—and it applies to everyone lawfully in the country, not just to citizens. Many of the rights the Constitution guarantees are, like the First Amendment, general limitations on what the government can do. Others, like the Due Process Clause, apply to all "persons" or all those accused of a crime and so cover citizens and noncitizens alike. Very few constitutional protections (like the Fourteenth Amendment's hard-to-define "privileges and immunities") are reserved only for citizens.

United States citizens are, of course, just as subject to the material support laws as Sami al-Hussayen. Even if the prosecution's theory in the *al-Hussayen* case does not seem to threaten the average American with prosecution, it threatens our shared fundamental rights. The attempt to build a wall between the American people and hateful ideas is inherently inconsistent with one of the First Amendment's core ideas. The First Amendment represents a commitment to trusting Americans, in this instance to confront the marketplace of ideas without having the government prescreen those ideas for us. The patronizing notion that the government should remove potentially dangerous ideas from the marketplace misconceives the Constitution's underlying view of the relationship of the government and the individual. The material support law, read as broadly as it was in this case, transfers immense power to the government to control ideas and disempowers the people.

Choosing constitutional principle over a fear-driven conviction, this Idaho jury of ordinary Americans took only two or three hours—after a nine-week trial—to agree to acquit Sami on all of the terrorism-related charges. They were not deterred by the fact that Sami was a Saudi citizen also charged with immigration fraud. The jurors debated the alleged immigration violations separately, finding those charges much more difficult. Whether Sami's statements on the immigration forms were intentionally misleading and whether the forms themselves were unclear were hot topics of debate among the jurors for six days in a discussion so intense that some jurors were reduced to tears. The jury voted to acquit Sami on three of the immigration charges but was unable to reach consensus on the other eight.

Is this a *Twelve Angry Men* happy ending?[27] Sami's life was ravaged notwithstanding the decisive acquittals on the material support charges. He had been locked up and held in solitary confinement for seventeen months and his family was forced to return to Saudi Arabia without him. The fact that the jury had deadlocked on eight of the

20

---

[27] "*a* Twelve Angry Men *happy ending*": In Reginald Rose's 1954 teleplay *Twelve Angry Men*, a jury is forced by a lone dissenter to reconsider its verdict, eventually deciding to acquit the defendant of the charge of murder.

immigration charges meant that the government could retry him on those charges. With that prospect hanging over his head, Sami decided to drop his appeal from the immigration court's deportation order and return to Saudi Arabia to rejoin his family. And although he had escaped conviction under the dragnet material support law, this law remained available to ensnare other law-abiding people—including American citizens—and to cast a shadow on our First Amendment rights.

From the government's point of view, it is easy to understand why broad laws like this one can seem desirable. The material support laws are designed to enable criminal prosecutions in situations where the government does not have proof that someone they suspect is a terrorist, or has conspired with terrorists, or is attempting to help terrorists. This expanded dragnet might conceivably catch an actual terrorist who could not otherwise be caught, although we have no way to estimate the likelihood of that happening. But what about the costs—the collateral damage to individual people, to the First Amendment, and to our concept of our relationship to our government—when these laws can capture the innocent and intimidate everyone else?

The desire to wield this broad a net, regardless of how great the potential costs might be, is typical of the Just Trust Us philosophy prevalent after 9/11. We are asked to assume that prosecutors won't use the net against the wrong people and so the costs of this strategy can be controlled. But that optimistic assumption, as Sami's case shows, doesn't always work out so well in practice. Investigators are not immune to wishful thinking, no matter who is president. The investigators in Sami's case wanted so much to find and disrupt a terrorist-financing network that they did not seem to notice that they were molding the facts in a procrustean[28] fashion—or that their theory of the case was a severe threat to First Amendment values. And so they made a serious mistake in this case. But even if prosecutors were superhumanly able to make only the wisest choices in deciding whom to charge, the very existence of this statute stifles free speech. Why would other students or computer experts agree to help run a chat room or post controversial materials if the result could be criminal prosecution? Will people become fearful that informing themselves by reading the ravings of terrorists, or associating themselves with any Islamic charity no matter how legitimate that charity is, might leave them in Sami's position—a focus of the government's attention even if they have not done anything other than add to a conversation? What if the next jury isn't as thoughtful as John Steger and his neighbors?

The government got this one wrong but these Idaho jurors, with this trial as their crash course in First Amendment law and values, stood up to defend the Constitution. Ultimately, the Constitution itself

---

[28] *procrustean:* Involving a ruthless arbitrariness or disregard of individual differences, from the Greek myth of Procrustes, a bandit who terrorized wayfarers by stretching or cutting off their limbs to fit the size of an iron bed.

gets the credit for providing the fail-safe of jury trials. In Article III of the Constitution as well as in the Sixth Amendment, the framers expressed their trust in the American people by empowering us to protect our rights by deciding whether someone the government has charged with a crime should be convicted. We are not told to just trust the government; we are asked to think for ourselves. As the Constitution's Preamble promises, we *are* the government. John Steger and his fellow jurors vindicated the Constitution's faith in the American people. They resisted any urge they might have had to lock up Sami al-Hussayen just in case the government's suspicions about him were right after all despite the lack of evidence—a victory for due process; they resisted the idea that a person can be prosecuted for making hateful ideas accessible to others—a victory for the First Amendment; and they resisted lowering their due process and First Amendment standards because Sami was an Arab, a Muslim, and a foreigner—a victory for the guarantee of equal protection of the laws. But the expanded material support law still remains available for use or misuse on other occasions.

Sami is back in Saudi Arabia, teaching at a university and continu- 25 ing his computer work. Profoundly affected by these events, he is still trying to reconcile his own experience with his lifelong belief that the United States stands for what is good and right. As for the residents of Moscow, Idaho, Liz Brandt says that watching these events unfold brought the liberals and libertarians of that community together. The liberals were already suspicious of the Patriot Act, which, she says, made this all possible because it did not provide enough protection against the government "running amok." To the libertarians, she says, the vision of armed federal agents in flak jackets occupying the Idaho campus due to a mistake, and then not backing off even as their case fell apart, was chilling. "This just looked like huge government, because it was." ...

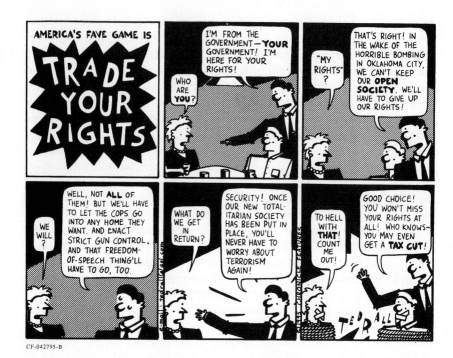

CF-042795-B

ENGAGING THE TEXT

1. To what extent were you surprised by the government's ability under the USA Patriot Act to collect information about Sami? In your view, does national security justify practices like monitoring a person's bank records, e-mail account, and phone calls? Why or why not?

2. What role, in your opinion, did Sami's nationality and ethnicity play in the charges that were brought against him? If he had not been a Muslim, do you think he would have been charged with supporting terrorism? Should the government be allowed to base its "drag net" investigations on race or ethnicity?

3. How do you think the experience Herman describes affected Sami, his wife, and their families? To what extent should we accept cases like Sami's as unfortunate but unavoidable "collateral damage" in the war on terror?

4. Why, according to Herman, does the "expanded material support" provision of the Patriot Act threaten freedom of speech? Should Americans be allowed to visit terrorist and terrorist-affiliated Web sites? Why or why not?

5. To what extent, according to Herman, do the provisions of the Bill of Rights extend to noncitizens in the United States? Why do you think the courts have extended the Bill's protections to noncitizens — and even to undocumented immigrants?

EXPLORING CONNECTIONS

6. How many different provisions of the Bill of Rights (p. 628) did the government appear to compromise or violate as it sought to build a case against Sami? Does the Bill of Rights explicitly guarantee a right to "privacy"? Should it? How might such a right be worded?

7. To what extent does Sami's story both support and challenge Naomi Wolf's assessment of the way Americans interpret the promises made in the Declaration of Independence (p. 625)? How do you think people at your college and in your community would respond to Sami's situation?

EXTENDING THE CRITICAL CONTEXT

8. Go online to learn more about the controversy surrounding the USA Patriot Act in its original and current forms. Why do groups like the ACLU, the American Library Association, the League of Women Voters, and the Libertarian Party view it as a threat to our civil liberties? To what extent do you think it's necessary to give up some privacy—and some rights—in order to guarantee public safety?

9. Break into groups to research some or all of the following topics. Report your findings in class and debate whether these activities represent a threat to American freedoms.

   • Domestic spying by the Central Intelligence and National Security Agencies

   • Sneak and peek searches

   • National Security Letters

   • Government data mining of bank, library, and bookstore records

   • Government surveillance of e-mail and computer searches

   • Indefinite detention of suspected terrorists without charges

   • The use of torture or "enhanced interrogation techniques"

   • Extraordinary rendition

10. Brainstorm a list of all the Middle Eastern characters you can recall portrayed in recent movies and television shows. To what extent do they tend to reinforce racial stereotypes of the terrorist?

VISUAL PORTFOLIO

READING IMAGES OF FREEDOM

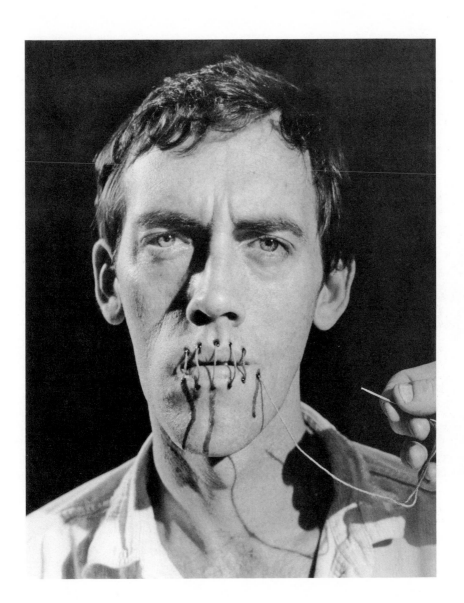

VISUAL PORTFOLIO

READING IMAGES OF FREEDOM

1. What does the photo from the 1963 March on Washington, DC, on page 698 suggest about the way Martin Luther King Jr., and other members of the civil rights movement viewed the economics of freedom? Can people be free, in your view, if they don't have access to jobs?

2. Since 1998 members of the Westboro Baptist Church have picketed at the funerals of U.S. military personnel who died in the service of their country (see p. 699). In 2011 the U.S. Supreme Court decided that the church's protests deserved "special protection under the First Amendment." To what extent would you agree with the Court? Should protestors have the right to exercise their right to free speech at funerals, in residential neighborhoods, or near health clinics and places of worship?

3. In 2002 Juneau, Alaska high school principal Deborah Morse suspended Joseph Frederick for displaying a banner saying "Bong Hits 4 Jesus" (p.700) during the Olympic Torch Relay. In a 6–3 decision in 2007, the U.S. Supreme Court ruled that school officials hadn't violated Frederick's free speech rights because the sign was part of a school event and "school speech" can be suppressed if it promotes illegal activity or undermines the school's mission or student safety. Do you agree that school officials have a special responsibility to monitor students' speech? Why or why not?

4. In 2002 the U.S. government opened a controversial detention camp for prisoners in the "War on Terror" on the grounds of the Guantanamo Bay Navel Base, Cuba (p.701). Of the 779 men who have been imprisoned at Guantanamo, 169 remain a decade after its opening. Reports on camp conditions by organizations like the International Red Cross, Human Rights Watch, and Wikileaks include allegations of torture, sleep deprivation, beatings, and prolonged solitary confinement. In your view, can a government hold prisoners in such conditions indefinitely without charges and still claim to represent the spirit of liberty to the rest of the world?

5. What's your reaction to the photo (p.702) of a Transportation Safety Administration officer patting down a young traveler at a U.S. airport? How effective do you think TSA security measures are in general? Have Americans been too willing to compromise their rights in order to feel secure in a post-9/11 world?

6. In 2010, directors of the Smithsonian Institution removed footage of artist David Wojnarowicz's film "A Fire in My Belly" (p.703) from the exhibit "Hide/Seek: Difference and Desire in American Portraiture." Wojnarowicz's video, containing images of gay couples, men in chains, Ellen DeGeneres holding her breasts, and ants crawling on a crucifix, had come under fire from the Catholic Church and politicians like House Speaker John Boehner, who threatened to cut off federal

funding to the Smithsonian. In your view, should public institutions bow to pressure from religious groups? Should controversial works of art be supported by public funds? Why or why not?

7. A video of University of California, Davis police pepper spraying students involved in the Occupy Wall Street protests (p.704) went viral in November 2011 and sparked calls for the firing of the officers involved and the university's president. Do you think college administrators and security officers should lose their jobs for incidents like this? In your opinion, when should campus police be allowed to use force to control student protests?

GEORGE ORWELL... MEET
MARK ZUCKERBERG

LORI ANDREWS

In the novel *1984*, George Orwell envisions a nightmare society where "Big Brother" controls every move his citizens make. The "Thought Police" in Orwell's dystopian masterwork keep the population under constant surveillance through the use of "telescreens," two-way televisions that report every action and conversation directly to the authorities. Today Orwell's warnings about the dangerous combination of technology and totalitarian control may seem more relevant than ever. As Lori Andrews explains in this selection, social networks and smartphones are funneling our personal information to "data aggregators," massive companies that track every aspect of our lives online, from the things we "like" — or "don't like" — to the Web sites we search and the e-mail we send our friends. The result is the creation of a virtual "double" of every American, a second online self that marketers, businesses, and employers can use when making crucial decisions about our future opportunities and choices. Andrews (b. 1953) is Distinguished Professor of Law and Director of the Institute for Science, Law, and Technology at the Illinois Institute of Technology. An internationally recognized expert on biotechnology and the legal aspects of genetic engineering, she has published ten books, including *Future Perfect: Confronting Decisions About Genetics* (2001), *Genetics: Ethics, Law and Policy* (2002), and *I Know Who You Are and I Saw What You Did: Social Networks and the Death of Privacy* (2011) the source of this selection.

ON A SUNDAY MORNING, I fire up my laptop and compose a memo to my co-counsel about a pro bono case we are considering filing against a biotechnology company. I attach it to an email and send it to him, carefully writing, "Confidential—Legal Mail" in the subject line and putting a few key ideas in the text of the email. Then I log on to the Southwest Airlines site, enter my credit card information, and buy a ticket for Florida. I enter a governmental website, run by the Florida Fish and Wildlife Conservation Commission, and type in my Social Security number to obtain a fishing license. I realize I'll be away on my sister's birthday and send her some books from Amazon. I check my emails and click through to a website that lists job openings for university professors. One is in a town I haven't heard of, so I Google it to find out if it will be urban enough for me. The town's name brings up a link to a local newspaper article about a poisoning and I save that information to my hard drive, thinking I might use it in the next mystery book I write. I read an email from my doctor telling me she changed my prescription electronically and the new drug is waiting for me at my neighborhood CVS. Before leaving the house to pick it up, I log on to Facebook to contact friends in Florida and let them know when I'll arrive. Elsewhere on my Facebook page, I check my news feed and indicate I liked the movie I saw the previous night. Someone has tagged me in a Halloween photo from years ago, when I was a Yale undergrad. I am wearing a belly dancer's costume and I am with someone dressed like a bottle of Imperial Single Malt Scotch. I untag myself from the photo. If I do interview for a new job, I don't want someone to say to me, "Well, Ruth Bader Ginsburg[1] would never have shown her navel."

All in all, I feel good about the security of my morning's travels across the Web. I haven't responded to any wealthy widows seeking my legal help for their $50 million estates, nor to emails purportedly from friends whose wallets and passports were stolen in London. I haven't given my credit card to anyone with a sketchy foreign email address who offers me an iPad for $30, nor have I opened the missive that tells me I've exceeded my email limit. I've only dealt with websites I trust.

But every action I've taken has been surreptitiously chronicled and analyzed by data aggregators, who then sell the information to companies, including perhaps the one I am contemplating suing. And not only have I not been informed about this invasion of my privacy and security, there's almost nothing I can do about it.

That stunning fact is completely at odds with the offline world. I care deeply about the type of information I've entered. I wouldn't leave my Social Security number or my credit card number lying on my desk at work where someone could copy it—nor would I send that information on a postcard through the mail. I wouldn't broadcast my medical condition or my desire to find a new job to the world. But that information about me is bought and sold daily by corporations that deal with data aggregators.

If someone broke into my home and copied my documents, he'd be guilty of trespass and invasion of privacy. If the cops wanted to wiretap my conversation, they'd need a warrant. But without our knowledge or consent, virtually every entry we make on a social network or other website is surreptitiously being tracked and assessed. The information is just as sensitive. The harms are just as real. But the law is not as protective.

The guiding force behind this enormous theft of private information is behavioral advertising. The covert collection of personal information is an exploding industry, fueled in part by the lust of advertisers for personal data about people's habits and desires. "Online behavioral advertising," notes the Federal Trade Commission, "involves the tracking of consumers' online activities in order to deliver tailored advertising. The

5

---

[1]*Ruth Bader Ginsberg*: Ruth Joan Bader Ginsberg (b. 1933) is an Associate Justice of the U.S. Supreme Court. [Eds.]

practice, which is typically invisible to consumers, allows businesses to align their ads more closely to the inferred interests of their audience."[2] But the unregulated amassing of personal information about people has also been used in ways that cause them harm.

Behavioral advertising was used by 85% of ad agencies in 2010.[3] They're drawn to it because it works—63% of ad agencies say targeted ads increased their revenue, with 30% of agencies reporting that behavioral advertising increased their revenue by $500,000 or more. In 2010, internet advertising revenues exceeded that of newspapers by $3.2 billion.[4] During the first quarter of 2010, internet users in the United States received 1.1 trillion display ads, which cost the ad sponsors about $2.7 billion.[5]

"It's a digital data vacuum cleaner on steroids, that's what the online ad industry has created," Jeff Chester, executive director of the Center for Digital Democracy, told *The New York Times.* "They're tracking where your mouse is on the page, what you put in your shopping cart, what you don't buy. A very sophisticated commercial surveillance system has been put in place."[6]

It's through data aggregation that Facebook makes its money. Facebook sits on a mountain of information worth a fortune. It's expected that in 2012 Facebook will be valued at $100 billion.[7] Currently the company generates most of its revenue by acting as an intermediary between advertisers and its database of users' personal information. Facebook will use information about my status, likes and dislikes, and the recent post about my travel plans to update its digital portrait of me. When an airline or outdoor clothing company pays Facebook to post an ad for traveling adults, Facebook will use its new information about me to post the ad on my Facebook page. This commercialization of my private data—the information I think I'm only posting to friends—is the reason Facebook earned an estimated $1.86 billion in 2010 from the

[2]Federal Trade Commission, "FTC Staff Report: Self-Regulatory Principles for Online Behavioral Advertising—Behavioral Advertising: Tracking, Targeting, & Technology," 2009 WL 361109 at 4 (February 2009). [All notes are Andrews', except 1, 10, and 51.]

[3]Audience Science Press Release, "State of Audience Targeting Industry Study: 50% of Advertisers Set to Boost Spending on Audience Targeting in 2011," Jan. 11, 2011, www.audiencescience.com/uk/press-room/press-releases/2011/state-audience-targeting -industry-study-50-advertisers-set-boost-spen.

[4]Internet Advertising Bureau, Internet Advertising Revenue Report, 2010 Full Year Results, April 2011, www.iab.net/insights_research/947883/adrevenuereport.

[5]ComScore Press Release, "Americans Received 1 Trillion Display Ads in Q1 2010 as Online Advertising Market Rebounds from 2009 Recession," May 13, 2010, www.comscore .com/Press_Events/Press_Releases/2010/5/Americans_Received_1_Trillion_Display_Ads_in _Q1_2010_as_Online_Advertising_Market_Rebounds_from_2009_Recession.

[6]Louise Story, "F.T.C. to Review Online Ads and Privacy," *The New York Times*, Nov. 1, 2007, at C1, www.nytimes.com/2007/11/01/technology/01Privacy.html?ref=technology.

[7]Nicholas Carlson, "Facebook Expected to File for $100 Billion IPO This Year," June 13, 2011, www.businessinsider.com/facebook-ipo-could-come-in-q1-2012-after-october-filing -cnbc-reports-2011-6.

display ads, 90% of its total revenue, and was expected to bring in $4.05 billion in advertising revenue the following year.[8]

Facebook uses its citizens' demographic information, interests, likes, friends, websites frequented, and even contact information as the foundation of its advertising platform. Facebook encourages users to disclose more information about themselves through "very powerful game-like mechanisms to reward disclosure," said media activist Cory Doctorow, co-editor of Boing Boing.[9] Doctorow compares Facebook's mechanisms to the famous Skinner box[10] used in psychology experiments.[11] But instead of a lab rat rewarded with a food pellet each time it pushes a lever in the box, a Facebook user is rewarded with "likes" and attention from friends and family each time that person posts more information.

"And this is not there because Facebook thinks that disclosing information is good for you necessarily," says Doctorow. "It's in service to a business model that cashes in on the precious material of our social lives and trades it for pennies."

But the collection and marketing of personal information are far more insidious, and profitable, than just the actions of Facebook. Mark Zuckerberg's brainchild makes up only 14.6% of the behavioral advertising market. And some of the other advertisers use tactics that make Zuckerberg's seem tame. Every single action I undertook that Sunday morning was potentially seized by a data aggregator through some means or another. In California, consumers are suing the company NebuAd, which contracted with 26 internet service providers, including Delaware's Cable One, New York's Bresnan Communications, and Texas's CenturyTel, to install NebuAd's hardware on those internet service providers' networks without ISP users' consent.[12] The hardware allowed NebuAd to use deep packet inspection—a mechanism to intercept and copy all the online transmissions of the ISPs' subscribers and transmit them to NebuAd's headquarters.[13] All of them.

Everything you post on a social network or other website is being digested, analyzed, and monetized. In essence, a second self—a virtual interpretation of you—is being created from the detritus of your life that exists on the Web. Increasingly, key decisions about you are based

---

[8]Stephanie Reese, "Quick Stat: Facebook to Bring in $4.05 Billion in Ad Revenues This Year," April 26, 2011, www.emarketer.com/blog/index.php/tag/facebook-ad-revenue/.

[9]Cory Doctorow, Talk at TEDx Observer, 2011, http://tedxtalks.ted.com/video /TEDxObserver-Cory-Doctorow.

[10]*Skinner box*: A laboratory apparatus designed by behavioral psychologist B.F. Skinner (1904–1990), used to test stimulus response conditioning on animals. [Eds.]

[11]Ibid.

[12]Complaint at 2, *Valentine v. NebuAd, Inc.*, No. C08-05113 TEH (N.D. Cal. Nov. 10, 2008); Karl Bode, "Infighting at ISPs over Using NebuAD," May 29, 2008, www.dslreports. com/shownews/Infighting-At-ISPs-Over-Using-NebuAD-94835; *Valentine* v. *NebuAd, Inc.*, 2011 WL 1296111 (N.D. Cal. 2011).

[13]Complaint at 2, *Valentine v. NebuAd, Inc.*, No. C08-05113 TEH (N.D. Cal. Nov. 10, 2008).

on that distorted image of you. Whether you get a mortgage, a kidney, a lover, or a job may be determined by your digital alter ego rather than by you.

In the late 1960s, sociologist John McKnight, then Director of the Midwest Office of the U.S. Commission on Civil Rights,[14] coined the term "redlining" to describe the failure of banks, supermarkets, insurers, and other institutions to offer their services in inner city neighborhoods.[15] The term came from the practice of banks, which drew a red line on a map to indicate where they wouldn't invest.[16] But use of the term expanded to cover a wide array of racially discriminatory practices in general, such as not offering home loans to African Americans, even if they were wealthy or middle class.

Now the map used in redlining is not a geographic map but the map of your travels across the Web. A new term, "weblining," covers the practice of denying certain opportunities to people due to observations about their digital selves. Sometimes redlining and weblining overlap, such as when a website uses zip code information from a social network or an online purchase elsewhere to deny a person an opportunity or charge him a higher interest rate.

"There's an anti-democratic nuance to all of this," says New York University sociologist Marshall Blonsky. "If I am Weblined and judged to be of minimal value, I will never have the products and services channeled to me — or the economic opportunities — that flow to others over the Net."[17]

Data aggregation is big business. The behemoth in the industry, Acxiom, has details on everything from your Social Security number and finances to your online habits.[18] Its former CEO, John Meyer, described it as "the biggest company you've never heard of."[19] Rapleaf is another data aggregator that combines online data, including usernames and social networks, and offline data from public records.[20] One of its competitors, ChoicePoint, has acquired more than 70 smaller database companies and will sell clients one file that contains an individual's credit report, motor vehicle history, police files, property records, court records, birth and death certificates, and marriage and divorce

---

[14]John L. McKnight, Curriculum Vita, www.northwestern.edu/ipr/people/jlmvita.pdf.

[15]Shirley Sagawa and Eli Segal, *Common Interest, Common Good: Creating Value Through Business and Social Sector Partnerships* (Boston: Harvard Business Press, 2000), 30.

[16]D. Bradford Hunt, "Redlining," The Electronic Encyclopedia of Chicago, www.encyclopedia.chicagohistory.org/pages/1050.html.

[17]Marcia Stepanek, "Weblining," April 3, 2000, www.businessweek.com/2000/00_14/b3675027.htm.

[18]David Goldman, "These Data Miners Know Everything About You," Dec. 16, 2010, http://money.cnn.com/galleries/2010/technology/1012/gallery.data_miners/index.html.

[19]Rowena Mason, "Acxiom: the Company That Knows if you Own a Cat or if You're Right-Handed," April 27, 2009, www.telegraph.co.uk/finance/newsbysector/retailandconsumer/5231752/Acxiom-the-company-that-knows-if-you-own-a-cat-or-if-youre-right-handed.html.

[20]Goldman, "These Data Miners Know Everything About You."

decrees.[21] Yet ChoicePoint didn't do a great job of keeping that information secure. In 2005, identity thieves who submitted false applications to ChoicePoint claiming to be small businesses were given access to ChoicePoint's database that contained financial records of more than 163,000 consumers.[22] The Federal Trade Commission attributed the security breach to a lack of proper security and record handling procedures and, as part of a settlement with ChoicePoint, required the company to implement a comprehensive information security program and to pay $10 million in civil penalties and $5 million to reimburse the consumers affected by the identity theft.[23] That same year, hackers targeted LexisNexis (an aggregator which later bought ChoicePoint for $4.1 billion in cash), and accessed the personal information of 310,000 customers.[24]

Weblining goes further than traditional redlining. Sometimes an individual's credit card limit is lowered, midcourse, based on data from aggregators, even when the cardholder has done nothing wrong. Kevin Johnson, a condo owner and businessman, held an American Express card with a $10,800 limit. When he returned from his honeymoon, he found that the limit had been lowered to $3,800. The switch was not based on anything Kevin had done but on aggregate data. A letter from the company told him: "Other customers who have used their card at establishments where you recently shopped have a poor repayment history with American Express."[25]

Not only does weblining affect what opportunities are offered to you (in the form of advertisements, discounts, and credit lines), it also affects the types of information you see. When you open Yahoo! News or go to other news websites, you get a personalized set of articles, different from your spouse's or neighbor's. That may sound like a good thing, but you may be losing out on the big picture. With the physical version of *The New York Times,* you'd at least see the headlines about what was going on in the world, even if you were skimming the paper to get to the movie reviews. But world news may disappear entirely from your browser if you have indicated an interest in something else. Ever since I clicked on a story about the royal wedding, the world news stories I used to receive when I logged on to my email have been replaced by celebrity breakup and fashion stories. But if we are all read-

---

[21]Ian Ayres, *Super Crunchers* (New York: Bantam Dell, 2007), 134.

[22]Complaint at 4, *U.S. v. ChoicePoint,* No. 06-CV-0198 (N.D. Ga. Jan. 30, 2006).

[23]Ibid at 4-6; Stipulated Final Judgment and Order for Civil Penalties, Permanent Injunction, and Other Equitable Relief, *U.S. v. ChoicePoint,* No. 06-CV-0198 (N.D. Ga. Feb. 10, 2006).

[24]Marcia Savage, "LexisNexis Security Breach Worse Than Thought," April 12, 2005, www.scmagazineus.com/lexisnexis-security-breach-worse-than-thought/article/31977/; Toby Anderson, "LexisNexis Owner Reed Elsevier Buys Choice-Point," Feb. 21, 2008, www.usatoday.com/money/industries/2008-02-21-reed-choicepoint_N.htm.

[25]Chris Cuomo, Jay Shaylor, Mary McGuirt, and Chris Francescani, "'GMA' Gets Answers: Some Credit Card Companies Financially Profiling Customers," Jan. 28, 2009, http://abcnews.go.com/GMA/GetsAnswers/Story?id=6747461.

ing a different, narrow range of articles, how can we participate in a civic democracy?

"Ultimately, democracy works only if we citizens are capable of thinking beyond our narrow self-interest. But to do so, we need a shared view of the world we cohabit," says Eli Pariser in *The Filter Bubble: What the Internet Is Hiding from You.* Pariser explains that the internet initially seemed like the perfect tool for democracy. But now, he points out, "Personalization has given us something very different: a public sphere sorted and manipulated by algorithms, fragmented by design, and hostile to dialogue."[26]

Most people have no idea how much information is collected surreptitiously about them from social networks and other websites. When asked about behavioral advertising, only half of the participants in a 2010 study believed that it was a common practice.[27] One respondent said, "Behavioral advertising sounds like something my paranoid friend would dream up, but not something that would ever really occur in real life."

People have a misplaced trust that what they post is private: A Consumer Reports poll found that "61% of Americans are confident that what they do online is private and not shared without their permission" and that "57% incorrectly believe that companies must identify themselves and indicate why they are collecting data and whether they intend to share it with other organizations."[28]

When people realize that websites and advertising companies are collecting extensive information about them, many want legal change. A telephone survey found that 66% of adult Americans opposed being targeted by behavioral advertising and are troubled by the technologies used to enable it.[29] Also, 68% of Americans opposed being "followed" on the Web and 70% of Americans supported the idea of requiring hefty fines to be paid by a company that collects or uses someone's information without his or her consent. Most people — 92% — believe that websites and advertising companies should be required to delete all information stored about an individual if requested to do so.

Your ability to protect yourself against unwanted data collection depends largely on the technique being used to acquire information. With some methods, companies use your own computer against you by instructing your internet browser to store information on your computer's

[26]Eli Pariser, *The Filter Bubble: What the Internet Is Hiding from You* (New York: Penguin, 2011), 164.

[27]Aleecia M. McDonald and Lorrie F. Cranor, "Americans' Attitudes About Internet Behavioral Advertising Practices," *Proceedings of the 9th Workshop on Privacy in the Electronic Society WPES*, Oct. 4, 2010, 6.

[28] "Consumer Reports Poll: Americans Extremely Concerned About Internet Privacy," Sep. 25, 2008, www.consumersunion.org/pub/core_telecom_and_utilities/006189.html.

[29]Joseph Turow, Jennifer King, Chris Jay Hoofnagle, Amy Bleakley, and Michael Hennessy, "Contrary to What Marketers Say, Americans Reject Tailored Advertising and Three Activities That Enable It," September 2009, at 3, www.ftc.gov/os/comments /privacyroundtable/544506-00113.pdf.

hard drive that data aggregators can use to track your movement online and build a profile of your online behaviors. Other methods tap the information as it travels from your computer to the recipient's website or email address. (See "Web Tracking Chart.")

The collection of information from websites and social networks 25 began modestly enough. Social networks asked you if you'd like to have your password stored. Websites like Amazon.com began to keep track of your purchases on their sites to make recommendations and to allow you the convenience of not re-entering a password or credit card number each time you visit the site. Now tracking technologies with names like cookies, Flash cookies, web beacons, deep packet inspection, data scraping, and search queries allow advertisers to create a picture of you by noting what you look at, look up, and buy across the internet. Sometimes this information is even linked to offline purchases and activities you engage in.

Until I started writing this book, I had no idea that Comcast, my internet service provider, installed more than a hundred tracking tools.[30] Dictionary.com (one of my favorite websites, which I use more often than Facebook) installed 234 tracking tools on a user's computer without permission, only 11 from Dictionary.com itself and 223 from companies that track internet users.[31] The vast majority of these tools, according to a report by *The Wall Street Journal*, did not allow users to decline tracking. Among the 50 top sites assessed in this study by *The Wall Street Journal*, Dictionary.com "ranked highest in exposing users to potentially aggressive surveillance."

Increasingly ingenious and troubling technologies are used to learn ever more about you. Two apps on the iPhone and Android devices—Color and Shopkick—activate your phone's microphone and camera to collect background sound and light patterns from your location, be it a bar, your office, or your home. Using the same type of program that allows your iPhone to name a song based on just a few notes, Color makes assessments about your location to alert you if other people in your social network are nearby and Shopkick assesses if the store you've entered has a bargain to offer you. Silicon Valley blogger Mike Elgan points out the wealth of information marketers can collect about you through these phone apps: "Your gender, and the gender of people you talk to; your approximate age, and the ages of the people you talk to; what time you go to bed, and what time you wake up; what you watch on TV and listen to on the radio; how much of your time you

[30]Julia Angwin and Tom McGinty, "Sites Feed Personal Details to New Tracking Industry," *The Wall Street Journal*, July 30, 2010, at A1, http://online.wsj.com/article/SB10001424052748703977004575393173432219064.html.
[31]"Tracking The Companies That Track You Online," Dave Davies's interview with Julia Angwin, *Fresh Air*, Aug. 19, 2010, www.npr.org/templates/story/story.php?storyId=129298003; Julia Angwin, "The Web's New Gold Mine: Your Secrets," *The Wall Street Journal*, July 30, 2010, at W1, http://online.wsj.com/article/SB1000142405274870394090457539507351298940 4.html.

spend alone, and how much with others; whether you live in a big city or a small town; what form of transportation you use to get to work."[32] . . .

Even the games you play and the apps you use on Facebook can collect and transmit personal information about you. In 2007, Facebook launched a platform that let software developers build applications that run on the site. By 2011, there were more than 550,000 apps, and those apps have become an industry, with social games, the biggest category of apps, having a projected revenue of $1.2 billion annually.[33] Facebook reported in 2010 that 70% of its users run at least one app each month.[34]

A 2010 investigation by *The Wall Street Journal* found that many of the most popular applications on Facebook were transmitting identifying information about users and their friends to advertisers and internet tracking companies, which is a violation of Facebook's privacy policy.[35] *The Wall Street Journal* analyzed the ten most popular Facebook apps, including Zynga's FarmVille, with 59 million users, and Zynga's Mafia Wars, with 21.9 million users, and found that they were transmitting Facebook user IDs to data aggregators. When a data aggregator has a Facebook ID, it can access any public information on a person's Facebook page (which could include the person's name, age, residence, occupation, and photos). The Zynga applications were sharing Facebook users' IDs with the internet tracking company Rapleaf, which then added the information to its own database of internet users for enhanced behavioral advertising.[36]

Rather than focusing on an individual's interaction with a website, some data aggregators use a method known as "scraping" to extract all the data that anyone has posted on a particular website, analyze it, and sell it. Web scrapers copy information from websites through specially coded software.[37] These software programs are also referred to as web robots, crawlers, spiders, or screen-scrapers. Scrapers are designed to search through the HTML code that makes up a website and extract desired information. If a certain website includes a discussion by new moms (or by people considering buying cars), the data scraper can sell that information and the people's email addresses or IP addresses to advertisers who want to target ads to those types of consumers.

Web scrapers "are capable of making thousands of database searches per minute, far exceeding what a human user of a website

30

[32]Mike Elgan, "Snooping: It's Not a Crime, It's a Feature," April 16, 2011, www .computerworld.com/s/article/print/9215853/Snooping_It_s_not_a_crime_it_s_a_feature.

[33]Jami Makan, "10 Things Facebook Won't Say," Jan. 10, 2011, www.smartmoney .com/spend/technology/10-things-facebook-wont-say-1294414171193/.

[34]Emily Steel and Geoffrey A. Fowler, "Facebook in Privacy Breach," *The Wall Street Journal*, Oct. 18, 2010, at A1, http://online.wsj.com/article/SB1000142405270230477280457 5558484075236968.html.

[35]Ibid.

[36]Ibid.

[37]"Web Scraping Tutorial," March 7, 2009, www.codediesel.com/php/web-scraping -in-php-tutorial/. CodeDiesel is a web development journal.

could accomplish," says attorney Sean O'Reilly, who previously worked in the software industry. "Web vendors have a difficult time detecting a difference between consumers accessing this information for their own benefit, and aggregators accessing the information to return to their own databases."[38]

Search engines such as Google, Yahoo!, and Bing also collect, store, and analyze information about individual users through their search queries. Search engines maintain "server logs," which, according to Google's Privacy Policy, include your "web request, Internet Protocol address, browser type, browser language, the date and time of your request and one or more cookies that may uniquely identify your browser."[39] Microsoft's search engine, Bing, adds that it also "will attempt to derive your approximate location based on your IP address."[40] Search engines use this information to optimize their search algorithms and to record an individual's preferences.[41] Though Google uses these logs for fraud prevention and to improve search results, it also analyzes the logs to generate more revenue through targeted advertising.[42] Yahoo! also uses this information to personalize advertising and page content. Yahoo! acknowledges that it also allows other companies to display ads on its pages and those ads may "set and access cookies on your computer" that are not subject to Yahoo!'s privacy policy.[43]

In 2006, AOL made public 20 million queries entered into its search engine from 658,000 users on its website research.aol.com.[44] AOL's release contained all of those users' searches over a three-month period and detailed whether they clicked on a result, what the result was, and where it was in the list of results.[45] An AOL researcher, Abdur Chowdhury, explained the release of the queries as an effort to facilitate "closer collaboration between AOL and anyone with a desire to work on interesting problems."[46] But the project ended up breaching people's privacy. In some instances, people could be identified through the types of searches they undertook.

[38]Sean O'Reilly, "Nominative Fair Use and Internet Aggregators: Copyright and Trademark Challenges Posed by Bots, Web Crawlers and Screen-Scraping Technologies," 19 *Loyola Consumer Law Review* 273 (2007).

[39]"Google Privacy FAQ," www.google.com/intl/en/privacy/faq.html#toc-terms-server-logs.

[40]"Bing Privacy Supplement," January 2011, http://privacy.microsoft.com/en-us/bing.mspx.

[41]"Google Privacy FAQ."

[42]Omer Tene, "What Google Knows: Privacy and Internet Search Engines," 2008 *Utah Law Review* 1433, 1454 (2008).

[43]"Yahoo! Privacy Policy," http://info.yahoo.com/privacy/us/yahoo/details.html.

[44]Tene, "What Google Knows: Privacy and Internet Search Engines."

[45]Michael Arrington, "AOL Proudly Releases Massive Amounts of Private Data," Aug. 6, 2006, http://techcrunch.com/2006/08/06/aol-proudly-releases-massive-amounts-of-user-search-data/.

[46]Abdur Chowdhury, Email sent to SIG-IRList newsletter, Aug. 3, 2006, http://sifaka.cs.uiuc.edu/xshen/aol/20060803_SIG-IRListEmail.txt.

A quick look at some of the leaked AOL search logs makes it easy to imagine how damaging a search log can be when linked to a party in a criminal, civil, or divorce case.

User 11574916:
> cocaine in urine
> asian mail order brides
> states reciprocity with florida
> florida dui laws
> extradtion from new york to florida
> mail order brides from largos
> will one be extradited for a dui
> cooking jobs in french quarter new orleans
> will i be extradited from ny to fl on dui charge

User 336865:
> sexy pregnant ladies naked
> nudist
> sexy feet
> child rape stories
> tamagotchi town.com
> preteen sex stories
> illegal child porn
> incest stories
> 10 year old nude pics
> preteen nude models
> illegel anime porn
> yu-gi-oh

User 59920:
> cats skinned in fort lupton co
> cats killed in fort lupton co
> jonbenets autopsy photos
> crime scene photos of the crawl space and duffle bag in ramseys house
> sexy bathing suits
> what a neck looks like after its been strangled
> pictures what a neck looks like after it was strangled
> pictures of murder victims that have been strangled
> pictures of murder by strangulation
> knitting stitches
> what jonbenet would look like today
> new jersey park police
> jonbenet in her casket
> ransom note in the movie obsession what did it read
> movie ransom notes
> scouting knots
> manila rope and its uses
> brown paper bags cops use for evidence
> rope to use to hog tie someone
> body transport boulder colorado

User 1515830:
> chai tea calories
> calories in bananas

aftermath of incest
how to tell your family you're a victim of incest
pottery barn
curtains
surgical help for depression
oakland raiders comforter set
can you adopt after a suicide attempt
who is not allowed to adopt
i hate men
medication to enhance female desire
jobs in denver colorado
teaching positions in denver colorado
how long will the swelling last after my tummy tuck
divorce laws in ohio
free remote keyloggers
baked macaroni and cheese with sour cream
how to deal with anger
teaching jobs with the denver school system
marriage counseling tips
anti psychotic drugs[47]

Your web searches provide data on which you can be judged, er- 35
roneously or not. If you've looked up the side effects of antidepressants,
that information might be used against you by an employer or a college
admissions officer. Your search for a divorce lawyer, advice about green
cards, or information about sexually transmitted diseases might also be
used in ways that harm you.

Your second self on the Web is likely a distortion of your offline self.
The person whose leaked AOL searches related to extradition might
have been writing a mystery, rather than covering up a crime. The
woman who was seeking information on AOL about incest might have
been trying to help a friend, rather than dealing with her own troubled
past.

When AOL released the supposedly anonymous queries, it was easy
for reporters from *The New York Times* to identify Thelma Arnold as
searcher 4417749 due to her searches for other Arnolds and her searches
about Lilburn, Georgia.[48] After discussing her queries for 60-year-old
single men, queries about her three dogs, and queries researching her
friends' ailments, Thelma said, "My goodness, it's my whole personal
life. I had no idea somebody was looking over my shoulder."[49]

But "in user search query logs, what you see is not always what you
get," notes Omer Tene, a professor at a law school in Rishon Le Zion,

---

[47]Declan McCullagh, "AOL's Disturbing Glimpse into Users' Lives," Aug. 7, 2006,
http://news.cnet.com/AOLs-disturbing-glimpse-into-users-lives/2100-1030_3-6103098.html
#ixzzlM56yaUU2.
    [48]Michael Barbaro and Tom Zeller, Jr., "A Face Is Exposed for AOL Searcher 4417749,"
The New York Times, Aug. 9, 2006, at A1, www.nytimes.com/2006/08/09/technology/09aol
.html?pagewanted=all.
    [49]Ibid.

Israel. Anyone who had access to Thelma Arnold's logs saw searches for "hand tremors," "nicotine effects on the body," "dry mouth," "bipolar," and "single dances in Atlanta." However, those were searches Thelma conducted for others and do not paint an accurate picture of her life or health.[50]

The attributes of your digital doppelgänger[51] may have more influence on what opportunities you receive than any of your offline characteristics. Rather than expanding opportunities for you, the targeted ads that you see may actually deny you certain benefits. You might be shown a credit card with a lower credit limit, not because of your credit history but because of your race, sex, zip code, or the types of websites you visit. As a consequence of weblining, the information collected by data aggregators is often sold to the public at large (through websites such as Spokeo) and might later hamper your efforts to get a job, qualify for a loan, adopt a child, or fight for your rights in a criminal trial.

As behavioral advertisers increasingly dictate a person's online and 40 offline experiences, stereotyped characterizations may become self-fulfilling. Rather than reflecting reality, behavioral analysis may inevitably define it. When young people from "poor" zip codes are bombarded with advertisements for trade schools, they may be more likely than their peers to forgo college. And when women are routinely shown articles about cooking and celebrities, rather than stock market trends, they will likely disclaim any financial savvy in the future. Behavioral advertisers are drawing new redlines, refusing to grant people the tools necessary to escape the roles that society expects they play. Our digital doppelgängers are directing our futures and the future of society....

ENGAGING THE TEXT

1. What kinds of information about herself does Andrews expose during the typical morning online she describes at the beginning of this selection (para. 1)? Which of the bits of information she divulges strike you as the most risky or dangerous to share online? Which, if any, seem relatively safe? Why?

2. In Andrews's view, what's wrong with data-mining companies collecting information about us online? Why does it matter if marketers and others can find out your marriage history, the gender of your friends, your favorite bars and restaurants, when you go to bed, or how you get to work?

3. Why does Andrews believe that "weblining" is potentially "undemocratic"? How might this practice limit opportunities and reinforce stereotypes? Why

---

[50]Tene, "What Google Knows: Privacy and Internet Search Engines."

[51]*doppelgänger*: German word for a "double" or "look-a like" of a person, often with negative or ominous characteristics. [Eds.]

might weblining and behavioral advertising pose a greater threat to democracy than traditional print or television advertising?

4. Working in groups, create alternative profiles for the AOL users associated with each of the four search histories that Andrews offers. How might you explain the pattern of searches in each case? Should public safety officials have access to this kind of online information? Why or why not?

5. Drawing on all the information you post on social media sites, a week's worth of Internet searches, recent purchases, and other forms of online activity, compose a profile of your online "doppelgänger." How do you appear to the world online? If you were an online decisionmaker, would you recommend your "digital self" as a potential marriage partner, for a job or loan, or as an adoptive parent? Why or why not?

EXPLORING CONNECTIONS

6. Write a dialogue between Andrews and Peggy Orenstein (p. 446) about the impact of the Internet on privacy and our ability to control our personal images. How might the online habits of the teens Orenstein discusses lead to serious problems later in life because of data aggregation?

7. Using Andrews and Juan Williams's analysis of political correctness (p. 648) as your point of departure, write an essay on the decline of a shared civic culture in the United States. In your view, do modern technologies like cable television and the Internet threaten to undermine the shared values that make democracy possible?

8. How might Andrews respond to Eric Liu and Nick Hanauer's (p. 750) enthusiastic support of social networks as a new form of citizenship? How might social networks actually undermine citizenship and democratic action?

EXTENDING THE CRITICAL CONTEXT

9. Go online to read more about data-aggregating companies like Acxiom, Rapleaf, and ChoicePoint. How much data do such corporations gather each year, and on how many Americans? What kinds of data do they collect? How is this data used, and by whom? Based on your research, how serious a threat to privacy and individual liberty is the data-aggregating industry?

10. Visit the Web site of Acxiom or other data-mining companies to learn more about the socio-economic categories they use to classify those they track. Who do you think you'd find in the following sampling of the seventy categories used by Acxiom? Which would you want — and not want — to belong to? How might these classifications affect the types of information and opportunities their members encounter online? Does the use of such categories amount to a legal form of discrimination? Why or why not?

Savvy Single	Collegiate Crowd
Solo & Stable	Modest Means
Toys & Tots	Cash & Carriers
Shooting Stars	Dynamic Duos
Humble Homes	Trucks & Trailers
Resilient Renters	Flush Families
Blue Collar Bunch	Platinum Oldies
Established Elite	Rural Rovers

11. Visit Lori Andrews's "Social Network Constitution" site on the Internet, and review the ten rights and freedoms it specifies for life online. Then take the interactive poll associated with the site. Which of the ten rights listed do you support? Which do you feel are most important for safeguarding privacy and freedom online? Which seem less important, and why? You can find the "Social Network Constitution" at: www.socialnetworkconstitution .com/the-social-network-constitution.html.

SLAVERY IN THE LAND OF THE FREE
KEVIN BALES AND RON SOODALTER

For most Americans, slavery may not seem like a serious threat to civil rights — at least not since 1865 when the Thirteenth Amendment to the Constitution abolished involuntary servitude. So it may come as a shock that slavery still thrives in today's United States. In fact, according to the authors of this selection, permanently indentured servants can be found in every American neighborhood and industry, washing our floors, building our houses, and picking the fruit and vegetables we eat. Slavery, it seems, is one of the fastest growing sectors of the national and world economies. Kevin Bales is founder of Free the Slaves, a Washington-based nonprofit organization dedicated to ending slavery around the world. He is also Emeritus Professor of Sociology at Roehampton University in London, England. His publications include *Disposable People: New Slavery in the Global Economy* (1999) and *Understanding Global Slavery: A Reader* (2005). Ron Soodalter is a respected historian who serves on the board of the Abraham Lincoln Institute. He is co-author, with Kevin Bales, of the *The Slave Next Door: Human Trafficking and Slavery in America Today* (2009), the source of this excerpt.

The Old Slavery and the New

> *The great thought of captains, owners, consignees, and others, was to make the most money they could in the shortest possible time. Human nature is the same now as then.*
> —FREDERICK DOUGLASS, *The New National Era*, August 17, 1871,
> recalling the Atlantic slave trade

CERTAIN THINGS we know to be true. We know that slavery is a bad thing, perpetrated by bad people. We also know that slavery not only exists throughout the world today but flourishes. With approximately twenty-seven million people in bondage, it is thought to be the third most profitable criminal enterprise of our time, following only drugs and guns. In fact, more than twice as many people are in bondage in the world today than were taken from Africa during the entire 350 years of the Atlantic slave trade. And we know that slavery is alive and more than well in the United States, thriving in the dark, and practiced in many forms in places where you'd least expect it.

Meet Sandra Bearden. Sandra was a twenty-seven-year-old home-maker in a comfortable suburb of Laredo, Texas—a neighborhood of solid brick homes and manicured lawns. Married, the mother of a four-year-old son, she lived a perfectly normal middle-class existence. By all accounts, Sandra was a pleasant woman, the sort you'd chat with at the mall or the supermarket...the sort who might live next door. Yet she is currently serving a life sentence, convicted of multiple offenses, includ-ing human trafficking and slavery.

It started innocently enough. At first, all Sandra wanted was a maid—someone to do the housework and help with her small son—but she didn't want to pay a lot. So she drove across the border to a small, dirt-poor village near Vera Cruz, Mexico, where she was introduced to Maria and her parents. Maria was only twelve when she met Sandra Bearden. She had very little schooling and dreamed of getting an edu-cation—a dream that her parents encouraged but could do nothing to achieve. Over coffee in their small kitchen, Bearden offered Maria a job, as well as the chance to attend school, learn English, and taste the rich life of "el Norte." The work, as Bearden described it, was much like what Maria was already doing at home, and, with the promise of educa-tion and opportunity, Sandra's offer made a very enticing package. The fact that Sandra herself was Mexican born helped Maria's parents feel they could trust her, and they gave their permission. Sandra smuggled Maria across the border in her expensive car and drove her to her home in Laredo.

On arrival, Maria was dragged into hell. Sandra Bearden used vio-lence and terror to squeeze work and obedience from the child. From early morning till midafternoon, Maria cooked, cleaned, scrubbed, and polished. If Maria dozed off from exhaustion, or when Sandra decided she wasn't working fast enough, Sandra would blast pepper spray into Maria's eyes. A broom was broken over the girl's back and a few days later, a bottle against her head. At one point, Bearden tortured the twelve-year-old by jamming a garden tool up her vagina. That was Maria's workday; her "time off" was worse.

When Maria wasn't working, Sandra would chain her to a pole in the backyard without food or water. An eight-foot concrete fence kept her hidden from neighbors. After chaining her, Sandra would sometimes force Maria to eat dog feces. Then Maria would be left alone, her arms chained behind her with a padlock, her legs chained and locked together till the next morning, when the work and torture would begin again. Through the long afternoon and night Maria would fade in and out of consciousness from dehydration, and in her hunger she would sometimes scoop dirt into her mouth. Like most slaves in America, Maria was in shock, disoriented, isolated, and dependent. To maintain control, Bearden kept Maria hungry and in pain.

About one-third of the handful of slaves freed in the United States each year come to liberty because an average person sees something he or she just can't ignore. Luckily, one of the Beardens' neighbors had to do some work on his roof, and that probably saved Maria's life. Looking down over the high concrete wall into the Bearden's backyard, the neighbor saw a small girl chained up and whimpering; he called 911.

The police found Maria chained hand and foot, covered in cuts and bruises, and suffering from dehydration and exposure. She was too weak to walk and had to be carried to freedom on a stretcher. Her skin was badly burned from days in the sun. (In Laredo, Texas, the *average* summer temperature is ninety-eight degrees.) Photos taken at the time show one of her eyes bloodied and infected and thick welts and scars on her skin where the chains had cut into her. She had not eaten in four days. The district attorney said, "This is the worst case I've ever seen, worse than any murder. It's tragic all the way around." Later, at Bearden's trial, the policeman who found Maria wept. "She was shaking and crying and had a scared look in her eyes. She was in severe pain," Officer Jay Reece testified. He explained that he had tried to remove the chains from Maria's arms with bolt cutters but couldn't. As he tried to move her arm to cut the chains, she twisted and whimpered because she was in so much pain. "I've never seen anything like it before," Reese said, and sitting in the witness box, this policeman began to cry.

It is hard to imagine, but Maria was one of the lucky slaves. In America, most slaves spend four to five years in bondage; Maria's enslavement lasted only seven months. Sandra Bearden was arrested, and the Mexican government brought Maria's parents up from Vera Cruz. Her father blamed himself for what had happened. "We made a decision that we thought would be good for our child, and look what happened. I made a mistake, truly, and this is all my fault," he said.[1] Unlike

---

[1] "Girl Reunited with Parents," *Laredo Morning Times*, May 17, 2001. [All notes are Bales' and Soodalter's, except 7, 8, 11, and 17.]

most slaveholders in America, Bearden was caught and convicted. Like most slaves, Maria got nothing, except the fare for the twelve-hour bus ride home. She had just turned thirteen.[2]

We all ask, "How could someone so abuse a child—to stake her in the sun, feed her excrement, beat her bloody....Surely, only a monster could do this." Yet Sandra Bearden's treatment of Maria is not unusual....

Equal Opportunity Slavery

Most Americans' idea of slavery comes right out of *Roots*[3]—the chains, 10 the whip in the overseer's hand, the crack of the auctioneer's gavel. That was one form of bondage. The slavery plaguing America today takes a different form, but make no mistake, it is real slavery. Where the law sanctioned slavery in the 1800s, today it's illegal. Where antebellum masters took pride in the ownership of slaves as a sign of status, today's human traffickers and slaveholders keep slaves hidden, making it all the more difficult to locate victims and punish offenders. Where the slaves in America were once primarily African and African American, today we have "equal opportunity" slavery; modern-day slaves come in all races, all types, and all ethnicities. We are, if anything, totally democratic when it comes to owning and abusing our fellow human beings. All that's required is the chance of a profit and a person weak enough and vulnerable enough to enslave.

This is capitalism at its worst, and it is supported by a dramatic alteration in the basic economic equation of slavery. Where an average slave in 1850 would have cost the equivalent of $40,000 in modern money, today's slave can be bought for a few hundred dollars. This cheapness makes the modern slave easily affordable, but it also makes him or her a disposable commodity. For the slaveholder it's often cheaper to let a slave die than it is to buy medicine to keep the slave alive. There is no form of slavery, past or present, that isn't horrific; however, today's slavery is one of the most diabolical strains to emerge in the thousands of years in which humans have been enslaving their fellows.

So How Many Slaves Are We Talking About?

According to a U.S. State Department study, some 14,500 to 17,500 people are trafficked into the United States from overseas and enslaved *each year*.[4] They come from Africa, Asia, India, China, Latin America, and the former Soviet states. Nor are native-born Americans immune from slavers; many are stolen from the streets of their own cities and towns. Some sources, including the federal government, have put out

---

[2]"Woman Sentenced to Life in Prison for Torturing 12-Year-Old Maid," *Amarillo Globe News*, October 20, 2001.

[3]*Roots*: Award-winning 1977 television mini-series on slavery in the United States.

[4]U.S. Department of State, *Trafficking in Persons Report*, June 2006, www.state.gov/g /tip/rls/tiprpt/2006/.

extremely high estimates of the number of U.S. citizens—primarily children—caught in slavery. The fact is, the precise number of slaves in the United States, whether trafficked in from other countries or enslaved from our own population, is simply not known. Given the hidden nature of the crime, the best numbers on offer are rough estimates. We do know that slaves in America are found—or rather, *not* found—in nearly all fifty states, working as commercial sex slaves, fruit pickers, construction workers, gardeners, and domestics. They work in restaurants, factories, laundries, and sweatshops. Each year human trafficking and slavery in America generate millions upon millions of dollars for criminals who prey on the most vulnerable: the desperate, the uneducated, and the impoverished immigrant seeking a better life. Brutalized and held in slavery for years, those who survive face indifference, official confusion, stigma, and shame as they struggle to regain control over their stolen and deeply damaged lives.

While no one knows for sure how many people are enslaved in America, a conservative estimate would be around fifty thousand and growing. Even for those who have worked in this area for years, these numbers are staggering. More astounding is the fact that this is a crime that, as a rule, goes unpunished. This lack of punishment is reflected in a remarkable parallel in American crime rates. If we accept the government's estimates, about seventeen thousand people are trafficked into slavery in the United States in any given year; coincidentally about seventeen thousand people are murdered in the United States each year. Obviously, murder is the ultimate crime, but slavery comes a close second, especially considering the other crimes associated with it, such as rape and torture. Note that the national success rate in solving murder cases is about 70 percent; around eleven thousand murders are "cleared" each year. But according to the U.S. government's own numbers, the annual percentage of trafficking and slavery cases solved is less than 1 percent. If 14,500 to 17,500 people were newly enslaved in America in 2006, the fact is that in the same year the Department of Justice brought charges against only 111 people for human trafficking and slavery; 98 of them were convicted.[5] And those figures apply only to people trafficked from other countries; no measures exist for domestic slavery victims.

In July 2004 then-President Bush[6] talked about the rate of arrests and convictions for human trafficking in the United States: "Since 2001, we've charged 110 traffickers. That's triple the number charged in the previous three years. We're beginning to make good, substantial progress. The message is getting out: We're serious. And when we catch you,

[5]U.S. Department of Justice, *Attorney General's Annual Report to Congress on U.S. Government Activities to Combat Trafficking in Persons for Fiscal Year 2006*, May 2007, www.usdoj.gov/olp/human_trafficking.htm, 17. Other cases were brought by Immigration and Customs Enforcement.

[6]*then-President Bush*: George Walker Bush (b. 1946), 43rd president of the United States from 2001 to 2009.

you'll find out we're serious. We're staying on the hunt." Strong words, but the unvarnished truth is, with less than 1 percent of the offenders apprehended and less than 1 percent of the victims freed, the flow of human "product" into America continues practically unchecked....

Slaves in the Pastures of Plenty

> *California, Arizona, I harvest your crops,*
> *Then it's north up to Oregon to gather your hops.*
> *Dig the beets from your ground, cut the grapes*
> *from your vine*
> *To set on your table your light sparkling wine.*
> —WOODY GUTHRIE, "Pastures of Plenty"

A Study in Contrasts

About thirty miles due south of the Southwest Florida International 15 Airport is the town of Naples. It sits on its own bay off the Gulf of Mexico, not far from Sanibel, Vanderbilt Beach, and the Isles of Capri. Naples is a lovely town—a rich town—attracting wealthy retirees and men of industry. A palm-lined walk down Fifth Avenue will take you past art galleries offering everything from contemporary sculpture to portraits of your pets; chic restaurants featuring a variety of ethnic and exotic cuisines; high-end clothing and jewelry stores; and a fair smattering of Bentleys and Rolls Royces.

A small tour boat offers a sunset cruise of the bay. The area is rich in animal and bird life, brightly colored flowers, and lush plants, but the guide points out only the houses and properties, proudly ticking off for the tourists the astronomical values of each. No number is below seven figures, and several are higher. One empty lot, we are told, recently sold for $18,000,000. It sits, like a missing tooth, between two massive structures of questionable taste but stunning worth. Many of these houses serve as second, third, or fourth homes and are occupied for only a few weeks a year.

The boats that line the pier are studies in sleekness and speed. Long, shark-shaped Cigarettes and Scarabs,[7] with their two and three outboards of 250 horsepower each, give the illusion of motion even at the dock. Looming over the pier walk are elegant new apartment buildings, painted various pastel shades, as are many of the homes and shops of Naples. There is nothing here to jar the senses. There is everywhere an air of money and complacency.

If, however, you left the airport and drove forty minutes to the south-*east,* along narrow state roads, you would enter the town of Immokalee. You could never confuse the two.

---

[7] *Cigarettes and Scarabs:* Types of powerboats.

Driving into Immokalee, you become instantly aware that this is not a town concerned with its appearance. There is no movie theater, no outward indication of social activity, except for the Seminole Casino, where out-of-towners from Naples and Fort Myers come to gamble. Many of the buildings of Immokalee are low, basic, carelessly maintained. Most of the signs—many roughly hand-painted—are in Spanish, as well as a language that looks familiar, almost French, but spelled phonetically. This is Haitian Creole. In many of Immokalee's homes, English is neither spoken nor understood. The languages are Spanish, Creole, and more than a sprinkling of indigenous tongues—Quiche, Zapotec, Nahuatl, Ttzotzil, Mam, Mixtec, Kanjobal.[8]

There is a handful of restaurants—mostly Mexican—with names like la Michoacana, el Taquito, Mi Ranchita. The décor is minimalist, the food just acceptable; dining out is not a major activity in Immokalee. There are a couple of nail and hair salons, housed in tiny storefronts. One turquoise-and-yellow painted structure advertises "Mimi's Piñatas." Chickens run wild, their crowing a backdrop you stop hearing after a while, and the vultures crowd the roads outside of town in such profusion that they present a driving hazard. Many who live here walk from point to point or ride one-speed bicycles. They can't afford cars. There is not much vehicle traffic in Immokalee itself, with the exception of the trucks that haul the produce to the packinghouses and the long school-type buses that carry the workers to and from the fields.

The Price of Tomatoes

Immokalee is a migrant town—actually, "more a labor reserve than a town."[9] There are many such communities in Florida, but this is the epicenter. Immokalee—an unincorporated community—was built in the first decades of the twentieth century for the growing, picking, packing, and shipping of tomatoes and oranges. Old-timers can still remember the days when teamsters drove horse-drawn wagons from Fort Myers to haul the produce from the fields.[10] There are other crops—lemons, grapefruit, watermelon—but these are the big two, and the tomato crop is the biggest by far. The crews who work in the fields come from Mexico, from Guatemala, from Haiti. Most are young—in their early twenties—small in stature and dark skinned, both by birth and by long exposure to the sun. Many have the Mayan features of the "Indio puro."[11] There is a shyness—a reserve—shown a stranger and, usually, a smile.

Immokalee's year-round population of twenty-five thousand swells to forty thousand during the nine-month harvest season. There are

20

[8]*Quiche, Zapotec, Najuatl, Ttzotzil, Mam, Mixtec, Kanjobal*: Languages of native Mesoamerican tribal peoples. Laura Germino, Coalition of Immokalee Workers (CIW), interview, January 6, 2007.

[9]Greg Asbed, "Coalition of Immokalee Workers: '¡Golpear a Uno Es Golpear a Todos!' To Beat One of Us Is to Beat Us All," in vol. 3 of *Bringing Human Rights Home*, ed. Cynthia Soohoo, Martha F. Davis, and Catherine Albisa (New York: Praeger, 2007), 1–24.

[10]Lucas Benitez, CIW, interview, January 7, 2007.

[11]*"Indio puro"*: Spanish for "pure Indian," indicating 100 percent Indian heritage.

surprisingly few women among Immokalee's farmworkers; around 95 percent of the workforce is male. They have left their home countries and crossed our borders into Texas, Arizona, or New Mexico—most with the help of a *coyote*, or "guide"—in the hope of finding a way to support their families, since no such opportunities exist at home. Instead, they have found jobs that are unrelentingly hard, under the rigid control of crew leaders, for the lowest wages imaginable. Every day, often seven days a week, the workers walk through the 4:00 a.m. darkness to begin gathering at parking lots around town; here they wait for buses that will take them—at least some of them—to the fields. Some carry their lunch from home in white plastic bags, while others choose to buy their daily food in one of the several convenience stores, with names like La Fiesta #3 and La Mexicana #2, that open early to accommodate them. The prices are high, often twice what they are elsewhere; the workers have no choice.

Nor do they have much option as to where they live. The town is honeycombed with parks of broken-down trailers, enclaves of tiny huts, and depressing little apartments. The rents are staggering. A dilapidated single-wide trailer, with dented, dingy yellow corrugated siding that is separating from the frame, accommodates twelve men, who sleep on bare mattresses abutting each other on the floor. Each of them pays a rent of $50 a week. There are perhaps fifteen such trailers on a single lot. The few individuals who own most of these enclaves would qualify as slumlords in any community in America, but their tenants pay the rents and live in their hovels; again, they have no choice.

Picking tomatoes is brutal; it requires working bent over in the southern sun for hours on end, straightening only long enough to run 100 to 150 feet with a filled thirty-two-pound bucket and literally throw it up to the worker on the truck. Lunch is a hurried affair, and water breaks are few. But at least nowadays there's clean water; not so very long ago, it wasn't uncommon for pickers to be obliged to drink from the canals and ditches, taking in the bacteria and the runoff of insecticides and fertilizer along with the water. And until fairly recently, a picker ran the risk of being beaten if he stopped picking long enough to drink.[12]

The pickers are not free to decide when or how much to work; they must work however many hours and days a week the crew chief mandates or weather and conditions permit. For this, they are paid a piece rate—so much per full bucket. The going rate—which has barely changed in nearly thirty years, despite the steady rise in the cost of living—is $25 per ton of tomatoes picked. This means filling around 125 buckets of tomatoes a day just to gross $50. But to make the equivalent of minimum wage, the worker has to fill around *two hundred* buckets—or two and a half tons—of tomatoes; this often entails working twelve or thirteen hours a day, if and when the work is available.

[12]Ibid.

Why aren't these workers paid the minimum wage? The term *minimum wage* is misleading; realistically, although the 2008 rate in Florida is $6.79 per hour, the worker stands no real guarantee of earning it. Conditions are against him. There are no fixed hours, and what records are kept are often doctored in favor of the crew leader and the grower. The worker is also at the mercy of the weather; the market; pestilence; the availability of harvesting equipment; the yield due to the relative richness of a field's soil; the number of times a field has been picked; the distance from the picker to the truck; personal stamina; and, most frustrating, time lost traveling to and from the field and waiting unpaid hours on the bus for the dew to dry or the weather to change.

Because harvesting is by nature unpredictable, the picker must be available every day at around five in the morning; if it turns out there is no work that day, he's just out of luck. This precludes his ability to take a second job. And on days when the work is slack and few pickers are required, he's likely to go home with nothing in his pocket. If he gets to the field and it rains, he earns nothing. The days spent on buses to other regions when the local crops have been picked is unpaid time; and if he and his fellow workers arrive at the new fields before they are ready for picking, they're paid nothing as they wait for the crops to ripen. They are paid only when they are picking, and they are paid little at that. It is no wonder that the Department of Labor (DOL) has described farmworkers as a labor force in "significant economic distress."[13]

The only true measure of the pickers' compensation is their annual earnings: workers average $7,000 to $10,000 per year. On a good day, the best they can accomplish is to reach the poverty level, but their yearly earnings are well below it. There are no benefits—no overtime, no health care, no insurance of any kind. "You can only get sick in Immokalee," says Coalition of Immokalee Workers (CIW) co-founder Lucas Benitez, "between 8:00 a.m. and 4:00 p.m., which are the hours of the clinic." If a picker does get sick, he works nonetheless. If he becomes seriously ill or breaks a limb, not only is he without income, but he must pay his medical bills himself—more often than not an impossibility, since nearly all his money goes to food and rent, with perhaps a few dollars put aside to send home. "You wait until you are half dead to go to a doctor."[14]

Score One for the Dixiecrats

There is no point in looking to the government for help: farm labor is practically the only type of work not covered by the National Labor Relations Act of 1935, the law that protects workers, gives them the right to organize without fear of retaliation, and fixes wage, health, and safety rules. Yes, farmworkers can organize a union or strike for better pay, but they can be fired for doing so. This exclusion of farmworkers from the rights given to almost all other American workers came

---

[13]Greg Asbed, CIW, interview, January 8, 2007.
[14]Lucas Benitez, interview, January 7, 2007.

from the power of Deep South congressmen in 1935, when the law was passed. These Dixiecrat politicians were adamant that black field hands should never be allowed to organize. Not surprisingly, household servants were also excluded from full rights. Some DOL wage and hour rules do apply to farmworkers, but with only two wage and hours inspectors for the entire Southwest Florida region—which includes tens of thousands of farmworkers, as well as other types of laborers—there is little hope of help there either.[15] For years, the local inspector for that section of Florida generally spoke only English—in the midst of workers who did not—and spent more time in the grower's office than in the fields, where he might witness firsthand the treatment of the pickers. With the law on their side, the crew leaders and the growers hold all the cards.

With conditions so dismal, and the pay so low, why would anyone come to Immokalee to work? Or to nearby towns like Lake Placid, Wimauma, or LaBelle? There is simply no real choice: wherever a worker goes to pick America's crops, he meets similar conditions. With the trend toward consolidation and expansion of agribusinesses, it has become increasingly difficult to find work on the old-style family-owned farms of twenty-five years ago. Instead, the small farms are being gobbled up by huge companies. Competing with each other and with foreign suppliers, these megagrowers are themselves being caught in a cost/price squeeze. On the one hand, they face constantly rising costs of gasoline, pesticides, fertilizer, and a couple dozen other items necessary for production. On the other hand, the buyers—fast-food giants such as McDonald's, Subway, Taco Bell, and Burger King, and market corporations like Shop Rite, Wal-Mart, and Costco—are dictating the prices they are willing to pay for tomatoes and other crops. The buyers have turned their corporate backs on the small growers who supplied them faithfully for years. In the words of one worker advocate, the buyers "each have a purchasing company, looking to buy high volume at the lowest possible price. They are price *setters*, not price *takers*."[16] Rather than purchase from several smaller growers, as in the past, these megabuyers have decided to work with the largest suppliers, who can provide ready, uniform, year-round supplies of product. Only the huge agribusinesses, such as Gargiulo, Pacific, Nobles Collier, and the Six L's, can meet the demanding production requirements while weathering the rising costs and the squeeze on their profit margin. Size counts: even with the cost/price pressure they manage to make a tremendous amount of money, and they are growing exponentially.

As large as these agribusinesses are, they pale in the shadow of the companies that supply their needs—giants such as Exxon, John Deere, and Monsanto. Against these multinational corporations the growers

---

[15]John Norris, U.S. DOL wage and hours inspector, Ft. Myers, FL, interview, March 28, 2007.

[16]Greg Asbed, CIW, interview, January 8, 2007.

have no bargaining power. So, with nothing to say about their escalating costs or the buyers' shrinking prices, the only way they can hold on to profits is by cutting labor costs. Their aim is to keep at gutter level the amount they pay—and for decades have paid—their workers, and they do. As a 2004 Oxfam America[17] report put it, "Squeezed by the buyers of their produce, growers pass on the costs and risks imposed on them to those on the lowest rung of the supply chain: the farmworkers they employ."[18] And because these privately held Florida-based grower corporations are constantly expanding, a worker can move to North Carolina, Delaware, California, or even Puerto Rico and still be working in the same grower's fields—for the same pay, and under the same conditions. There is no refuge. While the large grower corporations compete, they have also banded together to control the labor market by forming the Florida Tomato Committee. The committee and the Florida Fruit and Vegetable Association are powerful lobbies with the state government; this is not surprising, since some of the large growers are themselves members of the Florida legislature.

This situation is not new. In her excellent history of Atlantic Coast farmworkers, Cindy Hahamovitch writes of Florida in the 1930s: "While the rest of growers' expenses rose over the course of the decade—the cost of seed, fertilizer, and equipment all went up—farm wages remained stagnant or fell, depending on the crop.... As a veteran of harvests in thirty-three states put it, 'Florida is the sorriest wages in the United States.'"[19] In those days, the workers were mostly African American and Bahamian; today they are most likely to be Latino. Otherwise little has changed, with one ugly exception.

Slavery in the Fields

As bad as most pickers have it, there is a rung on the ladder that is lower still—the *enslaved* farmworker. Antonio Martinez came from a family of five younger siblings, in Hidalgo, Mexico. His parents were sickly, and Antonio was unable to make a sufficient living to support them all. He met with a contractor—a *coyote*—who promised that he would smuggle Antonio into the United States and find him construction work in California for a fee of 16,000 pesos—about $1,700 American. Antonio told the man that he didn't have that much money, but the *coyote* assured him that he could pay it off once he started to work. Two weeks later, he was on a bus along with forty others, heading north toward the border.

[17]*Oxfam America*: A nonprofit organization dedicated to ending poverty, hunger, and social injustice around the world.

[18]Oxfam America, "Like Machines in the Fields: Workers without Rights in American Agriculture," Report, March 2004, www.oxfamamerica.org/newsandpublications/publications/research_reports/art7011.html/OA-Like_Machines_in_the_Fields.pdf, 36.

[19]Cindy Hahamovitch, *The Fruits of Their Labor: Atlantic Coast Farmworkers and the Making of Migrant Poverty, 1870–1945* (Chapel Hill: University of North Carolina Press, 1997), 123.

When the bus arrived at a sparse border camp in the Sonora desert, the workers were separated and given to other *coyotes.* The man in charge of Antonio's group was called Chino. He led them through the desert for three days, despite having water and supplies for only one day, crossing the border to a whistle-stop called Tres Puntas. From there they were driven to a house in Tucson, where Chino demanded additional money from them or their families, on pain of violence. Some of the others complied, but Antonio had no money to give. At this point, without money or papers, under violent threat, he realized he was trapped.

Antonio was told that instead of going to a construction site in   35
California he would be put to work in the tomato fields of South Central Florida, at the pay rate of $150 per day. The promised amount went far toward allaying his misgivings. Chino then handed him over to a van driver, or *raitero,* called "el Chacal" — the jackal. Antonio was crowded into the back of the van along with seventeen other Mexican workers. On the long drive to Florida, the van stopped only for gasoline; the migrants in the back were told to urinate in a bottle when the need arose. Twice on their journey police stopped the van; on neither occasion did the officer question the presence of eighteen Mexicans packed like cargo in the back.

When el Chacal arrived in Florida, he drove to the camp of two labor contractors, Abel and Basilio Cuello. Here, Antonio overheard el Chacal negotiating with the Cuello brothers for the sale of the workers. El Chacal was demanding $500 apiece, whereas the Cuellos were willing to pay only $350. At this point, Antonio realized, "We were being sold like animals." [20]

Antonio's life was tightly controlled. The door of the shack in which he and the other workers slept was locked at night and was unlocked in the morning by Abel Cuello only when it was time to go to the fields. Cuello never left them alone; he stayed with them as they picked and threatened violence and death should they attempt to escape. The promised pay was whittled away to practically nothing as Cuello deducted for rent, food, water, even the cost of transportation to and from the fields. With the tiny amount left to them, the workers bought food or toiletries when taken by the bosses on rare trips to a small local grocery store.

After four months in slavery, Antonio saw his chance. While he and a few others were shopping, Cuello, on guard outside the market, dozed off, and the workers ran to the highway and escaped. The subsequent case against the Cuello trafficking operation was one of Florida's first contemporary cases of forced labor. Cuello was convicted and sentenced to prison on slavery charges.

Antonio still works with the crops — but under his own volition, and not with tomatoes. He also travels throughout the country, speaking about the slavery in America's fields and in the food we eat. He

[20] *Dying to Leave,* dir. Chris Hilton, "Wide Angle" special, PBS, 2003.

has marched in several campaigns against corporate abuse and partici- pated in the ten-day hunger strike against Taco Bell. At one point, he taught a training session to law enforcement officers and government officials in Chiapas, Mexico, through the U.S. Department of Justice (DOJ). This author spoke with Antonio while he was participating in a late-2007 workers' march against Burger King, and his motivation was clear. Taking action against the offending corporations, he said, "is ex- tremely important; there is more and more consumer participation in the struggle, and it makes the campaign that much stronger. The big companies buy so much produce that they must take responsibility for the conditions under which the people who harvest it are suffering. It infuriates me that some of these corporations are still ignoring the plight of the farmworkers.

"I just want you to know," he states, "why I'm out here today. For 40 four and a half months, I was held in forced labor in the fields against my will, and it seemed like an eternity for me. They were watching me all the time, controlling all I did. I thought I was going to die. Thanks to God, I was able to escape, and it allowed me to become more and more aware. I'm out here learning more every day."[21] ...

"Guests" in the Fields

It's bad enough when slavery exists and the government is either un- aware or unwilling to address it. But how about an ongoing federal program that makes it much too easy to bring people into the United States to be enslaved? Welcome to the "Guest Worker Program," also known as the H-2 program, after the type of visas assigned. Temporary agricultural workers from Latin America, Asia, eastern Europe, and the Caribbean are lured here by the *official guarantee* of good work- ing conditions: so many hours a week at a fixed and acceptable wage, government-inspected living conditions, and medical benefits, includ- ing "payment for lost time from work and for any permanent injury." Guest workers are also entitled to "federally funded legal services for matters relating to their employment." According to the rules, any em- ployer who receives DOL approval to import guest workers must com- pensate them for their travel expenses—the plane or bus fare and food costs incurred on the way to the promised job. Finally, the worker is guaranteed three-fourths of the total hours promised in his contract for the period of employment specified.[22] The conditions of the program also stipulate that the worker is obligated to stay with the employer who sponsored him; he cannot leave to seek a job elsewhere. Some employers adhere to the conditions of the law. But in a large number of cases, not a single one of these promises is honored because of employer abuses and government neglect.

---

[21]Antonio Martinez, CIW, interview, December 2, 2007.
[22]Mary Bauer, "Close to Slavery: Guestworker Programs in the United States," report, Southern Poverty Law Center, 2007, www.splcenter.org/pdf/static/SPLCguestworker.pdf, 7.

The Guest Worker Program is not a new concept: the United States has been taking in foreign workers almost since its inception. Our attitude toward them—at least over the last hundred years—has been ambivalent. America welcomed them when we needed them—during the two World Wars, for example, when most of the permanent workforce was in the service—and limited or simply ousted them when we didn't. In 1943, to provide workers for the southern sugar cane fields, the government established the H-2 program. From its beginning it was characterized by inequity and brutality. As recently as 1986, cane cutters who attempted a work stoppage over poor conditions were beset by armed police with dogs, acting at the employers' behest. The incident became known as the "Dog Wars." In that same year, the H-2 program was expanded to include nonagricultural workers, but the number of mainly Asian and Latin American guest workers arriving for farm work under the program is still significant. The number of foreign workers certified by DOL as agricultural—or H-2A—laborers went from forty-eight thousand in 2005 to nearly seventy-seven thousand in 2007.[23]

The viability of a guest worker program has been endlessly debated, but one thing is clear: its lack of oversight provides a splendid opportunity for mistreatment and enslavement. In the words of Mary Bauer of the Southern Poverty Law Center, "The very structure of the program...lends itself to abuse."[24] Increasingly, employers use labor contractors to recruit guest workers for them. In this way they avoid technical responsibility for the workers, legally distancing themselves from any abuses that follow. The brokers recruit the workers in their home countries. Unrestricted by law or ethics, they make promises of work and wages that far exceed the provisions of the program—so much so that the workers go into massive debt, often in excess of $10,000, to pay the recruiter's inflated fee.

Employers often bring in more workers than they need. They exaggerate the number required, as well as the period of employment, since they know the government isn't paying attention. Employers know they can get away with not paying the three-fourths of the wages or meeting the other conditions the contract stipulates. The worker, heavily in debt and doomed to few work hours and pay fraud, is indentured even before he leaves home. When he arrives in America, he finds himself at the mercy of his employer. The promised forty-hour week turns out to be only twenty-five hours, and his looming debt becomes instantly insurmountable. Sometimes the workweek is eighty hours long, but the promised pay is withheld or radically reduced. The "free housing in good condition" can turn out to be a lightless, heatless shack with no bed or blankets, and sometimes no windows to keep out the cold, shared with twenty or thirty other workers. In some cases, he is locked

[23]Mary Bauer, director of Southern Poverty Law Center's Immigrant Justice Project, interview, July 23, 2008.
[24]Bauer, "Close to Slavery," 42.

in or kept under armed guard.[25] If transportation to the job is required, a travel fee is deducted from his pay. Fees are illegally charged for food and sometimes rent, both of which are guaranteed him by law. The program also promises him worker's compensation for hospital or doctor's costs and lost wages, but the moment he gets sick or hurt on the job he finds this is a lie. Ignorant of the system and the language, he has no clue how to seek medical help, and his employer, far from being solicitous in the face of losing a laborer, pushes him to keep working.

To enforce control, the employer confiscates or destroys the guest worker's passport and visa, making him an illegal alien. In this way, he faces the threat of arrest and deportation should he attempt to leave or refuse to work. If he manages to escape and find his way to the local police, the likelihood of the authorities taking the word of an undocumented migrant worker, with little or no English, over that of an established local grower is slim to none. Without his papers, the worker is at considerably greater risk than his employer. And once he has made waves, he runs the risk of being blacklisted and destroys any chance of coming back in the future for a decent job.[26] The Carnegie Endowment for International Peace reported in 1999, "Blacklisting of H-2A workers appears to be widespread, is highly organized, and occurs at all stages of the recruitment and employment process."[27] The large North Carolina Growers Association has blatantly kept a blacklist, which in 1997 was titled "NCGA Ineligible for Rehire Report," listing over a thousand workers' names.[28]

All in all, there is little about this that doesn't fall under the definition of slavery. Workers are often kept against their will, held by the threat of violence, paid as little as their employers wish, and denied every basic right guaranteed by law. In fact, there is little to distinguish these thousands of guest workers from the crews held in slavery by Miguel Flores—except for the stunning fact that this particular form of bondage occurs within a government-sponsored program. Admittedly, this scenario doesn't play itself out in every instance: many employers honor the conditions of the H-2A laws, providing the work promised at the agreed-upon wage. Nonetheless, this doesn't change the fact that because of the program's lack of oversight the result can be coercion and peonage....

Slavery in Your Face

At the very beginning of the trans-Atlantic slave trade some Africans were tricked into slavery.[29] A slave ship might sail upriver and find an isolated village; if the people didn't run away, the slaver might trade with them and invite them on board the ship. He might tell them about

[25]Ibid., 39.
[26]Ibid., 15–17.
[27]Quoted in ibid., 27.
[28]Ibid., 17.
[29]Robert J. Allison, "The Origins of African-American Culture," *Journal of Interdisciplinary History* 30 (Winter 1999): 475–81.

the land on the other side of the water where food was abundant, land was there for the taking, and everyone lived like kings. Excited about the chance to see the enormous "canoe" up close, villagers would flock aboard, and while they were being shown the lower decks, they would be captured, beaten, and chained. The trap was set with lies and sprung with violence, and the new slaves would be on their way to the fields of North America. Once sold to farmers, the slaves who survived would usually be put to work growing and gathering crops: cotton, sugar, fruit, vegetables, timber, all to supply the growing nation's demand for food, clothing, and building materials. All over the United States, in slave states and free states, families would eat the food grown and picked by slaves in the South.

Today, the same things occur. Farmworkers are being ensnared by deception and enslaved through violence. And we Americans obliviously munch away on the slave-picked fruit and vegetables we bring home from the grocery store or order in fast-food restaurants. The slaves tend to come from Asia and Central and South America instead of Africa, but they are tricked with the same sorts of lies and promises. And while the U.S. government tended to just ignore the illegal antebellum slave trade, today it swings through the bipolar reaction of prosecuting some cases while propping open the door to human trafficking through the Guest Worker Program.

The idea of putting slave-grown food in the mouths of our children should make us sick. Putting a stop to this travesty should be an immediate concern. The good news is, we know how to bring this slavery to an end — through greater public awareness, an enhanced system of government inspection, a complete overhaul of the Guest Worker Program, a governmental willingness to root out and prosecute cases of trafficking in the fields, and — most vital — a solid respect for the rights and humanity of the people whom we put to growing and harvesting our crops. But none of this will happen until we all decide that slave-picked food is just too bitter to swallow.

ENGAGING THE TEXT

1. Bales and Soodalter note that most people think of slavery in terms of plantations and the Old South. How does this selection challenge your own thinking about the institution of slavery? Where do you think you might find slaves working in your state or region?

2. According to the authors, the price of a slave has dropped dramatically since the nineteenth century. Can you think of any reasons why human beings might be cheaper — and more expendable — today than in the past?

3. Given that slavery is roughly as common as homicide in the United States, how might you explain why the authorities and the media don't treat it as an urgent civil rights or public safety issue?

4. To what extent would you agree with Bales and Soodalter that modern slavery is an example of "capitalism at its worst"? In what sense is human trafficking similar to capitalism? How is capitalism different from slave trading?

5. Why, in the authors' view, is the U.S. Guest Worker Program not much better than slavery? Given their description of the program, do you think the government should continue to sponsor it? What could be done to improve the lot of guest workers?

6. According to the U.S. Department of Agriculture, the average daily pay of a fieldworker was $10.49 in 2010. How many students in your class would take a fieldworker job for this level of pay? How much would it take to tempt you to pick crops for a living under the conditions described in this selection?

EXPLORING CONNECTIONS

7. How might the theories of prejudice outlined by Vincent N. Parillo (p. 504) help to explain why an "average" American housewife could treat a young girl like Maria so inhumanely? Do you think it's likely that, as Bales and Soodalter claim, today's slaves come from all races and ethnicities?

8. How do the working conditions of employees like the waitresses described by Barbara Ehrenreich (p. 267) or the factory workers described by Adam Davidson (p. 333) compare with those of the migrant fieldworkers described in this selection? To what extent are all low-wage workers "indentured to their employers"?

EXTENDING THE CRITICAL CONTEXT

9. Do some research to learn more about how widespread the problem of human trafficking is in the United States. How does the United States compare with other nations in terms of human trafficking? What types of jobs are typically involved in the American slave market? Who are the new slaves and slave masters? What is being done to address the problem of American and global slavery?

10. Research the working and living conditions of employees in the foreign megamanufacturing plants that produce consumer electronics, clothing, athletic shoes, and household goods for companies like Abercrombie & Fitch, Ikea, Kohl's, Walmart, Gap Inc., GUESS?, Levi's, DKNY, Apple, Sony, Disney, and Nike. How are employees treated in these foreign megafactories? How much are they paid? How much control or choice do they have in their lives? In what ways do megafactory complexes mirror the conditions of slavery? To what extent do American consumers bear responsibility for these conditions?

THE NEW JIM CROW
MICHELLE ALEXANDER

"Jim Crow" is the term used to describe the legally-sanctioned disenfranchisement of freed slaves following the Civil War. From 1865 until the end of the civil rights era, Jim Crow laws allowed state and local governments to deprive African Americans of their most basic freedoms — from the right to vote to the right to choose where to live, work, or go to school. The "separate but equal" society sustained by Jim Crow officially ended with passage of the Voting Rights Act in 1965. But as Michelle Alexander argues in this selection, the spirit of Jim Crow didn't die: it simply assumed a new guise. In Alexander's view, we've been living in a new Jim Crow era ever since the beginning of the war on drugs, which led to the mass incarceration and stigmatization of unprecedented numbers of black and brown men in America. Imprisonment for minor drug offenses, she warns, threatens to create a permanent underclass of black men cut off from any hope of "Life, Liberty, and the pursuit of Happiness." A graduate of Stanford Law School and Vanderbilt University, Alexander (b. 1970) served for several years as director of the Racial Justice Project at the American Civil Liberties Union of Northern California before assuming the position of associate professor in the Moritz College of Law at Ohio State University. Her publications include *The New Jim Crow: Mass Incarceration in the Age of Colorblindness* (2010), the source of this selection.

IT WAS NO ORDINARY SUNDAY MORNING when presidential candidate Barack Obama stepped to the podium at the Apostolic Church of God in Chicago. It was Father's Day. Hundreds of enthusiastic congregants packed the pews at the overwhelmingly black church eager to hear what the first black Democratic nominee for president of the United States had to say.

The message was a familiar one: black men should be better fathers. Too many are absent from their homes. For those in the audience, Obama's speech was an old tune sung by an exciting new performer. His message of personal responsibility, particularly as it relates to fatherhood, was anything but new; it had been delivered countless times by black ministers in churches across America. The message had also been delivered on a national stage by celebrities such as Bill Cosby and Sidney Poitier.[1] And the message had been delivered with great passion by Louis Farrakhan,[2] who more than a decade earlier summoned

---

[1] *Bill Cosby and Sidney Poitier:* Two famous and highly respected African American entertainers. [All notes are Alexander's, except 1–3 and 7.]

[2] *Louis Farrakhan:* Louis Farrakhan Muhammad Sr. (b. 1933), leader of the African American religious movement known as the Nation of Islam.

one million black men to Washington, D.C., for a day of "atonement" and recommitment to their families and communities.

The mainstream media, however, treated the event as big news, and many pundits seemed surprised that the black congregants actually applauded the message. For them, it was remarkable that black people nodded in approval when Obama said: "If we are honest with ourselves, we'll admit that too many fathers are missing—missing from too many lives and too many homes. Too many fathers are MIA. Too many fathers are AWOL.[3] They have abandoned their responsibilities. They're acting like boys instead of men. And the foundations of our families are weaker because of it. You and I know this is true everywhere, but nowhere is this more true than in the African American community."

The media did not ask—and Obama did not tell—where the missing fathers might be found.

The following day, social critic and sociologist Michael Eric Dyson published a critique of Obama's speech in *Time* magazine. He pointed out that the stereotype of black men being poor fathers may well be false. Research by Boston College social psychologist Rebekah Levine Coley found that black fathers not living at home are more likely to keep in contact with their children than fathers of any other ethnic or racial group. Dyson chided Obama for evoking a black stereotype for political gain, pointing out that "Obama's words may have been spoken to black folk, but they were aimed at those whites still on the fence about whom to send to the White House.[4] Dyson's critique was a fair one, but like other media commentators, he remained silent about where all the absent black fathers could be found. He identified numerous social problems plaguing black families, such as high levels of unemployment, discriminatory mortgage practices, and the gutting of early-childhood learning programs. Not a word was said about prisons....

The fact that Barack Obama can give a speech on Father's Day dedicated to the subject of fathers who are "AWOL" without ever acknowledging that the majority of young black men in many large urban areas are currently under the control of the criminal justice system is disturbing, to say the least. What is more problematic, though, is that hardly anyone in the mainstream media noticed the oversight....Hundreds of thousands of black men are unable to be good fathers for their children, not because of a lack of commitment or desire but because they are warehoused in prisons, locked in cages. They did not walk out on their families voluntarily; they were taken away in handcuffs, often due to a massive federal program known as the War on Drugs.

---

[3]*MIA...AWOL:* Military acronyms standing for "Missing in Action" and "Absent Without Leave."

[4]Michael Eric Dyson, "Obama's Rebuke of Absentee Black Fathers," *Time*, June 19, 2008.

More African American adults are under correctional control today—in prison or jail, on probation or parole—than were enslaved in 1850, a decade before the Civil War began.[5] The mass incarceration of people of color is a big part of the reason that a black child born today is less likely to be raised by both parents than a black child born during slavery.[6] The absence of black fathers from families across America is not simply a function of laziness, immaturity, or too much time watching *SportsCenter.*[7] Thousands of black men have disappeared into prisons and jails, locked away for drug crimes that are largely ignored when committed by whites.

The clock has been turned back on racial progress in America, though scarcely anyone seems to notice. All eyes are fixed on people like Barack Obama and Oprah Winfrey, who have defied the odds and risen to power, fame, and fortune. For those left behind, especially those within prison walls, the celebration of racial triumph in America must seem a tad premature. More black men are imprisoned today than at any other moment in our nation's history. More are disenfranchised today than in 1870, the year the Fifteenth Amendment was ratified prohibiting laws that explicitly deny the right to vote on the basis of race.[8] Young black men today may be just as likely to suffer discrimination in employment, housing, public benefits, and jury service as a black man in the Jim Crow era—discrimination that is perfectly legal, because it is based on one's criminal record.

This is the new normal, the new racial equilibrium.

The launching of the War on Drugs and the initial construction of the new system required the expenditure of tremendous political initiative and resources. Media campaigns were waged; politicians blasted "soft" judges and enacted harsh sentencing laws; poor people of color were vilified. The system now, however, requires very little maintenance or justification. In fact, if you are white and middle class, you might not even realize the drug war is still going on. Most high school and college students today have no recollection of the political and media frenzy surrounding the drug war in the early years. They were young children when the war was declared, or not even born yet. Crack is out; terrorism is in.

Today, the political fanfare and the vehement, racialized rhetoric regarding crime and drugs are no longer necessary. Mass incarceration has been normalized, and all of the racial stereotypes and assumptions

[5]One in eleven black adults was under correctional supervision at year end 2007, or approximately 2.4 million people. See Pew Center on the States, *One in 31: The Long Reach of American Corrections* (Washington, DC: Pew Charitable Trusts, Mar. 2009). According to the 1850 Census, approximately 1.7 million adults (ages 15 and older) were slaves.

[6]See Andrew J. Cherlin, *Marriage, Divorce, Remarriage*, rev. ed. (Cambridge, MA: Harvard University Press, 1992), 110.

[7]*SportsCenter*: A daily sports news program on the ESPN cable network.

[8]See Glenn C. Loury, *Race, Incarceration, and American Values* (Cambridge, MA: MIT Press, 2008), commentary by Pam Karlan.

that gave rise to the system are now embraced (or at least internalized) by people of all colors, from all walks of life, and in every major political party. We may wonder aloud "where have the black men gone?" but deep down we already know. It is simply taken for granted that, in cities like Baltimore and Chicago, the vast majority of young black men are currently under the control of the criminal justice system or branded criminals for life. This extraordinary circumstance—unheard of in the rest of the world—is treated here in America as a basic fact of life, as normal as separate water fountains were just a half century ago.

States of Denial

The claim that we really know where all the black men have gone may inspire considerable doubt. If we know, why do we feign ignorance? Could it be that most people really don't know? Is it possible that the roundup, lockdown, and exclusion of black men en masse from the body politic has occurred largely unnoticed? The answer is yes and no.

Much has been written about the ways in which people manage to deny, even to themselves, that extraordinary atrocities, racial oppression, and other forms of human suffering have occurred or are occurring. Criminologist Stanley Cohen wrote perhaps the most important book on the subject, *States of Denial*. The book examines how individuals and institutions—victims, perpetrators, and bystanders—know about yet deny the occurrence of oppressive acts. They see only what they want to see and wear blinders to avoid seeing the rest. This has been true about slavery, genocide, torture, and every form of systemic oppression.

Cohen emphasizes that denial, though deplorable, is complicated. It is not simply a matter of refusing to acknowledge an obvious, though uncomfortable, truth. Many people "know" and "not-know" the truth about human suffering at the same time. In his words, "Denial may be neither a matter of telling the truth nor intentionally telling a lie. There seem to be states of mind, or even whole cultures, in which we know and don't know at the same time."[9]

Today, most Americans know and don't know the truth about mass 15 incarceration. For more than three decades, images of black men in handcuffs have been a regular staple of the evening news. We know that large numbers of black men have been locked in cages. In fact, it is precisely because we know that black and brown people are far more likely to be imprisoned that we, as a nation, have not cared too much about it. We tell ourselves they "deserve" their fate, even though we know—and don't know—that whites are just as likely to commit many crimes, especially drug crimes. We know that people released from prison face a lifetime of discrimination, scorn, and exclusion, and yet

[9]Stanley Cohen, *States of Denial: Knowing About Atrocities and Suffering* (Cambridge, UK: Polity, 2001), 4–5.

we claim not to know that an undercaste exists. We know and we don't know at the same time.

Upon reflection, it is relatively easy to understand how Americans come to deny the evils of mass incarceration. Denial is facilitated by persistent racial segregation in housing and schools, by political demagoguery, by racialized media imagery, and by the ease of changing one's perception of reality simply by changing television channels. There is little reason to doubt the prevailing "common sense" that black and brown men have been locked up en masse merely in response to crime rates when one's sources of information are mainstream media outlets. In many respects, the reality of mass incarceration is easier to avoid knowing than the injustices and sufferings associated with slavery or Jim Crow. Those confined to prisons are out of sight and out of mind; once released, they are typically confined in ghettos. Most Americans only come to "know" about the people cycling in and out of prisons through fictional police dramas, music videos, gangsta rap, and "true" accounts of ghetto experience on the evening news. These racialized narratives tend to confirm and reinforce the prevailing public consensus that we need not care about "those people"; they deserve what they get....

How It Works

Precisely how the system of mass incarceration works to trap African Americans in a virtual (and literal) cage can best be understood by viewing the system as a whole.... Only when we view the cage from a distance can we disengage from the maze of rationalizations that are offered for each wire and see how the entire apparatus operates to keep African Americans perpetually trapped.

This, in brief, is how the system works: The War on Drugs is the vehicle through which extraordinary numbers of black men are forced into the cage. The entrapment occurs in three distinct phases,...The first stage is the roundup. Vast numbers of people are swept into the criminal justice system by the police, who conduct drug operations primarily in poor communities of color. They are rewarded in cash—through drug forfeiture laws and federal grant programs—for rounding up as many people as possible, and they operate unconstrained by constitutional rules of procedure that once were considered inviolate. Police can stop, interrogate, and search anyone they choose for drug investigations, provided they get "consent." Because there is no meaningful check on the exercise of police discretion, racial biases are granted free rein. In fact, police are allowed to rely on race as a factor in selecting whom to stop and search (even though people of color are no more likely to be guilty of drug crimes than whites)—effectively guaranteeing that those who are swept into the system are primarily black and brown.

The conviction marks the beginning of the second phase: the period of formal control. Once arrested, defendants are generally denied meaningful legal representation and pressured to plead guilty whether they are or not. Prosecutors are free to "load up" defendants with extra charges, and their decisions cannot be challenged for racial bias. Once convicted, due to the drug war's harsh sentencing laws, drug offenders in the United States spend more time under the criminal justice system's formal control—in jail or prison, on probation or parole—than drug offenders anywhere else in the world. While under formal control, virtually every aspect of one's life is regulated and monitored by the system, and any form of resistance or disobedience is subject to swift sanction. This period of control may last a lifetime, even for those convicted of extremely minor, nonviolent offenses, but the vast majority of those swept into the system are eventually released. They are transferred from their prison cells to a much larger, invisible cage.

The final stage has been dubbed by some advocates as the period of invisible punishment.[10] This term, first coined by Jeremy Travis, is meant to describe the unique set of criminal sanctions that are imposed on individuals after they step outside the prison gates, a form of punishment that operates largely outside of public view and takes effect outside the traditional sentencing framework. These sanctions are imposed by operation of law rather than decisions of a sentencing judge, yet they often have a greater impact on one's life course than the months or years one actually spends behind bars. These laws operate collectively to ensure that the vast majority of convicted offenders will never integrate into mainstream, white society. They will be discriminated against, legally, for the rest of their lives—denied employment, housing, education, and public benefits. Unable to surmount these obstacles, most will eventually return to prison and then be released again, caught in a closed circuit of perpetual marginality.

In recent years, advocates and politicians have called for greater resources devoted to the problem of "prisoner re-entry," in view of the unprecedented numbers of people who are released from prison and returned to their communities every year. While the terminology is well intentioned, it utterly fails to convey the gravity of the situation facing prisoners upon their release. People who have been convicted of felonies almost never truly re-enter the society they inhabited prior to their conviction. Instead, they enter a separate society, a world hidden from public view, governed by a set of oppressive and discriminatory rules and laws that do not apply to everyone else. They become members of an undercaste—an enormous population of predominantly black and brown people who, because of the drug war, are denied basic rights and privileges of American citizenship and are permanently relegated to an inferior status. This is the final phase, and there is no going back.

[10]See Marc Mauer and Meda Chesney-Lind, eds., *Invisible Punishment: The Collateral Consequences of Mass Imprisonment* (New York: The New Press, 2002); and Jeremy Travis, *But They All Come Back: Facing the Challenges of Prisoner Reentry* (Washington, DC Urban Institute Press, 2005).

Nothing New?

...Today, the War on Drugs has given birth to a system of mass incarceration that governs not just a small fraction of a racial or ethnic minority but entire communities of color. In ghetto communities, nearly everyone is either directly or indirectly subject to the new caste system. The system serves to redefine the terms of the relationship of poor people of color and their communities to mainstream, white society, ensuring their subordinate and marginal status. The criminal and civil sanctions that were once reserved for a tiny minority are now used to control and oppress a racially defined majority in many communities, and the systematic manner in which the control is achieved reflects not just a difference in scale. The nature of the criminal justice system has changed. It is no longer concerned primarily with the prevention and punishment of crime, but rather with the management and control of the dispossessed. Prior drug wars were ancillary to the prevailing caste system. This time the drug war is the system of control.

If you doubt that this is the case, consider the effect of the war on the ground, in specific locales. Take Chicago, Illinois, for example. Chicago is widely considered to be one of America's most diverse and vibrant cities. It has boasted black mayors, black police chiefs, black legislators, and is home to the nation's first black president. It has a thriving economy, a growing Latino community, and a substantial black middle class. Yet as the Chicago Urban League reported in 2002, there is another story to be told.[11]

If Martin Luther King Jr. were to return miraculously to Chicago, some forty years after bringing his Freedom Movement to the city, he would be saddened to discover that the same issues on which he originally focused still produce stark patterns of racial inequality, segregation, and poverty. He would also be struck by the dramatically elevated significance of one particular institutional force in the perpetuation and deepening of those patterns: the criminal justice system. In the few short decades since King's death, a new regime of racially disparate mass incarceration has emerged in Chicago and become the primary mechanism for racial oppression and the denial of equal opportunity.

In Chicago, like the rest of the country, the War on Drugs is the engine of mass incarceration, as well as the primary cause of gross racial disparities in the criminal justice system and in the ex-offender population. About 90 percent of those sentenced to prison for a drug offense in Illinois are African American.[12] White drug offenders are rarely arrested, and when they are, they are treated more favorably at every stage of the criminal justice process, including plea bargaining and 25

[11]Paul Street, *The Vicious Circle: Race, Prison, Jobs, and Community in Chicago, Illinois, and the Nation* (Chicago Urban League, Department of Research and Planning, 2002).

[12]Street, *Vicious Circle*, 3.

sentencing.[13] Whites are consistently more likely to avoid prison and felony charges, even when they are repeat offenders.[14] Black offenders, by contrast, are routinely labeled felons and released into a permanent racial undercaste.

The total population of black males in Chicago with a felony record (including both current and ex-felons) is equivalent to 55 percent of the black adult male population and an astonishing 80 percent of the adult black male workforce in the Chicago area.[15] This stunning development reflects the dramatic increase in the number and race of those sent to prison for drug crimes. From the Chicago region alone, the number of those annually sent to prison for drug crimes increased almost 2,000 percent, from 469 in 1985 to 8,755 in 2005.[16]

When people are released from Illinois prisons, they are given as little as $10 in "gate money" and a bus ticket to anywhere in the United States. Most return to impoverished neighborhoods in the Chicago area, bringing few resources and bearing the stigma of their prison record.[17] In Chicago, as in most cities across the country, ex-offenders are banned or severely restricted from employment in a large number of professions, job categories, and fields by professional licensing stat-utes, rules, and practices that discriminate against potential employ-ees with felony records. According to a study conducted by the DePaul University College of Law in 2000, of the then ninety-eight occupations requiring licenses in Illinois, fifty-seven placed stipulations and/or re-strictions on applicants with a criminal record.[18] Even when not barred by law from holding specific jobs, ex-offenders in Chicago find it ex-traordinarily difficult to find employers who will hire them, regardless of the nature of their conviction. They are also routinely denied public housing and welfare benefits, and they find it increasingly difficult to obtain education, especially now that funding for public education has been hard hit, due to exploding prison budgets.

The impact of the new caste system is most tragically felt among the young. In Chicago (as in other cities across the United States), young black men are more likely to go to prison than to college.[19] As of June 2001, there were nearly 20,000 more black men in the Illinois state prison system than enrolled in the state's public universities.[20] In fact, there were more black men in the state's correctional facilities that year *just on drug charges* than the total number of black men enrolled

[13]Alden Loury, "Black Offenders Face Stiffest Drug Sentences," *Chicago Reporter*, Sept. 12, 2007.

[14]Ibid.

[15]Street, *Vicious Circle*, 15.

[16]Donald G. Lubin et al., *Chicago Metropolis 2020: 2006 Crime and Justice Index* (Washington, DC: Pew Center on the States, 2006), 5, www.pewcenteronthestates.org/report _detail.aspx?id=33022.

[17]Ibid., 37.

[18]Ibid., 35.

[19]Ibid., 3; see also Bruce Western, *Punishment and Inequality in America* (New York: Russell Sage Foundation, 2006), 12.

[20]Street, *Vicious Circle*, 3.

in undergraduate degree programs in state universities.[21] To put the crisis in even sharper focus, consider this: just 992 black men received a bachelor's degree from Illinois state universities in 1999, while roughly 7,000 black men were released from the state prison system the following year just for drug offenses.[22] The young men who go to prison rather than college face a lifetime of closed doors, discrimination, and ostracism. Their plight is not what we hear about on the evening news, however. Sadly, like the racial caste systems that preceded it, the system of mass incarceration now seems normal and natural to most, a regrettable necessity.

Mapping the Parallels

Those cycling in and out of Illinois prisons today are members of America's new racial undercaste. The United States has almost always had a racial undercaste—a group defined wholly or largely by race that is permanently locked out of mainstream, white society by law, custom, and practice. The reasons and justifications change over time, as each new caste system reflects and adapts to changes in the social, political, and economic context. What is most striking about the design of the current caste system, though, is how closely it resembles its predecessor. There are important differences between mass incarceration and Jim Crow, to be sure...but when we step back and view the system as a whole, there is a profound sense of déjà vu. There is a familiar stigma and shame. There is an elaborate system of control, complete with political disenfranchisement and legalized discrimination in every major realm of economic and social life. And there is the production of racial meaning and racial boundaries....

Symbolic production of race. Arguably the most important parallel   30
between mass incarceration and Jim Crow is that both have served to define the meaning and significance of race in America. Indeed, a primary function of any racial caste system is to define the meaning of race in its time. Slavery defined what it meant to be black (a slave), and Jim Crow defined what it meant to be black (a second-class citizen). Today mass incarceration defines the meaning of blackness in America: black people, especially black men, are criminals. That is what it means to be black.

The temptation is to insist that black men "choose" to be criminals; the system does not make them criminals, at least not in the way that slavery made blacks slaves or Jim Crow made them second-class citizens. The myth of choice here is seductive, but it should be resisted. African Americans are not significantly more likely to use or sell prohibited drugs than whites, but they are *made* criminals at drastically higher

[21]Ibid.
[22]Ibid.

rates for precisely the same conduct. In fact, studies suggest that white professionals may be the most likely of any group to have engaged in illegal drug activity in their lifetime, yet they are the least likely to be made criminals.[23] The prevalence of illegal drug activity among all racial and ethnic groups creates a situation in which, due to limited law enforcement resources and political constraints, some people are made criminals while others are not. Black people have been made criminals by the War on Drugs to a degree that dwarfs its effect on other racial and ethnic groups, especially whites. And the process of making them criminals has produced racial stigma.

Every racial caste system in the United States has produced racial stigma. Mass incarceration is no exception. Racial stigma is produced by defining negatively what it means to be black. The stigma of race was once the shame of the slave; then it was the shame of the second-class citizen; today the stigma of race is the shame of the criminal....

It is precisely because our criminal justice system provides a vehicle for the expression of conscious and unconscious antiblack sentiment that the prison label is experienced as a racial stigma. The stigma exists whether or not one has been formally branded a criminal, yet another parallel to Jim Crow. Just as African Americans in the North were stigmatized by the Jim Crow system even if they were not subject to its formal control, black men today are stigmatized by mass incarceration—and the social construction of the "criminalblackman"—whether they have ever been to prison or not. For those who have been branded, the branding serves to intensify and deepen the racial stigma, as they are constantly reminded in virtually every contact they have with public agencies, as well as with private employers and landlords, that they are the new "untouchables."

In this way, the stigma of race has become the stigma of criminality. Throughout the criminal justice system, as well as in our schools and public spaces, young + black + male is equated with reasonable suspicion, justifying the arrest, interrogation, search, and detention of thousands of African Americans every year, as well as their exclusion from employment and housing and the denial of educational opportunity. Because black youth are viewed as criminals, they face severe employment discrimination and are also "pushed out" of schools through racially biased school discipline policies.[24]

For black youth, the experience of being "made black" often begins with the first police stop, interrogation, search, or arrest. The experience carries social meaning—*this is what it means to be black.* The

[23]Whites are far more likely than African Americans to complete college, and college graduates are more likely to have tried illicit drugs in their lifetime when compared to adults who have not completed high school. See U.S. Department of Health and Human Services, Substance Abuse and Mental Health Services Administration, *Findings from the 2000 National Household Survey on Drug Abuse* (Rockville, MD: 2001). Adults who have not completed high school are disproportionately African American.

[24]See Julia Cass and Connie Curry, *Americq's Cradle to Prison Pipeline* (New York: Children's Defense Fund, 2007).

story of one's "first time" may be repeated to family or friends, but for ghetto youth, almost no one imagines that the first time will be the last. The experience is understood to define the terms of one's relationship not only to the state but to society at large. This reality can be frustrating for those who strive to help ghetto youth "turn their lives around." James Forman Jr., the cofounder of the See Forever charter school for juvenile offenders in Washington, D.C., made this point when describing how random and degrading stops and searches of ghetto youth "tell kids that they are pariahs, that no matter how hard they study, they will remain potential suspects." One student complained to him, "We can be perfect, perfect, doing everything right and still they treat us like dogs. No, worse than dogs, because criminals are treated worse than dogs." Another student asked him pointedly, "How can you tell us we can be anything when they treat us like we're nothing?"[25] . . .

[25]James Forman Jr., "Children, Cops and Citizenship: Why Conservatives Should Oppose Racial Profiling," in *Invisible Punishment*, ed. Mauer and Lind, 159.

Federal Bill Would Give America's Hens Bigger Cages

ENGAGING THE TEXT

1. Why, according to Alexander, are so many black men "missing" from contemporary American society? How, in her view, does the war on drugs make this possible? Would you agree that most Americans accept the mass incarceration of black men as a "basic fact of life"?

2. In Alexander's opinion, what role do the media play in reinforcing the "state of denial" that characterizes the attitudes of most Americans toward the mass incarceration of men of color? How might TV police dramas, music videos, gangsta rap music, and local nightly news programs help people see mass incarceration as a matter of "common sense"?

3. As Alexander sees it, how does "the system" strip black and brown men of their constitutional rights, both in and out of prison? Do you think that convicted felons should enjoy the same rights as law-abiding citizens? Would you agree with Alexander that denying felons certain rights is a form of "legalized discrimination"?

4. Should convicted felons who have served their time have the right to keep their criminal records private? Is requiring a felon to report his criminal record on applications for employment, housing, or college admission a matter of "common sense" or, as Alexander suggests, a matter of legalized "apartheid"?

5. To what extent would you agree that the modern mass incarceration of black men has symbolically defined being black as being "criminal"? Does the stigma of mass incarceration extend, as Alexander contends, to other men of color as well?

EXPLORING CONNECTIONS

6. Drawing on Erin Aubrey Kaplan's analysis of "the idea of President Obama" (p. 540) and Alexander's explanation of the "symbolic production of race" (para. 30), write a journal entry or essay on the what it means to be a black man in contemporary America.

7. How might Cheryl I. Harris and Devon W. Carbado's notion of "frames" (p. 524) help explain why most Americans accept the mass incarceration of black and brown men? How effectively, in your view, does Alexander force us to question what Harris and Carbado would term our "color blindness"? To what extent does Alexander challenge the claim that facts alone won't help us move beyond racism?

8. In your view, is drug use a matter of what Katherine Mangu-Ward would call "positive" or "negative" liberty (p. 659)? How might Alexander explain why Mangu-Ward omits mention of the war on drugs in her discussion of the "war on negative liberty"?

9. Compare the lot of the free and enslaved Latino migrant workers described by Kevin Bales and Ron Soodalter (p. 721) or that of the parolees and

welfare/workfare recipients discussed by Kathleen Arnold (p. 342) to the situation of felons as depicted by Alexander. To what extent do these selections challenge the notion that America is the home of the free? Would you agree that freedom is a relative and not an absolute value in American society? Why or why not?

EXTENDING THE CRITICAL CONTEXT

10. Go online to learn more about current incarceration rates for different racial and ethnic groups in the United States. How accurate is Alexander's portrayal of the mass incarceration of black men? How many of the black, brown, and white men currently in jail are there for relatively minor offenses like drug possession? What differences do you see in the crime rates and the lengths of sentences for members of different races?

GREAT CITIZENSHIP
ERIC LIU AND NICK HANAUER

Since the first Arab Spring uprisings in 2010 in Tunisia, Egypt, and Libya, the Internet and social media have emerged as powerful weapons in the arsenal of liberty. Beginning in 2011, the worldwide Occupy movement seemed to confirm the role of social networking as a source of collective resistance to power. Of course it should come as no surprise that revolutions are created by collective action and not by rugged individualists and self-reliant loners. As the authors of the following selection remind us, we draw strength from our connectedness and from the networks we belong to. Eric Liu and Nick Hanauer see social networks as a powerful tool for transforming America. They believe that our collective participation in networks offers a new way to look at individuality and freedom — and a new way of thinking about what it means to be a citizen. The son of Taiwanese immigrants, Eric Liu (b. 1968) is an author, educator, and entrepreneur who served in the Clinton Whitehouse. Along with Nick Hanauer, he is cofounder of the True Patriot Network, a progressive political action organization based in Seattle, Washington. Nick Hanauer (b. 1958) is a venture capitalist, Internet entrepreneur, philanthropist, and civic activist who has coauthored two books with Eric Liu: *The True Patriot* (2007) and *The Gardens of Democracy: A New American Story of Citizenship, the Economy, and the Role of Government* (2011), the source of this selection.

TOO OFTEN IN AMERICA TODAY, to call someone a good citizen is to treat her like a saint who's gone to some special length to help another—or like a sucker who forgot to look out for herself.

Either way, what's assumed so much of the time is that being a good citizen is something either beyond or against self-interest. The very word "citizenship" has a musty, 1950s feel to it, evoking a time when people tried hard to be seen as pro-social, when scouts got badges for it. The memory of that time can stir nostalgia or disparagement. But it does often seem like that time has passed.

America has high rates of volunteerism and charity and we respond swiftly to disasters at home and abroad. But at the same time, too many Americans today live their everyday lives by an ethic of "that's not my problem." The "not my problem" mindset is a problem. It is both the source and the result of an ideology that exalts individual autonomy at all costs. It is also, as we will explain below, highly contagious and quickly corrosive. And thus it is part of a feedback loop in which the disavowal of problems creates the very problems being disavowed.

Our argument... is that there's no such thing as "not my problem." We don't mean that all problems are equal or equally our burden, which would be paralyzing. We mean simply that great citizenship treats civic life as a garden demanding constant tending and the willingness to see all problems as interconnected.

It is an accepted axiom of corporate life that great companies create a culture where any problem the company faces is every employee's problem. These are cultures where employees compete to identify and solve problems, rather than avoid them. In this way, problems are quickly identified and solved, or even better, headed off completely. By contrast, a corporate culture where problems are avoided or blamed on others inevitably leads to infighting, suboptimization, and failure.

So it seems obvious to us that we must create a civic culture that mirrors such high-performance organizational cultures—where every problem the society faces is everyone's problem. As we will explain below, a culture where every problem is everyone's problem predictably has very few problems.

The Squeeze on Citizenship

In too many American communities today, such a culture of civic ownership does not prevail. Robert Putnam has documented the decades-long decimation of Tocqueville's little platoons of democracy,[1] the voluntary associations from bowling leagues to Elks clubs that once comprised a vibrant civic ecosystem. National measures of civic health—from volunteering to neighborliness to social connectedness—have all declined substantially since the 1970s.

All around us, in less measurable ways, there has been a slow and quiet seepage of trust and responsibility. For instance, not until you stop

[1]*Tocqueville's little platoons of democracy:* In his 1835 work *Democracy in America*, French historian Alexis de Tocqueville (1805–1859) documented the tendency of Americans to form civic "associations" for almost any public purpose. [All notes are the editors' unless otherwise indicated.]

and think about it might this seem odd: today we have a federal law requiring chief executives of public corporations to declare affirmatively in their corporate reports that they are not lying. Perhaps you find it outrageous that private security guards in a public bus tunnel in Seattle would stand by and watch a vicious beating of one teenager by another—and that the guards would justify their passivity by pointing out that the law forbade them from intervening like police officers. But then you move on. This is how it is.

The two of us don't believe that great citizenship has been killed just yet. We do believe, however, that it has been crowded out—by the market on one side and by the state on the other. Nowadays, too many people think of their responsibilities of citizenship as limited mainly to basic compliance with the law, or perhaps jury duty or voting—and, of course, only half of us even vote.

The market is the first force that has led to the shriveling of citi-   10 zenship. The classic case is the Wal-Mart effect. A town has a Main Street of small businesses and mom-and-pop shops. The shopkeepers and their customers have relationships that are not just about economic transactions but are set in a context of family, neighborhood, people, and place. Then Wal-Mart comes to town. It offers lower prices. It offers convenience. Because of its scale and might in the marketplace, it can compensate its workers stingily and drive out competition.

The presence of Wal-Mart leads the townspeople to think of themselves primarily as consumers, and to shed other aspects of their identities, like being neighbors or parishioners or friends. As consumers first, they gravitate to the place with the lowest prices. Wal-Mart thrives. The small businesses struggle and lay off workers. They cut back on their sponsorship of tee ball, their support of the food bank. As the mom-and-pops give way to the big box, and commutes become necessary, lives become more frenetic and stressful. People see each other less often. The sense of mutual obligation that townsfolk once shared starts to evaporate. Microhabits of caring and sociability fall away. In this tableau of libertarian citizenship, market forces triumph and everyone gets better deals—yet everyone is now in many senses poorer.

Two things have happened in such a scene, which, by the way, is not about Wal-Mart alone but about an ideology that treats everything—including people—like costs to be reduced. When we see ourselves as consumers above all, we start thinking of citizenship as grumpy customerhood—as suspicious, skeptical, "what's-in-it-for-me" consumerism. Globalization and pressures on the middle class accelerate these effects. Throw in the scarcity mindset and anxieties of the Great Recession[2] and the harm compounds. The insidious marketization of life distorts—indeed, corrupts—our politics and our civic lives.

---

[2]*the Great Recession:* The economic downturn that affected the United States and nations around the world beginning in 2007.

Meanwhile, on another front, the state has encroached increasingly into arenas of civic action, reducing the space that people have to show up for one another. What used to be the sort of thing you or I might just do because it needed doing, we now see as someone else's job. What used to be left to common sense is now prescribed by law. What used to be undertaken by self-organizing citizens is now too often delegated to the state. Elinor Ostrom's classic *Governing the Commons* depicts these dynamics in societies around the world.

But for direct evidence we need examine only our own schools. Somewhere between the one-room schoolhouse of the 19th century and the assembly-line high school of the 20th, Americans came to accept the tacit notion that the walls of the school are to keep kids in and others out. As public education has become more bureaucratized and rule-bound, and the actual work of teaching more test-driven, it's become easier for parents to drop their children off and check out of the process of education. At the same time, it's become harder for parents — or, for that matter, neighbors or grandparents or mentors — to enter the classroom and become a truly integrated part of the schooling experience, let alone to improve the actual quality of the school.

A norm now prevails in most public schools that education is the job 15
of professional educators. Rules have arisen to support that norm. There were probably good reasons for such rules, and certainly teachers are professionals to be respected. But one unintended consequence of all this is that the state gives us permission to treat education — even of one's own child — as someone else's job (or problem). When challenges arise in a public school, it's rare or only on the margins that families or the community are permitted to come up with solutions or innovations.

What's lost in such crowding-out and such shifts of power?

Quality of life, for one thing. In the case of the decimated Main Street, the glue of neighborliness disappears when everyone drives to the superstore. Eye contact, touch, presence, and smiles: all decline and disappear. In the case of the school-as-fortress, children get a desiccated experience of what it means to live in community. No adult outside the school owes them any special support or concern, and they in turn don't owe any back. Our schools are worse for it.

What's lost is the willingness of people to make judgments in situations that are not formulaic but are messy and human, and then to trust each other to make the best calls we can. As Philip Howard has argued powerfully, in a society that over-relies on laws and rules to govern everyday interactions — one where much is prescribed and proscribed and "what is not prohibited is permitted" — people forget how to exercise both rights and responsibilities.

What's lost, in short, is citizenship. By "citizenship" we do not mean legal documentation status. We mean living in a pro-social way at every scale of life. We mean showing up for each other.

Citizenship matters because it delivers for society what neither the 20
market nor the state can or should. Citizenship isn't just voting. Nor

is it just Good Samaritanism. A 21st-century perspective forces us to acknowledge that citizenship is, quite simply, the work of being in public. It encompasses behaviors like courtesy and civility, the "etiquette of freedom," to use poet Gary Snyder's phrase. It encompasses small acts like teaching your children to be honest in their dealings with others. It includes serving on community councils and as soccer coaches. It means leaving a place in better shape than you found it. It means helping others during hard times and being able to ask for help. It means resisting the temptation to call a problem someone else's.

Central to our conception of citizenship is an ethic of sacrifice—and a belief that sacrifice should be *progressive*. That is to say, being a citizen is not just about serving others and contributing when it's convenient but also when it's inconvenient. And the scale of the contribution should grow in proportion to the ability of the person to contribute. Just as progressive taxation[3] asks those who can pull the most weight to do so, progressive civic contribution asks those who have the most civic capacity—and who have benefited most from our civic culture—to take the most responsibility.

Citizen Gardeners

In the opening section of this book, we laid out a new story of self-interest. It is an obliteration of the myth of rugged individualism. The self-made person may be a great American icon but he is also a fairy tale. Ask that individualist who made the bootstraps she is pulling up. Ask her who paved the road that she walked on to be able to see you, who taught her the very language she uses to assert her independence.

Citizenship is a recognition that we are interdependent—that there are values, systems, and skills that hold us together as social animals, particularly in a tolerant, multiethnic market democracy. More than that, citizenship is a rejection of what Francis Fukuyama[4] has labeled "the Hobbesian fallacy,"[5] the ahistorical notion that humans began as individuals and only later rationally calculated that it made sense to band together in society. In fact, humans have been social from the very start; individualism is a creation of recent centuries.

The old story of self-interest is a product—and perpetuator—of Machinebrain. The new story is an exemplar of Gardenbrain.

Machinebrain held that citizens are automatons, mindlessly seeking advantage over one another, colliding like billiard balls, and that the best to be hoped for in civic life is that we should channel our 25

---

[3]*progressive taxation:* Taxation based on relative income level, which reduces the burden on those in lower income brackets and raises it on those who have more ability to pay.

[4]*Francis Fukuyama:* Yoshihiro Francis Fukuyama (b. 1952) is an American political scientist and political economist.

[5]*Hobbesian fallacy:* Refers to the theories of Thomas Hobbes (1558–1679), the English philosopher who introduced the idea that governments originally formed when individuals agreed to limit some of their natural rights for mutual security via a "social contract."

irredeemable self-seeking into a machinery of checks and balances that can set one interest or faction against another. Machinebrain uses malevolence to cancel out malevolence in the hopes of generating benevolence. This is the political and civic culture that has dominated American politics since the early 19th century.

Gardenbrain, by contrast, sees citizens as gardeners, tending to the plots we share—and also as organisms within a greater garden, each affecting the next. We form each other. We are bound up in each other's choices. We are not separate. As Paul said in Corinthians,[6] "the eye cannot say unto the hand, I have no need of thee: nor again the head to the feet, I have no need of you." We are deeply, irretrievably interdependent. We cannot pretend that our acts and choices happen in isolation. When we start with this recognition, we have to accept more responsibility. For everything.

If this sounds weird to you, perhaps that is because you live in a society that is, to use the acronym coined by moral psychologist Jonathan Haidt, WEIRD: Western, educated, industrialized, rich, and democratic. In other parts of the world, Haidt shows in *The Righteous Mind*, people have always paid far more attention than we Americans do to relationships among things and people than to the separateness of all objects. Gardenbrain sees systems. It tempers autonomy with community.

Creating Civic Contagions

Yet Gardenbrain also enables us to claim more individual power—much more power than conventional theories of citizenship attribute to us as individuals. For one of the central facts of life on an interdependent web is that every action and omission is potentially powerfully contagious. When you are compassionate and generous, society can become compassionate and generous. When you are violent and hateful, society can become violent and hateful. *You* can be the original cause of that contagion.

Why? Because humans are copying machines. As the philosopher Eric Hoffer once said, "When people are free to do as they please, they usually imitate each other." What this means is not that you are powerless but that you can set off a new chain of copying—and you do—every day with every act.

In their groundbreaking book on social networks, *Connected,* Nicholas Christakis and James Fowler document the powerful and remarkable effect social networks have on us, and we on them. Exploring a variety of social phenomena, from obesity to home-buying to happiness, Christakis and Fowler show that "social networks affect every aspect of our lives. Events occurring in distant others can determine the shape of our lives, what we think, what we desire, whether we fall ill or die."

30

---

[6]*"As Paul said in Corinthians..."*: The *First Epistle to the Corinthians* is the seventh book of the New Testament of the Bible, written by Paul the Apostle (written about 5–67 CE).

This is to be taken not as generalized ethical precept but rather as a reporting of social fact. Just because you don't immediately, or perhaps ever, see the virus of behavior leap from host to host doesn't mean it isn't leaping. It is, relentlessly. Most people are wired for strong reciprocity, which means we repay good with good and bad with bad, and are willing to repay bad with bad even at some personal cost, just to reinforce group norms.

As a result, even when good behavior is the minority choice in a bad setting, those who hew to good behavior can eventually prevail—and they are not suckers for doing so, but rather players of the long game over the short.

This law of enlightened citizenship also makes it insufficient for us merely to complain about social trends we don't like. When you read in the news about teenage pregnancies or greedy Wall Street CEOs or steroid-taking athletes, you cannot say that those people are bringing America down. You cannot distance yourself from the trend that you decry. You own it—either because you contributed to that contagion or because you didn't contribute enough to stopping it. Either way, permission from someone else for you to act was never required.

Understanding the world as networked, complex, and adaptive frames our perspective. Any human population will have a wide range of behaviors, from completely altruistic to totally sociopathic. Some people will be criminal and dishonest, many others will simply be what social scientists call "free riders." Free riders accept the benefits of their environment without being willing to pay the costs to create those benefits. This is well understood. What is now just as well understood is the destabilizing effect their behavior has on the group. Free riders gain initial competitive advantage over non-free riders, and thus put pressure on them. Companies that are allowed to cheat destroy industries by forcing all competitors into a race to the bottom. People who are free riders destroy communities by forcing citizens into the same behaviors.

Anti-social contagions spread more readily than pro-social ones, for 35 the same reason that it is easier to push things downhill than up, and easier to fall into vice than into virtue. The challenge is how to generate the right kinds of contagions.

Five Rules

There are five rules we lay out for pro-social citizenship, and they reflect our epidemiological way of looking at civic life.

Small acts of leadership compound. Participating in a town meeting on a proposed new highway. Leading a corps of afterschool reading tutors. Persuading other voters to support a ballot measure. These are forms of citizenship. So is turning off a running faucet. Picking up a candy wrapper. Helping someone with a heavy load. True citizenship is about treating even the most trivial choice as a chance to shape your society and be a leader. It is laying down habits that scale up throughout society. It is not just setting an example; it is actively leading others to copy you. The science of complex adaptive systems teaches us that small acts, tiny everyday choices, accrue and compound into tipping points. We believe that the systems of the body politic, like the systems of the human body, are fractally[7] interrelated. Just as the tiniest capillaries ramify into like-shaped webs of arteries, so too do the smallest pathways of civic action yield similar patterns of politics and common life. Tiny acts of responsibility are replicated, scale upon scale, and thus every act is inherently an act of leadership—either in a pro-social or anti-social way. Every one of us can set off a cascade. Understood thus, the habits and culture of citizenship aren't good for social health; they are essential for it. In schools, homes, firms, and every domain, adults have to be more comfortable talking about and modeling *character* in the most modest-seeming of acts. And as we will discuss more below, government at every turn should be helping citizens take responsibility in small ways too.

Infect the supercarriers.   If we look at good citizenship as a contagion, but as a contagion we want to accelerate rather than contain, then it behooves us to search out the supercarriers—the nodes of networks in every community whose influence and reach are disproportionate. Then it behooves us to infect them. We ensure that they model the kind of pro-social behavior we want, talk about it, and reward it in their own networks. The supercarriers need not be the obvious and most visible leaders; in every circle, there are those who, regardless of station, are so trusted by others that they can make a meme[8] spread very rapidly. Whether you are a neighborhood activist or a youth organizer or a marketer, it has become more necessary than ever to learn and to teach the skills of reading network maps, identifying the nodes, and developing educational and other persuasive strategies for activating those nodes.

Bridge more than bond.   For some Americans, citizenship is expressed by clustering with people very much like oneself. There's of course a fulfilling place for that in life. But we believe in what Mark Granovetter called "the strength of weak ties." What sustains the ecosystem of citizenship is not reinforcing old and already strong ties with, say, fellow liberals or soccer fans or Brooklynites, but instead building new and somewhat weaker ties with conservatives or baseball fans or Manhattanites. In every latticework, whether chemical or physical or human, it's the links that connect a tight ring to another tight ring that add the greatest collective value and make the network bigger and more powerful. Or to put it in terms used by Robert Putnam, *bridging* social capital is better than *bonding*. Great citizens build

---

[7]*fractally:* A fractal is a mathematical concept referring to a type of complex, repeating natural pattern.
    [8]*meme:* An idea, behavior, or style that spreads, like a virus, from person to person within a culture.

bridges between unacquainted realms, more than they reinforce bonds among people already close. Bridging spreads trust while bonding concentrates it. This is why, as Putnam described long before he wrote of "bowling alone," southern Italy with its more tribal blood loyalties has long been a less functional and prosperous social milieu than northern Italy, where weak ties and openness prevail. But because people tend naturally toward building strong ties, they often have to be encouraged to develop the habit of creating weaker ones. In this light, programs like a universal draft or required national civilian service are necessary for diverse democracies. These experiences connect us in ways that the tribalism of everyday life does not.

Create Dunbar units. We believe that one of the great forces that 40 feeds both citizen apathy and the citizen rage of the Tea Party phenomenon[9] is bigness, and the powerlessness it engenders: big government fighting big business as reported by big media, all fueled by big money, and leaving most of us on the sidelines. The antidote is smallness. Our vision of citizenship is moral and philosophical, but it comes to life only on a face-to-face human scale. There is reason why, across all cultures and time periods, the maximum size of a coherent community has always been about 150. This is known as Dunbar's number, after the social scientist Robin Dunbar, who named the phenomenon. As a matter of both public policy and private self-organization, we should be de-chunking ourselves into units of no more than 150, and then connecting the chunks. A neighborhood or a housing project of 1000 units is not really a neighborhood. A neighborhood consisting of 10 sets of 100 houses, each set linked to the others—that's more like it. Since vast cities and vast national organizations create deserts of citizenship, we believe in localizing globally—every chance we get, making little Dunbar units and getting them to identify as such, bridging with one another, sometimes competing in a healthy way with one another. When one's civic action consists of being just a dues-paying member of a vast national organization, one is only a fraction as powerful and empowered as when it consists of being a leader in a local network, particularly one tied to other local networks. A small-town ethos situated in a high-tech web...makes for effective 21st-century citizenship.

Make courtesy count. Courtesy—a cooperative consideration of, and deferral to, the needs of others—is the start of true citizenship. It is what we practice when we don't live on an island alone. And that is why we believe courtesy should be actively encouraged in American civic life, not as ritual or routine but as mindful practice. When you open doors for others, let others into traffic, say "please" and "thank you," you are watering the garden of social life. These kinds of choices can

---

[9]"*the Tea Party phenomenon...*": The Tea Party movement is a conservative, populist American political movement that has supported limited government since its birth in 2007.

be named and promoted. Though courtesy connotes something courtly and quaint, it is actually one of the most vital and fluid forces in any civic ecology. That is because, at bottom, courtesy is about subordinating the self, even if momentarily. It breeds trust, and trust is everything in civic life.

Trust in trust. Trust is foremost among the social virtues that make healthy societies. Alas, we note its absence more readily than its presence. When market actors behave in ways that erode the trust that citizens have in one another—as Wall Street banks did in peddling financial time bombs during the housing boom—they send a signal that "dumb money" deserves its fate. When the state acts in ways that erode the trust that citizens have in one another—by codifying a presumption of deceptiveness, as the CEO affirmations do, or by requiring teachers to teach certain pages of a text on certain days—it is not just responding to a depletion of trust; it's contributing to it. By contrast, every act of great citizenship adds to the social stocks of trust. Designing experiences where people come to know each other, where they can expect to encounter one another repeatedly, and where the quality of life is increased for all if each individual thinks of himself as a steward—or trustee—of the experience: this is what life is like, say, in a neighborhood library branch, and we believe great citizens behave as if every space they are in is a public library.

Trust, in short, is the DNA to be found in all the other habits of citizenship. It is what fuels the fractal impact of small acts of leadership. It is what empowers supercarriers to infect others. It is what makes weak ties useful. It is why we need to preserve a human scale for citizenship. And it is why courtesy counts.

The Power of One

We recognize that there are latent dangers in the networked ethics we advocate. One is what might be called "hivemind,"[10] the tendency for individuals to lose their voice and identity in the midst of the collective. The other is simple bullying, the fear the Framers had in mind when they drafted the Constitution, that majorities might create great waves of opinion that swamp minorities.

As to the first fear, we are no champions of group-driven dehumanization. But citizenship of the kind we describe is the *opposite* of dehumanizing conformity. When any one person can be an agent of contagion, and can set off cascades of new thought or action, that is a truly empowering situation. Yes, that one person needs to have some savvy about how complex systems tip, and not everyone has that. But the fact is that in our story of citizenship, the individual has even more

45

---

[10] *"hivemind"*: Refers to collective consciousness or social action of insects, such as ants and bees.

power than she does in the more atomized, solipsistic account of citizenship—and far more than in some collectivist dystopia. The corollary to always being influenced by others (which we are) is always being able to influence others—a power we dramatically underutilize.

As to the second fear, of majoritarian bullying, what we value is cooperation, and there is a crucial distinction between cooperation and conformity. Cooperation presumes difference—and derives its moral value from the fact that joint action is undertaken out of difference rather than out of sameness. That said, we do believe it's perfectly appropriate for majorities to squeeze out anti-social behavior. The trick is being clear about what constitutes anti- and pro-social behavior. By anti-social we do not mean "deviant" and "unlike others," as communism or homosexuality were once tagged. We mean behavior that is pathologically selfish, that breaks down group trust and cooperation in pursuit of egotism.

How *You* Behave

When one person behaves like it's OK to litter, others do as well, and the behavior of littering goes viral. Or take another example. You're at the park enjoying a picnic with family and friends and a boom box. Another group at a nearby table turns up their music. Now you feel you've got to turn up your music so that it isn't drowned out. Then the other group feels the same, and turns up *their* music.

In the study of sound they call this the Lombard effect, the ratcheting-up of noise levels as everyone fights to be heard over the din of everyone else. There is a civic Lombard effect as well. And in a world where the operating mode is to do what you want to do, damn the consequences to anyone else, we get Lombard-esque cycles of discourtesy and disregard.

The new science we spoke of in the introduction reveals that in a networked environment, where behaviors are contagious and can lead to cascades of anti-social one-upsmanship, there is only one way to stop the spiral. And that is to stop the spiral. Or to put it another way, it is to recognize that *society becomes how you behave*—not anyone else but you.

This is a deceptively profound idea. To assume that society becomes how you behave is to leave behind forever the myth of social externalities—that you don't have to bear the costs of your bad or selfish behavior. To assume that society becomes how you behave is to leave behind also the myth that you are just one in a billion, that somewhere out there is some good person whose acts can cancel out your bad ones, thus creating no net social harm.

To assume that society becomes how you behave is to take on the responsibility of everyday "small 1" leadership. This is more than acknowledging that on an individual basis, character counts and virtue matters. It's acting as if the character of a community will, sooner or later, *exactly* reflect your own character: because it will. Collective character is real and something each of us shapes.

So, for instance, when you are cut off in traffic and feel the chemical rush of road rage, play out two scenarios. The first is the commonly expected one, in which the rest of your drive is dedicated to exacting revenge against the offending driver or to paying his ruthlessness forward and cutting off another driver.

The alternative scenario is one in which you catch yourself and choose not to compound one person's discourtesy with your own. Here, you recognize that if you make the small decision to let drivers into traffic, even if it feels like an affront to your dignity, then other people will do the same.

Because the first scenario is indeed the common one, and everyone 55 assumes its rules are the rules of the freeway, gridlock and awful traffic jams are the inevitable result. But when we let the second scenario play out, traffic flows more smoothly. Gridlock does not occur. We get where we want to get faster.

This is not just parable. It is hard science. People who study complex adaptive systems—using computer models of traffic going along two axes (north-south and east-west)—can demonstrate and compare the effects of these two scenarios. Lesson one: others will act the way you act. Lesson two: when you act in a pro-social way, the net result for you and everyone else is better.

This may seem counterintuitive, the notion that slowing down gets you there faster, that to yield now is to advance later. The reason, again, is our ingrained and too-narrow idea about what constitutes our self-interest. In a onetime transaction with someone who won't exist after the transaction (and here, we are describing the parameters of neoclassical economics), you might rightly think that screwing that person is the best way to achieve your own interest. At a minimum, you'd be safe to think you could get away with it. You would think that someone else's problem is someone else's problem.

If, however, we allow for the possibility that the other person in the transaction may still exist after the transaction, then we think differently. If we allow for the possibility that the other person will not only reciprocate vis-à-vis you but will also carry your behavior virally to others, then we must act differently. If we allow for the possibility that someone else's problem is eventually your problem too, then we must act differently.

This possibility is called real life.

We acknowledge that this vision of true citizenship is challenging. 60 The picture we paint here is not of the path of least resistance. Our vision requires people to lean forward and engage rather than lean back and let things happen. Left to themselves, many Americans—indeed, most humans—choose convenience over participation. But while it seems convenient to cede responsibility for the common good to the market or the state, that convenience is penny-wise and pound-foolish.

It diminishes our feeling of enfranchisement, and our actual power. And while it seems inconvenient to show up and participate, that inconvenience pays dividends in material benefit and in the purposeful enjoyment of life. Why? Because participation, freely chosen rather than incentivized or delegated, springs from intrinsic motivation—and intrinsic motivation yields the kind of happiness that money can't buy and laws can't create....

ENGAGING THE TEXT

1. Do you think the authors are right when they say that today the idea of citizenship seems "musty" and out-of-date or that a "good citizen" is just "a sucker who forgot to look out for herself"? Would you agree that we, as a nation, suffer from "an ideology that exalts individual autonomy at all costs"? Are Liu and Hanauer suggesting that modern Americans are actually too free?

2. To what extent would you agree with Liu and Hanauer's assertion that big business and big government have both worked against the interests of citizenship in recent years? What examples can you think of that support or challenge this claim?

3. Assess Liu and Hanauer's claim that we have grown beyond the era of "Machine Brain" self-interest and have entered into the new era of "Garden Brain" interdependence. What evidence can you see to support the notion that we are no longer "rugged individualists" but members of increasingly complicated social networks?

4. How, according to Liu and Hanauer, does mutual interdependence empower us? To what extent do you agree that individual actions today can have enormous impact by means of "network contagion"? How, exactly, might this "contagion" work?

5. How might the idea that "society becomes how you behave" change your behavior today? If you knew that your actions would be imitated by millions around the world, what would you do in the next 24 hours and why?

EXPLORING CONNECTIONS

6. Do you think the schools described by John Taylor Gatto (p. 141), Mike Rose (p. 151), and Jonathan Kozol in Chapter Two (p. 201) would create the kinds of "great citizens" that Liu and Hanauer describe? In what ways did you learn about citizenship, formally and informally, in your own school experience?

7. Compare the idea of "great citizenship" to the kind of "real patriot" that Naomi Wolf identifies with the Declaration of Independence (p.625). Is it possible to see the Declaration itself as a proclamation of interdependence?

8. Compare the visions of American culture presented by Liu and Hanauer and Juan Williams (p. 648). Is American society becoming "tribal" and

polarized as Williams suggests, or are we becoming more "open" and interconnected? Do you see more "bridging" going on around you, or more conflict and competition — or both?

9. Are the ice-cream-banning moms that Katherine Mangu-Ward describes (p. 659) examples of "great citizenship"? How does the notion of the networked self presented by Liu and Hanauer complicate the ideal of "negative liberty"?

10. How might Michelle Alexander (p. 738) or Kevin Bales and Ron Soodalter (p. 721) respond to the idea that Americans are more interdependent than ever today? To what extent might the social problems they describe affect all Americans? How responsible is every American for what happens in U.S. prisons and on factory farms?

EXTENDING THE CRITICAL CONTEXT

11. Interview five or more friends or students in other classes to learn about their views of citizenship. What do they associate the idea of citizenship with? What does it mean to them personally?

12. Liu and Hanauer suggest that a universal draft, or required national civilian service, might be necessary in a diverse democracy. Hold a class debate on whether requiring all citizens to participate in such experiences would benefit America.

13. Research the role that the Internet and social networking have played in recent acts of resistance and rebellion worldwide — from the Arab Spring uprisings to the Occupy Wall Street movement. How have social networks and the Internet been used in these protests? How do you think social media will transform the role of citizens and the way governments work in the future?

FURTHER CONNECTIONS

1. Some social media activists have argued that "information wants to be free," meaning that the Internet should not be subject to the same intellectual property laws that regulate the ownership of books, works of art, inventions, and consumer products. Research the current state of the copyright wars surrounding online content. How successful have major corporations been in limiting the free distribution of music, films, videos, books, and other forms of content on the Internet? How have hackers, crackers, phreakers, and other Internet anarchists attempted to subvert corporate interests? To what extent have the "open-source" or "free culture" movements succeeded in maintaining an open Internet? Based on your findings, would you agree that free access to information is an important human right? Why or why not?

2. Research the growth of mass surveillance in modern American society. How has government surveillance of the general population increased in response to terrorist threats and the development of new electronic crime-fighting technologies? How have federal and local government agencies used any or all of the following innovations to monitor the activities of American citizens:

   • Data-mining bank and bookstore records

   • Tracking and data-mining Internet searches and social-media site use

   • TV surveillance cameras

   • Facial recognition systems

   • Mobile-phone tracking and wiretapping

   • Mobile-phone and vehicle GPS tracking

   • DNA databases

   • Unmanned aerial vehicles

   To what extent do you think such activities threaten the privacy and personal freedom of American citizens?

3. Do some online research to learn more about how corporations are exploiting online social networks and new electronic technologies like the Radio Frequency Identification (RFID) chip to gather data about their customers. What kinds of information can Internet corporations like Google, Facebook, or Twitter gather about their users? What

kinds of information do data-mining companies like Acxiom, eXelate, Intellidyn, and RapLeaf collect about consumers? How might data mining threaten individual liberties? What can be done to limit the erosion of privacy rights in an age of digital communications?

4. Research the impact of the Supreme Court's 2010 *Citizens United v. Federal Election Commission* decision, which extended the right of free speech to corporations. What impact has this decision had on U.S. politics? Do you think corporations and unions should enjoy the same legal rights as individual citizens? Why or why not?

5. Learn more about the costs and benefits of the "war on drugs" that the United States has been engaged in since the term was coined in 1971. Drawing on the information you gather, hold a debate in class on whether drugs should be legalized or decriminalized. Should Americans have the right to choose for themselves on this issue, or is state control of intoxicants a matter of "the general Welfare," as expressed in the Preamble to the Constitution? Is state regulation of drug use simply another "nanny state" attempt to protect us from our own "bad inclinations"? Or is banning drugs a matter of the common good, like regulating pollutants in drinking water and mandating seat belts in cars?

6. In 1975 philosopher Peter Singer published *Animal Liberation*, a book that is often recognized as the beginning of the contemporary animal rights movement. Learn more about organizations associated with animal rights, like the Animal Liberation Front and People for the Ethical Treatment of Animals (PETA). What are the objectives of animal rights groups and what arguments do they make to support them? In your view, should animals have "rights" in the same way that human citizens have them? If so, what rights should they have?

Connecting to the e-Pages. (See bedfordstmartins.com/rereading /epages for access to these materials.)

1. View *A Declaration of Interdependence* at the Bedford e-Pages site and compare this Declaration with that of the Founders. Which of the ideas or principles in *A Declaration of Interdependence* strike you as the most important or meaningful? Which would you include if you were revising the American Declaration of Independence for the twenty-first century and why?

2. Read Chris Norwood's *The Rise of Mass Dependency*, and do some online research to learn more about the growth of what Norwood

calls the "medical industrial complex" in the United States. How has medical spending as a percent of gross national product increased over the last forty to fifty years? Why might this increase be seen as a serious threat to the nation?

3. After reading Norwood, research the arguments for and against universal, government-mandated healthcare. How would you expect Norwood to react to the idea of taxpayer-funded healthcare for all Americans? In your view, do all American citizens have a right to healthcare? Why or why not?

ACKNOWLEDGMENTS

Text Acknowledgments

ACKNOWLEDGMENTS

Susan N. Herman, *Taking Liberties: The War on Terror and the Erosion of American Democracy*. Copyright © 2011 Oxford University Press. Reprinted with permission.

Ines Hernández-Ávila, "Para Teresa" in *Con Razon Corazon*. Reprinted with permission of the author.

Erin Aubry Kaplan, "Barack Obama: Miles Traveled, Miles to Go" from *Black Talk, Blue Thoughts, and Walking the Color Line: Dispatches from a Black Journalist*. Copyright © 2011. University Press of New England. Reprinted with permission.

Diana Kendall, "Framing Class" from *Framing Class: Media Representations of Wealth and Poverty in America*. Copyright © 2011. Reprinted with permission of Rowman & Littlefield.

Jean Kilbourne, "Two Ways a Woman Can Get Hurt: Advertising and Violence" from *Can't Buy My Love: How Advertising Changes the Way We Think and Feel*. Copyright © 1999 by Jean Kilbourne. All rights reserved.Reprinted with the permission of The Free Press, a Division of Simon & Schuster, Inc.

Michael Kimmel, "Bros Before Hos," from *The Guyland: The Perilous World Where Boys Become Men* by Michael Kimmel. Copyright © 2009 Michael Kimmel. Reprinted with permission of HarperCollins Publishers.

Jamaica Kincaid, "Girl" from *At the Bottom of the River*. Copyright © 1983 by Jamaica Kincaid. Reprinted with permission of Farrar, Straus & Giroux, LLC.

Jonathan Kozol, "Still Separate, Still Unequal" from *The Shame of the Nation*. Copyright © 2006 Jonathan Kozol. Reprinted with permission of Crown Publishers, a division of Random House, Inc.

Eric Liu and Nick Hanauer, "Great Citizenship," *The Gardens of Democracy: A New American Story of Citizenship, the Economy, and the Role of Government*. Copyright © 2011 Sasquatch Books. Reprinted with permission.

Malcolm X, "Learning to Read" from *The Autobiography of Malcolm X*. Copyright © 1964 by Alex Haley and Malcolm X. Copyright © 1965 by Alex Haley and Betty Shabazz. Reprinted with permission of Random House, Inc.

Katherine Mangu-Ward, "The War on Negative Liberty," *New Threats to Freedom*. Copyright © 2010 Templeton Press. Reprinted with permission.

Gregory Mantsios, "Class in America—2009" from *Race, Class and Gender in the United States*, edited by Paula Rothenberg. Copyright © 2007 Worth Publishers. Reprinted with permission.

Rubén Martinez, "The Crossing," *Crossing Over: A Mexican Family on the Migrant Trail*. Copyright © 2001 by Ruben Martinez. Published in paperback by Picador USA, and originally in hardcover by Metropolitan Books/Henry Holt & Co. All rights reserved. Reprinted with permission of Susan Bergholz Literary Services, New York, NY and Lamy, NM.

Kay Givens McGowen, "Weeping for the Lost Matriarchy," *Daughters of Mother Earth: The Wisdom of Native American Women*. Copyright © 2006 Praeger. Reprinted with permission.

Michael Moore, "Idiot Nation" from *Stupid White Men ... And Other Sorry Excuses for the State of the Nation by Michael Moore*. Copyright © 2002 Michael Moore. Reprinted with permission of HarperCollins Publishers.

Charles Murray, "The New American Divide," *The Wall Street Journal*, January 21, 2012. Reprinted by permission of the author, Charles Murray, the WH Brady Scholar at the American Enterprise Institutute.

Katherine S. Newman, excerpt from *The Accordion Family: Boomerang Kids, Anxious Parents, and the Private Toll of Global Competition*. Copyright © 2012 Beacon Press. Reprinted with permission.

Timothy Noah, "Introduction" and "Rise of the Stinking Rich," *The Great Divergence: America's Growing Inequality Crisis and What We Can Do About It*. Copyright © 2012 Bloomsbury Press. Reprinted with permission.

Martha C. Nussbaum, "Whether from Reason or Predjudice: Taking Money for Bodily Services," *Liberty for Women: Freedom and Feminism in the Twenty-First Century*. Copyright © 2002 Ivan R. Dee. Reprinted with permission.

Theodore B. Olson, "The Conservative Case for Gay Marriage: Why Same-sex Marriage Is an American Value," *The Daily Beast*, Jan 8, 2010. Copyright © 2010 by Theodore Olson. Reprinted with permission.

ACKNOWLEDGMENTS

94   Yana Paskova for New York Times

96   Robert Leighton/The New Yorker Collection/www.cartoonbank.com

CHAPTER 2, LEARNING POWER

103   Yeko Photo Studio/BigStock

120   Lloyd Dangle

140   From Love is Hell © 1986 by Matt Groening. All Rights Reserved. Reprinted by permission of Pantheon Books, a division of Random House, Inc., NY. Courtesy of Acme Features Syndicate.

150   From Love is Hell © 1986 by Matt Groening. All Rights Reserved. Reprinted by permission of Pantheon Books, a division of Random House, Inc., NY. Courtesy of Acme Features Syndicate.

180   Works by Norman Rockwell printed by permission of the Norman Rockwell Family Agency Copyright © 2013 The Norman Rockwell Family Entities.

181   Works by Norman Rockwell printed by permission of the Norman Rockwell Family Agency Copyright © 2013 The Norman Rockwell Family Entities.

182   Jon Chase/Harvard Public Affairs

183   © Homer W Sykes / Alamy

184   © Erik S. Lesser/The New York Times/Redux

185   Pablo Yanez, 2012

186   AP Photo/Jacquelyn Martin

197   THE BOONDOCKS © 2000 Aaron McGruder. Dist. BY UNIVERSAL UCLICK. Reprinted with permission. All rights reserved.

217   Jeff Danziger

227   Candorville used with the permission of Darrin Bell, the Washington Post Writers Group and the Cartoonist Group. All rights reserved.

236   Copyright © Ted Rall 2012. All Rights Reserved.

CHAPTER 3, MONEY AND SUCCESS

241   Image Source/Getty Images

259   LALO ALCARAZ © 2011. Dist. By UNIVERSAL UCLICK. Reprinted with permission. All rights reserved.

263   THE BOONDOCKS © 2000 Aaron McGruder. Dist. BY UNIVERSAL UCLICK. Reprinted with permission. All rights reserved.

273   Copyright ©David McLain/Aurora Photos

297   Joel Pett Editorial Cartoon used with the permission of Joel Pett and the Cartoonist Group. All rights reserved.

307   Copyright © Paul D'Amato. Used by permission.

308   Reuters/Lucy Nicholson/Landov

309   AP Photo/John Minchillo

310   Copyright © Michael Siluk/The Image Works

311   John Moore/Getty Images

312   Mario Tama/Getty Images

315   Roz Chast/The New Yorker Collection/www.cartoonbank.com

330   Copyright © Tom Tomorrow

351   Copyright © Lloyd Dangle/Troubletown. Used with permission.

367   William Hamilton/The New Yorker Collection/ www.cartoonbank.com

CHAPTER 4, TRUE WOMEN AND REAL MEN

375   Photo by Carolyn Jones

395   Robert Mankoff/The New Yorker Collection/www.cartoonbank.com

409   Mike Keefe, The Denver Post and InToon.com

411 Photo © Michael A. Messner

412 Claudia Janke

413 © Megan Maloy/Getty Images

414 © Digital Vision/Getty Images

415 iStockphoto

416 © Eli Reed/Magnum Photos

417 David Lewis/AP Photo

453 Distributed by UniversalUclick/GoComics.com

463 THINK AGAIN (David John Attyah and S.A. Bachman)www.agitart.org

489 Candorville used with the permission of Darrin Bell, the Washington Post Writers Group and the Cartoonist Group. All rights reserved.

CHAPTER 5, CREATED EQUAL

493 Copyright © Eric Gay/AP Photo

502 Joel Pett Editorial Cartoon used with the permission of Joel Pett and the Cartoonist Group. All rights reserved.

507 Candorville used with the permission of Darrin Bell, the Washington Post Writers Group and the Cartoonist Group. All rights reserved.

525 left © Dave Martin/AP Photo

525 right © Chris Graythen/Getty Images

538 David Sipress/The New Yorker Collection/www.cartoonbank.com

552 Joel Pett Editorial Cartoon used with the permission of Joel Pett and the Cartoonist Group. All rights reserved.

554 © Roberto Gonzalez/AP Photo

555 © Jean-Yves Rebeuf/Image Works

556 Photo by Roland Charles 1992

557 Solomon D. LittleOwl

558 Michael Ainsworth/The Dallas Morning News

559 © Todd Bigelow/Aurora Photos

560 © A. Ramey/PhotoEdit

561 European Press Agency/Michael Reynolds

562 © Justin Sullivan/Getty Images

569 LALO ALCARAZ © 2003. Distributed by UNIVERSAL UCLICK. Reprinted with permission. All rights reserved.

591 BORS ©2012 Distributed by UNIVERSAL UCLICK. Reprinted with permission. All rights reserved.

594 Candorville used with the permission of Darrin Bell, the Washington Post Writers Group and the Cartoonist Group. All rights reserved.

609 © Christophe Vorlet

CHAPTER 6, LAND OF LIBERTY

617 Works by Norman Rockwell Printed by permission of the Norman Rockwell Family Agency. Copyright © 2013 The Norman Rockwell Family Entities

629 Copyright © John Jonik

637 Created by Tracie Harris. Published by the Athiest Community of Austin. http://www.atheist-community.org

646 McCoy © 2012 Distributed by UNIVERSAL UCLICK. Reprinted with permission. All rights reserved.

659 Copyright © Tom Tomorrow

668 Barry Deutsch, leftycartoons.com

e-Pages Acknowledgments

INDEX OF AUTHORS AND TITLES

Missing something?

To access the e-Pages that accompany this text, visit **bedfordstmartins
.com/rereading/epages**. Students who do not buy a new book can purchase access to e-Pages at this site.

Inside the e-Pages for *Rereading America*

Chapter 1

Roger Jack, *An Indian Story*

Susan Saulny, Shayla Harris, and Matthew Orr, *Just a Family* (video)

Chapter 2

Richard Rodriguez, *The Achievement of Desire*

Adam B. Ellick and Natasha Singer, *The Commercial Campus* (video)

Chapter 3

Studs Terkel, *Stephen Cruz*

Tim Kasser, *The High Price of Materialism* (video)

Chapter 4

Jesse Green, *S/He*

Megan Chiplock, *Speaking Out: Kevin Downs* (video)

Chapter 5

Maysan Haydar, *Veiled Intentions: Don't Judge a Muslim Girl by Her Covering*

Todd County High School Students, *More Than That...* (video)

Chapter 6

Chris Norwood, *The Rise of Mass Dependency*

Tiffany Shlain, *A Declaration of Interdependence: A Crowdsourced Short Film*
  (video)